Strategic Financial Management Casebook

Strategic Financial Management Casebook

Rajesh Kumar
Professor of Finance
Institute of Management Technology
Dubai International Academic City
Dubai, UAE

AMSTERDAM • BOSTON • HEIDELBERG • LONDON
NEW YORK • OXFORD • PARIS • SAN DIEGO
SAN FRANCISCO • SINGAPORE • SYDNEY • TOKYO
Academic Press is an imprint of Elsevier

Academic Press is an imprint of Elsevier
125 London Wall, London EC2Y 5AS, United Kingdom
525 B Street, Suite 1800, San Diego, CA 92101-4495, United States
50 Hampshire Street, 5th Floor, Cambridge, MA 02139, United States
The Boulevard, Langford Lane, Kidlington, Oxford OX5 1GB, United Kingdom

Notices
Knowledge and best practice in this field are constantly changing. As new research and experience broaden our understanding, changes in research methods, professional practices, or medical treatment may become necessary.

Practitioners and researchers must always rely on their own experience and knowledge in evaluating and using any information, methods, compounds, or experiments described herein. In using such information or methods they should be mindful of their own safety and the safety of others, including parties for whom they have a professional responsibility.

To the fullest extent of the law, neither the Publisher nor the authors, contributors, or editors, assume any liability for any injury and/or damage to persons or property as a matter of products liability, negligence or otherwise, or from any use or operation of any methods, products, instructions, or ideas contained in the material herein.

British Library Cataloguing-in-Publication Data
A catalogue record for this book is available from the British Library

Library of Congress Cataloging-in-Publication Data
A catalog record for this book is available from the Library of Congress

ISBN: 978-0-12-805475-8

For Information on all Academic Press publications
visit our website at https://www.elsevier.com

Working together
to grow libraries in
developing countries

www.elsevier.com • www.bookaid.org

Publisher: Nikki Levy
Acquisition Editor: Scott Bentley
Editorial Project Manager: Susan Ikeda
Production Project Manager: Jason Mitchell
Designer: Mark Rogers

Typeset by MPS Limited, Chennai, India

Dedication

To
T.P. Sankunni Nair and K. Chandralekha

Contents

Preface

Strategic Finance is the critical link between strategic management and financial management for value creation. Finance is the main link between strategic plans and their implementation. In the pursuit for value creation all planning leads to financial planning. Value drivers must be linked to shareholder value creation and which in turn are measured by both financial and operational Key Performance Indicators. Stock price maximization is one of the significant factors for value maximization objectives. The concept of measuring and managing shareholder value is of great significance basically on account of the increasing relevance of capital markets and corporate governance. Identification of how corporate performance is related to strategic and financial decisions facilitates cross-fertilization in theory building and applied research. The value drivers for shareholder wealth creation depend on the investment, financing, operating and dividend decisions undertaken by the firms. Intangibles are a critical driver for innovation and creation of organizational value. Corporate Restructuring which encompasses mergers, acquisitions, divestitures, spin off, split off, equity carve out, joint ventures, share buyback are all strategic initiatives which companies adopt for wealth maximization objectives. Sources of financing like going in for Initial Public offerings are important strategic finance decisions taken by companies. Corporate governance refers to both the structure and relationships which determine corporate direction and performance. Corporate sustainability is aligning an organization's products and services with stakeholder expectations and in the process creating economic, environmental, and social value. CSR meant a commitment to developing policies which integrate practices into daily business operations and report the progress made towards implementing these practices.

This book on strategic finance uses integrative case studies to provide a framework for understanding the different perspectives of strategic financial management. The book presents a holistic perspective to comprehend and analyze the strategic growth perspectives of the world's largest wealth creators. The book develops strategic analyzes of financial structures by evaluating policies, decisions and models. The book suggests a conceptual framework for integrating strategy and finance for value creation. The case studies presented in this book analyzes the wealth created by large companies in different industry sector. Each chapter explores in depth the stock market performance since the day of the firm's listing in stock market along with operating and financial performance of these largest companies over a decade. The framework of analysis involve discussion on the operating segments, strategies of growth, restructuring strategies, analysis of ownership structure, dividend and share buyback strategies. Each chapter also highlights the corporate governance practices, citizenship and sustainability issues and risk management practices adopted by firms.

Chapter 1, Perspectives on Strategic Finance, provides the theoretical framework for discussion on strategic perspectives of finance. Chapter 2, Wealth Creation by Coca-Cola—A Strategic Perspective, discusses the strategic perspective of growth of Coca Cola which is the world's largest beverage company. Cola Cola is one of the most valuable and recognizable brands in the world. Chapter 3, Wealth Creation by Johnson & Johnson, analyses the wealth created by Johnson & Johnson which is one of the largest company in the health care sector. The J&J Family of Companies is organized into several business segments comprised of franchises and therapeutic categories. Chapter 4, Wealth Creation by Microsoft, discusses the strategy of growth and wealth creation of Microsoft which is the world leader in software, services, devices, and solutions. Microsoft develops, manufactures, licenses, supports and sells computer software, consumer electronics, personal computer, and services. Chapter 5, Wealth Creation by Exxon Mobil, discusses the wealth creation of Exxon Mobil. Exxon Mobil is one of the largest integrated refiners, marketers of petroleum products and chemical manufacturers. Over a period of 125 years, Exxon Mobil has evolved from a regional marketer of kerosene in United States to become the largest publicly traded integrated oil company in the world. Chapter 6, Wealth Creation—A Case Analysis of Apple, focuses on wealth creation by Apple which transformed itself from a computer company to a leader in the consumer electronics and media sales industry. Apple focuses on innovation as the strategic pursuit for growth. Chapter 7, Wealth Creation—Analysis of Google, discusses the strategy of growth and wealth creation by Google, the American multinational technology company which specializes in internet related services and products. The products and services offered by Google include online advertising technologies, search, cloud computing, and software. Chapter 8, Wealth Analysis of General Electric, analyses the wealth created by General Electric Company (GE) which is one of the world's largest digital industrial company with focus on software defined machines and solutions. GE is one of the world's best infrastructure and technology company with secondary focus on financial services division. Chapter 9, Strategies of Wealth Creation by Berkshire Hathaway, highlights the strategies of wealth creation by Berkshire Hathaway the holding company which owns a number of subsidiaries in diversified business activities which includes insurance and reinsurance, freight rail transportation, utilities and energy, finance, manufacturing, services and retailing. Chapter 10, Analysis of Wealth—Walmart, analyses the wealth created by Walmart, the American multinational retail corporation which operates one of the world's largest chain of hypermarkets, discount department stores, and grocery stores. Chapter 11, Wealth Analysis of Facebook, focuses on wealth created by Facebook which enable people to connect and share through mobile devices and personal computers. Facebook facilitate people to share their opinions, ideas, photos, and videos. Chapter 12, Wealth Analysis of Procter and Gamble, deals with the wealth analysis of P&G which is a global leader in fast moving consumer goods sector. Chapter 13, Wealth Analysis of Wells Fargo, highlights the wealth creation of Wells Fargo & Company which is a diversified financial services company with over $1.8 trillion in assets. Chapter 14, Wealth Creation by Amazon, discusses the wealth created by Amazon which has emerged as the largest internet based retailer in the United States. In the year 2015, Amazon became the fastest company ever to reach $100 billion in annual sales. Chapter 15, Wealth Analysis of AT&T, focuses on wealth analysis of AT&T which is the largest communication company in the world. AT&T is a fully integrated service provider. AT&T offer advanced mobile services, next generation TV, high speed internet and smart solutions. Chapter 16, Wealth Creation by Boeing, analyzes the wealth created by Boeing which is the largest aerospace company in the world which manufactures commercial jetliners, defense, space and security systems. In 2016, Boeing completes one century of flying in the sky. Chapter 17, Analysis of Wealth—Time Warner Inc., discusses the wealth created by Time Warner which is a global leader in media and entertainment with the focus on television networks and film and TV entertainment.

Acknowledgment

I would like to thank the production and editorial staff at Elsevier who guided this book through the publishing process. I wish to acknowledge the valuable guidance and support of Scott Bentley, Senior Acquisition Editor at Elsevier. My thanks to Susan Ikeda, Editorial Project Manager and her team for all cooperation and support for the publication of this book. I thank Jason Mitchell, Publishing Services Manager and his team for all the support. I also acknowledge the content of the various web sites and sources of information to which I referred.

Perspectives on strategic finance

1.1 Strategic role of finance

Strategy basically refers to how resources are to be deployed through a combination of products, markets and technologies. The basic purpose of the finance function is to ensure the timely acquisition and efficient utilization of funds so that strategic goals are achieved. Financial resources are the foundation of the strategic plan and financial value is the unifying factor which bonds products, market and operating decisions associated with strategic options. The financial aspects have a major role in strategic aspects like the type of assets the firm acquires, the rate at which they are acquired and the ultimate size of the firm. Investment, financing, operating, and dividends decisions are the major strategic financial decisions within a firm. The primary finance function is to identify and plan for the proper mix of financing to support strategic activity and to ensure that funds are employed to achieve expected returns.

The unifying financial goal for any profit seeking enterprise would be the maximization of the net present value of the projected cash flows, discounted at the cost of capital.

In modern world, the finance manager ought to be more skilled in managing people and managing risk rather than in aspects of financial reporting. The role of financial director in an organization is becoming increasingly relevant in the context of uncertainty, flexibility federalism, and downsizing [1]. Financial Director is the one director who would be frequently consulted on every strategic decision a company takes. In the context of the trend to reduce the size of the corporate headquarters, however lean and mean a company is, it must produce consolidated accounts and reports to shareholders and authorities. Hence there is a need for adequate financial staff to handle these tasks even in decentralized organizations. Finance function is the central fulcrum which holds businesses together, manages its controls and information in a decentralized step up. It can be argued that in the long run, all planning leads to financial planning. The role of financial directors has become more challenging and sophisticated while dealing with information systems, treasury management, authorities, shareholders, and investing institutions.

The strategic role of finance can be explained in the context of strategy implementation, strategic change and strategic flexibility. Finance is the main link between strategic plans and their implementation. The deployment of funds in capital expenditure programme is an example of how finance function becomes important in strategy implementation. Companies like ABB allows its finance department to play a proactive role in strategy implementation [1]. Financial management and information systems need to respond to organizational changes. Finance function has to respond fast to opportunities in the context of strategic flexibility. Finance department has to identify the essential information needs to the management. The major key elements of strategic finance function are strategic planning, establishment of the optimum capital structure, managing key financial relationship with outsiders, implementation of the financial policy, operational financial planning which includes capital expenditure programs, cash planning, and balance sheet planning. The other key elements include treasury management, debt structure and risk management. The economic viability measures include performance measures and budgeting systems. The element of quality control involves information systems, standards, and procedures. The finance team consists of Finance Director, the controller, the treasurer, senior departmental managers and, business unit financial managers. The finance director is a member of the top management team who is concerned with the strategic direction of the business. Controller is also a part of the core strategy making group which is involved in the implementation of strategic decisions. Finance functions also contain specialized departments like mergers and acquisition (M&A) team information departments. Finance function provided direct input into Unilever's long, medium and short term plans as well as their cost reduction programs and innovation projects. Unilever developed a culture in finance of innovative business partnering, continuous improvement and capability development which enabled the finance team to play an active role in delivering Unilever's growth strategy.

1.2 Managing risk

Investors are assumed to maximize investment return. In quantitative sense risk is the measurement of standard deviation of returns. Statistical techniques are used to manage risk. Historical risk estimates are used along with expected return forecasts to generate asset allocation strategies and portfolios which are optimal with respect to risk and return. Managing risk involves various dimensions of risks like competitive risk, project risk, exchange rate risk, and interest rate risks. International diversification is a technique for managing risk. The concept of global diversification ensured that different types of risk could be diversified improving the risk/return trade off.

1.3 Challenges

Modern businesses in the context of globalization, competition and decreasing margins have to focus on ways to drive business performance. Businesses rely on timely and relevant quantitative data to arrive at strategic decisions. It has become increasingly important to focus on value innovation which advocates on maintaining core business strengths while continuously developing new value additive ideas and strategies. Enhanced understanding of risk factors, updated competitive analysis tools, improved valuation, and projection models are all relevant in modern environment.

Modern financial managers must have understanding of control systems and operational risks. Cash management, capital budgeting, earnings volatility, and forecasting demand are the significant challenges faced by managers. The context of increased contagion in the global financial markets creates challenges of managing interrelated employment, debt reduction, monetary policy, and exchange rate policies when companies plan expansion, treasury hedging and capital management, and acquisition strategies.

1.3.1 Strategic value drivers

Mills [2] identify seven value drivers—sales growth rate, operating profit margin, cash tax rate, fixed capital needs, working capital needs, planning period, and cost of capital. The selection of an appropriate planning period is vital for generating future cash flows based on short term and long term perspective. The estimation of the planning period can be explained in terms of five forces identified by Michael Porter. The planning period needs to be explained in the context of potential entrants, possibility of substitute products, relative power of suppliers and buyers and by the degree of competitive rivalry within the industry in which it exists. For example, in the context of planning period, the company may incorporate the threat of new entrant in the market within a five-year period as the present barriers to entry act as a competitive advantage for the company. Organizations which focus on relative performance creates the most value. The strategic value analysis approach must have a long planning period aimed at creating good sales potential and free cash flow.

Competitive advantage is the result of the core competences nurtured by an organization. It results from the collective learning of the company in terms of diverse production skills, integration of different streams of technology, patterns of communication and managerial rewards. Strategic value creation results from the creation of a strategic architecture. Strategic architecture involves identification and development of technical and production linkages across business units which in turn leads to development of distinct skills and capabilities which cannot be replicated easily by other organizations.

John Kay have identified four aspects of core capabilities—reputation, architecture, innovation, and strategic assets. Reputation facilitates companies to follow price differential strategy whereby they could charge premium price for products or gain larger market share at a competitive price. The unique structure of relational contracts that may exist within or around firms is referred to as architecture. Airline industry develops networks through strategic alliances which in turn provides cost effective ways of providing international services to customers. Marks and Spencer's strategy of growth is based on the development of its supplier architecture. Innovation is also a major source of competitive advantage. Companies like Apple creates value through successful product innovations. Strategic assets are sources of competitive advantage based on the market position.

Fundamental value is based on the present value of expected free cash flows. Shareholder value is firm value minus the value of outstanding debt. Firm value can be based on book value or market value. Market value is based on the stock market performance of a company. The most widely used practical measure of shareholder value is Total Shareholder Return (TSR) which is based on stock price appreciation plus dividends. Companies create value by means of investing capital at a higher rate of return when compared to its cost of capital. Companies with higher returns and higher growth are valued more highly in the stock market.

Knowledge assets are organizational resources which are integral for company's value creation. The strategic relevance of knowledge assets has led to the generation of new concepts and models for managing a company's knowledge assets. Intellectual Capital has emerged as a key concept to evaluate the intangible dimension of an organization. The modern economic world is based on the foundation of new technologies, globalization, and increased relevance of intangible assets. Value creation is often perceived as the future value captured in the form of increased market capitalization. The new global economy has led to the emergence of new business models where companies are combining both old and new economy assets. New processes and tools are required to manage the risks on account of new business models. The greatest challenge a company's face today is identification of the combination of tangible and intangible assets which create the greatest amount of economic value (EV).

Every asset, financial as well as real has value. The key to fundamental aspect of investing and managing assets lies in understanding of not only what value is, but also the sources of value. A value driver is a performance variable which impacts the results of a business such as production effectiveness or customer satisfaction. The metrics associated with value drivers are called key performance indicators (KPIs). Value drivers should be directly linked to shareholder value creation and measured by both financial and operational KPIs which must cover long term growth and operating performance.

The three commonly cited financial drivers of value creation are sales, costs and investments. Earnings growth, cash flow growth and return on invested capital are specific financial drivers. Profitability, growth, and capital intensity are considered as important drivers of free cash flow and value of a firm. The KPIs also include financial measures such as sales growth and earnings per share (EPS) as well as nonfinancial measures. The nonfinancial performance measures include product quality, workplace safety, customer loyalty, employee satisfaction and customer's willingness to promote products.

The finance functions in large organizations had earlier focused on cost control, operating budgets and internal reporting. Institutional and managerial forces shape the critical functions of financing, risk management and capital budgeting. Multinational firms exploit internal capital markets to gain competitive advantage.

1.3.2 Strategic models of valuation

Value-based management (VBM) focuses on the application of valuation principles. In VBM system, the components of the employees' work should be identified and linked to profitability, growth and capital intensity. The actual performance should be measured, evaluated and rewarded in terms of targets for profitability, growth, and capital intensity.

Value creation is traditionally considered as a chain of activities. The field of corporate finance was revolutionized by introduction of mathematical models of capital asset pricing model and the Black Scholes Merton option pricing model. Value based business strategy was adapted by A Brandenburger. Harborne Stuart applied mathematics to the evaluation of strategic decisions through mathematical linkages. Value capture model (VCM) defines competition in an industry as a tension between the value generated from transactions that a firm undertakes with a given set of agents and the forgone value it could have generated from transactions with other agents. Cooperative game theory could be applied effectively in studying competitive dynamics. VCM model of competition allows a firm to identify potential payoffs to investments in resources and capabilities supported by big data. The resources and capabilities which influence value are deployed with competitive intent.[1]

1.4 Strategic financial planning

Goodstein et al. [3, p. 2] define strategic planning as "the process by which an organization envisions its future and develops the necessary procedures and operations to achieve that future". Strategic Planning involves the selection of the most important choices of organization in terms of objectives, mission, policies, programs, goals, and major resource allocations. The long term perspective for assessment of value creating opportunities with the strategic framework is essential for the firm's future. Gluck et al. [4] suggest that firms evolve through at least four stages in developing capacity for effective strategic management. The first stage of simple financial planning focuses on developing annual budgets, financial objectives which are driven by activity schedules aimed at meeting budgets and objectives. The second stage is forecast based planning which is dominated by multiyear budgets and driven by attempts to forecast the future. The third stage termed strategic planning consists of situation analysis, environmental assessment, and identification of strategic alternatives in the context of strategic thinking. The final stage encompasses the evolution of strategic management stage which is influenced by explicitly articulated strategic vision and leadership, supportive structure and systems, staff, and skills. Taylor [5] suggest five key strategic planning modes of central control system, framework for innovation, strategic management, political planning, and futures research.

[1] M.D. Ryall, The new dynamics of competition. *Harvard Business Review* 2013, 80−87.

1.4.1   Stock price maximization

Stock price maximization is one of the significant factor for value maximization objectives. Stock prices are the most observable of all measures which can be used to judge the performance of a listed company. Stock prices are constantly updated to reflect new information about a firm. Thus managers are constantly judged about their actions with the benchmark being the stock price performance. Book value measures like sales and earnings are obtained only at the end of year or in each quarter. Stock prices reflect the long term effects of a firm's business decisions. When firms maximize their stock prices, investors can realize capital gains immediately by selling their shares in the firm. An increase in stock price is often automatically attributed to management's value creation performance. At the same time, the stock price might have increased due to macro-economic factors.

1.4.2   Shareholder value and wealth creation

The concept of measuring and managing shareholder value is of paramount importance on account of the increasing relevance of capital markets and corporate governance. In the era of globalization of markets, investors have easy accessibility to raise funds. The shareholders of the company desires transparency in the operations of the company and places much significance to the corporate governance practices. Today no underperforming company is safe as always there is the threat of hostile takeovers. Hence the managers of firms have to perform to improve the value of the company. The criticism with accounting measures such as EPS and profit or growth in earnings is that they do not consider the cost of investment made for running the businesses.

Shareholder is the main pivotal stakeholder or fulcrum of the business activity. Firms which don't create value for shareholders faces challenges like risk of capital flight, higher interest rates, lower efficiency and productivity and threat of hostile takeovers. Maximization of shareholder wealth is the main objective of any value creating organization. The value perspective is based on measurement of value from accounting based information while wealth perspective is based on stock market information.

Economist's viewpoint suggests the firms create value when management generates revenues over and above the economic costs to generate these revenues. The economic costs are attributed to sources like employee wages and benefits, materials, economic depreciation of physical assets, taxes, and opportunity cost of capital. Value creation occurs when management generates value over and above the costs of resources consumed, including the cost of using capital. A company which loses its value faces the daunting task of attracting further capital for financing expansion as the declining share price becomes a detrimental factor for value creation. In such a scenario, the company is compelled to pay higher interest rates on debt or bank loans.

Wealth creation refers to changes in the wealth of shareholders on a periodic (annual) basis. In the case of stock exchange listed firms, changes in shareholder wealth occurs from changes in stock prices, dividends, equity issues during the period. Stock prices reflect the investors' expectation about future cash flows of the firm. Shareholder wealth is created when firms take investment decisions with positive NPV values.

The real or true value of a stock or intrinsic value includes all aspects of company in terms of both tangible and intangible factors which affect the value of a company and subsequently the perceived value of a share of stock.

1.4.3 Value drivers for shareholder wealth creation

Value drivers are variables which affect the value of the organization. The main value drivers for shareholder wealth creation are intangibles, operating, investment and financial. Increase in shareholder value results from improvement in cash flow from operations. Value enhancement can also result from minimizing the cost of capital by focusing on optimal capital structure decisions. The value drivers for increase in cash flow from operations are higher revenues, lower costs and income taxes and reduction in capital expenditure. No company can maintain their operation and produce great wealth for its shareholders without stable and rising revenue which comes from customer.

The strategic requirements for higher revenues consist of patent barriers to entry, niche markets, and innovative products. The strategic requirements for lower costs and income taxes are scale economies, captive access to raw materials, efficiencies in processes of production, distribution, and services. The strategic requirements for reduction in capital expenditure are efficient asset acquisition and maintenance, spin offs, higher utilization of fixed assets, efficiency of working capital, and divestiture of nonperforming assets.

The value drivers for reduction in capital charge are reduced business risk, optimization of capital structure, reduction of cost of debt, and cost of equity. The strategic requirements for reduced business risks are superior operating performance and long term contracts. The strategic requirement for optimal capital structure involve maintaining a capital structure that minimizes the overall costs which optimizes tax benefits. Companies often adopt different strategies for value creation. Companies like Sony, Apple, and Microsoft often introduce new products for enhancing shareholder value creation.

1.4.4 Measures of shareholder value creation

1.4.4.1 Economic value

EV as a performance measure has been popularized by multinational companies like Coca-Cola, AT&T, and Kellogg. EV is calculated as net operating income after taxes (NOPAT) minus the capital charge. The sequential steps for EV calculation are as follows:

- Calculation of NOPAT
- Estimation of Capital Employed
- Estimation of Weighted Average Cost of Capital (WACC)
- Calculation of capital charge and EV.

1.4.4.2 Equity spread

Equity Spread is a variation of the EV measures. Equity spread is the difference between the ROE and the required return on equity (cost of equity) as the source of value creation. Mathematically, the equity spread is expressed as:

Equity value creation = (Return on equity in % − Cost of equity in %) ∗ Equity Capital

1.4.4.3 Implied value

The implied value measure is similar to discounted future market value. This method is closely related to the Discounted cash flow [DCF] framework. If the difference between implied value at the beginning of the year and end of the year is positive, then management would have created value. Value would be created if the management's decisions generate cash flows over and above the cost of capital and is able to sustain this performance over a long period of time. The implied value measure is based on forecasts of future by making proforma income and balance sheet statements over a period of time.

1.4.4.4 Cash flow return on investment

Cash Flow Return on Investment (CFROI) represents the sustainable cash flow a business generates as a percentage of the cash invested in the business. This measure can be interpreted as the internal rate of return (IRR) over the economic life of the assets. The difference between this IRR and cost of capital represents the value creation potential of the firm. The calculation of CFROI involves conversion of income and balance sheet items into cash and calculating cash flows after adjusting for inflations and adjustments for monetary or near monetary assets such as inventories. The estimation of the normal life of assets is made. The value of the nondepreciating assets at the end of the horizon is also calculated.

NOPAT + Depreciation = Real Gross Cash Flow.

The capital employed is considered as the initial investment. Then IRR is calculated.

1.4.5 Measures of shareholder wealth creation

Wealth creation measures are based on stock market and doesn't require analysis of the financial statements of the firm. Hence these measures are applicable only to exchange listed firms and cannot be used for privately held firms. The price of a share of any company is basically considered to be the market's expectation about the firm's value creation potential. The higher the potential, higher will be the share price relative to the capital invested. Companies which create fundamental value in the operating performance are expected to create value in the market through rise in the stock prices.

The two major wealth creation measures are

a. Total Shareholder Return (TSR)

TSR is the rate of return earned by shareholder based on capital appreciation through price changes and dividends received. TSR enable measurement of a firm's contribution to the overall capital gain and dividend yield to investors. Return on Investment (ROI), free cash flow and growth in invested capital are the key value drivers of capital gains. Companies with higher returns on the invested capital are able to achieve stock price increases as these companies are able to invest more capital at high ROIs.

The annual TSR is calculated as the change in price plus any dividends divided by the initial price.

Mathematically, TSR can be expressed as:

$$\text{TSR} = (\text{Price}_{t+1} + \text{dividends}_{t+1} - \text{Price}_t)/\text{Price}_t$$

b. Annual Economic Return

Annual Economic Return (AER) is based on a firm's annual wealth creation performance. AER calculation is based on dividends and its timings and externally raised capital. The AER method involves estimation of the cost of equity based on the riskiness of the firm.

AER is calculated as a return by the firm after adjusting for dividends paid and external dividends paid and external capital.

1.4.6 Approaches to valuation

There are basically three approaches to Valuation. DCF valuation is based on the fundamental idea that the value of any asset is the present value of expected future cash flows on that asset. Relative valuation estimates the value of any asset by analyzing the pricing of comparable assets relative to a common variable such as earnings, cash flows, sales etc. The contingent claim valuation employs option pricing models to measure the value of assets which have option characteristics. DCF valuation consists of equity valuation and firm valuation.

1.5 Value-based management

VBM is an approach to management whereby the company's overall aspirations, analytical techniques, and management processes are aligned to help the company maximize its value by focusing management decision making on the key drivers of shareholder value. Coca-Cola is one of the pioneering company with VBM principles. The ultimate test of corporate strategy is to analyze whether strategic decisions creates EV for shareholders. VBM are used to assess firm value and shareholder value. According to the basic VBM model, the present financial value must be equal to the discounted future free cash flows from operations using the firm's weighted average cost of capital as discount rate.

1.6 Significance of shared value

Shared values are policies and operating practices which enhance the competitiveness of a company. In this concept, businesses have to focus on value with a societal perspective. Value is defined as benefits relative to costs. The approach to value creation have undergone transformational changes. Value creation is not just optimizing short term financial performance. Companies like GE, Google, IBM, Intel, Johnson & Johnson, Nestle, Unilever, and Walmart aims to create shared values by focusing on the interaction between societal needs and corporate performance. The next wave of innovation and productivity growth in the global economy will be based on shared value creation. Porter (2011) [6] suggests three key ways that companies can create shared value opportunities—a) By reconceiving products and markets b) By redefining productivity in value chain c) By enabling local cluster development. The concept of shared values focuses on societal needs instead of economic needs. Societal harms or weakness creates internal costs for firms such as wasted energy or raw materials.

1.7 Innovation and value creation

In R&D organizations, intangible assets are a key driver of innovation and organizational value. The allocation and deployment of intangible resources is an important strategic decision for organizations. Intangible assets are identified as key resource and driver of organizational performance and value creation.

Innovation is the successful conversion of new concepts and knowledge into new products and processes that deliver new customer value in the market place. The fundamental purpose of innovation is to create value which leads to value creation for different stakeholders of a company. Innovation is profitable, radical and needs speed. According to BCG survey 2013, technology and telecommunications top the list of most innovative companies. Apple, Google, Samsung, Microsoft, IBM, GE have been consistently ranked as top innovative companies. A study by Booze & Company lists Apple, Google, 3M, GE, Toyota, Microsoft, P&G, IBM, Samsung, and Intel as the most valuable companies in terms of innovation.

1.8 Role of technology

The information age has an important role for finance. Finance have the highest level of linkage access to information, strategy, economic targets and internal business processes. Performance metrics and performance enhancement play a key role in gauging progress and identification of opportunities for improvement of economic targets. The investments need to be prioritized and resources deployed according to EV which can be realized through achieving strategic improvement. Information technology in the form of enterprise resource planning systems provides companies with the ability to operate, manage and measure fundamental business activities as individual entities. Technology reshapes value chains. Technology becomes central to the mix as powerful new database, application, networking, and desktop tools increases the capabilities and expectations of users. The biggest challenge lies with respect to implementation of new processes and supporting technology as company acquires or divests business units, develops new models and reengineers the supply chain.

1.9   Behavioral finance

Behavioral finance is a modern area of study in finance which aims to combine behavioral and cognitive psychological theory with conventional economics and finance to provide explanations for the reasons why people make irrational financial decisions. The Efficient Market Hypothesis assumes that the competition between investors seeking abnormal profits drive prices to their "correct" value. The EMH does not assume that all investors are rational, but it does assume that markets make unbiased forecasts of the future. In contrast the behavioral finance assumes that financial markets are informationally inefficient. Specific applications of behavioral finance can be examined in phenomena like inflation and underpricing of IPOs. Behavioral finance theory holds that markets might fail to reflect economic fundamentals under conditions of irrational behavior, systematic patterns of behavior and limits to arbitrage in financial markets. Investors behave irrationally when they don't correctly process all the available information while forming their expectations of a company's future. When large group of investors share particular patterns of behavior (irrational systematic behavior), persistent price deviations do occur. Behavioral finance theory suggests that the patterns of overconfidence, overreaction and over representation are common to many investors and such groups can be large enough to prevent a company's share price from reflecting economic fundamentals.[2] When investors assume that a company's recent performance alone is an indication of future performance, they may start bidding for shares and drive up the price. The two observed phenomena are long term reversal in shares and short term momentum. In the phenomena or reversal, high performing stocks in the past few years will become low performing stocks of the next few years. According to behavioral finance theorists, this effect is caused by an overreaction on the part of investors. Momentum occurs when positive returns for stocks over the past few months are followed by several more months of positive returns. Behavioral finance still cannot explain why investors overreact under certain conditions such as IPOs and underreact in others such as earnings announcement. Under the assumption that a company's share price will eventually return to its intrinsic value in the long run, it would be beneficial for managers to benefit from using DCF valuation for strategic decisions.

---

[2] M. Gerhard, T. Keller, D. Wessels, Do Fundamentals or Emotions—Drive the Stock Market, Financial strategy, Chapter 2. John Wiley, pp. 52–53.

1.10   Corporate restructuring

Restructuring is the corporate management strategy of reorganizing a company for value creation and making it more efficient. Many companies undertake restructuring activities to focus on core businesses while divesting noncore business activities. Restructuring is a strategy through which a firm changes its set of business or financial structure.[3] From the 1970s through the 1990s divesting businesses from company portfolios and downsizing accounted for a large percentage of firms' restructuring strategies.[4] Restructuring includes such activities like change in corporate management, sale of underutilized assets like patents and brands, outsourcing of operations, relocation of manufacturing facilities to lower cost locations and reorganization of functions such as sales, marketing and distribution. Restructuring can also include refinancing of corporate debt to reduce interest payments and reduction of staff.

M&As are a part of corporate restructuring activities. Financial restructuring is basically aimed at optimizing the capital structure of the company. Generally, firms adopt three types of restructuring strategies: downsizing, down scoping, and leveraged buyout (LBO).

Downsizing is a reduction in the number of a firm's employees and sometimes in the number of its operating units. The objective of downsizing is to improve profitability through cost reductions and efficient operations. Downscoping refers to divestitures, spin off or some other means of eliminating businesses that are unrelated to a firm's core businesses. LBO is used as a restructuring strategy whereby a company buys all of a firm's assets in order to take the firm private. In summary corporate restructuring can be classified into portfolio restructuring, financial restructuring and organizational restructuring. Unilever is one of the largest consumer goods companies in the world. In September 1999, the company had announced its plan to restructure its brand portfolio by end of 2004. The plan involved cutting down its unwieldy portfolio of 1600 brands and focusing on top 400 brands. Procter and Gamble was transformed from a structure of four business units based on geographic regions to seven global business units based on product lines.

1.10.1   Mergers and acquisitions

M&As represent a major force in modern financial and economic environment. Acquisitions remain the quickest route companies take to operate in new markets and to add new capabilities and resources. As markets globalize and the pace at which technology change continues to accelerate, more and more companies are finding M&A to be a compelling strategy for growth. M&A, by which two

[3] J.E. Bethel, J. Liebeskind, The effects of ownership structure on corporate restructuring. *Strategic Management Journal*, 1993, 14(Special Summer Issue), 15–31.

[4] A. Campbell, D. Sadtler, Corporate breakups. *Strategy &Business* 1998, 12, 64–73;

E. Bowman, H. Singh, Overview of corporate restructuring: trends and consequences. In: L. Rock, R.H. Rocks (eds.) *Corporate Restructuring*, New York: McGraw Hill, 1990.

companies are combined to achieve certain strategic and business objectives are transactions of great significance not only to the companies themselves but also to all other stakeholders like employees, competitors, communities and the economy. Their success or failure has enormous consequences for shareholders and lenders as well as the above constituents. The Great Merger Movement was a predominantly US business phenomena that happened from 1895 to 1905. This wave followed the 1903–1904 market crash and the First World War. It is estimated that during this wave characterized by the period of economic growth and stock market boom, about 12,000 firms disappeared. The merger activity increased after the end of the Second World War and peaked during the 1960s. The third wave resulted in a massive shift in the business composition of US firms towards greater diversification. This merger period is known as the period of conglomerate merger movement. The 1980s witnessed one of the most intense periods of merger activity in the US economic history. The fourth wave specifically featured the hostile takeover and the corporate raider. This period also witnessed the rapid growth and decline of the LBO—the use of debt capital to finance a buyout of the firm's stock. The fifth wave deals of 1990s are not highly leveraged hostile transactions that were common in the 1980s. They can be categorized as strategic mergers.

A merger is a combination of two companies into one larger company. These actions involve stock swap or cash payment to the target. In a merger the acquiring company takes over the assets and liabilities of the merged company. All the combining companies are dissolved and only the new entity continues to operate.

Acquisitions are more general term enveloping in itself range of acquisition transactions. It could be acquisition of control leading to takeover of company. It could be acquisition of tangible assets, intangible assets, rights and other kind of obligations. They could be independent transactions and may not lead to any kind of takeovers or mergers.

An acquisition also known as a takeover is the buying of one company (the target) by another. An acquisition can be friendly or hostile. In a friendly takeover the companies proceed through negotiations. In the latter case, the takeover target is unwilling to be bought or the target's board has no prior knowledge of the offer. Horizontal mergers take place when two merging companies produce similar product in the same industry. In other words, a horizontal merger occurs when two competitors combine. For example, in 1994 two defense firms Northrop and Grumman combined in a $12.7 billion merger. A vertical merger refers to a firm acquiring a supplier or distributor of one or more of its goods or services These are combinations of companies that have a buyer seller relationship. Vertical mergers occur when two firms, each working at different stages in the production of the same good combine. Vertical mergers take place between firms in different stages of production operation.

Five wealth increasing motivation for M&As[5] can be explained in terms of a) increase in efficiency by creating economies of scale, or by disciplining inefficient

[5] J.T. Severiens, Creating value through mergers and acquisitions: some motivations. *Managerial Finance* 1991, 17(1).

managers b) Exploitation of asymmetric information between acquiring firm managers and acquiring or target firm shareholders c) Solution to agency problems associated with the firm's free cash flow d) Increase of Market power e) Utilization of tax credits. The operating and financial economies of scale and scope are certainly major determinants of merger activity. Mergers occur because when incompetent managers reduce the value of the firm's shares to the point where it is profitable for outsiders to gain control. Mergers then can be viewed as an effective discipline over management.

The operating synergy theory postulates economies of scale or of scope and that mergers help achieve levels of activities at which they are obtained. It includes the concept of complementarity of capabilities. For example, one firm might be strong in R&D but weak in marketing, while another has a strong marketing department without the R&D capability. Merging these two firms may result in operating synergy.

The financial synergy theory hypothesizes complementarities between merging firms in the availability of investment opportunities and internal cash flows. A firm in the declining industry will produce large cash flows since there are few attractive investment opportunities. A growth industry has more investment opportunities than cash with which to finance them. The merged firm will have a lower cost of capital due to lower cost of internal funds as well as possible risk reduction, savings in floatation costs and improvement in capital allocation. The debt capacity of the combined firm can be greater than the sum of the two firm's capacities before the merger and this provides tax savings on investment income.[6]

1.10.1.1 Synergies in mergers

Synergic effect occurs when two substances or factors combine to produce a greater effect together than the sum of those together operating independently. The principle of synergy (2 + 2 = 5) aims to maximize the shareholder value of the merged entity. Synergy is the ability of a merged company to create more shareholder value than standalone entity.

If synergy is perceived to exist in a takeover, the value of the combined firm should be greater than the sum of the values of the bidding and target firms, operating independently.

$$V(AB) > V(A) + V(B)$$

where

    $V(AB)$ = Value of a firm created by combining A and B (Synergy)
    $V(A)$ = Value of firm A, operating independently
    $V(B)$ = Value of firm B, operating independently

[6] J. Fred Weston, K.S. Chung, S.E. Hoag, Mergers, Restructuring and Corporate Control. Prentice Hall, 2006 Edition, pp. 75–79.

Two types of synergy need to be distinguished—cost based and revenue based. Cost based synergy focuses on reducing incurred costs by combining similar assets in the merged businesses. Cost synergy can typically be achieved through economies of scale, particularly when it comes to sales and marketing, administrative, operating, and/or research and development costs. Revenue based synergy focus on enhancing capabilities and revenues, combining complementary competencies. Revenue based synergy can be exploited if merging businesses develop new competencies that allow them to command a price premium through higher innovation capabilities (product innovation, time to market, etc.) or to boost sales volume through increased market coverage (geographic and product line extension).

Operating synergies are those synergies that allow firms to increase their operating income, increase growth or both. Operating synergy results from economies of scale that may arise from the merger, allowing the combined firm to become more cost-efficient and profitable. The sources of operating synergy could be attributed to greater pricing power from reduced competition and higher market share, which should result in higher margins and operating income. The combination of different functional strengths will also result in operating synergy. For example, a firm with a good product line being acquired by a firm with strong marketing skills may result in operating synergy.

Integration planning is one of the most difficult tasks of a successful merger or acquisition. Merger teams must process the information from due diligence and develop an integration process that helps to ensure that merger synergies are resulted. Most successful companies' link effective strategic formulation, pre-merger planning, and post-merger integration. Basically an acquirer integrates five core functions: (1) Information Technology; (2) Research and Development; (3) Procurement; (4) Production and networks; and (5) Sales and Marketing. GE Capital Services acquisition integration process has been codified as the Path Finder Model. The major components of the path finder model are pre acquisition, foundation building, rapid integration and assimilation phase. In the preacquisition phase, emphasis is on cultural compatibility, assessment of strengths/weakness of business and function leaders, development of integration plan by GE, and target acquired company. The rapid integration phase would involve continual assessment of progress and adjustment of the integration plan. The post implementation phase is viewed as the assimilation phase where integration effort is assessed. The integration of business requires those involved with the finance function to identify and safeguard the existing and acquired assets.

1.10.1.2 Research perspectives on M&A success

There are two main research approaches to measure the impact of M&A success. The first method called event studies examines the abnormal returns to shareholders in the period surrounding the announcement of a transaction. The abnormal or excess return is the raw return less a benchmark of what investors required that day, which typically would be the return on a large market index, or the benchmark return specified by the capital asset pricing model. The analysis involving the

Table 1.1 **Biggest blockbuster deals in the world**

Deal	Year value	Value
Vodafone buys Mannesmann	2000	$202.8 billion
AOL mergers with time warner, spun off	2001	$181.6 billion
Altria shareholders spin off Philip Morris	2008	$113 billion
RFS holdings buys ABN Amro Holdings	2007	$98.2 billion
AT&T merges with Bell South	2006	$89.4 billion

difference between return on stock and return on market index is known as market return method. In the market model method, the expected rate of return on security is found using the market model. The model parameters are estimated by regressing daily stock returns on market index over the estimation period. Residual analysis basically tests whether the return to the common stock of individual firm or groups of firms is greater or less than that predicted by general market relationship between return and risk. Event studies yield insights about market based returns to target firm shareholders, buyers and combined entity. The findings of 25 empirical studies show that the M&A transaction delivers a premium return to target firm shareholders. The pattern of findings about market based returns to the buyer firm's shareholders is mixed. The accounting studies examine the reported financial results of acquirers before and after the acquisition to see how financial performance changes. These studies are structured as matched sample comparisons in which acquirers' performance is set against that of nonacquirers of similar size that operate in the same industry. Out of a group of 15 M&A studies on profit margins, growth rates and return on assets, capital and equity, two reported significantly negative post-acquisition performance, four reported significantly positive performances and the rest showed insignificant results. Table 1.1 gives the highlights of the biggest blockbuster deals in corporate history.

1.10.2 Divestitures

Divestitures have been traditionally seen as the opposite of M&As. The 1980s were known as the decades of M&As whereas the 1990s will be known as the decade of divestitures. Divestitures are means through which companies can undo earlier diversification efforts. Divestitures involve selling of assets, product lines, division or subsidiary for cash or stock or both. Divestitures can be used to focus on core areas while disposing of underperforming assets or declining businesses. Alcan of Canada the second largest producer of Aluminum in the world had divested 40 businesses with more than 100 plants worldwide with combined sales of 2.5 billion.

There are number of transactions in divestitures like, spin offs, split offs, split ups, and equity carve outs. Equity Carve out is a method of selling a division in which the parent company creates a new publicly traded company out of one of its division and sells that stock to the public in an Initial Public Offering (IPO).

1.10.2.1   Spin off, split up, and split off

A spin-off involves the pro rata distribution of a controlled corporation's stock to the distributing corporation's shareholders without their surrendering any distributing corporation stock. A spin off occurs when a subsidiary becomes an independent entity. The parent firm distributes shares of the subsidiary to its shareholders through a stock dividend. Mckinsey research[7] have showed that the parent company spin off takes place when the parent company is no longer in the best position to create the greatest value from its business through skills, systems, or synergies. One reason for the 1996 spin-off of EDS from GM was the desire to free EDS from constraints that prevented it from pursuing certain deals. Spin-offs can increase the strategic flexibility of businesses by allowing a subsidiary to form relationships with companies that do not want competitive information to flow to its parent. After being spun off from AT&T, Lucent was better able to do business with international telecommunications companies that perceived its parent as a rival. The Lehman Brothers was formed from the spun off of American Express in 1984. In the year 1997, PepsiCo spun off KFC, Pizza Hut, and Taco Bell into a separate Corporation-Tricon Global Restaurants Inc. The Company spun off 100% of the restaurant unit to stockholders who received shares in the new company. The spin off was aimed at better focus on its Pepsi beverage operations and Frito Lay snack business.

In a split up the existing corporation transfers all assets to two or more new controlled subsidiaries in exchange for subsidiary stock. The parent distributes all stock of each subsidiary to existing shareholders in exchange for all outstanding parent stock and liquidates. In other words, a single company splits into two or more separately run companies. One of the classical examples for split up is the split up of AT&T into four separate units—AT&T Wireless, AT&T Broadband, AT&T Consumer, and AT&T Business. It could be termed as one of the biggest shake up in the US Telecommunications industry since 1984. Another notable example of a split up was the 1995 breakup of ITT into three businesses—diversified industrial, insurance, and hotels and gaming.

A split off is a type of corporate reorganization whereby the stock of a subsidiary is exchanged for shares in a parent company. Split off are basically of two types. In the first type, a corporation transfers part of its assets to a new corporation in exchange for stock of the new corporation. The original corporation then distributes the same stock to its shareholders, who in turn surrender part of their stock in the original corporation. In the second type, a parent company transfers stock of a controlled corporation to its stockholders in redemption of a similar portion of their stock. "Control" refers to the ownership of 80% or more of the corporation whose shares are being distributed. A split-off differs from a Spin off in that the shareholders in a split-off must relinquish their shares of stock in the parent corporation in order to receive shares of the subsidiary corporation whereas the shareholders in

---

[7] P.L. Anslinger, S.J. Klepper, S. Subramaniam, Breaking Up is good to do. Restructuring through spin offs, equity carve outs and tracking stocks can create shareholder value. *The Mckinsey Quarterly*, 1999, 1, 16–27.

a spin-off need not do so. In 1994, five big companies took up the split up route. They included Cooper Industries, Eli Lily, Price/Costco, Viacom, and GM. Viacom announced a split off of its interest in Blockbuster in 2004 whereby Viacom offered its shareholders stock in Blockbuster in exchange for an appropriate amount of Viacom stock. In 2008, Krafts Foods had split off its Post Cereal business. The split-off transaction is in connection with the merger of Cable Holdco, Inc., a wholly owned subsidiary of Kraft that will own certain assets and liabilities of the Post cereals business, and a subsidiary of Ralcorp Holdings.

1.10.2.2   Equity carve out

Equity carve-outs are an IPO of a stake in a subsidiary. Although a carve-out technically is an IPO, economically it is an asset sale to public shareholders as opposed to a single buyer, where the parent firm typically remains a controlling shareholder after the offering[8]. Equity carve out (also known as partial public offering) are transactions in which firm sells a minority interest in the common stock of a previously wholly owned subsidiary. A noted example of a substantial carve-out is DuPont's IPO of Conoco, in October 1998. DuPont raised $4.2 billion for a 30% stake in its subsidiary.

1.10.2.3   Sell off

Asset sell off involves the sale of tangible or intangible assets of a company to generate cash. Normally sell offs are done because the subsidiary doesn't fit into the parent company's core strategy. Sell offs often aims to sharpen the corporate focus by spinning off (or divesting) units which are a poor fit with the remainder of the parent company's operations. Philips sold of its car and audio navigation equipment division to the German Engineering giant Mannesmann in a $760 million deal. In July 2008, Citi had decided to sell seven of its Citi Capital equipment finance business lines to General Electric GE Capital for an undisclosed price.

1.10.3   Leveraged buyout

In general a LBO is defined as the acquisition financed largely by borrowing, of all the stock, or assets of a hitherto public company by a small group of investors. This buying group may be sponsored by buyout specialists (e.g. Kohlberg, Kraves, Robert &Co) or investment bankers that arrange such deals. Once the buy-out group owns the stock, they de-list the firm and make it a private, rather than a publicly traded, company, which is the origin of the term going-private transactions. In an LBO, debt financing typically represent 50% or more of the purchase price. Basically there are four stages in a LBO operation[9]. The first stage of the operation consists of raising the cash required for the buyout and devising a management

---

[8] J.W. Allen, J.J. McConnell, Equity carve-outs and managerial discretion. *Journal of Finance* 1998, 53, 163−186.

[9] J. Fred Weston, et al., Mergers, Restructuring and Corporate Control, Chapter 16, Going Private and Leveraged Buy outs, pp. 400−401.

incentive system. In the second stage of the operation, the organizing sponsor buys all the outstanding shares of the company and takes it private or purchases all the assets of the company. In the third stage, the management tries to increase profits and cash flow by cutting operating costs and changing marketing strategies. In the fourth stage the investor may take the company public again if the company emerges financially stronger. This reverse LBO is affected through public equity offering, referred to as secondary initial public offering (SIPO).

1.10.4 Employee stock option plans

Development of organizational capability based on skill and motivated human resource is a vital source of competitive advantage in business in the context of rapid advances in technology, financial markets and marketing strategies. Broad-based employee stock option plans (ESOPs) are now an option is the norm in high technology companies and are becoming popular in other industries as well, as part of an overall equity compensation strategy.

1.10.5 Strategic alliances/joint ventures

Joint Venture is a type of business combination. Joint venture may be organized as partnership, a corporation or any other form of business organization the participating firms might choose to select. The joint venture has been formed basically for entry strategy. Joint Venture provides a lower risk option of entering a new country. The joint ventures provide opportunity for both the partners to leverage their core strengths and increase the profits. Finance plays an important role in establishing and monitoring strategic alliances. According to Deloitte Research, the number of corporate alliances is growing by as much as 25% each year and now accounts for nearly a third of many companies' revenues and value. Cisco Systems and Fujitsu have a strategic alliance which focusses on delivering value through comprehensive customer focused IT, communications and network-ing solutions. Pharmaceutical giants Astra Zeneca and Bristol Myers Squibb have an alliance to develop and commercialize two compounds for the treatment of Type 2 diabetics. The two companies decided to share the costs and profits equally.

1.11 Value creation through financing[10]

Investment decision is considered as the first among equals. Managers focus more on investment than on financing decisions. Modigliani and Miller showed that in perfect markets, with no corporate taxes, neither dividend policy nor capital structure changes add to the value of the firm. Later Modigliani and Miller showed

[10] M.J. Barclay, C. Smith, The capital structure puzzle, another look at the evidence, Financial Strategy 2nd ed., Wiley, pp. 125–145.

that in the presence of corporate taxes, capital structure did matter. The 1980s and 1990s witnessed dramatic rise in LBOs by companies through rearranging their own capital structure through share repurchases, using debt to repurchase equity and increase leverage. Steward Myers suggested that managers form a pecking order in which retained earnings are preferred to outside financing and debt is preferred to equity when outside funding is required. Myers termed this conflict among different theories as the "capital structure puzzle". Most of the competing theories of optimal capital structure are not mutually exclusive. The corporate financial policy can be categorized into three broad sectors. 1) Taxes 2) Contracting costs 3) information costs. The greatest advantage of debt is the deduction of interest payment. Hence higher debt addition to the company's capital structure lowers its expected tax liability and increases its after tax cash flows. In the context of only corporate profits tax and no individual taxes on corporate securities, the value of the levered firm would be equal to that of an identical all equity firm plus the present value of its interest tax shield. In terms of contracting costs, conventional capital structure analysis holds that financial managers set leverage targets by balancing the tax benefits of higher leverage against the greater probability and hence the higher expected cost of financial distress. The direct expenses associated with the administration of the bankruptcy process appear to be quite small relative to the indirect costs. In scenario of bankruptcy, the underinvestment problem arises in which managers postpone major capital projects, cutbacks in R&D, maintenance and advertising. Information asymmetry between managers and investors have led to the theory of pecking order and signaling. With better information, managers of undervalued companies can raise the share prices by communicating the information to managers. Adding more debt to capital structure may serve as a credible signal of higher future cash flows. Signaling theory suggests that companies are more likely to issue debt than equity when they are undervalued due to large information costs associated with equity offerings. A constructive capital structure theory must include a broad array of corporate financial policy choices which include dividends, compensation hedging and leasing policies.

1.12   Real options strategy

The real options valuation is a dynamic approach to valuation in terms of flexibility and growth opportunities. The real options approach is an extension of financial options theory. Options are contingent decisions that provide an opportunity to make decisions after uncertainty become relevant. A number of strategic decisions can be considered as real options. Investments in computer business, valuation of an aircraft purchase option, development of commercial real estate are all examples for real options before firms. Mining companies might acquire rights to an ore mine which could be turned profitable if the price of products increases. The development of a worn out farmland would become a strategic option for a real estate developer to build a shopping mall if a new highway becomes feasible in the region.[11] The acquisition of patent to market a new drug is a viable strategic option for a pharmaceutical company.

Firms choose projects with positive NPV projects. But managers are prone to reject projects which are very risky even though the NPV is positive. Real options are also used by companies in evaluating investment opportunities and associated risks. The strength of the real option is the value of its flexibility. The flexibility of real options facilitate companies to plan their investment and operating strategies. Unavoidable investment situations can be avoided by waiting.

The value of flexibility of an investment project is basically a collection of real options, which can be valued with the techniques estimated for financial options.

Strategic investment options by pioneering firms like development of technology provides such firms with cost or timing advantage which could lead into value creation. Valuation of a gold mine concession license to develop a mine can be considered as considered as analogous to the valuation of a simple call option. The multistage R&D Investment can be considered as a compound option.

Strategic investments facilitate firms to invest or divest in subsequent periods of time on the basis of new opportunities. Like financial options, these strategic investments provide the firms different options on the future market conditions. These strategic options which are based on value of real assets called strategic real options. Unlike financial options, real options require the purchase the sale or restructuring of the real or nonfinancial assets. These investment opportunities also involve investment in intangibles like Intellectual Property Rights and Patents. Amazon has the ability to adapt rapidly to the digital business environment. Amazon is more than an internet book seller as it delivers a broad range of products to customers. Amazon provided a wide range of IT based business initiatives in collaboration with other firms. Amazon developed the ability to acquire strategic digital options and nurture them by capitalizing on those likely to prove successful while exercising discipline to eliminate nonprofitable ones.

The value of the option is the present value of the expected cash flows plus the value of new growth opportunities. The value of growth options can be estimated as the difference between the total market capitalization of a firm and its capitalized value of its earnings which includes estimated earnings. Growth options are more valuable for small high growth companies which market innovative products. At the time of its IPO, Genentech had revenues of $9 million. The IPO was priced at $35 per share. After listing, its market capitalization value was $262 million which was basically attributed to the value of the growth option.[12]

Real options valuation in R&D Investment projects is mainly applicable in pharmaceutical industry. Regulation also has important effects on the cost of innovation in the pharmaceutical industry. The average span of new drug development is between 10 and 12 years. In US, the average time from discovery to Food and Drug Administration (FDA) approval is around 15 years. The odds of a compound

[11] R.A. Brealey, S.C. Myers, *Journal of Applied Corporate Finance*, 2008, 20(4), 58–71.
[12] W.C. Kester, Today's options for tomorrow's growth, *Harvard Business Review*, 1984, 62(2), 153–160.

making it through this process are around one in 10,000 while the cost of getting it through is around $200 million. The cost of research process is increasing significantly as many of the drugs are focusing on complex and difficult targets.

Real options valuation is applicable in natural resources investment projects. The valuation of mining and other natural resources project have option characteristics since traditional valuation methods are difficult on account of uncertainty of output prices.

Real options have become a truly cross disciplinary area of research with great potential to improve corporate decision making. Real options are used by companies in evaluating investment opportunities and associated risks. The focus on real options is due to its value of flexibility. Managers get the opportunity to plan investment and operating strategies in response to new information over time. Corporate real investment opportunities which appear unprofitable when managerial flexibility is ignored in the evaluation analysis often have positive value when viewed as growth options. In the context of risk and return perspective, the risk profiles of projects often differ on account of the fact that the projects are early stage investments in creating options or later stage expenditures which involve exercising options to complete investment in a project.

The first major area of application was in valuing investments in the exploration and development of natural resource reserves like minerals and energy. The life science industry including pharmaceutical industry along with technology industry have successfully implemented real options.

1.12.1 Dividend strategy

The investment, financing and dividend decisions are the three main pillars of decision making in corporate finance. The dividend principle assumes that when firms don't have enough investments that earn their minimum required return or hurdle rate, then firms have to return the cash generated to the owners in the form of dividends. Basically there are three schools of thoughts on dividend policy. The dividend irrelevance theory advocated by Miller and Modigliani states that dividends do not affect the firm value. This theory is based on the assumption that dividends is not a tax disadvantage for an investor and firms can raise funds in capital markets for new investments without much issuance costs. The proponents of second school assumes that dividends are bad as they have a tax disadvantage for average shareholder and hence value of firm decreases when dividends are paid. Dividends create a tax disadvantage for investors who receive them when they are taxed much more heavily than price appreciation (capital gains). According to this viewpoint, dividend payments should reduce the returns to stockholders after personal taxes. The third school of thought states that dividends are good and can increase the value of the firm. Investors prefer dividends to capital gains since dividends are certain and capital gains are not. Risk averse investors will therefore prefer dividends. The clientele effect suggests that stockholders tend to invest in firms whose dividend policies match their preferences. This clustering of stocks in companies with dividend policies that match their preferences is called the client effect. Dividends also operate as an information signal to financial markets. The empirical evidence concerning price reactions to dividend increases and decreases is consistent at least on average with this signaling theory.

The proportion of firms paying dividends have dropped sharply during the 1980s and 1990s. The major factors which affect companies propensity to pay dividends are profitability, growth and size. Larger and profitable companies tend to pay dividends. High growth companies are less likely to pay dividends. Dividend payers typically have higher measured profitability than nonpayers. It is often stated that firms which have never paid dividends have the strongest growth. Companies like Google and Amazon aggressively invest in future growth initiatives and have never paid dividends. Berkshire Hathway doesn't pay dividends.

1.12.2 Share buyback strategy

In the context of economic recovery, share buyback programs are gaining relevance. Announcements of companies buying back their shares is often seen as a good sign by Wall Street and market investors. Management often goes for share buyback since they believe that their shares are undervalued. Buying back shares of stocks allows the company to reduce the extra cash that it has on its balance sheet. Share buyback is an indirect way of insider buying. Buyback can be perceived more as an investment decision rather than a capital structure or payout decision.

Treasury stock basically captures the cumulative effects of stock repurchases and reissues and is not affected by new issues of stock (seasoned equity offerings).

It is the re acquisition by a company of its own stock. The company can buy shares directly from the market or offer its shareholder the option to tender their shares directly to the company at a fixed price. In 2004, buyback by companies were a hit. In 2015, General Electric announced $50 billion buyback.

In November 2015, German industrial giant Siemens AG announced a new share buyback program as it reported a 33% slide in fourth quarter net profit. According to S&P Capital IQ statistics, in 2014, the companies in the S&P 500 spent over $553 billion for buy back of stocks. In 2007, stock buybacks from S&P 500 companies amounted to $589 billion. In past big buyback programs were announced by Exxon Mobil, General Electric, Intel Corp, IBM, Microsoft, Procter & Gamble. In 2013, Apple issued bonds worth $17 billion to fund the share buyback program amounting to $100 billion.

A buyback's impact on share price comes from changes in a company's capital structure and from the signals the buyback sends. Buyback of shares boosts EPS. However, a company's fixation on buybacks might come at the cost of investments in its long term health. The buyback deconsolidates the firms into two distinct entities: an operating company and one that holds cash.

Markets often react favorably when investors learn that companies don't intend to make unwise acquisition or poor capital expenditure with excess cash and instead buy back shares. Market often responds to announcements of buybacks as they offer new information about a company's future and hence its share price. Management often believes that buyback sends a positive signal that stock is undervalued. Another positive signal that is perceived is that the company doesn't need the cash to cover future commitments such as interest payments and capital expenditures. The negative signal send out to market by buyback may be due to the perception that few investment opportunities exist in future.

Share buybacks are gaining significance due to different factors. Buybacks are more flexible in the context that highly cash generative companies can return cash to investors whenever it is excess and retain the amount if adequate investment opportunities arises. When companies pay dividends, it becomes like a contract and it would be difficult for company to reduce it as stock market react harshly to dividend cuts. Share buybacks also provide flexibility to investors as they can opt to not take part in the program. On the other hand dividends force all share-holders to participate in the cash dividend and thus incur tax. Dividends provides income for shareholders and share buyback provide them capital gains. In many countries capital gains are taxed at a lower rate than income tax. Thus repurchases are more efficient than dividends as a way for returning cash. Buybacks can also lead to reduction in transaction costs.

1.13   IPO strategy

An IPO is the first sale of a company's share to the public and listing of shares on a stock market. It facilitates companies to raise capital to build businesses by creating and selling new shares. Fast growing companies can use IPO as a superior route to fund growth. The feasibility of IPO is a function of factors like business model and management capability, growth potential and market size, financial track record, valuation, shareholder objectives, company life cycle, prospects and position within industry, investor base, and analyst coverage. Other alternatives like sale to a strategic buyer through M&A market, sale to a private equity firm, private placement, joint ventures and strategic alliances are other strategic options before considering an IPO. Timing of IPOs is also crucial for pricing with an optimal valuation. Quality of management is also an important nonfinancial factor when evaluating new offerings. Robot infrastructure can facilitate regulatory compliance and protect against risk exposure. The IPO process takes from four to eight months. The investment banker will handle the details of IPO, facilitate SEC filing and road show where senior management team meets investors prior to the offering and pricing of stock. Most IPOs are backed by an investment banking underwriting guarantee where the investment bank guarantees the offering price in return for an underwriting fee. Underpricing of IPOs is a worldwide phenomenon. Underpricing of IPOs is the frequent incidence of large initial returns due to price changes measured from the offering price to the market price on the first trading accruing to investors in the IPOs of common stock. The average underpricing for IPOs in the US was 14.8% during the period 1990–1998, 51.4 per cent during the period 1999–2000 and 12.1% during the period 2001–2009. Over the last 50 years, the IPOs in the United States have been underpriced by 16.8% on average. The underpricing in China have averaged 137.4% during the period 1990–2010. IPO underpricing occurs due to informational asymmetry. On account of the fact that a more or less fixed number of shares are sold at a fixed offering price, rationing will result if demand is unexpectedly strong. If some investors are more likely to attempt to buy shares, when an issue is underpriced, then the amount of excess demand will be higher when there is more underpricing. The information asymmetry theory assumes that the IPO pricing is a product of information disparities. Uninformed investors bid without considering the quality of IPO. Informed investors bid based on the information of superior returns. In the case of weak IPO only uninformed investors bid and lose money. The underwriters need the uninformed investors to bid since informed investors do not exist in sufficient numbers. In order to solve this problem, the underwriter reprices the IPO to ensure that uninformed investors bid and underpricing results. Another perspective of informational based theory suggest that IPO underpricing is due to informational revelation. This theory is applied to the book building process in which underwriter assess demand and obtain information from potential buyers about the price buyers are willing to pay. In order to incentivize investors to disclose sufficient information about the price, underwriters allocate lesser shares to potential purchasers who bid low. Underpricing can be termed as a dynamic strategy employed by issuing firms to overcome the asymmetry of information between issuing firms and outside investors. A good firm may underprice its issue to attract outside investors. Another perspective is that management allows underpricing to ensure that there are many purchasers of the shares and no large shareholders created as a result of IPO may be incentivized to replace management.

Alibaba Group's staggering IPO of $25 billion was the largest IPO. The company went public on September 18, 2014 at a whopping $21.8 billion. Four days after, underwriters exercised an option to sell more shares bringing the total IPO to $25 billion. Agriculture Bank of China went public on July 7 2010 at an initial offering raising $19.228 billion. The follow on green shoe offerings from underwriter Goldman Sachs Asia brought the total offerings to over $22 billion. Industrial and Commercial Bank of China which went public on October 20, 2006 raised a total of $19.092 billion. NTT, the Tokyo based telecommunication company was listed on Oct 22, 1998 raising $18.099 billion and underwritten by Goldman Sachs Asia. Visa was listed on March 18 2008 and raised $17.86 billion in the public market. AIA, the Hong Kong based investment and insurance company raised $17.816 billion through IPO. Facebook IPO raised $16 billion in the year 2012. It was the largest technological IPO in US history. Facebook IPO was one of the hyped IPOs. After listing the share prices crashed by more than 50 per cent over the next couple of months. It took more than a year for the shares to trade above the $38 listing price. In Nov 2010, General Motors raised $15.77 billion in its IPO after emerging from a bankruptcy filing one year earlier. Nippon Tel, the Tokyo based telecommunication provider raised $15.301 billion during February 1987.

1.14 Risk management

The use of treasury computer systems was made to ensure the correct market valuations and compliance with the risk management controls on market, operational and credit risks. The impact of changes in exchange rates on operating profit expressed in home currency is called operating exposure. In economic terms, the contractual items on the company's balance sheet such as debt, payables and receivables are exposed to changes in exchange rates. The effect of changes in exchange rates on operating profits can be separated into margin effects and volume effects.

Value at risk is a summary statistic which quantifies the exposure of an asset or portfolio to market risk or the risk that a position declines in value. VAR is the method of measuring the financial risk of an asset, portfolio or exposure over some specified period of time. VAR is described as an approximation of the "maximum reasonable loss," a company can expect to realize from all of its financial exposures. Commercial banks use VAR measures to quantify current trading exposures and compare them to establish counterparty risk limits. Credit derivatives are swap, forward and option contracts which transfer risk and return from one counterparty to another without actually transferring the ownership of the underlying assets. The major types of credit derivatives are default swaps, total rate of return swaps and credit spread put options. Default swaps basically transfer the potential loss on a "reference asset" that can result from specific credit events such as default, bankruptcy, insolvency and credit rating downgrades. Default swaps are one of the largest component of the global credit derivatives market. Total rate of return swaps transfers the returns and risks on an underlying reference asset from one party to another. Credit linked notes are securities that effectively embed default swaps within a traditional fixed income structure. In return for a principal payment when the contract is made, they typically pay periodic interest plus, at maturity, the principal minus a contingent payment on the embedded default swap.

1.15 New valuation tools

New primary tools for management to assess are EVA (Economic Value added), Market Value Added (MVA) and CFROI. The new economic tools enable executives to view the entire enterprise and to redeploy assets to generate the greatest yield. The emergence of high tech information exchanges called shared service centers are changing the traditional command and control structure of finance and accounting. Sophisticated systems permit processing of sales, inventory and essential data to be consolidated. EV can be a better predictor of return to shareholders since it takes into account return on capital. EVA concept was developed by Stern Stewart firm. Many companies like Coca Cola, Monsanto and Procter & Gamble have adapted the EVA concept. CFROI was promoted by BCG and HOLT. This ROI measure compares a firm's cash flows with the inflation adjusted capital used to produce them. Stern Stewart proposed the MVA which is a measure of overall corporate value.

The MVA takes into account the total capital of the firm which includes equity, loans and retained earnings and deduct this from the value of its share capital and debt. The TSR is the change in the firm's value over a period of one year plus dividends paid to shareholders, expressed as a percentage of its initial value.

1.16 The balanced score card

The balanced score card is the strategic planning and management system which is used extensively in business and industry to align business activities to the vision and strategy of the organization. The concept of balanced score card was introduced as a performance measurement framework by Kaplan and Norton to add strategic nonfinancial performance measures to traditional financial metrics to give a focused balanced view of organizational performance. The four perspectives in the score-card are financial, customer, internal business processes, and learning and growth. The financial strategy in terms of growth, profitability and risk are viewed from the perspective of the shareholder. The customer perspective focuses on creating value and differentiation from the perspective of the customer. The internal business process emphasizes the strategic priorities for various business processes that create customer and shareholder satisfaction. The learning and growth perspective provides the priorities to create a climate that supports organizational change, innovation and growth. Companies increase EV through revenue growth and productivity. Customer value proposition is the core of any business strategy which highlights the unique mix of product, price, service, relationship, and image of the company. Companies differentiate their value proposition by selecting among operational excellence, customer intimacy and product leadership. Mc Donald and Dell Computers were known for operational excellence. Intel and Sony were known for their product leadership.[13]

1.17 Governance and ethics

Corporate governance refers to both the structure and relationships which determine corporate direction and performance. The board of directors is the central pillar to the corporate governance structure. Shareholders and management are the other pillars of the system. The other participants include employees, customers, suppliers and creditors. The corporate governance framework also involves the legal, regulatory, institutional and ethical environment. The modern management is focused on governance practices. Corporate governance refers to broad range of policies and practices which stockholders, executive managers

[13] R.S. Kaplan, D.P. Norton, Transforming the balanced scorecard from performance measurement to strategic management, *Accounting Horizons*, 2001, 15(1), 87–104.

and board of directors use to manage themselves and fulfill their responsibilities to investors and other stakeholders. Corporate governance has been the subject of increasing stakeholder attention and scrutiny. Shareholder activists composed of large institutional investors, socially responsible investment groups uses a variety of vehicles to influence board behavior which includes creating corporate governance standards and filing shareholder resolutions. The topics of importance include board diversity, independence, compensation, accountability. The other areas of importance include social issues like employment ethics practices, environmental policies and community involvement. Ethics is at the core of corporate governance. The management must reflect accountability for their actions on a global community scale. It is found that corporate ethics and shareholder desires for profitability are not always aligned. It is the responsibility of management to ensure ethics supersede profitability. In the simplest form, corporate ethics is a legal matter. Abiding by laws protecting workers rights and appropriate compensation is a top priority for management.[14]

1.18   Corporate social responsibility

Corporate responsibility refers to fulfilling the responsibilities or obligations that a company has toward its stakeholders. Corporate responsibility facilitate to distinguish between a stakeholder expectation and corporate obligation. Issues like profit maximization at the cost of environment are topics of concern in corporate social responsibility (CSR). CSR stress upon the obligations the company has towards community with respect to charitable activities and environmental stewardship. Socially responsible business practices strengthen corporate accountability with focus on ethical values in the interest of all stakeholders. Socially responsible business practices empower people and invest in communities where business operates. Corporate sustainability is aligning an organization's products and services with stakeholder expectations and in the process creating economic, environmental and social value. CSR meant a commitment to developing policies which integrate practices into daily business operations and report the progress made towards implementing these practices. Earlier CSR activities focused on philanthropy as the driver of CSR. The concept of CSR now focuses on addressing issues related to governance and ethics; worker hiring, opportunity and training, purchasing and supply chain policies, energy, and environmental impact. The emphasis of CSR has been on social, environmental, and economic sustainability.

[14] Boundless. "The Challenge of Ethics and Governance." *Boundless Management*. Boundless, 21 Jul. 2015. Retrieved 15 Dec. 2015. Available from: https://www.boundless.com/management/textbooks/boundless-management-textbook/introduction-to-management-1/current-challenges-in-management-21/the-challenge-of-ethics-and-governance-134-10569/.

References

[1] T. Sheridan, A new frame for financial management. *Management Accounting: Magazine for Chartered Management Accountants*, 1994, 72(2), 00251682.

[2] R. Mills, Strategic value analysis: linking finance and strategy. *Management Accounting: Magazine for Chartered Management Accountants*, 1995, 73(4), 00251682.

[3] L.D. Goodstein, J.W. Pfeiffer, T.M. Nolan, Applied strategic planning: A new model for organizational growth and vitality, in: J.W. Pfeiffer (Ed.), Strategic planning: selected readings, University Associates, Inc, San Diego, CA, 1986, pp. 1–25.

[4] F.W. Gluck, S.P. Kaufman, A.S. Walleck, Strategic management for competitive advantage, Harvard Business Review 58 (5) (1980) 154–164.

[5] B. Taylor, An overview of strategic planning styles, in: W.R. King,, D.I. Cleland (Eds.), Strategic planning and management handbook, Van Nostrand Reinhold Co, New York, 1987, pp. 21–35.

[6] M.E. Porter, M.R. Kramer, Creating Shared Value, Harvard Business Review 89 (1/2) (2011) 62–77.

Further reading

[1] J.R. Squires, A paradigm for teaching strategic planning in the finance case course. *Journal of Education for Business*, 1991, 66(1), 08832323.

[2] R. Dobbs, W. Rehm, The value of share buybacks, Mckinsey Quarterly, 2005 Available from: http://www.mckinsey.com/insights/corporate_finance/the_value_of_share_buybacks.

[3] Companies With the Largest Stock Buybacks of All Time − General Electric Company (NYSE:GE) - 24/7 Wall St. Available from: http://247wallst.com/investing/2015/04/13/companies-with-the-largest-stock-buybacks-of-all-time/#ixzz3rXprwpYu.

[4] N.A. Ronald, J. Lawrence, C. Suzanne, Making the deal real: how GE capital integrates acquisitions., Harvard Business Review 76 (1) (1998) 165–170.

Wealth creation by Coca-Cola—a strategic perspective

2.1 Introduction

Coca-Cola had its origin in downtown Atlanta, Georgia in 1886. Coca-Cola Company is the world's largest beverage company. Coca-Cola is one of the most valuable and recognizable brands in the world. The company's portfolio features 20 billion dollar brands. The major brands of Coca-Cola include Diet Coke, Fanta, Sprite, Coca-Cola Zero, vitamin water, POWERADE, Minute Maid, Simply, Georgia, Dasani, FUZE TEA, and Del Valle. Coca-Cola is the world's largest provider of sparkling beverages, ready to drink coffees, juices, and juice drinks. Coca-Cola has the largest beverage distribution system in the world serving consumers in more than 200 countries. Coca-Cola offers beverages at a rate of 1.9 billon servings a day. Coca-Cola along with its nearly 250 bottling partners rank among the world's largest 10 private employers with more than 700,000 system associates. Coca-Cola own and market four of the world's top five nonalcoholic sparkling beverage brands namely Coca-Cola, Diet Coke, Fanta, and Sprite. Finished beverage products with trademarks, sold in the United States since 1886, are now sold in more than 200 countries. Coca-Cola owns or licenses and market more than 500 nonalcoholic beverages brands which are mostly sparkling beverages and variety of still beverages such as waters, enhanced waters, juices and juice drinks, ready to drink teas and coffees and energy and sports drinks.

It can be said that if all the Coca-Cola ever produced were to cascade down Niagara Falls at its normal rate of 1.6 million gallons per second, it would flow for nearly 83 hours.[1] Coca-Cola is one of the most-admired and best-known trademarks in the world. If all the Coca-Cola ever produced were in eight-ounce contour bottles, and these bottles were laid end to end, they would reach to the moon and back 2051 times. Consumers use Coca-Cola company products 1.7 billion times every single day which amounts to 19,400 beverages every second. Coca-Cola has the strongest portfolio of brands in the nonalcoholic beverage industry with 20 brands which generate more than $1 billion in annual retail sales. In year 2014, company owned bottlers represented 26% of bottling operations globally in terms of unit case volume. The 10 largest bottling partners including CCR and BIG represented nearly 70% of global volume. The company employed approximately 130,600 and 129,200 employees in 2013 and 2014, respectively.[2]

---

[1] Coca-Cola website.
[2] Coca-Cola Annual Report 2015.

The Coca-Cola Company manufactures and sells concentrates, beverage bases and syrups to the bottling partners. The bottling partners manufacture, package, merchandise and distribute the final branded beverages to the customers and vending partners. The finished product operations of Coca-Cola consist of sparkling beverages, still beverages like juices and juice drinks, energy and sports drinks, ready to drink teas and coffees, and certain water products. In United States, Coca-Cola manufacture fountain syrups and sell them to fountain retailers such as restaurants and convenience stores who uses the fountain syrups to produce beverages for current consumption. Water is the main ingredient of Coca-Cola products. The other principal raw materials are nutritive and nonnutritive sweeteners. The principal nutritive sweetener is high fructose corn syrup which is nutritionally equivalent to sugar. The principal nonnutritive sweeteners used are aspartame, acesulfame potassium, saccharin, cyclamate, and sucralose.

2.1.1 Timelines

Year	Milestones
1886	On May 8, 1886, Coca-Cola was created by John S. Pemberton and served at Jacobs' Pharmacy. Nine drinks a day are sold during this year
1887	Coca-Cola registers "Coca-Cola Syrup and Extract" label as a copyright with the U.S. Patent Office
1892	Asa Candler which initiated the acquisition of the Coca-Cola Company in 1888, acquired the company and incorporated the Coca-Cola Company as a Georgia Corporation
1893	The company paid first dividend to investors at the Company's second annual meeting
1900	The second bottling plant began production under the 1899 contract opened in Atlanta
1904	Annual sales of Coca-Cola reached the one million-gallon mark
1906	Bottling operations begin in Canada, Cuba, and Panama
1911	The annual advertising budget for The Coca-Cola Company surpasses $1 million for the first time
1912	Coca-Cola expands into Asia with bottling operations in Philippines
1919	Coca-Cola establishes the first bottling plants in Europe in Paris and Bordeaux. The Coca-Cola Company is purchased by a group of investors led by Ernest Woodruff for $25 million
1923	The introduction of the first six-bottle carton is a significant innovation for the beverage industry. The carton is patented the following year
1930	The Coca-Cola Export Corporation was established to market Coca-Cola outside the United States
1941	The first paper cups for Coca-Cola are introduced
1945	"Coke" becomes a registered trademark of The Coca-Cola Company
1950	Coca-Cola becomes the first product to appear on the cover of Time magazine
1955	King size bottles were introduced in the United States in addition to the standard 6.5 ounce bottles. Consumers could now purchase Coke in 10-, 12-, and 26 ounce bottles

Year	Milestones
1956	McCann-Erickson, Inc., replaces the D'Arcy Advertising Company as the official advertising agency for the Company
1957	Sales outside the United States accounted for about 33% of revenue
1960	The Coca-Cola Company acquires The Minute Maid Corporation, which dealt with a line of juice products
1961	Coca-Cola celebrates its 75th Anniversary. New lemon lime beverage is introduced
1963	The first diet drink TaB is introduced
	The advertising campaign "Things Go Better with Coke "advertising campaign begins
1970	Coca-Cola introduces its first sports drink in the United States
1972	The first bottling operations open in Poland
1978	Coca-Cola reenter the China market after a nearly 30-year absence. Hi-C soft drinks are introduced
1980	Diet Coke is introduced as the first extension of the trademarks Coca-Cola and Coke
1982	The Coca-Cola Company purchases Columbia Pictures Industries, Inc.
1985	Coca-Cola begins operation in Russia. The formula for Coca-Cola is changed for the first time in 99 years
	Coca-Cola becomes the first soft drink to be consumed by astronauts abroad the space shuttle Challenger
1986	Marks hundredth anniversary of Coca-Cola
1989	The Company sells Columbia Pictures
1993	The Company reenters India after leaving the country in 1977 when the company refused to reveal the secret formula of Coca-Cola
1995	The Coca-Cola Company acquires the Barq's root beer brand
1996	Coca-Cola creates Coca-Cola Olympic City as part of Centennial Olympic Games in Atlanta
1998	The Coca-Cola Company enters into a 100-year partnership with the NationalBasketball Association
1999	The Coca-Cola Company acquires Peruvian soft drink Inca Kola and Schweppes beverages
2000	The Coca-Cola Company sponsors the Olympic Games in Sydney, Australia
2001	The Coca-Cola Company and Nestle establish a new company, Beverage Partners Worldwide, to market ready to-serve coffee and tea beverages
	Coca-Cola introduces a not—from-concentrate orange juice named Simply Orange
	The Coca-Cola Company acquires Odwalla Inc., a producer of premium refrigerated fruit beverage
2002	Vanilla Coke is introduced in the United States
2004	Diet Coke with Lime is introduced
2005	Coca-Cola Zero, a zero-calorie cola, is introduced in the market
2006	Coca-Cola establishes the Bottling Investments Group to manage the operations of company owned bottling plants around the world
2008	Sprite becomes the third company product to cross sales over two billion cases after Coca-Cola and Diet Coke/Coca-Cola light
2009	Simply becomes a billion-dollar brand
2010	The Coca-Cola Company acquires the entire North American bottling operations of Coca-Cola Enterprises
2011	The Coca-Cola Company celebrates 125 years of brand Coca-Cola

Source: Coca-Cola_125_years_booklet.pdf.

Company registered net operating income of $46 billion in year 2014. The net income amounted to $7.1 billion. The company paid $8 billion as returns to shareholders in the form of dividends and share repurchases in year 2014. As of year 2015, Coca-Cola offered 53 consecutive years of dividend increases.[3]

The worldwide unit case volume mix geographically composed of 20% North America, 29% of Latin America, 13% of Europe, 16% of Eurasia and Africa and 22% Asia Pacific. Coca-Cola is among the top most admired company ranked by Fortune 2015. The company offers 3600 plus products throughout the world. The company has 23 million customer outlets throughout the world. The company has invested $60 billion along with partners since the year 2010.

2.2 Growth strategies

By 1899, the Coca Company started franchised bottling operations in the United States and in 1906, the operations were expanded internationally.

The Company envisages its 2020 Vision document as a roadmap for doubling revenues in the decade with the focus on key areas of profit, people, portfolio, and partners. Coca-Cola have more than 500 brands and more than 3600 beverage products which include more than 1000 low and no calorie products, new product offerings.

Coca had focused on its marketing efforts as a part of advertising strategies. In 1887 Coca-Cola introduced its first marketing efforts through coupons which promoted free samples of beverages. Later initiatives like newspaper advertising, distribution of promotion items bearing the Coca-Cola script to participating pharmacies were introduced. The advertising campaign was focused to create a brand connected with fun, friends and good times. In the 1970s, the company focused on such popular advertising campaigns like "I'd Like to Buy the World a Coke," and "Have a Coke and a Smile." The 1980s featured slogans like Coke is It!," "Catch the Wave" and "Can't Beat the Feeling." In 1993, the popular campaign "Always Coca-Cola" campaign was launched in a series of advertisements featuring animated polar bears. In 2009, "the Open Happiness" Campaign was introduced globally. The "Open Happiness" message was spread out in stores, billboards, TV spots and printed advertising along with digital and music components. The open happiness theme was featured in the Vancouver Olympic Games which was followed by a 2010 social media extension initiative wherein three happiness ambassadors travel to 206 countries in 365 days with the mission to determine what makes people happy.

The Coca-Cola Company's core is the production, marketing, and selling of the beverages. The Bottling Investments Group (BIG) is the central part of the Coca-Cola System. BIG had been strategically investing in select bottling operations. BIG operates in five continents and employs more than 100,000 people. BIG have

[3] http://www.coca-colacompany.com/our-company/infographic-coca-cola-at-a-glance/.

an operating income margin of ten percent over the past ten years. BIG manages bottling operations in 19 markets which represent more than 25% of the system volume. BIG is the largest global bottler for the Coca-Cola company. BIG through a strategic framework implemented key strategic initiatives in supply chain, sales, revenue and profit generation. In 2010, Coca-Cola Company acquired the former North American business of Coca-Cola Enterprises (CCE) Inc. Coca-Cola company had also entered into an agreement with Dr. Pepper Snapple Group to distribute certain DPSG brands in territories where DPSG brands had been distributed by CCE prior to the CCE transaction.

The optimal menu of company product offerings is determined by consumer demand which varies from place to place. Coca-Cola company business strategy focuses on building its existing brands and broadening of is family of brands, products, and services. The factors which affect unit case volume and concentrate sales volume are seasonal fluctuations, bottlers inventory practices, supply point changes, timing of price increases, new product introductions and changes in product mix.[4] One of the unique strength of Coca-Cola's strategy is that the Coca-Cola system is the world's largest beverage distribution system which involves making the branded beverage products available to consumers in more than 200 countries through the network of company owned or controlled bottling and distribution operations as well as independent bottling partners, distributors and retailers. The Coca-Cola system sold 28.6 billion, 28.2 billion, and 27.7 billion unit cases of products in the year 2014, 2013, and 2012, respectively. Sparkling beverages comprised of 73%, 74%, and 75% of the worldwide unit case volume[5] for Coca-Cola during the period 2014, 2013, and 2012, respectively. Trademark Coca-Cola beverages accounted for 46%, 47%, and 48% of the worldwide unit case volume for Coca-Cola during the period 2014, 2013, and 2012, respectively.[6]

The operating segments of Coca-Cola are classified into the following groups: Eurasia and Africa; Europe; Latin America; North America; Asia Pacific; Bottling Investments and Corporate. Generally finished product operations have higher net operating revenues but lower gross profit margins than concentrate operations.

In 2014, the unit case volume outside the United States represented 81% of the company's worldwide unit case volume for the year 2014. The countries outside the United States which contributed to maximum unit case volumes were Mexico, China, Brazil, and Japan which accounted for 31% of the Worldwide unit case volume of Coca-Cola.

Coca-Cola have separate agreements with bottling partners with respect to manufacture and sale of company products. The bottlers are required to purchase its entire requirement of concentrates or syrups for the designated company trademark

---

[4] 2014 Annual Report.

[5] Unit case volume means the number of unit cases (or unit case equivalents) of company beverage products directly or indirectly sold by the Company and its bottling partners (the "Coca-Cola system") to customers. Unit case volume primarily consists of beverage products bearing Company trademarks.

[6] Annual Report 2014.

beverages from the company or company authorized suppliers. The company has implemented an incidence based pricing model for sparkling and still beverages in which the concentrate price charged is impacted by a number of factors which include bottler pricing, channels in which the finished products are sold and package mix.

The core capabilities of Coca-Cola are consumer marketing, commercial leadership, franchise leadership, bottling and distribution operations. Successful marketing investments basically aims to produce long-term growth in unit case volume, per capital consumption and worldwide share of nonalcoholic beverage sales. The marketing strategies is also aimed to drive volume growth in emerging markets and increase of brand value in developed markets. Most of the company beverage products are manufactured, sold and distributed by independent bottling partners. The company also focuses on acquiring bottlers in underperforming markets.

The company focuses on global initiatives to fight obesity by offering low or no calorie beverage options and other initiatives like no advertising to children under 12. The company has a robust water stewardship and management program.

The safety and quality compliance are maintained through unannounced audits of the manufacturing facilities around the world. The Supplier Management Program is designed to identify and assess potential supplier risk. It provides assurance and documentation that the suppliers are capable of consistently providing ingredients and packaging materials that meet the company's stringent specifications.

In February 2012, the Company announced a four-year productivity and reinvestment program. This program was designed to strengthen the brands and reinvest the resources to drive long-term profitable growth. The first component of this program is a global productivity initiative that will target annualized productivity of $350 million to $400 million. This initiative focuses on four primary areas: global supply chain optimization; global marketing and innovation effectiveness; operating expense leverage and operational excellence; and data and information technology systems standardization. The second component of the productivity and reinvestment program relates to additional integration initiative in North America on account of acquisition of CCE's former North America business. The company expects that the expanded productivity initiatives will generate incremental $2 billion in annualized productivity. The expansion of productivity initiatives focuses on key areas of restructuring the company's global supply chain which includes manufacturing in North America; implementing zero based budgeting and streamlining the company's operating model.

The nonalcoholic beverage segment of the commercial beverage industry is highly competitive. PepsiCo is one of the major competitor for Coca-Cola. The other competitors include Nestle, DPSG, Group Danone, Mondele-z International Inc., Kraft Foods Group, Suntory Beverage and Food Ltd. and Unilever Group. The major strength of Coca-Cola are its leading brands, worldwide network of bottlers and distributors of company products Table 2.1 provides the highlights of major brands of Coca Cola.

Table 2.1 **Billion dollar brands of Coca-Cola**

SL	Brands	Highlights
1	Coca-Cola	Introduced in year 1886 by Dr John S Pemberton and patented in year 1887. It is the most popular and biggest selling soft drink in history
2	Fanta	Fanta was introduced in year 1940 and is the second oldest brand of Coca-Cola. Fanta Orange is the leading flavor in the brand
3	Sprite	Sprite was introduced in year 1961. It is the world's leading lemon lime flavored drink. It ranks as the number 3 soft drink worldwide and is sold in more than 200 countries
4	Diet Coke/Coca-Cola light	Diet Coke is a sugar and calorie free soft drink introduced in year 1982. It uses the Coca-Cola Trademark. The brand is sold in more than 185 markets globally
5	Coca-Cola Zero	The Coke Zero (Sugar Zero) which was launched in year 2005 obtained billion dollar sales target in year 2007
6	Minute Maid	Minute Maid was acquired from Minute Maid Corporation in year 1960 by Coca-Cola
7	Georgia Coffee	Georgia Coffee is the No. 1 ready to drink coffee introduced in Japan in 1975. It includes more than 100 varieties of cold and hot coffees sold in Japan. The brand has been expanded to other Asian markets like China, South Korea, Singapore, and India
8	Powerade	Sport drinks which contains carbohydrates and electrolytes
9	Del Valle	Acquired by Coca-Cola Company in year 2007. The brand has a diverse juice portfolio which ranges from 100% juices and nectars to juice drinks
10	Schweppes	The mineral water brand is owned by The Coca-Cola Company in more than 100 countries except in the United States, Canada, Mexico, Australia, and other European Union Countries
11	Aquarius	Aquarius was launched in Japan and is the number one selling sports drink in the Japan
12	Minute Maid Pulpy	The brand was launched in China in year 2005
13	Dasani	Dasani is purified water brand enhanced with minerals. Launched in year 1999. Dasani is distributed in Plant Bottle made up of 30% plant based materials
14	Simply	Simply brand offers premium, not from concentrate 100% juices as well as variety of juice drinks. The juices have no added preservatives or artificial flavors. The product was launched in year 2001. Available in the United States and Canada
15	Glacéau	Glacéau vitaminwater provides range of flavored waters with added vitamins and minerals. Coca-Cola company acquired vitamin water in 2007

(Continued)

Table 2.1 **(Continued)**

SL	Brands	Highlights
16	BonAqua	BonAqua brand provides water with enhanced minerals. The major markets for BonAqua are Russia, Hong Kong, South Africa, Germany, and Azerbaijan
17	Ayataka	Ayataka Green tea was introduced in year 2007 and achieved billion dollar status in year 2012
18	Gold Peak	This ready to drink iced tea brand was introduced in the United States in year 2006
19	I Lohas	I Lohas is the number 1 natural mineral brand sold in Japan which was launched in year 2009
20	Fuze Tea	It was the first global tea brand from the Coca-Cola Company. It was introduced in 14 countries during the year 2012. Presently the brand has presence in 40 markets, making it one of the fastest brands of Coca-Cola to reach billion-dollar status

2.3 Challenges

Increased public concern about the health problems associated with obesity may affect demand for some of the Coca-Cola products. Coca-Cola also face the challenge of quality water scarcity in future due to unprecedented challenges from overexploitation of water for consumer and industrial products. The beverage industry is witnessing trends of consolidation in the retail channel particularly in the markets of Europe and the United States. The Coca-Cola system's profitability may be affected if large retailers seek lower prices and bottling partners may demand increased marketing or promotional expenditures. The fluctuations in exchange rates may also impact Coca-Cola's profitability. With respect to debt financing, changes in interest rates will adversely affect the company's cash flows. The company uses derivative financial instruments to reduce the exposure to interest rate risks. The company's profitability could also be affected by introduction of numerous duties like import duties, excise duties, sales or value added taxes on sugar sweetened beverages, property taxes and payroll taxes by local or state governments. Net operating revenue growth rates are impacted by sales volume; structural changes; price, product and geographic mix; and foreign currency fluctuations.

2.4 Corporate social responsibility activities[7]

Coca have joint United Nations Program on HIV/AIDS termed UNAIDS. Coca-Cola Foundation and Coca-Cola bottlers contribute $12 million in disaster relief following the September 11 terrorist attacks in the United States. In 2014, the company

[7] Source: 2014/2015 Sustainability Report Coca Cola.

supported more than 330 active healthy living programs in 112 markets. The company had introduced more than 400 beverage options of which 100 are reduced low or no calorie. In 77 countries, low or no calorie products are introduced which represent 20% of the local product portfolio. Based on responsible marketing policy, Coca-Cola do not buy advertising placements that target children defined as audiences with 35% or more of viewers under the age of 12. The Coca-Cola Foundation was awarded nearly $22 million to support nutrition and physical activity programs in 40 countries across the global system. In support of FIFA World Cup, overall 376 games were played in 55 countries and more than 5600 associates participated as team members or active supporters. Coca-Cola Foundation offered $1 million as unrestricted grant to EIN'S new OPEN Project which will advance 13 community based initiatives in Europe. The product manufacturing and distribution policies, requirements and specifications are managed through the integrated quality management program called the Coca-Cola Operating Requirements (KORE). 5by20 initiative is aimed to enable the economic empowerment of five million women entrepreneurs throughout the Coca-Cola Value Chain by 2020. In 2014, the company enabled approximately 313,000 women, making a total of nearly 865,000 since 2010. In December 2014, Coca-Cola became the first consumer goods company to join Better Than Cash Alliance which advocates for the transition from cash to digital payments in order to achieve inclusive growth and reduce poverty. In 2011, the Coca-Cola Company formally endorsed the United Nations Guiding Principles on Business and Human Rights. The Coca-Cola Africa Foundation committed $30 million to improve safe access to drinking water to two million African people by year 2015. The Coca-Cola System have contributed more than $1.25 million to the Ebola response and relief efforts in West Africa. The company aims to improve access to medical supplies through "Project Last Mile." The Project Last Mile partners consisting of Coca-Cola Company and its Foundations, USAID, the Global Fund and the Bill & Gates Foundation committed more than $21 million over five years to implement Project Last Mile in African Countries.

The company contributed 1.3% which amounted to $126 million in communities worldwide in 2014. In terms of charitable contributions, 28% of funds were allotted to Water Stewardship, 26% to health initiatives and 23% to education in year 2014. During the period 2005−2014, through 209 community water partnership projects in 61 countries, the company balanced an estimated 94% of the equivalent amount of water used in the finished beverages estimated on 2014 sales volume. This totaled approximately 153.6 billion liters of water replenished to communities and nature. Approximately 12.4% of the packaging materials are currently made with recycled or renewable material. With respect to climate protection, Coca-Cola aims to reduce the carbon footprint of the "drink in your hand" by 25% by the year 2020. The company have plans to reduce greenhouse gas emissions across the value chain by making changes in manufacturing processes, packaging formats, delivery fleet, refrigeration equipment and ingredient sourcing. The Behavior based Energy Efficiency (BEE) of the company aims to transform energy management practices at 900 manufacturing sites. The Company's Sustainable Agriculture Guiding Principles (SAGP) focuses on sustainable methods of sourcing and lay out expectations for suppliers in the areas of human and workplace rights, environmental stewardship and responsible farm management.

2.4.1 Strategic alliances

In February 2014, Coca-Cola entered into a 10-year global strategic agreement with Green Mountain Coffee Roasters for the introduction of global brand portfolio for use in Keurig's at home beverage system. Coca-Cola provide marketing support for the sales of other nonalcoholic beverage brands through licenses, joint ventures and strategic partnerships. The company produces and/or distribute certain other third party brands like DPSG brands in designated territories. Coca-Cola company also have a joint venture with Nestle SA named Beverage Partners Worldwide (BPW) which markets and distributes Nestea products (ready to drink tea) in Europe, Canada and Australia on basis of agreement with the bottlers. This 50:50 joint venture was established in year 2001. This joint venture was created to focus in markets of Europe and Canada. In Taiwan and Hong Kong, the Coca-Cola Company entered into a license agreement with Nestle for the Nestea brand. Nestlé and The Coca-Cola Company also cooperated in a joint venture called Coca-Cola and Nestlé Refreshments.

Coca-Cola have a strategic partnership with Aujan Industries Company, one of the largest independent beverage companies in the Middle East. Coca-Cola distributes certain brands of Monster Beverage Corporation basically Monster Energy in designated territories in the United states and Canada. Coca-Cola entered into a definitive agreement with Monster for long-term strategic relationship in global energy drink market in the year 2014.

2.4.2 Acquisitions

In 1960, Minute Maid was acquired by Coca-Cola. During this time, Minute Maid has expanded into orange juices and also marketed the Hi C line of canned fruit drinks. In 1982, the Coca-Cola company entered into an agreement to acquire Columbia Pictures Industries in a $750 million transaction. In previous years, Coke had diversified into fields like ocean farming and orange groves. The offer called for a payment of $74 a share in cash and stock which was twice the current value of the stock for Columbia's 10.7 million shares outstanding. Coke spun off its entertainment holdings and sold it to Tri Star Pictures for $3.1 billion. In the new entity named Columbia Pictures Entertainment Inc, Coke had 49% ownership. The root beer brand of the Barq was acquired by the Coca-Cola company in year 1995. Coca-Cola had also acquired Ica Kola in Peru, Maaza, Thums Up and Limca in India. In 1998, Coca-Cola company acquired Cadbury Schweppes beverage brands in more than 120 countries around the world in for approximately $1.85 billion. The brands acquired included Schweppes and Canada Dry mixers, Dr. Pepper, Crush, and other regional brands. The transactions did not apply to the the the United States, France and South Africa. In 1999, Coca-Cola purchased 50% of the shares of Inca Kola for $200 million and subsequently took control of overseas marketing and production for the brand. The Lindley Corporation was permitted to retain ownership of the soft drink within Peru. Coca-Cola had adopted a defensive strategy through acquisition of Inca Kola. Instead of trying to ruin the brand or do away with it, Coca-Cola allied itself with Inca Kola. In 1993, Coke Cola bought Parle's four leading soft drinks Thums Up, Limca, Gold Spot, and Maaza. In India, these acquisitions gave Coca-Cola an instant 60% share of Indian soft drinks market. At that time, PepsiCo had less than 30% market share in Indian market. Thums Up was the largest selling soft drink in India.

In 2001, Coca-Cola acquired Odwalla Inc, a producer of premium refrigerated juices and other products for about $181 million and the assumption of about $5 million in debt. Coca-Cola paid $15.25 for each Odwalla shares which included 11 million shares outstanding and 1.7 million shares to options. Odwalla became the unit of Coca-Cola's juice division Minute Maid. The acquisition gave Coca-Cola a strong foot hold in the super premium chilled juice category. In 2007, Jugos Del Valle, the leading juice company in the Latin American region was acquired in a joint venture by the Coca-Cola Company and Coca-Cola FEMSA, with further participation in the joint venture by an additional 12 bottlers in Mexico. In the same year the Coca-Cola Company bought Glaceau, the maker of Vitaminwater for $4.2 billion in cash. The acquisition of these energy brands enabled Coca-Cola to upgrade its portfolio of noncarbonated beverages. In 2015, Coca-Cola acquired 30% minority stake in the organic cold pressed juice maker Suja Life. By 2011, Vitaminwater grew from $350 million in annual revenues to more than $1 billion. Del Valle sales also grew to $1 billion by year 2010. During the period 2012, Coca-Cola had acquired Sacramento Coca Bottling Co and bottling operations in Vietnam, Cambodia and Guatemala.

2.5 Ownership structure

In February 2015, there were 232,496 shareowner accounts of record. Currently equity composed of 36 per cent and debt comprised 64% of the capital structure. Financial Institutions held approximately 68% of the ownership structure while the mutual funds held 31% and promoters held approximately one per cent of the equity ownership of the company. The top ten funds held approximately 9 per cent of the total shares while the top ten financial institutions 32.8% of the total shares Tables 2.2–2.3 gives the details of equity ownership of major funds and financial institutions in Coca Cola.

Table 2.2 Top major funds

SL	Fund	Percent of share held
1	Vanguard Total Stock Market Index	1.62
2	VA CollegeAmerica WA Mutual 529B	1.32
3	Vanguard 500 Index Inv	1.08
4	Vanguard Institutional Index I	0.97
5	SPDR S&P 500 ETF	0.90

Table 2.3 **Top financial institutions**

SL	Financial institutions	Percent of share held
1	Berkshire Hathaway Inc	9.20
2	Vanguard Group Inc	5.88
3	Capital World Investors	3.77
4	State Street Corp	3.71
5	BlackRock Fund Advisors	2.63

2.6 Stakeholder engagement, business ethics, and governance[8]

Effective and ongoing stakeholder engagement is a core component of the business and sustainability. The Coca-Cola Company uses Golden Triangle partnership for stakeholder engagement with focus on public, private and civil sectors. The foundations of corporate governance approach are laid out in the company's certificate of incorporation, By-Laws and Corporate Governance Guidelines. The Board serves as the ultimate decision-making body of the Company. The Board currently have 15 members of which 14 are not employees of Coca-Cola Company. Out of 15 members 11 are men and four are women. The Board implements its risk oversight function both as a whole and through delegation to Board Committees. The company has published a code of business conduct for NonEmployee Directors and Other Directors. The company has also published the Supplier Code of Business Conduct and Supplier Guiding Principles on how suppliers are expected to conduct businesses. With respect to Public engagement, the Coca-Cola Company and its Political Action Committees comply with US laws regarding contribution to political organization. In 2013, the coke company was the first company to sign an anticorruption Memorandum of Understanding with Government of Cambodia. With respect to sustainability the company draws guidance from three prominent frameworks namely Millennium Development Goals, the United Nations Global Compact (UNGC) and the UNGC CEO Water Mandate.

2.7 Financial highlights

The Table 2.4 compares the five-year cumulative total return among the Coca-Cola Company, Peer Group Index and the S&P 500 Index as of December 31st of the period of analysis. The total return specified is stock price plus the reinvested dividend. The total return analysis is based on a $100 investment on December 31, 2009. It is assumed that dividends are reinvested daily. The Peer Group Index is a self-constructed peer group of companies which are included in the Dow Jones Food and Beverages Group and the Dow Jones Tobacco Group of Companies.

[8] Guiding our Performance, Governance, Ethics and Business Principles, Sustainability Report, pp. 53–55.

Table 2.4 **Performance analysis**

Year	2009	2010	2011	2012	2013	2014
The Coca-Cola Company	$100	$119	$130	$139	$163	$171
Peer Group Index	$100	$119	$142	$156	$198	$229
S&P 500	$100	$115	$117	$136	$180	$205

Source: Page 28, Annual Report 2014.

Table 2.5 **Financial highlights in million dollars except per share data**

	2010	2011	2012	2013	2014
Net operating revenues	35,119	46,542	48,017	46,854	45,998
Net Income	11,787	8584	9019	8584	7098
Total Assets	72,921	79,974	86,174	90,055	92,023
Total Debt	14,041	13,656	14,736	19,154	19,063
Basic EPS	$2.55	$1.88	$2.0	$1.94	$1.62
Cash Dividends	$0.88	$0.94	$1.02	$1.12	$1.22

Source: Annual Report 2014.

Table 2.6 **Net operating revenues by segment in year 2014**

Region	Percent of revenues
Eurasia & Africa	5.9
Europe	10.5
Latin America	10
North America	46.7
Asia Pacific	11.4
Bottling Investment	15.2
Corporate	0.3
Total	100

Source: Annual Report 2014.

The financial highlights are based on 31st December every year (Table 2.5). The 2013 financial results include the impact of deconsolidation of the Brazilian and Philippine bottling operations. In 2010, Coca-Cola company acquired CCE'S former North America business and sold the Norwegian and Sweden bottling operations to new CCE.

Sixty-two percent of the net operating revenues in 2014 were attributed to finished product operations and 38% were attributed to concentrate product operations. The intangible assets amounted to 29% of the total assets in year 2014. Table 2.6 gives the net operating revenues of Coca Cola region wise during the year 2014. Table 2.7 provides the capital expenditure incurred by Coca Cola segment wise during the period 2014.

Table 2.7 **Capital expenditure in different regions in the year 2014**

Region	Percent of capital expenditure
Eurasia & Africa	1.3
Europe	2.2
Latin America	2.3
North America	53.7
Asia Pacific	3.2
Bottling Investment	26.1
Corporate	11.2
Total	100

2.8 Debt financing

The company does not raise capital through the issuance of stock. The company uses debt financing to lower the overall cost of capital. The debt financing include the use of an extensive commercial paper program as a part of cash management strategy. The company reviews its optimal mix of short-term and long-term debt regularly and would replace certain amounts of commercial paper, short-term debt and current maturities of long-term debt with new issuances of long-term debt in future.

In 2014, the long-term debt was rated AA by Standard & Poor's, Aa3 by Moody', and A+ by Fitch. The commercial paper program was rated "A-1+" by Standard & Poor's, "P-1" by Moody's and "F-1" by Fitch. In 2014, the company had $7677 million in lines of credit available for general corporate purposes. In 2014, the Company had issuances of debt of $41,674 million, which included net issuances of $317 million of commercial paper and short-term debt with maturities of 90 days or less and $37,799 million of issuances of commercial paper and short-term debt with maturities greater than 90 days.

During 2014, the Company made payments of $36,962 million, which included $35,921 million for payments of commercial paper and short-term debt with maturities greater than 90 days or less and long-term debt payments of $1041 million. The company had $7677 million in lines of credit for general corporate purposes as of December 31, 2014. These backup lines of credit expire at different times from 2015 through 2019.

2.9 Dividend decision

2.9.1 Issuances of stock

The issuances of stock in 2014, 2013, and 2012 were primarily related to the exercise of stock options by company employees.

2.9.2 Dividends

By 2015, Coca-Cola had its 53rd consecutive annual increase in dividends. The company paid common stock dividend of $1.02, $1.12, and $1.22, respectively during the period 2012, 2013, and 2014, respectively. The dividend per share increased by 10% in year 2013 and 9% in year 2014.

2.9.3 Share repurchases

Coca-Cola's initial share repurchase program was initiated in the year 1984. The latest repurchase program was initiated in year 2014. During this period of 1984–2014, Coca-Cola had purchased 3.2 billion shares of the company at an average price per share of $14.66. In 2006, the company initiated share repurchase program of up to 600 million shares of the company's stock. Approximately 43 million shares were yet to be repurchased under the 2006 program. In 2012, the Board of Directors authorized a new share repurchase program of up to 500 million shares. In 2013 and 2014, approximately 121 and 98 million shares were repurchased at average share price of $39.84 and $40.97, respectively.

2.9.3.1 Off balance sheet activities

In 2014, the contingent liabilities amounted to $565 million of which $155 million was related to VIEs. These guarantees were primarily related to third party customers, bottlers, vendors, and container manufacturing operations.

2.10 Risk management

The international operations of Coca-Cola are subject to currency fluctuations and governmental actions. In 2014, the company used 71 functional currencies. In 2014, the Brazilian real depreciated 10% against US dollar. The Mexican peso and Australian dollar depreciated by 4% and 7% against dollar in the year 2014. The company recorded foreign exchange losses of $2 million, $162 million and $569 million, respectively in year 2012, 2013, and 2014, respectively. In 2014, the company generated $26,235 million of the net operating revenues from operations outside the United States. Venezuela has been considered as a hyperinflationary economy. Coca-Cola uses derivative financial instruments to reduce the net exposure to foreign currency fluctuations. The company have derivative positions in forward exchange contracts and currency options. The currency options are principally denominated in euros and Japanese yen. Collars are also used to hedge certain part of forecasted cash flows denominated in various foreign currencies. Coca-Cola have foreign exchange contracts to offset the earnings impact related to foreign currency fluctuations on certain monetary assets and liabilities. Coca-Cola enters into foreign exchange contracts to hedge net investments in international operations. The total notional values of foreign currency derivatives were $15,341 million and $23,553 million respectively during 2013 and 2014. In 2014 the 10% weakening of the US dollar would have eliminated net unrealized gains and an unrealized loss of $103 million.

The company enters into interest rate swaps to manage exposure in interest rate fluctuations. Coca have exposure in interest rate risk related to investments in highly liquid securities. The company policy guideline stipulates investments to be investment grade in order to minimize the potential risk of principal loss. The investment policy limits the amount of credit exposure to any one issuer.

The company is exposed to market risk with respect to commodity price fluctuations particularly purchase of sweeteners, metals, juices, PET and fuels. Fuels are used to operate the extensive fleet vehicles. Coca-Cola manages commodity risk exposures through use of supplier pricing agreements. Coke also uses derivative financial instruments to manage exposure to commodity risks. The commodity derivatives which qualified for hedge accounting had notional values of $26 million and $9 million in year 2013 and 2014, respectively. Open commodity derivatives which don't qualify for hedge accounting had notional values of $1441 million and $816 million in year 2013 and 2014, respectively.

2.11 Trend analysis

Table 2.8 shows the financial highlights of Coca Cola during the ten year period 2005−2014. Revenues, operating income, net income, and capital expenditure are given in millions of dollars.

The year on year comparison reveals that revenue growth was highest in the period 2011 when revenues increased by approximately 32% in year 2011. The revenue growth was approximately 20% in year 2007 compared to the previous year. In 2010 the growth rate of revenues was 13%. The growth rate of revenues in year 2012 was approximately 3%. Coca-Cola registered negative growth rates of revenues in the year 2013 and 2014 respectively. The average growth rate of revenues was approximately 9% during the period 2005−2010. At the same time, the average growth rate of revenues was approximately 8% during the period 2011−2014. The average gross margin during the period 2005−2009 was 64.6% while the average gross margin during the five-year period 2010−2014 decreased to 61%. The year on year comparison reveals that operating income registered the highest growth rate of 20% in year 2011. The average growth rate of operating income which was 7% during the period 2005−2010 declined to 4% during the period 2011−2014. The year on year comparison shows that net income registered a growth rate of approximately 18% in year 2007 and 2009. The highest growth rate of net income of approximately 73% was recorded in year 2010 during the 10-year period of analysis. The average growth rate of net income during the period 2005−2010 was approximately 22%. The average growth rate of net income was −11% during the period 2010−2014. EPS increased by 72% in year 2010. DPS had the highest growth rate of 11.7% in year 2008. In 2006, the capital expenditure grew by 56.5% compared to the previous year 2005. The growth rate of capital expenditure was 31.8% in year 2011. The capital expenditure which was $899 million in 2005 increased to $2406 million in 2014. The average growth rate of capital expenditure was 21% during the period 2005−2010. During the period 2011−2014, the average growth rate of capital expenditure declined to 3%.

The comparison of the profitability position of the company during the ten-year period of analysis reveals that the profitability ratios peaked during the year 2010 (Table 2.9). The net profit margin and return on assets (ROA) was 33.6% and

Table 2.8 Financial highlights during the 10-year period 2005–2014

Year	2005	2006	2007	2008	2009	2010	2011	2012	2013	2014
Revenues	23,104	24,088	28,857	31,944	30,990	35,119	46,542	48,017	46,854	45,998
Gross Margin in %	64.5	66.1	63.9	64.4	64.2	63.9	60.9	60.3	60.7	61.1
Operating Income	6085	6308	7252	8446	8231	8449	10,154	10,779	10,228	9708
Net Income	4872	5080	5981	5807	6824	11,809	8572	9019	8584	7098
EPS	1.02	1.08	1.29	1.25	1.47	2.53	1.85	1.97	1.9	1.6
DPS	0.56	0.62	0.68	0.76	0.82	0.88	0.94	1.02	1.12	1.22
Capital Expenditure	899	1407	1648	1968	1993	2215	2920	2780	2550	2406

Table 2.9 Profitability trends

Year	2005	2006	2007	2008	2009	2010	2011	2012	2013	2014
Net Profit Margin in %	21.09	21.09	20.73	18.18	22.02	33.63	18.42	18.78	18.32	15.43
ROA in %	16.04	17.11	16.33	13.86	15.3	19.42	11.21	10.86	9.74	7.8
ROE in %	30.18	30.53	30.94	27.51	30.15	42.32	27.37	28	26.03	22.36
ROIC in %	21.59	23.42	23.39	19.35	20.79	26.69	14.87	14.27	12.58	9.86

19.4% during the year 2010. The return on equity (ROE) and return on invested capital (ROIC) was 42% and 27% approximately during the year 2010. The average net profit margin during the two five period of analysis 2005−2009 and 2010−2014 were approximately 21%. The average ROE during the above period of analysis was approximately 29%. The average ROA which was 15.7% during the period 2005−2009 declined to 11.8% during the period 2010−2014. The ROIC which was 21.7% during the period 2005−2009 decreased to 15.65 per cent during the period 2010−2014.

The solvency ratios for Coca Cola during the ten year period is given in Table 2.10. The average financial leverage during the period 2005−2009 was 1.9 while the average financial leverage during the 2010−2014 increased to 2.65. The debt equity ratio increased from 0.13 during the period 2005−2009 to 0.51 during the period 2010−2014. The ability of the firm to meet its fixed interest obligations was sound as reflected by the interest coverage ratio during the 10-year period of analysis. The ICR increased from 17.98 in 2008 to 26.2 in 2009, and peaked in year 2012 when ICR was 30.75.

The current ratio and quick ratio peaked in year 2009 (Table 2.11). The average current ratio during the period 2005−2009 was 1.03 while the average current ratio during the period 2010−2014 was 1.09. The average quick ratio improved from 0.69 during the period 2005−2009 to 0.822 during the period 2010−2014.

The average receivables turnover ratio was 9.82 during the period 2005−2009 which declined slightly to 9.61 during the period 2010−2014 on an average basis. The average inventory turnover ratio improved from 5.3 to 5.73 during the two five year periods of comparison. The assets and fixed asset turnover ratios have declined on average basis during the above period of comparison. The average payment period declined from 89 days to 41 days during the period 2010−2014 compared to the period 2005−2009. Table 2.12 gives the efficiency ratios of Coca Cola during the ten year period of analysis.

2.12 Stock wealth creation

The cumulative return analysis of Coca-Cola's stock price based on monthly returns during the 53-year period 1962−2015 shows that the company had recorded cumulative monthly returns of 885% during the period of analysis. During the same 53-year period consisting of 648 months, the market index S&P 500 registered cumulative monthly returns of approximately 400 per cent. The data for analysis was taken from yahoo finance (Fig. 2.1).

Coca-Cola had higher cumulative returns compared to S&P 500 in all the period of analysis.

Coca-Cola had excess returns during three years (2010, 2011, and 2015) compared to S&P 500 Index (Table 2.13). The company recorded the highest excess returns over the S&P 500 of 8.36% during the year 2011. Coca-Cola registered highest average yearly returns of 18.72% in year 2010. Coca-Cola had average

Table 2.10 **Long-term solvency position**

Year	2005	2006	2007	2008	2009	2010	2011	2012	2013	2014
Financial Leverage	1.8	1.77	1.99	1.98	1.96	2.35	2.53	2.63	2.71	3.04
Debt Equity Ratio	0.07	0.08	0.15	0.14	0.2	0.45	0.43	0.45	0.58	0.63
Interest Coverage Ratio				17.98	26.2	20.43	28.43	30.75	25.79	20.31

Table 2.11 **Liquidity position**

Year	2005	2006	2007	2008	2009	2010	2011	2012	2013	2014
Current Ratio	1.04	0.95	0.92	0.94	1.28	1.17	1.05	1.09	1.13	1.02
Quick Ratio	0.72	0.58	0.58	0.62	0.95	0.85	0.78	0.77	0.9	0.81

Table 2.12 **Efficiency position**

Year	2005	2006	2007	2008	2009	2010	2011	2012	2013	2014
Receivables Turnover	10.38	9.9	9.78	9.97	9.05	8.58	9.96	9.92	9.73	9.85
Inventory Turnover	5.76	5.33	5.39	5.16	4.88	5.07	6.34	6	5.63	5.61
Fixed Assets Turnover	3.89	3.8	3.75	3.8	3.47	2.89	3.14	3.26	3.18	3.11
Asset Turnover	0.76	0.81	0.79	0.76	0.69	0.58	0.61	0.58	0.53	0.51
Payables Period	195.44	121.2	40.5	44.12	45.76	47.4	40.67	39.66	38.66	41.03

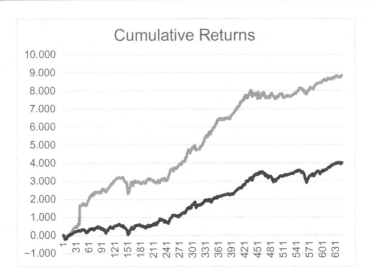

Figure 2.1 Cumulative monthly returns during the period 1962−2015.

Table 2.13 Average yearly returns in percent: Coca-Cola versus S&P 500

Year	Coca-Cola	S&P 500	Excess returns
2010	18.72	13.80	4.92
2011	9.50	1.15	8.36
2012	7.39	13.16	−5.77
2013	16.69	26.54	−9.86
2014	6.76	11.14	−4.38
2015	7.17	0.93	6.23

yearly returns of 16.69% in year 2013. But S&P 500 index outperformed Coca-Cola in the same year. In 2015, Coca-Cola outperformed the S&P 500 index with excess returns of 6.23%.

Holding period yield assumes that stock is purchased and held for a period of one year. The stock is purchased in January and sold off in December every year. The analysis is based on monthly stock price (Table 2.14). Coca-Cola had the highest holding period yield in year 2010. In 2014, Coca-Cola had holding period yield of approximately 15%. The five-year annual holding period yield was approximately 18% during the period 2010−2015.

The market value and book value of equity are given in millions of dollars (Table 2.15). The average book value as percent of market value was approximately 19% during the period 2010−2014. The market value of equity peaked with value of US$162 billion in year 2012. The excess value is estimated as the difference between market value and book value of equity. The market capitalization is based on year-end

Table 2.14 **Holding period yield**

Year	Holding period yield in percent
2010	25
2011	14.5
2012	10.4
2013	14.1
2014	14.98
2015	9.27

Table 2.15 **Excess value creation**

Year	2010	2011	2012	2013	2014
Market Cap	150,745	158,342	162,001	181,847	184,333
Book Value	31,003	31,635	32,790	33,173	30,320
Excess Value	119,742	126,707	129,211	148,674	154,013
BV as percent of MV	20.6	20	20.2	18.2	16.4

values The excess value generated was highest in year 2014 with value of $154 billion. In the same year book value was only 16% of the market value of the equity.

2.13   Valuation

In this section Coca-Cola is valued using discounted cash flow valuation models and relative valuation. The discounted cash flow valuation models used are dividend discount model, free cash flow to equity and free cash flow to firm.

2.13.1   Cost of capital estimation

Cost of capital is the weighted average cost of capital where weights are based on the market value of equity and debt. The market value of equity is the market capitalization and the market value of debt is estimated by multiplying the ratio of price of a long-term bond to face value of bond with book value of debt. Interest bearing liabilities are taken as book value of debt. Cost of equity is estimated using the Capital Asset Pricing Model (CAPM).

Cost of equity = Risk free rate + beta*Risk premium.

The average yield to maturity on the 30 year US Treasury bond during the three year period 2013−2015 is assumed as the risk free rate.[9] The risk free rate is assumed as 3.26%.

[9] http://www.federalreserve.gov/releases/h15/data.htm.

Beta is estimated by regressing the daily stock returns of Coca-Cola on the daily returns of market index S&P 500 during the three-year period 2013−2015.

Beta = 0.64

Risk Premium = Return on market Index-Risk free rate.

Return on market index is estimated using the three-year average returns given by S&P 500 during the period 2013−2015. Return on market index is estimated as 13.49%.

Risk Premium = 13.49 − 3.26 = 10.23%

Cost of equity = 3.26 + 0.64 * 10.23 = 9.81 %.

Weighted Average Cost of Capital (WACC)

The yield to maturity on a long-term bond maturing in 2093 is taken as the cost of debt. The bond which matures on 29/7/2093 with fixed coupon rate of 7.375% have yield to maturity of 5.32%. The price of this bond is $137.9. This bond has a rating of Aa3, AA and A + given by Moody's, S&P and Fitch Rating.[10]

Cost of debt = 5.32%

Tax rate = 35%[11]

After tax cost of debt = 5.32(1 − 0.35) = 3.46%

Estimation of debt in year 2014

Short-term debt = 22,682 million dollars

Long-term debt = 19,063 million dollars

Book Value of debt = 22,682 + 19,063 = 41,745 million dollars

Market Value of debt = Book Value of debt *Ratio of long-term bond price to the face value of bond.

Ratio = 137.9/100 = 1.379

Market Value of debt = 41,745 * 1.379 = 57566.36 million dollars.

Market Value of Equity = 184,333 million dollars. (Year-end market capitalization.)

Total Capital = 184,333 + 57,566.36 = 241,899.40 million dollars.

Weight of Equity = 184,333/241,899.40 = 0.76

Weight of Debt = 57,566.36/241,899.40 = 0.24

Weighted Average Cost of Capital (WACC) = Cost of Equity*Weight of Equity + After tax Cost of debt* Weight of debt.

WACC = 9.81 * 0.76 + 3.46 * 0.24 = 8.30%

Weighted Average Cost of Capital = 8.30%

2.13.2 Dividend discount model valuation

In this model of valuation, the future expected dividends are discounted by the cost of equity to arrive at the value of Coca-Cola.

2.13.2.1 Historical growth rate estimation

The historical growth rate of earnings analysis reveal that the average growth rate of earnings per share during the period 2006−2015 was approximately 4% while the average growth rate of earnings per share during the five-year period 2011−2015

---

[10] http://finra-markets.morningstar.com/BondCenter/Results.jsp; http://quicktake.morningstar.com/StockNet/bonds.aspx?Symbol=KO&Country=USA.

[11] https://home.kpmg.com/xx/en/home/services/tax/tax-tools-and-resources/tax-rates-online/corporate-tax-rates-table.html.

Table 2.16 Estimation of DPO

Year	2010	2011	2012	2013	2014	2015
EPS	2.53	1.85	1.97	1.9	1.6	1.56
DPS	0.88	0.94	1.02	1.12	1.22	1.3
DPO	0.35	0.51	0.52	0.59	0.76	0.83
Average	0.59					

Table 2.17 Estimation of growth rate from fundamentals for DDM

Year	2010	2011	2012	2013	2014	2015
Retention Ratio	0.65	0.49	0.48	0.41	0.24	0.17
ROE	0.42	0.27	0.28	0.26	0.22	0.23
Growth Rate	0.27	0.13	0.14	0.11	0.05	0.04

was approximately -9%. The average growth rate of dividends per share during the period 2006–2015 was approximately 9%. The average growth rate of dividends per share during the five-year period 2011–2015 was approximately 8%. The average dividend payout (DPO) during the five-year period 2011 2015 was 64%. The average growth rate of DPO during the period 2006–2015 was 4% while the average growth rate of DPO during the period 2011–2015 was approximately 19%. The average DPO during the period 2010–2015 was 59% (Table 2.16).

The average growth rate of earnings during the period 2010–2015 was 12%.

Retention Ratio = 1-DPO
Growth Rate = Retention Ratio*Return on Equity.

The growth rate estimated from fundamentals is assumed as the growth rate of dividends in the high growth period estimation of the dividend discount model (DDM) (Table 2.17).

2.13.2.2 Two-stage DDM

In this two stage DDM, the earnings per share are expected to grow at growth rate of 12% during the high growth phase and then at the stable phase growth rate which is assumed to be the growth rate of world economy.

2.13.2.3 High growth phase inputs

Growth Period = 10 years
Cost of Equity = 9.81%
DPO = 59% (The average DPO during the period 2010–2015 was 59%.)
Current EPS = 1.60
EPS in the first year of high growth period = 1.60 * 1.12 = 1.79

The present value of dividends per share in the high growth phase = $10.54 (Table 2.18).

Table 2.18 Present value of dividends in high growth phase

Year	1	2	3	4	5	6	7	8	9	10
EPS	1.79	2.01	2.25	2.52	2.82	3.16	3.54	3.96	4.44	4.97
DPO	0.59	0.59	0.59	0.59	0.59	0.59	0.59	0.59	0.59	0.59
DPS	1.06	1.18	1.33	1.49	1.66	1.86	2.09	2.34	2.62	2.93
PV	$0.96	$0.98	$1.00	$1.02	$1.04	$1.06	$1.08	$1.11	$1.13	$1.15
Sum	**$10.54**									

2.13.2.4 Stable period inputs

The growth rate of Coca-Cola in the stable period is assumed to be the growth rate of US Economy.

The average growth rate of US GDP during the period 2011−2014 was 2.13%.[12]

The retention ratio in the stable phase is estimated through the relationship given below:

Growth Rate = Retention Ratio*Return on Equity of industry (Nonalcoholic beverage industry.)

The current ROE of the nonalcoholic beverage industry is 22.6%.[13]

2.13% = Retention Ratio*22.6%

Retention Ratio = 2.13/22.6 = 9.42%

DPO in stable period = 1 − 0.094 = 0.906

EPS at the end of high growth period = $4.97

EPS in stable period = 4.97 * 1.0213 = $5.08

DPO during the stable period = 1 − 0.0942 = 0.906

DPS in stable period = 5.08*0.906 = $4.60

Terminal Value = DPS in stable period/(Cost of equity-growth rate in stable period)

= 4.60/(0.0981 − 0.0213) = $59.88

Present Value of terminal value = $23.49

Value of Coca-Cola = Present Value of dividends in high growth phase + Present Value of terminal price in stable phase.

Value of Coca-Cola share = 10.54 + 23.49 = $34.03.

Coca-Cola was trading at $42 on 31/12/2014 in NYSE. The 52-week range was $36.56−$43.91.

2.13.3 Free cash flow to equity model

The historical average growth rate of net income was 4.3% during the period 2006−2015 and average historical growth rate of net income during the period 2010−2015 was only 0.8%.

---

[12] http://data.worldbank.org/indicator/NY.GDP.MKTP.KD.ZG.

[13] http://www.morningstar.com/stocks/XNYS/KO/quote.html.

Table 2.19 Estimation of adjusted capital expenditure in millions of US dollars

Year	2010	2011	2012	2013	2014
Capex	2920	2780	2550	2406	2458
Deprec	1954	1982	1977	1976	1942
Net Acquisitions	562	2189	519	−241	−2044
Adjusted Capex	**1528**	**2987**	**1092**	**189**	**− 1528**

Table 2.20 Estimation of change in working capital in millions of US dollars

Year	2009	2010	2011	2012	2013	2014
Current Assets	17,551	21,579	25,497	30,328	31,304	32,986
Cash and Marketable Securities	9151	11,337	14,035	16,551	20,268	21,675
Non cash current assets	8400	10,242	11,462	13,777	11,036	11,311
Current Liabilities	13,721	18,508	24,283	27,821	27,811	32,374
Interest bearing current liabilities	6749	9376	14,912	17,874	17,925	22,682
Noninterest bearing current liabilities	6972	9132	9371	9947	9886	9692
NonCash Working Capital	1428	1110	2091	3830	1150	1619
Change in Working Capital		−318	981	1739	−2680	469

In the next section, growth rate is estimated from fundamentals.

Growth Rate = Reinvestment Rate * Return on Equity

Estimation of Reinvestment rate.

Reinvestment = Net Adjusted Capital Expenditure + Change in Working Capital
Adjusted Capital Expenditure = Capital Expenditure-Depreciation + Net Acquisitions (Table 2.19).
Noncash Working Capital = Non cash current Assets-Noninterest bearing current liabilities (Table 2.20).
Noncash current assets = Current Assets-Cash and Marketable Securities
Noninterest bearing current liabilities = Current Liabilities-Interest bearing current liabilities.

Increase in working capital is a cash outflow while decrease in working capital is a cash inflow.

Free Cash Flow to Equity (FCFE) = Net Income-Adjusted Net Capital Expenditure − Change in NonCash Working Capital + Debt Issued − Debt Repaid (Table 2.21).

The free cash flow to equity have been fluctuating over the five-year period of analysis.

When net debt issued was included in the estimation, the reinvestment rate was negative. Hence net debt issued was not included in final reinvestment rate calculation (Table 2.22). See Coca Cola.xlsx for detailed calculations.

The average growth rate of earnings based on geometric mean was 2.7% (Table 2.23).

2.13.3.1 One stage or stable stage FCFE model

Since the growth rate of net income was approximately equal to the growth rate of US economy, the stable stage FCFE model is used to value Coca-Cola. The model assumes that the growth rate of earnings of Coca-Cola would be equal to the growth rate of US economy since the estimated value of growth rate of net income was 2.7%.

Table 2.21 Estimation of FCFE in millions of US dollars

Year	2010	2011	2012	2013	2014
Net Income	11,809	8572	9019	8584	7098
Adjusted Net Capex	1528	2987	1092	189	−1528
Change in Working Capital	−318	981	1739	−2680	469
Debt Issued	15,251	27,495	42,791	43,425	41,674
Debt Repaid	13,403	22,530	38,573	38,714	36,962
FCFE	12,447	9569	10,406	15,786	12,869

Table 2.22 Estimation of reinvestment rate for FCFE model

Year	2010	2011	2012	2013	2014
Net Income	11,809	8572	9019	8584	7098
Adjusted Net Capex	1528	2987	1092	189	−1528
Change in Working Capital	−318	981	1739	−2680	469
Reinvestment	1210	3968	2831	−2491	−1059
Reinvestment rate	0.10	0.46	0.31	−0.29	−0.15

Table 2.23 Estimation of growth rate from fundamentals for FCFE model

Year	2010	2011	2012	2013	2014
Reinvestment Rate	0.10	0.46	0.31	−0.29	−0.15
ROE	0.42	0.27	0.28	0.26	0.22
Growth Rate	0.04	0.12	0.09	−0.08	−0.03

FCFE in current year (2014) = \$12,869 million
Growth Rate = 2.7%
Cost of equity = 9.81%
FCFE in stable phase = 12,869*1.0217 = \$13,216.46 million
Present Value of FCFE = 13,216.46/(0.0981−0.027) = \$185,885.56 million
Cash and cash equivalents = \$21,675 million
Value of Coca-Cola = 185,885.56 + 21,675 = \$207,560.56 million
Number of Shares = 4387 million
Value per share = 207,560.56/4387 = \$47.31

Coca-Cola was trading at \$43.54 on 26/12/2015 with market capitalization of 189.36 billion US dollars.

2.13.4   Free cash flow to firm valuation model

Reinvestment = Adjusted Net Capital Expenditure + Change in NonCash Working Capital
Reinvestment Rate = Adjusted Net Capital Expenditure + Change in NonCash Working Capital/EBIT(1-T)

The average reinvestment rate is 7% during the period 2010−2014 based on geometric mean (Table 2.24).

Free Cash Flow to Firm (FCFF) = EBIT(1-T)-Adjusted Net Capital Expenditure-Change in NonCash Working Capital (Table 2.25).

The average growth rate of earnings of Coca-Cola as estimated from fundamentals during the five-year period 2010−2014 was 2.5% (Table 2.26).

Table 2.24 Estimation of reinvestment rate for FCFF Model

Year	2010	2011	2012	2013	2014
EBIT(1-T)	6065	7349	8056	7377	7507
Adjusted Net Capex	1528	2987	1092	189	−1528
Change in NonCash Working Capital	−318	981	1739	−2680	469
Reinvestment	1210	3968	2831	−2491	−1059
Reinvestment Rate	0.20	0.54	0.35	−0.34	−0.14

Table 2.25 Estimation of FCFF in millions of US dollars

Year	2010	2011	2012	2013	2014
EBIT(1-T)	6065	7349	8056	7377	7507
Adjusted Net Capex	1528	2987	1092	189	−1528
Change in NonCash Working Capital	−318	981	1739	−2680	469
FCFF	4855	3381	5225	9868	8566

Table 2.26 Estimation of growth rate from fundamentals for FCFF model

Year	2010	2011	2012	2013	2014
Return on Invested Capital	0.27	0.15	0.14	0.13	0.10
Reinvestment Rate	0.20	0.54	0.35	−0.34	−0.14
Growth Rate	0.05	0.08	0.05	−0.04	−0.01

2.13.4.1   One stage or stable stage FCFF model

Since the growth rate of earnings is approximately equal to the US GDP growth rate, it is assumed that Coca-Cola is in the stable growth stage and one stage FCFF model is used to value Coca-Cola.

Current Year FCFF = 8566
Stable period growth rate = 2.5%
FCFF in stable period = 8566 * 1.025 = $8780.15 million
Weighted Average Cost of Capital = 8.30%
Present Value of FCFF = 8780.15/(0.083 − 0.025) = $173056.89 million dollars
Value of operating assets = $151381.90 million
Value of Coca-Cola = Value of operating assets + cash and cash equivalents in 2014
= 151,381.90 + 21,675 = $173,056.90 million dollars
Value of Equity = Value of Firm-Value of debt = 173,056.90 − 41,745 = $131,311.90 million dollars.
Number of shares = 4387 million
Value per share = $29.93

Summary of Discounted Cash Flow Valuation

Two Stage DDM
Value of Coca-Cola share = $34.03.
One Stage or Stable Stage FCFE Model
Value per share = $47.31
One Stage or Stable Stage FCFF Model
Value per share = $29.93

Coca-Cola was trading at $43.54 on 26/12/2015 with market capitalization of 189.36 billion US dollars. Coca-Cola was trading at $42 on 31/12/2014 in NYSE. The 52-week range was $36.56−$43.91.

2.14   Relative valuation

The values except ratios are given in millions of US dollars (Table 2.27). The values given are for the latest year. The revenues, net income and market capitalization are for the year end 2015. The total assets values are for year 2014. The ratio

Table 2.27 Comparison with peer group in 2015

SL	Name	Market cap	Revenues	Net income	Total assets	P/S	P/B	P/E	Div yield%
1	Coca-Cola	189,354	45,166	6884	92,023	4.3	7.3	27.9	3
2	PepsiCo	146,471	64,419	5045	70,509	2.3	10.9	29.8	2.8
3	Monster Beverage Group	30,169	2683	533	1939	10.3	6.5	51.6	
4	Dr Pepper Snapple	17,740	6245	729	8273	2.9	8.1	24.9	2

Table 2.28 Comparison of price multiples with industry average

	Coca-Cola	Industry average
P/S	4.3	2.9
P/B	7.3	7
P/E	27.9	28.7
Div Yield %	3	2.7

Source: Data from Morningstar.

Table 2.29 Price multiple trends

Year	2010	2011	2012	2013	2014	2015
P/E	13	12.9	18.4	21.4	23.4	27.9
P/B	4.9	4.8	4.9	5.7	5.5	7.3
P/S	4.4	3.5	3.5	4	4.1	4.3
P/CF	16.1	17.9	15.6	17.8	17.4	17.4

Source of data: Morningstar.

values are for current year 2015. Coca-Cola had the highest market capitalization of $189.35 billion among the peer companies. PepsiCo had the second highest market capitalization of $146.47 billion. Coca-Cola was the net income and asset maximizer among all the peer group. Coca-Cola also had the highest dividend yield among all the companies.

The price multiples of Coca-Cola are compared with industry average in year-end 2015 (Table 2.28). Coca-Cola has higher price to sales and price to book ratio compared to the industry average. Coca-Cola also had higher dividend yield compared to the industry average.

It can be observed from the Table 2.29 that the price earnings ratio for Coca-Cola has been increasing over the period 2010−2015. Price to Book ratio has also showed increasing trend except in year 2014. Price to sales and price to cash flow have been fluctuating over the period of analysis.

Table 2.30 **Enterprise value multiples**

Company	Coca-Cola	PepsiCo	Monster Beverage	Dr. Pepper Snapple
REVENUES	45,998	66,683	2465	6121
EBITDA	11,784	12,291	773	1417
EBIT	9708	9581	748	1180
Debt	41,745	28,897	0	0
Market Value of Equity	184,333	140,705	18,173	13,831
Cash and Cash Equivalents	21,675	8726	1151	237
Enterprise Value (EV)	204,403	160,876	17,022	13,594
EV/REVENUES	4.44	2.41	6.91	2.22
EV/EBITDA	17.35	13.09	22.02	9.59
EV/EBIT	21.06	16.79	22.76	11.52

Enterprise Value = Book Value of debt + Market Value of Equity-Cash and Cash Equivalents (Table 2.30).

Lower the enterprise value multiples, the more undervalued are the stocks. These stocks are attractive to be purchased.

All detailed calculations of financial performance analysis and valuation are given in excel worksheet CocaCola.xlsx.

Further reading

[1] Annual Reports Coca-Cola.

Wealth creation by Johnson & Johnson

3

3.1 Introduction

The family of companies under Johnson & Johnson (J&J) is engaged globally in research and development, manufacture, and sale of a wide range of products in the health care sector. J&J was incorporated in the State of New Jersey in the year 1887. J&J was listed as one of the top Fortune Magazine's 2016 World's Most Admired Companies List. J&J was also listed as a top company in the 17th annual Harris Poll Reputation Quotient. J&J has more than 250 companies located in 60 countries around the world. The J&J Family of Companies is organized into several business segments comprised of franchises and therapeutic categories. There are 24 brands and platforms which generate over $1 million in sales for J&J.

J&J and its Family of Companies is the largest and most diversified health care company in the world. J&J family consists of 265 operating companies with presence in 60 countries. The Company involves more than 78,000 suppliers and 500 external manufacturers for assisting the manufacturing of products worldwide. J&J have 389,000 products and product variations which serve more than one billion people every day. The company is headquartered in New Brunswick, New Jersey USA. The company has been listed on New York Stock Exchange since 1944 under the symbol JNJ. The total number of employees worldwide was 126,500 and the total net sales worldwide was $74.3 billion in the year 2015.

3.1.1 Major milestones

Year	Milestones
1886	Three Johnson brothers establish J&J in New Jersey, USA
1888	J&J publish "Modern methods of Antiseptic Wound Treatment" for practice of sterile surgery. J&J introduces the first commercial first aid kits
1894	J&J introduces maternity kits and baby powder
1896–97	J&J introduces the first mass produced sanitary protection products for women
1898	Introduces the first mass dental floss for teeth protection
1901	J&J publishes the First Aid Manuals
1921	Brand Adhesive Bandages introduced
1924	First overseas operating company established in United Kingdom
1930–31	Expands operations into Mexico, South Africa, and Australia
1931	Introduces the first prescription gel as part of family planning products

Strategic Financial Management Casebook.

Year	Milestones
1937	Expands business operations to Argentina and Brazil
1944	J&J goes for IPO with listing on NYSE. Dr. Philip Levine the discoverer of the human Rh factor joins Ortho Research Lab
1949	Ethicon Inc. is established for the company's heritage suture business
1954	Baby shampoo introduced
1957	J&J enters Indian market
1959	J&J acquires McNeil Lab in United States and Cilag Chemie AG in Europe which gave company presence in pharmaceutical medicines. The McNeil product Tylenol is the first prescription aspirin free pain reliever
1961	J&J acquires Janssen Pharmaceutical NV of Belgium
1963–73	During this period, the operating companies introduces new treatments for schizophrenia, family planning, and personal care
1978	J&J forms public private partnership to modernize the New Brunswick city
1976–89	J&J expands into new areas like vision care, mechanical wound closure, and diabetics management. J&J expands operations into China and Egypt
1987	J&J becomes the founding partner of the global campaign Safe Kids Worldwide. The vision care business division introduces the first disposable contact lenses - ACUVUE Brand Contact Lenses
1989–2002	J&J expands into Russia and Eastern Europe. J&J acquires Neutrogena Corporation, Kodak's Clinical Diagnostics business, Cordis Corporation, and Centocor
1990s	Ethicon Endo surgery pioneers minimally invasive surgery
1994	The introduction of the first coronary stent revolutionizes cardiology
2002	J&J enters into new therapeutic areas such as HIV/AIDS, Health, and wellness. J&J acquires Tibotec-Virco BVBA to focus on AIDS and tuberculosis
2006	J&J acquires Pfizer Consumer Healthcare and adds consumer brands like Listerine antiseptic to its portfolio of products
2010	J&J becomes sponsor for the UN Millennium Development goals to improve the health of mothers and children in developing countries
2011	The company celebrates 125 years of establishment
2013	Opens innovation centers in Boston, Menlo Park, London, and Shanghai

3.2   Organization structure of J&J

J&J is structured as decentralized organization. The Executive committee of J&J is central pillar responsible for the strategic operations and allocation of resources of the J&J family of companies. The operating companies of J&J are basically categorized into three business segments of consumer, pharmaceutical, and medical devices. Group operating committee consisting of key managers in specialized functional departments coordinates the activities of domestic and international companies in each of the business segment.

J&J is divided into three business segments-pharmaceutical, medical devices, and consumer segments. The pharmaceutical segment focusses on five therapeutic areas of immunology, infectious diseases, neuroscience, oncology, cardiovascular, and metabolic diseases. The medical devices segment provides products in the orthopedic, surgical care, specialty surgery, cardiovascular care, diagnostics, diabetics care, and vision care markets. The consumer segment offers a wide range of products in the baby care, oral care, skin care, over the counter (OTC) pharmaceutical, women's health, and wound care markets. The sales of pharmaceutical segment amounted to $32.3 billion, the medical segment sales amounted to $27.5 billion and the consumer segment accounted for $14.5 billion in the year 2014.

3.2.1   Major subsidiaries of J&J

Advanced sterilization products	ALZA corporation	ANIMAS corporation
Baby Center LLC	Biosense Webster Inc.	Centocor Ortho Biotech Inc.
Children with Diabetics Inc.	Cilag	Codman & Shurtleff Inc.
Crucell NV	DePuy Inc.	Ethicon Endo Surgery Inc.
Ethicon Inc.	Global Pharmaceutical Supply Group	Group Vendome SA
Gynecare	Health Media	Independence Technology LLC
Information Technology Services	Janssen Pharmaceutica	Janssen Pharmaceutica Products, L P
J&J Group of Consumer Companies Inc.	J&J Health Care Systems Inc.	J&J-Merck Consumer Pharmaceuticals Co.
J&J Pharma Research & Development LLC	J&J Pharmaceutical Services LLC	Life Scan Inc.
McNeil Consumer Healthcare	McNeil Nutritionals	Mentor Worldwide LLC
Noramco Inc.	OraPharma	Ortho Clinical Diagnostics
Ortho McNeil Pharmaceutical	Ortho Neutrogena	Personal Products Company
Penaten	Pharmaceutical Group Strategic Marketing	Penisula Pharmaceuticals Inc.
PriCara Inc.	Scios Inc.	Synthes
Tasmanian Alkaloids	Tibotec	Transform Pharmaceuticals Inc.
Veridex LLC	Vistakon	

3.3   Strategic pursuits of J&J

The pharmaceutical business of J&J is one of the top 10 pharmaceutical businesses in the United States, Europe, and Japan. The medical devices segment has introduced over 50 major new products since the year 2012. The division aims to introduce 30 major new filings by end of the year 2016. In 2015, approximately 25% of sales were from new products launched between 2010 and 2014. J&J is one of the top ranked healthcare companies in terms of patents.

In 2014, the research and development expenses amounted to $8.5 billion. The pharmaceutical segment has launched 14 new medicines during the period 2009–14.

On account of patent expiry, the company adopted a strategic refocus on five therapeutics areas of immunology, oncology, cardiovascular and metabolism, neuroscience, and infectious diseases. These therapeutic areas have strategic focus on discovery, research, early development, late development, and life cycle management. The research and development activities on diseases are reviewed yearly and major competitive review is done after every 3 years. J&J have in depth research capabilities in biotechnology, medicinal chemistry, vaccine platforms, research operations, and diagnostics. J&J also focuses on external innovation strategy to build collaborations with leading scientists in the world. In the year 2013, J&J established four regional hub innovation centers for development of new health care solutions. In 2015, Janssen launched three new research platforms which focuses on disease prevention, disease interception, and microbiome.

Medical devices segment has achieved leadership position in areas of orthopedics, surgery, diabetics care, and vision care due to acquisitions and divestitures. The segment is also focusing on key platforms in emerging markets and new go to market models. The strategy of the medical division is to direct resources toward the highest patient value opportunities for R&D. Medical devices segment has launched over 50 major new products since the year 2012. J&J is expected to launch 30 new major medical device product filings between 2014 and 2016 and more than 10 major new pharmaceutical filings and more than 40 line extensions by year 2019. Research and development of global surgery focuses on four therapeutic areas of cardiovascular disease, thoracic, metabolic, and colorectal oncology. Research and development focuses on development of transformative and innovative solutions in the areas of sutures, staplers, energy devices, trocars, and hemostats. Global orthopedics focus areas are trauma, knees, sports medicine, hips, shoulders, cranio maxifacial, spine, power tools, and value segment products in emerging markets. J&J have a clear strategy to leverage scale and innovation to grow in targeted medical device segments.

In the consumer segment, R&D initiatives focuses on critical need areas in the OTC medicines as well as oral care, baby, and skin care markets. R&D of the consumer segment focuses on diseases like Psoriasis, skin care, and eczema. Consumer segment have projects which include market specific development of oral care products, OTC smoking cessation, and co development of orally dissolved tablets. The clinical trials are conducted to evaluate the efficacy and safety of medicines and medical devices according to regulatory requirements. J&J companies sponsor and support clinical trials in more than 40 countries. The ethical code for the conduct of research and development provides standards of conduct and behavior for physicians. J&J sponsored studies are carried out in accordance with current international guidelines on Good Clinical Practice (GCP) and applicable regulatory and country specific requirements.

3.4   Strategic collaborations

The company had entered into 100 strategic partnerships, licenses, and acquisitions in pharmaceutical, medical devices, and consumer segments.[1] J&J enters into collaborative arrangements, typically with other pharmaceutical companies or biotechnology companies, to develop and commercialize drug candidates or intellectual property. Collaborations are extended to more than one activity by these parties in areas of research and development, marketing, and selling and distribution. These collaborations require upfront, milestone and royalty or profit share payments, contingent upon the occurrence of certain future events linked to the success of the asset in development.

J&J also focuses on cross segment innovative collaborations. J&J established Lung Cancer Center in China to analyze disease from multiple and integrated perspectives. Pharmaceutical and Consumer vision care collaboration is aimed to treat Age related Macular Degeneration through stem cell therapy. The introduction of EVARREST for treatment of problematic bleeding during surgery is a classic example of how J&J leveraged its pharmaceutical expertise in biologics with polymers to assist the development of solution for surgery.

Janssen Biotech Inc. and J&J Innovation have formed research collaboration with Weill Cornell Medical College for developing compounds for understanding the function of lymphoma causing protein. J&J Innovation and DePuy Synthes Products, LLC formed a strategic collaboration with medical device company Tissue Regeneration Systems, Inc. (TRS) to develop patient specific resorbable implants for orthopedic oncology. The collaboration was aimed at creating synergy using DePuy Synthes's expertise and market leadership with TRS's 3D printing technologies and development expertise. The neuroscience therapeutic area of Janssen Research and Development, LLC have an agreement with UK Dementias Research Platform to fight Alzheimer's disease. The research platform is a major initiative of public private partnership with six industry and eight leading academic institutions.

Ethicon Endo Surgery have a research collaboration with BrainStem Biometrics with respect to development of medical devices to detect minute eye movements in patients undergoing anesthesia. This technology is aimed to distinguish safe and unsafe levels of sedation for patients around the world. Janssen Pharmaceutica NV, J&J Innovation, and the Janssen neuroscience have established a research collaboration with Minerva Neurosciences for treatment of patients with insomnia and neuropsychiatric disorders. J&J have collaborated with biotechnology firm Energesis Pharmaceuticals for identification of biological compounds for treating metabolic diseases. J&J consumer companies, J&J Innovation have collaboration with scientists from the University of Manchester to explore potential applications of probiotic extracts for prevention and treatment of skin, oral, and respiratory conditions.

---

[1] J&J Annual Report 2014.

J&J have formed the J&J Quality & Compliance organization to ensure the standardization and consistent implementation of quality standards. The Quality Policy implies that J&J's operating companies must ensure that the design, make up and delivery of products are made in a consistent way.

J&J had associated with healthcare regulators to launch affordable blood glucose monitoring device for millions of Indians with diabetics. J&J Supply Chain (JJSC) has developed a global enterprise wide capability to collect direct commercial customer feedback on a regular basis on supply chain performance. J&J Office of Health Care Compliance & Privacy (HCC&P) and US Law department have developed enterprise wide standards for anticorruption laws. J&J require anticorruption training for those employees with relevant job responsibilities. In 2014, J&J through a collaboration with Yale University School of Medicine's Open Data Access (YODA) became the first company to share clinical trial data for pharmaceutical products. The YODA project became the independent authority to decide what clinical trial data would be shared with researchers. In 2015, J&J extended the agreement to cover clinical trials by medical devices companies. Janssen Pharmaceutica have partnered with the International AIDS Society for Pediatric HIV Education and Research program.

3.5 Sustainability initiatives

The three main strategic pillars of sustainability adopted by J&J are advancing human health and well-being, stewarding healthy environment, and leading a dynamic and growing business responsibly. The major areas of focus in advancing human health are global health, research and development, access and development. Collaboration is the engine of innovation at J&J. J&J have collaborations with consortia of nongovernmental organizations and national research programs to expand the Ebola vaccine program. J&J have collaboration with US Agency for International Development for programs like TB Partnership's Global Drug Facility. J&J also have entered into collaboration with the international partnership for microbicides for worldwide development and commercialization of dapivirine for fighting HIV in women.

To achieve the objective of healthy environment, J&J have established the goal to significantly increase on site renewable and clean technology energy capacity. In 2015, the company entered into an extended agreement with the Yale Open Data Access (YODA) project to provide access to varied portfolio of medical device products.[2] J&J have programs to communicate important health information to new and expectant mothers in South Africa. J&J have a global partnership Program-Save the Children which aims to help improve the health of children under the age of five. J&J focuses on building healthy communities through innovative and impactful health care solutions and partnerships. J&J also aims to unite scientific

---

[2] 2014 Sustainability and Citizenship Report, http://www.jnj.com/sites/default/files/pdf/cs/2014-JNJ-Citizenship-Sustainability-Report.pdf.

capabilities and innovative access models to address unmet health needs. In 2014, Janssen Pharmaceutical Companies launched Janssen Global Public Health to develop and deliver transformational medicines to combat critical diseases like multi drug address resistant tuberculosis, neglected tropical diseases, and HIV. J&J through Janssen GPH has associated with Harvard Medical School to support research for pediatric and adult drug resistant TB treatment. J&J medicines for HIV are available in 112 countries at special effort or reduced pricing if local regulatory systems allow import prior to registration. J&J medicines like PREZISTA (darunavir), SIRTURO (bedaquiline), and OLYSIO (simeprevir) are included on WHO's Essential Medicines List. In 2014, J&J provided more than 181 million doses of VERMOX for distribution to affected children in 15 countries. During the period 2004–14, the weighted average compound annual growth rate of the company's net price increases for health care products was below the US consumer price index (CPI).[3] J&J is one of the founding members of Together Rx Access which have assisted more than 2.5 million American people who have no access to prescription drug coverage and not eligible for Medicare.

J&J have been targeting health education programs in targeted communities around the world. In 2014, six new education programs were launched across China, Philippines, and India to reach 22 million people. J&J have a mobile health partnership termed mMitra with the Mobile Alliance for Maternal Action, USAID, the UN Foundation, BabyCenter, J&J, and ARMMAN, a Mumbai-based NGO. The program sends preventive-care voice messages to pregnant women and new mothers twice a week. The messages go directly to their mobile phones in their chosen language and preferred time slot corresponding to the stage of their pregnancy or the developmental stage of their child. The mMitra program have enrolled more than 40,000 women since its launch in November 2014, and about 10,000 women are added monthly. J&J have partnership with Nurse.com for providing educational campaign on Ebola risks. In 2014, J&J have provided more than 181 million doses of Vermox for distribution to affected children in 15 countries.

3.5.1 Community engagement

J&J UK have established Social Impact through Procurement Initiative to help sustainable employment for disadvantaged group. Bridge to Employment (BTE) is another global initiative program aimed at academic development of under privileged sections of society. J&J Vision Care Inc., business Sight for Kids is one of the longest running community programs in partnership with the Lions Clubs International Foundation (LCIF). In 2014, 650 employees of J&J Diabetics Solutions engaged in over 40 volunteerism projects. In 2014, J&J partnered with Stop Hunger Now to address global child hunger. Through the Earthwards process, J&J focus on improving the impacts of the products. J&J has implemented five targeted demand-side efficiency efforts designed to optimize the largest

---

[3] Annual Report 2015.

energy-using systems in intensive manufacturing process. J&J aims for 20% absolute reduction in facility carbon dioxide emissions by 2020.

3.6 Corporate governance

J&J is governed by the principles of values set forth in credo which was created by General Robert Wood Johnson in year 1943. The principles of corporate governance are based on these credo values. The credo principles of J&J define the responsibilities of the company towards patients, consumers, employees and the communities.

All members of director board are elected annually by the shareholders. The directors select, oversee and monitor the performance of the senior management team. The chairman of the Board with participation by the Lead Director will set the agenda for Board meetings. Executive sessions of independent directors are held at least four times a year without the participation of nonindependent directors. The lead director chairs these executive sessions. Every year the board will select a member of Board to serve as the Chairman of the Board of Directors. Annually the independent directors would select an independent member of the board to serve as Lead Director. Directors and every employee must avoid business, financial, or other direct or indirect interests or relationships which conflict with the interests of the company. A director who serves as a chief executive officer or similar position should not serve more than two public company boards including the J&J board. Other directors should not serve on more than five public company boards which include the J&J board. The company aims that at least two-thirds of directors should be independent. The directors of the company have full and free access to officers and employees of the company. The nonemployee directors of the company are compensated. The Compensation and Benefits Committee annually review and approve changes to the compensation of directors. The general policy adopted by the company is that all major decisions are considered by board as a whole. The Board of J&J have the following committees: Audit Committee, Compensation & Benefits Committee, Nominating & Corporate Governance Committee, Regulatory Compliance & Government Affairs Committee, Science, Technology & Sustainability Committee, and Finance Committee. The Board and committees have an annual self-evaluation. The company conducts a comprehensive orientation program for all the new nonemployee directors. The Board have stipulated minimum share ownership guidelines which are applicable for all nonemployee directors and designated members of senior management. The CEO is required to own share or share units in value to six times the annual salary. Each Executive committee member is required to own share or share units equal to three times the annual salary. The responsibility to review the share ownership guidelines is entrusted with the Nominating and Corporate Governance Committee. The mandatory retirement age is 72. In 2014, J&J have 13 Board members of whom 12 are independent based on the criteria set by New York Stock Exchange. Three of them were women.

Table 3.1 **Timeline of major acquisitions by J&J**

Year	Acquisitions
1959	McNeil Lab in the United States and Cilag Chemie AG in Europe which gave the company a foothold in pharmaceutical medicines
1961	Janssen Pharmaceutica NV of Belgium
2001	Baby Center
2002	J&J acquires Tibotec-Virco BVBA to focus on AIDS and tuberculosis
2005	J&J acquires Peninsula Pharmaceuticals and Transform Pharmaceuticals
2006	J&J acquires Pfizer Consumer Healthcare
2008	J&J acquires Health Media and Omrix Bio pharmaceuticals
2009	Acclarent
2011	Crucell
2012	Calibra Medical and Synthes
2013	Aragon Pharmaceuticals
2014	Alios Biopharma and Covagen AG
2015	XO1 and Novira Therapeutics

3.7 Corporate restructuring activities—acquisitions

Table 3.1 lists the major acquisitions done by J&J. In 2001, J&J acquired BabyCenter from eToys Inc.BabyCentre.com is the largest and best known online parenting resource. J&J was attracted to the superior content and personalized relationship that BabyCenter had created for millions of parents.

In 2002, J&J acquired the assets of Tibotec Virco, a privately held biopharmaceutical company focused on the development of antiviral treatments including infectious diseases like HIV. The transaction was valued at $320 million in cash and debt. J&J incurred one-time charge of approximately $145 million, or $0.05 per share which reflected the write off in process research and development costs. The acquisition was aimed to provide a good strategic fit to the R&D operations of J&J. This all cash transaction was valued at approximately $10 million.

In 2005, Ortho McNeil Pharmaceutical Inc., the subsidiary of J&J acquired Peninsula Pharmaceuticals Inc., a privately held biopharmaceutical company focused on developing and commercializing antibiotics to treat life threatening infections. Before the completion of the acquisition, Peninsula had to spun out PPI-0903, a fifth generation broad spectrum cephalosporin into Cerexa Inc the new company. The cash deal was valued at $245 million. At the time of announcement of the deal, the lead product of Peninsula was a broad spectrum antibiotic in six late stage clinical trials. In 2005, J&J had acquired Trans Form Pharmaceuticals which specializes in the discovery of superior formulations and novel crystalline forms of drug molecules. This cash deal was valued at approximately $230 million. Transform was a strong strategic addition to J&J's pharmaceutical research, discovery and development model.

In 2006, J&J acquired Pfizer Consumer Healthcare for $16.6 billion in cash. The acquisition enabled J&J to add diverse portfolio of enduring brands which created leadership position for the company in nine additional categories including large new segments such as smoking cessation and mouthwash. The addition of LISTERINE, the world's No. 1 mouthwash transformed J&J's oral health care business by more than tripling it into a franchise with sales in excess of one billion dollars. The Pfizer consumer healthcare brands complement J&J's well known consumer and OTC products. The acquisition provided significant opportunities to leverage the sales, administration, and supply chain of both organizations globally.

In 2008, J&J had acquired Ann Arbor's Health Media which specializes in online health counseling and web interventions. The site's suite of services provides automated coaching for topics on wellness, disease management, behavioral health, and medication. This acquisition by J&J was aimed to focus on health and wellness by using Health Media's programs to reduce per capita health plan costs and improve employee health and productivity. J&J purchased Omrix Biopharmaceuticals for $438 million in cash. The price of $25 per share offered to Omrix represented a premium of 18% to the target company's price at the time of announcement. Omrix the producer of bio surgical products fitted well with the portfolio of J&J's Ethicon.

Acclarent Inc. was acquired by Ethicon, Inc. of J&J in an all cash transaction for approximately $785 million. The innovative ENT products of the Acclarent have been used to treat more than 95,000 patients by 2011. The acquisition boosted J&J's presence in the ear, nose, and throat treatment business.

J&J acquired Dutch vaccine manufacturer Crucell for 1.75 billion euro ($2.4 billion) in 2011. It gave J&J access to the global vaccine market worth $22.1 billion. The acquisition was aimed to provide a cost effective vaccine platform for J&J which can drive long term growth with limited generic exposure. In 2009, J&J held 18% of Crucell. Crucell's focus is on the development, production, and marketing of vaccines, proteins, and antibodies that prevent and/or treat infectious disease. Crucell has a robust preclinical research program, and also licenses a human cell-line based manufacturing system for high-yield, large-scale production of vaccines, recombinant proteins, and gene therapy products. J&J had acquired 98.89% of the issued shares in Crucell.

In 2012, J&J completed the acquisition of Synthes for a total purchase price of $19.7 billion in cash and stock. Synthes was integrated with the DePuy franchise to establish the DePuy Synthes Companies of J&J. The acquisition was aimed to create the world's most innovative and comprehensive orthopedics business in the world. Under the terms of the agreement, each shares of Synthes common stock was exchanged for CHF 55.65 in cash and 1.7170 shares of J&J common stock. Cash was also provided for fractional share. In the same year, J&J's Life Scan acquired Calibra Medical, maker of the Finesse "insulin patch pen" for type 1 and type 2 diabetics.

In 2013, J&J completed its acquisition of Aragon Pharmaceuticals Inc., a privately held pharmaceutical discovery and development company focused on drugs to treat hormonally driven cancers. The acquisition was aimed at strengthening the prostrate cancer pipeline with second generation potentially best in class compound.

In 2014, J&J acquired privately held clinical stage biopharmaceutical company Alios Bio Pharma Inc. which focuses on developing therapies for viral diseases. The total purchase price of the deal was approximately $1.75 billion in cash. With the acquisition, Alios Bio Pharma became part of the infectious diseases therapeutic area of Janssen Pharmaceutica Companies of J&J. The acquisition enabled J&J to have access to Alios Bio Pharma's portfolio of potential therapeutics for viral infections with the promising compound AL-8176 which is an orally administered antiviral therapy currently in Phase 2 Studies for the treatment of infants with respiratory syncytial virus (RSV). RSV is a major pediatric disease which have no effective therapy. J&J also acquired two early stage compounds for hepatitis C (HCV) which could potentially augment Janssen's existing HCV portfolio.

In 2014, Covagen AG the biopharmaceutical company which specializes in the development of multi specific protein therapeutics were also acquired by J&J. In the same year, J&J acquired the ORSL electrolyte ready-to-drink brand from Jagdale Industries Ltd. In 2014, J&J completed the divestiture of its Ortho Clinical Diagnostics (OCD) business to the Carlyle Group for approximately $4 billion. OCD is the global provider of solutions for screening, diagnosing, monitoring and confirming diseases. The division had generated net sales of approximately $1.9 billion in year 2013. J&J decided to divest OCD as it belonged to logistically wise more complex industry as well.

In 2015, Janssen Pharmaceuticals Inc. (Janssen) acquired XO1 Ltd., a privately held asset centric virtual biopharmaceutical company which was founded to develop the antithrombin antibody ichorcumab. The acquisition facilitates Janssen to acquire leadership position in the fields of anticoagulation and biologics. The acquisition adds to the Janssen's cardiovascular portfolio. In 2015, J&J entered into a definitive agreement with Novira Therapeutics to treat chronic HBV infection. Novira's lead candidate is in Phase I testing to treat chronic HBV infection. The compound is an oral small molecule inhibitor of the HBV core protein.

3.8   Share buyback

In July 2014, J&J announced a share repurchase program which authorizes the company to purchase up to $5 billion of the company's shares of common stock. By December 2014, shares worth $3.5 billion were repurchased under the program. The share repurchases is expected to take place on the open market from time to time based on market condition. The repurchase program has no limit and may be suspended for periods or discontinued at any time. The company intends to finance the share repurchase program through available cash.

3.9   Risk management

J&J uses financial instruments to manage the impact of foreign exchange rate changes on cash flows. J&J uses forward foreign exchange contracts to protect the value of certain foreign currency assets and liabilities. The company basically hedges future foreign currency transactions primarily related to product costs. J&J hedges exposure to fluctuations in currency exchange rates with currency swap contracts. In 2014, it was estimated that 1% change in the spread between United States and foreign interest rates on the company's interest rate sensitive financial instruments would either increase or decrease the unrealized value of the company's swap contracts by approximately $145 million. J&J does not use financial instruments for trading or speculative purposes. J&J have a policy of entering into contracts with parties that have at least an "A" or (equivalent) credit rating. The counter parties to these contracts are major financial institutions. The company do not have significant concentration of exposure with any one counter party. In 2014, J&J secured a new 364-day credit facility. Interest charged on borrowings under credit facility is based on either bids provided by banks, the prime rate or London Interbank Offered Rates (LIBOR) plus applicable margins. The Company's contractual obligations are primarily for leases, debt, and unfunded retirement plans.

3.10   Stock compensation

J&J provides stock options to employees. On the basis of equity instrument, the fair value is estimated on the date of grant using either the Black Scholes option valuation model or a combination of both the Black Scholes option valuation model and Monte Carlo valuation model. The input assumptions used in determining fair value are the expected life, expected volatility, risk free rate, and the dividend yield.

3.11   Risk factors

J&J faces a number of risk factors such as interest rate and currency exchange rate fluctuations, challenges to patents, obtaining regulatory approvals, impact of patent expirations, uncertainty of commercial success of new drug development, financial instability of nations, financial distress of purchasers of health care products. In February 2016, J&J was ordered by a Missouri state jury to pay $72 million of damages to the family of a woman whose death from ovarian cancer was linked to the use of the company's talc based Baby Powder and Shower to Shower for several decades.[4] J&J and some of its subsidiaries are involved in various lawsuits and claims with regard to product liability, intellectual property, commercial and other matters, governmental investigations, and other legal proceedings. As of December 28, 2014, in the United States there were approximately 11,200 plaintiffs with direct claims in pending lawsuits regarding injuries allegedly due to the ASR XL Acetabular System and DePuy ASR Hip Resurfacing System, 7300 with respect to

[4] http://www.theguardian.com/world/2016/feb/24/johnson-johnson-72-millon-babuy-talcum-powder-ovarian-cancer.

the PINNACLE Acetabular Cup System, 36,600 with respect to pelvic meshes, and 1200 with respect to RISPERDAL.[5] In August 2010, DePuy Orthopaedics, Inc. (DePuy) announced a worldwide voluntary recall of its ASR XL Acetabular System and DePuy ASR Hip Resurfacing System used in hip replacement surgery. There have been claims for personal injury which have been made against Janssen Pharmaceuticals, Inc. and J&J arising out of the use of RISPERDAL, which has been used for the treatment of schizophrenia, acute manic, or mixed episodes associated with bipolar disorder and irritability associated with autism, and related compounds. Law suits were also filed against Ethicon, Inc. and J&J as claims for personal injury arising out of Ethicon's pelvic mesh used to treat stress urinary incontinence and pelvic organ prolapse.[6]

3.12   Ownership structure

In 2015, the equity amount amounted to $71,554 million while the debt amount was $19,750 million. Equity constituted 78% of the capital structure while debt amounted to 22% of the capital structure.

Financial institutions hold 66.9% of the equity ownership. Mutual Funds hold 32.9% of the equity capital ownership. The insiders hold 0.2% of the equity capital of J&J (Table 3.2). The top 10 mutual funds hold 7.8% of the equity ownership. The top ten institutions hold 23% of the total share holdings (Tables 3.3 and 3.4).

Table 3.2 **Equity ownership in year 2015**

Type	Value in million dollars
Institutions	197,141.52
Mutual funds	97,072.19
Insiders	73.79

Table 3.3 **Major financial institutions with stakes in equity capital**

SL	Mutual funds	Percentage of share held
1	Vanguard Group Inc.	6.21
2	State Street Corp.	5.38
3	BlackRock Fund Advisors	3
4	Fidelity Management and Research	1.72
5	State Farm Mutual Automobile Ins Co.	1.37

[5] Johnson & Johnson Annual Report 2014. p. 64.
[6] Johnson & Johnson Annual Report 2014. p. 64.

Table 3.4 **Major mutual funds with stakes in equity capital**

	Name	Percentage of share held
1	Vanguard Total Stock MARKET Index	1.89
2	Vanguard 500 Index	1.24
3	Vanguard Institutional Index	1.09
4	SPDR S&P 500 ETF	1.02
5	Healthcare Select Sector SPDR ETF	0.49

3.13   Financial highlights

In 2014, J&J had registered full year sales of $74.3 billion and adjusted net earnings of $17.1 billion. The pharmaceutical sales registered operational growth rate of approximately 16.5%. J&J's pharmaceutical segment has been the fastest growing of the top 10 pharmaceutical businesses in the United States, Europe, and Japan. By 2014, the company had 53 consecutive years of dividend increases. By this time the company had 31 consecutive years of adjusted earnings increases. J&J is one of the three industrial companies to hold AAA ratings. J&J have 24 brands and platforms which generate sales over $1 billion. J&J have various retirement and pension plans which include defined benefit, defined contribution and termination indemnity plans. In 2014, the free cash flow amounted to $14.8 billion. These plans are based on assumptions for the discount rate, expected return on plan assets, mortality rates, expected salary increases, and health care cost trends. The Company also provides post-retirement benefits, primarily health care, to all eligible US retired employees and their dependents. Each pension plan is overseen by a local committee or board that is responsible for the overall administration and investment of the pension plans.

J&J includes highly liquid investments with stated maturities of greater than three months from the date of purchase as current marketable securities. The company invests in products of commercial institutions which have at least an A or equivalent credit rating. The cash reserves are invested in reverse repurchase agreements, government securities and obligations, corporate debt securities, and money market funds. The advertising expenses amounted to $2.6 billion in year 2014. The company have plans that it would cut 3000 jobs at its medical devices unit as part of a restructuring effort designed to save up to $1 billion a year in costs.[7]

Table 3.5 estimates the economic value generated by J&J during the period 2011-2014. Tables 3.6–3.8 gives the operating highlights of J&J. Table 3.9 gives the R&D Expenses .During the period 2012–14, R&D as% of sales was approximately 11% of sales.

3.13.1   Shareholder return analysis

According to J&J 2014 Annual Report, the 5-year CAGR of J&J was 13.8%, while that of S&P 500 was 15.4%, while that of S&P Pharma was 17.5%. The 10 year

---

[7] http://www.ft.com/intl/cms/s/0/19cf178e-c43e-11e5-b3b1-7b2481276e45.html#axzz41AL6waLk.

Table 3.5 Economic value retained in billions of US dollars

Year	2011	2012	2013	2014
Revenues	65,030	67,224	71,312	74,331
Operating, employee, and other costs	48,364	48,821	48,898	52,459
Payment to providers of capital	6727	7146	7768	8301
Community investments	706	966	993	1080
Economic value retained	9233	10,291	13,653	12,491

Source: 2014 Citizenship and sustainability report.

Table 3.6 Major consumer franchise sales trends

Values in million dollars	2012	2013	2014
OTC	3766	4028	4106
Skin care	3618	3704	3758
Baby care	2254	2295	2239
Oral care	1624	1622	1647
Wound care/other	1560	1480	1444
Women's health	1625	1568	1302
Total consumer sales	14,447	14,697	14,496

Source: Annual report 2014.

Table 3.7 Major pharmaceutical therapeutic area sales

Values in million dollars	2012	2013	2014
Total immunology	7874	9190	10,193
Total infectious diseases	3194	3550	5599
Total neuroscience	6718	6667	6487
Total oncology	2629	3773	4457
Total other	4936	4945	5577
Total	25,351	28,125	32,313

Source: Annual Report 2014.

CAGR for J&J was 8.3% while that of S&P 500 was 7.7%. The analysis compares the returns of J&J with Standard & Poor's 500 Stock Index, the Standard & Poor's Pharmaceutical Index and the Standard & Poor's Health Care Equipment Index. The analysis is based on the assumption that $100 was invested on December 31, 2004 in each of the company's common stock, the standard and Poor's 500 Stock Index, the Standard & Poor's Pharmaceutical Index, the Standard and Poor's Health Care Equipment Index, and that all dividends were reinvested (Table 3.10).

Table 3.8 **Major medical devices franchise sales**

Values in million dollars	2012	2013	2014
Orthopedics	7799	9509	9675
Surgical care	6483	6269	6176
Specialty surgery/other	3478	3504	3541
Vision care	2996	2937	2818
Cardiovascular care	1985	2077	2208
Diabetics care	2616	2309	2142
Diagnostics	2069	1885	962
Total medical sales	27,426	28,490	27,522

Source: Annual Report 2014.

Table 3.9 **R&D expenses**

Values in million dollars	2012	2013	2014
Consumer	622	590	629
Pharmaceutical	5362	5810	6213
Medical devices	1681	1783	1652
Total R&D	7665	8183	8494

Source: Annual Report 2014.

3.14 Trend analysis

The values given are in millions of US dollars. The number of employees given are in thousands (Table 3.11). The revenues have increased from $47.348 billion in year 2004 to $74.331 billion in year 2014. The operating income increased from $12.33 billion in year 2004 to $20.959 billion in year 2014. The net income increased from $8.18 billion in year 2004 to $16.323 billion in year 2014. The 10-year average growth rate of revenues during the period 2005−14 was approximately 5%. The average increase in cost of goods sold during the ten-year period was 5.5%. The average growth rate of operating income and net income during the ten-year period 2005−14 was 5.7% and 8.5%. The total assets increased by 9.4% on an average basis during the 10-year period of analysis. The average increase in total debt during the 10-year period of analysis was 9.4%. The average increase in R&D expenses during the 10-year period was 5%. R&D as % of revenues was approximately 12% on an average basis during the period 2004−14. The cost of goods sold as % of revenues was approximately 30% during the above ten-year period of analysis. The average gross margin during the 11-year period was approximately 70% while the operating margin during the period 2004−14 was approximately 25%.

Table 3.10 **Return analysis—amount in US dollars**

Year	2004	2005	2006	2007	2008	2009	2010	2011	2012	2013	2014
J&J	100	96.64	108.68	112.61	103.92	115.64	114.97	126.34	139.98	188.34	220.99
S&P 500 Index	100	104.91	121.48	128.15	80.74	102.11	117.48	119.97	139.16	184.22	209.42
S&P Pharmaceutical Index	100	96.64	111.96	117.17	95.85	113.69	114.57	134.91	154.38	208.76	255.14
S&P Healthcare Equipment Index	100	100.05	104.18	109.52	79.25	102.06	99.29	98.50	115.51	147.49	186.25

Source: Johnson &Johnson 2014, Annual Report, p. 69.

Table 3.11 **Trend analysis of operating performance**

Year	2004	2005	2006	2007	2008	2009	2010	2011	2012	2013	2014
Revenues	47,348	50,514	53,324	61,095	63,747	61,897	61,587	65,030	67,224	71,312	74,331
Cost of goods sold	13,474	14,010	15,057	17,751	18,511	18,447	18,792	20,360	21,658	22,342	22,746
Sales and advertising expenses	16,174	17,211	17,433	20,451	21,490	19,801	19,424	20,969	20,869	21,830	21,954
R&D expenses	5344	6462	7125	7680	7577	6986	6844	7548	7665	8183	8494
Operating income	12,331	13,009	13,150	13,661	15,988	15,590	16,527	16,153	15,869	18,377	20,959
Net income	8180	10,060	11,053	10,576	12,949	12,266	13,334	9672	10,853	13,831	16,323
Total assets	54,039	58,864	70,556	80,954	84,912	94,682	102,908	113,644	121,347	132,683	131,119
Total debt	2565	2017	2014	7074	3120	8223	9156	12,969	11,489	13,328	15,122
Number of employees (in thousands)	109.9	115.6	122.2	119.2	118.7	115.5	114	117.9	127.6	128.1	126.5

Source: J&J Annual report 2014.

The comparison of variables during the two five-year period 2005–09 and 2010–14 reveals that the average growth rate of revenues declined from 5.7% during the period 2005–09 to 3.8% during the period 2010–14. The average increase in cost of goods sold declined from 6.7% during the period 2005–09 to 4.3% during the period 2010–14. The average rate of increase in R&D expenses during the period 2005–09 decreased from 6% to 4% during the period 2010–14. The average growth rate of net income declined from 9% to 7.8% during the two periods of comparison. The average growth rate of total assets decreased from 12% to 6.8% during the period of analysis. The average debt amount registered a decline of 49.2% to 14.2% during the two periods of comparison.

The per share data values are given in dollar amounts (Table 3.12). EPS increased from $2.74 in 2004 to $5.7 in 2014 signifying an increase of almost 2.4 times. The DPS increased from $1.09 in 2004 to $ 2.76 by 2014. The shareholder equity increased from $10.95 to $25.06. The market price per share increased from $63.42 in 2004 to $105.06 in year 2014. The average growth rate of earnings per share during the 11-year period 2004–14 was approximately 9%. The average increase in dividend per share and book value per share was approximately 10% and 9% during the period 2004–14. The average returns based on year end closing price was approximately 6% during the period of analysis.

3.15   Ratio analysis

The average net margin during the period 2005–14 was 19.28%. The ROA and ROE during the above period was 13.41% and 24.29%, respectively. The return on invested capital was approximately 20% during the 10-year period 2005–14. The profitability ratios have declined in the post 2009 period compared to pre 2009 period. The average net margin decreased from 19.76% during the 2005–09 period to 18.8% during the period 2010–14. The average return on assets declined from 15.8% to 10.98% during the two periods of comparison. The average return on equity declined from 28% to 20.4% during the above period. The return on invested capital decreased from 23% to 16.4% during the two periods of comparison (Table 3.13).

The gross, net and operating margins were fluctuating over the 10-year period. The average gross margin during the 10-year period was approximately 70%. The average operating margin during the 10-year period was 25.23%. The average net margin was 19.4% during the 10-year period 2006–15 (Table 3.14).

The average 10-year EBITDA per share value was $6.9 while the average free cash flow per share was $4.6 (Table 3.15).

The average current ratio during the period 2005–14 was 1.96 while the quick ratio during the above period was 1.41 (Table 3.16).

The average payable period during the 10-year period was 116.5 days. The average receivable period during the above period was 55 days. The average inventory turnover, fixed assets and total assets turnover was 3.4, 4.4, and 0.7, respectively during

Table 3.12 Per share data

Per share data	2004	2005	2006	2007	2008	2009	2010	2011	2012	2013	2014
Earnings per share	2.74	3.35	3.73	3.63	4.57	4.4	4.78	3.49	3.86	4.81	5.7
Dividend per share	1.095	1.275	1.455	1.62	1.795	1.93	2.11	2.25	2.4	2.59	2.76
Shareholder equity per share	10.95	13.01	13.59	15.25	15.35	18.37	20.66	20.95	23.33	26.25	25.06
Market price per share (year end close)	63.42	60.1	66.02	67.38	53.56	64.41	61.85	65.58	69.48	92.35	105.06

Table 3.13 Profitability ratios

Year	2005	2006	2007	2008	2009	2010	2011	2012	2013	2014
Net margin in percent	20.61	20.73	17.31	20.31	19.82	21.65	14.87	16.14	19.4	21.96
Return on assets in percent	18.7	17.19	13.96	15.61	13.66	13.5	8.93	9.24	10.89	12.38
Return on equity in percent	29.88	28.64	25.6	30.17	26.35	24.88	17.02	17.81	19.92	22.7
Return on invested capital in percent	26.81	24.22	21.16	24.26	21	19.65	13.39	14.22	16.39	18.47

Table 3.14 Margins in percent

Year	2006	2007	2008	2009	2010	2011	2012	2013	2014	2015
Gross margin	71.76	70.95	70.96	70.2	69.49	68.69	67.78	68.67	69.4	69.27
Net margin	20.73	17.31	20.31	19.82	21.65	14.87	16.14	19.4	21.96	21.99
Operating margin	24.66	22.36	25.08	25.19	26.84	24.84	23.61	25.77	28.2	25.78

Table 3.15 **Cash flow per share**

Year	2006	2007	2008	2009	2010	2011	2012	2013	2014	2015
EBITDA per share	5.68	5.62	7.12	6.81	7.29	5.8	6.39	6.97	8.73	8.35
Free cash flow per share	3.88	4.15	4.2	5.09	5.02	4.11	4.43	4.8	5.15	5.6

Table 3.16 **Liquidity ratios**

Year	2005	2006	2007	2008	2009	2010	2011	2012	2013	2014
Current ratio	2.48	1.2	1.51	1.65	1.82	2.05	2.38	1.9	2.2	2.36
Quick ratio	1.83	0.67	0.95	1.08	1.34	1.62	1.88	1.34	1.59	1.76

Table 3.17 **Efficiency ratios**

Year	2005	2006	2007	2008	2009	2010	2011	2012	2013	2014
Payables period in days	124.8	121.28	129.54	142.09	129.05	108.42	101.72	97.38	98.81	111.52
Receivable period in days	49.32	53.10	53.49	54.14	56.34	56.78	56.34	58.63	58.06	54.96
Inventory turnover	3.62	3.4	3.55	3.64	3.61	3.56	3.49	3.14	2.91	2.83
Fixed assets turnover	4.75	4.47	4.49	4.47	4.25	4.2	4.44	4.36	4.35	4.53
Asset turnover	0.91	0.83	0.81	0.77	0.69	0.62	0.6	0.57	0.56	0.56

the above period of analysis. The average payable period declined from 129 days during the period 2005—09 to 103.6 days during the period 2010—14. The average receivable period increased from 53 days during 2005—09 to 57 days during the period 2010—14. The inventory turnover ratio declined from 3.6 to 3.2 during the period of analysis. The fixed assets turnover ratio declined from 4.5 to 4.4 during the above period (Table 3.17).

The ratio of long-term debt to total assets provides a general measure of the financial position of a company, including its ability to meet financial requirements for outstanding loans.

The average long-term debt to total assets ratio during the 10-year period 2006—15 was 0.093. The average debt equity ratio during the 10-year period 2006—15 was 0.265.

Table 3.18 **Leverage ratios**

Year	2006	2007	2008	2009	2010	2011	2012	2013	2014	2015
Long term debt to total assets ratio	0.03	0.09	0.1	0.09	0.09	0.11	0.1	0.1	0.12	0.1
Debt equity ratio	0.17	0.22	0.28	0.29	0.3	0.34	0.25	0.25	0.27	0.28
Interest coverage ratio	208.73	46.15	36.75	34.57	36.32	28.29	29.83	38.13	39.32	32.73

The leverage ratios had been fluctuating over the 10-year period of analysis. The average interest coverage ratio (ICR) during the 10-year period was 53. On the basis of ICR, it can be interpreted that J&J's financial strength is strong (Table 3.18).

3.16   Estimation of WACC

The first step in the estimation of WACC is the estimation of cost of equity. The cost of equity is estimated using the dividend growth model and capital asset pricing model.

Cost of equity using dividend growth model
Cost of equity = (Dividend next period/Market price) + Growth rate.
Dividend in year 2015 = $2.90
The average growth rate of dividends during the 5-year period 2010−14 was 7.4%.
Dividend in year 2015 = $2.90
Dividend next period = Current dividend × (1 + growth rate)
    = 2.90 × (1 + 0.074) = $3.11
Market Price at end of year 2015 = $105.06
Cost of Equity = 2.96/105.06 + 7.4% = 10.36%

The cost of equity using dividend growth model is estimated as 10.36%.
Estimation of cost of equity using CAPM

Required rate of return = Risk free rate + Beta × (Return on market index − Risk free rate)

The risk free rate is assumed as the average yield to maturity on the 30-year treasury bond during the 2-year period 2014−16.[8]

Year	Yield to maturity on 30-year treasury bond
2014	3.55
2015	2.63
2016	2.63
Average	2.94%

[8] https://www.treasury.gov/resource-center/data-chart-center/interest-rates/Pages/Historic-Yield-Data-Visualization.aspx.

The risk free rate is estimated as 2.94%. Beta is estimated by regressing the daily returns of J&J stock on the daily returns on market index S&P 500 during the period January 2014 to December 2015. The beta value estimated is 0.84.

The average yearly return on market index S&P 500 is estimated to be 9.15%.

Cost of equity = 2.94 + 0.84 × (9.51−2.94)
Cost of equity = 2.94 + 0.84 × (6.21) = 8.09%.

For the estimation purposes, we take the average of the cost of equity obtained from dividend discount model and CAPM

Final estimated cost of equity = (10.36 + 8.09)/2 = 9.23%.

Estimation of cost of debt

The yield to maturity on the long term bond issued by J&J maturing in the year 2038 is 3.684%.[9]
The yield to maturity on the long term bond issued by J&J is assumed to be the cost of debt. The effective tax rate in 2015 is estimated as 20%.
After tax cost of debt = Cost of debt (1 − Tax Rate) = 3.684 × (1 − Tax Rate) = 3.684 × (1−0.20) = 3.684 × 0.80 = 2.95%

Market value weights

Book value of debt in year 2015 = $19,861 million

To find the market value of debt, the price of the long term bond maturing in year 2038 is estimated. Then the ratio of the price of this long term bond to the face value of bond is estimated.

Ratio = 132.81/100 = 1.382
Market value of debt = 19,861 × 1.382 = $26,377.39 million
Market value of equity based on year end 2015 values = $284,220 million
Total value of capital = $310,597.4 million
Weight of equity = 284,220/310,597.4 = 0.92
Weight of debt = 26,377.39/310,597.4 = 0.08
Weighted average cost of capital (WACC) based on market value weights = Weight of Equity × Cost of equity + Weight of debt × After tax cost of debt
        = 0.92 × 9.23 + 0.08 × 2.95 = 8.73%
Weighted Average Cost of Capital for J&J in year 2015 = 8.73%

3.17   Shareholder wealth analysis

The average monthly returns based on period 1970−February 2016 consisting of 554 months was 1.18% Based on the above calculation the average yearly returns during the 46-year period was approximately 14%. The cumulative monthly return during the 554 months (1970−2016) period was 652 % (Fig. 3.1). Suppose an

[9] http://finra-markets.morningstar.com/BondCenter/Results.jsp.

investor made an investment of $1000 in the shares of J&J during January 1970. In a 46-year period this investment would have grown from $1000 to $7520 on the basis of cumulative monthly returns.

The cumulative monthly returns during the six-year period 2010–15 was approximately 75%. The average compounded monthly returns during the period Jan 2010–Feb 2016 was approximately 34.6%.

J&J outperformed the index S&P in four out of six years of analysis on the basis of average yearly returns. The abnormal returns generated by J&J over the S&P 500 index was 9.23% in year 2011. In year 2013 and 2014, J&J generated excess returns of 4.71% and 5.64%, respectively. The performance of S&P 500 was better than J&J in 2010 and 2012 (Table 3.19).

The holding period yield analysis is based on the assumption that a J&J stock is purchased in the beginning of every year and sold by the end of the year. The holding period yield was highest in the year 2013 when J&J had holding period yield of 27.67%. In 2014, the holding period yield was 21.48%. J&J's share price in the first week of January 2010 was $51.44. By end of December 2015, the stock price rose to $101.98. The six year holding period yield was 98.24% (Table 3.20).

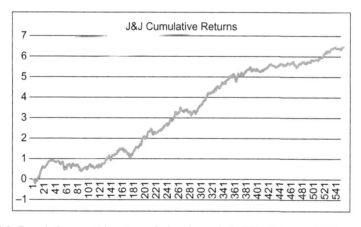

Figure 3.1 Cumulative monthly returns during the period 1970–February 2016.

Table 3.19 Average yearly returns in percent

Year	J&J	S&P	Excess return
2010	0.35	19.09	− 18.74
2011	10.38	1.15	9.23
2012	10.8	13.16	− 2.36
2013	31.25	26.54	4.71
2014	16.77	11.13	5.64
2015	1.89	0.11	1.78

Table 3.20 **Holding period yield in %**

Year	Holding period yield in %
2010	1.86
2011	13.71
2012	10.29
2013	27.67
2014	21.48
2015	5.62

Table 3.21 **Market value added in millions of dollars**

Year	2011	2012	2013	2014	2015
MV of equity	179,089	194,772	258,341	291,042	284,220
BV of equity	57,080	64,826	74,053	69,752	71,150
BV as % of MV	32	33	29	24	25
Excess market value	122,009	129,946	184,288	221,290	213,070

The average book value as % of market value of equity during the five-year period 2011−15 was 29%. Excess market value generated is estimated as the difference between market value of equity and book value of equity. The book value as % of market value was only 24% in year 2014. The excess market value created was highest in year 2014 (Table 3.21).

3.18   Valuation perspectives

3.18.1   Estimation of economic value of J&J

The value is estimated for year 2015.

Economic value is estimated as net operating income after taxes (NOPAT) − Capital charge.
Profit before interest and tax-income tax = NOPAT.
Capital employed = Stock holder equity + Long term debt
Capital charge = Capital employed × WACC
Economic value (EV) = NOPAT − Capital charge

Estimation of economic value (EV)

Net operating income after taxes (NOPAT) = PBIT − Taxes
NOPAT in 2015 = 18,065 − 3787 = $14,278 million
Stock holder equity in year 2015 = $71,150 million
Long term debt in year 2015 = $12,857 million

Capital employed = \$71,150 + \$12,857 = \$84,007 million.
WACC = 8.73%
Capital charge = 84,007 × 8.73% = \$7333.811 million
Economic value = NOPAT − Capital charge
    = 14,278 − 7333.811 = \$6944.189 million
Economic value created for J&J in year 2015 = \$6944.189 million.

3.18.2 Equity spread

Equity spread is a variation of the EV measures. Equity spread is the difference between the ROE and the required return on equity (cost of equity)

Equity Spread = (Return on equity−Cost of equity) × Equity capital
Return on equity in year 2015 = 19.87%
Cost of equity = 9.23%
Equity spread = (19.87% − 9.23%) × 71,150 million = \$7570.36 million.

The equity spread estimated for J&J is \$7570.36 million.

3.18.3 Valuation-dividend discount model

The net income growth rate during the 5-year period 2011−15 was approximately 3% based on geometric mean average. The earnings per share growth rate during the above period was 2.7%.

3.18.3.1 DDM two-stage model

The average growth rate of earnings estimated from fundamentals is estimated as 9%. We use two stage Dividend Discount Model (DDM) to value J&J stock. First it is assumed that J&J will grow at the fundamental earnings growth rate of 9% for a period of 10 years followed by the stable growth rate of US economy (Tables 3.22 and 3.23).

High growth period = 10 years
Growth rate in the high growth period = 9% (Estimated from fundamentals)
Current EPS = \$5.48

Table 3.22 Estimation of retention ratio

Year	2011	2012	2013	2014	2015
EPS	3.49	3.86	4.81	5.7	5.48
DPS	2.25	2.4	2.59	2.76	2.95
DPO	0.64	0.62	0.54	0.48	0.54
RR	0.36	0.38	0.46	0.52	0.46

Retention ratio (RR) = 1 − DPO
Average DPO = 57%

Table 3.23 Estimation of growth rate from fundamentals

Year	2011	2012	2013	2014	2015
RR	0.36	0.38	0.46	0.52	0.46
ROE	0.17	0.1781	0.1992	0.227	0.2187
Growth rate	0.06	0.07	0.09	0.12	0.10

Growth rate = Retention ratio × Return on equity.

Table 3.24 Present value of dividends in high growth phase

Year	1	2	3	4	5	6	7	8	9	10
EPS	5.97	6.51	7.10	7.74	8.43	9.19	10.02	10.92	11.90	12.97
DPO	0.57	0.57	0.57	0.57	0.57	0.57	0.57	0.57	0.57	0.57
DPS	3.40	3.71	4.05	4.41	4.81	5.24	5.71	6.22	6.78	7.39
PV	$3.12	$3.11	$3.10	$3.10	$3.09	$3.08	$3.08	$3.07	$3.06	$3.06
SUM	$30.88									

The average DPO in the high growth period is taken as the average DPO during the 5-year period 2011−15 that is 57% (Table 3.24).

Cost of equity = 9.23%

The present value of dividends of J&J in the high growth phase is estimated as $30.88.

3.18.3.2 Stable phase inputs

Growth rate in stable period is assumed to be the growth rate of US economy. The average growth rate of US GDP for two year period 2013−14. The GDP growth rate is estimated as 2.3%.[10]

Growth rate in stable phase = 2.3%
Return on equity of pharma industry sector = 23.3%[11]
Growth rate in stable period = Retention ratio × Return on equity of the industry sector.
2.3% = Retention ratio × 23.3%
Retention ratio = 2.3%/23.3%
Retention ratio in stable period = 9.9%
DPO in stable period = $1 - 0.099 = 0.901$
EPS at end of high growth period = $12.97
EPS at beginning of stable period = $12.97 \times (1 + g)$ where g is the growth rate of earnings in stable period.
EPS at beginning of stable period = $12.97 \times 1.023 = 13.27
DPS in stable period = EPS × DPO = $13.27 \times 0.901 = 11.96

[10] http://data.worldbank.org/indicator/NY.GDP.MKTP.KD.ZG.

[11] http://www.morningstar.com/stocks/xnys/jnj/quote.html.

Terminal value of dividends in stable period = DPS in stable period/(Cost of equity-Growth rate in stable period)
Terminal Value of dividends = 11.96/(0.0923 − 0.023) = \$172.56
Present value of terminal value of dividends = \$71.37
Value of J&J stock = Present value of dividends in high growth phase + Present value of terminal value of dividends in stable phase
   = \$30.88 + \$71.37 = \$102.25

The value of J&J stock is estimated as \$102.25. J&J was trading at \$105.78 in NYSE on 26/2/2016.

3.18.4 Free cash flow to equity valuation

Free cash flow to equity valuation (FCFE) is the residual cash flow available to shareholders. It is a measure of the potential dividends which a firm can pay to its shareholders. It is the residual cash flow after taxes, interest expenses, and reinvestment needs.

FCFE = Net income − Capital expenditure + Depreciation and amortization − Change in noncash working capital + New debt issued − Debt repayment.

Since J&J is a research intensive company, the following adjustments are made in the FCFE Valuation.

> *Net capital expenditure = Capital expenditure − Depreciation and Amortization.*
> *Adjusted net capital expenditure = Net capital expenditure + R&D expenses in current period − Amortization of research asset + Net acquisitions.*
> *Adjusted depreciation and amortization = Depreciation and amortization + Amortization of research asset.*
> *Adjusted net income = Net income + Current year's R&D expense − Amortization of research asset.*
> *Adjusted operating income = Operating income + Current year's R&D expenses − Amortization of research asset.*
> *Adjusted book value of equity = Book value of equity + Value of research asset.*

Research assets are amortized linearly over time. The life of research asset is assumed to be 10 years and 10% is amortized each year. The value of research asset and amortization expense calculation for the current year 2015 are given below (Tables 3.25−3.26). The details of the calculations are given in the sheet FCFE of *J&J.xlsx.*
Adjusted net capital expenditure = Net capital expenditure + R&D expenses in current period−Amortization of research asset + Acquisitions (Table 3.27).

Noncash working capital = Noncash current assets − noninterest bearing current liabilities (Table 3.28).
Noncash current assets = Total current assets − cash and cash equivalents

Table 3.25 **Estimation of amortization and value of research asset in year 2015**

Year			Unamortized portion		Amortization this year (million dollars)
			%	(million dollars)	
Current	9046		100	9046	
−1	8494		90	7644.6	849.4
−2	8183		80	6546.4	818.3
−3	7665		70	5365.5	766.5
−4	7548		60	4528.8	754.8
−5	6844		50	3422	684.4
−6	6986		40	2794.4	698.6
−7	7577		30	2273.1	757.7
−8	7680		20	1536	768
−9	7125		10	712.5	712.5
−10	6462		0	0	646.2
	Value of research asset			43,869.3	
	Amortization expense current year				7456.4

Table 3.26 **R&D expenses, value, and amortization of R&D in millions of dollars**

Year	R&D expenses	Value of R&D	Amortization of R&D
2014	8494	42,279.7	7141.4
2015	9046	43,869.3	7456.4

Table 3.27 **Estimation of adjusted net capital expenditure in millions of dollars**

Year	2014	2015
Capex	3714	3463
Depreciation and amortization	3895	3746
Net Capex	−181	−283
R&D expenses in current period	8672	9046
Amortization of research asset	7141.4	7456.4
Adjusted Net Capex	1349.6	1306.6
Adjusted Net Income	17,675.6	16,998.6
Net capex as % of adjusted net income	0.076	0.076
Average	0.076	

Net capital expenditure as per cent of adjusted net income was 7.6% during the 2-year period 2014−15.

Table 3.28 **Estimation of noncash working capital**

Values in million dollars	2013	2014	2015
Total current assets	56,407	59,311	60,210
Cash and cash equivalents	29,206	33,089	38,376
Noncash current assets	27,201	26,222	21,834
Total current liabilities	25,675	25,085	27,747
Short term debt	4852	3638	7004
Noninterest bearing current liabilities	20,823	21,447	20,743
Noncash working capital	6378	4775	1091
Change in noncash working capital		−1603	−3684

Table 3.29 **Estimation of FCFE in year 2015**

	Values in millions of dollars
Adjusted net income	16,998.6
Adjusted net capex	1306.6
Change in noncash working capital	−3684
Net debt issued	1379
FCFE in millions of dollars	20,755

Noninterest bearing current liabilities = Total current liabilities − short term debt

Estimation of growth rate from fundamentals require the estimation of reinvestment rate. Reinvestment rate is estimated by dividing the amount spend for capital expenditure divided by the adjusted net income. The growth rate estimated in year 2015 as the product of the reinvestment rate and adjusted return on equity was approximately 1%. Hence it is assumed that the growth rate for cash flows for J&J would be approximately equal to the US GDP growth rate of 2.3% estimated in the above section. The constant growth model is used for FCFE valuation.

Constant growth FCFE Valuation model

FCFE = Adjusted Net income−Adjusted net capex − Change in noncash working capital + Net debt issued.
Net debt issued = Debt issued − Debt repayment.

The FCFE value is estimated to be $20,755 million in year 2015 (Table 3.29).

FCFE in stable period = FCFE in year 2015 × (1 + g).

Where g is the growth rate in stable period. The growth rate in stable period is assumed to be the growth rate of US GDP growth rate.

Value of equity = FCFE2015 × (1 + growth rate)/(Cost of Equity − growth rate)
   = 20,775 × (1.023)/(0.0923 − 0.023) = $306,383.33 million
Number of shares = 2813 million
Value per share = $108.92

Value of J&J according to FCFE Constant growth model is arrived at $108.92. The 52 week range for J&J during the year 2015 was $81.79–$106.92.

3.18.5 FCFF valuation model

The estimation of growth rate from fundamentals yields the growth rate as approximately 1%. Hence we use the constant growth FCFF model for valuation in this section.

Estimation of FCFF in 2015

Adjusted EBIT (1−T)	15,867.6
Adjusted net capex	1306.6
Change in noncash working capital	−3684
FCFF	18,245

Free cash flow to firm (FCFF) in year 2015 = $18,245 million

3.18.5.1 Constant growth FCFF model

FCFE in stable period = FCFE in year 2015 $\times$ (1 + g)

where g is the growth rate of cash flows in the stable period. This growth rate is assumed to be the growth rate of US GDP of 2.3%.

FCFF in stable period = 18,245 $\times$ 1.023 = $18,664.64 million
Value = FCFF in stable period/(WACC − growth rate)
WACC = 8.73%
Value = 18,664.64/(0.0873 − 0.023) = $290,274.3 million
Value of operating assets of J&J = $290,274.3 million

Value of operating assets	290,274.3
Cash and cash equivalents	38,376
Value of J&J	328,650.3
Value of debt	19,861
Value of equity	308,789.3
No of shares	2813
Value of equity per share	109.77

The number of shares = 2813 million. The value of operating assets of J&J is estimated as $290.274 billion. Adding cash and cash equivalents of $38.376 billion, the value of J&J is arrived at $328.65 billion. Deducting the value of debt, the value of equity is arrived at $308.789. Dividing the value of equity by the number of shares, the value of equity per share is arrived at $109.77.

Summary of Discounted Cash Flow Valuation

DDM Two stage growth model
Value of J&J share = $102.25
Constant growth FCFE valuation model

> *Value of J&J share = $108.92. Market value of equity = $306.38 billion*
> Constant growth FCFF model
> *Value of J&J share = $109.77*
>
> *J&J was trading at $105.78 in NYSE on 26/2/2016. The 52 week range for J&J during the March 2016 was $81.79–$106.92. The market capitalization of J&J as on 1/3/2016 was $290.3 billion.*

3.18.6 Relative valuation

All values except EPS are given in millions of dollars. The financial highlights of the year 2015 reveal that Pfizer Inc had the highest total assets which amounted to $167.46 billion followed by J&J with value amounted to $133.411 billion (Table 3.30). Bristol Myers and J&J were the lowest debt intensive companies among the peer group of companies. J&J incurred the maximum R&D expenses of $9.046 billion. Novartis was the second most R&D intensive company with expenses amounting to $8.9 billion. In year 2015, J&J had registered the highest revenues amounting to $70.07 billion. Novartis had achieved the second highest revenues of $50.387 billion. J&J had been the highest cash flow maximizer among the peer firms. J&J had the highest cash reserves among the peer group of companies. J&J had a cash reserve of $38 billion dollars compared to cash reserve of $23.29 billion dollars for Pfizer.

In relative valuation, J&J is compared with the peer group of companies like J&J, Pfizer, Novartis, Merck, and Bristol Myers.

The current peer comparison is based on data in March 2016 (Table 3.31). The source of data was Morningstar.com. The market capitalization and net income are given in millions of dollars. J&J had the highest market capitalization with $295.86 billion among the peer companies. J&J has the second highest price to sales and price to book ratio after Bristol Myers. Bristol Myers had the highest price multiples among the peer group of companies. Bristol Myers PE ratio was 68.9. J&J had the highest ICR of 35.8 among the peer group of companies.

Table 3.30 Financial highlights of the peer companies in year 2015

Company	J&J	Pfizer	Novartis	Merck	Bristol Myers
Total assets	133,411	167,460	131,556	101,779	31,748
Total debt	19,861	38,978	21,931	26,514	6689
R&D expenses	9046	7690	8935	6704	5920
Revenues	70,074	48,851	50,387	39,498	16,560
Cash flow	23,494	15,321	8977	12,448	2637
Cash and cash equivalents	38,376	23,290	3847	13,427	4270
EPS	5.56	1.13	7.4	1.58	0.94

Table 3.31 **Peer group-market value, net income and price multiples comparison**

SL	Company	Market capitalization	Net income	P/S	P/B	P/E	Div yield %	ICR
1	J&J	295,858	15,409	4.2	4.1	19.2	2.8	35.8
2	Pfizer	185,436	8360	3.9	2.8	22.6	3.8	9.7
3	Novartis AG	172,914	17,783	3.5	2.2	25.3	3.8	13.2
4	Merck & Co	143,619	10,781	3.7	3.2	33.1	3.5	24.6
5	Bristol Myers	107,212	1565	6.5	7.5	68.9	2.3	12.3

Table 3.32 **Price multiple comparison with Industry and market index**

Price multiples	JNJ	Industry average	S&P 500
P/E	19.6	17.6	18.1
P/B	4.2	3.5	2.5
P/S	4.3	3.6	1.7
P/cash flow	15.6	15.9	11.1
Dividend yield%	2.8	3.7	2.4

Table 3.32 highlights J&J's price multiple comparison with industry and market index. The data values are based on the current year 2016. The data was sourced from morning star.com. J&J had higher P/E, P/B, P/S than the industry sector and S&P 500. The price to cash flow (P/cash flow) and dividend yield for J&J was higher than for S&P 500.

The price to earnings multiple for J&J peaked in year 2013. The price to book and price to sales ratio has steadily improved over the five-year period 2011−15. The price to sales ratio peaked in the year 2015. The price to cash flow multiple was highest in the year 2014.

The earnings yield is an indication of how much return shareholders' investment in the company earned over the past 12 months. The higher the earnings yield is, the better (Table 3.33).

The revenues, EBITDA, EBIT, debt, market value of equity, cash and cash equivalents, and enterprise value are given in millions of dollars (Table 3.34).

Enterprise value = Market value of equity + Debt − Cash and cash equivalents

The enterprise value multiples of EV/Revenues were lower for J&J, Novartis and Merck compared to Pfizer and Bristol Myers. Lower the enterprise value multiples, the more undervalued the stocks and hence attractive. J&J had the lowest EV/EBITDA and EV/EBIT multiples compared to the peer companies. Hence J&J is an attractive stock.

Table 3.33 **Trend analysis of price multiples of J&J**

Year	2011	2012	2013	2014	2015
P/E	16	18.2	20.4	17.3	19.7
P/B	2.9	3	3.7	3.8	4
P/S	2.8	2.9	3.7	4	4.1
P/CF	12.4	12.8	15.8	16.4	15.6
Earnings yield in %	6.3	5.5	4.9	5.8	5.1

Table 3.34 **Enterprise value multiples in current year**

Company	J&J	Pfizer	Novartis	Merck	Bristol Myers
Revenues	70,074	48,851	50,387	39,498	16,560
EBITDA	23,494	15,321	8977	12,448	2637
EBIT	18,065	11,824	8803	6928	1890
Debt	19,861	38,978	21,931	26,514	6689
Market value of equity	295,858	185,436	172,914	143,619	107,212
Cash and cash equivalents	38,376	23,290	3847	13,427	4270
Enterprise value (EV)	277,343	201,124	190,998	156,706	109,631
EV/revenues	3.96	4.12	3.79	3.97	6.62
EV/EBITDA	11.80	13.13	21.28	12.59	41.57
EV/EBIT	15.35	17.01	21.70	22.62	58.01

3.18.6.1 Comparative growth rate analysis

The analysis of average growth rates of revenues and operating income in year 2015 reveals that J&J had positive growth rate in terms of 5 and 10-year average growth rates. The 5-year average growth rate of J&J's revenues was 2.62%. The 10-year average growth rate of J&J revenues was 3.33%. The 5-year average growth rate of revenues for Bristol Myers, Merck, Novartis, and Pfizer had been negative. Merck had a 10-year average growth rate of revenues of 6.02% while Novartis had growth rate of 4.58%. The average 5-year growth rate of operating income for J&J was 1.8% while the 10-year average growth rate was 3.34%. The 5-year average growth rate of operating income of Merck had been 23% while the 10-year growth rate was 2.27%. The average 5-year growth rate of operating income of Pfizer had been 4.65%.

3.18.6.2 PEG ratio

PEG ratio is obtained by dividing P/E ratio by the growth rate of cash flow proxied by EBITDA (Earnings before interest, tax, and depreciation). The growth rate used is the 4-year average EBITDA growth rate. The average growth rate of EBITDA during the period 2011–15 was 9.9%. The PE ratio is 2015 was 19.7. The value of PEG ratio calculated is 1.99. Peter Lynch who suggested the PEG ratio opines that a company with P/E ratio equal to its growth rate is fairly valued (Table 3.35).

Table 3.35 **PEG ratio comparison**

Company	J&J	Pfizer	Novartis	Merck	Bristol Myers
P/E	19.7	22.6	25.3	33.1	68.9
Growth rate of EBITDA	9.90%	− 10.10%	− 6%	− 5.35%	− 24%
PEG	1.99	− 2.24	− 4.22	− 6.19	− 2.87

The PE ratios were for the year 2015. The average growth rate of EBITDA was for the 4-year period 2011−15. Only J&J had positive PEG ratio.

3.19 Performance indicator analysis

3.19.1 Altman Z score

NYU Stern Finance Professor, Edward Altman developed the Altman Z score formula in the year 1967. In the year 2012, he released an updated version called the Altman Z Score Plus which can be used to evaluate both public and private companies. Investors can use Altman Z score to decide if they should buy or sell a particular stock based on the company's financial strength. The Altman Z score is the output of a credit strength test which gauges a publicly traded manufacturing company's likelihood of bankruptcy. Z score model is an accurate forecaster of failure up to two years prior to distress.

$$\text{Z-Score} = 1.2\,A + 1.4B + 3.3C + 0.6D + 1.0E$$

where:

A = Working capital/total assets
B = Retained earnings/total assets
C = Earnings before interest & tax/total assets
D = Market value of equity/Total liabilities
E = Sales/total assets

The zones of discrimination are such that when Z Score is less than 1.81, it is in distress zones. When the Z score is greater than 2.99, it is in safe zones. When the Z Score is between 1.81 and 2.99, the company is in Grey Zone.

The calculations are based on the year 2015 (Table 3.36). The Z score of 5.09 for J&J indicates that the score is strong and the company is in safe zone.

3.19.2 Piotroski score

The Piotroski score is a discrete score between 0 and 9 which is an indicator of the firm's financial position. The score was named after the Chicago accounting

Table 3.36 Estimation of Altman Z Score for J&J

Ratios	Values	Constant	Score
Working capital/total assets	0.24	1.2	0.29
Retained earnings/total assets	0.78	1.4	1.09
Operating income/total assets	0.14	3.3	0.45
Market value of equity/total liabilities	4.56	0.6	2.74
Sales/total assets	0.53	1	0.53
		Z Score	5.09

professor Joseph Piotroski. The cumulative points suggest whether the stock is a value stock or not. If the company achieves a score of 8 or 9, the stock can be considered strong. If the score ranges between 0−2, then the stock is considered weak.

3.19.2.1 Criteria for Piotroski score

SL	Profitability scores	Score points	Score for J&J
1	Positive return on assets in current year	1	1
2	Positive operating cash flow in current year	1	1
3	Higher ROA in current year compared to previous year	1	0
4	Return on cash flow from operations greater than ROA	1	1
	Leverage, liquidity, and sources of funds		
5	Lower ratio of long term debt to average total assets in current year compared to previous year	1	1
6	Higher current ratio in this year compared to previous year	1	0
7	No new shares were issued in the last year	1	1
	Operational efficiency ratios		
8	A higher gross margin compared to the previous year	1	0
9	A higher asset turnover ratio compared to the previous year	1	0
Total		9	5

J&J have a Piotroski score of 5 out of 9. The analysis based on the current year reveals that J&J is a stable firm.

3.19.3 Peter Lynch Fair valuation

Peter Lynch Fair value is fundamentally applicable to growth companies. The ideal range for the growth rate is between 10% and 20% a year. According to this valuation criteria, the fair P/E value for a growth company must equals its growth rate that is PEG = 1. The earnings are the trailing twelve month (TTM) earnings.

J&J's Peter Lynch Fair value is calculated in the following manner.

Peter Lynch Fair Value = PEG × 5 year EBITDA growth rate × EPS

The five year EBITDA growth rate during the period 2011−2015 is arrived at 3.8%. The price to earnings ratio (PE) is 19.7.

PEG = 19.7/3.8 = 5.18. The TTM EPS in year 2015 was 5.56.
Peter Lynch Fair Value = 5.18 × 3.8 × 5.56 = $109.5

According to Peter Lynch fair value model, the value of J&J stock is $109.5.

3.19.4   Graham number

It is a conservative method used for valuing a stock. It is a figure which measures a stock's fundamental value by taking into account the company's earnings per share and book value per share. Graham number is the upper bound of the price range which a defensive investor should pay for the stock. According to Graham number theory, any stock price below the Graham number is considered undervalued and hence worth investing in. Graham number is a combination of asset valuation and earnings power valuation.

EPS in year 2015 = 5.56
Book value per share = 25.86

$$\text{Graham number} = \sqrt{22.5 \times (\text{earning per share}) \times (\text{book value per share})}$$
$$= \$56.88$$

Wealth creation by Microsoft

4

4.1 Introduction

Microsoft is the worldwide leader in software, services, devices, and solutions. It was founded in the year 1975 by Paul Allen and Bill Gates to develop and sell basic interpreters for Altair 8800. In the 1980s, Microsoft rose to dominate the personal computer operating system market with MS-DOS and then followed by Microsoft windows. The company was listed in Nasdaq in the year 1986. The initial public offering and subsequent rise in share prices created three billionaires and an estimated 12,000 millionaires among Microsoft employees. Microsoft research is one of the world's largest computer science research organizations and works in close collaboration with top universities in the world.[1]

Microsoft has operations in more than 100 countries. Microsoft develops, manufactures, licenses, supports and sells computer software, consumer electronics, personal computer, and services. The best known software products are the Microsoft windows line of operating systems, Microsoft office suite, Internet Explorer, and Edge web browsers. The flagship hardware products are the Xbox game consoles and the Microsoft surface tablet lineup. It is one of the world's largest software maker by revenue. The services offered by Microsoft include cloud based services to consumers and businesses. Microsoft design, manufacture and sell devices which are integrated with the cloud based services. Microsoft is headquartered in Redmond, Washington.

The products offered include operating systems for computing devices, servers, phones, and other intelligent devices. Microsoft offers server applications for distributed computing environment, business solution applications, desktop and server management tools, software development tools, video games, and online advertising. Microsoft design and sell hardware which includes PCs, tablets, gaming and entertainment consoles, phones, and related accessories. The cloud based solutions of Microsoft facilitate customers with software, services, and platforms. Microsoft also provide consultancy services, product and solution support services, train and certify computer system integrators and developers. Microsoft have operations centers which support all operations like customer contract, order processing, credit and collections, information processing, vendor management, and logistics. The regional centers are located in Ireland, Singapore, Fargo, North Dakota, Fort Lauderdale, Florida, Puerto Rico, Redmond, Washington, Reno, and Nevada. The data centers operate in Americas, Australia, Europe, and Asia. The production and customization of phones are basically done in Vietnam. The Xbox consoles, surface, first party video games, Microsoft PC accessories and other hardware are manufactured by third party contract manufacturers. Microsoft is market dominant in both the IBM PC compatible operating system.

---

[1] Annual Reports , Microsoft.

In 2006, Microsoft had 71,553 employees. By 2015, the employee count increased to 118,000. 60,000 employees are based in United States. Approximately 39,000 employees were employed in product research and development, 29,000 in sales and marketing, 32,000 in product support and consulting services, 8000 in manufacturing and distribution and 10,000 in general and administration. In 2015, Microsoft had generated revenues of $93.6 billion, $60.5 billion of gross margin, $18.2 billion in operating income and $12.2 billion in net income. In 2015, the company returned cash worth $23.3 billion to shareholders which represented an increase of 50% compared to the previous year. Microsoft Office 365 is now deployed in four out of five Fortune 500 enterprises. Microsoft adds over 50,000 small and medium sized enterprises customers every month. By 2015, Microsoft served more than 17,000 Enterprise Mobility Services customers. By 2015, Microsoft attained over eight million paid dynamics seats and enhanced Microsoft dynamics ERP products. Microsoft have currently more than 15 million Office 365 consumer subscribers with the trend that new customers are signing up at a current pace of one million per month. In 2015, Microsoft surpassed 150 million downloads of Office mobile to iOS and Android devices. By 2015, Bing's market share exceeded 20% in the US market share. Table 4.1 lists the historical milestones achieved by Microsoft.

Table 4.1 Milestones

Year	Event
1975	Microsoft is founded
1981	Microsoft Incorporated. IBM introduces personal computer with Microsoft's 16 bit operating system, Ms DOS 1.0
1986	Microsoft goes public and is listed in NASDAQ
1990	Microsoft launches Windows 3.0
1995	Microsoft launches Windows 95
1998	Windows 98 is launched
2000	Windows 2000 launched
2001	Microsoft launches Office XP, Windows XP, and Xbox
2002	Microsoft and partners launch Tablet PC
2003	Microsoft launches Windows Server 2003, Microsoft Office System
2004	Microsoft announces plans to pay $75 billion to shareholders in dividends and stock buybacks
2005	Microsoft launches Xbox 360
2006	Microsoft authorizes additional share repurchase program of up to $20 billion within 5-year period
2007	Microsoft launches Windows Vista and 2007 Microsoft Office System
2008	Microsoft launches Windows Server 2008, SQL Server 2008 and Visual Studio 2008
2009	Bing decision engine and Windows 7 introduced
2010	Office 2010, Kinect for Xbox 360, Windows Phone 7,
2011	Microsoft launches Office 365, Completes acquisition of Skype
2012	Acquires Yammer, Launches Windows Server 2012, Visual Studio 2012. Microsoft launches Windows 8, Microsoft Surface, Windows Phone 8
2013	Microsoft launches Windows 8.1, Surface 2 and Surface Pro 2, Xbox One
2014	Microsoft launches Office for iPad and Surface Pro 3. Microsoft completes acquisition of Nokia devices and service business. Microsoft offers apps for Android tablets
2015	Microsoft launches Surface 3, Windows 10, Office 2016, Surface Book, Surface Pro 4, Microsoft Band 2, Lumia 950 and Lumia

4.2 Operating segments

The operating segments of Microsoft consists of devices and consumer (D&C) segments and commercial segments. The D&C segment include D&C Licensing, Computing and Gaming hardware, phone hardware and D&C other. In 2014, Microsoft acquired all of Nokia's Corporation's ("Nokia") Devices and Services Business ("NDS").

4.2.1 Devices and consumer (D&C) segment

D&C segment of Microsoft is involved in the development, manufacturing, marketing and support of products and services. The major products and services of D&C licensing segment are "Windows OEM," licensing of the windows operating system, nonvolume licensing of Microsoft Office, Windows Phone operating system. The major products and services offered by the Computing and Gaming Hardware segment are Xbox gaming and entertainment consoles and accessories, second party and third party video game royalties, Xbox Platform, Surface devices and accessories and Microsoft PC accessories. Xbox Platform provides variety of entertainment choices by means of devices, peripherals, content and online services. Xbox Platform consists of products like Xbox 360 and Xbox One. Surface devices facilitate students and consumers to be more effective. The main products offered by the phone hardware segment are Lumia phones and other nonLumia phones. Lumia phones run windows. The main products and services offered by D&C other segment consists of retail resale products, 365 Consumer consisting of Office 365 Home and Office 365 Personal, studios consisting of first party video games and nonMicrosoft products sold in retail stores.

4.2.2 Commercial segment

This segment is made up of the commercial licensing and commercial other segments. The principal products and services offered by the commercial licensing agreement consists of server products like Windows server, Microsoft SQL server, Visual Studio, System center, and related client access licenses. The Microsoft Office for business consists of products which includes Office, Exchange, SharePoint, Skype for businesses etc. Windows commercial includes volume licensing of the Windows operating system, excluding academic.

The main products offered by the commercial other segment are commercial cloud and enterprise services. The commercial cloud consists of Office 365 commercial, Microsoft Azure, dynamics CRM online and other Microsoft online offerings. The enterprise services offer premium support services and Microsoft consulting services. The online services offering of Office 365 commercial include Microsoft Office, Exchange SharePoint, and Skype for business which is available across a variety of devices and platforms. Microsoft Azure is a scalable cloud platform with computing, networking, storage, database, and management. Microsoft Azure also provides advanced services such as analytics and comprehensive solutions like enterprise mobility suite. Microsoft Azure also facilitates developers to build and manage enterprise mobile and web applications for any platform or device. Dynamics CRM online facilitates customer relationship management and analytical applications for organizations. Enterprise services help customers in developing and managing Microsoft server and desktop solutions. Enterprise services also provide training and certification to professionals on various Microsoft products.

4.2.3 Key growth strategies [2]

Microsoft's three major strategic initiatives for growth are based on reinventing productivity and business processes, building intelligent cloud platform and create more personal computing experiences. The strategy of Microsoft focuses on building best in class platforms and productivity services for a "mobile first, cloud first world." In this era of generational change, the cloud is emerging as the most significant technology shift. Connected supply chains powered by cloud hubs are changing the way the businesses are operated. Big data technology through cloud deployment will facilitate businesses to analyze huge volume of data and take better informed decisions.

The cloud computing and storage solutions provide users and enterprises with capabilities to store and process their data in third party data centers. The Research and development strategy focuses on reinventing productivity and business processes, building intelligent cloud platform, and personal computing. Microsoft offers broad portfolio of communication, productivity and information services that spans devices and platforms. The major business process tools offered by Microsoft include Skype, One Drive, One Note, Outlook, Word, Excel, PowerPoint, Bing, and Dynamics. The business process tools of Office 365 facilitate cloud services which enables access from anywhere. Microsoft is strategically involved in building the intelligent cloud platform. Microsoft focused on innovation strategy and became one of the largest providers of cloud computing. The key drivers of the strategic shift towards cloud platform is driven by important economies of scales with respect to large data centers. Large data centers can engage computational resources at significantly lower cost per unit. Large data centers can improve the utilization of computing, storage, and network resources. Microsoft focuses on providing big data solution to a billion people by facilitating easy access to all data. Microsoft is focusing on capturing an unprecedented volume of information using vast amounts of unstructured data such as files, images, videos, blogs, clickstreams, and geo spatial data. New technologies such as Apache Hadoop can store and analyze petabytes of unstructured data. HD Insight is Microsoft's new Hadoop based service, built on the Hortonworks Data Platform which offers 100% compatibility with Apache Hadoop.

Microsoft is one of the very few cloud vendors which is capable of meeting the needs of businesses of all sizes and complexities. The combination of Azure and

---

[2] https://www.microsoft.com/investor/reports/ar15/index.html#shareholder-letter.

Windows server created distinctive competitive advantage for Microsoft as it emerged as the only company with a public, private and hybrid cloud platform. Microsoft focuses on continuing investment in data centers. The introduction of Windows 10 aims to create a more effective personal computing experience for users. The introduction of Windows 10 is an important step towards the realization of a single, unified Windows operating system. Microsoft is in the process of developing new input/output methods like speech, pen, gesture, and reality holograms to improve personal computing experiences. Microsoft is investing resources to deliver new productivity, entertainment and business processes. Microsoft is also engaged in establishing windows platforms across the PC, tablet, phone, server, and the cloud to provide effective ecosystems of information technology. In 2015, Microsoft undertook a change in organization structure as part of the transformation in the mobile first, cloud first world.

The major determinant of the Windows revenue is the number of Windows operating system licenses purchased by OEM. Some other critical factors which determine the windows revenues are the mix of computing devices based on form and screen size, differences in device market demand between developed markets and emerging markets. Customer mix between consumer, small and medium sized businesses and large enterprises, changes in inventory levels are other factors which affect windows revenue. The productivity of versions of Office in D&C licensing segment are improved through a range of programs, services and software solutions. Windows commercial revenue is affected mainly by the demand from commercial customers for volume licensing and software assurance. Microsoft faced huge challenge in competing with rivals like Apple and Google in smart phone operating system. As a result, in year 2010, Microsoft revamped their aging flagship mobile operating system, Windows Mobile and replaced it with new Windows Phone OS. Microsoft adopted a new strategy of collaborations with smartphone makers like Nokia to provide user experience across smartphones using Microsoft's Windows Phone OS. In 2016, Microsoft merged its PC and Xbox divisions with the focus on Universal Windows Application as the future of Microsoft's gaming businesses.

4.2.4 R&D strategy

Microsoft have a focused R&D strategy. The company spends around 13% of its revenues on R&D activities. The R&D expenses amounted to $12 billion, $11.4 billion and $10.4 billion respectively during the 3-year period 2013−15. Microsoft is a world leader in innovation among technology companies on account of patents introduced. Currently Microsoft have a portfolio of over 57,000 US and international patents and over 35,000 are in process. Microsoft also engage in outbound and inbound licensing of specific patented technologies which are incorporated into licensees' or Microsoft products. Microsoft also enter into cross license agreements with other technology firms covering entire groups of patents. Microsoft also purchase or license technology which are incorporated into products or services. Microsoft focuses on investment in a wide spectrum of emerging technologies, tools and platforms like cloud computing and devices operating systems.

The products and services offered by Microsoft are developed internally by the three engineering groups. The applications and service engineering group develops broad applications and services, core technologies in productivity, communication, education, search, and information categories. The cloud and enterprise engineering group focuses on development of cloud infrastructure, server database, CRM, enterprise resource planning, management, and development tools. Windows and devices engineering group develops windows platform across devices of hardware components which include Xbox consoles, surface devices, Lumia phones, nonlumia phones, and other hardware products and accessories.

4.2.5 Distribution and marketing strategy

Microsoft market and distribute products and services through channels like OEMs, distributors and resellers, online, and Microsoft retail stores. Microsoft distribute software through OEMs which pre install the software on new PCs, tablets, servers, phones, etc. The largest segment of the OEM business is the Window's operating system preinstalled on computing devices. Microsoft also market services through OEMs and service bundles like Windows with Bing or Windows with Office 365 subscription. Microsoft have distribution agreements covering one or more products with all multinational OEMs which include Acer, ASUSTek, Dell, Fujitsu, Hewlett Packard, Lenovo, Samsung, Toshiba, and other regional OEMs. Microsoft also have enterprise agreements with organizations which license its products and services. Organizations license Microsoft's products and services indirectly through license solution partners, distributors, value added resellers, system builder channels, and retailers. The Microsoft dynamics software offerings are licensed to organizations through global network of channel partners which provide vertical solutions and specialized services. Microsoft's retail packaged products are distributed basically through independent nonexclusive distributors, authorized replicators and retail outlets. Microsoft's hardware products like Surface, Xbox, and PC accessories are distributed through third party retailers and Microsoft retail stores. Microsoft's phones are distributed through global wireless communications carriers. Microsoft provide online content services through Bing, MSN portals and channels, Office 365, Windows Phone Store, Xbox Live, Outlook.com, OneDrive, Skype, and Windows Store.

4.2.6 Investment strategy

The total cash, cash equivalents and short term investments totaled $96.5 billion as of June 30 2015. In 2014, the cash, cash equivalents and short term investments totaled $85.7 billion. The short term investments are basically to facilitate liquidity and capital preservation. Microsoft consider all highly liquid interest earning investments with a maturity of three months or less at the date of purchase to be cash equivalents. Investments with original maturities of greater than three months and remaining maturities of less than one year are classified as short term investment.

Microsoft invests in highly liquid investment grade fixed income securities which are diversified across industries. These investments are predominantly in US dollar denominated securities. Microsoft also invests in foreign currency denominated securities for diversifying risks. In year 2015, the amount of cash, cash equivalents and short term investments held by the foreign subsidiaries of Microsoft amounted to $2.1 billion. Microsoft also lend certain fixed income and equity securities to increase investment returns. The level 1 nonderivative investments consist of US government securities, domestic and international equities and actively traded mutual funds. The level 1 derivative assets and liabilities include those actively traded on exchanges. The level 2 nonderivative investments basically consist of corporate notes and bonds, common and preferred stock, mortgage and asset backed securities, US government and agency securities and foreign government bond. The level 2 derivative assets and liabilities primarily include over the counter option and swap contracts. The level 3 nonderivative assets consist of investments in common and preferred stock. The level 3 derivative assets and liabilities include equity derivatives. Microsoft uses quoted prices in active markets for identical assets or liabilities to determine the fair value of the financial instruments. This pricing methodology is used to value level 1 investments. The level 2 investments are valued at quoted prices. The majority of investments are priced by pricing vendors.

4.3   Mergers and acquisitions strategy

4.3.1   Key acquisitions

Microsoft has acquired 148 companies during the period 1987–2011. Microsoft made the first acquisition in 1987. The company acquired Forethought which developed presentation program which was later known as Microsoft PowerPoint. In 1997 Microsoft acquired Hotmail for $500 million and integrated it into its MSN group of services. Since 1987, Microsoft have made five acquisitions worth over one billion dollars. These were the acquisition of Skype, aQuantive; Fast Search & Transfer, Navision, and Visio Corporation. In 2015, Microsoft completed 16 acquisitions which included Mojang Synergies AB.

In 2009, Microsoft acquired the technology assets of Interactive Supercomputing (ISC) which specialized in bringing the power of parallel computing to the desktop and making high performance computing more accessible to end users. ISC's products and technology enabled faster prototyping, iteration and deployment of large scale parallel solutions. In 2009, Microsoft acquired Opalis Software, a Toronto based private company which was a leader in IT process automation software. Opalis became a wholly owned subsidiary of Microsoft. The synergy of the deal was that the acquisition brought together the deep datacenter automation expertise of Opalis with the integrated physical and virtual datacenter management capabilities of Microsoft system center. Table 4.2 provides the major investment made by Microsoft. Table 4.3 highlights the major deals of Microsoft.

Table 4.2 List of investments[a]

Year	Company
1994	TCI technology ventures
1995	UUNET, Vanstar, DreamWorks SKG, Wang, Digital Individual Inc., NBC
1996	Black Entertainment Television, MTel (SkyTel), Helicon Publishing Ltd., Tandem, Entex, Single Trac Entertainment Technologies, WebTV, VDOnet, Verisign, CMG, Proginet
1997	Digital Anvil, Comcast, First Data, RealNetworks, Navital, Apple Computer, eFusion, TRADOS, Lernout &Hauspie, E-Stamp Corp, Wildlife Communications, Digital Sound Corporation
1998	General Magic, Accel Partners, Reservation Works LLC, Tut Systems, Avid Technology, Softimage, Road Runner, Pluto Technologies, OpenPort, Wireless Knowledge, Quest Communications, CMGI
1999	Banyan Systems, NTL, United Pan Europe Communications, Dialogic, Reciprocal, Audible. com,ThingsWorld.com, Rhythms, Portugal Telecom, NorthPoint Communications, AT&T, TeleWest, Nexetel, @home solutions, WebMD, CareerBuilder, DEN,Wink Communication, Concentric Network, Rogers Communication, TickMaster CitySearch, DSL.net, Global Cabo, United Global Communications, Fairmarket Inc., Asia Global Crossing, Akamai, USWeb, Telmex, Data Return, Teligent, Expedia.com, RadioShack, GigaMedia Ltd., Korea Thrunet Co, Equinix, Best Buy, DiscoverMusic.com, Commtouch
2000	Diagex, Yam Digital Technology, VerticalNet, Jato Comm, Keen.com, Corio, Intertainer, CompUSA, Interland, CSI Inc, ITRAN Comm, Gilat, BroadBand Office, MyPlant.com, Radiant Systems, SRS Labs, Avande, RealNames, MBNS, Interliant, HomeAdvisor Technologies, Evoke, TITUS Comm, ContentGuard, CAIS Internet, Plural, SeaChange International, CommVault. Hitachi, Ameranth Tech, Digital Island, Futurelink, VenturrCom, Blixer, eLabor, Hutchison Global Crossing, Big Huge Games, Corel, US internet working, Chyron
2001	Cpa2biz, MediaWave, American City Business Journals, SMART, Extreme Logic, Ecompys, Blackboard, Commerce One, Telecom New Zealand, Sendo, Groove Networks, Amicore, i-Deal, Infolibria, KT
2003	Immersion Corp.
2007	Facebook
2009	N-trig
2012	24/7 Inc.

[a]https://www.microsoft.com/investor/Stock/InvestmentHistory/All/default.aspx.

Table 4.3 Biggest deals

Year	Company	Business	Value in billion dollars
2011	Skype communications	Telecommunications	8.5
2007	aQuantive	Digital marketing	6.3
2000	Visio Corp.	Wholesale drawing software	1.375
2002	Navision	Software program	1.33
2008	Fast search and transfer	Enterprise search	1.191
2000	Titus communications	Cable TV	0.9448
2001	Great plain software	Business management software	0.939
1997	Hotmail	Internet software	0.5
2008	Danger	Mobile Internet software	0.5

In 2012 Microsoft and Yammer Inc. entered into a definitive agreement under which Microsoft acquired Yammer a leading provider of enterprise social networks for $1.2 billion in cash. The purchase price consisted of goodwill of $937 million and identifiable intangible assets of $178 million. The acquisition of Yammer was aimed at adding a best in class enterprise social networking service to Microsoft's portfolio of complementary cloud services. Established in year 2008, Yammer had more than five million corporate users at 85% of the Fortune 500. The acquisition of PhoneFactor in year 2012 helped Microsoft to bring effective and easy to use multifactor authentication to the cloud services and on premises applications. In 2014, Microsoft acquired Mojang the Stockholm based game developer and the company's iconic "Minecraft" franchise for $2.5 billion. The purchase price consisted of $1.8 billion in goodwill and identifiable intangible assets of $928 million. "Minecraft" is one of the most popular video games with more than 100 million downloads on PC alone by players since its launch in the year 2009. This acquisition provided value addition for Microsoft's gaming portfolio across Windows and Xbox. In 2014, Microsoft acquired all of Nokia Corporation's Nokia devices and services businesses for a total purchase price of $9.4 billion which included the cash acquired of $1.5 billion of the target acquisition. The acquisition was aimed to accelerate the growth of D&C business of Microsoft. In 2015, Microsoft wrote off $7.6 billion as impairment charge on Nokia acquisition which was nearly the full amount the company paid for Nokia's smartphone business and patents. This write off was Microsoft's largest ever write off suggesting that the acquisition was overpaid. Along with the write off, Microsoft also announced that it would lay off about 7800 employees working in its device division particularly the phone group. In 2016, Microsoft signed an agreement to acquire Xamarin, a leading platform provider for mobile app development. Xamarin have more than 15,000 customers in 120 countries which included more than one hundred Fortune 500 companies. Microsoft entered into definitive agreement to acquire SwiftKey whose software keyboard and SDK powers more than 300 million Android and iOS devices.

4.3.2   Acquisition of Skype communications

In October 2011, Microsoft acquired the Internet communications company Skype for $8.5 billion. Skype is the world's leading provider of real time Internet video and video communications services and technology. Skype became the new division of Microsoft. Skype was founded in 2003. eBay Inc. bought Skype in 2005 for around $3.1 billion, but took a $1.4 billion charge for the transaction in 2007 when the acquisition failed to realize the expected synergy from the deal. Later in 2009 eBay sold 70% stake in Skype to a group of investors led by private equity firm Silver Lake Partners for $2.75 billion.

This deal was the most expensive acquisition made by Microsoft. But Skype was not yet profitable. Despite its widespread use, it has been slow to convert users into paying customers and generate profits. It had a net loss of $7 million in 2010. Skype lets people make free phone calls between computers or pay pennies-a-minute to make overseas calls from traditional phones. Increasingly it is being used in the form of an application on smart phones to avoid paying higher fees to wireless carriers for phone calls.

In 2010, Skype had 170 million connected users and over 207 billion minutes of voice and video conversations.

Microsoft management believes that Skype acquisition is a perfect fit for Microsoft's strategic vision to connect millions of people and provide then with innovative ways to communicate through PCs, phones, the Xbox and applications like office and Lync. Microsoft estimated to accelerate Skype's reach to one billion users daily. The combination of Microsoft and Skype was expected to extend Skype's world class brand and networked platform thereby adding value to Microsoft's existing portfolio of real time communications products and services. Plans were in place to integrate Skype into Microsoft devices and systems such as Xbox and Kinect, Xbox Live, the Windows Phone, Lync, Outlook, Hotmail, and Messenger.

Microsoft also expected to turn around its fortunes in the mobile phone market with Skype acquisition. Phones running Microsoft software were just 7.5% of the Smartphone market lagging far behind Apple Inc. and Google. This acquisition comes at a time when the technological growth is facilitated by the exponential growth of social network sites like Face book and innovative devices such as Apple's iPad and iPhone reshaping the cell phone and computer markets.

One interesting fact to be highlighted in this acquisition is that Microsoft had planned to purchase Skype with cash held overseas, money that it could not otherwise bring back to the United States without paying repatriation taxes of more than 30%. The majority of Microsoft's roughly $50 billion in cash is held overseas.

4.3.3 Acquisition of aQuantive

In the year 2007, Microsoft acquired online advertising agency aQuantive for $6 billion in a cash deal. Microsoft paid $66.50 a share which represented an 85% premium over the previous day share price of aQuantive on announcement.

The acquisition was a strategic move by Microsoft to strengthen its position against Google and Yahoo in the online advertising sector. The acquisition came after Google bought DoubleClick for $3.1 billion and Yahoo acquired competitor Right Media for $680 million. The deal was significant as many online services that Microsoft offers from software to video games were increasingly dependent on online advertising revenues Through the acquisition, Microsoft was able to better monetize inventory and sell display advertisements on third party sites. The acquisition was done with a strategic aim to provide the advertising industry with world class advertising platform across devices and media. This becomes more relevant in the context that advertisement market is increasingly being shifted to the world of online and IP served platforms. In 2012, Microsoft undertook an impairment charge of $6.2 billion to account for its purchase of aQuantive suggesting the expected synergy doesn't materialize.

4.3.4   Acquisition of Visio Corporation

In 2000, Microsoft acquired Visio Corp. which is the leading supplier of enterprise wide business diagramming and technical drawing software with an installed base of more than three million users worldwide. Visio's product lines have become worldwide standard for graphical solutions in business. The products are available in 12 language versions and sold in more than 45 countries. The merger was structured as exchange of common stock where each share of Visio was exchanged for 0.45 shares of Microsoft. The deal was valued at approximately $1.3 billion. Visio and Microsoft had long term partnership relationship with respect to both Windows and Office Products. The Visio products were rebranded as MS vision and consists of Microsoft office application like Microsoft Project.

4.3.5   Navision acquisition

In 2002, Microsoft acquired Navision the Danish mid-market business applications vendor. The acquisition created a global business application team that focused on the mid-market sector with businesses having annual revenues between $1 million and $800 million. Navision was absorbed into the Microsoft Business Solutions division. Earlier Microsoft acquired Great Plains. The transaction was structured as a hybrid of cash and stock based on an offer of $37.1 per share with estimated transaction value of $1.3 billion. One of the major motive of the acquisition was to gain a strong hold in the business applications market especially in the European market. Approximately 86% of Navision revenue came from Europe. Through Navision, Microsoft got access to an extensive network of European partnerships. Partners are considered to be a critical factor in selling to SME sector. Navision with its 2,400 Navision Solutions Centers had proven network in more than 94 countries.

4.3.6   Acquisition of fast search and transfer

In 2008, Microsoft acquired fast search and transfer, the Norwegian based enterprise search and business intelligence provider for $3.54 per share which totaled $1.2 billion in value. Enterprise search software and applications help employees locate documents and other data often hidden deep inside corporate networks and databases. The acquisition was aimed to facilitate the growth of Microsoft in the high end search development platform.

4.3.7   Acquisition of Titus communications

In 2010, Microsoft acquired MediaOne International's stake in Titus Communications, the second largest broadband provider in Japan. This acquisition was in tune with Microsoft's vision for broadband deployment and voice, data, video convergence through a leading Japanese broadband provider.

4.3.8   Acquisition of great plain software

In 2000, Microsoft acquired great plain software basically for entry into small and medium business application market. This acquisition was also an important part of Microsoft's strategy to deliver the power of the .NET platform to small and medium companies. The acquisition gave Microsoft the ability to give the medium to large enterprise customers "one stop shopping" under the Microsoft brand, with the combination of Windows 2000, Microsoft Exchange, Microsoft SQL Server, and Great Plains business functions.

4.3.9   Acquisition of Hotmail

In 1998, Microsoft bought Hotmail, the web mail pioneer for approximately 500 million dollars. This acquisition completed the lineup for Microsoft as the company was missing a search engine and free email on the MS Network portal. The acquisition facilitated the Hotmail users to use various sites of Microsoft. Hotmail became an important component of the Microsoft Network of online communication and information services that Microsoft offers free to all Internet users; it includes sites for news, travel, investment, car buying, games, computing, and shopping. With this deal, Microsoft Network boosted its traffic substantially as Hotmail members were added to its collective sites. The Hotmail web centric email services complemented Microsoft's family of email and collaboration clients. Hotmail was in need for new services for its members like personalized information, ecommerce, multimedia content. Table 4.4 provides the major acquisition history of Microsoft.

4.3.10   Strategic alliances

Microsoft have a partnership with Yahoo! to provide algorithmic and paid search platform for Yahoo! websites worldwide. In the year 2015, Microsoft entered into agreement with AOL and AppNexus to outsource display sales efforts.

4.4   Corporate governance

The board oversees the strategic risk management at the company. The ideal board size is considered to be 9–14 members. Currently in 2015 the board have 11 members of which nine are independent. Four committees assist the board of directors in carrying out its oversight functions. These committees are designated as audit committee, compensation committee, governance and nominating committee, and regulatory and public policy committee. The directors who serve on each of the four committees are independent. The audit committee oversee the accounting and financial reporting processes of the company. The compensation committee's responsibilities are related to compensation of the company's executive officers and adoption of policies which govern the company's compensation. The governance and nominating committee determine the slate of director nominees for election

Table 4.4 **Major acquisitions history**[a]

Year	Company
1994	SOFTIMAGE, Altamira, NextBase, One Tree Software
1995	RenderMorphics Ltd., SNMP Technology from Network Managers, Dare to Dream Intertainment, The Blue Ribbon SoundWorks Ltd., Interoperability Technology, Expertise from Netwise Inc., Bruce Artwick Organization Ltd.
1996	Vermeer Technologies Inc., Colusa and Aspect, aha! software, EXOS Inc., eShop Inc., Electric Gravity Inc., OLAP technology from Panorama Software, ResNova Software, NetCarta
1997	Interse, WebTV Networks, Dimension X, Cooper & Peters, LinkAge Software, VXtreme, Hotmail
1998	Flash Communications, Firefly Network, The MESA Group, Valence Research, LinkExchange
1999	CompareNet, Access Software, Jump Networks, ShadowFactor, OmniBrowse, Sendit, ZOOMIT, STNC, Visio, Softway Systems, Entropic
2000	Peach Networks, Driveoff.com, Bungie software, NetGames USA, Mongo Music, Pacific Microsonics Inc., WebAppoint, Digital Anvil, Great Plains Software
2001	Design Intelligence, NCompass Lab, Ensemble Studios
2002	Navision, XDegrees, Rare, Vicinity
2003	PlaceWare, Connectix
2004	ActiveViews, GIANT Company Software
2005	Sybari Software Inc., Groove Networks Inc., FrontBridge Technologies, Telep Inc., media-streams.comAG, FolderShare, Alacris Inc.
2006	Motion Bridge, Onfolio Inc., Apptimum Inc., ProClarity Corp., Lionhead Studios, Massive Inc., Whale Communications, Softricity, Winternals, Azvxxi, Colloquis
2007	Medstory Inc., Tellme Networks, Inc., ScreenTonic, aQuantive Inc., AdECN Inc., Parlano, Global Care Solutions, Multimap
2008	Fast Search and Transfer ASA, Calista Technologies, Caligari Corporation, Danger Inc., YaData, Credentica, Kidaro, RaptInc, Komoku, Farecast, Navic Networks, MobiComp, Powerset, Zoomix, DATAAllegro Inc., Greenfield Online Inc.
2009	BigPark Inc., Interactive Super Computing, LS Retail and To Increase, Teamprise, Sentillion, Opalis Software
2010	Sentillion, AVIcode, Canesta Inc.
2011	Skype, Prodiance, VideoSurf Inc.
2012	Yammer Inc., Perceptive Pixel Inc., PhoneFactor Inc., MarketingPilot, StorSimple Inc., R2 Studios
2013	Pando Networks, MetricsHub, NetBreeze, InRelease, Apiphany
2014	Parature, GreenButton, Capptain, SyntaxTree, InMage, Moiang, Aorato, Acompli, HockeyApp
2015	Equivio, Revolution Analytics, Sunrise, Datazen Software, 6Wunderkinder, BlueStripe, FieldOne Systems LLC, Incent Games Inc., VoloMetrix, Adallom, Adxstudio Inc., Havok, Mobile Data Labs, Secure Islands, Metanautix
2016	Xamarin, SwiftKey

[a]https://www.microsoft.com/investor/Stock/AcquisitonHistory/All/default.aspx.

to the company's board of directors and evaluate the company's corporate governance. The regulatory and public policy committee assists the board of directors in overseeing the company's policies and programs with respect to legal, regulatory and compliance matters. The board members are elected annually by the shareholders. The governance and nominating committee makes recommendation to the board regarding the candidature of directorship for nomination and election at the annual shareholder's meetings. The board considers many factors in evaluation of individual candidates for board membership like general understanding of marketing, finance and other disciplines. The retirement age for board of directors is 75. There is no limit to overall length of service an individual may serve as a director. The board will generally hold four regular meetings and hold special meetings as necessary. The chairman of the board directs the full board in the annual CEO performance evaluation.

Microsoft is a leader in adopting standards to increase accountability to shareholders which includes early adoption of majority voting for board directors, say on pay advisory votes on executive compensation and a proxy access bylaw. In the context of shareholder engagement, the independent members of the board and senior management conducted outreach program for shareholders who own approximately 40% of outstanding shares. In the first cycle of year, the governance cycle begins with reviewing governance best practices, regulatory developments, and own policies and practices. This analysis involves annual update of the governance framework and policies. In the second cycle, the significant changes to the governance practices are communicated to the shareholders. In the third cycle, the annual communications to the shareholders and other stakeholders are prepared in the form of annual reports, proxy statements, and citizenship report. The cycle concludes with the annual board and committee evaluations based on the feedback received from shareholders. Under the principles for engagement in the public policy process in the United States, Microsoft discloses a semiannual list of election campaign expenditures consisting of financial and in kind contributions made by the company to candidates, political parties and committees. The compensation committee have adopted formal stock ownership and holding requirement whereby each covered officer is required to maintain minimum equity stake in the company. The minimum share ownership levels for covered officers are determined by base pay multiples, base pay rate at the end of fiscal year and average daily closing price of the 12 months' period ending on June 30.

4.5   Citizen initiatives[3]

Microsoft actively participates in relevant human rights focused collaborative initiatives such as the EICC and the GNI. In the year 2015, Microsoft made more than $922 million in technology donations to more than 120,000 nonprofit

[3] Microsoft 2015 Citizen Report.

organizations worldwide. In 2015, Microsoft employees contributed $117 million to nearly 20,000 nonprofits organization through the corporate giving campaign. Microsoft established the YouthSpark initiative for creation of opportunities for education, employment and entrepreneurship for approximately 307 million youth worldwide. Microsoft has plans to commit $75 million to the next generation of the YouthSpark initiative to increase access to computer science education for all youth worldwide. Microsoft offers several programs that provide students in grades K-12 with opportunities to interact with modern technology and careers in industry. Microsoft DigiGirlz which is a part of the Microsoft YouthSpark initiative which provides high school girls with opportunities to learn about careers in technology. DigiGirlz program now span 16 countries and have reached 26,000 participants. In 2009, Microsoft had spent more than US $ one billion dollars working with 1255 suppliers which are women owned, minority owned and veteran owned businesses.

In 2015, Microsoft surpassed the 3-year goal for the YouthSpark initiative by creating opportunities for education, employment and entrepreneurship for 307 million youth worldwide. Over the next three years, Microsoft have plans to commit $75 million to the next generation of the YouthSpark initiative to increase access to computer science education for all youth worldwide, especially those from underrepresented backgrounds. The annual giving by Microsoft crossed $ one billion each during the period 2014 and 2015. Microsoft launched a free cloud based version of PhotoDNA which could identify and remove child sexual abuse images from internet.

In 2014, Microsoft completed 314 third party audits and Microsoft assessments of 138 Tier 1 and high and medium risk Tier 2 hardware suppliers. Microsoft also met its carbon neutrality commitment through internal efficiency projects by purchasing more than three billion kilowatt hours (KWh) of renewable energy and carbon offset project portfolio which represent more than 600,000 metric tons of carbon dioxide (CO_2) emissions. The Microsoft's office of legal compliance is responsible for the business conduct and compliance program. Microsoft offers employees and external parties multiple ways to report compliance issues like toll free telephone integrity hotline which is staffed 24 hours a day throughout the week, submission of online report and emailing directly the office of legal compliance. Microsoft prohibits corruption of government officials and the payment of bribes or kickbacks while dealing with public officials or individuals in the private sector. Microsoft's supplier code of conduct includes strong ethics and anticorruption provisions. Microsoft conducts risk assessment to identify third party representatives and certain suppliers to pursue legitimate businesses. In 1993, Microsoft became the first Fortune 500 Company to provide same sex domestic partnership benefits for Microsoft lesbian, gay, bisexual and transgender employees. Microsoft's partnership with Code.org have enabled the company to reach 52 million youth in a period of 18 months. During the period 2014−15, Microsoft were able to connect 6000 students in 131 high schools through the Technology Education and Literacy in Schools (TEALS) program. Microsoft Office 365 is free for all students and teachers around the world. The Anudip Foundation for

Social Welfare establishes women run cooperatives in rural India and provides them technology and skills training. Silatech's Youth Works Employment Initiative is aimed to empower one million Arab youth through training, job placement and self-employment resources.

Microsoft's free online digital literacy curriculum is which available in 10 languages covers a broad range of technology skills at basic, standard and advanced levels. The Microsoft technology and human rights center conducts due diligence and identify emerging risks and opportunities related to human rights. Microsoft is one of the founding member of the GNI which is a collaborative effort between ICT companies, civil society organizations, investors and academics. In year 2015, Microsoft certified its first ENERGY STAR and EPEAT registered product, Surface Pro 3. The shift to Microsoft cloud services for Microsoft Exchange, Microsoft SharePoint, and Microsoft dynamics facilitates businesses to reduce energy use and carbon emissions by 30−90% per user. Microsoft CityNext partners provide solutions in areas spanning energy, water, building, infrastructure, and transportation to help modernize cities in sustainable ways.

4.6   Risk management

Microsoft faces risks from foreign exchange rates, interest rates, credit risks, equity prices, and commodity prices. Some forecasted transactions, assets and liabilities are exposed to foreign currency risks. Derivative instruments are used by Microsoft to manage risks due to foreign currencies, equity prices, interest rates and credit; enhance investment returns and facilitate portfolio diversification.

Microsoft monitor the foreign currency exposures daily and utilize hedges to offset the risks. The principal currencies hedged include the euro, Japanese yen, British pound, Canadian dollar, and Australian dollar. The foreign currency risks related to nonUS dollar denominated securities are hedged using foreign exchange forward contracts.

Microsoft's fixed income portfolio is diversified across credit sectors and maturities. The fixed income portfolio primarily consists of investment grade securities. The credit risk and average maturity of the fixed income portfolio is managed to obtain economic returns benchmarked against some global and fixed income indices using exchange-traded option and futures contracts and over-the-counter swap and option contracts. The company also uses forward purchase agreements of mortgage backed assets to gain exposure to agency mortgage backed securities. Microsoft uses credit default swap which are not designated as hedging instruments to manage credit exposures.

Microsoft faces market price risk on account of the equity portfolio of Microsoft which consists of developed and emerging market securities. The company manages these securities relative to certain global and domestic indices by using convertible preferred investments, options, futures and swap contracts which are not designated as hedging instruments. To hedge price risk, Microsoft use equity derivatives which includes puts, calls, swaps, and forwards. The investment portfolio of Microsoft has exposure to a variety of commodities like precious metals, energy and food grains. Microsoft uses swaps, futures and option contracts not designated as hedging instruments to manage commodity risks. Microsoft manages these exposures relative to global commodity indices. Microsoft uses a value-at-risk (VaR) model to estimate and quantify the market risks. The distribution of the potential changes in total market value of all holdings is computed based on the historical volatilities and correlations among foreign exchange rates. The liquidity, operational and legal risks are not captured in the VaR model. The total one day VaR for the combined risk categories was $237 million in year 2015.

4.7 Licensing options

Microsoft permits customers to acquire multiple licenses of products and services. Customer licensing programs can be categorized into open licensing, Microsoft products and service agreement, select plus licensing. Open licensing is basically designed for small and medium enterprises in which customers can acquire perpetual or subscription licenses over a specified period of time. Customers can acquire licenses only or licenses with software assurance, and/or new software assurance upon the expiration of other existing volume licensing agreements. Microsoft products and services agreement provides small and medium enterprise customers the ability to purchase online services subscriptions, software licenses with software assurance and renewals of software assurance through a single agreement. The Select Plus Licensing allows customers of medium and large enterprises, the right to acquire perpetual licenses and software assurance over a specified time period of maximum three years. Enterprise agreement licensing is designed primarily for medium and large sized enterprises which acquire licenses to online services, software products and software assurance. Microsoft online subscription agreement is designed to enable small and medium enterprises to purchase Microsoft online services. Microsoft cloud solution provider program facilitate partners to directly manage their Microsoft cloud customer life cycle. The Microsoft services provider license agreement program allows service providers and independent software vendors to provide software services and hosted applications to their end customers. Independent software vendor royalty program facilitate partners to use Microsoft software in their own software programs.

4.8 Challenges from competitors

The market for software, devices and cloud based services is dynamic and highly competitive. Microsoft faces challenges from competitors who are developing new software and devices and deploying cloud based services.

The Windows operating system faces competition from various software products and from alternative platforms and devices basically from Apple and Google. The versions of Office in D&C licensing faces competition from global application vendors like Apple and Google, variety of web based and mobile application competitors and local application developers in Europe and Asia. Apple distributes preinstalled application software like email, note taking and calendar products through its PCs, tablets, and phones. Google provides messaging and productivity suite. Windows Phone operating system faces strong competition from iOS, Android, and Blackberry operating systems. The Xbox Platform of Microsoft faces competition from console platforms of Sony and Nintendo. The average life cycle for gaming and entertainment consoles ranges from 5−10 years. The Surface devices offered by Microsoft faces competition from Apple and other computer hardware and tablet manufacturers. The phone hardware system faces competition basically from Apple, Samsung, and other mobile device manufacturers which run Android operating systems. The resale products and services offered by Microsoft faces competition from various online companies like Amazon, Apple, and Google. The search and display advertising business of Microsoft competes with websites like Google and other social platforms like Facebook and portals like Yahoo!. The server products of Microsoft faces competition from vertically integrated computer manufacturers like Oracle, Hewlett Packard, and IBM who offer their own versions of the Unix operating systems preinstalled on server hardware. Most of the computer manufacturers offer server hardware for the Linux operating system. Linux operating systems' competitive position have been strengthened as large number of compatible applications are now being produced by a large number of commercial and noncommercial developers. IBM and Oracle focusses on the Java Platform Enterprise. The system management solutions of Microsoft faces competition from server management and server virtualization platform facilitators like BMC, CA Technologies, Hewlett Packard, IBM, and VMware. The database, business intelligence and data warehousing solutions product offerings faces competition from products of companies like IBM, Oracle, and SAP. Microsoft's products for software developers faces competition from Adobe, IBM, Oracle, and open source projects. The Office commercial application products of Microsoft faces competition from software application vendors such as Adobe Systems, Apple, Cisco Systems, Google, IBM, Oracle, SAP, and other web based and mobile application competitors. Microsoft dynamics product offerings of Microsoft faces competition from vendors like Oracle and SAP and divisions of global enterprises. Skype faces competition from a wide range of instant messaging, voice and video communication providers. Microsoft Azure faces competition from companies like Amazon, Google, IBM, Oracle, and Salesforce.com, VMware and open source offerings. Dynamics CRM online faces competition primarily from Salesforce.com's on demand CRM offerings. The enterprise service business of Microsoft faces competitive pressures from consultancy firms which focus on business planning, application development and infrastructure services. Small niche businesses which focus on specific technologies also emerge as competitors for enterprise service business of Microsoft.[4]

---

[4] https://www.microsoft.com/investor/reports/ar15/index.html#operating-segments.

4.9 Patent claims and litigation issues

In 2010, Microsoft filed patent infringement complaints against Motorola mobility with International Trade Commission and in US District Court in Seattle for infringement of nine Microsoft patents by Motorola's Android devices. There are approximately 70 other patent infringement cases pending against Microsoft. A large number of antitrust and unfair competition class action lawsuits were filed against Microsoft in various courts on behalf of direct and indirect purchasers of PC operating systems and certain software products during the period between 1999 and 2005. Microsoft obtained dismissals or reached settlements of all claims made in the United States. As of June 30 2015 Microsoft accrued aggregate legal liabilities of $614 million in other current liabilities and $20 million in other long term liabilities.[5]

4.10 Equity ownership

In year 2015, equity accounted for 63% and debt constituted 37% of the capital structure.

Financial institutions held 64% of the equity ownership while mutual funds held 34% of the equity ownership. Insiders held 2% of the equity ownership (see Table 4.5).

The top ten institutions held 31% of the total shares (see Table 4.6).

The top ten funds held 10% of the shares (see Table 4.7).

4.11 Operational highlights segment wise

All values are given in millions of dollars. The total revenues from D&C segment increased from $32 billion in 2013 to $41.5 billion in 2015. The revenues from licensing declined from $19.427 to $14.969 billion during the period 2013−15. The revenues from computing and gaming hardware increased from $6.149 billion

Table 4.5 Current equity ownership

	Value in millions of dollars
Institutions	327,506.9
Mutual funds	173,427.71
Insiders	11,246.52
Total	512,181.13

[5] https://www.microsoft.com/investor/reports/ar15/index.

Table 4.6 Top financial institutions with equity ownership

SL	Top institutions	Percent of shares held
1	Vanguard Group Inc.	6.12
2	BlackRock Advisors	5.69
3	Capital World Investors	4.51
4	State Street Corp.	3.79
5	BlackRock Fund Advisors	2.9
6	T. Rowe Price Associates, Inc.	2.15
7	Wellington Management Company LLP	1.97
8	Fidelity Management and Research Company	1.61
9	Northern Trust Investments N A	1.3
10	State Street Global Advisors (Aus) Ltd.	0.96

Table 4.7 Top mutual funds with equity ownership

SL	Mutual funds	Percent of shares held
1	Vanguard Total Stock Mkt Idx	1.83
2	Vanguard 500 Index Inves	1.26
3	VA CollegeAmerica WA Mutual 529B	1.11
4	Vanguard Institutional Index	1.11
5	SPDR S&P 500 ETF	1.06
6	VA CollegeAmerica Fundamental Invs 529E	0.8
7	VA CollegeAmerica Inc Fund of Amer 529E	0.78
8	VA CollegeAmerica Amercn Bal 529E	0.77
9	Powershares QQQETF	0.79
10	VA CollegeAmerica Growth Fund of America 529F	0.56

Table 4.8 Devices and consumer segment

Year	2013	2014	2015
Licensing	19,427	19,528	14,969
Computing and gaming hardware	6,149	9,093	10,183
Phone hardware	0	1982	7524
Others	6431	7014	8825
Total devices and consumer	32,007	37,617	41,501

Source: Annual Report.

to $10.183 billion during the above period registering an increase of approximately 66% (see Table 4.8).

Table 4.9 lists the commercial segment revenues of Microsoft. All values are given in millions of dollars. The total revenues from commercial increased from $45.439 billion in year 2013 to $51.875 billion in year 2015.

Table **4.9** **Commercial segment**

Year	2013	2014	2015
Licensing	39,778	42,085	41,039
Other	5,661	7,546	10,836
Total commercial	45,439	49,631	51,875

Source: Annual Report.

The average sales and marketing expenses as apercent of revenues as 18% during the 3-year period 2013–15. The average general and administrative expenses as per cent of revenues was 5% during the period 2013–15.

4.11.1   Research and development expenses

R&D expenses amounted to $12.046 billion in year 2015. The average R&D expenses as per cent of revenues was 13% during the period 2013–15. R&D expenses include payroll, employee benefits, stock based compensation expense and other headcount related expenses associated with product development. R&D expenses also include third party development and programming costs, localization costs incurred to translate software for international markets and amortization of purchased software code. [6]

4.11.2   Debt

Debt issuances are used to for general purposes like funding for working capital, capital expenditures, repurchases of capital stock, acquisitions, and repayment of existing debt.

The total principal payment contractual obligations amounted to $30.463 billion. The total operating leases obligations amounted to $5.153 billion. The total contractual obligations amounted to $67.140 billion. (see Table 4.10)

4.12   Share repurchases

In 2013, board of directors approved a share repurchase program authorizing up to $40 billion in share repurchases. The repurchase program has no expiration date. As of June 2015, $21.9 billion out of $40 billion share repurchase program remained outstanding. In 2015, Microsoft repurchased 295 million shares for $13.2 billion. In year 2014, 175 million shares were repurchased for $6.4 billion In 2013, 128 million shares worth $4.9 billion were repurchased under the $40 billion repurchase program announced in year 2013. During the fiscal year 2013, approximately 158 million

[6] Annual Report 2015.

Table **4.10** **Contractual obligations in millions of dollars**

Year	2016	2017–18	2019–20	Thereafter	Total
Long term debt					
Principal payment	2500	1050	3750	23,163	30,463
Interest payment	855	1641	1552	11,412	15,460
Construction commitments	681	0	0	0	681
Operating leases	863	1538	1135	1617	5153
Purchase commitments	13,018	989	164	261	14,432
Other long-term liabilities	0	237	75	639	951
Total contractual obligations	17,917	5455	6676	37,092	67,140

Source: Annual Report 2015.

shares worth $4.6 billion were repurchased under the share repurchase program announced on September 2008. All repurchases were carried out using the cash resources. During the 5-year period 2010–14, Microsoft had returned approximately $73 billion to investors in the form $40 billion in share buybacks and $32.5 billion in common dividends.

4.13 Stock option plans

Stock based compensation is a key component of the rewards programs at Microsoft. Approximately 85% of Microsoft employees are eligible for an annual stock award.

Microsoft grants stock based compensation to directors and employees. By June 30 2015, an aggregate of 294 million shares were authorized for future grant under the stock plans. Stock awards are grants which entitle the holder to shares of Microsoft common stock as the award vests. Stock awards generally vest over a four or five-year period. Under the executive incentive plan, the compensation committee awards SAs to executive officers and certain senior executives. Microsoft have an employee stock purchase plan for eligible employees under which the stock may be purchased by employees at three month intervals at 90% of the fair market value on the last trading day of each three-month period. Employees may purchase shares having a value not exceeding 15% of their gross compensation during an offering period. Microsoft have a savings plan in the United States which qualifies under Section 401(k) of the internal revenue code and a number of savings plans in international locations. The participating US employees can contribute up to 75% of their salary, but not more than the statutory limit. Employee stock purchase plan offers employees discounted shares of Microsoft stock.

Table 4.11 Dividend history

Year	2003	2004	2005	2006	2007	2008	2009	2010	2011	2012	2013	2014	2015
Dividend per share	0.08	0.16	3	0.34	0.39	0.43	0.5	0.52	0.61	0.76	0.89	1.07	1.21

4.14 Microsoft dividends

In an extraordinary move, Microsoft paid one-time dividend of $32 billion to its shareholders in the year 2005. In that year, the company also announced that it would buy back up to $30 billion of the company's stock over the next four years. The plans which Microsoft had valued up to $75 billion over 4-year period was considered to be the largest corporate cash disbursement in history. During that period Microsoft held a stockpile of approximately $60 billion in cash and short term investments. However, the share price during that period had been nearly flat during 6-year period. The $32 billion one-time dividend payment came to $3 for each share of Microsoft stock Table 4.11. Individuals who owned approximately 30% of Microsoft's shares received roughly $9 billion from the special dividend. Bill Gates was the largest single beneficiary who received one-time payment of more than $3 billion. The 10-year dividend growth rate is 14.70%. The 5-year dividend growth rate was 18.90%. In March 2016, the dividend yield was 2.58%.

The average dividend payout (DPO) during the 10-year period 2006−15 was 31.5%. The average DPO during the 5-year period 2011−15 was 36% (Table 4.12).

4.15 Microsoft stock splits

In year 2003, Microsoft approved a two for one split on its common stock. The number of common shares after the split was approximately 10.8 billion. This was the ninth time Microsoft's common stock has split since the initial public offering in year 1986. After the ninth split, one original share equaled 288 shares (See Table 4.13).

4.16 Trend analysis

The revenues for Microsoft increased from $44.282 billion in 2006 to $93.580 billion during the year 2015. It can be observed that growth rate of revenues was 111% during the period 2006−15. The average year on year growth rate of revenues during the period 2007−15 was approximately 9% while the year on year average growth rate of revenues during the 5-year period 2011−15 was approximately 8%. The operating cash flow increased from $14.404 billion to $29.080 billion during the 10-year period 2006−15. The operating income increased from $16.472 billion in year 2006 to $18.161 billion in year 2015. The total cash in terms of cash, cash

Table 4.12 **Dividend payout trends**

Year	2006	2007	2008	2009	2010	2011	2012	2013	2014	2015
DPO (%)	28.4	27.5	23	30.9	24.7	22.6	26.3	44.5	38.3	49

Table 4.13 **Stock splits**[a]

Year	Type of split	Closing price before split	Closing price after
1987	2 for 1	$114.50	$53.50
1990	2 for 1	$120.75	$60.75
1991	3 for 2	$100.75	$68
1992	3 for 2	$112.50	$75.75
1994	2 for 1	$97.75	$50.63
1996	2 for 1	$152.88	$81.75
1998	2 for 1	$155.13	$81.63
1999	2 for 1	$178.13	$92.38
2003	2 for 1	$48.30	$24.96

[a]https://www.microsoft.com/investor/InvestorServices/FAQ/default.aspx#section_4.

Table 4.14 **Financial highlights in millions of dollars**

Year	2006	2007	2008	2009	2010	2011	2012	2013	2014	2015
Revenues	44,282	51,122	60,420	58,437	62,484	69,943	73,723	77,849	86,833	93,580
Operating cash flow	14,404	17,796	21,612	19,037	24,073	26,994	31,626	28,833	32,231	29,080
Operating income	16,472	18,524	22,492	20,363	24,098	27,161	21,763	26,764	27,759	18,161
Net income	12,599	14,065	17,681	14,569	18,760	23,150	16,978	21,863	22,074	12,193
Capital expenditure	1578	2264	3182	3119	1977	2355	2305	4257	5485	5944
R&D expenditure	6584	7121	8164	9010	8714	9043	9811	10,411	11,381	12,046
Total cash	34,161	23,411	23,662	31,447	36,788	52,772	63,040	77,022	85,709	96,526
Long term debt	0	0	0	3746	4939	11,921	10,713	12,601	20,645	27,808
Total assets	69,597	63,171	72,793	77,888	86,113	108,704	121,271	142,431	172,384	176,223

equivalents and marketable securities increased from $34.161 billion in year 2006 to $96.526 billion in year 2015 which represented an increase of 2.83 times. The average yearly growth rate of operating cash flow during the period 2007−15 was approximately 9% which fell to 4.5% during the 5-year period 2011−15. The average growth rate of net income during the period 2007−15 was 3.4%. The capital expenditure increased by 3.76 times and the research and development expenses increased by 1.83 times during the 10-year period 2006−15. The company didn't raise any long term debt during the 3-year period 2006−8. The long term debt amounted to $27.808 billion in year 2015. The average yearly growth rate in assets during the period 2007−15 was approximately 11% (see Table 4.14).

Table 4.15 **Per share ratio**

Year	2006	2007	2008	2009	2010	2011	2012	2013	2014	2015
EPS	1.2	1.42	1.87	1.62	2.1	2.69	2	2.58	2.63	1.48
DPS	0.34	0.39	0.43	0.5	0.52	0.61	0.76	0.89	1.07	1.21
DPO (%)	28.4	27.5	23	30.9	24.7	22.6	26.3	44.5	38.3	49
Book value per share	3.99	3.73	3.97	4.44	5.33	6.82	8.19	9.21	10.61	11.23
Revenue per share	4.21	5.17	6.38	6.5	7	8.14	8.67	9.19	10.34	11.34
EBITDA per share	1.65	2.01	2.74	2.55	3.12	3.62	3.01	3.69	4	3.06
Debt per share	0	0	0	0.65	0.69	1.42	1.43	1.87	2.75	4.4

The average growth rate of EPS during the period 2006−15 was 6.2% while the growth rate of DPS during the above period was 15%. The average DPO ratio during the 10-year period was approximately 31%. The average growth rate of EBITDA per share during the above period was 11.8% (see Table 4.15).

4.17 Ratio analysis

The average profitability ratios are compared for two 5-year periods 2006−10 and 2011−15. The average profitability ratios declined in the period 2011−15 compared to the period 2006−10. The average gross margin of 80.4% during the period 2006−10 declined to 72% during the period 2011−15. The average operating margin of 36.7% during the period 2006−10 declined to 30.8% during the period 2011−15. The average net profit margin declined from 28% to 24.5% during the two five periods of comparison. The average return on assets and return on equity (ROE) declined from 21.5% and 40.5% during the period 2006−10 to 15.23% and 28.59% during the period 2011−15. The average return on invested capital during the period 2006−10 declined from 37.4% to 23.38% during the 5-year period 2011−15 (see Table 4.16).

The inventory turnover ratio and days sales outstanding on average basis have improved during the period 2006−10 compared to the 2011−15 period. The inventory turnover ratio improved from 11.65 during the period 2006−10 to 13.098 during the period 2011−15. The average days' sales outstanding improved from 73 days to 75.6 days during the two 5-year period of analysis. The average fixed assets turnover ratio declined from 11.67 during the period 2006−10 to 8.13 during the period 2011−15. The average asset turnover also declined from 0.766 to 0.608 during the two periods of comparison. The average payables period declined from 111.49 to 85.03 days during the two periods of comparison (see Table 4.17).

The company had a high interest coverage ratio as reflected by the average ICR ratio of 56.30 during the 5-year period 2011−15. The average debt equity ratio was

Table 4.16 **Profitability ratios in per cent**

Year	2006	2007	2008	2009	2010	2011	2012	2013	2014	2015
Gross margin	82.72	79.08	80.8	79.2	80.16	77.73	76.22	73.99	68.98	64.7
Operating margin	37.2	36.07	36.86	34.85	38.57	38.83	29.52	34.38	31.97	19.41
Net profit margin	28.45	27.51	29.26	24.93	30.02	33.1	23.03	28.08	25.42	13.03
Return on assets	17.95	21.19	26.01	19.34	22.88	23.77	14.77	16.58	14.02	7
Return on equity	28.56	39.51	52.48	38.42	43.76	44.84	27.51	30.09	26.17	14.36
Return on invested capital	28.56	36.92	50.52	33.36	37.45	37.4	22.62	25.07	21.11	10.71

0.26 during the 5-year period 2011−15. The average long term debt to total assets was 0.11 during the period 2011−15 (see Table 4.18).

The liquidity position on average basis have improved during the period 2011−15 compared to the period 2006−10. The average current ratio increased from 1.85 to 2.58 during the two period of comparison. The average quick ratio increased from 1.63 during the period 2006−10 to 2.38 during the period 2011−15 (see Table 4.19).

4.17.1 Stock highlights

When Microsoft went public in year 1986, the opening stock price was $21. After the trading, the price closed at $27.75. The stock price peaked at $119 in year 1999. By 2010 the company had nine splits. Microsoft started paying dividends in the year 2003. Standard and Poor's and Moody's have both given a AAA rating to Microsoft. In 2011, Microsoft had released a corporate bond amounting to $2.25 billion with relatively low borrowing rates compared to government bonds.

The market capitalization of Microsoft increased from $234.44 billion in 2006 to $354.392 billion by year 2015 (see Table 4.20).

4.18 Stock wealth analysis

Microsoft was listed on NASDAQ on March 13 1986. The monthly stock return analysis shows that cumulative return for Microsoft for 30-year period comprising 361 months was 856%. The analysis was based on adjusted closing price sourced from yahoo finance. Suppose an investor invested $1000 in Microsoft shares during March 1986. By March 2016, the value of his investment would have become $9556.36 based on cumulative returns. The adjusted closing price of Microsoft was $0.066 on March 13 1986. By March 1 2016, the adjusted closing price of

Table 4.17 Efficiency ratios

Year	2006	2007	2008	2009	2010	2011	2012	2013	2014	2015
Inventory turnover	7.77	8.21	10.98	14.28	17.01	14.75	13.97	13.17	11.72	11.88
Fixed assets turnover	16.43	13.83	11.41	8.48	8.24	8.86	8.97	8.53	7.55	6.75
Asset turnover	0.63	0.77	0.89	0.78	0.76	0.72	0.64	0.59	0.55	0.54
Payables period	119.16	105.07	114.57	110.48	108.2	96.33	87.16	81.14	83.07	77.46
Days sales inventory	46.97	44.46	33.23	25.55	21.45	24.74	26.12	27.71	31.16	30.72
Days sales outstanding	67.99	73.73	75.29	77.39	70.7	73.06	76.16	77.98	77.83	73.04

Table 4.18 Leverage ratios

Year	2006	2007	2008	2009	2010	2011	2012	2013	2014	2015
Debt to equity ratio	0	0	0	0.15	0.13	0.21	0.18	0.2	0.25	0.44
Long term debt to total assets	0	0	0	0.05	0.06	0.11	0.09	0.09	0.12	0.16
Interest coverage ratio	0	0	210.1	535.87	159.59	92.07	57.27	62.39	46.5	23.25

Table 4.19 Liquidity ratio

Year	2006	2007	2008	2009	2010	2011	2012	2013	2014	2015
Current ratio	2.18	1.69	1.45	1.82	2.13	2.6	2.6	2.71	2.5	2.5
Quick ratio	1.94	1.46	1.25	1.58	1.9	2.35	2.41	2.53	2.31	2.3

Table 4.20 Market capitalization in million dollars

Year	2006	2007	2008	2009	2010	2011	2012	2013	2014	2015
Market capitalization	234,445	276,296	251,744	211,743	199,451	217,776	256,375	287,732	343,566	354,392

Microsoft was $53.86. The stock price increased by approximately 814 times during the 30-year period. The cumulative returns for NASDAQ Composite during the 30-year period based on the analysis of monthly returns was 331%. On the basis of cumulative returns, it is observed that Microsoft outperformed the market index NASDAQ during the entire period of analysis.

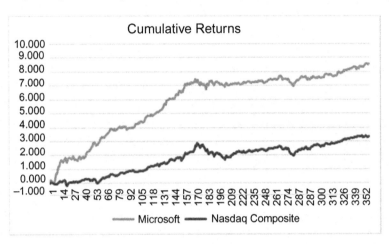

The graph above gives the cumulative returns of Microsoft and Nasdaq Composite during the 30-year period of analysis. The cumulative returns of Microsoft during the period January 2010–March 2016 was approximately 90%. The compounded annual growth rate of Microsoft stock's returns during the 6-year period was approximately 15%.

The average monthly returns were estimated and then the yearly returns were calculated. During the period 2013–15, Microsoft outperformed the market index Nasdaq Composite. In the first three years of comparison, Microsoft underperformed with respect to market index Nasdaq Composite. The excess return generated by Microsoft was highest in the year 2014 when the excess return amounted to 11.86%. Microsoft had generated the highest return of 39.11% in year 2013, but the Nasdaq index had registered return of 33.19% during the same year (see Table 4.21).

Table 4.21 Average yearly returns inpercent

Year	Microsoft	Nasdaq composite	Excess returns
2010	−2.23	18.17	−20.4
2011	−3.63	−0.63	−3
2012	7.84	15.86	−8.02
2013	39.11	33.19	5.92
2014	24.98	13.12	11.86
2015	26.06	6.67	19.39

Table 4.22 **Holding period yield**

Year	Holding period yield inpercent
2010	1.1
2011	− 3.89
2012	− 6.99
2013	40.4
2014	26.12
2015	32.95

Table 4.23 **Excess wealth created in millions of dollars**

Year	2010	2011	2012	2013	2014	2015
MV of equity	199,451	217,776	256,375	287,732	343,566	354,392
BV of equity	46,175	57,083	66,363	78,944	89,784	80,083
BV as percent of MV	0.23	0.26	0.26	0.27	0.26	0.23

In holding period yield calculation, it is assumed that an investor buys a stock of Microsoft every year in January and sells the stock in December end of the year. The holding period yield of 40.4% was highest in the year 2013. The holding period yield was negative in the year 2011 and 2012. The annual holding period yield on the investment period horizon of six years (January 2010−March 2016) was approximately 15% (see Table 4.22).

The market value of Microsoft increased from $199.45 billion in year 2010 to $354.39 billion in year 2015. The book value of equity increased from $46.175 billion in year 2010 to $80.083 billion by year 2015. The average book value as per cent of market value was 25%. The book value as per cent of market value was 23% during the period 2010−15 (see Table 4.23).

4.19 Estimation of weighted average cost of capital (WACC)

The cost of equity is first estimated through the CAPM Model.

Estimation of cost of equity using CAPM

Required rate of return = Risk free rate + Beta × (Return on market index − Risk free rate)

The risk free rate is assumed as the average yield to maturity on the 30-year treasury bond during the 2-year period 2014−16.[7]

---

[7] https://www.treasury.gov/resource-center/data-chart-center/interest-rates/Pages/Historic-Yield-Data-Visualization.aspx.

Year	Yield to maturity on 30 year treasury bond
2014	3.55
2015	2.63
2016	2.63
Average	2.94%

The risk free rate is estimated as 2.94%. Beta is estimated by regressing the monthly returns of Microsoft on the monthly returns on market index NADAQ Composite during the period 5-year period 2011−15. The beta value estimated is 0.84. The annual market returns are estimated on the basis of the average monthly returns of market index NASDAQ during the 5-year period 2011−15. The market return = 11.77%

Cost of equity = Risk free rate + Beta × Risk premium.
Risk premium = Average return on market index − Risk free rate = 11.74−2.94 = 8.83%
Cost of equity = 2.94 + 0.84 × 8.83 = 10.36%.
The yield to maturity of the long term bond which matures in August 2 2041 is assumed as the cost of debt. The yield to maturity on this long term bond was 3.901%. The price of this bond on March 23 2016 was 122.13[8].
The pretax income in year 2015 was $18,507 million and the tax expenses amounted to $6314 million. Hence the effective tax rate was 34%.
After tax cost of debt = Cost of debt (1 − Tax rate) = 3.901 × (1−0.34) = 2.57%.
Market value weights.
Market value of equity in year 2015 = $354,392 million.
Book value of debt = Short term debt + long term debt = 7484 + 27,808 = $35,292 million.
Market value of debt = (Book value of debt) × (Ratio of price of the long term bond to the face value of bond).
Ratio = 122.13/100 = 1.22.
Market value of debt = 35,292 × 1.22 = $43,056.24 million.
Total value = 354,392 + 43,056.24 = $397,448.24 million.
Weight of equity = 354,392/397,448.24 = 0.89.
Weight of debt = 43,056.24/397,448.24 = 0.11.
WACC = Weight of equity × Cost of equity + Weight of debt × After tax cost of debt.
= 0.89 × 10.36 + 0.11 × 2.57 = 9.51%.
The weighted average cost of capital (WACC) for Microsoft is estimated as 9.51%.

4.20   Valuation perspectives

4.20.1   Estimation of economic value

The EV estimated is for year 2015.
Economic value is estimated as net operating income after taxes (NOPAT) − Capital charge.
Profit before interest and tax(PBIT) − Income tax = NOPAT.
Capital employed = Stock holder equity + Long term debt

[8] http://finra-markets.morningstar.com/BondCenter/Results.jsp.

Capital charge = Capital employed × WACC
Economic value (EV) = NOPAT − Capital charge
Estimation of EV
PBIT in year 2015 = $18,161 million
Income tax in year 2015 = 6314 million
NOPAT = 18161 − 6314 = $11,847 Million
Stock holder equity = $80,083 million
Long term debt = $27,808 million
Capital employed = $107,891 million
WACC = 9.51%
Capital charge = 107,891 × 0.0951 = $10,260.43
EV = 11,847 − 10,260.43 = $1587 million.
The EV for Microsoft is estimated as $1587 million.

4.20.2 Equity spread

Equity spread is a variation of the EV measures. Equity spread is the difference between the ROE and the required ROE (cost of equity).

Equity spread = (Return on equity − Cost of equity) × Equity capital
Return on equity in year 2015 = 14.36%
Cost of equity = 10.36%
Equity spread = (14.36% − 10.36%) × 80,083 million = $3203.32 million.

The value of equity spread for Microsoft is $3203.32 million in year 2015.

4.20.3 Discounted cash flow valuation

The discounted cash flow valuation models used are dividend discount model (DDM), Free Cash Flow to Equity (FCFE) and Free Cash Flow to Firm (FCFF).

4.20.3.1 Dividend discount model (DDM)

The average DPO during the period 2010−15 was 39% (see Table 4.24).
   Growth rate = Retention Ratio (RR) × ROE. The average growth rate of fundamentals estimated for the period 2010−15 was 19.9% during the period 2010−15.

High growth period assumptions and inputs
High growth period = 10 years

Table 4.24 Dividend trends

Year	2010	2011	2012	2013	2014	2015
EPS	2.1	2.69	2	2.58	2.63	1.48
DPS	0.52	0.61	0.76	0.89	1.07	1.21
DPO	0.248	0.227	0.380	0.345	0.407	0.818

Table 4.25 **Estimation of growth rate of fundamentals**

Year	2010	2011	2012	2013	2014	2015
RR	0.752	0.773	0.620	0.655	0.593	0.182
ROE	0.4376	0.4484	0.2751	0.3009	0.2617	0.1436
Growth rate	0.3292	0.3467	0.1706	0.1971	0.1552	0.0262

Table 4.26 **Present value of dividends in high growth phase**

Year	1	2	3	4	5	6	7	8	9	10
EPS	1.775	2.128	2.551	3.059	3.667	4.397	5.272	6.321	7.579	9.088
DPO	0.39	0.39	0.39	0.39	0.39	0.39	0.39	0.39	0.39	0.39
DPS	0.692	0.830	0.995	1.193	1.430	1.715	2.056	2.465	2.956	3.544
PV	$0.63	$0.68	$0.74	$0.80	$0.87	$0.95	$1.03	$1.12	$1.22	$1.32
SUM	$9.37									

Average DPO = 39%
Cost of equity = 10.36%
Average growth rate of earnings estimated from fundamentals = 19.9% (Table 4.25)
EPS in current year (2015) = 1.48
EPS in first year of high growth period = $1.48 \times 1.199 = \$1.775$
Present value of dividends in high growth period = $9.37 (Table 4.26).

4.20.4 Stable phase inputs

Growth rate in stable period is assumed to be the growth rate of US economy. The average growth rate of US GDP for 2-year period 2013−14. The GDP growth rate is estimated as 2.3%.[9]

The ROE of industry sector is 15%.[10]
Growth rate in stable period = 2.3%
Growth rate = RR × Industry ROE
2.3% = RR × 15%
RR = 2.3/15 = 15%
DPO = 85%
EPS at end of high growth period = $9.088
EPS at beginning of stable period = $9.088 \times (1 + g) = 9.088 \times 1.023 = \$9.30$
DPO = 0.85
DPS in stable period = $9.30 \times 0.85 = \$7.87$
Terminal value = DPS in stable period/(Cost of equity − growth rate in stable period) = 7.87/(0.1036−0.023) = $97.66
Present value of terminal value = $36.44

[9] http://data.worldbank.org/indicator/NY.GDP.MKTP.KD.ZG.
[10] http://www.morningstar.com/stocks/XNAS/MSFT/quote.html.

Value of Microsoft stock = PV of dividends in high growth phase + PV of dividends in stable phase = 9.37 + 45.81 = $45.81

Value of Microsoft stock based on two stage DDM is $45.81.

4.20.4.1 FCFE valuation model

Adjustments for FCFE valuation

Net capital expenditure = Capital expenditure − Depreciation and amortization

Adjusted net capital expenditure = Net capital expenditure + R&D expenses in current period − Amortization of research asset + Net acquisitions

Adjusted net income = Net income + Current year's R&D expenses − Amortization of research asset.

Adjusted book value of equity = Book value of equity + Value of research asset.

The research assets are amortized linearly over time. The life of research asset is assumed to be 5 years. The research assets are amortized 20% each year. The value of research asset and amortization expense for the year 2015 is given in the table (see Tables 4.27−4.28). The calculations for the rest of the years are detailed in the FCFE worksheet of *Microsoft.xlsx*.

Table 4.27 Estimation of amortization and value of research asset in year 2015

Year	R&D expenses	Unamortized portion		Amortization this year (million $)
		%	(mil dollars)	
Current	12046	100	12,046	
−1	11,381	80	9104.8	2276.2
−2	10,411	60	6246.6	2082.2
−3	9811	40	3924.4	1962.2
−4	9043	20	1808.6	1808.6
−5	8714	0	0	1742.8
	Value of research asset		33,130.4	
	Amortization expense current year			9872

Table 4.28 Amortization and value of research assets

Year	R&D expenses	Value of R&D	Amortization of R&D
2011	9043	26,110	7918.6
2012	9811	27,510.6	8410.4
2013	10,411	28,973.2	8948.4
2014	11,381	30,956.4	9397.8
2015	12,046	33,130.4	9872

Table 4.29 Adjusted net income in millions of dollars

Year	Net income	R&D expenses	Amortization	Adjusted net income
2011	23,150	9043	7918.6	24,274.4
2012	16,978	9811	8410.4	18,378.6
2013	21,863	10,411	8948.4	23,325.6
2014	22,074	11,381	9397.8	24,057.2
2015	12,193	12,046	9872	14,367

Table 4.30 Adjusted book value of equity in millions of dollars

Year	Book value of equity	Value of research asset	Adjusted book value of equity
2011	57,083	26,110	83,193
2012	66,363	27,510.6	93,873.6
2013	78,944	28,973.2	107,917.2
2014	89,784	30,956.4	120,740.4
2015	80,083	33,130.4	113,213.4

Table 4.31 Adjusted ROE

Year	Adjusted ROE in percent
2012	22.09
2013	24.85
2014	22.29
2015	11.90

The values are given in millions of dollars.

Adjusted ROE = Adjusted net income in year t/Adjusted book value of equity in year t − 1 (see Tables 4.29−4.31).

Adjusted net Capex = Net Capex + R&D expenses in current period −Amortization of research asset + Net acquisition (see Table 4.32).

Net Capex = Capex − Depreciation and amortization.

Noncash current assets = Total current assets − Cash and cash equivalents
Noninterest bearing current liabilities = Total current liabilities − Short term debt
Noncash working capital = Noncash current assets − Noninterest bearing current liabilities (see Table 4.33).

Reinvestment = Adjusted net capex + Change in noncash working capital.
Reinvestment rate = Reinvestment/Adjusted net income (see Table 4.34).
The average reinvestment rate during the 5-year period 2011−15 is 22.7% based on geometric mean.

Table 4.32 **Adjusted net Capex in millions of dollars**

Year	2011	2012	2013	2014	2015
Capex	2355	2305	4257	5485	5944
Dep and amortization	2766	2967	3755	5212	5957
Net Capex	− 411	− 662	502	273	− 13
R&D expenses in current period	9043	9811	10,411	11,381	12,046
Amortization of research asset	7918.6	8410.4	8948.4	9397.8	9872
Net acquisitions	71	10112	1584	5937	3723
Adjusted net Capex	784.4	10,850.6	3548.6	8193.2	5884

Table 4.33 **Estimation of noncash working capital in millions of dollars**

Year	2011	2012	2013	2014	2015
Total current assets	74,918	85,084	101,466	114,246	124,712
Cash and cash equivalents	52,772	63,040	77,022	85,709	96,526
Non cash current assets	22,146	22,044	24,444	28,537	28,186
Total current liabilities	28,774	32,688	37,417	45,625	49,858
Short term debt	0	1231	2999	2000	7484
Noninterest bearing current liabilities	28,774	31,457	34,418	43,625	42,374
Noncash working capital	−6628	−9413	−9974	−15,088	−14,188
Change in noncash working capital	−369	−2785	−561	−5114	900

Table 4.34 **Estimation of reinvestment rate**

Year	2011	2012	2013	2014	2015
Adjusted net Capex	784.4	10850.6	3548.6	8193.2	5884
Change in noncash working capital	−369	−2785	−561	−5114	900
Reinvestment	784	8066	2988	3079	6784
Adjusted net income	24,274.4	18,378.6	23,325.6	24,057.2	14,367
Reinvestment rate	0.032	0.439	0.128	0.128	0.472

Growth rate in net income = Adjusted ROE × Reinvestment rate (see Table 4.35) The average growth rate of earnings from fundamentals is estimated as 5.3%.

FCFE = Adjusted net income − Adjusted net Capex − Change in noncash working capital + new debt issued-debt repaid (see Table 4.36). The average FCFE generated by the company was $21,568 million during the period 2011−15.

Table 4.35 Estimation of growth rate from fundamentals

Year	2012	2013	2014	2015
Adjusted ROE	0.22	0.25	0.22	0.12
Reinvestment rate	0.44	0.13	0.13	0.47
Growth rate	0.10	0.03	0.03	0.06

Table 4.36 Estimation of FCFE in millions of dollars

Year	2011	2012	2013	2014	2015
Adjusted net income	24,274.4	18,378.6	23,325.6	24,057.2	14,367
Adjusted net Capex	784.4	10,850.6	3548.6	8193.2	5884
Change in noncash working capital	0	−2785	−561	−5114	900
New debt issued	6774		4883	10,350	10,680
Debt repaid	814		1346	3888	1500
FCFE	29,450	10,313	23,875	27,440	16,763

4.20.5   FCFE valuation model

Two stage FCFE model is used for valuation of Microsoft in this section. It is assumed that Microsoft's earnings will grow at a growth rate of 5.03% for 10-year period and then at the stable growth rate of 2.3% (US GDP growth rate).

High growth period inputs
Growth rate of net income in high growth period = 5.3%
High growth period = 10 years
Adjusted net income at initial stage = $20,881 million[11]
Cost of equity = 10.36%; Reinvestment rate = 22.7%

The present value of FCFE in high growth phase is calculated as $125,823.4 million (see Table 4.37).

Stable phase inputs
Growth rate in stable period = 2.3%(average US GDP growth rate during the period 2013−14)
Growth rate in stable period = Reinvestment rate × Industry ROE
Industry sector ROE = 15%
2.3% = Reinvestment rate × 15%
Reinvestment rate = 15.3%

---

[11] The adjusted net income in year 2015 was $14,367 million which was very low compared to the previous years. Hence the average of adjusted net income for the 5-year period 2011−15 was taken for estimation.

Table 4.37 Present value of FCFE in the high growth phase period

Year	1	2	3	4	5	6	7	8	9	10
Adjusted net income	21,987.7	23,153.0	24,380.2	25,672.3	27,032.9	28,465.7	29,974.4	31,563.0	33,235.8	34,997.3
Reinvestment	4991.2	5255.7	5534.3	5827.6	6136.5	6461.7	6804.2	7164.8	7544.5	7944.4
FCFE	16,996.5	17,897.3	18,845.9	19,844.7	20,396.5	22,004.0	23,170.2	24,398.2	25,691.3	27,052.9
PV	15,400.9	14,694.8	14,021.1	13,378.2	12,764.8	12,179.5	11,621.1	11,088.3	10,579.9	10,094.8
Sum	125,823.4									

Adjusted net income at the end of high growth 34,997.3 period = $34,997.3 million
Adjusted net income in stable period = 34,997.3 × 1.023 = $35,802.28 million
Reinvestment = 35,802.28 × 0.153 = $5477.75 million
FCFE in stable period = 35,802.28 − 5477.75 = = $30,324.53 million
Terminal value of FCFE = FCFE in stable period/(Cost of equity − growth rate in stable period) = 30,324.53/(0.1036 − 0.023) = $37,6234.84 million.
Present value of FCFE in stable period = $140,391.91 million
Value of operating assets = PV of FCFE in high growth period + PV of FCFE in stable period = 125,823.4 + 140,391.91 = $266,215.34 million
Add cash and cash equivalents in year 2015 = $96,526 million
Value of Microsoft = 266,215.34 + 96,526 = $362,741.34 million
Number of shares = 8254 million
Value per share = $43.95
Value of Microsoft stock on basis of FCFE two stage model is estimated as $43.95.

4.20.5.1   FCFF valuation model

In this section, Microsoft is valued using two stage FCFF model. It is assumed that the operating earnings of Microsoft will grow at the high growth rate of earnings estimated from fundamentals for 10 years and then at the stable growth rate of US economy. In FCFF valuation, the discount rate used is WACC.

In general form,

FCFF = EBIT(1 − T) − Net capital expenditure − Change in working capital.
For valuation of Microsoft, the following adjustments are made
Adjusted EBIT(1 − T) = EBIT(1 − T) + R&D expenses − Amortization of research asset (see Table 4.38).
Adjusted book value of capital = Adjusted book value of equity + Debt (see Table 4.39)
Adjusted book value of equity = Book value of equity + Value of research asset
FCFF = Adjusted EBIT(1 − T) − Adjusted net capital expenditure − Change in working capital.

The values are given in millions of dollars.
Adjusted ROCE = Adjusted EBIT(1 − T) in year t/Adjusted book value of capital in year t − 1 (see Table 4.40).

Reinvestment rate = Reinvestment/Adjusted EBIT(1 − T) (see Table 4.41).
Reinvestment = Adjusted net Capex + Change in noncash working capital.
The average reinvestment rate during the period 2011−15 based on geometric mean was 23%.

The average growth rate of operating income during the 4-year period is calculated as 4.6% (see Table 4.42).
The average FCFF during the 5-year period was $16,192.4 million (see Table 4.43).

Valuation using two stage FCFF
High growth period inputs
High growth period = 10 years
Growth rate of operating income = 4.6%

Table 4.38 Adjusted operating income after taxes

Year	EBIT	Taxes	EBIT (1 − T)	R&D expenses	Amortization of research asset	Adjusted EBIT(1 − T)
2011	27,161	4921	22,240	9043	7918.6	23,364
2012	21,763	5289	16,474	9811	8410.4	17,875
2013	26,764	5189	21,575	10,411	8948.4	23,038
2014	27,759	5746	22,013	11,381	9397.8	23,996
2015	18,161	6314	11,847	12,046	9872	14,021

Table 4.39 Adjusted book value of capital (million dollars)

Year	Book value of equity	Value of research asset	Adjusted book value of equity	Debt	Adjusted book value of capital
2011	57,083	26,110	83,193	11,921	95,114
2012	66,363	27,510.6	93,873.6	11,944	105,817.6
2013	78,944	28,973.2	107,917.2	15,600	123,517.2
2014	89,784	30,956.4	120,740.4	22,645	143,385.4
2015	80,083	33,130.4	113,213.4	35,292	148,505.4

Table 4.40 Adjusted ROCE

Year	Adjusted ROCE
2012	0.19
2013	0.22
2014	0.19
2015	0.10

Table 4.41 Estimation of reinvestment rate

Year	2011	2012	2013	2014	2015
Adjusted net Capex	784.4	10,850.6	3548.6	8193.2	5884
Change in noncash working capital	−369	−2785	−561	−5114	900
Reinvestment	415	8065.6	2987.6	3079.2	6784
Adjusted EBIT (1 − T)	23,364.4	17,874.6	23,037.6	23,996.2	14,021
Reinvestment rate	0.02	0.45	0.13	0.13	0.48

Table 4.42 Estimation of growth rate of operating income from fundamentals

Year	2012	2013	2014	2015
Adjusted ROCE	0.19	0.22	0.19	0.10
Reinvestment rate	0.45	0.13	0.13	0.48
Growth rate	0.085	0.028	0.025	0.047

Reinvestment rate in high growth period = 23%
WACC = 9.5%
The average EBIT(1 − T) during the 5-year period 2011–15 = $16,192.4 million [12]
EBIT(1 − T) in the first year of high growth period = 16,192.4 × 1.046 = $16,937.3 million

The present value of FCFF during the high growth period is $ 97722.3 million (see Table 4.44).

Stable phase inputs
Growth rate in stable period = US GDP growth rate = 2.3%
The return on capital employed for software and programming industry is 15.42%.[13]

Growth rate = Reinvestment rate × Return on capital employed for software and programming industry.

Reinvestment rate = 2.3/15.42 = 15%
EBIT(1 − T) at end of high growth period = $25,388 million
EBIT (1 − T) in stable period = 25,388 × 1.023 = $25,971.90 million
Reinvestment = 0.15 × 25,971.90 = $3895.78 million
FCFF in stable period = 25,971.90 − 3895.78 = $22,076.11 million
Terminal value = FCFF in stable period/(WACC − growth rate in stable period) = 22,076.11/(9.51% − 2.3%) = $306187.43 million
Present value of terminal value = $123,438.20 million
Value of operating assets = PV of FCFF in high growth phase + PV of FCFF in stable phase = 97,722.3 + 123,438.20 = $221,160.46 million
Add cash and cash equivalents in year 2015 = $96,526 million
Value of Microsoft = 221,160.46 + 96,526 = $317,686.46 million
Subtracting the value of debt in year 2015 = $35,292
Value of Microsoft equity = 317,686.46 − 35,292 = $282,394.46 million
Number of shares = 8254 million
Value per share = 282,394.46/8254 = $34.21

The value per share for Microsoft is estimated as $34.21 per share according to FCFF two stage valuation model.

---

[12] Since the operating income after tax fluctuations are high, the average value is used for estimation.
[13] http://csimarket.com/Industry/industry_ManagementEffectiveness.php?ind=1011.

Table 4.43 **FCFF in million dollars**

Year	2011	2012	2013	2014	2015
Adjusted EBIT(1 − T)	23,364.4	17,874.6	23,037.6	23,996.2	14,021
Adjusted net Capex	784.4	10,850.6	3548.6	8193.2	5884
Change in noncash working capital	−369	−2785	−561	−5114	900
FCFF	22,949	9809	20,050	20,917	7237

Table 4.44 **PV of FCFF in high growth phase**

Year	1	2	3	4	5	6	7	8	9	10
EBIT(1 − T)	16,937.3	17,716.4	18,531.3	19,383.8	20,275.4	21,208.1	22,183.7	23,204.1	24,271.5	25,388.0
Reinvestment rate	0.23	0.23	0.23	0.23	0.23	0.23	0.23	0.23	0.23	0.23
Reinvestment	3895.6	4074.8	4262.2	4458.3	4663.3	4877.9	5102.2	5336.9	5582.4	5839.2
FCFF	13,041.7	13,641.6	14,269.1	14,925.5	15,612.1	16,330.2	17,081.4	17,867.2	18,689.0	19,548.7
PV	11,909.1	11,375.2	10,865.1	10,378.0	9912.7	9468.2	9043.7	8638.2	8250.9	7881.0
Sum	97,722.3									

Summary of Discounted Cash Flow Valuation Models

Two stage DDM
Value of Microsoft share based on two stage DDM is $45.81.
Two stage Free Cash to Equity (FCFE)
Value of Microsoft equity = $362.741 billion
Value of a Microsoft share based on two stage FCFE is estimated as $43.95
Two stage FCFF
Value of Microsoft firm = $317.686 billion
Value of Microsoft equity = $282.394 billion
Value of a Microsoft stock based on two stage FCFF is estimated as $34.21

*Microsoft was trading at **$54.21** in NASDAQ on March 26 2016 with market capitalization of $428.8 billion. The 52 week range for Microsoft was **$39.72– $56.85.***

4.20.6 Relative valuation

The peer companies used for comparison are Oracle, ACI Worldwide, Activision Blizzard, and Adobe Systems. Market capitalization and net income values are given in millions of dollars. Oracle Corporation has the highest net income among the peer companies. Adobe Systems and Microsoft were the P/E and P/B maximizers (see Table 4.45).

The price multiples like price to earnings, price to book, price to sales, price to cash flow and dividend yield of Microsoft are compared with industry average and S&P 500 values. Microsoft had higher price multiple ratios compared to industry and S&P 500 price multiples. The analysis was for the period March 2016. The source of data was Morningstar.com (see Table 4.46).

The 10-year period (2006–15) analysis of price multiples shows that the price earning multiple (P/E) peaked in the year 2015 (see Table 4.47). The average P/E ratio during the 10-year period was 16.47. The price to book ratio was highest in year 2007. The average P/B ratio was 5.09. The PEG ratio was highest in the year 2015. The PEG ratio is obtained by dividing the P/E ratio divided by the growth rate.

Table 4.45 Current peer group comparison

Company	Market cap	Net income	P/E	P/S	P/B
Microsoft	428,763	11,408	36.3	4.91	5.6
Oracle Corp	170,019	8844	20.2	4.81	3.71
ACI Worldwide	2,313,608	85	29.97	2.42	3.89
Activision Blizzard	23,674,286	892	26.8	6.11	2.93
Adobe Systems	46,105,492	630	74.7	9.66	6.51

Table 4.46 **Relative valuation comparison**

Ratios	Microsoft	Industry average	S&P 500
P/E	38.6	30.8	17.7
P/B	5.6	4.4	2.5
P/S	5	4.6	1.7
P/CF	14.4	13.6	11
Dividend yield (%)	2.5	2	2.5

Table 4.47 **Price multiple trends**

Year	2006	2007	2008	2009	2010	2011	2012	2013	2014	2015
P/E	19.48	20.7	14.66	14.67	10.95	9.68	15.29	13.3	15.85	30.16
P/B	5.85	8.88	6.94	5.35	4.32	3.82	3.86	3.64	3.83	4.43
P/S	5.57	5.72	4.32	3.66	3.29	3.19	3.52	3.75	4.03	3.91
PEG	3.03	1.3	0.59	0.62	0.64	0.6	1.4	2.55	2.35	12.44
P/CF	19.22	18.79	14.14	13.39	9.3	9.07	8.86	11.89	13.09	15.81

Table 4.48 **Enterprise value multiples**

Company	Microsoft	Oracle	Adobe systems
Revenues	93,580.0	38,226.0	4796.0
EBITDA	25,245.0	16,838.0	1277.0
EBIT	18,161.0	13,871.0	903.0
Debt	35,292.0	41,958.0	1907.0
Market value of equity	428,763.0	170,019.0	46,105,492.0
Cash and cash equivalents	96,526.0	54,368.0	3988.0
Enterprise value (EV)	367,529.0	157,609.0	46,103,411.0
EV/REVENUES	3.9	4.1	9612.9
EV/EBITDA	14.6	9.4	36,102.9
EV/EBIT	20.2	11.4	510,55.8

The average 5-year growth rate of EBITDA was used for the analysis. The average P/S ratio was 4.09 during the 10-year period of analysis. The average PEG ratio was 2.55 during the ten-year period of analysis. The average price to cash flow during the 10-year period of analysis was 13.36. The cash flow used for analysis was free cash flow which is an important measure considered by value investors.

The table 4.48 gives the enterprise value multiples of Microsoft and peer companies like Oracle and Adobe System. Enterprise value is market capitalization

Table 4.49 **Enterprise value multiple trends**

Year	2006	2007	2008	2009	2010	2011	2012	2013	2014	2015
EV/revenues	4.5	5.0	3.8	3.2	2.7	2.5	2.8	2.9	3.2	3.1
EV/EBITDA	11.5	12.7	8.8	8.1	6.1	5.7	7.9	7.3	8.3	11.6
EV/EBIT	12.2	13.7	9.5	9.1	6.7	6.2	8.9	8.2	9.9	15.2

plus debt minus cash and cash equivalents. Lower the enterprise value multiples, the more undervalued the stock is. Based on enterprise value multiples, Microsoft and Oracle is more undervalued compared to Adobe Systems.

The enterprise value multiples of Microsoft have been fluctuating over the 10-year period of analysis (see Table 4.49). The average EV/revenues, EV/EBITDA, and EV/EBIT was 3.4, 8.8, and 10, respectively.

4.21 Performance indicator analysis

4.21.1 Altman Z score

NYU Stern Finance Professor, Edward Altman developed the Altman Z score formula in the year 1967. In the year 2012, he released an updated version called the Altman Z Score Plus which can be used to evaluate both public and private companies. Investors can use Altman Z score to decide if they should buy or sell a particular stock based on the company's financial strength. The Altman Z score is the output of a credit strength test which gauges a publicly traded manufacturing company's likelihood of bankruptcy. Z score model is an accurate forecaster of failure up to two years prior to distress.

$$\mathbf{Z - Score = 1.2A + 1.4B + 3.3C + 0.6D + 1.0E}$$

Where:

A = Working capital/Total assets
B = Retained earnings/Total assets
C = Earnings before interest and tax/Total assets
D = Market value of equity/Total liabilities E = Sales/Total assets

The zones of discrimination are such that when Z Score is less than 1.81, it is in distress zones. When the Z score is greater than 2.99, it is in safe zones. When the Z Score is between 1.81 and 2.99, the company is in Grey Zone (see Table 4.50).

The calculations are based on the year 2015. The Z score of 4.13 for Microsoft indicates that the score is strong and the company is in safe zone.

Table 4.50 Estimation of Altman Z score for Microsoft

Ratios	Values	Constant	Score
Working capital/Total assets	0.42	1.2	0.51
Retained earnings/Total assets	0.05	1.4	0.07
Operating income/Total assets	0.10	3.3	0.34
Market value of equity/Total liabilities	4.46	0.6	2.68
Sales/Total assets	0.53	1	0.53
		Z score	4.13

4.21.2 Piotroski score

The Piotroski score is a discrete score between 0 to 9 which is an indicator of the firm's financial position. The score was named after the Chicago accounting Professor Joseph Piotroski. The cumulative points suggest whether the stock is a value stock or not. If the company achieves a score of 8 or 9, the stock can be considered strong. If the score ranges between 0 and 2, then the stock is considered weak.

Criteria for Piotroski score

SL	Profitability scores	Score points	Score for Microsoft
1	Positive return on assets in current year	1	1
2	Positive operating cash flow in current year	1	1
3	Higher ROA in current year compared to previous year	1	0
4	Return on cash flow from operations greater than ROA	1	1
	Leverage, liquidity and sources of funds		
5	Lower ratio of long term debt to average total assets in current year compared to previous year	1	0
6	Higher current ratio in this year compared to previous year	1	1
7	No new shares were issued in the last year	1	1
	Operational efficiency ratios		
8	A higher gross margin compared to the previous year	1	0
9	A higher asset turnover ratio compared to the previous year	1	0
Total		9	5

J&J have a Piotroski score of 5 out of 9. The analysis based on the current year 2015 reveals that Microsoft is a stable firm.

4.21.3 Graham number

It is a conservative method used for valuing a stock. It is a figure which measures a stock's fundamental value by taking into account the company's earnings per share and book value per share. Graham number is the upper bound of the price range which a defensive investor should pay for the stock. According to Graham number theory, any stock price below the Graham number is considered undervalued and hence worth investing in. Graham number is a combination of asset valuation and earnings power valuation.

EPS in year 2015 = 1.49
Book Value per share = 11.23

$$\text{Graham number} = \sqrt{22.5 \times (\text{Earning per share}) \times (\text{Book value per share})}$$
$$= \$19.40$$

The detailed calculation for all the analysis are given in the resources file *Microsoft.xlsx*.

Further reading

[1] Microsoft Corporation Mergers and Acquisitions. Thomson Financial.
[2] http://www.alacrastore.com/mergers-acquisitions/Microsoft_Corporation-1011097.
[3] Microsoft Annual Reports.

Wexalth creation by Exxon Mobil

5.1   Introduction

Exxon Mobil is the world's premier petroleum and petrochemical company. Over a period of 125 years, Exxon Mobil has evolved from a regional marketer of kerosene in United States to become the largest publicly traded integrated oil company in the world. Exxon Mobil has the industry's leading inventory of resources. Exxon Mobil is one of the largest integrated refiners, marketers of petroleum products and chemical manufacturers. The global economic flows from Exxon Mobil amounted to $196 billion in the year 2014. The government taxes and duties paid amounted to $8.3 billion. The capital and exploration expenditures was $39 billion in 2014. The distributions of dividends amounted to $24 billion. The production expenses amounted to $50 billion in year 2014. In 2014, Exxon Mobil had four million oil equivalent barrels of net oil and gas production per day in the year 2014.The company had 5.9 million barrels of petroleum product sales per day. The company had 24.2 million metric tons of prime product sales in year 2014.

5.1.1   Major timelines

Year	History
1859	The first successful oil well was drilled in Pennsylvania
1870	Standard oil company with largest refining capacity was established by Rockfeller and his associates
1879	Standard oil purchases three quarter interest in Vacuum oil company
1882	Standard oil trust consisting of standard oil company of New York and standard oil company of New Jersey formed
1903	The Wright brothers use Jersey Standard fuel and Mobil oil (Vacuum) lubricants for their historic first flight at Kitty Hawk, North Carolina
1911	Based on landmark US Supreme court decision, standard oil breaks into 34 unrelated companies which included Jersey Standard, Socony, and Vacuum Oil
1919	Jersey Standard acquires 50% interest in humble oil and refining company of Texas
1920	Researchers at Jersey standard produce the first commercial petrochemical—isopropyl alcohol(rubbing) alcohol
1936	First commercial unit in a cat cracking refinery begins operation at Socony's New Jersey refinery.
1942	The World's first fluid catalytic cracker established at Louisiana Standard Baton Rouge refinery

Year	History
1958	Pan American airways flies its first trans-Atlantic Boeing 707 flight from New York to London fueled by Mobil aviation fuel
1966	Vacuum oil company renamed to Mobil oil corporation and celebrates 100 years
1972	Jersey standard officially changes its name to Exxon corporation
1975	Mobil participates in completion of Beryl A, the world's first concrete production platform
1982	Exxon celebrates 100 years since the formation of the standard oil trust in 1882
1995	Exxon establishes the save the tiger fund in partnership with the national fish and wildlife foundation
1999	Exxon and Mobil joined to form Exxon Mobil Corporation
2005	Exxon Mobil and Qatar Petroleum with other joint venture partners expanded the development of the North Field offshore Qatar, the largest nonassociated gas field in the world
2007	Exxon Neftegas, a subsidiary of Exxon Mobil Corporation completed the drilling of the Z-11 well, the longest measured depth extended reach drilling ERD well in the world
2009	Exxon Mobil Corporation and Synthetic Genomics announced the opening of greenhouse facility for research and testing algae biofuels program
2010	Exxon Mobil entered into an agreement with XTO energy to establish a new organization to focus on global development and production of unconventional resources
2011	Two major oil discoveries and gas discovery in the deep water Gulf of Mexico made by Exxon Mobil

Source: http://corporate.exxonmobil.com/en/company/about-us/history/overview.

5.2 Economic scenario

In the last century many nations developed due to transition to modern energy and technology. Developed economies (OECD) consumed more than 50% of the world's energy though having only 20% of its population. Global energy consumption is expected to rise by about 35% from 2010 to 2040. The future trends would include shift to low carbon fuels, a plateau in carbon dioxide, emissions, and new energy options such as unconventional oil and natural gas in North America. China and India are expected to account for half the growth in global energy demand. The other key countries which would contribute to growth in energy needs are Brazil, Mexico, South Africa, Nigeria, Egypt and Turkey, Saudi Arabia, Iran, Thailand, and Indonesia.

In the future ahead, the energy sources will evolve and diversify driven by changes in technology, consumer needs, and public policies. Crude oil is expected to remain as the single biggest source of energy while natural gas will play an increasingly relevant role in meeting the global energy demands. The demand for oil is expected to grow by approximately 30% through 2040 due to increased commercial transportation activity. A major share of this demand will be met through sources like deep water, oil sands, and tight oil on account of advanced technology.

By 2040, natural gas will be the fastest growing major energy source. Liquefied natural gas volumes are expected to triple by 2040 contributing almost 20% of global gas supply. The residential/commercial sector accounts for only about 15% of global energy consumption but about 50% of electricity demand.[1]

Natural gas is expected to see demand growth of about 65% positioning to the second spot in the overall energy mix. Oil and gas is expected to meet about 65% of the global energy demand growth by the year 2040. Oil is expected to remain the world's primary energy source. The global population is projected to rise to 9 billion in 2040, as global economic output is expected to more than double.

The current global energy demand is estimated to be about 550 quadrillion BTUs, which is equivalent in energy to more than 12 billion gallons of gasoline daily. Energy demand will increase by 35%. Oil is expected to remain the world's primary energy source, with demand expected to rise by almost 30% on account of growth in commercial transportation requirements and chemical industry's need for feedstock.

5.3 Business operations

Exxon Mobil's diversified and balanced portfolio of high quality assets, projects and resources span across upstream, downstream, and chemical businesses.

5.3.1 Upstream operations

The upstream business include exploration, development, production, natural gas marketing, and research activities. The upstream business of Exxon Mobil involves a portfolio of world class projects. Exxon Mobil have an active exploration or production presence in 36 countries. The total resource base is 92 billion oil equivalent barrels which includes addition of 3.2 billion oil equivalent in year 2014. Proved reserve base of Exxon Mobil comprise approximately 27% of the resource base or 25 billion oil equivalent barrels.

Recently Exxon Mobil completed eight major operations which included Papua New Guinea liquefied Natural gas, Arkutun Dagi in Russia, Cold Lake Nabiye Expansion in Canada, Lucius in the Gulf of Mexico, Cravo Linio Orquidea Violeta (CLOV) in Angola. Focus is on for higher margin liquid production across the Permain, the Bakken, and the Ardmore/Marietta. Exxon Mobil aims to grow total production to 4.3 million oil equivalent barrels per day by the year 2017.

In 2014, resources were added in Angola, Argentina, Australia, Canada, Nigeria, Norway, Tanzania, and the United States. The largest components of Exxon Mobil's resource base comprise conventional oil and heavy oil/oil sands, which comprise 72% of the total. Approximately 13% of the total resource base was LNG. The remaining 15% of the resources is made up of Artic and acid/sour gas resources.

ExxonMobil is a leading reserves holder and producer of oil and natural gas in the United States. The company has significant position in all major producing

---

[1] Annual report Exxon Mobil.

areas which include offshore Gulf of Mexico, the Gulf Coast, the Rockies, the mid-continent, California, Alaska. The US portfolio includes mature conventional assets, emerging unconventional developments, and new deep water developments.

5.3.2   Downstream operations

Exxon Mobil is one of the world's largest integrated refiners and manufacturers of lube stocks. The company is also the leading supplier of petroleum products and finished lubricants. Exxon Mobil have refining facilities in 17 countries. Exxon Mobil have an ownership interest in 30 refineries with distillation capacity of over 5.2 million barrels per day and lube base stock capacity of 131 thousand barrels per day. About 75% of the refineries are integrated with chemical or lubricant manufacturing facilities. Exxon Mobil branded products has presence in more than 120 countries. The fuel products are sold in more than 35 countries and Mobil branded lubricants are sold in more than 120 countries. The average return on capital employed for downstream operations was 26% for the past 10 years.

5.3.3   Chemical operations

Exxon Mobil is the one of the largest chemical companies in the world. The company manufactures high quality chemical products in 16 countries. The specialty business generated annual sales of more than 24 million tons of prime products. Exxon Mobil are among the top producers of butyl polymers, specialty elastomers, and adhesive polymers. The specialty businesses generate annual sales of more than 24 million tons of prime products. Exxon Mobil are among the largest global manufacturers of aromatics which include paraxylene and benzene, as well as olefins such as ethylene and propylene. Exxon Mobil is the largest producer of polyethylene.

5.4   Strategy of growth of Exxon Mobil

Exxon Mobil obtains synergy from the integrated model as technology advances in the upstream, downstream and chemical businesses. The adoption of best practices of proven project management system facilitated Exxon Mobil to manage global project portfolio from initial discovery phase to production startup. Exxon Mobil focus on improving long term profitability by investing in higher margin barrels, maximizing production of installed capacity and driving cost efficiencies through productivity and efficiency gains. Exxon Mobil focuses on achieving operational efficiency by diversifying feed stocks through flexible and integrated systems, expanding logistics capabilities and maximizing sales of high value lubricant, diesel and chemical products. Exxon Mobil's operations integrity management system (OIMS) framework for excellence includes 11 elements. Each element contains an underlying principle and set of expectations. These elements consist of management leadership, commitment and accountability, risk assessment and management, personnel and training, third party services, facilities, design and construction, operations and maintenance, incident investigation and analysis, information and documentation, management of change, community awareness and emergency preparedness, and operations integrity assessment and improvement. Exxon Mobil growth strategy is driven by a strong acreage position and operational expertise. Exxon Mobil has initiated another phase of liquid growth from the oldest producing regions of West Texas and New Mexico by deploying substantial water flood, carbon dioxide and unconventional operations. As a result, net production surpassed 100 thousand oil equivalent barrels per day in year 2014. The company is also expanding production capacity by progressing water and gas handling improvement initiatives.

The Banyu Urip project is expected to produce up to 165 thousand barrels of oil per day. The integrated model of the value chain adopted by Exxon Mobil aims to maximize the overall profitability. The investments in downstream assets is aimed at increasing high value product yields, improve feedstock flexibility, expand logistics capability and increased operational efficiency. This focus on high value products is important in the context that demand for petroleum products like gasoline and fuel oil is expected to decline while the demand for higher value products such as ultra-low Sulphur diesel, jet fuel, chemical feedstock, and lubricants are expected to grow in future. In 2014, the Clean Fuel Project at Saudi Aramco Mobil Company Ltd was established to reduce Sulfur levels in gasoline and diesel.

Exxon Mobil has the largest combined mid-continent and Gulf Coast refining capacity in the industry which would benefit its refineries due to increased north American crude oil supply. In North America, the company is strengthening its crude oil and product logistics capabilities. The company have initiated a joint venture rail terminal with Kinder Morgan Canada terminal to provide cost advantaged export logistics for supply of Western Canada crude oil.

Exxon Mobil also focuses on portfolio optimization by continuous assessment. The company has reduced its refining capacity by more than one million barrels per day by divesting or restructuring 23 less competitive facilities. The company has also divested or restructured more than 6000 miles of pipeline, over 200 fuel terminals, 38 lubricant plants and over 15,000 retail service stations. With these steps the company aims to improve its downstream return on average capital employed.

Exxon Mobil have been successful in introducing price advantaged US tight oil and Canadian heavy oil crudes.

Exxon Mobil is making strategic investments in its chemical businesses. It uses proprietary technologies to capture advantaged feed stocks, deploy lower cost processes and increased premium product sales. The proposed ethane steam cracker in Baytown Texas is Exxon Mobil's largest ever chemical investment in United States. The Baytown Plant is the largest integrated refining and chemical manufacturing site in United States. Exxon Mobil had early mover advantage in capturing abundant affordable supplies of energy in North America.

In its Singapore petrochemical plants, the company have initiated a project to add production of halobutyl rubber and premium resins for adhesive applications.

The demand for these product lines is expected to double in the next 15 years. There is a growing demand for halobutyl rubber used in tyre inner liners as the global number of cars and light trucks are expected to double by 2040. The company with its joint venture partner Saudi Basic Industries is expected to build first of its kind specialty elastomers facility in Saudi Arabia.

ExxonMobil is one of the leading oil and gas producers in Canada, Europe and Africa. In Asia, ExxonMobil is participating in the development of some of the world's largest oil and gas projects.

In May 2014, ExxonMobil and Rosneft completed joint venture agreements for seven blocks in the Russian Arctic, stretching across the Kara, Laptev, and Chukchi Seas as an extension of the Strategic Cooperation Agreement.

5.5 Corporate governance

The business affairs of Exxon Mobil are managed by or under the direction of its Board in accordance with New Jersey law. According to ExxonMobil's by laws, the board may have no fewer than 10 and no more than 19 members. Majority of these directors are independent. No director may stand for election after reaching age 72 unless the board approves an exception to the guidelines on a case by case basis. To avoid any potential conflict of interest, the directors will not accept a seat on any additional company board without first reviewing the matter with the Board Affairs Committee. Review of ExxonMobil's operations are presented by appropriate executives from time to time as part of the agenda of regular board meetings. The standing committees of the board are the Executive Committee, Audit Committee, Board Affairs Committee, Compensation Committee, Finance Committee, and Public Issues and Contribution Committee. The Board Affairs Committee, Audit Committee, and Compensation Committee will consist solely of independent directors. By 2014, the common shareholders held 83% of the company's shares which amounted to approximately 3.56 billion shares. In 2014 the company had 37 shareholder dialogs with labor, religious organizations, pension funds, and institutional investors. The Public Issues and Contributions Committee (PICC) of ExxonMobil's board of directors oversees the corporation's contributions, public engagement, and safety and environmental performance.

5.6 CSR activities

Exxon Mobil have taken initiatives for cleaner energy. In Saudi Arabia Exxon Mobil had commissioned a project to reduce sulfur levels in gasoline and diesel at the refinery in Yanube. The company is also expanding its range of chemical specialty products in the region along with its partner Saudi Basic Industries Corporation. In its European refinery located at Antwerp, Exxon Mobil have decided to install a delayed Coker to produce cleaner transportation fuels. Exxon Mobil have helped in meeting the risk of climatic change by supplying cleaner burning natural gas by reducing US greenhouse gas emissions to 1990 levels by developing emissions reducing technologies. Exxon Mobil have received various safety excellence awards. The rigorous Product Stewardship Information Management System applies common global processes and computer systems to capture and communicate information on the safe handling, transport, use and disposal of the products, as well as emergency contact information. It also ensures compliance with regulations in more than 150 countries. Local water management efforts at key sites have contributed to the gradual decline in the company's water consumption since 2011. For example, the wastewater treatment facility at the Singapore chemical plant uses state-of-the-art membrane bioreactor (MBR) technology to treat wastewater, enabling it to be reused as cooling water. The company is focusing on developing and implementing local water management strategies which include the use of freshwater alternatives like recycled municipal and industrial wastewater, seasonal water management and rain water harvesting. Approximately 7200 acres of land have been managed for wildlife over a period of 10 years. Exxon Mobil with the engagement of different stakeholders like policymakers, investors, consumers and public focusses on climate change issues which are of relevance to society. The company contributed $835 million to education programs worldwide. Exxon Mobil invests in education program related to science, technology, engineering and mathematics. Women account for about 28% of the worldwide workforce.

The company provides fund for the economic empowerment of women. The company's efforts are also directed to combat malaria and other infectious diseases. The development of Banyu Urip project in Indonesia saw the participation of over 10,000 individuals. More than 70,000 community members people benefitted from education, health and community development programs.

5.7   Mergers and acquisitions

5.7.1   Exxon Mobil merger highlights

In the year 1998—the merger of Exxon and Mobil took place. In 2009, Exxon Mobil announced plans to acquire XTO Energy for $40 billion.

The Exxon Mobil merger reunited the major disintegrated divisions of the standard oil which controlled almost 90% of all oil produced in United States. In 1911 the Supreme Court of United States broke up standard oil into 33 companies of which eight were retained under the standard oil. After series of name changes, standard oil of New York became Mobil in 1966. By 1972, the once standard oil of New Jersey had evolved into Exxon.

On Nov 30 1999 Exxon and Mobil merged to form Exxon Mobil. The deal saw the world's largest energy company Exxon acquiring Mobil, the second biggest US and Oil gas group. The merger created the largest oil company in the world. At the time of merger, the combined Exxon Mobil was the third largest company in the world behind GE and Microsoft in terms of market capitalization. The merger led to approximately 9000 job losses or 7% of the group's workforce around the world.

5.7.2   Strategic reasons for merger

Consolidation of oil companies were taking place on account of high production costs and weak oil prices. The merger brought together two complementary businesses that fitted well in the exploration and production of petroleum and chemicals. By combining complementary assets, Exxon Mobil was able to expand their presence in regions of high potential for future oil and gas discoveries. The merger facilitated the combination of Exxon's rich experience in deep water exploration with Mobil's production and exploration acreage in Nigeria and Equatorial Guinea. In the Caspian region, Exxon's presence in Azerbaijan coupled with Mobil's presence in Kazakhstan particularly in the Tengiz field was expected to yield merger benefits. Complementary exploration and production operations also existed in South America, Russia, and Eastern Canada. Cost synergy resulted from the merger due to elimination of duplication facilities and excess capacity. The general and administrative costs were also reduced. Moreover, synergy benefits were realized from applying each company's best business practices across their worldwide operations. By 2002 Exxon realized project synergies of $7 billion. The merger resulted in an increase of market share by 23%. The merger expected savings of about $2.8 billion per year.

5.7.3   Terms of the deal

Exxon paid 1.32 shares for each share of Mobil. Since Mobil had 780 million shares outstanding, Exxon paid 1030 million shares times the $72 share price of Exxon for a total of $74.2 billion. This was a 26.4% premium over the $58.7 billion Mobil market capitalization at the time of merger announcement. The new company was owned by 70% of Exxon's existing shareholders.

Exxon and Mobil sold off 24,131 gas stations primarily in the northeastern United States, California and Texas as required by the federal trade commission for approval of the merger.

5.8   Acquisition of XTO energy

In 2009, Exxon Mobil acquired XTO energy in an all-stock deal valued at $41 billion. Exxon Mobil issued 0.7098 of a share of common stock for each common share of XTO. The deal represented a 25% premium to XTO stockholders. This acquisition was the largest acquisition made by Exxon Mobil after the Mobil acquisition. The acquisition was significant in the context of the growing relevance of natural gas as the source for clean energy. XTO energy had been active in extracting natural gas from shale formations in the region spread between Pennsylvania, New York and West Virginia in Texas and North Dakota. The company has proven reserves of 13.9 trillion cubic feet of gas and total reserves of 45 trillion cubic feet. Consolidation has been active as biggest players in the field were on the lookout

Table 5.1 **Stock restructuring trends**

Year	Events
1922	Cash dividend of $5 plus 400% stock dividend
1926	Cash dividend of $1.125 plus warrants
1927	$25 par value common stock becomes capital stock
1951	Stock split 2 for 1
1956	Stock split 3 for 1
1957	Cash dividend of $2.25 plus warrants
1970	Cash dividend of $3.75 plus warrants
1976	Stock split two for 1
1981	Stock split two for 1
1987	Stock split two for 1
1997	Stock split two for 1
2001	Stock split two for 1

Table 5.2 **Dividend trends**

Year	2005	2006	2007	2008	2009	2010	2011	2012	2013	2014	2015
DPS in $	1.14	1.28	1.37	1.55	1.66	1.74	1.85	2.18	2.46	2.70	2.15

for independent producers which suffered on account of low gas prices. The acquisition was basically meant to enhance Exxon Mobil's position in the development of unconventional natural gas and oil resources. Earlier, energy companies burned off natural gas as a waste product. With the realization of its value as an energy source aided with technology, natural gas trapped in vast shale oil fields have been freed with a technique called fracking. Both Exxon Mobil and XTO have established presence in Piceance Basin in Colorado. XTO's resource base consists of 45 trillion cubic feet of gas and includes shale gas, tight gas, coal bed methane and shale oil. These assets are expected to complement the assets of Exxon Mobil's holdings in the United States, Canada, Germany, Poland, Hungary and Argentina.

During the past 125 years of its existence, Exxon Mobil had undertaken stock splits seven times (see Table 5.1).

Exxon Mobil's dividend payment to shareholders have grown at an average annual rate of 6.4% over the past 32 years. The average growth rate of dividend per share (DPS) was 7.07% during the 10-year period 2006−15. In the year 2015 DPS was up to month September (see Table 5.2). The dividends have been consistently increasing over the last decade. In 1911 the par value of common stock was $100. In the same year, Exxon Mobil paid a dividend of $37 (see Table 5.3). The average dividend payout (DPO) during the period 2005−2015 was approximately 28%. The average DPO during the period 2005−9 was approximately 24%. The average DPO during the period 2010−14 was approximately 27%.

Table 5.3 **Cash dividends in past decades**

Year	Cash dividends
1911	$37, par value of common stock was $100
1920	$20. In 1920, par value was changed to $25 and four $25 par value certificates was issued for each $100 certificate
1930	$2
1940	$1.75
1950	$5. In 1951 par value changed to$15 par value
1960	$2.25. In 1956, par value becomes $7
1970	$3.75
1980	$5.40
1990	$2.47, In 1997 stock split 2 for 1
2000	$1.76. In 2001, stock split 2 for 1
2010	$1.74
2015	$2.15

Table 5.4 **Upstream statistics**

Year	2010	2011	2012	2013	2014
Earnings (millions of dollars)	24,097	34,439	29,895	26,841	27,548
Liquids production (net, thousands of barrel per day)	2422	2312	2185	2202	2111
Natural gas production for sale (net, millions of cubic feet per day)	12,148	13,162	12,322	11,836	11,145
Oil equivalent production (net, thousands of barrels per day)[a]	4447	4506	4239	4175	3969
Proved reserved replacement ratio[b]	211	116	124	106	111
Return on average capital employed (%)	23.3	26.5	21.4	17.5	16.7

[a]Natural gas converted to oil equivalent at six million cubic feet per one thousand barrel.
[b]The reserves replacement ratio is calculated for a specified period utilizing the applicable proved oil-equivalent reserves additions divided by oil-equivalent production.

5.9 Operational statistics

The following section discusses the operational trends of Exxon Mobil during the period 2010–14 (see Tables 5.4–5.8).

The net income registered an increase of approximately 35% in the year 2012 compared to the previous year 2011. In 2012, the net income growth rate fell to 9%. In 2013 the net income registered negative growth of 27% and in 2014 the net income growth rate was—0.18%. In 2011, the cash flow from operations increased by 28%. The capital and exploration expenses increased by 14%, 8%, and 6.7%, respectively during the period 2011, 2012, and 2013. The market valuation had been fluctuating during the period 2010–14. The market valuation increased by 10% in 2011 and fell

Table 5.5 **Downstream statistics**

Year	2010	2011	2012	2013	2014
Earnings in millions of dollars	3567	4459	13,190	3449	3045
Refinery throughput (thousands of barrel per day)	5253	5214	5014	4585	4476
Petroleum product sales (thousands of barrel per day)	6414	6413	6174	5887	5875
Return on average capital employed (%)	14.8	19.1	54.9	14.1	12.7

Source: 2014 Exxon Mobil operating and financial review.

Table 5.6 **Chemical business statistics**

Year	2010	2011	2012	2013	2014
Earnings (millions of dollars)	4913	4383	3898	3828	4315
Prime product sales (thousands of tons)	25,891	25,006	24,157	24,003	24,235
Return on average capital employed (%)	26.3	22.1	19.3	18.5	19.4

Source: 2014 Exxon Mobil operating and financial review.

Table 5.7 **Capital and exploration expenditures (millions of dollars)**

Year	2010	2011	2012	2013	2014
Upstream	27,319	33,091	36,084	38,231	32,727
Downstream	2505	2120	2262	2413	3034
Chemical	2215	1450	1418	1832	2741
Others	187	105	35	13	35
Total	32,226	36,766	39,799	42,489	38,537

Table 5.8 **Capital and exploration expenditures by geographical region (millions of dollars)**

Year	2010	2011	2012	2013	2014
USA	7797	11,654	12,157	11,072	12,436
Canada/Latin America	5732	6186	8616	12838	8189
Europe	3901	2914	3111	3045	2851
Africa	4915	4291	3907	4220	4187
Asia	6693	7066	6704	6734	7330
Australia/Oceania	3188	4655	5304	4580	3542
Total worldwide	32,226	36,766	39,799	42,489	38,537

Table 5.9 **Financial highlights in millions except as noted**

Year	2010	2011	2012	2013	2014
Net income attributable to Exxon Mobil	30,460	41,060	44,880	32,580	32,520
Cash flow from operations and asset sales	51,674	66,478	63,825	47,621	49,151
Capital and exploration expenses	32,226	36,766	39,799	42,489	38,537
Research and development costs	1012	1044	1042	1044	971
Total debt at year end	15,014	17,033	11,581	22,699	29,121
Average capital employed	145,217	170,721	179,094	191,575	203,110
Market valuation at year end	364,035	401,249	389,680	438,684	388,398
Regular employees at year end (thousands)	83.6	82.1	76.9	75	75.3

Source: 2014 Exxon Mobil operating and financial review.

Table 5.10 **Key financial ratios**

Year	2010	2011	2012	2013	2014
Return on average capital employed (percent)	21.7	24.2	25.4	17.2	16.2
Earnings to average Exxon Mobil share of equity (percent)	23.7	27.3	28	19.2	18.7
Debt to capital (percent)	9.0	9.6	6.3	11.2	13.9
Net debt to capital (percent)	4.5	2.6	1.2	9.1	11.9
Current ratio (times)	0.94	0.94	1.01	0.83	0.82
Fixed-charge coverage (times)	42.2	53.4	62.4	55.7	46.9

by 3% approximately during the period 2012. The market capitalization increased by 12.5% in year 2013 and fell by 11% in year 2014 (see Table 5.9). Table 5.10 gives the key financial ratios of Exxon Mobil during the period 2010-2014.

5.10   Ownership details

In November 2015, equity and debt comprised 83% and 17% of the total capital, respectively. The total number of shares outstanding was 4163 million. The total value of holdings of $168,911 million. The institutional ownership amounted to 50.4%. There are 2103 institutional holders. Financial Institutions, Mutual fund, and promoter's equity ownership stake was 68.8%, 31%, and 0.24%, respectively in year 2015 (see Table 5.11).

The top 10 major fund holders account for 7.45% of the total shares held in year 2015.Vanguard stock market index and Vanguard 500 index investment held 3% of the total shares.

Table 5.11 **Major 10 equity institutional holders in year 2015**

SL	Financial institution	Percentage of share held
1	The Vanguard Group	5.96
2	Vanguard Group Inc.	6.16
3	State Street Corp.	4.33
4	BlackRock Fund Advisors	2.96
5	Northern Trust Investments	1.41
6	Wellington Management Co.	1.39
7	State Street Global Advisors	1
8	Govt Pension Fund Norway	0.68
9	State Farm Mutual Auto Ins.	0.89
10	Geode Capital Management LLC	0.83
	Total share	25.61

Source: Morning star.

Table 5.12 **Peer comparison in year 2015**

Company	Exxon Mobil	Royal Dutch shell	British petroleum	Total Fina
Market capitalization	338,239	159,334	107,011	118,122
Revenues	296,351	306,146	247,695	157,863
Net income	19,940	1595	−7449	1055
Total assets	349,493	353,116	284,305	229,798
Number of institution owners	3181	999	1032	651
Percent owned by institution owners	55.68	8.95	10.95	5.63

Values in millions of US dollars otherwise stated.

Exxon Mobil had the highest market capitalization among the peer group. The net income of Exxon Mobil was 12.5 times that of the next highest competitor Royal Dutch Shell. Approximately 56% of the equity stake was owned by institutional owners which was highest among the peer group (see Table 5.12).

5.11 Wealth creation by Exxon Mobil

The average monthly returns based on period 1970–2015 involving 550 months was 1.2%. Based on the above calculation the average yearly returns during the 45-year period was approximately 14%. The cumulative monthly return during the 550 months (1970–2015) period was 660%. The average yearly returns for S&P 500 index (calculations based on monthly returns) was approximately 8%. The cumulative monthly returns during the 550-month period for S&P 500 index was approximately 371% during the above period.

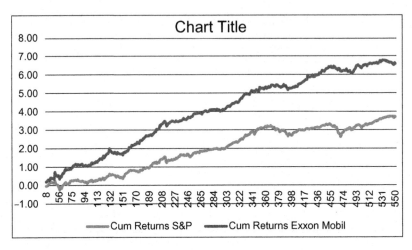

Figure 5.1 Cumulative monthly returns during the period 1970−2015.

Table 5.13 Average yearly returns in percent: Exxon Mobil versus S&P 500

Year	Exxon Mobil	S&P 500	Excess returns
2010	11.3	13.8	−2.5
2011	18.8	1.1	17.7
2012	5.6	13.2	−7.6
2013	19.3	26.5	−7.2
2014	−5.2	11.1	−16.3
2015	−13.3	−1	−12.3

The cumulative return analysis shows that Exxon Mobil outperformed the market index S&P 500 during the entire 45-year period of analysis (see Fig. 5.1).

The table 5.13 compares the average yearly returns of Exxon Mobil with that of S&P 500 during the period 2010−15. The average monthly returns are found out and then average yearly returns are estimated. Excess returns are estimated as the difference between the average yearly returns of Exxon Mobil and S&P 500. Except in year 2011, S&P 500 outperformed Exxon Mobil in all other years. The highest yearly returns of Exxon Mobil were in year 2013 (return of 19.3%). In the same year S&P 500 made a yearly return of 26.5%. The highest excess return for Exxon Mobil was in year 2011.

Holding period yield for Exxon Mobil is estimated for each year based on the assumption that the stock is bought on the first month of every year and sold in the last month of the year. The holding period yield was highest in the year 2010 and 2011, respectively. The holding period yield was −8% in year 2015 (see Table 5.14).

Table 5.14 **Holding period yield**

Year	Holding period yield in%
2010	17
2011	2
2012	6
2013	16
2014	3
2015	−8

Table 5.15 **Excess value creation**

Year	2010	2011	2012	2013	2014
Market Cap USD Mil	364,064	401,254	389,648	438,702	388,382
Book value USD Mil	146,839	154,396	165,863	174,003	174,399
Excess value	217,225	246,858	223,785	264,699	213,983
BV as% of MV	40	38	43	40	45

Excess value is estimated as the difference between the market capitalization and book value of equity during the period 2010−14. On an average the market value was approximately 2.4 times as that of book value of equity during the period 2010−14. The book value as per cent of market value was 45% during the year 2014 (see Table 5.15).

5.12 Operating performance analysis

The revenues of Exxon Mobil increased from $370.68 billion in year 2005 to $411.94 billion in year 2014. The operating income decreased from $91.5 billion in year 2005 to $51.63 billion in year 2014. The capital spending increased from $13.83 billion in year 2005 to $32.95 billion by year 2014. The geometric mean based average growth rate of revenues during the period 2005−14 was 1.2%. The average growth rate of operating income and net income during the above period was approximately −6 % and −1 %. The operating cash flow average growth rate was −0.7%. Based on geometric mean, the capital expenditure growth rate was approximately 10% during the period 2005−14. The year on year growth rate analysis reveal that the revenue growth rate peaked in year 2011 with growth rate of approximately 27%. The net income growth rate peaked in year 2010 with growth rate of approximately 58% compared to the previous period. The growth rate of capital expenditure was highest in year 2010 with growth rate of approximately 19% compared to previous year (see Table 5.16).

Table 5.16 Operating highlights during the period 2005−4 (values in million US dollars)

Year	2005	2006	2007	2008	2009	2010	2011	2012	2013	2014
Revenues	370,680	377,635	404,552	477,359	310,586	383,221	486,429	482,295	438,255	411,939
Operating income	91,469	69,107	103,607	118,578	34,777	52,959	73,257	78,726	57,711	51,630
Net income	36,130	39,500	40,610	45,220	19,280	30,460	41,060	44,880	32,580	32,520
Operating cash flow	48,138	49,286	52,002	59,725	28,438	48,413	55,345	56,170	44,914	45,116
Capital spending	13,839	15,462	15,387	19,318	22,491	26,871	30,975	34,271	33,669	32,952

The average gross margin during the period 2005–15 period was 39%. The average operating margin and net margin during the above period was 17% and 9%, respectively. The average return on assets and return on equity during the period 2005–15 was 13% and 26% approximately. The average return on capital employed during the 11-year period 2005–15 was 24%. The average profitability ratios have declined in the period 2010–14 compared to the period 2005–9. The average gross margin declined from 42% in the period 2005–9 to 37% during the period 2010–14. The average operating margin was 21% during the period 2005–9. In 2010–14, the average operating margin was reduced to 14%. The average net margin which was 9% during the period 2005–9 slightly declined to 8% during the period 2010–14. The average return on assets was 16% during the period 2005–9 while it was 11% during the period 2010–14. The average return on equity declined from 32% to 23% during the two period of comparison. The average return on capital employed also declined from 30% to 23% during the two comparative periods of analysis (see Table 5.17).

The average EPS during the period 2005–15 was 6.94. The average EPS during the period 2005–9 was 6.5 while the average EPS during the period 2010–14 was 7.9 (see Table 5.18).

The liquidity position has declined over the period 2005–15. The average current ratio during the 11-year period was 1.14. The average quick ratio during the above period was 0.82. The average current ratio during the 5-year period 2005–9 was 1.1 while the average current ratio during the 5-year period 2010–14 was 0.91. The average quick ratio which was 1.1 during the period 2005–9 declined to 0.6 during the period 2010–14 (see Table 5.19).

The long term solvency position of the firm is found to be good. Exxon Mobil has very low financial risk as the average debt equity ratio is only 0.07 during the period 2005–15. The average financial leverage during the 11-year period was 2. Exxon Mobil have very high Interest Coverage Ratio (ICR) (see Table 5.20).

The average payable period during the period 2005–14 was 37 days. The average receivables turnover ratio was 14.78 during the above period. The average inventory turnover ratio during the period 2005–14 was 20.31. The average fixed assets turnover and asset turnover ratio during the above period was 2.69 and 1.56. The average payable period during the period 2005–9 was 46.8 while average payable period was 24.72 during the period 2010–14. The average receivable turnover ratio during the period 2005–9 was 14.45 while the average receivable turnover ratio was 15.1 during the period 2010–14. The average inventory turnover ratio which was 21.3 during the period 2005–9, declined to 19.2 during the period 2010–14. The average fixed assets turnover ratio declined from 3.3 to 2.06 during the two period of comparison. The average asset turnover ratio declined from 1.75 to 1.38 during the two periods of comparison (see Table 5.21).

Table 5.17 **Profitability trends**

Year	2005	2006	2007	2008	2009	2010	2011	2012	2013	2014	2015
Gross margin (%)	42.54	43.53	42.44	39.5	40.17	39	36.93	37.04	35.04	35.23	39.42
Operating margin (%)	24.68	18.3	25.61	24.84	11.2	13.82	15.06	16.32	13.17	12.53	9.51
Net margin (%)	9.75	10.46	10.04	9.47	6.21	7.95	8.44	9.31	7.43	7.89	6.73
Return on assets (%)	17.9	18.49	17.61	19.24	8.36	11.37	12.96	13.5	9.57	9.34	5.75
Return on equity (%)	33.93	35.11	34.47	38.53	17.25	23.67	27.26	28.03	19.17	18.67	11.35
Return on capital employed (%)	31.79	33.27	32.24	35.99	16.19	21.72	24.74	25.84	17.42	16.34	9.9

Table 5.18 **EPS**

Year	2005	2006	2007	2008	2009	2010	2011	2012	2013	2014	2015
EPS	5.71	6.62	7.28	8.69	3.98	6.22	8.42	9.7	7.37	7.6	4.74

Table 5.19 **Liquidity position**

Year	2005	2006	2007	2008	2009	2010	2011	2012	2013	2014	2015	Average
Current ratio	1.58	1.55	1.47	1.47	1.06	0.94	0.94	1.01	0.83	0.82	0.86	1.14
Quick ratio	1.21	1.17	1.22	1.16	0.74	0.64	0.66	0.69	0.53	0.5	0.48	0.82

Table 5.20 **Long term solvency position**

Year	2005	2006	2007	2008	2009	2010	2011	2012	2013	2014	2015	Average
Financial leverage	1.87	1.92	1.99	2.02	2.11	2.06	2.14	2.01	1.99	2	2	2.01
DER	0.06	0.06	0.06	0.06	0.06	0.08	0.06	0.05	0.04	0.07	0.12	0.07
ICR						205.5	297.6	241.8	6413.3	181.5	89.3	1238.17

Table 5.21 **Efficiency position**

Year	2005	2006	2007	2008	2009	2010	2011	2012	2013	2014	Average
Payable period	58.16	52.38	55.14	44.24	24.3		20.21	20.41	19.82	38.44	37.01
Receivable turnover	14.03	14.37	13.15	17.31	13.4	12.79	13.72	14.39	16.12	18.5	14.78
Inventory turnover	22.65	21.29	21.36	25.41	16.02	19.06	21.91	20.54	18.56	16.26	20.31
Fixed assets turnover	3.44	3.42	3.45	3.94	2.38	2.26	2.35	2.18	1.86	1.66	2.69
Asset turnover	1.84	1.77	1.75	2.03	1.35	1.43	1.54	1.45	1.29	1.18	1.56

5.13   Valuation of Exxon Mobil

In this section Exxon Mobil is valued using discounted cash flow valuation models and relative valuation models. The discounted cash flow valuation models used are dividend discount model, free cash flow to equity and free cash flow to firm models.

5.13.1   Dividend discount model

The dividends are considered as the residual cash flows to the firm in this model. The future expected dividends are estimated and discounted by the cost of equity to arrive at the value of the share. The cost of equity is estimated using the Capital Asset Pricing Model (CAPM).

5.13.2   Cost of equity

Expected return = Risk free rate + beta × Risk premium.
   The average yield to maturity on the 30 year US Treasury bond during the 3-year period 2013−15 is assumed as the risk free rate.[2] The risk free rate is assumed as 3.26%.
   Beta is estimated by regressing the weekly stock returns of Exxon Mobil on the weekly returns of market index during the 3-year period 2013−15.

Beta = 1.05
Risk premium = Return on market Index-Risk free rate.

Return on market index is estimated using the 3-year average returns given by S&P 500 during the period December 2012−December 2015. Return on market index is estimated as 13.45%.

Risk premium = 13.46−3.26 = 10.20%
Cost of equity = 3.26 + 1.05 × 10.20 = 13.97%

5.13.3   Cost of debt estimation

The cost of debt is taken as the yield to maturity on a long term debt of Exxon Mobil. The Exxon Mobil bond which matures on March 6 2045 rated AAA by S&P have yield to maturity of 3.8%. Hence the cost of debt is assumed to be 3.8%. The price of this bond was $95.02 on the day of estimation. The marginal tax rate is 35%.[3]

After tax cost of debt = 3.8(1−0.35) = 2.47%.
Weighted Average Cost of Capital (WACC)

---

[2] http://www.federalreserve.gov/releases/h15/data.htm.
[3] https://home.kpmg.com/xx/en/home/services/tax/tax-tools-and-resources/tax-rates-online/corporate-tax-rates-table.html.

WACC is estimated on the basis of market value weights of equity and debt. Only interest bearing liabilities are considered as part of debt.

Book value of debt = \$29121 million.

Market value of debt is calculated by multiplying the ratio of the price of the selected long term bond of Exxon Mobil to the face value of the bond.

Ratio = 95.02/100 = 0.9502
Market value of debt in 2014 = 0.9502*29,121 = \$ 27,670.77 million.
Market value of equity in 2014 = \$388,382 million
Total capital = 27,670.77 + 388,382 = \$416,052.8 million
Weight of equity = 388,382/416,052.8 = 0.93
Weight of debt = 27,670.77/416,052.8 = 0.07
WACC = Weight of equity × Cost of equity + Weight of debt × After tax cost of debt
WACC = 0.93 × 13.97 + 0.07 × 2.47 = 13.21
WACC = 13.21%

5.13.4 Dividend discount model

The 10-year average EPS (2006−11) based on geometric mean was −5% approximately. The 5-year average EPS (2011−15) based on geometric mean was approximately −1.8%. The average growth rate of DPS during the 10-year period (2006−15) and (2011−15) was approximately 10%. The average DPO during the 10-year and 5-year period of analysis was approximately 28% (see Table 5.22).

The average DPO during the 5-year period 2010−14 was 28%.

Retention ratio = 1-DPO.

The average growth rate of earnings estimated from fundamentals during the period (2010−15) was 15% (see Table 5.23).

Two stage dividend discount model valuation.

Table 5.22 Estimation of DPO

Year	2010	2011	2012	2013	2014	2015
EPS	6.22	8.42	9.7	7.37	7.6	4.74
DPS	1.74	1.85	2.18	2.46	2.7	2.84
DPO	0.28	0.22	0.22	0.33	0.36	0.60

Table 5.23 Estimation of growth rate from fundamentals

Year	2010	2011	2012	2013	2014	2015
Retention ratio	0.72	0.78	0.78	0.67	0.64	0.40
ROE	0.24	0.27	0.28	0.19	0.19	0.11
Growth rate	0.17	0.21	0.22	0.13	0.12	0.04

Table 5.24 Present value of dividends in high growth phase

Year	1	2	3	4	5	6	7	8	9	10
EPS	8.74	10.05	11.56	13.29	15.29	17.58	20.22	23.25	26.74	30.75
DPO	0.28	0.28	0.28	0.28	0.28	0.28	0.28	0.28	0.28	0.28
DPS	2.45	2.81	3.24	3.72	4.28	4.92	5.66	6.51	7.49	8.61
PV	$2.15	$2.17	$2.19	$2.21	$2.23	$2.25	$2.27	$2.29	$2.31	$2.33
Sum	$22.37									

The growth rate of Exxon Mobil's earnings (based on EPS) estimated from fundamentals was 15%. Hence we assume that Exxon Mobil would grow at 15% for the next 10 years and then grow at the steady growth rate which is considered to the growth rate of US economy.

Assumptions of high growth period.
High growth period = 10 years.
High growth rate = 15%.
Current EPS (based on year 2014)[4] = $ 7.6.
The average DPO during the high growth period is assumed to the average DPO during the 5-year period 2010−14.
DPO in the high growth period = 28%.
EPS in the first year of estimation = 7.6 × 1.15 = $8.74.
Cost of equity = 13.97%.
The present value of dividends in the high growth phase = $22.37 (see Table 5.24).
Stable period inputs.
Stable growth rate of Exxon Mobil = Growth rate of US economy.
The average growth rate of US GDP during the period 2011−14 was 2.13%.[5]
The retention ratio in the stable phase is estimated through the relationship given below:
Growth rate = Retention ratio × Return on equity of industry (oil sector).
Return on equity of the oil and gas industry sector = 5.44%.[6]
2.13% = Retention ratio × ROE.
2.13% = Retention ratio × 5.44%.
Retention ratio = 2.13%/5.44% = 39.15%.
The retention ratio of earnings of Exxon Mobil during the stable period = 39.15%.
DPO during the stable period = 1−0.39 = 0.61.
EPS in stable phase period = 30.75 × 1.0213 = $31.40
DPO = 0.61.
DPS in stable period = $31.40 × 0.61 = $19.15.
Terminal value = DPS in stable period/(Cost of equity-growth rate in stable period).
Terminal value = 19.15/ (0.1397−0.0213) = $161.78.
Present value of terminal price = $43.75.

---

[4] We assume the year 2014 since the annual report for 2015 was not available during the period of calculation.
[5] http://data.worldbank.org/indicator/NY.GDP.MKTP.KD.ZG.
[6] http://csimarket.com/Industry/industry_ManagementEffectiveness.php?ind=603.

Value of Exxon Mobil = Present value of dividends in high growth phase + Present value of dividends in the stable phase.
Value of Exxon Mobil share = 22.37 + 43.75 = $66.12.

Based on two stage dividend discount model, the value of Exxon Mobil is arrived at $66.12. On December 2 2015, Exxon Mobil was trading at $80.60 in New York Stock Exchange. On the basis of comparison, it can be stated that Exxon Mobil is overvalued. The 52 week range for Exxon Mobil in year 2015 was $66.55–$95.33.

5.13.5 Free Cash Flow to Equity (FCFE) valuation

On the basis of historical growth rates, the average growth rate of net income during the period 2005–14 was 4.5% on the basis of arithmetic mean and −1.2% on the basis of geometric mean. The historical growth rate of net income during the period 2010–14 was 14.9% on the basis of arithmetic mean and 11% on the basis of geometric mean.

For estimation of growth rate of net income in high growth period, we estimate the growth rate of net income from fundamentals.

5.14 Estimation of growth rate of net income from fundamentals

Growth rate in net income = Reinvestment rate × Return on equity.
Reinvestment rate = Adjusted net capital expenditure + Change in noncash working capital −Net debt issued/Net income.
Net capital expenditure (Net Capex) = Capital expenditure − Depreciation.
Adjusted net capital expenditure = Net capital expenditure + Acquisitions.
Net debt issued = Debt issued − Debt repaid.
Noncash working capital = Noncash current assets − Noncash current liabilities (see Table 5.25).

Table 5.25 Estimation of change in working capital in millions of dollars

Year	2009	2010	2011	2012	2013	2014
Current assets	23,670	58,984	72,963	64,460	59,308	52,910
Cash and marketable securities	4660	7827	12,664	9582	4644	4616
Noncash current assets	19,010	51,157	60,299	54,878	54,664	48,294
Current liabilities	22,310	62,633	77,505	64,139	71,724	64,633
Interest bearing current liabilities	1060	2787	7711	3653	15,808	17,468
Noninterest bearing current liabilities	21,250	59,846	69,794	60,486	55,916	47,165
Noncash working capital	−2240	−8689	−9495	−5608	−1252	1129
Change in working capital		−6449	−806	3887	4356	2381

Table 5.26 **Estimation of reinvestment rate**

Year	2010	2011	2012	2013	2014
Capex	26,871	30,975	34,271	33,669	32,952
Depreciations	14,760	15,583	15,888	17,182	17,297
Acquisitions	3261	11,133	7655	2707	4035
Adjusted Net Capex	15,372	26,525	26,038	19,194	19,690
Change in noncash working Capital	−6449	−806	3887	4356	2381
Net debt issued	−6919	396	−2682	−408	4917
Reinvestment	15,842	25,323	32,607	23,958	17,154
Net Income	30,460	41,060	44,880	32,580	32,520
Reinvestment Rate	0.52	0.62	0.73	0.74	0.53

Table 5.27 **Estimation of growth rate from fundamentals**

Year	2010	2011	2012	2013	2014
Reinvestment rate	0.52	0.62	0.73	0.74	0.53
ROE	0.24	0.27	0.28	0.19	0.19
Growth rate	0.12	0.17	0.20	0.14	0.10

Noncash current assets = Current assets − Cash and marketable securities.

Noncash current liabilities = Current liabilities − Interest bearing current liabilities.

Reinvestment = Adjusted net Capex + Change in noncash working Capital − Net debt issued.
Reinvestment rate = Reinvestment/Net income (see Table 5.26).
The average reinvestment rate based on geometric mean was 62% during the 5-year period 2010−14.
Estimation of growth rate from fundamentals.

Growth rate of earnings = Reinvestment rate × Return on equity of Exxon Mobil (see Table 5.27).
The average growth rate of net income based on geometric mean during the period 2010−14 was 14.6%.
FCFE = Net income−Adjusted net Capex − Change in noncash working capital + Debt issued − Debt repaid (see Table 5.28).

5.14.1 Two stage FCFE model

In this section, Exxon Mobil is valued using two stage FCFE model in which it is assumed that Exxon Mobil's net income will grow at a growth rate of 14.6% during the high growth period of 10 years and thereafter at the steady growth rate equal to growth rate of US economy.

High growth period inputs.
Net income in 2014 = $32520 million.

Table 5.28 Estimation of Free Cash Flow to Equity (FCFE) in million dollars

Year	2010	2011	2012	2013	2014
Net income	30,460	41,060	44,880	32,580	32,520
Adjusted net Capex	15,372	26,525	26,038	19,194	19,690
Change in noncash working capital	−6449	−806	3887	4356	2381
Debt issued	1741	1765	1953	361	5731
Debt repaid	8660	1369	4635	769	814
FCFE	14,618	15,737	12,273	8622	15,366

Growth rate in high growth period = 14.6% (average value estimated from fundamentals) High growth period = 10 years.

Reinvestment rate = 62% (average reinvestment rate during the period 2010–14).

Present value of FCFE in high growth period = $127,396.05 million (see Table 5.29). Stable growth period inputs. Stable period growth rate = US GDP growth rate = 2.13% (based during period 2011–14). Return on equity of industry sector = 5,4%. Reinvestment rate = 2.13%/5.4% = 39%.

The average reinvestment rate during the stable period is estimated as 39%.

Net income at end of high growth period	**127,056.45**
Net income in stable period ($127,056.45 \times 1.0213$)	129,762.75
Reinvestment	50,607.47
FCFE in stable period	79,155.28
Terminal value of FCFE	FCFE in stable period/(cost of equity-growth rate in stable period) 668,541.2018
PV of terminal value	$180,810.10

Value of Exxon Mobil = Present value of Exxon Mobil in high growth phase + Present value of terminal value of Exxon Mobil in stable phase.

= $127,396.05 + $180,810.10 = $308,206.15 million. Number of shares = 4282 million. Value per share = $71.98.

Exxon Mobil was trading at $78.42 on December 3 2015. On the basis of two stage FCFE model, Exxon Mobil was slightly overvalued in the market. The market value of equity was $328.3 billion on December 4 2015.

5.14.2 Free Cash Flow to Firm (FCFF) valuation model

Exxon Mobil is valued using two stage FCFF Valuation model. In two stage FCFF model, the present value of Exxon Mobil is estimated on the basis of assumption that

Table 5.29 Present value of FCFE in the high growth period

Year	1	2	3	4	5	6	7	8	9	10
Net income	37,267.92	42,709.036	48,944.56	56,090.4607	64,279.67	73,664.4995	84,419.516	96,744.766	110,869.5	127,056.45
Reinvestment rate	0.62	0.62	0.62	0.62	0.62	0.62	0.62	0.62	0.62	0.62
Reinvestment	23,106.11	26,479.60	30,345.62	34,776.09	39,853.39	45,671.99	52,340.10	59,981.75	68,739.09	78,775.00
FCFE	14,161.81	16,229.43	18,598.93	21,314.38	24,426.27	27,992.51	32,079.42	36,763.01	42,130.41	48,281.45
PV of FCFE	$12,425.91	$12,494.60	$12,563.66	$12,633.11	$12,702.95	$12,773.17	$12,843.8	$12,914.8	$12,986.2	$13,057.9
Sum	$127,396.05									

Table 5.30 **Estimation of reinvestment rate**

Year	2010	2011	2012	2013	2014
EBIT(1 − T)	52,959	73,257	78,726	57,711	51,630
Adjusted net Capex	15,372	26,525	26,038	19,194	19,690
Change in noncash working capital	−6449	−806	3887	4356	2381
Reinvestment	8923	25,719	29,925	23,550	22,071
Reinvestment rate	0.17	0.35	0.38	0.41	0.43

Table 5.31 **Estimation of FCFF during 2010−14 in million dollars**

Year	2010	2011	2012	2013	2014
EBIT(1 − T)	52,959	73,257	78,726	57,711	51,630
Adjusted net Capex	15,372	26,525	26,038	19,194	19,690
Change in noncash working capital	−6449	−806	3887	4356	2381
FCFF	44,036	47,538	48,801	34,161	29,559

Table 5.32 **Estimation of growth rate from fundamentals**

Year	2010	2011	2012	2013	2014
Return on invested capital	0.22	0.25	0.26	0.17	0.16
Reinvestment rate	0.17	0.35	0.38	0.41	0.43
Growth rate	0.04	0.09	0.10	0.07	0.07
Average growth rate	0.07				

the earnings (EBIT(1 − T)) grows at a high growth rate for a period of 10 years and thereafter at the stable growth rate which was equal to the growth rate of US economy.

Reinvestment = Adjusted net Capex + Change in noncash working capital
Reinvestment rate = Reinvestment/EBIT(1 − T).

The average reinvestment rate during the period 2010−14 was 34.4% (see Table 5.30).

FCFF = EBIT(1 − T) − Adjusted net Capex − Change in working capital (see Table 5.31).

The average growth rate of earnings during the 5-year period 2010−14 was 7% (see Table 5.32).
High growth period inputs.
High growth period = 10 years.
Growth rate in high growth period = 7% (based on growth rate estimation from fundamentals).
Reinvestment rate = 34.4% (based on average reinvestment rate during 2010−14).

Current EBIT$(1 - T)$ = \$51,630 million.

WACC = 13.21%.

The present value of FCFF in the growth period = \$251,615.24 million (see Table 5.33). Stable period inputs.

The growth rate in stable period is assumed to the growth rate of the US economy.

Growth rate of Exxon Mobil earnings in stable period = 2.13%.

Return on capital employed for oil and gas sector = 6.03%. [7]

Reinvestment rate = 2.13/6.03 = 35%

EBIT$(1 - T)$ at the end of high growth period = \$101,564.02 million

EBIT$(1 - T)$ at beginning of stable period = 101,564.02 × 1.0213 = \$103,727.34 million

Reinvestment = 103,727.34 × 0.35 = \$36,304.57 million.

FCFF in stable period = 103,727.34 − 36,304.57 = \$67,422.77 million.

Terminal value of FCFF in stable period = FCFF in stable period/(WACC−Growth rate in stable period).

= 67,422.77/(0.1321−0.0213) = \$608,508.75 million.

Present value of terminal value = \$175,962.01 million.

Value of operating assets of Exxon Mobil = Present value of operating assets of Exxon Mobil in high growth phase + Present value of Exxon Mobil's operating assets in stable phase period.

Value of operating assets of Exxon Mobil = 251,615.24 + 175,962.01 = \$427,577.25 million.

Value of Exxon Mobil = Value of operating assets + Cash and cash equivalents in current year.

Value of Exxon Mobil = 427,577.25 + 4616 = \$432,193.25 million.

Less value of interest bearing debt in current year = \$29,121 million.

Less value of minority interests = \$6665 million.

Less value of pension obligations = \$25,802 million.

Value of Equity = \$370,605.25 million.

Number of shares in 2014 = 4282 million.

Value per share = \$86.55.

Summary of Discounted Cash Flow Valuation

Two stage dividend discount model
Value of Exxon Mobil per share = \$66.12.
Two stage FCFE
Value of Exxon Mobil per share = \$71.98
Value of equity = \$308.21 billion
Two stage FCFF
Value of Exxon Mobil's operating assets = \$432193.25 million
Value of equity = \$370.61 billion
Value per share = \$86.55

The 52 week range for Exxon Mobil in year 2015 was \$66.55–\$95.33. Exxon Mobil was trading at \$78.42 on December 3 2015. The market capitalization of Exxon Mobil was \$328.3 billion on December 3 2015.

---

[7] http://csimarket.com/Industry/industry_ManagementEffectiveness.php?ind = 603. Estimation based on average of last five quarters.

Table 5.33 Present value of FCFF in high growth phase

Year	1	2	3	4	5	6	7	8	9	10
EBIT(1 − T)	55,244.1	59,111.2	63,249.0	67,676.4	72,413.7	77,482.7	82,906.5	88,710.0	94,919.6	101,564.0
Reinvestment	19,004.0	20,334.2	21,757.6	23,280.7	24,910.3	26,654.1	28,519.8	30,516.2	32,652.4	34,938.0
FCFF	36,240.1	38,776.9	41,491.3	44,395.7	47,503.4	50,828.7	54,386.7	58,193.7	62,267.3	66,626.0
PV of FCFF	32,011.4	30,255.5	28,595.8	27,027.3	25,544.7	24,143.5	22,819.1	21,567.4	20,384.3	19,266.2
SUM	$251,615.24									

5.15 Relative valuation of Exxon Mobil

In relative valuation, Exxon Mobil is compared with peer companies like Royal Dutch, Petro china, Total SA, and British Petroleum (see Table 5.34).

The market based multiples used for analysis are price to sales ratio, price to book ratio, price to earnings and dividend yield. Exxon Mobil had the highest P/S and P/B ratio among the peer group. The price to sales and price to book ratio was higher for Exxon Mobil compared to the industry average. Exxon Mobil has lower P/E and dividend yield compared to the industry average.

All price multiple ratios have been fluctuating over the 6-year period of analysis (see Table 5.35).

The enterprise value multiples are estimated based on year 2014. The values of the financial data are given in millions of dollars. Lower the enterprise value multiples, the more undervalued the stocks would be and hence the more attractive the stocks. On basis of EV/Sales, British Petroleum is the most undervalued stock. On the basis of EV/EBITDA, Royal Shell is the most attractive stock and on basis of EV/EBIT, Chevron and Exxon Mobil are the most undervalued stocks (see Table 5.36).

Table 5.34 **Relative valuation based on price multiples in year 2015**

Company	P/S	P/B	P/E	Dividend yield (%)
Exxon Mobil	1.1	1.9	16.6	3.6
Chevron corporation	0.5	1	97.3	7.7
Petro China	0.5	0.7	19.3	3.6
Total SA	0.7	1.2	118.4	5.8
BP PLC	0.4	1	–	7.4
Royal Dutch shell	0.5	1	96.6	7.8
Industry average	0.6	1	68.2	5

Source: Data from Morningstar.com.

Table 5.35 **Price multiple trends**

Year	2010	2011	2012	2013	2014	2015
P/E	11.8	10.2	8.9	13.2	11.6	16.6
P/B	2.5	2.6	2.3	2.6	2.2	1.9
P/S	0.9	0.9	0.8	1	0.9	1.1
P/CF	7.4	7.3	7.1	9.4	8.3	9.9

Table 5.36 **Enterprise value multiples**

Company	Exxon Mobil	Royal shell	Chevron	British petroleum
SALES	411,939	431,344	211,970	358,678
EBITDA	69,213	54,617	47,995	21,261
EBIT	51,916	28,314	31,202	6098
Debt	28,648	45,540	27,750	52,854
Market value of equity	388,382	210,726	210,859	115,852
Cash and cash equivalents	4616	21,607	13,207	30,092
Enterprise value (EV)	412,414	234,659	225,402	138,614
EV/SALES	1.00	0.54	1.06	0.39
EV/EBITDA	5.96	4.30	4.70	6.52
EV/EBIT	7.94	8.29	7.22	22.73

Further reading

[1] M. Mehta, Exxon Mobil acquires XTO Energy for $31 billion. Available from: http://www.123jump.com/market-update/Exxon-Mobil-Acquires-XTO-Energy-for-$31-Billion/35661.

[2] F. Weston, Exxon Mobil Merger, an archetype. J. Appl. Finance. Financial Management Association.

[3] Data from Morningstar, Yahoo finance and Google Finance.

Wealth creation—A case analysis of Apple

6

6.1 Introduction

On 1 April 1976, Apple Computer was founded by Steve Jobs and Stephen Wozniak. For 30 years, Apple was predominantly a manufacturer of personal computers which included the Apple II, Macintosh, and Power Mac lines. With the successful introduction of iPod music player in 2001 and iTunes Music Store in 2003, Apple transformed itself from a computer company to a leader in the consumer electronics and media sales industry. The company is well known for its iOS range of smart phone, media player, and tablet computer products that began with the iPhone, followed by the iPod Touch and then iPad. In the 1970 s Apple I and Apple II were introduced. Apple III was introduced in May 1980. On December 12 1980, Apple was listed in stock market through its IPO. By 1981 Apple was one among the three largest microcomputer companies in the world. The Macintosh was introduced in October 1983. In 1985, Jobs left Apple and founded NeXT Inc with futuristic designs. Apple gave its first corporate stock dividend in the year 1987 under the leadership of John Sculley. In 1987, Apple registered the Apple.com domain name. By the year 1983, the PC of IBM surpassed the Apple II as the best-selling personal computer. In 1991 Apple established AIM alliance with competitors IBM and Motorola to create a new computing platform known as PReP which would use IBM and Motorola hardware and Apple Software. Using this platform, Apple started the Power Macintosh line in year 1994. In the year 1993, Apple introduced the Newton an early personal digital assistant (PDA). In 1996 Apple purchased Steve Jobs company Next paving the way for the return of Jobs back to Apple. Steve Jobs became the CEO of Apple and continued till August 2011. In 1997, Apple introduced the Apple Store which is an online retail store based on the WebObjects. In 1997, Apple entered into a partnership with Microsoft to release Microsoft for Macintosh. In 1999, Apple introduced the Power Mac G4 and iBook. In 2000, Apple introduced its iTools service. In 2001, Apple introduced Mac OSX which was an operating system based on NeXT and its first iPod portable digital audio player. In 2003, Apple launched the Power Mac G5 based on IBM 'S G5 processor and iTunes Music Store. In the year 2007, Apple Computer shortened its name to Apple Inc. highlighting the transformation of Apple from a computer company to consumer electronics company.

In 2001, Apple introduced Mac OS X, an operating system based on NeXT's NeXTstep and its first iPod portable digital audio player. In 2003, Apple launched

Strategic Financial Management Casebook.

the Power Mac G5 based on IBM's G5 processor. The iTunes Music Store was launched in April 2003, with two million downloads in the first 16 days. Tim Cook became the CEO in the year 2011. In 2012, Apple unveiled the iPad's second generation iPad2.

6.2 Growth strategy of Apple

Apple's products and services compete in a highly competitive global market which is characterized by price cuts, downward pressure on gross margins, quick introduction of new products, short product life cycle, rapid adoption of technological, and product advancements by competitors and price sensitivity on the part of consumers. The company follows on the strategy of introduction of innovative new products with the focus on the design and development of the entire solution for its products which includes the hardware, operating systems software applications and other services. Apple have a minority market share in the smartphone market.

Apple focuses on innovation as the strategic pursuit for growth. The company focuses on designing its own operating systems, hardware, application software, and services. The company has expanded its platform for the discovery and delivery of third party digital content and applications through the iTunes Store. The iTunes Store, the Company's App Store and iBook's Store facilitate customers to download applications and books through either a Mac or Windows based computer or through iPhone, iPad and iPod Touch devices ("iOS devices"). Through Apple's Mac App Store, customers can discover, download and install Mac applications. Apple Company also provides support for the development of third-party software and hardware products and digital content that complement the Company's offerings. The company also emphasizes expanding its own retail and online stores and third party distribution network to provide sales and after sales services. The company also invests in discretionary expenditures like R&D for development of innovative products. Apple's ability to focus on continuous innovation and forward focus helps the firm to maintain an edge over its competitors. Apple follows a strategy which allows the company to capture high margins with early adopters and then focuses on price conscious customers. When Apple launched its most recent iPhone, it reduced the price of its 3 G version to $99. Similarly, when new iPad was launched, the price of iPad was reduced by $100. Apple had been focusing on organic growth as its acquisition had averaged only one acquisition per year during the past 25 years (till 2014) compared to other competitors in the technology sector.

Apple manages its business primarily on a geographical basis. The major regions are Americas, Europe, Greater China, Japan, Rest of Asia Pacific, and Retail. North and South America region are included in the Americas segment. European segment includes countries like India, Middle East and Africa. The Greater China region include China, Hong Kong, and Taiwan.

Apple's customers are basically in the consumer, Small and medium businesses, education, enterprise, and government market segments. The company sells its products and resells third party products directly to consumers through direct sales force, retail, and online stores, indirect distribution channels like third party cellular network carriers, wholesalers and retailers. In 2014, the indirect distribution channels accounted for 72% of total net sales. During the 3-year period 2012–14, Apple spend $13.4 billion in research and development. Apple holds rights to patents and copyrights relating to certain aspects of its hardware devices, accessories, software, and services.

6.3 Mergers and acquisitions strategy

Apple Inc. had acquired many companies over the years (see Table 6.1). Most of them were software companies. The acquisition strategy of Apple focusses on acquiring smaller businesses which could be quickly integrated into the company and applied for future products or features. Apple acquired Siri whose features were integrated into iOS. In 2012, Apple purchased Authen Tec for $356 million for acquiring sensing technology. This acquisition facilitated Apple to use the Touch ID feature in the iPhone 5 s.

Table 6.1 Notable acquisitions of Apple Inc.

Year	Companies
1988	Nashoba Systems, Styleware, Orio Network Systems, Network Innovations
1989	Coral
1997	Next, Power Computing Company
1998	KeyGrip
1999	Xemplar Education, Raycer Graphics
2000	NetSelector, Astarte
2001	SoundJam MP, Blue buzz, Spruce Technologies, PowerSchool
2002	Nothing Real, Zayante, Silicon Grail Corp, Propel Software, Prismo Graphics, Magic
2005	Fingerworks, Schemasoft
2006	Silicon Color, Proximity
2007	Common Unix Printing System
2008	PA Semi
2009	Placebase, Lala
2010	Polar Rose, IMSense, Poly9, SiriInc, Intrinsity
2011	Anobit, C3 Technologies
2012	Color Labs, Particle, Authen Tec, Redmatica, CHOMP
2013	WifiSLAM, Match.tv, Locationary, HopStop.com Inc., Passif Semiconductor, Embark Inc, Algo Trim, Cue, PrimeSense, Topsy, Broad Map, Catch.com, Novauris
2014	Snappy Labs, Burstly, LuxVue, Beats Music & Beats Electronics, Spotsetter, BookLamp, Concept.io, Semetric, linX Computational Imaging

In 2013 Apple acquired Beats Music and Beta Electronics for $3 billion. The Beats acquisition enabled Apple to acquire a music streaming service so that iTunes could compete with Spotify and Google Play. In the year 2013 Apple acquired mapping companies like Broad Map, Embark, Hopstop, Locationary, and WifiSlam. The other acquisitions in 2013 included 3D Company, Prime Sense, and the speech recognition company Novauris.

In 2014, Apple purchased 29 companies. This includes acquisition of LuxVue Technology, Spotsetter, Snappy Labs which produced burst mode photo app and Burstly which provided Testflight iOS beta testing platform.

6.4 Products and services

iPhone is the Apple's line of smartphones which combines a phone, music player and internet device in one product, and is based on Apple's iOS Multi-Touch operating system.

iPad is the Apple's line of multipurpose tablets based on Apple's iOS Multi-Touch operating system, which includes iPad Air and iPad Mini. iPad has an integrated photo and video camera and photo library app. Pad works with the iTunes Store, the iBooks Store and the App Store for purchasing, organizing and playing music, movies, TV shows, podcasts, books, and apps.

Mac is Apple's line of desktop and portable personal computers. Macs feature Intel microprocessors, the OS X operating system and include Mail, Safari web browser, Messages, Calendar, Reminders, Contacts, and the iLife apps. The Company's iWork apps are also available as free downloads with all new Macs. The Company's desktop computers include IMac, Mac Pro and Mac mini. Apple' portable computers include MacBook Pro, MacBook Pro with Retina display and MacBook Air. In the year 2014, Apple introduced the 27-inch iMac with Retina 5k display. iTunes and the iTunes Store Apple's iTunes are available for iOS devices.

Mac App store enable customers to discover, download and install Mac applications. The Mac App Store offers applications in education, games, graphics and design and lifestyle. iCloud is Apple's cloud service which stores music, photos, applications, contacts, calendars, and mail and are available to multiple iOS devices, Mac and Windows personal computers and Apple TV. iCloud services include iTunes in the Cloud, iCloud DriveSM, iCloud Photo Sharing, Family Sharing, Find My iPhone, iPad or Mac, and iCloud Backup for iOS devices. In 2014, Apple released Apple Pay in the United States which makes mobile payment easy. iOS is the Company's Multi-Touch operating system that serves as the foundation for iOS devices. In 2014, Apple released iOS 8. The Mac operating system is built on an open source UNIX based foundation. iLife for Mac is the firm's consumer-oriented digital lifestyle software application suite included with all Mac computers. iWork for Mac is the Apple's integrated productivity suite designed to help users create, present and publish documents, presentations and spreadsheets. The other application software includes Final Cut Pro, Logic Pro X and its FileMaker Pro database software.

Apple sells variety of Apple-branded and third-party Mac-compatible and iOS-compatible accessories, including Apple TV, headphones, cases, displays, storage devices, and various other connectivity and computing products and supplies. In July 2014, the company acquired Beats Electronics, LLC, which makes Beats headphones, speakers and audio software. In 2014, Apple introduced Apple Watch which uses new precision watch technology with an iOS-based user interface.

Apple's iOS and Mac Developer Programs support app developers with the development, testing and distribution of iOS and Mac apps through the App Store and the Mac App Store. AppleCare provides a range of support options for the Company's customers. These include assistance that is built into software products, printed, and electronic product manuals, online support including comprehensive product information as well as technical assistance, the AppleCare Protection Plan ("APP") and the AppleCare + Protection Plan ("AC + ").

6.5   Risk factors

The products and services faces risk with respect to global and economic conditions as consumers and businesses postpone spending in response to tighter credit, higher unemployment, financial market volatility, and austerity programs of government institutions. The worldwide demand could also be affected by increases in fuel and energy costs, conditions in real estate and mortgage markets.

6.6   Ownership structure

In book value terms, equity accounts for 75% and debt accounts for 25% of the capital structure. Institutions hold 67.7% and mutual funds hold 32.2% of the ownership structure of the company. The insiders hold 0.1% of the ownership of the company. The number of institution owners were 3752 and fund owners were 5577, respectively.

6.7   Stock wealth creation

Apple launched the initial public offering of its stock on December 12 1980. The stock is listed in NASDAQ. The closing price was $0.52 on December 12 1980. On May 1 2015, the stock was trading at $128.77. During the 35-year period, the stock price increased 246.7 times. The holding period return (HPR) was 24,663%. The total cumulative returns based on the monthly stock prices during the 34 year and 5-month period (December 12 1980—May 1 2015) was 948%. The total cumulative return during the five and half year period 2010—mid 2015 was approximately 170% (see Fig. 6.1).

During the last six years Apple Stock had the highest yearly returns in the year 2010. The average yearly returns during the 6-year period was approximately 32% (see Table 6.2).

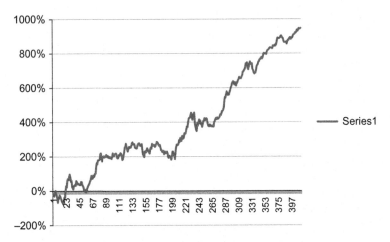

Figure 6.1 Cumulative returns of Apple stock for past 35 years.

Table 6.2 **Average returns in percent**

Year	Monthly returns	Yearly returns
2010	3.9	46.8
2011	2.1	25.2
2012	2.7	32.4
2013	1	12
2014	3.1	37.2
2015	3.4	40.8
Average		32.4

The cumulative monthly returns for approximately 414 months representing the period 1980–2015 mid-year reflects the exponential increase in the returns of Apple since 1980. The stock price data was taken from yahoo finance. The analysis starts from the month the stock is listed in the stock market.

In 2014, the highest closing price of Apple stock was $625.71 which was the closing price on 27/5/2014. This price was $11.58 up from the previous close. The share price of Apple reached an all-time high of $700 in September 2012 and then declined in late 2012 and early 2013. In the first week of June 2014, the shares of Apple went for a 7 for 1 split. The existing shareholders who bought in before the deadline were awarded six additional shares of Apple stock and the split adjusted trading began on June 9th 2014.

Holding Period Yield (HPY)
HPR is obtained as the ratio of the ending value of investment divided by the beginning value of investment.
HPR = Ending value of investment/Beginning value of investment.
HPR can be converted into an annual percentage return which is known as HPY.

Table 6.3 **Holding period yield**

Year	Holding Period Yield (HPY) (%)
2010	50
2011	23
2012	29
2013	2
2014	44

HPY = HPR-1

Annual HPR = (HPR)^1/n where n is the number of years the investment is held.

The HPR analysis assumes that an investment is made in an Apple share in the beginning of the year and sold off at the end of the year. For example, an Apple share is bought on January 4 2010 and sold off on December 31 2010. The closing price of Apple share on January 4 2010 was $214.50 and on December 31 2010 was $322.56.

HPR = $322.56/ $214.50 = 1.50

HPY = 1.50−1 = 0.50.

The HPY was 50% in the year 2010 (see Table 6.3).

The HPY was 50% in year 2010. In 2014, the HPY was 44%. The yield was lowest in the year 2013. The stock price of Apple in January 2013 was $549.03.

Assume that an investor bought an Apple stock which was trading at $214.50. His investment period was five years. The stock was trading at $110.38 on December 31 2014. Note that the stock had undergone 7 for 1 stock split in year 2014. Hence we can consider the actual value as $772.66 (110.38 × 7).

HPR = Ending value of investment/Beginning value of investment = $772.66/$214.50 = 3.6

Annual HPR = (3.6) ^1/5 = 1.29

Annual HPY = 1.29−1 = 0.29

The annual HPY for Apple for the 5-year investment period 2010−14 was 29%.

The market capitalization has increased over the 6-year period. The market capitalization which was $299.04 billion in the year 2010 reached $763.57 billion by May 2015. The year on growth rate in market capitalization was approximately 27% in the year 2011 and 2012, respectively. In 2013, the market capitalization increased by approximately 4%. In the year 2014, the market capitalization increased by approximately 33%. The average growth rate of market capitalization was approximately 21% during the five and half year period of 2010−mid May 2015. The market capitalization is based on the share price and number of shares outstanding. The share prices are the December end share price in each year (see Table 6.4).

The excess value is obtained as the difference between the market capitalization and book value of equity each year. The highest excess value amounted to $557 billion in the year 2014.The average book value as% of market value was

Table 6.4 Market capitalization during the period 2010–May 2015

Year	Market capitalization
2010	$299.04 billion
2011	$378.95 billion
2012	$482.57 billion
2013	$503.31 billion
2014	$668.53 billion
May-15	$763.57 billion

Table 6.5 Excess market value added

Year	2010	2011	2012	2013	2014
Book value of equity	47.8	76.6	118.2	123.5	111.5
Market value of equity	299.0	379.0	482.6	503.3	668.5
Excess value	251.2	302.3	364.4	379.8	557.0
BV as percentage of MV	16.0	20.2	24.5	24.5	16.7
Average in percentage	20.4				

Table 6.6 Comparative stock performance

Year	2009	2010	2011	2012	2013	2014
Apple Inc.	$100	$160	$222	$367	$272	$407
S&P 500 index	$100	$110	$111	$145	$173	$207
Dow Jones US technology supersector index	$100	$112	$115	$150	$158	$205
S&P information technology index	$100	$111	$115	$152	$163	$210

Source: Annual Report 2014.

only 20.4% during the 5-year period 2010–14. The book value was 16% and 16.7% of market value of equity during the period 2010 and 2014, respectively. This signifies higher market valuation of Apple Stock (see Table 6.5).

The table 6.6 shows the comparative performance of Apple Inc. in comparison to the indexes like Dow Jones US technology super sector index and S&P information technology index. The assumption involves the initial investment of $100 in stock or index in the last week of September of the year 2009.The calculation is based on cumulative total shareholder return, calculated on a dividend reinvested basis. On the basis of calculation, Apple stock had registered a return of 307% while S&P 500 registered return of 107%.

Table 6.7 **Stock dividends**

Year	Stock dividends
1987	2-for-1 stock split
2000	2-for-1 stock split
2005	2-for-1 stock split
2014	7-for-1 -stock split

Table 6.8 **Regular cash dividends**

Year	Regular cash dividends
1987	0.2
1988	0.34
1989	0.41
1990	0.45
1991	0.48
1992	0.48
1993	0.48
1994	0.48
1995	0.48
2012	5.3
2013	11.8
2014	7.28

Source: Annual Reports.

6.8 Dividend policy of Apple

During the period 1987−2015, Apple have paid both regular cash and stock dividends.

Apple had stock split in the year 1987, 2000, 2005, and 2014. The company had a 7 for 1 stock split in the year 2014 (see Table 6.7).

Apple paid constant dividend per share during the period 1992−95. During the 16-year period 2006−11, Apple paid no dividends. In 1988 the dividend per share increased by 7% compared to the previous year. On the year on year basis the DPS increased by 21% in the year 1989. In 1990, the DPS increased by 10%. In 2013, the DPS increased by 123% and fell by 38% in year 2014 (see Table 6.8).

6.9 Share buyback scheme

Apple announced its initial capital return program of $45 billion in March 2012. The program was increased to $100 billion in April 2013 which included $60 billion share buyback. The amount increased to over $130 billion in April 2014 and increased to $200 billion in April 2015.By September 2014, $67.9 billion of the $90 billion had been utilized. Apple's share repurchase program does not obligate the company to acquire any specific number of shares. Under the program the shares can be repurchased in privately negotiated and /or open market transactions which include plans complying with Rule 10b5-1 under the Securities Exchange Act of 1934. Apple had also entered into four accelerated share repurchase (ASRs) arrangements with financial institutions effective from August 2012.

In exchange for up-front payments, the financial institutions deliver shares of the company's common stock during the purchase periods of each ASR. The total number of shares ultimately delivered, and therefore the average repurchase price paid per share, will be determined at the end of the applicable purchase period of each ASR based on the volume weighted-average price of the company's common stock during that period. The shares received are retired in the periods they are delivered, and the up-front payments are accounted for as a reduction to shareholders' equity in the company's consolidated balance sheet in the periods the payments are made.

6.10 ESOP program

6.10.1 Stock option plans

The employee stock option plan 2003 was a shareholder approved plan which provided for broad-based equity grants to employees, including executive officers. The 2003 plan permitted the granting of incentive stock options, nonstatutory stock options, Restricted Stock Units (RSUs), stock appreciation rights, stock purchase rights and performance-based awards. Options granted under the 2003 plan generally expire seven to ten years after the grant date and generally become exercisable over a period of four years, based on continued employment, with either annual, semi-annual or quarterly vesting. In 2014 employee stock plan was adopted by the company after the termination of the 2003 plan. RSUs granted under the 2014 plan generally vest over four years, based on continued employment, and are settled upon vesting in shares of the company's common stock on a one-for-one basis. As of September 27 2014, approximately 492.6 million shares were reserved for future issuance under the 2014 plan. The 1997 director stock plan (the "Director Plan") is a shareholder approved plan that (i) permits the company to grant awards of RSUs or stock options to the company's nonemployee director. The company's 401(k) plan is a deferred salary arrangement under section 401(k) of the internal revenue code. The company's matching contributions to the 401(k) plan were $163 million, $135 million and $114 million in 2014, 2013, and 2012, respectively.

The company had 6.6 million stock options outstanding as of September 27 2014, with a weighted-average exercise price per share of $21.99 and weighted-average remaining contractual term of 1.4 year. Total intrinsic value of options at time of exercise was $1.5 billion, $1.0 billion and $2.3 billion for 2014, 2013, and 2012, respectively.

6.11   Financial analysis

The values are given in millions of dollars except per share data like EPS (see Table 6.9). The financial highlights are given for the 10-year period 2005—14. The net sales have increased from $13,931 million in year 2005 to $182,795 million in year 2014. The year on year growth rate analysis of net sales reveal that growth rate was highest in the year 2011 with approximately 66% growth rate. The net sales increased by 56% in the year 2008. The net sales grew by approximately 7% in year 2014. The net income registered the highest growth rate of 85% in the year 2011. The net income grew by approximately 75% in the year 2007 and 2008, respectively. The net income declined by 11% in year 2013 and then increased by 7% in year 2014. The total cash, cash equivalents and short term investments registered the highest growth rate of approximately 60% in year 2011. The cash and cash equivalents grew by approximately 6% in the year 2014. The total assets registered the highest growth rate of 58% in the year 2010. On an average basis, the total cash and cash equivalents was 67% of the total assets. The total shareholder equity registered the highest growth rate of 60% and 54% in year 2011 and 2012, respectively. EPS grew by 82% in the year 2011.

The table 6.10 gives the average growth rate of financial parameters in three time frames—the period 2005—14, the 4-year period 2006—09 and the 5-year period 2010—14. The average growth rate of net income, total cash and cash

Table 6.9 Financial highlights 2005—14

Year	2005	2006	2007	2008	2009	2010	2011	2012	2013	2014
Net sales	13,931	19,315	24,006	37,491	42,905	65,225	108,249	156,508	170,910	182,795
Net income	1328	1989	3496	6119	8235	14,013	25,922	41,733	37,037	39,510
Total cash and equivalents	8261	10,110	15,386	24,490	33,992	51,011	81,570	121,251	146,761	155,239
Total assets	11,516	17,205	25,347	36,171	47,501	75,183	116,371	176,064	207,000	231,839
Long term debt	0	0	0	0	0	0	0	0	16,960	28,987
Total shareholder equity	7428	9984	14,532	22,297	31,640	47,791	76,615	118,210	123,549	111,547
EPS	1.64	2.36	4.04	6.94	9.22	2.2	4.01	6.38	5.72	6.49

Source: Annual Reports.

Table 6.10 Average growth rate in percent

Period	2006—14	2006—09 (4 year)	2010—14 (5 year)
Net sales	34.7	33.4	35.7
Net income	49.6	58.9	42
Total cash and equivalents	39.8	43	37
Total assets	40.5	43	39
Total shareholder equity	37	44	32
EPS	32	54	13.6

equivalents, total assets, total shareholder equity, and EPS have decreased in the period 2010–14 compared to the period 2006–09.The average growth rate of net sales was higher in the period 2010–14 compared to the period 2006–09.

On an average, the Americas region contributed 36% of the total net sales during the 3-year period 2012–14. The Europe region contributed 23% of the total net sales during the 3-year period 2012–14. Greater China, Japan, and rest of Asia had 29% average market share during the period 2012–14. The retail sector have an average market share of 12% during the 3-year period (see Table 6.11).

iTunes, softwares and services include revenue from iTunes Store, the App Store, the Mac App Store, the iBook's Store, AppleCare, licensing, and other services. The accessories include sale of Apple branded and third party accessories for iPhone, iPad, Mac, and iPod. iPhones accounted for 53% of net sales based on average values during the 3-year period 2012–14. iPad and Mac sales accounted for 18% and 14% of the net sales during the period 2012–14. On an average basis, iPhone, iPad, and Mac sales accounted for 85% of the total net sales during the above period. iTunes, softwares and services accounted for 9% of the net sales. Accessories and iPod contributed 3% and 2% of net sales during the 3-year period. iPhones sales registered a growth rate of 16% in 2013 compared to previous year and 12% in the year 2014. iPad sales increased by 3% in year 2013 and declined by 5% in year 2014 compared to year 2013. Mac sales improved by 12% in 2014 though it fell by 7% in 2013. iPod growth rate declined by 21% in 2013 and 48% in 2014. The iTunes, softwares and services sales grew by 25% in 2013 and 13% in 2014. Accessories growth rate improved by 11% in 2013 and 7% in 2014 (see Table 6.12).

Table 6.11 **Net sales by operating segment (in millions of dollars)**

Year	2012	2013	2014
Americas	57,512	62,739	65,232
Europe	36,323	37,883	40,929
Greater China	22,533	25,417	29,846
Japan	10,571	13,462	14,982
Rest of Asia Pacific	10,741	11,181	10,344
Retail	18,828	20,228	21,462
Total net sales	156,508	170,910	182,795

Table 6.12 **Net sales by products (million dollars)**

Net sales by products	2012	2013	2014
iPhone	78,692	91,279	101,991
iPad	30,945	31,980	30,283
Mac	23,221	21,483	24,079
iPod	5615	4411	2286
iTunes, Softwares and services	12,890	16,051	18,063
Accessories	5145	5706	6093
Total net sales	156,508	170,910	182,795

6.12   Ratio analysis

The average gross margin during the 10-year period was approximately 37%. The gross margin improved from 33% during the period 2005−09 to 40% during the period 2010−14. The average net margin during the 10-year period 2005−14 was approximately 18%. The average net margin improved from 13.7% during the period 2005−09 to 23% during the period 2010−14. The average return on assets during the 10-year period was 19%. The average return on assets during the period 2005−09 was 15.5% which improved to 23% during the period 2010−14. The average return on equity during the 10-year period 2005−14 was 31.5%. The average ROE which was 26% during the period 2005−09 increased to 36% during the period 2010−14. The average return on invested capital was 30% during the 10-year period 2005−14. The 5-year average return on invested capital was 26% during the period 2005−09. The average return on invested capital increased to 34.7% during the period 2010−14. It can be stated that the profitability position of Apple has improved during the period 2010−14 compared to the period 2005−09 (see Table 6.13).

The cost of goods sold as per cent of sales have decreased over the 10-year period. The average cost of goods sold during the 5-year period 2005−09 was 66.7 per cent of sales. The figure decreased to 60% of sales during the period 2010−14 (see Table 6.14).

Capital expenditure as percent of sales had been increasing till 2011 and then fluctuating (see Table 6.15).

The highest growth rate in EPS was in the year 2011while the EPS grew by 83% and 69% in year 2009. In 2007 EPS grew by 75% (see Table 6.16).

The average current ratio during the 10-year period was 2.06 while the average quick ratio for the above period was 1.76. The liquidity position of Apple declined in the period 2010−14 compared to the period 2005−09. The average current ratio which was 2.55 in the 5-year period 2005−09 decreased to 1.58 in the 5-year period 2010−14. The 5-year quick ratio which was 2.21 in the period 2005−09 decreased to 1.31 in the period 2010−14 (see Table 6.17).

The average payable period during the two five-year period of comparison (2005−09) and (2010−14) was approximately 78 days. The average receivable period of 22 days in 2005−09 improved to 23 days during the period 2010−14. The average fixed assets turnover ratio of 16.6 times in the period 2005−09 declined to 13 times in the period 2010−14 (see Table 6.18).

6.13   Valuation of Apple using FCFF model

Estimation of Weighted Average Cost of Capital (WACC).
Cost of equity estimation

Beta for Apple Stock is estimated by regressing the daily stock returns of Apple on the market index NASDAQ Composite Index during the period 3-year period 2012−14.
Beta = 1.008.

Table 6.13 Profitability ratios

Year	2005	2006	2007	2008	2009	2010	2011	2012	2013	2014
Gross margin (%)	29	29	34	34.3	40.1	39.4	40.5	43.9	37.6	38.6
Net margin (%)	9.58	10.3	14.56	14.88	19.19	21.48	23.95	26.67	21.67	21.61
Return on assets (%)	13.62	13.83	16.43	14.89	18.92	22.84	27.07	28.54	19.34	18.01
Return on equity (%)	21.29	22.8	28.52	27.19	31.27	35.28	41.67	42.84	30.64	33.61
Return on invested capital (%)	21.29	22.8	28.52	27.19	31.27	35.28	41.67	42.84	26.94	27.1

Table 6.14 Cost of goods sold trend

Year	2005	2006	2007	2008	2009	2010	2011	2012	2013	2014
COGS as per cent of sales	70.98	71.02	66.03	65.69	59.86	60.62	59.52	56.13	62.38	61.41

Table 6.15 Capital expenditure as per cent of sales

Year	2005	2006	2007	2008	2009	2010	2011	2012	2013	2014
Cap Ex as a percent of sales	1.87	3.4	4.11	3.69	2.83	3.25	6.88	6.01	5.31	5.37

Table 6.16 EPS and growth rate

Year	2005	2006	2007	2008	2009	2010	2011	2012	2013	2014
EPS	0.22	0.32	0.56	0.77	1.3	2.16	3.95	6.31	5.68	6.45
Growth rate		0.45	0.75	0.38	0.69	0.66	0.83	0.60	−0.10	0.14

Table 6.17 Liquidity position

Year	2005	2006	2007	2008	2009	2010	2011	2012	2013	2014
Current ratio	2.96	2.24	2.36	2.46	2.74	2.01	1.61	1.5	1.68	1.08
Quick ratio	2.63	1.76	2.09	2.07	2.48	1.72	1.35	1.24	1.4	0.82

Table 6.18 Efficiency position

Year	2005	2006	2007	2008	2009	2010	2011	2012	2013	2014
Payables period	59.62	68.77	96.25	89.74	79.02	81.31	75.48	74.39	74.54	85.45
Receivable period	21.57	20.01	21.66	22.50	24.25	24.47	18.09	18.75	25.32	30.10
Fixed assets turnover	18.28	18.41	15.42	15.15	15.85	16.89	17.26	13.48	10.67	9.82

Assuming the risk premium to be 5.5% (based on historical average values given by academic studies), the cost of equity is estimated using the CAPM.

Cost of equity = Risk free rate + Beta × Risk premium

Risk free rate is based on the annual average yield of 30-year Treasury bond rate during the period 2012−14.[1] Risk free rate is estimated as 3.24%.

Cost of equity = Risk free rate + beta × Risk premium

= 3.24% + 1.008 × 5.5 = 8.78%

Cost of debt estimation

The yield to maturity of a long term bond of Apple maturing in year 2023 is taken as the cost of debt. The cost of debt is taken as 2.82%.[2]

The corporate tax rate in United States is estimated to be 35%.[3]

Cost of debt for Apple = 2.82%

After tax cost of debt = 2.82 × (1−0.35) = 1.83%

Market value of equity in 2014 = 643,120 million

Book value of debt in 2014 = 28,987 million

Total value = 672107 million

Market value weights

Weight of equity = 0.96

Weight of debt = 0.04

WACC = 0.96 × 8.78 + 0.04 × 1.83 = 8.48%

The weighted average cost of capital is estimated as 8.48%.

Valuation

The Free Cash Flow to Firm (FCFF) discounted cash flow method have been used to value Apple.

One of the most important adjustment to be made is the adjustment of research and development expenses. The research and development expenses need to be capitalized. Thus the capital expenditure need to be adjusted. The operating earnings and book value of equity are also adjusted.

Adjusted operating earnings = Operating earnings + Current year's R&D expense − Amortization of research asset.

Adjusted book value of capital = Adjusted book value of equity + Debt.

Adjusted book value of equity = Book value of equity + Research value of asset.

The research assets are amortized linearly over time. The life of research asset is assumed to be 5 years. The value of research asset and amortization expense calculation for the year 2014 is given below (see Table 6.19). The detailed calculation of the values for the previous years are given in the worksheet *Valuation of Apple.xlsx*.

The table 6.20 gives the amount of R&D expenses, value of R&D asset and amortization of R&D asset value each year during the time period 2008−14.

---

[1] http://www.federalreserve.gov/releases/h15/data.htm.

[2] http://quicktake.morningstar.com/StockNet/Bondsquote.aspx?
cid = 0C00000ADA&bid = d85cbb7dc2dfa4f872c5cfea9d1ba185&bname=Apple + 2.4%25 + %
7C + Maturity%3A2023&ticker=AAPL&country=USA&clientid=dotcom.

[3] http://www.kpmg.com/global/en/services/tax/tax-tools-and-resources/pages/corporate-tax-rates-table.
aspx.

Table 6.19 Estimation of amortization and value of research asset in 2014

Year		Unamortized portion		Amortization this year (million $)
		%	(million dollars)	
Current	6041	100	6041	
−1	4475	80	3580	895
−2	3381	60	2028.6	676.2
−3	2429	40	971.6	485.8
−4	1782	20	356.4	356.4
−5	1300	0	0	260
	Value of research asset		12,977.6	
	Amortization expense current year			2673.4

Table 6.20 Value of research and development and amortization expenses in millions of dollars

Year	R&D expenses in millions of dollars	Value of R&D	Amortization of R&D
2008	1100	2464.6	597.8
2009	1300	3041	723.6
2010	1782	3937.2	885.8
2011	2429	5231	1135.2
2012	3381	7133.4	1478.6
2013	4475	9610	1998.4
2014	6041	12,977.6	2673.4

Adjusted book value of equity = Book value of equity + Value of R&D asset

Adjusted capital = Adjusted book value of equity + debt. The values are given in millions of dollars (see Table 6.21).

The adjusted operating income values are given in millions of dollars.

Adjusted ROCE = EBIT(1 − t) in year t/Capital employed in year t − 1 (see Table 6.22). The values are in millions of dollars.

Net capital expenditure = Capital expenditure − Depreciation and amortization

Adjusted net capital expenditure = Net capital expenditure + R&D expenses in current year−Amortization of research asset + Net acquisitions (see Table 6.23).

Table 6.24 shows estimation of non cash working capital. The values of FCFF are given in millions of dollars.

FCFF = EBIT(1 − T) − Adjusted net capex − change in noncash working capital (see Table 6.25).

Total current assets − total cash = Noncash current assets

Table 6.21 Estimation of adjusted book value of capital

Year	Book value of equity	Value of R&D asset	Adjusted book value of equity	Debt	Adjusted capital
2008	22,734	2464.6	25,198.6		25,198.6
2009	31,872	3041	34,912.98		34,912.98
2010	47,791	3937.2	51,728.2		51,728.2
2011	76,615	5231	81,846		81,846
2012	118,210	7133.4	125,343.4		125,343.4
2013	123,549	9610	133,159	16,960	150,119
2014	111,547	12,977.6	124,524.6	35,295	159,819.6

Table 6.22 Estimation of adjusted operating income and return on capital employed

Year	EBIT	Taxes	EBIT (1 − T)	R&D expenses	Amortization	Adjusted operating income	Adjusted capital	Adjusted ROCE
2008	6275	2061	4214	2464.6	597.8	6080.8	25,198.6	
2009	7658	2280	5378	3041	723.6	7695.4	34,912.98	0.305
2010	18,385	4527	13,858	3937.2	885.8	16,909.4	51,728.2	0.484
2011	33,790	8283	25,507	5231	1135.2	29,602.8	81,846	0.572
2012	55,241	14,030	41,211	7133.4	1478.6	46,865.8	125,343.4	0.573
2013	48,999	13,118	35,881	9610	1998.4	43,492.6	150,119	0.347
2014	52,503	13,973	38,530	12,977.6	2673.4	48,834.2	159,819.6	0.325

Table 6.23 Adjusted net capital expenditure

Year	Capex	Dep and amortization	Net Capex	R&D expenses	Amortization	Net acquisition	Adjusted net Capex
2008	1199	473	726	2464.6	597.8	220	2812.8
2009	1213	703	510	3041	723.6		2827.4
2010	2005	1027	978	3937.2	885.8	638	4667.4
2011	4260	1814	2446	5231	1135.2	244	6785.8
2012	8295	3277	5018	7133.4	1478.6	350	11,022.8
2013	8165	6757	1408	9610	1998.4	496	9515.6
2014	9571	7946	1625	12,977.6	2673.4	3765	15,694.2

Total current liabilities − short term debt = Noninterest bearing current liabilities.

Noncash working capital = Noncash current assets − Noninterest bearing current liabilities.

Reinvestment = EBIT (1 − T)−Adjusted net Capex − Change in noncash working capital.

Reinvestment rate = Reinvestment/EBIT (1 − T) (see Table 6.26).

The 5-year average (2010−14) reinvestment rate is estimated as 27% of EBIT (1 − T) on the basis of geometric mean.

Table 6.24 Estimation of noncash working capital (values in million dollars)

Year	2008	2009	2010	2011	2012	2013	2014
Total current assets	32,311	36,265	41,678	44,988	57,653	73,286	68,531
Cash, cash equivalents and short term marketable securities	22,111	23,464	25,620	25,952	29,129	40,546	25,077
Noncash current assets	10,200	12,801	16,058	19,036	28,524	32,740	43,454
Total current liabilities	14,092	19,282	20,722	27,970	38,542	43,658	63,448
Interest bearing current liabilities	0	0	0	0	0	0	6308
Noninterest bearing current liabilities	14,092	19,282	20,722	27,970	38,542	43,658	57,140
Noncash working capital	− 3892	− 6481	− 4664	− 8934	− 10,018	− 10,918	− 13,686
Change in noncash working capital		− 2589	1817	− 4270	− 1084	− 900	− 2768

Table 6.25 Estimation of Free cash flow to the firm (FCFF) 2009−14

Year	2008	2009	2010	2011	2012	2013	2014
EBIT(1 − T)	4214	5378	13,858	25,507	41,211	35,881	38,530
Adjusted net Capex	2812.8	2827.4	4667.4	6785.8	11,022.8	9515.6	15,694.2
Change in noncash working capital		− 2589	1817	− 4270	− 1084	− 900	− 2768
FCFF		5139.6	7373.6	22,991.2	31,272.2	27,265.4	25,603.8

Table 6.26 Estimation of reinvestment rate

Year	2009	2010	2011	2012	2013	2014
EBIT(1 − T)	5378	13,858	25,507	41,211	35881	38,530
Adjusted net Capex	2827.4	4667.4	6785.8	11,022.8	9515.6	15,694.2
Change in noncash working capital	−2589	1817	−4270	−1084	−900	−2768
Reinvestment	238.4	6484.4	2515.8	9938.8	8615.6	12,926.2
Reinvestment rate	0.04	0.47	0.10	0.24	0.24	0.34

The historical growth rate of earnings on the basis of geometric mean during the 5-year period 2010−2014 was 48%.

Growth rate = Reinvestment rate × Adjusted ROCE

The average growth rate from fundamentals during the 5-year period 2010−14 was 12% (see Table 6.27).

Table 6.27 Estimation of growth rate from fundamentals

Year	2010	2011	2012	2013	2014
Reinvestment rate	0.47	0.10	0.24	0.24	0.34
Adjusted ROCE	0.48	0.57	0.57	0.35	0.33
Growth rate	0.23	0.06	0.14	0.08	0.11

FCFF valuation model

Two stage valuation model is used for valuing Apple. It is assumed that Apple will grow at 12% for the next 10 years and then at the stable growth rate of the US economy for ever.

High growth period inputs

High growth period = 10 years

Growth rate = 12%

Reinvestment rate = 27%

WACC = 8.48%

EBIT(1 − T) in year 2014 = $38,530 million

EBIT(1 − T) in year 2015 (start of high growth period) = $43,153.6 million.

Value of Apple in the high growth phase = $336,684.4 million dollars (see Table 6.28).

Stable phase inputs

The growth rate in the stable phase is assumed to be the growth rate of the US economy (see Table 6.29).

Growth rate in stable period = Reinvestment rate × Return on capital employed of consumer electronics industry.

Return on invested capital in consumer electronics industry is taken as 5.4% based on the average value during the period 2006−13.[4]

2.15% = Reinvestment rate × Return on invested capital

2.15% = Reinvestment rate × 5.4%

Reinvestment rate = 40%.

EBIT(1 − T) at the end of high growth period = $119,668.33 million

Growth rate in stable period = 2.15%

EBIT(1 − T) in stable period = 119,668.33 × 1.0215 = $122,241.20 million

Reinvestment rate = 40%

Reinvestment = $48,896.48 million

FCFF in stable period = $73,344.72 million

Terminal value of FCFF in stable period = FCFF in stable period/(WACC − growth rate) = 73,344.72/(5.53% − 2.15%) = $1158,684.366 million.

Present value of terminal value of FCFF in stable period = $676,403.37 million.

Value of operating assets of Apple = Present value of operating assets in high growth phase + Present value of operating assets in stable phase = 336,684.4 + 676,403.37 = $1,013,087.78 million

Value of operating assets of Apple = $1,013,087.78 million

Add cash and equivalents in 2014 = $25,077 million

Value of Apple in 2014 = $1,038,164.78 million

Table 6.28 Present value of FCFF in high growth period

Year	1	2	3	4	5	6	7	8	9	10
EBIT(1 − T)	43,153.6	48,332.0	54,131.9	60,627.7	67,903.0	76,051.4	85,177.6	95,398.9	106,846.7	119,668.3
Reinvestment	11,651.5	13,049.6	14,615.6	16,369.5	18,333.8	20,533.9	22,997.9	25,757.7	28,848.6	32,310.4
FCFF	31,502.1	35,282.4	39,516.3	44,258.2	49,569.2	55,517.5	62,179.6	69,641.2	77,998.1	87,357.9
PV of FCFF	29,039.6	29,981.9	30,954.7	31,959.2	32,996.2	34,066.8	35,172.3	36,313.5	37,491.9	38,708.4
Sum of PV	336,684.4									

Table 6.29 Estimation of growth rate in stable period

Year	Annual GDP growth rate
2010	2.5
2011	1.6
2012	2.3
2013	2.2
Average	2.15

Source: http://data.worldbank.org/indicator/NY.GDP.MKTP.KD.ZG.

Table 6.30 Relative value peer comparison in year 2015

	Apple	HPQ	Samsung	Google	Sony
P/E	16.4	12.9	14.1	27.5	6.8
P/B	5.9	2.3	1.2	3.5	0.5
P/S	3.7	0.6	0.9	5.6	0.1
P/cash flow	10.3	6.3	4.6	15.5	1.5
Dividend yield (%)	1.5	1.9	1.36		0.3

Less debt of Apple in 2014 = $35,295 million
Less lease commitments in 2014 = $4987 million
Value of equity in year 2014 = $997,882.78 million
Number of shares in year 2014 = 6522 million
Value per share = $153

The market value of equity in year 2014 was $668.5 billion. Apple was trading at $109.48 on December 31, 2014. Based on this FCFF valuation model it can be stated that Apple was undervalued at the time of analysis.

6.14 Relative valuation

The relative values used for comparison are price multiples like Price to Earnings ratio (P/E), Price to Book ratio (P/B), Price to Sales (P/S), Price to Cash Flow (P/CF), dividend yield and enterprise value multiples.

The peer competitors selected for comparison are HPQ, Google, Samsung, and Sony (see Table 6.30).

The price multiples are fluctuating over 5-year period of analysis. The price to earnings ratio declined from 18 in the year 2010 to 11.5 in year 2011 and then showing increasing trend. The P/S, P/B, and P/CF ratios were also fluctuating over the 5 years (see Table 6.31).

Apple had the highest price to book ratio among the peer companies. Google had the highest P/E, P/S, and price/cash flow multiple values among the peer group. HPQ had the highest dividend yield (see Table 6.32).

Table 6.31 Price multiples trends

Year	2010	2011	2012	2013	2014
P/E	18	11.5	12.1	13.9	14.9
P/B	5.4	4.2	3.9	3.9	5.2
P/S	3.9	3	3.1	3	3.3
P/CF	13.2	8.4	8.9	9.8	9.4

Source: Data from Morningstar.

Table 6.32 Enterprise value multiples in year 2014

EV multiples	Samsung	Sony	Google	HPQ	Apple
EV/revenues	0.7	1.8	4.6	0.7	3.6
EV/EBITDA	2.9	12.0	13.5	6.8	10.6
EV/EBIT	5.1	276.3	18.3	10.9	12.4

The table 6.32 highlights the enterprise value multiples of the peer competitors during the period 2014. Lower the enterprise value ratios, the more attractive the stock would be.

*The financial data and the detailed calculation of each section is given in the excel file **Apple.xlsx**.*

Further reading

[1] www.Apple.com.
[2] http://www.inc.com/karl-and-bill/3-strategies-to-adopt-from-apple.html.
[3] "Apple Investor Relations FAQ". Apple Inc. Retrieved January 29, 2015.
[4] "Apple Computer, Inc. Finalizes Acquisition of NeXT Software Inc.". Apple Inc.
[5] http://www.macrumors.com/2014/07/22/apple-29-companies-fiscal-2013/.
[6] http://9to5mac.com/2014/03/10/apple-looking-to-boost-ma-team-with-acquisition-integration-analysts/.
[7] www.morningstar.com.

Wealth creation—analysis of Google

7

7.1 Introduction

Google is an American multinational technology company which specializes in internet related services and products. The products and services offered by Google include online advertising technologies, search, cloud computing, and software. Google was founded by Larry Page and Sergey Brin when they were Ph.D. students at Stanford University. Google was incorporated in California in September 1998 and reincorporated in August 2003. Google provide products and services in more than 100 languages and in more than 50 countries. The innovations in search and advertising had catapulted Google as one of the most recognized brands in the world. Google generate revenues by primarily delivering online advertising. By 2014, Google had 53,600 full-time employees: 20,832 in research and development, 17,621 in sales and marketing, 7510 in general and administrative, and 7637 in operations.

7.2 Ownership and capital structure

Google's ownership structure consists of 95% equity and 5% debt. The equity ownership is held by financial institutions and mutual funds. There are 2906 institution owners who own 36.69% of the equity ownership. There are 4433 fund owners who own 19.22% of the equity ownership. The top institutions having equity ownership stakes in Google include Vanguard Group, Fidelity Management and Research financial Company, State Street Corp, BlackRock Fund Advisors, and T. Rowe Price Associates. The top funds having equity ownership include Vanguard Total Stock Market Index, Fidelity Contra fund, VA College America Growth Fund, Vanguard 500 Index, and Vanguard Institutional Index. The major bond ownership funds are Vanguard Total Bond Market Index fund, iShares 1−3 Year Credit bond, SA Global fixed income fund and KLP Obligasion Global 1. Larry and Sergey together own about 14% of the shares but control 56% of the stockholder voting power through super voting stock. Google had issued $3 billion of unsecured senior notes in three tranches in the year 2011. Google issued unsecured senior notes of $1 billion in the year 2014. In 2014, Google repaid $1.0 billion on the first tranche of the 2011 notes upon their maturity.

7.3   Stock details

Google's board of directors have authorized three classes of stock—Class A, Class B common stock, and Class C capital stock. The rights of the holders of stock are identical except with respect to voting rights. Each share of Class A common stock is entitled to one vote per share. Each share of Class B common stock is entitled to 10 votes per share. Class C capital stock has no voting rights, except as required by applicable law. Shares of Class B common stock may be converted at any time at the option of the stockholder and automatically convert upon sale or transfer to Class A common stock. In 2012, the nonvoting capital stock (Class C Capital stock) was created through amendments to the incorporation which authorized 3 billion shares of Class C capital stock and increased the authorized shares of Class A common stock from 6 billion to 9 billion. In 2014, the company approved the distribution of shares of the Class C capital stock as dividends to the holders of Class A and Class B common stock. In this stock split, share and per share amounts were retroactively adjusted to reflect the effects of the stock split. Google's Class A common stock has been listed on the Nasdaq Global Select Market under the symbol "GOOG" since August 19, 2014. The symbol was changed to "GOOGL" since April 3, 2014. The Class B stock is neither listed nor traded. The Class C capital stock has been listed on the Nasdaq Global Select Market under the symbol GOOG since April 3, 2014. By 2014, there were approximately 2448 and 2507 stockholders of Class A and Class C capital stock and 73 stock holders of Class B common stock.

7.4   Main products and services of Google

The main products and services of google are discussed below.

7.4.1   Google web search

Google.com focuses on building products and services on websites whereby users could find relevant information quickly and easily. Google web search with integrated special features provide easy access to billions of web pages which help people find exactly what they look for on the web. The Google.com search experience include items like search option panels, rich snippets, music search, real time search, Google suggest, search personalization, advanced search functionality, web page translation, integrated tools, cached links, movie, music, and weather information. Google Suggest shows related query suggestions as users type searches in 153 domains and 52 languages. Web Page Translation supports 51 languages and automatically translates between any two of these languages, with a total of 2550 language translation pairs. The other features include news, finance, maps, image, video, book, blogs, and groups information.

Google images are the searchable index of images found across the web. Google Books enable users to search full text of collection of books. Google Books links bring users to pages containing bibliographic information and several sentences of the search term in context, sample book pages, or full text, depending on author and publisher permissions and book copyright status. By 2009, Google have scanned and indexed over 12 million books for search.[1] Google Scholar provides the platform for broad search for relevant scholarly literature consisting of peer reviewed research papers, theses, books, abstracts, and articles. Google Finance provides real time stock quotes and charts, financial news, currency conversions, business, and enterprise headlines for companies. Google News facilitate gathering information from thousands of news sources worldwide and provides new stories in a searchable format within minutes of their publication on the web. Google Videos is the searchable index of videos found across web. The Google Blog Search index includes every blog that publishes a site feed. iGoogle connects users to the information which can be used in a customizable format. Google Product Search enable users to search for product information which is submitted electronically by sellers or automatically identified by Google software. Google Merchant Centre facilitate merchants to submit product listings which they would like to share on Google web sites. Google Custom Search allows communities of users familiar with particular topics to build customized search engines. Google Trends provides users with the ability to track the popularity of keyword searches over time on Google. Google Music Search provides music discovery service for users searching for music. Google Webmaster Tools enables webmasters to understand their sites' performance in Google's search results.

7.4.2 Applications

Google Docs allows the users to create, view, edit, and share documents, spreadsheets, and presentations from anywhere using a browser. Calendar is a free online shareable calendar service offered by Google. Gmail is Google's free webmail service with built in Google search technology which allows for searching of emails and have over seven gigabytes of storage. Google Groups is a free service that helps groups of people connect to information and people. Google Reader is the free service which lets users subscriber to feeds and receive updates from multiple web sites in a single interface.

Orkut enables users to search and connect to other users through networks of friends. Blogger is a web-based publishing tool that lets people publish to the web instantly using blogs. Google Sites allows users to easily create, update, and publish content online without technical expertise, with control over who can see and update the site. YouTube is an online community that lets users worldwide upload, share, watch, rate, and comment on videos, from user generated to niche professional to premium videos.

[1] Google Annual Report 2015.

7.4.3 Client

Google Toolbar is a free application that adds a Google search box to web browsers (Internet Explorer and Firefox). Google Chrome is an open-source browser for Windows, Mac, and Linux which combines a minimal design with technologies to make the web faster, safer, and easier to navigate. Google Chrome OS is an open source operating system for users. Google Pack is a free collection of safe and useful software programs from Google. Picasa is a free service that allows users to view, manage, and share their photos. Google Desktop lets people perform a full-text search on the contents of their own computer, including email, files, instant messenger chats, and web browser history.

7.4.4 Google Geo

Google Local Search powers local queries on Google.com, Google Maps, Google Earth, and mobile. Google Maps helps users explore the world from their desktop or phone using global mapping data, satellite imagery, and Google Street View imagery. Panoramio enables users to upload photos and locate them on the earth using Google Maps. Google Earth offers an immersive, three-dimensional (3D) way to explore mapping data and imagery. Google Earth includes detailed maps of the earth's ocean floors and Sky, an astronomical imagery library with images of over 100 million stars and 200 million galaxies. Google SketchUp is a free tool that enables users to model buildings in 3D.

7.4.5 Android

It is a free open-source mobile software platform that allows developers to create applications for mobile devices and for handset manufacturers to install. There are 26 Android devices supported by 60 carriers in 49 countries and 19 languages.

7.4.6 Google Mobile

Google Mobile provides mobile specific features like voice input and location based technology to mobile phone users. Google Checkout is a service offered to users, merchants, and advertisers to make online shopping and payments more streamlined and secure.

7.4.7 Google Labs

Google Labs is the test bed for Google engineers and adventurous Google users. On Google Labs, the product prototypes are posted and feedback on how the technology could be used or improved is solicited.

7.5 Strategies of growth

The continuing shift from an offline to online world has contributed to the growth of Google's business. Advertising revenues are generated increasingly from mobile phones and new advertising formats. The maximum revenues for Google are obtained from AdWords which is an online advertising service that places advertising near the list of search lists.

Google generate revenue primarily by delivering both performance advertising and brand advertising. Performance advertising delivers relevant advertisement which users click and results in direct engagement with advertisements. The performance advertisers generally pay on a cost per engagement basis. The websites of Google Network and AdWords, the primary auction based advertising program facilitate simple text based advertisement. Brand advertising is facilitated by delivering advertisers products and services through videos, text images, and interactive advertisements which run across devices.

Google have expanded scope of business outside United States and have been focusing on developing localized versions of products and relevant advertising programs. The share of international revenues has increased from 55% of total revenues in the year 2013 to approximately 57% in year 2014.

Nonadvertising revenues have increased from 9% of total revenues in 2013 to 11% in 2014. Google sources of nonadvertising revenues are primarily from sales of digital content products, hardware sales, and licensing. Google have invested in an ambitious project called Project Loon to enhance internet connectivity for millions of people across people in remote places. Google have invested billions of dollars for developing new products and services through research and development. Google research and development expenses were $6.1 billion, $7.1 billion, and $9.8 billion in 2012, 2013, and 2014, respectively. Google invested $900 million in SpaceX which is a space exploration and space transport company in year 2015.

7.6 Challenges

Google have many competitors in different industries, including general purpose search engines and information services, vertical search engines and e-commerce websites, social networks, providers of online products and services, other forms of advertising. Google faces major challenges on account of rapid changes as well as new and disruptive technologies. Google faces competition from general purpose search engines and information services like Yahoo, Microsoft's Bing, Yandex, Baidu, Naver, Webcrawler, and MyWebSearch. The competition also comes from vertical search engines and ecommerce websites like Kayak which deals with travel queries, LinkedIn for job queries, WebMD for health related queries, Amazon, and eBay for ecommerce. Users may navigate directly to such content, websites and applications rather than using Google directly to access information. Social network sites like Facebook and Twitter are also competitors for Google as users rely on social networks for products or service referrals. Google also faces competition from online advertising platforms and networks like Criteo, AppNexus, and Facebook. Google faces challenges from these competitors who constantly develop innovations in search, online advertising, wireless mobile devices, and operating systems. Google also faces the risk of losing advertisers who could terminate their contracts at any time. Google generated about 89% of their revenues in 2014 from their advertisers. Google 's operating margins would come down if greater percentage of revenues comes from advertisement placed on Google Network. Members earn revenues which are generated through advertisements placed directly on Google websites. The margins on revenues from Google network members is significantly less than the margin on revenues generated from advertisements from traditional formats. Foreign exchange fluctuations also impact the international revenues of Google. The international revenues are favorably impacted as the US dollar weakens relative to other foreign currencies and revenues decrease when the US dollar strengthens relative to other foreign currencies. Google uses foreign currency options to hedge foreign exchange impacts on forecasted earnings.

7.7   Mergers and Acquisitions strategy

Acquisition is an important strategy of growth for Google. Google has emerged as the one of the biggest and most successful acquirers in the technology industry. Its core search advertising platform and biggest new businesses like Android and YouTube and display advertising have all resulted from acquisitions. Google had spent more than $28 billion for acquiring 163 companies since 2001. These acquisitions can be estimated as one company per month.

The largest acquisition made by Google was the purchase of Motorola Mobility, a mobile device manufacturing subsidiary of Motorola. This acquisition was nearly four times larger than the previous largest purchase of online advertising company DoubleClick for $3.2 billion. It can be said that Google on average had acquired more than one company per week since 2010.

7.7.1   Acquisition of Motorola Mobility

In May 22, 2012, Google acquired Motorola Mobility Holdings Inc. which consists of the Motorola Home and Motorola Mobile businesses. In the 1990s, Motorola had a leading position in the analog cell phone market, but was unable to capture the digital technology market, making the way for global rivals such as Nokia and Samsung. Motorola had shifted its operating system from their proprietary software to Google's Android operating system in year 2009. Under the definitive agreement, Google acquired Motorola Mobility for $40 per share in cash or a total of about $12.5 billion which represented a premium of 63% to the closing price of Motorola Mobility shares on August 12, 2011.The acquisition included a sizeable portfolio of patents owned by Motorola. In 2011, Motorola Mobility held approximately 14,600 granted patents and 67,000 pending applications worldwide.

Motorola deal information

Target:	Motorola Mobility
Acquirer:	Google Inc.
Acquisition date	22-05-2012
Acquirer fiscal year end prior to acquisition	31-12-2011
Stub year fraction	0.39
Offer price per share	$40.00
Target stock price	$24.45
Stock price as of (mm/dd/yyyy)	12-08-2011
Premium	63.0%
Acquirer stock price as on 12/08/2011	$563.77

Of the $12.4 billion total purchase price, $2.9 billion was cash acquired, $5.5 billion was attributed to patents and developed technology, $2.6 billion to goodwill, $730 million to customer relationships, and $670 million to other net assets acquired.

The acquisition of Motorola enabled Google to supercharge the Android ecosystem which would enhance competition in mobile computing. Google expected to enhance its competitive advantage as Motorola Mobility had formidable strength in Android smartphones and devices along with market leadership position in the home devices and video solutions business. Google's strategy for the acquisition rationale was to build up the company's patent portfolio in order to protect Android from anticompetitive threats from Microsoft, Apple, and other companies. Android which is open source software is vital to competition in the mobile device space. It has to be noted that Google had lost the bid for Nortel patents.

The transaction was subject to regulatory approvals from United States, Europe and other jurisdictions. The Motorola acquisition is considered as a means of protecting the viability of Android. Android system has been under the centre of controversy involving patent infringement in which Android manufacturers HTC, Motorola, and Samsung were sued by Microsoft, Oracle, and Apple. More than 150 million Android devices have been activated worldwide through a network of about 39 manufacturers and 231 carriers in 123 countries.

Motorola had a successful stint as hardware integrator in the mobile industrial design world. The acquisition was aimed to create better user experience at reduced costs through hardware and software integration through innovation in mobile computing. The acquisition also fit into Google's strategy to enter home networking market via Motorola's connected home business. The Android market is heavily fragmented and the developers face problems for designing applications. This acquisition was expected to provide Google a better Android system with lot of applications. This acquisition also provided the opportunity to Google to diversify into focused hardware products and mobile computing. Google could access all the product lines of MMI cell phones, set top boxes, and tablets.

In 2013, Motorola home business was sold to Arris Group Inc. The deal was done for approximately $2412 million in cash. The deal also included approximately $175 million in Arris common stock. Subsequent to the transaction, Google owned 7.8% of the outstanding shares of Arris. In 2014, Motorola Mobile business was sold to Lenovo Group for a total purchase price of approximately $2.9 billion which comprised of $660 million in cash and $750 million in Lenovo ordinary shares. The remaining $1.5 billion was paid in the form of an interest free 3-year pre payable promissory note.

Google had acquired Android Mobile software for $50 million which is the best smart phone operating system in the world. Table 7.1 lists the major acquisitions done by Google.

7.7.2 Acquisitions in year 2013

In 2013, Google acquired Waze Ltd. the provider of mobile map application which offers turn by turn navigation and real time traffic updates powered by incidents and route information submitted by community of users. The acquisition was for a cash consideration of $969 million. Of the total purchase price $841 million was attributed to goodwill and $193 million was attributed to intangible assets. Google also entered into a collaboration agreement with Calico a life science company to harness advanced technologies to increase understanding of the biology which controls lifespan.

7.7.3 Acquisitions in year 2014

In 2014, Google completed the acquisition of Nest Labs in which earlier Google had 12% stake. Nest Labs is involved in the making of reinvent devices in the home such as thermostats and smoke alarms. The acquisition was aimed at enhancing Google's suite of products and services. The purchase price amounted to $2.6 billion.

Google had acquired Dropcam for approximately $517 million in cash. Dropcam enable consumers and businesses to monitor homes and offices through video. Google acquired Skybox, the satellite imaging company for approximately $478 million in cash. The acquisition was aimed to equip Google Maps with up to date imagery, improve internet access and disaster relief.

7.8 Google IPO

In August 1998, Andy Bechtolsheim co-founder of Sun Microsystems made a contribution of $100,000 as the first funding for Google. In the year 1999, major investors and venture capital firms Kleiner Perkins, Caufield, and Byers and Sequoia Capital invested $25 million in Google. Google went public on August 19, 2004. The company offered 19,605,052 shares at a price of $85 per share. The shares were sold in an online auction format using a system built by Morgan Stanley and Credit Suisse who were the underwriters of the deal. The market capitalization of Google was $23 billion at that time. By January 2014, the market capitalization of Google increased to $397 billion.

Table 7.1 Major acquisitions by Google

SL	Year	Target firm	Value	Strategic reasons
1	2011	Motorola	$12.5 billion	The acquisition was basically aimed to acquire the patents of Motorola
2	2014	Nest Labs	$3.2 billion	The acquisition was made for expansion in consumer homes for smart thermostats and smoke detectors
3	2007	DoubleClick	$3.1 billion	The acquisition was aimed for expansion in online advertising world. Google acquired the software of DoubleClick and obtained the relationship with web publishers, advertisers and agencies of the company
4	2006	Youtube	$1.65 billion	Google acquired Youtube 1 year after its launch and transformed it into the second biggest search engine in the world after Google
5	2013	Waze	$966 million	This is a GPS based navigation application company which emerged as a strategic fit for Google
6	2009	Admob	$750 million	Facilitated Google to achieve a major foothold in mobile advertising platform
7	2010	ITA Software	$700 million	ITA is a major player in the travel reservations software industry. This acquisition was aimed at gaining infrastructural facilities
8	2007	Postini	$625 million	This acquisition provided Google the email and web security service
9	2014	Dropcam	$555 million	This deal was aimed at acquiring Dropcam's video monitoring and security technology to facilitate Nest Lab to increase home automation products
10	2014	Skybox	$500 million	Skybox's satellite technology would help Google acquire accurate and update imagery for Google Maps
11	2014	DeepMind Technologies	$650 million	Strategic fit for data mining and artificial intelligence
12	2013	Boston Dynamics	$500 million	The company makes robots for Google which would facilitate delivery of packages
13	2011	Zagat	$150 million	Google's purchase of Zagat helped Google to enhance various services of Google which included Maps, search and Earth

7.8.1   Dividends

Google had never declared or paid any cash dividend on the common or capital stock.

7.9   Financial analysis

7.9.1   Operating performance analysis

The following section discusses the operating performance analysis.

The values of the financial parameters are given in millions of dollars except per share data of EPS. The revenues of Google increased from $3189.22 million in year 2004 to $66,001 million in year 2014. It means that revenues increased by approximately 20 times during the period 2004–14. The income from operations improved from $640.19 million in year 2004 to $16,496 million in year 2014 registering a growth rate of 2476% during the period. Net income improved from $399.11 million in year 2004 to $14,444 million in year 2014. The net income rise during the two comparative years was 36 times. The total cash which includes cash, cash equivalents and marketable securities increased from $2132.29 million dollars in 2004 to $64,395 million dollars in 2014. The total cash increased 30 times during the period. The total assets of Google increased from $3313.35 million in year 2004 to $131,133 million in year 2014. The total stock holder equity increased from $2929 million dollars in the year 2004 to $104,500 million dollars in year 2014. This represented an increase of value of approximately 36 times (Table 7.2).

The financial parameters registered maximum growth rate in the year 2005 (see Table 7.3). The net income registered growth rate of 267% in the year 2005 compared to the previous year 2004. The average growth rate of revenues during the 10-year period 2005–14 was 38%. The average growth rate in income from operations, net income and EPS during the above period was 46%, 56%, and 35%, respectively. The average growth rate in total cash, total assets, and total stock holder equity have been 52%, 51%, and 51%, respectively during the 10-year period.

The comparative analysis between the two 5-year periods (2005–9) and (2010–14) reveals that the operating performance have declined in the period 2010–14 compared to the period 2005–14. The average growth rate in revenues during the period 2005–9 was 52% compared to the growth rate of 23% in the period 2010–14. The average growth rate of income from operations which was 78% in the period 2005–9 declined to 15% in the period 2010–14. The average net income growth rate of 94% in the period 2005–9 declined to 17% in the period 2010–14. The average EPS growth rate of 67% in the period 2005–9 had declined to 3% during the period 2010–14. The average growth rate of total cash of 82% during the period 2005–9 declined to 22% during the period 2010–14. The average growth rate of total assets during the period 2005–9 was 76%. The average growth rate of total assets fell to 27% during the period 2010–14. The average growth rate

Table 7.2 Financial highlights (millions of dollars) 2004–14

Year	2004	2005	2006	2007	2008	2009	2010	2011	2012	2013	2014
Revenues	3189.22	6138.56	10,604.9	16,593.9	21,795.5	23,650.5	29,321	37,905	46,039	55,519	66,001
Income from operations	640.19	2017.27	3549.99	5084.4	6631.96	8312.18	10,381	11,742	13,834	15,403	16,496
Net income	399.11	1465.39	3077.44	4203.72	4226.85	6520.44	8505	9737	10,737	12,920	14,444
EPS (per dollar)	2.07	5.31	10.21	13.53	13.46	20.62	13.35	15.09	16.41	19.41	21.37
Total cash	2132.29	8034.24	11,243.91	14,218.61	15,845.77	24,484.77	34,975	44,626	48,088	58,717	64,395
Total assets	3313.35	10,271.81	18,473.35	25,335.81	31,767.57	40,496.77	57,851	72,574	93,798	110,920	131,133
Total stock holder equity	2929.056	9418.95	17,039.84	22,689.67	28,238.86	36,004.22	46,241	58,145	71,715	87,309	104,500

Table 7.3 **Year on year growth rate**

Year	2005	2006	2007	2008	2009	2010	2011	2012	2013	2014
Revenues (%)	92	73	56	31	9	24	29	21	21	19
Income from operations (%)	215	76	43	30	25	25	13	18	11	7
Net income (%)	267	110	37	1	54	30	14	10	20	12
EPS (per dollar) (%)	157	92	33	−1	53	−35	13	9	18	10
Total cash (%)	277	40	26	11	55	43	28	8	22	10
Total assets (%)	210	80	37	25	27	43	25	29	18	18
Total stock holder equity (%)	222	81	33	24	27	28	26	23	22	20

Table 7.4 **Sources of revenues in million dollars**

	2009	2010	2011	2012	2013	2014
Advertising revenues						
Google websites	15,723	19,444	26,145	31,221	37,422	45,085
Google network members websites	7166	8792	10,386	12,465	13,125	13,971
Total advertising revenues	22,889	28,236	36,531	43,686	50,547	59,056
Other revenues	762	1085	1374	2353	4972	6945
Total revenues	23,651	29,321	37,905	46,039	55,519	66,001

of stock holder equity which was 78% during the period 2005−9 fell to 24% during the period 2010−14.

The total advertising revenues increased from $22,889 million in year 2009 to $59,056 million by year 2014 (see Table 7.4). The advertising revenues from Google websites improved from $15,723 million in year 2009 to $45,085 million by year 2014. The Google website's contribution of advertising revenues to the total revenues was 68% on average basis during the period 2009−14. Google members advertising revenues was 27% of the total revenues during the period 2009−14 on average basis. The 6 year average of advertising revenues as percent of total revenues was 94%. The average growth rate of total advertising revenues during the 5-year period 2010−14 was 21%.

The revenues from Google Network member's websites include revenues generated primarily through advertising programs including AdSense for search and content, Ad Exchange, Ad Mob, and Double Click Bid Manager.

7.9.2   Cost of revenues

The cost of revenues incurred by Google consisted of acquisition costs which are the advertising revenues shares with the Google network members and the amount paid to the distribution partners. These amounts are primarily based on the revenue share and fixed fee arrangements with Google network members and distribution partners. The cost of revenues also include expenses associated with the operation

Table 7.5 **Cost of revenues in millions of dollars**

Year	2010	2011	2012	2013	2014
Traffic acquisition costs	7317	8811	10,956	12,258	13,497
Other cost of revenues	2799	4589	6220	9735	12,194
Total cost of revenues	10,116	13,400	17,176	21,993	25,691

Table 7.6 **R&D expenses and sales and marketing expenses**

Year	2010	2011	2012	2013	2014
R&D expenses	3762	5162	6083	7137	9832
Sales and marketing expenses	2799	4589	5465	6554	8131

Table 7.7 **Percent of revenues by geographic region**

Year	2009	2010	2011	2012	2013	2014
US	47	48	46	46	45	43
UK	13	11	11	11	10	10
Rest of world	40	41	43	43	45	48

of data centers which include labor, energy and bandwidth costs, credit card and transaction fees related to processing customer transaction which include Google checkout transactions, amortization of acquired intangible assets, and content acquisition costs (Table 7.5).

The average increase in traffic costs during the period 2010−14 was 17%. The average total cost of revenues as per cent of revenues was 37% during the 5-year period 2010−14.

The R&D expenses increased from $3762 million in year 2010 to $9832 million in 2014. The sales and marketing expenses increased from $2799 million in year 2010 to $8131 million in year 2014. The average R&D expenses as percent of revenues was 13% during the period 2010−14. The average sales and marketing expenses as percent of revenues was 12% during the 5-year period 2010−14 (Table 7.6).

The proportion of contribution from the rest of world has shown increasing trend during the period 2009−14. The contribution from United Kingdom is showing a constant trend (Table 7.7).

7.10   Ratio analysis

The average gross margin during the period 2005−9 slightly improved from 60.24% to 61.3% during the period 2010–14. The average operating margin during the period 2005−9 declined from 32.5% to 28.02% during the period 2010−14.

Table 7.8 **Profitability ratios**

Year	2005	2006	2007	2008	2009	2010	2011	2012	2013	2014
Gross margin (%)	58.1	60.2	59.9	60.4	62.6	64.5	65.2	58.9	56.8	61.1
Operating margin (%)	32.9	33.5	30.6	30.4	35.1	35.4	31	25.4	23.3	25
Earnings per share	2.51	4.97	6.65	6.66	10.21	13.17	14.89	16.17	19.08	21.02
Return on assets (%)	21.57	21.41	19.19	14.8	18.05	17.3	14.93	12.91	12.62	11.93
Return on equity (%)	23.73	23.26	21.16	16.6	20.3	20.68	18.66	16.54	16.25	15.06

Table 7.9 **Liquidity ratios**

Year	2005	2006	2007	2008	2009	2010	2011	2012	2013	2014
Current ratio	12.08	10	8.49	8.77	10.62	4.16	5.92	4.22	4.58	4.8
Quick ratio	11.7	9.63	8.12	8.03	10.08	4	5.7	3.95	4.28	4.52

The average EPS during the period 2005−9 improved from 6.2 to 16.87 during the period 2010−14.

The average return on assets and return on equity has declined during the 5-year period 2010−14 compared to the previous 5-year period 2005−9. The average return on assets declined from 19% during the period 2005−9 to 13.9% during the period 2010−14. The average return on equity declined from 21% during the period 2005−9 to 17.44% during the period 2010−14 (Table 7.8).

The liquidity position of Google has declined during the period 2010−14 compared to the period 2005−9. The average current ratio which was 9.99 during the period 2005−9 declined to 4.74 during the period 2010−14. The average quick ratio which was 9.51 during the period 2005−9 declined to 4.49 during the period 2010−14 (Table 7.9).

The average days' sales outstanding which was 37.56 during the period 2005−9 improved to 48.58 during the period 2010−14. The average payable period which was 11.21 days during the period 2005−9 increased to 22.24 days during the period 2010−14. The average receivable and asset turnover ratios also declined during the five period 2010−14 compared to the previous 5-year period 2005−9. The average receivable turnover ratio during the period 2005−9 was 9.91 while the average receivable turnover ratio during the period 2010−14 was 7.53. The average asset turnover ratio of 0.76 during the period 2005−9 declined to 0.58 during the period 2010−14 (see Table 7.10).

7.11 Stock wealth creation

Google had its IPO listed on NASDAQ stock exchange on August 19, 2004. The closing price on the day of first listing was $102.37. The Google stock was trading

Table 7.10 **Efficiency ratios**

Year	2005	2006	2007	2008	2009	2010	2011	2012	2013	2014
Days sales outstanding	29.72	34.6	38.33	40.23	44.92	46.25	46.6	48.42	51.15	50.5
Payables period	10.52	14.11	13.54	9.74	8.13	12.24	14.82	23	31.51	29.61
Receivables turnover	12.28	10.55	9.52	9.07	8.13	7.89	7.83	7.54	7.14	7.23
Asset turnover	0.9	0.74	0.76	0.76	0.65	0.6	0.58	0.6	0.58	0.55

Table 7.11 **Average returns in percent**

Year	Monthly returns	Yearly returns
2005	7	84
2006	1.3	16
2007	3.8	45
2008	−5.7	−69
2009	6.1	73
2010	0.2	2.4
2011	1.0	13
2012	1.0	12
2013	4.0	48
2014	−4.4	−52
2015[a]	0.5	7

[a]The yearly returns for the year was based on 5 months' average returns (January–June) and then the yearly average was obtained by multiplying by 12.

at $547.47 on June 1, 2015. The stock price increased by 5.34 times during the 11-year period. The holding period return (HPR) based on the day of listing and first of June 2015 was approximately 435%. The total cumulative monthly returns during the 11 years (2004–mid 2005) comprising 130 months was approximately 250% (see Fig. 7.1). The total cumulative monthly returns for the 5.5 year period (2010–mid 2015) was approximately 26%.

The average yearly returns during the period 2005–mid 2015 was 16%. The average yearly returns during the period five and half year period 2010–mid 2015 was 5%. Google stock gave average negative returns of 69% in year 2008 and 52% in year 2014. The highest yearly average returns was registered in the year 2005 with returns of 84%. In 2009, Google stock documented average yearly returns of 73% (see Table 7.11).

The cumulative daily returns during since the date of listing to mid-June 2015 was 243.83%. The cumulative returns were based for the period 2004–15 comprising 2722 days of stock trading (Fig. 7.1).

The cumulative monthly returns for approximately 130 months during the period 2004–15 mid-year was 251%. The stock price data was taken from yahoo finance. The analysis starts from the month the stock is listed in the stock market (August 2014).

Figure 7.1 Cumulative returns of Google since listing.

Table 7.12 **Holding period yield**

Year	Holding period yield (HPY) (%)
2010	−5
2011	6.8
2012	6.3
2013	55
2014	−52

Holding Period Yield (HPY)

HPR is obtained as the ratio of the ending value of investment divided by the beginning value of investment.

HPR = Ending value of investment/Beginning value of investment.

HPR can be converted into an annual percentage return which is known as HPY.

HPY = HPR − 1

Annual HPR = (HPR)^1/n where n is the number of years the investment is held.

The HPR analysis assumes that an investment is made in a Google share in the beginning of the year and sold off at the end of the year. For example, a Google share is bought on January 4, 2010, and sold off on December 31, 2010. The closing price of Google share on January 4, 2010, was $626.75 and on December 31, 2010, was $593.97.

HPR = $593.97/$626.75 = 0.947

HPY = 0.947−1 = −0.053

The HPY was −5% in the year 2010 (Table 7.12).

The HPY has been fluctuating over the 5-year period. The HPY was highest in the year 2013 with maximum yield of 55%. In the year 2014, the yield was the lowest with −52%.

Table 7.13 Market capitalization in millions of dollars

Year	Market capitalization in $ million
2010	190,843
2011	209,850
2012	233,421
2013	376,370
2014	361,436

Table 7.14 Excess value added

Year	2010	2011	2012	2013	2014	2015
Market value of equity	190,843	209,850	233,421	376,370	361,436	372,643
Book value of equity	46,241	58,145	71,715	87,309	104,500	109,185
Excess value	144,602	151,705	161,706	289,061	256,936	263,458
BV as percent of MV (%)	24	28	31	23	29	29

Assume that an investor bought a Google stock which was trading at 626.75 on January 4, 2010. His investment period was 5 years. The stock was trading at $530.66 on December 31 2014.

HPR = Ending value of investment/Beginning value of investment = $530.66/$626.75 = 0.84.
Annual HPR = (0.84) ^1/5 = 0.96.
Annual HPY = 0.96−1 = −0.04.

The annual HPY for Google for the 5-year investment period 2010–14 was −4%.

The market capitalization increased from $190.84 billion in year 2010 to $361.43 billion by 2014. The market capitalization increased by approximately 10% in the year 2011 compared to the previous year 2010. The increase in market capitalization had been 11% in the year 2012. The maximum increase in market capitalization was registered in year 2013 when the market capitalization increased by approximately 61% compared to the previous year. In 2014, the market capitalization fell by approximately 4% (Table 7.13).

The book value was 24% of the market value in the year 2010. By 2015, the book value as percent of market value increased to 29%. The average book value was 27% of the market value during the period 2010–15. It can be said that on an average 73% of the value is not found in the books and attributed to wealth creation in the market. The excess value is obtained as the difference between the market value of equity and book value of equity. The excess value increased from$144.6 billion in year 2010 to $263.46 in year 2015 (Table 7.14).

Table 7.15 Estimation of amortization and value of research asset in 2014

Year	R&D expenses	Unamortized portion		Amortization this year (million $)
		%	(million $)	
Current	9832	100	9832	
−1	7952	80	6361.6	1590.4
−2	6793	60	4075.8	1358.6
−3	5162	40	2064.8	1032.4
−4	3762	20	752.4	752.4
−5	2843.027	0	0	568.6054
	Value of research asset		23,086.6	
	Amortization expense current year			5302.4054

The values are given in millions of dollars.

7.12 Valuation using Free Cash Flow to Firm (FCFF) model

The Free Cash Flow to Firm (FCFF) discounted cash flow method have been used to value Google.

One of the most important adjustment to be made is the adjustment of R&D expenses. The R&D expenses need to be capitalized. Thus, the capital expenditure need to be adjusted. The operating earnings and book value of equity are also adjusted.

Adjusted operating earnings = Operating earnings + Current year's R&D expense − Amortization of research asset.
Adjusted book value of capital = Adjusted book value of equity + Debt.
Adjusted book value of equity = Book value of equity + Research value of asset.

The research assets are amortized linearly over time. The life of research asset is assumed to be 5 years. The value of research asset and amortization expense calculation for the year 2014 is given in Table 7.15. The detailed calculation of the values for the previous years are given in the worksheet *Valuation of Google.xlsx*.

The Table 7.16 gives the amount of R&D expenses, value of R&D asset and amortization of R&D asset value each year during the time period 2008−14. Table 7.17 estimates the adjusted book value of capital. Table 7.18 shows the calculation of adjusted operating income and ROCE.

Table 7.19 gives the estimation of adjusted net capex. Table 7.20 gives the estimation of non cash working capital. Table 7.21 shows the FCFF calculation . Table 7.22 gives the reinvestment rate calculation.

Table 7.16 Value of R&D and amortization expenses

Year	R&D expenses	Value of R&D	Amortization of R&D
2008	2793.192	5545.17	913.78
2009	2843.027	6960.91	1427.29
2010	3762	8806.05	1916.86
2011	5162	11,418.69	2549.36
2012	6793	14,875.65	3336.04
2013	7952	18,557.01	4270.64
2014	9832	23,086.6	5302.41

The values are given in millions of US dollars.

Table 7.17 Estimation of adjusted book value of capital

Year	Book value of equity	Adjusted book value of equity	Debt	Adjusted capital
2008	28,239	33,784.17		33,784.17
2009	36,004	42,964.91		42,964.91
2010	46,241	55,047.05	3465	58,512.05
2011	58,145	69,563.69	4204	73,767.69
2012	71,715	86,590.65	5537	92,127.65
2013	87,309	105,866.01	5245	111,111.01
2014	104,500	127,586.60	5237	132,823.60

The values are given in millions of US dollars.
Adjusted book value of equity = Book value of equity + Value of R&D asset
Adjusted capital = Adjusted book value of equity + Debt

Growth rate = Reinvestment rate × Adjusted ROCE.

The average growth rate from fundamentals during the 5-year period 2010–14 was 17% (see Table 7.23).

WACC estimation

The cost of equity is estimate using the CAPM. The beta is estimated by regressing the daily Google stock returns on the market index NASDAQ Composite index (IXIC) during the 3-year period 2012–14.

Beta for Google = 1.04.

Risk free rate is based on the monthly average yield of 10-year Treasury bond rate during the period 2012–14. Risk free rate is estimated as 2.18%.[2]

Cost of equity = Risk free rate + beta × Risk premium.

Risk premium is assumed to be 5.5% based on historical average values.

= 2.18 + 1.04 × 5.5 = 7.9%.

Cost of debt calculation

The yield to maturity of a long term bond of Google maturing in year 2024 is taken as the cost of debt. The cost of debt is taken as 2.86% [3]

---

[2] http://www.treasury.gov/resource-center/data-chart-center/interest-rates/Pages/TextView.aspx?data=yieldYear&year=2014.

[3] http://quicktake.morningstar.com/StockNet/bonds.aspx?Symbol=GOOGL&Country=USA.

Table 7.18 Estimation of adjusted operating income and return on capital employed

Year	EBIT	Taxes	EBIT (1 − T)	R&D expenses	Amortization	Adjusted operating income	Adjusted capital	Adjusted ROCE
2008	6632	1790.64	4841.36	2793.192	913.78	6720.78	33,784.17	
2009	8312	1828.64	6483.36	2843.027	1427.29	7899.10	42,964.91	0.23
2010	10,381	2291	8090	3762	1916.86	9935.14	58,512.05	0.23
2011	11,742	2589	9153	5162	2549.36	11,765.64	73,767.69	0.20
2012	12,760	2598	10,162	6793	3336.04	13,618.96	92,127.65	0.18
2013	13,966	2282	11,684	7952	4270.64	15,365.36	111,111.01	0.17
2014	16,496	3331	13,165	9832	5302.41	17,694.59	132,823.60	0.16

Values are in millions of dollars.
Adjusted ROCE = EBIT(1 − t) in year t/Capital employed in year t − 1.

Table 7.19 **Adjusted net capital expenditure**

Year	Capex	Depreciation and amortization	Net Capex	R&D expenses	Amortization	Net acquisition	Adjusted net Capex
2008	2358	1499.88	858.12	2793.192	913.78	3320.299	6057.835
2009	810	1524.25	−714.25	2843.027	1427.29	108.02	809.509
2010	4018	1396	2622	3762	1916.86	1067	5534.1394
2011	3438	1851	1587	5162	2549.36	1900	6099.6414
2012	3273	2962	311	6793	3336.04	10,568	14,335.9592
2013	7358	3939	3419	7952	4270.64	−1077	6023.3562
2014	10,959	4979	5980	9832	5302.41	4502	15,011.5946

The values are in millions of dollars.
Net capital expenditure = Capital expenditure − Depreciation and amortization.
Adjusted net capital expenditure = Net capital expenditure + R&D Expenses in current year −Amortization of research asset + Net acquisitions.

Table 7.20 **Estimation of noncash working capital**

Year	2008	2009	2010	2011	2012	2013	2014
Total current assets	20,178.18	29,166.96	41,562	52,758	60,454	72,886	80,685
Total cash	15,845.77	24,484.78	34,975	44,626	48,088	58,717	64,395
Noncash current assets	4332.41	4682.18	6587	8132	12,366	14,169	16,290
Total current liabilities	2302.09	2747.47	9996	8913	14,337	15,908	16,805
Interest bearing current liabilities	0	0	3465	1218	2549	3009	2009
Noninterest bearing current liabilities	2302.09	2747.47	6531	7695	11,788	12,899	14,796
Noncash working capital	2030.32	1934.71	56	437	578	1270	1494
Change in noncash working capital		−95.61	−1878.71	381	141	692	224

The values are given in millions of dollars.
Total cash includes cash, cash equivalents, and marketable securities.
Total current assets − total cash = Noncash current assets.
Total current liabilities − short term debt = Noninterest bearing current liabilities.
Noncash working capital = Noncash current assets − Noninterest bearing current liabilities.

The marginal corporate tax rate in United States is estimated to be 35%.[4]
Cost of debt for Google = 2.86%.
After tax cost of debt = $2.86 \times (1 - 0.35) = 1.86\%$
Market value of equity in 2014 = 372,643 million.
Book value of debt in 2014 = 5237million.
Total value = 377,880 million.
Market value weights
Weight of equity = 0.986.
Weight of debt = 0.014.
WACC = $0.986 \times 7.9 + 0.014 \times 1.86 = 7.82\%$.

[4] http://www.kpmg.com/global/en/services/tax/tax-tools-and-resources/pages/corporate-tax-rates-table.aspx.

Table 7.21 Estimation of free cash flow to the firm (FCFF) 2009–14

Year	2008	2009	2010	2011	2012	2013	2014
EBIT(1 − T)	4841.36	6483.36	8090	9153	10,162	11,684	13,165
Adjusted net Capex	6057.8	809.5	5534.1	6099.6	14,336.0	6023.4	15,011.6
Change in noncash working capital		−95.61	−1878.71	381	141	692	224
FCFF		5769.5	4434.6	2672.4	−4315.0	4968.6	−2070.6

The values of FCFF are given in millions of dollars.
FCFF = EBIT(1 − T) − Adjusted net capex − change in noncash working capital.

Table 7.22 Estimation of reinvestment rate

	2009	2010	2011	2012	2013	2014
EBIT(1 − T)	6483.36	8090	9153	10,162	11,684	13,165
Adjusted net Capex	809.5	5534.1	6099.6	14,336.0	6023.4	15,011.6
Change in noncash working capital	−95.61	−1878.71	381	141	692	224
Reinvestment	713.9	3655.4	6480.6	14,477.0	6715.4	15,235.6
Reinvestment rate	0.11	0.45	0.71	1.42	0.57	1.16

Reinvestment = EBIT(1 − T)−Adjusted net Capex−Change in noncash working capital.
Reinvestment rate = Reinvestment/EBIT (1 − T).
The 5-year average (2010–14) reinvestment rate is estimated as 82% of EBIT(1 − T) on the basis of geometric mean.

Table 7.23 Estimation of growth rate from fundamentals

Year	2010	2011	2012	2013	2014
Reinvestment rate	0.45	0.71	1.42	0.57	1.16
Adjusted ROCE	0.23	0.23	0.20	0.18	0.17
Growth rate	0.11	0.16	0.29	0.11	0.19

The weighted average cost of capital is estimated as 7.82%.

FCFF valuation model

Two stage valuation model is used for valuing Google. It is assumed that Google will grow at 17% for the next 10 years and then at the stable growth rate of the US economy forever.

High growth period inputs.

High growth period = 10 years.

Growth rate = 17%.

Reinvestment rate = 82%.

WACC = 7.82%.

EBIT$(1 - T)$ in year 2014 = \$13,165 million.

EBIT$(1 - T)$ in year 2015 (start of high growth period) = $13,165 \times 1.17 = \$15,403$ million.

Value of Google in the high growth phase = \$38,174 million (Table 7.24).

Stable phase inputs

The growth rate in the stable phase is assumed to be the growth rate of the US economy (Table 7.25).

Growth rate in stable period = Reinvestment rate $\times$ Return on capital employed of technology sector.

Return on invested capital in technology industry is taken as 13.79%.[5]

2.15% = Reinvestment rate $\times$ Return on invested capital

2.15% = Reinvestment rate $\times$ 13.79%

Reinvestment rate = 2.15/13.79 = 15.6%

The reinvestment rate in the stable period is assumed to be 15.6%.

EBIT$(1 - T)$ at the end of high growth period = \$63,281.90 million

Growth rate in stable period = 2.15%

EBIT$(1 - T)$ in stable period = $119,668.33 \times 1.0215 = \$64,642.46$ million

Reinvestment rate = 15.6%

Reinvestment = \$10,084.22 million

FCFF in stable period = \$54,558.23

Terminal value of FCFF in stable period = FCFF in stable period/(WACC − growth rate)
= 54,558.23/(7.86%−2.15%) = \$962,226.28 million

Present value of terminal value of FCFF in stable period = \$453,193.78 million.

Value of operating assets of Google = Present value of operating assets in high growth phase + Present value of operating assets in stable phase.
= \$38,174 + \$453,193.78 = \$491,367.44 million

Value of operating assets of Google = \$491,367.44
   Add cash and equivalents in 2014 = 64,395
Value of Google in 2014 = \$555,762.44
Less debt of Google in 2014 = 5237
Less lease commitments = 6183
Value of equity = \$544,342.4 billion
Value per share = \$792.3

The value of equity of Google is estimated as \$544.342 billion dollars as on the year 2014. The number of shares of Google in 2014 is 687 million. Hence the value per share = \$792.3. Google was trading at \$530.66 on December 31, 2014. The market capitalization on this date was \$364.56 billion dollars. Based on FCFF Valuation it can be stated that Google was undervalued in the stock market as the estimated value provided by the valuation was higher than the market capitalization prevailing in 2014. The market capitalization of Google on June 15, 2015, was \$365.63 billion.

[5] http://csimarket.com/Industry/industry_ManagementEffectiveness.php?s=1000&hist=1.

Table 7.24 Present value of FCFF in high growth period

Period	1	2	3	4	5	6	7	8	9	10
EBIT(1−T)	15,403	18,022	21,085	24,670	28,864	33,770	39,511	46,228	54,087	63,282
Reinvestment	12,631	14,778	17,290	20,229	23,668	27,692	32,399	37,907	44,351	51,891
FCFF	2773	3244	3795	4441	5195	6079	7112	8321	9736	11,391
PV of FCFF	2571	2790	3028	3286	3566	3869	4199	4556	4944	5365
Sum of PV	38,174									

Table 7.25 Estimation of growth rate in stable period

Year	Annual GDP growth rate
2010	2.5
2011	1.6
2012	2.3
2013	2.2
Average	2.15

Source: http://data.worldbank.org/indicator/NY.GDP.MKTP.KD.ZG.

Table 7.26 Price multiples trends

Year	2010	2011	2012	2013	2014
P/E	22.6	22	21.2	31.2	28.2
P/B	4.1	3.8	3.3	4.5	3.7
P/S	6.5	5.9	4.5	6.4	5.4
P/CF	17.3	14.9	13.7	20.3	17.1

7.13 Relative valuation

The relative values used for comparison are price multiples like Price to Earnings ratio (P/E), Price to Book ratio(P/B), Price to Sales (P/S), Price to Cash Flow (P/CF), and enterprise value multiples. The peer companies used for comparison are Facebook, Tencent Holdings Ltd., Baidu Inc., and Naspers Ltd. The source of data is Morningstar.com.

The price earnings ratio has been fluctuating over the period of 5 years. The P/E ratio, P/B, and P/CF ratio had peaked in the year 2013. The P/E ratio had improved from 22.6 in year 2010 to 28.2 in year 2014. The P/S ratio declined from 6.5 in year 2010 to 5.4 in year 2014. The price to cash flow declined from 17.3 in year 2010 to 17.1 in year 2014 (Table 7.26).

In the latest financial year 2015, Google had the highest market capitalization. Tencent Holdings Ltd. had the highest net income and P/B ratio among the peer companies. Facebook had the highest P/S ratio and P/E ratio among the peer companies (Table 7.27).

Enterprise value multiple

The EV multiples analyzed are EV/revenues, EV/EBITDA, and EV/EBIT.

Enterprise value is obtained as the sum of market capitalization and debt minus total cash (Table 7.28).

The values of Baidu Inc. and Tencent Holdings are in millions of CNY.

The EV/revenues multiple suggest that Baidu and Naspers Ltd. are the most undervalued companies among the peer group. Baidu Inc. and Tencent Holding are the most undervalued firms in terms of EV/EBITDA and EV/EBIT (Table 7.29).

The detailed calculation and data of each section is given in the excel file *Google.xlsx*.

Table 7.27 Current peer comparison

Company	Market capitalization	Net income	P/S	P/B	P/E
Google	371,057	14,578	5.5	3.4	27
Facebook	226,652	2810	16.3	6	78.7
Tencent Holding Ltd.	187,788	24,386	13.9	13.3	47.6
Baidu Inc.	72,258	13,101	8.6	8.7	34.5
Naspers Ltd.	61,318	11,576	11	9.8	65.4

The values of market capitalization and net income are given in millions of dollars.

Table 7.28 EV and revenue variables

Company	Google	Facebook	Tencent Holding	Baidu Inc.	Naspers Ltd.
Market capitalization	371,057	226,652	187,788	72,258	61,318
Debt	5237	0	35,584	25,767	30,915
Cash and cash equivalent	64,395	11,199	53,511	57,671	13,873
Enterprise value	311,899	215,453	169,861	40,354	78,360
Revenues	66,001	12,466	78,932	49,052	62,728
EBITDA	22,339	6176	34,697	19,075	14,730
EBIT	16,496	4994	25,656	12,804	2018

Data Source: Morningstar.com.

Table 7.29 Enterprise value multiples in year 2014

EV multiples	Google	Facebook	Tencent Holding	Baidu Inc.	Naspers Ltd.
EV/revenues	4.73	17.28	2.15	0.82	1.25
EV/EBITDA	13.96	34.89	4.90	2.12	5.32
EV/EBIT	18.91	43.14	6.62	3.15	38.83

Further reading

[1] www.google.com.
[2] Annual Reports Google.
[3] http://www.businessinsider.com/important-google-acquisitions-2014-8.
[4] www.morningstar.com.

Wealth analysis of General Electric

8

8.1 Introduction

General Electric (GE) company is one of the world's largest digital industrial companies with focus on software defined machines and solutions. GE is one of the world's best infrastructure and technology company with secondary focus on financial services division. GE is a global digital industrial company with presence in approximately 180 countries. The products and services offered by GE range from aircraft engines, power generation, oil and gas production equipment to medical imaging, financing and industrial products.

The origin of GE can be traced to Thomas A. Edison who had established the Edison electric light company in year 1878. GE was established in 1892 as a result of the merger of Edison General Electric Company and Thomson Houston Electric Company. GE is the only company which is listed in the Dow Jones Industrial Index today which was in the original index of 12 in the year 1896. GE is headquartered in Fairfield CT. GE have global locations in 170 countries. GE has approximately 307,000 employees. GE is listed on the New York Stock Exchange, London Stock Exchange, Euronext Paris and the Frankfurt Stock Exchange. GE was ranked as ninth among the Fortune's World's most admired companies in year 2015. GE was also ranked as the seventh world's most valuable brand in year 2014. GE was ranked #1 in the world on the 2014 Aon Hewitt top companies for leaders list.

GE has 10 research centers, 3000 plus engineers PhDs and scientists. About 3100 patents were filed in year 2015. GE has more than 300,000 employees. Approximately 125,000 people were employed in United States. In 2015, GE had orders worth more than one billion from 20 countries. GE also had $67 billion non US infrastructure orders in the latest financial year. Manufacturing operations are carried out at approximately 206 manufacturing plants located in 40 states in the United States and Puerto Rico. There are approximately 295 manufacturing plants located in 39 other countries. The total revenues amounted to $113.2 billion, $117.2 billion, and 117.4 billion in the year 2013, 2014, and 2015, respectively.

In 2015, GE made 18 deals worth over $140 billion. In 2015, GE finalized a landmark power contract with the Saudi electric company which was valued nearly one billion. In 2015, GE also had the largest ever deal in India for 1000 diesel locomotives to upgrade the 162-year-old Indian rail network. In 2015, GE had a mega deal for more than 2.6 GW of power in Egypt and more than $35 billion of deals at Paris and Dubai Airshow. Table 8.1 lists the major milestones achieved by GE.

Table 8.1 **Milestones of GE**

Year	Events
1878	Thomson Edison forms the Edison Electric Light Company
1879	Edison invents the carbon filament incandescent lamp; Edison and team develops dynamos of powering wide lighting systems.
1880	The first commercial installation of incandescent lights completed by Edison on the steamship "S S Columbia"
1882	Edison starts GE's power generation businesses; The world's first hydroelectric plant is operated using Edison bipolar generator
1888	Thomson Houston installs the first industrial electrical locomotive
1891	Edison invents the motion picture camera
1892	GE founded as the result of merger of Edison General Electric and Thomson Houston Electric Company. Machine molded incandescent bulbs replace the old hand blown type
1896	GE becomes the component of the Dow Jones Industrial Average. GE's Elihu Thomson build electric equipment for production of X-ray
1900	GE establishes the first lab in United States; GE monogram registered as a trademark
1902	GE gets patent for electric fan
1903	The largest steam turbine developed
1905	GE organizes The Electric Bond and Share Co to provide finance to small utilities. First electric toaster is introduced
1910	The Hotpoint the first electric range is manufactured
1913	Charles A Coffin becomes the first Chairman of GE. The first GE locomotive powered by an internal combustion engine is produced. GE produces the hot cathode high vacuum X-ray tube
1914	Electrical installation of Panama Canal done by GE
1915	GE launches a new slogan "Largest Electric Manufacturer" in world
1917	GE introduces the first hermetically sealed home refrigerators
1918	GE builds record capacity water wheel generator for Niagara Falls
1921	New world altitude of 40,800 feet set by a plane equipped with a GE supercharger
1922	GE hires advertising agency BBDO. In 94 years' time, GE and BBDO represents one of the longest standing client agency relationships in advertising history GE radio station WGY begins broadcast with its 1500 watt transmitter
1924	A portable electrocardiogram is developed
1927	GE brings TV into homes for the first time with a signal from GE's WGY in Schenectady
1930	The company develops moldable plastic and forms a new plastic division; Empire State Building is built with GE safety switchesThe company introduces the first electric cloth washer
1932	GE scientist, Irving Langmuir becomes the first US Industrial scientist to win Nobel Prize in surface chemistry. GE Credit Corporation is created to provide finance for purchase of GE appliances
1935	The first household electric food waste disposer
1938	GE invents the fluorescent lamp

(Continued)

Table 8.1 (Continued)

Year	Events
1939	Katherine Blodgett invents nonreflecting invisible glass which becomes the prototype for coatings on all camera lenses and optical devices
1941	GE builds the first US jet engine. A new mobile X-ray unit is developed for medical use
1943	GE engineer develop automatic pilot
1945	The first American turboprop engine GE-T31 is developed to power an aircraft
1947	GE unveils the first two door refrigerator freezer combination
1949	GE introduces the J 47 the most produced jet engine in history
1950	GE scientist, Arnold Spielberg designed the GE-225 mainframe computer which could develop basic programming language
1952	GE builds the world's largest circuit breakers
1953	GE publishes a series of "5 Blue Books" which outline GE's approach to management and decision making
1959	GE invents halogen lamp
1962	GE engineer, Nick creates the first visible LED. GE develops superconducting magnet which laid foundation of magnetic resonance imaging (MRI)
1963	The first electric drive system for off highway vehicles developed by GE
1971	GE introduces the first portable room air conditioner the Carry Cool
1973	GE's Dr. Ivar Giaever receives 1973 Nobel Prize for Physics for his discovery for superconductive tunneling
1974	GE introduces the first energy saving fluorescent bulb
1978	GE develops the prototype of electric car. GE becomes the first organization in world to be assigned the 50,000th US patent. GE develops a computed tomography scanner
1983	GE invents the SIGNA MRI system
1992	GE builds the Mars observer for NASA
1994	GE Plastics launches the first website and GE becomes the first company outside the computer industry to go online
1996	GE's corporate website www.ge.com is launched
1997	GE Capital generates approximately $33 billion in revenue and becomes largest equipment lessor
1998	GE introduced the new LightSpeed which enables doctors to capture multiple images at a speed which is six times faster than conventional single slice scanners
1999	GE introduces the first full field digital mammography for scanning cancer
2000	The company introduces the first diagnostic agent for objective identification of Parkinson disease. GE introduces the Innova 2000, the world's all digital X-ray cardiovascular imaging system
2002	GE enters wind business GE introduces the world's first 4D ultrasound system
2003	GE introduces the H system, the world's most advanced combined cycle system GE introduces GE profile ovens with Trivection technology
2004	Introduces the Ultra scan duo, GE launches development of GEnx to power the Boeing Company's new 787 Dreamliner aircraft
2004	GE introduces Vivid 1 a miniaturized cardiovascular ultrasound system
2005	GE becomes a worldwide Olympic partner; GE launches ecomagination
2006	GE introduces the world's first true 64 slice combination PET/CT medical imaging system

(Continued)

Table 8.1 (**Continued**)

Year	Events
2008	GE introduces LED general lighting for lamps and outdoor systems.GE and Vanderbilt University developed advanced cancer mapping technology. Introduces the world's first high definition CT scanner
2009	The firm invests $1 billion investment in American manufacturing.
2010	GE introduces energy smart LED bulb
2012	Introduces Durathon batteries
2013	Revolution CT is introduced
2014	GE completed the $2.9 billion IPO of GE money the US consumer finance business as synchrony financial
2015	GE power generation equipment creates a quarter of the world's electricity every day. Every two seconds, an aircraft powered with GE engine technology takes off. GE technologies help doctors save every year 3000 lives. GE introduces global strategic repositioning of GE Capital and sale of nonindustrial vertical platforms. GE Café introduces the first refrigerator with a Keurig Brewing system
2016	GE relocates headquarters to Boston

Source: http://www.ge.com/transformation.

8.2 Segment operations

8.2.1 Power

Major products of GE power division are power generation services, gas turbines, engines and generators, steam turbines and generators, nuclear reactors and water systems. The digital solutions offered by GE power are PowerOn Advantage, Operations Optimization and Asset Performance Management. In 2015, this segment contributed 20% of industrial segment revenues.

8.2.2 Renewable energy

The renewable energy major products are onshore and offshore wind turbines, hydropower plants, solar power plants, geothermal power plants, biomass power plants. The digital solutions are wind PowerUp, Wind Farm Wake Management, water and process insight. This new segment was created from the formerly power and water segment. This segment included the wind and hydro businesses acquired from Alstom.

8.2.3 Oil and gas segment

Oil and gas serves all segments of the oil and gas industry, from drilling, completion, production and oil field operations, to transportation via liquefied natural gas (LNG) and pipelines. The major products of the oil and gas division are surface and subsea drilling and production systems, floating production platform equipment, mechanical drives and compressors, high-pressure reactors, artificial lift solutions, sensing and inspection solutions. The digital solutions are Subsea systems optimization, intelligent pipeline solution, reliability max, field Vantage.

8.2.4 Energy management

The energy management sector provides industrial solutions, grid solutions, and power conversions.

The major products offered by this operational segment are electrical distribution and control, products and services, lighting and power panels, grid management products and grid modernization services, industrial automation and software solutions, advanced motor, drive and control technologies. The digital solutions offered are Grid IQ, Proficy Monitoring & Analysis and, SmallWorld.GE and Alstom joint venture, equips 90% of power utilities worldwide for power generation.

8.2.5 Aviation

Aviation segment designs and produces commercial and military aircraft engines, integrated digital components, electric power, and mechanical aircraft systems. The major products offered by aviation segment are jet and turboprop engines, components and integrated systems for commercial, military, business and general aviation aircraft and ship propulsion applications, global service network. The digital solutions include Flight Efficiency Services, Fuel Management, and Fleet Management.

8.2.6 Healthcare

Healthcare provides essential healthcare technologies and has expertise in medical imaging, software and information technology (IT), patient monitoring and diagnostics, drug discovery, biopharmaceutical manufacturing technologies, and performance improvement solutions. Products and services are sold globally to hospitals, medical facilities, pharmaceutical and biotechnology companies, and to the life science research market.

The major products offered include diagnostic imaging systems (MRI, CT, nuclear and molecular imaging, digital mammography), surgical imaging products, ultrasound, pharmaceutical research and production tools. The digital solutions offered are Centricity, Dose Management, Workforce Optimization, Asset Optimization, Health Cloud.

8.2.7 Transportation

The major products offered by this segment include locomotives, diesel engines, drilling motors, mining equipment and propulsion systems, motorized drive systems, software and analytics solutions to optimize rail and mining operations.

The digital solutions offered include Trip Optimizer, Locotrol Distributed Power, GoLINC, Railconnect, ShipperConnect, Movement Planner, Yard Planner, Smart Intermodal and Automotive Terminal, Customer Performance Analytics. Transportation segment's signaling business was sold off to Alstom. In 2015, a total of 756 Tier 4 compliant locomotives were shipped.

8.2.8 Appliances and lighting

The major products offered are major home appliances and lighting products and services which includes industrial scale lighting solutions. The major home appliances include refrigerators, freezers, electric and gas ranges, cooktops, dishwaters, dryers, microwave oven, room air conditioners, residential water system for filtration. GE sells a variety of energy efficient solutions for commercial, industrial, municipal and consumer applications using light emitting diode (LED), Fluorescent, halogen and high intensity discharge technologies. The digital solutions are intelligent cities and intelligent enterprises.

8.2.9 Capital

The capital segment provides industry focused financial services verticals like GE Aviation Services, Energy Financial Services and Industrial Finance which includes healthcare equipment finance. The financial services segment, previously referred to as GE Capital, is now called Capital.

8.3 Strategy[1]

GE has technical leadership and scale with growth market capabilities. Over the last decade GE's strategy had been on transforming the portfolio to focus on industrial leadership. In 2001, the portfolio consisted of 40% industrials, 40% on capital and insurance and 20% on appliances, NBC and plastics. By 2014, the portfolio consisted of 60% industrial and 40% capital. As a part of corporate restructuring, GE acquired Enron Wind Assets, Betz Dearborn in the year 2002. GE also acquired Amersham in year 2004. In 2013 GE acquired Lufkin and Avio. GE disposed of insurance, plastics in 2005 and NBCU in the year 2007. GE focuses on innovation strategy through investments in Research and Development. GE has a workforce of approximately 36000 technicians working in various business and global research centers. During the period 2005−14, the company had made investments worth $15 billion in Research and Development. GE Capital focuses on divestitures with plans to sell assets valued $200 billion by the end of year 2017. In 2015, GE launched GE Digital which was aimed to transform GE into the world's largest digital industrial company. In the same year GE sold off capital assets of GE

[1] http://www.ge.com/sites/default/files/Strategy_Page_121714.pdf.

Capital worth $200 billion. As a part of transforming its portfolio, GE exited most of its financial services by the year 2015. GE Capital have closed transactions valued at more than $100 billion and signed transactions which were valued at $154 billion. The company has successfully completed the $20.4 billion public offering of Synchrony Financial. The deal allowed GE to give approximately $90 billion as dividends and buybacks to shareholders. Recently GE undertook a major restructuring to create a unified digital business within the company called GE Digital.

GE has a well-connected multibusiness portfolio as competitive advantage. The diversity in business provides strength through disruptive events and commodity cycles. Capital verticals are connected to the industrials by means of financing infrastructure through energy financial services, GE Capital aviation services and industrial finance which includes healthcare finance. GE focuses on crowdsourcing innovation both internally and externally to improve customer value.

In response to 2001, 9/11 attacks, GE invested in next generation aircraft engines like GE90, GEnx, next gen CFM. In 2004, in response to US gas turbine cycle bottom, GE diversified into energy businesses. During the 2009 financial crisis, GE supported GE Capital with capital infusions. During the 2015 oil price drop crisis, GE restructured the oil and gas businesses and acquired Alstom. In a restructuring move, the distributed power business which provides turbines for oil and gas applications were realigned from the power segment to the oil and gas segment. GE focuses on digital innovation and solutions to increase revenues and reduce costs and risk in the onshore wind business. GE expanded its renewable energy portfolio through acquisition of Alstom's renewable business. The reduction in fuel costs is expected to increase airline profitability and improve the aviation segment's businesses. Healthcare segment focuses on life science business through bioprocess market growth and enterprise solutions.

8.4   GE Capital exit plan

On April 10, 2015, GE announced restructuring of GE Capital by announcing the GE Exit Plan. The plan was aimed to create more value for the company by reducing the size of its financial services businesses through the sale of the assets of GE Capital. The restructuring strategy of GE was to focus on retaining financial assets which support the verticals (industrial businesses). GE Capital is expected to release $35 billion in dividends and buybacks to the shareholders. By 2015, GE had signed agreements with buyers for $157 billion of ending net investment (ENI) which excludes liquidity of which $104 billion had been closed. In year 2015, GE completed the split off of the retail finance business (the American credit card business) to holders of GE common stock. This restructuring resulted in a $20.4 billion buyback of GE Common stock in year 2015. Along with cash dividends of $4.3 billion, GE Capital returned approximately $25 billion to shareholders in year 2015. The restructuring resulted in the merger of GE Capital into GE. The other highlights of the restructuring were the

guarantee by GE of GE Capital debt and exchange of $36 billion of GE Capital debt
for new GE notes. The restructuring exercise was aimed to convert GE portfolio into
more of a pure industrial company and move away from its financial business.
The motivation to divest the financial business could be due to regulatory factors.
GE along with GE Capital was a unique business of being a large industrial as
well as financial services company. By 2014, GE Capital's net investment was over
$360 billion and controlled assets worth $500 billion. As a result, GE Capital became
the seventh largest bank in United States and was viewed as a systemically important
financial institution by federal regulators. Hence GE was subject to tougher regulatory standards. During economic recession, GE Capital also received bailout package.
In the aftermath of recession, value of GE shares decreased as investors perceived
GE Capital to be risky and volatile. GE was forced to slash down its dividends for
the first time since 1938 which was not well received by shareholders. GE expects
that the divestiture of majority GE Capital would create more value for investors
and shareholders and achieve greater margins. The shrinking of earnings might
occur with the sale of GE Capital assets. For example, in year 2014, the real estate
business under GE Capital had generated earnings of $1 billion. The majority of
GE Capital's real estate debt and equity portfolio were sold off to funds managed
by the Blackstone Group which in turn sold of a part of this portfolio to Wells &
Fargo.

With the completion of GE Capital exit plan, GE aims to derive 90% of its
operating income from its industrial businesses. GE had announced a $50 billion
share buyback of common stock. GE expects to return more than $90 billion to
investors through dividends, buybacks and the synchrony spin off until 2018.[2]

8.5   Financial restructuring and exchange offers[3]

As part of the GE Capital Exit Plan, on September 21 2015, GE Capital
commenced private offers to exchange (the exchange offers) up to $30 billion of
certain outstanding debt for new notes with maturities of six months, five years,
10 years or 20 years. The offerings were increased by $6 billion with the aggregate
principal amount of $36 billion (representing $31 billion of outstanding
principal and $5 billion of premium) of outstanding notes being tendered for exchange
and settled on October 26 2015. The new notes that were issued at closing are
composed of $15.3 billion of 0.964% six month notes due April 2016, £0.8 billion of
1.363% six month notes due April 2016, $6.1 billion of 2.342% notes due 2020,
$2.0 billion of 3.373% notes due 2025 and $11.5 billion of 4.418% notes due
2035. Immediately prior to the reorganization, GE Capital had $5.0 billion in

[2] http://www.forbes.com/sites/greatspeculations/2015/06/02/understanding-ge-capitals-exit-plan/
#7ebf001f28cb.
[3] http://www.ge.com/ar2015/assets/pdf/GE_2015_Form_10K.pdf.

aggregate liquidation preference of series A, B, and C preferred stock outstanding. The holders who previously held GE Capital preferred stock were issued an aggregate liquidation preference of $5.9 billion of new GE series A, B, and C preferred stock. GE launched an exchange offer on December 18 2015 that allowed GE preferred stock investors to exchange their existing series A, B, and C preferred stock into a series D GE preferred stock. In August 2014, GE completed the initial public offering (IPO) of North American Retail Finance business. The net proceeds from IPO and underwriter options amounted to $2.8 billion and retained 84.6% of synchrony financial. In 2015, GE completed the split off of synchrony financial through which the company accepted 671,366,809 shares of GE common stock from its shareholders in exchange for 705,270,833 shares of synchrony.

8.6 Competitive challenges

GE is one of the leading firms in most of the major industries in which they operate. GE Capital faces competition from various types of financial institutions like banks, investment banks, leasing companies, finance companies associated with manufacturers and insurance, and reinsurance companies. GE faces challenges due to global economic factors, instability in certain regions, commodity prices, and foreign currency volatility. The long life cycle of product development and R&D expenditures are other major factors which are critical. In the power segment, GE faces challenges due to excess capacity in developed markets, pressure in oil and gas applications and macroeconomic and geopolitical environments result in greater uncertainty in this industry sector. Digitization of renewable energy is a critical factor for renewal energy which has become the mainstream option on an unsubsidized basis in many regions. The wind business of GE is subject to global policies and regulation which includes the US Production Tax Credit and incentive structures in China and various European countries. Renewable energy capacity additions account for approximately half of the power plant additions throughout the world. Oil and gas segment is sensitive to economic and political environment of each country in which business is conducted and are subject to regulation by US and non US energy policies. Lower prices of oil lead to lesser capital expenditures by oil companies which would affect GE businesses. Energy management segment faces competition from businesses with energy domain expertise. The challenges faced by products in energy management segment are subject to a number of regulatory specifications and energy industry standards. Energy management faces challenges as the US electrical grid load growth is expected to slow down in near future. Research and development expenditures are critical for aviation business. The health care segment products are subject to regulations by numerous government agencies like US Food and Drug Administration. Cost control and productivity are key challenges faced by appliances and lighting segment globally.

8.7 GE's ecomagination strategy[4]

Eco imagination is GE's growth strategy aimed to enhance resource productivity and reduce environmental impact at a global scale. GE focuses on investing in cleaner technology and business innovation and develops solution to enable growth. During the last decade the investments in clean R&D initiatives increased from $700 million to a cumulative $15 billion investments in R&D. These investments have yielded approximately $200 in revenues from Eco imagination solutions for sectors like power generation, energy management, water, transportation, and healthcare industries. Through sustainable practices, GE has cut GHG emissions by 32%, energy intensity by 31% and fresh water consumption by 45% thereby saving the company $350 million.

GE has recycled 5.5 million pounds of refrigerator material since the year 2009 as a part of the EPA's Responsible Appliance Disposal Program. During the period 2005−14, GE has reduced GHG emissions by 31% and decreased fresh water use by 42% for its operations.GE has installed 40 GW Clean energy initiatives during the last decade. GE has treated one billion gallons of waste water per day.

The eco imagination products and solutions include predix, solid oxide fuel cell, digital wind farms, CFM leap engines, 9HA turbines, Tier 4 locomotive engine. In 2015, GE invested $2.3 billion in cleaner technology R&D and generated $36 billion in revenues from Ecomagination technologies and solutions. In GE, more than 50,000 technologists work to develop solutions to transform millions of lives. The 2020 goals of GE Ecoimagination includes 20% reduction in GE's GHG emissions and reduction in water use from the 2011 baseline and $25 billion investment in cleaner technology and R&D.

In 2015, GE announced the formation of ecomagination 2020 partnerships to solve global resource challenges with industry leaders like Walmart, Total, Intel, Goldman Sachs, MWH Global, BHP Billiton, Masdar, and Statoil. GE ecoimagination and Aramco entrepreneurship have joint initiatives to develop solutions to improve the energy efficiency of sea water desalination. GE ecoimagination have plans to invest CAD $1 million in programs aimed at technology development for Canada's oil sands in order to reduce GHG emissions in oil sands. GE Oil & Gas and Statoil have a joint collaboration to develop low cost reduced carbon solutions for oil and gas operations. In 2014, GE Ventures and Ferus Natural Gas Fuels introduced a system called "Last Mile" to capture the natural gas released from being flared at oil wells for compression and use it as a fuel for powering oil field equipment.

In last one decade, ecomagination initiatives have saved approximately 41 billion gallons of diesel which resulted in fuel savings of $98 million. The GE wind fleet had generated 549 twh of energy during the last decade. Approximately 391 million tons of carbon dioxide emissions were avoided during the period. GE focuses on digital resource productivity by the integration of efficient hardware with internet enabled software. In this context, GE introduced the Powerup as a part of

---

[4] http://www.ge.com/about-us/ecomagination.

ecomagination's brilliant wind turbine platform to harness the industrial internet to drive higher output for wind farms. The RailEdge movement planner software solution of GE facilitate faster and efficient freight movements on existing rail lines. GE's internet enabled aviation navigation service provides more efficient design of flight patterns. The new products like Tier 4 locomotives decreases emissions by approximately 70% or more from Tier 3 technology and saved an estimated $1.5 billion in infrastructure costs. GE's HA-turbine is the largest and most fuel efficient gas turbine in the world. The LEAP jet engine is targeted for a 15% improvement in fuel efficiency in comparison to its predecessor along with double digit improvements in noise and emissions. In 2014, GE ventures introduced innovative portfolios like sungevity and stem. Sungevity provides homeowners with an instant installation quote and snapshot which demonstrates how much homeowners could save on their electricity bills using proprietary remote solar design technology. The product stem is a developer of cloud based energy solution which leverages real time data in the framework of cloud based predictive analytics.

8.8   GE's acquisition strategy

During the period 1981–2011, GE company has made 791 acquisitions while taking stakes in 261 companies. GE company had 620 divestitures during this period. In the year 1997, GE made the maximum acquisition of 58 companies. In 1986, GE purchased Radio Corporation of America (RCA), primarily for the NBC television network. Again in 1986, GE acquired Kidder, Peabody & Co. a United States based securities firm which after heavy losses was sold to Paine Webber in 1994. In 2002, GE bought the wind turbine manufacturing assets of Enron Wind after the Enron scandal. In 2004, GE bought 80% of universal pictures from Vivendi. In 2007, GE acquired Smiths Aerospace for $4.8 billion. The acquisition broadened GE's offerings for aviation customers by adding Smiths innovative flight management systems, electrical power management, mechanical actuation systems and airborne platform computing systems to GE Aviation's growing commercial and military aircraft engines and services. The Smith's Aerospace business has a significant presence on most commercial aircraft, including the Boeing 737 and Airbus A320, as well as many military aircraft. In 2010, GE had bought a $1.6 billion portfolio of retail credit cards from Citigroup. In 2010, GE announced acquisition of data migration and SCADA simulation specialists opal Software. In 2011, GE had made big ticket deals like the $3 billion acquisition of Dresser, the global energy infrastructure technology and service provider; $3.2 billion buyout of Converteam that specializes in energy from wind turbines and buyout of John Wood Group Plc for about $2.8 billion. GE plans to expand Dresser's presence in emerging markets such as Latin America and the Middle East, where the company has limited exposure, but where growth prospects are significant.

GE Capital's acquisition were basically portfolio purchases that add volume to businesses, consolidation of acquisitions that add an acquired business into an

Table 8.2 **Restructuring history**

Year	Events
1890	Edison Electric Light Co., Edison Lamp Co., Edison Machine Works, Bergmann Co. merge as Edison Electric Company
1892	GE founded as the result of merger of Edison General Electric and Thomson Houston Electric Company
1911	GE's light division absorbs National Electric Lamp Association (NELA)
1919	GE enters into negotiation to buy American Marconi company and incorporate Radio Corporation of America (RCA)
1920	GE acquires Victor Electric Co. and forms General Electric X-ray corporation
1974	CFM International a 50/50 joint company with Snecma of France is formed to produce CFM56 engine
1980	GE acquires Intersil, Calma and four software producers
1986	GE acquires Kidder, Peabody & Co. GE reacquires RCA primarily for NBC television network
1987	GE sells RCA television manufacturing businesses to French Company Thomson in exchange for Thomson's medical diagnostic businesses
1994	GE acquires Italian state owned energy conglomerate Nuovo Pignone and enters oil service businesses. GE sells Kidder, Peabody & Co. and PaineWebber
2001	Company acquires Heller Financial which provided commercial, financial, equipment, leasing, and real estate finance to small and medium sized companies
2002	GE acquirers Jenbacher AG expanding into gas engines and cogeneration.GE enters wind business through acquisition of Enron's wind assets. GE acquires Bently Nevada
2003	GE acquires Amersham Health Plc which enabled GE to enter the market for radiopharmaceuticals and contrast media agents
2004	GE spins off insurance business as Genworth Financial with the largest IPO of year 2004. GE acquires 80% of Universal Pictures from Vivendi
2005	Acquires Lonics to expand business into desalination of seawater and waste water treatment. World's first high definition magnetic resonance system is introduced
2007	GE Oil and Gas acquires Vetco Gray to expand operations in drilling, completion and production equipment for oil and gas fields. GE Aviation acquires Smiths Aerospace to add portfolio of flight management system and airborne platform computing systems
2008	GE acquires Well stream to expand deep water oil and gas exploration business. The company enters life sciences business by acquiring Whatman Plc. GE begins strategic exit of consumer finance business by selling Japanese platform to Shinsei bank
2011	GE Oil and Gas acquires Dresser Waukesha expanding GE portfolio of natural gas engines and fueling systems. GE acquires RMI to form Optimization Solution
2012	GE acquires ALBEO thereby strengthening GE's LED offerings. GE acquires Avio Aero to enhance GE's capabilities in mechanical transmission systems, low pressure turbines, and automation systems

(Continued)

Table 8.2 (**Continued**)

Year	Events
2013	Acquires Lufkin Industries for $3.3 billion which was a leading provider of artificial lift technologies for oil and gas industry and manufacturer of gears. GE Commercial Aviation Services acquires Avia solutions, the consultancy firm which focuses on active investment and development of regional airports and terminals. GE exits media business and sold remaining shares of NBC Universal to Comcast
2014	GE acquires Milestone Aviation. The acquisition provided GE access to market for approximately 2000 helicopter ferrying workers and supplies to offshore oil and gas platforms. Acquired Cameron reciprocating compression division for $0.6 billion
2015	The acquisition of Alstom became the biggest industrial investment in GE history. Completed the acquisition of Advantec group for $0.1 billion. The group provides subsea intervention equipment and services to the oil and gas industry

Source: http://www.ge.com/transformation.

existing GE Capital business, platform or strategic business where the acquisition operates in a sector that is new to the GE Capital and hybrid purchases where parts of the acquisitions fit into one or several GE Capital businesses (see Table 8.2). GE Capital services' acquisition integration process has been codified as the Path Finder Model. The major components of the Path Finder Model are preacquisition, foundation building, rapid integration and assimilation phase. In the preacquisition phase, the emphasis is on cultural issues. In the foundation phase the emphasis is on development of the integration plan by GE and the target company. The rapid integration stage involves the continual assessment of progress and adjustment of the integration plan. The post implementation phase of assimilation involves the assessment and evaluation of the long-term business plan.[5]

In 2002, GE acquired Bently Nevada which market equipment to monitor the condition of rotating equipment in machinery intensive industries. In 2015 GE sold of Clarient, one of its life science business.

8.9   Alstom acquisition

The acquisition of Alstom's energy and grid business was the largest industrial acquisition in the corporate history of GE. The acquisition provided the opportunity to connect GE's digital services to Alstom's global industrial footprint. The acquisition included Alstom's huge Haliade offshore wind turbines. On November 2 2015, GE closed its acquisition of Alstom's Thermal, Renewables & Grid businesses for

---

[5] N.A. Ronald, J. Lawrence, C. Suzzane, Making the deal real: how GE Capital integrates acquisitions. Harv. Bus. Rev. January–February 1998.

approximately $10.1 billion. The acquisition was complementary in technology, operations and geography to GE's businesses. The acquisition was aimed to yield efficiencies in supply chain, service infrastructure, new product development, and SG&A costs. The signaling business was sold to Alstom for approximately $0.8 billion. GE first offered to buy Alstom for about $13.5 billion. Finally, the value of the transaction fell to $10.1 billion on account of joint energy ventures, changes in the deal structure, price adjustments for the remedies, and net cash at close. In order to win clearance from the European Union, GE sold off some of the Alstom assets. Alstom Power and GE Power and Water combined to form GE Power. GE expects that the deal would be able to generate approximately 15−20 cents of EPS by the year 2018. GE expects target cost savings of $3 billion within five-year period due to this deal.[6]

8.10 Governance

The board of directors at GE have eight scheduled meetings a year in which the company reviews and discusses the performance of the company, its future plans and prospects. All director nominees other than CEO are independent. In 2015, all director nominees attended at least 75% of the meetings of the board. The retirement age is 75. Annual director elections are held at GE with majority voting standards. GE conducts annual board review of investor feedbacks. Periodic independent director meetings are held with investors. GE have 16 directors of which 15 are independent.

Capital allocation is a major responsibility of the board. GE Board implemented a new policy of proxy access at 3% for 3 years. GE also recently adopted a 15-year director term limit policy to achieve a balanced mix of director ages and tenures. The major committees are Audit, Governance and Public affairs, Management Development and Compensation, GE Capital, Technology and Industrial Risk. The recent focus areas of the Audit Committee are accounting, controls and disclosure of GE Exit Plan and new revenue recognition standard. The governance and public affairs focus areas are board refreshment and recruitment of directors. The management development and compensation committee oversees succession planning, CEO and senior executive performance evaluations and compensation. The new focus areas of the committee are new annual cash incentive programs, implementation of new long-term equity incentive program for senior executives and impact of GE Capital exit plan on compensation. The capital committee approve the company's and GE Capital's capital and liquidity framework, including GE Capital's annual capital, recovery and resolution plans, liquidity policy and contingency funding plan, regulatory capital and stress testing policies and ratios and internal capital adequacy assessment processes. The new focus areas of this committee are the risk oversight of execution of GE Capital exit plan, GE Capital reorganization, capital planning and liquidity.

[6] http://www.wsj.com/articles/ge-completes-alstom-power-acquisition-1446477255.

The technology and industrial risk committee focuses on technology, software and innovation strategies and R&D initiatives. The committee focuses on R&D funding, GE Digital and product management. The GE Board held 13 meetings in year 2015. Independent directors are encouraged to contact senior managers of the company without senior corporate management present.

GE provides a robust disclosure of its political and lobbying activities. GE provides equal opportunity employment and employs diverse workforce globally. GE provides no individual severance or change of control agreements or gross ups on excise taxes. GE does not allow hedging or pledging of GE stock. GE also do not provide lump sum payout of pension.

The governance framework at GE stipulates that all independent directors are required to hold at least $500,000 worth of GE stock and/or deferred stock units while serving as a director of GE. The directors have five years to attain this threshold ownership. The senior executive officers are also required to own specified amounts of GE stock which is set at a multiple of the officer's base salary rates. GE provides the forum to report integrity concerns through extensive ombudsperson process. GE have a global network of approximately 500 ombudspersons.

8.11   Healthymagination

The healthymagination focuses on investing in innovations to provide affordable and accessible healthcare to people around the world. This initiative is carried forward through the leadership of GE ventures, GE foundation, and GE healthcare businesses. New portfolio companies like Aver Software focus on re-engineering the complex reimbursement process between insurance payers and healthcare providers through data management and analytics platform for cost savings.GE also have partnership with governments, universities, industry leaders to find solutions for biggest healthcare challenges.GE have invested $8 million in partnership initiatives to promote research in the area of traumatic brain injury. GE is also a part of the "Neurodata Beyond Borders" initiative of the Kayli Foundation. The initiative with collaboration with researchers from research institutes aims to develop protocols and procedures necessary to share neurodata across many research platforms.

8.12   Risk management

The GE Board of Directors has oversight for risk management with a focus on significant risks like strategic, operational, financial and legal and compliance risks. The risk committee assists the Board in its oversight of the risk management framework. The three distinct lines of defense for risk management consists of business units, corporate risk management and internal audit function. The Enterprise Risk Management Committee has delegated the management of specific risks to various sub committees which includes the Operational Risk Management Committee, Asset-Liability Committee, Capital Planning Committee, Allowance and Valuation

Risk Committee, Credit and Investment Risk Committee, Model Risk Management Committee, New Product Introduction Committee and Compliance Committee. GE Capital monitors its capital adequacy through economic capital, regulatory capital, scenario analysis, and enterprise stress testing methodologies.

Approximately 55% of the current revenues of GE are attributed to operations outside United States. Hence the strategic business plans of GE are subject to global competitions and geopolitical risks. The strategic risk also arises due to restructuring activities, joint ventures, acquisitions, product demand, technology, and product innovation. The highly sophisticated products and specialized services offered by GE exposes the firm to operational risks. Cybersecurity is also another area of concern. GE uses a number of techniques like employee training, monitoring and testing, and maintenance of protective systems and contingency plans to manage operational risks. The reliance on third party suppliers, contract manufacturers and service providers, commodity markets for securing raw materials, components and subsystems exposes GE to supply chain risks due to volatility of process and availability of materials. The business and operating results of industrial business are affected by worldwide economic conditions in air and rail transportation, power generation, oil and gas, renewables, healthcare and other major industries. As a result, GE is exposed to different forms of financial risks. GE Capital is exposed to credit risk. Legal and compliance risk relates to risks arising from the government and regulatory environment and action on account of the Dodd Frank Wall Street Reform and Consumer Protection Act. There are 14 lawsuits relating to pending mortgage loan repurchase claims of GE Capital.

The non US activities of GE are affected by currency exchange. GE manages currency exchange rate fluctuations by means of selective borrowings in local currencies and selective hedging of significant cross currency transactions. The principal currencies used for hedging risk are the euro, the pound sterling, the Brazilian real and the Chinese renminbi. Exchange rate and interest rate risks are managed through match funding and derivatives. GE follows a policy to minimize exposure to interest rate changes. GE's hedging strategy involve funding the financial investments using debt or combination of debt and hedging instruments so that interest rates on borrowings are matched with the expected interest rates of assets. GE also minimizes currency exposures and conduct operations either within functional currencies or using protection of hedging strategies. GE manage counterparty credit risk according to the terms of the standard master agreements on an individual counterparty basis. The assets and liabilities which are measured at fair value every reporting period includes investment in debt and equity securities and derivatives. GE uses currency forwards as economic hedge of forecasted foreign cash flows under long-term contracts. GE uses cash flow hedges to reduce or eliminate the effects of foreign exchange rate changes on purchase and sale contracts of industrial businesses and to convert foreign currency debt in financial services businesses into the functional currency. Fair value hedges are used to hedge the effects of interest rate and currency exchange rate changes on debt which has been issued. In cases where fixed rate debt is used to fund floating rate assets,

GE uses interest rate swaps to manage changes in interest rates. Net investment hedges are used to hedge currency risk associated with investments in foreign operations. GE also uses interest rate forwards, swaps, and currency forwards to hedge risks.

8.13 Ownership structure

By December end 2015, equity comprised 33% and debt comprised 67 of the total capital structure. Financial institutions hold 67.5% of the equity ownership, while mutual funds hold 32.41% of the total equity ownership while insiders hold 0.04% of the equity ownership (see Table 8.3).

The top 10 funds currently hold 8.45% of the total shares held by the company. The top 10 financial institutions hold 24.63% of the total equity capital (see Tables 8.4, 8.5).

Table 8.3 **Equity ownership in millions of dollars**

Institutions	Value(million dollars)
Institutions	166,769.72
Mutual funds	80,013.15
Insiders	98.62
Total	246,881.49

Table 8.4 **Top financial institutions**

	Top institutions	Percent of shares held
1	Vanguard Group Inc.	5.88
2	GE Savings and Security Program	4.29
3	State Street Corp.	3.7
4	BlackRock Fund Advisors	2.57
5	Capital World Investors	1.87

Table 8.5 **Top mutual funds**

SL	Mutual fund	Percent of shares held
1	Vanguard Total Stock Mkt Index	1.93
2	Vanguard 500 Index Inv	1.26
3	SPDR S&P 500 ETF	1.12
4	Vanguard Institutional Index	1.11
5	VA College America Inc. Fund	0.83

8.14   Authorized shares

GE was initially established on April 15, 1892.GE have five million plus shareowners around the world. The corporation is authorized to issue 13,250,000,000 shares of common stock with a par value of $0.06 per share and 50,000,000 shares of preferred stock having a par value of $1 per share. As of January 31, 2016, there were approximately 458,000 shareowner accounts of record. As of December 31, 2014, GECC had outstanding 50,000 shares on noncumulative A, B, and C series perpetual preferred stock at an average dividend rate of 6.44% with a face value of $5000 million. As a part of the GE Exit Plan, in year 2015, these shares were converted into a corresponding series A, B, and C of fixed to floating rate noncumulative perpetual preferred stock issued by GE with face value of $2778 million, $2073 million, $1094 for a cumulative face value of $5944 million.

8.15   Dividends

GE has paid quarterly dividend for the last 100 years. In 2015, the firm has returned $33 billion to shareholders in year 2015. This included dividends of $9.3 billion, stock buyback of $3.3 billion and synchrony financial exchange of $20.4 billion.

8.16   Share repurchase

In 2015, GE Board of Directors had authorized new repurchase program of up to $50 billion in common stock. In November 2015, GE completed the split off of Synchrony Financial in which GE acquired 671,366,809 shares of GE common stock from shareholders in exchange for 705,270833 shares of Synchrony Financial stock. Under the GE share repurchase programs, GE repurchased shares of 432.6 million, 73.6 million, and 109.8 million, for a total of $10,375 million, $1901 million and $3320 million for the years 2013, 2014, and 2015, respectively.[7]

8.17   Stock options

Under the 2007 long-term incentive plan, GE grant stock options, restricted stock units and performance share units to employees. All these grants must be approved by the Management Development and Compensation Committee. Under the stock option program, the eligible employee can purchase GE shares in future at the market price of the stock on the date in which award is granted. The options become exercisable in equal amounts over a 5-year vesting period and expire 10 years from the grant date if the options are not exercised.

[7] GE Annual Report 2015.

8.18   Financial resources and charges

Most of the borrowings of GE are in financial services. GE Capital has historically relied on the unsecured term debt markets, the global commercial paper markets, deposits, secured funding, retail funding products, bank borrowings, and securitizations to fund its balance sheet. The operations of GE in United States are funded through the cash generated from the operating activities, dividend payments from GE Capital and commercial papers. With the GE Capital Exit Plan, GE has reduced the reliance on deposits and securitization. As of 2015, GE has reduced the commercial paper from $25 billion to $5 billion. GE plans to focus on excess cash positions, cash generated through dispositions, and cash flow from vertical businesses to fund debt maturities and operating and interest expense costs.[8]

The interest expense amounted to $2 billion, $1.6 billion, and $2.3 billion in years 2013, 2014, and 2015, respectively. The interest rates had been flat over the three-year period basically on account of a mix shift in funding sources. The GE Capital average composite effective interest rate (including interest allocated to discontinued operations) was 2.6% during the three-year period 2013−15. The average borrowings of GE Capital were $297.3 billion in year 2013, $267.6 billion in 2014 and $217.5 billion in year 2015, respectively. The liquidity policy of GE Capital requires GE Capital to maintain a contingency funding plan. In 2015, GE assumed $87.7 billion of senior unsecured notes and $4.9 billion of commercial paper upon merger with GE Capital. In 2015, $2 billion of long-term debt issued by GE had matured. Eight deposit taking banks outside United States were classified as discontinued operations. One deposit taking bank in the US, GE Capital Bank, an industrial bank (IB) was also classified as discontinued operations. In 2015, GE and GE Capital's long-term unsecured debt rating from S&P were AA+ and the short-term funding rating from S&P were A-1 + . In April 2015, Moody's downgraded the senior unsecured debt rating for GE from Aa3 to A1 due to the announcement of the GE Capital Exit Plan. The GE Capital Tier 1 common ratio estimate was 13 % and 14.5%, respectively in year 2014 and 2015, respectively.

Baby bonds are senior unsecured obligations of GE. These bonds are of minimum denomination of $2. Internotes are corporate bonds designed for individual investors which can be brought directly from over 300 plus nonaffiliated broker dealers and are underwritten by Bank of American Securities and Incapital LLC. GE also issues debt with maturities ranging from 1 to 30 years. GE have issued series D 5% fixed to floating rate noncumulative perpetual preferred stock. The commercial papers issued by GE are placed directly in currencies in US dollars, Indian rupees, euro, and British pound.

8.19   Investments

GE makes investments in corporate fixed income, government mortgage, and asset back securities. The corporate debt portfolio consists of securities issued by public

---

[8] GE Annual Report 2015.

and private companies in different industry sectors basically in the United States. GE invests in corporate debt securities which are rated investment grade by major rating agencies like S&P, Moody's etc. All of GE's investment securities are classified as available for sale and none are classified as held to maturity. GE also enter into reverse securities repurchase agreements, primarily for short-term investment with maturities of 90 days or less.

8.20   Operational highlights

Industrial segment revenues had decreased less than 1% in the year 2015, reflecting negative foreign currency impacts and the effects of dispositions, partially offset by organic growth of 3% and the effects of acquisitions (primarily Alstom). Table 8.6 gives the segment revenues in the year 2015.

Table 8.6 **Segment revenues in year 2015**

Segment	Revenues (%)
Power	18
Renewable energy	5
Oil and gas	14
Energy management	6
Aviation	21
Healthcare	15
Transportation	5
Appliance and lighting	7
Capital	9

Table 8.7 **Summary of operating revenues of GE segments**

Segment	2011	2012	2013	2014	2015
Power	20,335	20,364	19,315	20,580	21,490
Renewable energy	4924	7373	4824	6399	6273
Oil and gas	13,874	15,539	17,341	19,085	16,450
Energy management	6422	7412	7569	7319	7600
Aviation	18,859	19,994	21,911	23,990	24,660
Healthcare	18,083	18,290	18,200	18,299	17,639
Transportation	4885	5608	5885	5650	5933
Appliance and lighting	7692	7967	8338	8404	8751
Capital	11,843	11,268	11,267	11,320	10,801
Corporate items and elimination	3145	(1228)	(1405)	(3863)	(2211)
Consolidated revenues	110,062	112,588	113,245	117,184	117,386

Source: Annual Report 2015

Table 8.8 **Segment profits**

Segment	2011	2012	2013	2014	2015
Power	4213	4368	4328	4486	4502
Renewable energy	714	914	485	694	431
Oil and gas	1754	2064	2357	2758	2427
Energy management	78	131	110	246	270
Aviation	3512	3747	4345	4973	5507
Healthcare	2803	2920	3048	3047	2882
Transportation	757	1031	1166	1130	1273
Appliance and lighting	237	311	381	431	674
Capital	1469	1245	401	1209	−7983
Total segment profit	15,536	16,731	16,621	18,973	9983

The consolidated revenues are given in millions of dollars. The increase in revenues of power segment in year 2015 was primarily driven by higher volume, primarily at power services, as well as the effects of the Alstom acquisition (see Table 8.8).

The values given are in millions of dollars. The renewable segment accounted for 5% of segment revenues and 6% of industrial segment revenues. The oil and gas segment accounted for 15% of the industrial segment revenues in year 2015. Energy management contributed to 7% of the industrial segment revenues in year 2015. Aviation segment contributed 23% of the industrial segment revenues. Transportation and appliance and lighting sector contributed 5% and 8% towards the industrial segment revenue in year 2015. Capital contributed 9% of the segmental revenues in the year 2015. The non US revenues accounted for approximately 56% of the total consolidated revenues during the 3-year period 2013−15. The consolidated income tax rate for 2015 was greater than 35% due to charges associated with the GE Capital Exit Plan.

8.21 Financial highlights

The year on year comparison shows that the growth rate of revenues peaked in year 2007 and 2008 with growth rates of 6% approximately. During the period 2006−15, the year 2008 registered the highest revenues of value $182.515 billion. The revenues showed a declining trend from year 2009 onwards. By the year 2014, the revenues dropped down to $148.589 billion. The operating income, cash flow, and net income was fluctuating over the period 2006−15. The operating income registered the highest growth rate of 14% in the year 2007. The total cash reserves peaked in year 2013 with $132.53 billion. The year on year comparison reveals that maximum growth rate of total cash was 47% in year 2008. The total assets increased by 14% in year 2007 (see Table 8.9).

Table 8.9 Financial highlights in millions of dollars

Year	2006	2007	2008	2009	2010	2011	2012	2013	2014	2015
Revenues	163,391	172,738	182,515	156,783	150,211	147,300	147,359	146,045	148,589	117,386
Operating income	44,814	51,301	45,991	29,113	30,191	34,643	29,914	26,267	26,711	16,862
Net income	20,829	22,208	17,410	11,025	11,644	14,151	13,641	13,057	15,233	−6126
Operating cash flow	30,646	45,967	48,601	24,593	36,123	33,359	31,331	28,579	27,710	19,891
Capital expenditure	16,650	17,870	16,010	8634	9800	12,650	15,126	13,458	13,727	7309
Total cash	61,905	61,007	89,633	121,831	122,881	131,875	125,778	132,536	105,530	102,456
Long-term debt	260,752	319,013	322,847	337,631	312,842	262,003	258,500	242,742	190,226	147,466
Total assets	696,683	795,683	797,769	781,901	747,793	718,189	684,999	656,560	654,954	492,692

Market capitalization is estimated based on the year end price of the stock of GE in each year. The market capitalization declined from $382.421 billion in year 2006 to $292.165 billion by the year 2015. The year on year comparison reveals that the market capitalization declined by 3% and 6%, respectively in year 2007 and 2008. The highest increase in market capitalization was in year 2013 when the market capitalization increased by 29% compared to the previous year. The market capitalization increased by 20% and 15% respectively during the period 2010−12. The year on year growth rate of market capitalization reveals that the highest growth rate of market capitalization was in year 2013 when the market capitalization increased by approximately 29%. The market capitalization peaked in year 2006 with value of $382.421 billion (see Table 8.10).

8.22   Ratio analysis

EPS and DPS have been fluctuating over the 10-year period. EBITDA per share, revenue per share and book value per share also have been fluctuating over the 10-year period. The total debt per share have declined over the period 2006−15. EBITDA per share which was 4.87 in year 2006 declined to 1.65 by the year 2015. The revenue per share which was 14.58 in year 2006 declined to 11.72 per share by the year 2015. The book value per share peaked in year 2013 (see Table 8.11).

The profitability ratios have been fluctuating over the 10-year period. The average gross margin declined from 54.1% during the period 2006−10 to 45.1% during the period 2011−15. The average operating margin and average net margin declined from 24.2% and 9.9% during the 5-year period 2006−10 to 18.8% and 6.4% during the period 2011−15. The average ROA, ROE, and ROIC also declined from 2.2%, 14.7%,and 6% during 2006−10 to 1.4%, 7.8%, and 3.6%, respectively during the period 2011−15 (see Table 8.12).

The average dividend payout was approximately 54% during the period 2006−14. The dividend per share have been fluctuating over the period 2006−15 (see Table 8.13).

The average P/B ratio of 2.23 during the five-year period 2006−10 declined to 2.10 during the period 2011−15. The average P/E ratio during the five-year period 2006−10 was 15.26. The average P/E ratio increased to 25.38 during the period 2011−15. The average P/S ratio of 1.56 during the period 2006−10 increased to 1.74 during the period 2011−15. The average price to cash flow increased from 7.28 during the period 2006−10 to 9.02 during the period 2011−15. The growth rate for PEG calculation was based on five year EBITDA growth rate (see Table 8.14).

The average current ratio declined from 2.2 during the five-year period 2006−10 to 2.01 during the period 2011−15. The average quick ratio declined from 2.16 to 1.88 during the above two periods of comparison (see Table 8.15).

The comparison of average efficiency ratios in two periods 2006−10 and 2011−15 reveal that the days' payable declined from 95.7 days to 70.6 days. The

Table 8.10 Market capitalization in millions of dollars

Year	2006	2007	2008	2009	2010	2011	2012	2013	2014	2015
Market capitalization	382,421	370,240	161,278	161,332	194,155	189,363	218,414	282,006	254,150	292,165

Table 8.11 **Per share data**

Year	2006	2007	2008	2009	2010	2011	2012	2013	2014	2015
EPS	2	2.17	1.72	1.01	1.06	1.23	1.29	1.27	1.5	−0.62
DPS	1.03	1.15	1.24	0.61	0.46	0.61	0.7	0.79	0.89	0.92
EBITDA per share	4.87	6.03	5.65	3.67	3.7	4.1	3.69	1.67	1.77	1.65
Revenue per share	14.58	16.88	17.98	14.63	14.01	13.8	13.89	11.01	11.58	11.72
Book value per share	10.85	11.57	10.51	11	11.2	11.01	11.82	12.98	12.74	10.48
Total debt per share	42.11	51.48	48.91	44.07	41.57	38.81	35.33	32.77	25.99	21.14

Table 8.12 **Profitability ratios in percent**

Year	2006	2007	2008	2009	2010	2011	2012	2013	2014	2015
Gross margin	54.6	57.7	54.1	51.6	52.3	53.6	49.6	47.2	45.3	29.6
Operating margin	27.4	29.7	25.2	18.6	20.1	23.5	20.3	18	18	14.4
Net margin	12.75	12.86	9.5	6.84	7.55	8.91	9.26	8.94	10.25	−5.23
Return on assets	3.04	2.98	2.18	1.36	1.48	1.79	1.95	1.95	2.33	−1.08
Return on equity	18.79	19.49	15.74	9.66	9.6	11.15	11.39	10.3	11.78	−5.42
Return on invested capital	7.22	7.2	6.69	4.52	4.55	4.33	4.79	4.79	5.33	−1.07

Table 8.13 **Dividend history**

Year	2006	2007	2008	2009	2010	2011	2012	2013	2014	2015
DPS	1.03	1.15	1.24	0.61	0.46	0.61	0.7	0.79	0.89	0.92
DPO in percent	53	52.3	69.7	59.2	40	47.2	50.4	54.3	59.3	178.4

average days' inventory increased from 58.5 to 75.8 days. The days' sales outstanding declined from 834.1 days to 526.1 days. The average asset turnover ratio was same during the same two periods of analysis. The average inventory turnover ratio declined from 6.2 to 4.8 during the above period of analysis (see Table 8.16).

Table 8.14 **Price multiples**

Year	2006	2007	2008	2009	2010	2011	2012	2013	2014	2015
P/B	3.43	3.2	1.54	1.38	1.63	1.63	1.78	2.16	1.98	2.97
P/E	19.7	16.9	9.1	14.7	15.9	14.6	15.1	20	17	60.2
P/S	2.4	2.2	0.9	1	1.3	1.3	1.5	2	1.7	2.2
P/cash flow	12.9	8.2	3.4	6.5	5.4	5.6	7.1	10.2	9.3	12.9
PEG	3.88	1.47	0.65	3.29	0	0	0	0	0	0

The leverage position of the firm has improved over the 10-year period 2006−15. The average debt equity ratio was 3.38 while the average long-term debt to total assets ratio was 0.374 during the 10-year period. The average ICR during the 10-year period was 3.08. The average debt equity ratio declined from 4.41 in the period 2006−10 compared to 2.62 in the period 2011−15. The average long-term debt to total assets also declined from 0.406 to 0.34 during the above period of analysis. The average ICR increased from 1.93 to 4.23 during the above period of analysis (see Table 8.17).

8.23 Stock wealth analysis

The wealth analysis of GE stock was based on 54-year analysis involving 651 months during the period January 1962−April 2016. The analysis was done on the basis of adjusted closing price of GE stock. The data source was yahoo finance. The monthly stock returns were estimated and then the cumulative returns for the time span of the period 1962−2016 was estimated. The cumulative returns for GE Stock during the 652 months was estimated as 690%. If an investor invested $1000 in GE stock on January 2, 1962, his investment would have grown to $7900 on the basis of cumulative returns by April 1, 2016. The adjusted closing price of GE stock was $0.145 on January 2, 1962. By April 1, 2016, the adjusted closing price of the stock was $30.98. The stock price increased by approximately 213 times. In this context, suppose assume that an investment of $1000 was made in GE Stock during 1962. This investment would have increased to $213,220 by April 2016. The market index S&P 500 cumulative monthly returns during the same 651 months was approximately 400%. Hypothetically an investment of $1000 in the index during the 54-year period would have yielded $5000 based on cumulative returns.

On the basis of cumulative returns, it is observed the GE stock have outperformed the S&P 500 index during the entire 651 months of analysis (see Figure 8.1).

The cumulative monthly returns for GE during the period January 2010 to April 2016 was approximately 108%. The cumulative monthly returns for S&P 500 index during the above period was approximately 66%.

Table 8.15 Liquidity ratios

Year	2006	2007	2008	2009	2010	2011	2012	2013	2014	2015
Current ratio	1.97	1.99	2.3	2.4	2.4	2.08	2.35	2.53	1.48	1.61
Quick ratio	1.93	1.94	2.24	2.34	2.34	2.01	2.26	2.42	1.32	1.4

Table 8.16 Efficiency ratios

Year	2006	2007	2008	2009	2010	2011	2012	2013	2014	2015
Days payable	112.78	106.51	90.71	93.88	74.6	87.67	76.89	75.3	52.62	60.38
Days inventory	56.05	57.22	57.89	61.68	59.84	67.67	71.63	74.74	76.34	88.73
Days sales outstanding	862.74	877.96	804.09	822.16	803.38	767.04	709.19	878.11	133.76	142.58
Asset turnover ratio	0.24	0.23	0.23	0.2	0.2	0.2	0.21	0.22	0.23	0.21
Fixed turnover ratio	2.29	2.26	2.33	2.12	2.22	2.23	2.18	2.11	2.2	1.95
Inventory turnover	6.78	6.02	6.31	5.92	5.1	5.39	5.1	4.72	4.64	4.11

Table 8.17 Leverage positions

Year	2006	2007	2008	2009	2010	2011	2012	2013	2014	2015
DER	3.88	4.45	4.65	4.01	3.71	3.52	2.99	2.53	2.04	2.02
Long-term debt to total assets	0.37	0.4	0.41	0.43	0.42	0.37	0.38	0.37	0.29	0.3
ICR	2.28	2.16	1.77	1.55	1.91	2.4	2.4	5.39	6.11	4.87

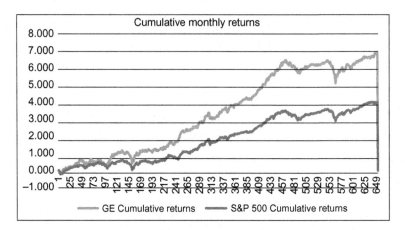

Figure 8.1 Cumulative monthly returns during 1962–2016.

Table 8.18 Average yearly returns inpercent

Year	GE	S&P500	Excess returns
2010	27.7	13.8	13.9
2011	−10.21	11.46	−21.67
2012	21.18	13.16	8.02
2013	33.53	26.54	6.99
2014	−5.95	11.13	−17.08
2015	26.77	0.11	26.66

The average yearly returns were based on the average monthly returns. During the six-year period 2010–16, GE stock had outperformed the market index S&P 500 in all years of analysis except in 2011 and 2014 where the excess return was −21.67% and −17.08% respectively. The maximum excess return for GE was in year 2015 when the stock registered average yearly return of 26.66% over the S&P 500 index returns. It has to be noted that GE had announced the restructuring program of GE Capital Exit Plan in year 2015. Both GE and S&P 500 recorded the highest average yearly returns of 33.53% and 26.54% in the year 2013 (see Table 8.18).

The holding period time horizon is assumed to be one year. An investor is assumed to buy the stock of GE in January every year and sell by December of that year. The holding period yield for GE was highest in 2015 with yield of 34.9%. Only in year 2011, the holding period yield was negative. In 2013 the holding period yield was 29.9%. The 6-year annual holding period yield was approximately 15% (see Table 8.19).

Excess value is estimated as the difference between the market value and book value of equity. The average book value as % of market value was 50% during the

Table 8.19 Holding period yield

Year	Holding period yield in percent
2010	16.9
2011	−8
2012	16.4
2013	29.9
2014	4.1
2015	34.9

Table 8.20 Excess wealth created in millions of dollars

Year	2011	2012	2013	2014	2015
Book value of equity	116,438	123,026	130,566	128,159	98,274
Market value of equity	189,363	218,414	282,006	254,150	292,165
BV asper cent of MV	0.61	0.56	0.46	0.50	0.34
Excess value	72,925	95,388	151,440	125,991	193,891

five-year period 2011−15. The maximum excess value was created in the year 2015 when the excess value amounted to $193.891 billion. In 2015, the book value as % of market value was only 34% (see Table 8.20).

8.24 Estimation of cost of capital

Cost of equity is estimated through the CAPM model
Cost of equity = Risk free rate + Beta × Risk premium

Beta is estimated by regressing the daily returns of GE on the market index S&P 500 during the two-year period 2014−15. The beta value obtained was 1.

Risk premium = Return on market index−Risk free rate. The return on market index is the yearly average return on market index S&P 500 during the two-year period 2014−15. The risk free rate is assumed as the average yield to maturity on the 30-year treasury bond during the 2-year period 2014−16.[9]

Year	Yield to maturity on 30 year treasury bond
2014	3.55
2015	2.63
2016	2.63
Average	0.0294

[9] https://www.treasury.gov/resource-center/data-chart-center/interest-rates/Pages/Historic-Yield-Data-Visualization.aspx.

Risk free rate = 2.94%

Beta = 1

Risk premium = Return on market index −risk free rate = 9.28−2.94 = 6.34%

Cost of equity = 2.94 + 1*6.34 = 9.28%.

The GE Capital average composite effective interest rate (including interest allocated to discontinued operations) of 2.6% during the three-year period 2013−15 is assumed as the cost of debt. The tax rate is assumed to be 35%.

After tax cost of debt = Cost of debt × (1−0.35) = 2.6 × (1−0.35) = 1.69%

Market value of equity in 2015 = $ 292,165 million

The price of the long-term bond of GE maturing on 2/2/2046 was 99.500. Ratio of this long-term bond to the face value of the bond = 99.5/100 = 0.995

Book value of total debt in 2015 = $198,276 million

Market value of debt = $198,276 × 0.995 = $197,284.6

Total value = Market value of equity + Market value of debt = $489,450 million

Weight of equity (WE) = 0.60; Weight of debt (WD) = 0.40

WACC = WE × Cost of equity + WD × after tax cost of debt = 0.60 × 9.28 + 0.40 × 1.69% = 6.22%

The WACC for GE is estimated as 6.22%.

8.25 Valuation

8.25.1 Economic value

The economic value for GE in year 2015 is estimated as follows.

Economic value is estimated as net operating income after taxes (NOPAT)−Capital charge.

Profit before interest and tax (PBIT) − Income tax = NOPAT.

Capital employed = Stock holder equity + Long-term debt

Capital charge = Capital employed × WACC

Economic value (EV) = NOPAT − Capital charge

Operating income = $16,862 million

Income tax = $1772 million

NOPAT = $15,090 million

Stockholder equity = $98,274 million

Long-term debt = $147,466 million

Capital employed = $245,740 million

WACC = 6.22%

Capital charge = $15285.03

Economic value = − $195 million.

8.25.2 Equity spread

Equity spread is a variation of the EV measures. Equity spread is the difference between the ROE and the required return on equity (cost of equity)

Equity spread = (Return on equity − Cost of equity) × Equity capital

Return on equity = 11.78%

Cost of equity = 9.28%

Equity spread = (11.78%−9.28%) × 98,274 million = $245,685 million.

8.26   Discounted cash flow valuation

The discounted cash flow valuation models used are dividend discount model (DDM), Free cash flow to firm (FCFF).

8.26.1   Dividend Discount Model (DDM)

In the first stage, the dividend payout ratio is analyzed (see Table 8.21).

The average DPO during the period 2010−14 was 54%. On account of restructuring of GE Capital in year 2015, the year was excluded from analysis.

Retention ratio (RR) = 1 − DPO.
Growth rate = Retention ratio × Return on equity.
The average growth rate estimated from fundamentals was 5% (see Table 8.22).
DDM Two stage growth model is used to value GE in this section. It is assumed that the EPS of GE will grow at 5% for the next 10 years and then at the GDP growth rate of US economy in the stable period.
High growth stage inputs
High growth period = 10 years
High growth rate = 5%
Cost of equity − 9.28 %
Average DPO = 0.54)
The present value of dividends in the first growth phase is estimated as $6.54 (see Table 8.23.
Stable phase inputs.
Growth rate in stable period is assumed to be the growth rate of US economy. The average growth rate of US GDP for 2-year period 2013−14. The GDP growth rate is estimated as 2.3%.[10]

Table 8.21 Dividend Trends

Year	2010	2011	2012	2013	2014	2015
EPS	1.06	1.23	1.29	1.27	1.5	−0.62
DPS	0.46	0.61	0.7	0.79	0.89	0.92
DPO	0.43	0.50	0.54	0.62	0.59	−1.48

Table 8.22 Estimation of growth rate from fundamentals

Year	2010	2011	2012	2013	2014
RR	0.57	0.50	0.46	0.38	0.41
ROE	0.096	0.1115	0.1139	0.103	0.1178
Growth Rate	0.054	0.056	0.052	0.039	0.048

[10] http://data.worldbank.org/indicator/NY.GDP.MKTP.KD.ZG.

Table 8.23 Present value of dividends in first growth phase

Year	1	2	3	4	5	6	7	8	9	10
EPS	1.58	1.65	1.74	1.82	1.91	2.01	2.11	2.22	2.33	2.44
DPO	0.54	0.54	0.54	0.54	0.54	0.54	0.54	0.54	0.54	0.54
DPS	0.85	0.89	0.94	0.98	1.03	1.09	1.14	1.20	1.26	1.32
PV	$0.78	$0.75	$0.72	$0.69	$0.66	$0.64	$0.61	$0.59	$0.57	$0.54
Sum	$6.54									

Table 8.24 Adjusted net capital expenditure in millions of dollars

Year	2010	2011	2012	2013	2014	2015
Capital expenditures	9800	12,650	15,126	13,458	13,727	7309
Depreciation and amortization	9786	9185	9346	9762	9283	4847
Net capital expenditures	14	3465	5780	3696	4444	2462
Net acquisitions	1212	2325	2389	2210	311	9744
Adjusted net capital expenditures	1226	5790	8169	5906	4755	12,206

The return on equity of industry sector is 9.1%.[11]
Growth rate = Retention ratio × ROE of the industry sector
2.3% = Retention ratio × 9.1%.
Retention ratio = 2.3/9.10 = 25.2%.
EPS at the end of high growth period = $2.44.
EPS at the beginning of the stable growth period = 2.44 × 1.023 = $2.50.
DPO = 1 − Retention ratio.
 = 1 − 0.252 = 0.748.
DPS in stable period = 2.50*0.748 = $1.87.
Terminal value = DPS in stable period/(Cost of equity − growth rate in stable period).
 = 1.87/(0.0928−0.023) = $26.8.
Present value of the dividends in stable phase = $11.03.
Value of GE stock = Present value of dividends in high growth phase + Present value of dividends in stable phase = 6.54 + 11.03 = $17.58.
Value of GE stock based on two stage DDM is arrived at $17.58.

8.26.2 FCFF valuation

Adjustments to capital expenditure.
Capital expenditure − Depreciation and amortization = Net capital expenditure.
Net capital expenditures + Net acquisitions = Adjusted net capital expenditure (see Table 8.24).

---

[11] http://www.morningstar.com/stocks/XNYS/GE/quote.html.

8.27 Noncash working capital

Total current assets-cash, cash equivalents and marketable securities = Noncash current assets.

Total current liabilities−short-term debt = Noninterest bearing current liabilities.

Noncash current assets − Noninterest bearing current liabilities = Noncash working capital (see Table 8.25).

The reinvestment rate has been positive only in year 2015. The reinvestment rate was 57.5% in year 2015 (see Table 8.26).

The growth rate for the year 2015 was estimated as 3.04% (see Table 8.27).

Table 8.25 **Noncash working capital in millions of dollars**

Year	2010	2011	2012	2013	2014	2015
Total current assets	463,611	453,624	426,156	422,303	166,162	170,827
Cash and cash equivalents	122,881	131,875	125,778	132,536	105,530	102,456
Non cash current assets	340,730	321,749	300,378	289,767	60,632	68,371
Total current liabilities	192,907	218,581	181,414	167,220	112,442	106,030
Short-term debt	128,458	148,325	109,099	86,937	71,198	50,810
Noninterest bearing current liabilities	64,449	70,256	72,315	80,283	41,244	55,220
Noncash working capital	276,281	251,493	228,063	209,484	19,388	13,151
Change in noncash working capital		−24,788	−23,430	−18,579	−190,096	−6237

Table 8.26 **Estimation of reinvestment rate**

Year	2011	2012	2013	2014	2015
EBIT	34,643	29,914	26,267	26,711	16,862
Taxes	5732	2504	676	1772	6486
EBIT(1 − T)	28,911	27,410	25,591	24,939	10,376
Adjusted net capex	5790	8169	5906	4755	12,206
Change in noncash WC	−24,788	−23,430	−18,579	−190,096	−6237
Reinvestment	−18,998	−15,261	−12,673	−185,341	5969
Reinvestment rate	−0.65712	−0.55677	−0.49521	−7.43177	0.57527

Table 8.27 **Estimation of growth rate from fundamentals**

Year	2015
Reinvestment rate	0.575
ROCE	0.053
Growth rate	0.0304

Table 8.28 **Estimation of Free Cash Flow to Flow (FCFF)**

Year	2011	2012	2013	2014	2015
EBIT(1 − T)	28,911	27,410	25,591	24,939	10,376
Adjusted net capex	5790	8169	5906	4755	12,206
Change in noncash WC	−24,788	−23,430	−18,579	−190,096	−6237
FCFF	47,909	42,671	38,264	210,280	4407

The values are given in millions of dollars. The free cash flow in year 2015 was $4407 million. The average FCFF during the period 2011−15 excluding the FCFF of year 2014 is taken for estimation purposes. In 2014, the FCFF was abnormally high (see Table 8.28).

Since the growth rate estimated from fundamentals was approximately 3%, the stable stage FCFF model of valuation was used for estimation purposes.

Average FCFF during 2011−15 (excluding 2014) = $33,312.75 million.
Growth rate = 3%.
WACC = 6.22%.
Value = FCFF × (1 + g)/(WACC − g) = $33,312.75 × 1.03/(0.0622−0.03)
 = $1,065,594.18 million.
Value of operating assets = $1,065,594.18.
Value of GE = Value of operating assets + Value of cash and cash equivalents.
$1,065,594.18 + $102,456 = $1,168,050.18 million.
 = Value of equity = Value of GE −Value of debt
 = $1,168,050.18 − $198,276 = $969,774.18.
Value of equity = $969,774.18 million.
Number of shares = $10,016.
Value per share = $96.82.

Summary of Discounted Cash Flow Valuation

Value of GE stock based on two stage DDM = $17.58
Value of GE stock based on stable stage FCFF model = $96.82

By April 7th 2016, the 52-week range was $19.37−32.05. The market capitalization was $288.3 billion.

8.27.1 Relative valuation

The source of data is Morningstar.com. The values except that of Interest Coverage Ratio (ICR) and Debt Equity Ratio (DER) are given in millions of dollars. The analysis is based on the year 2015 except market capitalization which is based on April 2016. GE achieved the maximum sales of $117.386 billion among the peer firms

Table **8.29** **Financial highlights—comparison with competitors**

Company	Sales	Net income	Market capitalization	ICR	Debt equity ratio
GE	117,386	−6126	288,315	3.4	1.5
Siemens AG	105,631	4833	100,926	46.8	0.8
Honeywell International	38,581	4768	86,979	22.2	0.3
3M Co.	30,274	7282	83,145	9.8	0.8
Danaher Co.	20,563	3357	64,482	21.4	0.5
ABB Ltd.	35,481	1133	42,166	10.9	0.4

Table **8.30** **Price multiples—comparison with competitors**

Company	P/S	P/B	P/E	Div. yield (%)
GE	2.6	2.9	181.8	3
Siemens AG	3.5	8.6	22	2.5
Honeywell International	2.3	4.8	18.7	2
3 M Co.	1	2.1	14.3	3.7
Danaher Co.	3.2	2.7	25.6	0.6
ABB Ltd.	1.2	2.9	22.1	

during the year 2015.3 M had the highest income among the competitor firms. GE had the highest market capitalization among the six competitor firms. Siemens AG had the highest ICR among the six firms. GE had the least ICR among the competitor firms. GE was the most leverage firm among the peer firms (see Table 8.29).

The price multiples are based on April 2016. Siemens Ltd. had the highest price to sales ratio and price to book ratio among the competitor firms. 3 M had the highest dividend yield among the competitor firms (see Table 8.30).

Enterprise value = Market value of equity total debt − Total cash.

Lower the enterprise value multiple, the more undervalued the stock becomes and hence attractive. In terms of enterprise value multiples like EV/Revenues, EV/EBITDA, and EV/EBIT. Siemens is the most attractive stock among the competitive firms (see Table 8.31).

The basis of comparison of growth rates is the year 2015. GE's 5- and 10-year growth rates of revenues was negative. The 5- and 10-year growth rates of Danaher was 9.27% and 9.92%. Siemens had the highest 10-year revenue growth rate of 11.25% (see Table 8.32).

Based on the year 2015, GE had negative average growth rates of operating income in 5 years and 10 year periods. Honeywell had the maximum average growth rate of operating income in the five-year period. Siemens had the maximum average growth rate of operating income in the 10-year horizon (see Table 8.33).

The enterprise value multiples have been fluctuating over the 10-year period of analysis (see Table 8.34).

Table 8.31 Enterprise value multiples

Company	GE	Siemens	Honeywell	3M	Danaher Co.	ABB Ltd.
Revenues	117,386	105,631	38,581	30,274	20,563	35,481
EBITDA	16,496	19,180	7779	8407	4538	4286
EBIT	16,862	15,466	6828	6946	3469	3099
Debt	198,276	252	12,068	10,797	12,870	7439
Market value of equity	288,315	100,926	86,979	83,145	64,482	42,166
Cash and cash equivalents	102,456	20,968	7558	1916	791	6198
Enterprise Value (EV)	384,135	80,210	91,489	92,026	76,561	43,407
EV/revenues	3.3	0.8	2.4	3.0	3.7	1.2
EV/EBITDA	23.3	4.2	11.8	10.9	16.9	10.1
EV/EBIT	22.8	5.2	13.4	13.2	22.1	14.0

Table 8.32 Comparison of growth rates of revenues

Growth rates in percent	ABB	Danaher	3M	Honeywell	Siemens	GE
5 Year	2.35	9.27	2.57	2.94	1.89	−4.81
10 Year	4.69	9.92	3.64	3.39	11.25	−2.4

Table 8.33 Comparison of growth rate of operating income

Growth rates	ABB	Danaher	3 M	Honeywell	Siemens	GE
5 Year	−5.47	9.87	3.26	16.85	6.94	− 11
10 Year	10.15	10.62	3.32	10.65	14.12	− 7.88

Table 8.34 Enterprise value multiples

Year	2006	2007	2008	2009	2010	2011	2012	2013	2014	2015
EV/revenues	4.9	4.8	3.1	3.3	3.5	3.2	3.2	4.3	3.5	3.3
EV/EBITDA	14.9	13.5	10.0	13.3	13.1	10.8	12.0	25.4	21.6	23.3
EV/EBIT	17.8	16.2	12.5	18.3	17.4	13.6	15.6	40.6	29.0	22.8

8.28 Performance indicator analysis

8.28.1 Altman Z score

Investors can use Altman Z score to decide if they should buy or sell a particular stock based on the company's financial strength. The Altman Z score is the output of a credit strength test which gauges a publicly traded manufacturing company's likelihood of bankruptcy. Z score model is an accurate forecaster of failure up to two years prior to distress.

$$Z\text{-Score} = 1.2A + 1.4B + 3.3C + 0.6D + 1.0E$$

where:

A = Working capital/Total assets
B = Retained earnings/Total assets
C = Earnings before interest and tax/Total assets
D = Market value of equity/Total liabilities
E = Sales/Total assets

The zones of discrimination are such that when Z score is less than 1.81, it is in distress zones. When the Z score is greater than 2.99, it is in safe zones. When the Z score is between 1.81 and 2.99, the company is in Gray Zone.

The financial values are given in millions of dollars

Total assets	492,692		
Total liabilities	394,418		
Sales revenues	117,386		
Operating income	16,862		
Retained earnings	140,020		
Market value of equity	288,315		
Working capital	64,797		
Ratios	Values	Constant	Score
Working capital/Total assets	0.13	1.2	0.16
Retained earnings/Total assets	0.28	1.4	0.40
Operating income/Total assets	0.03	3.3	0.11
Market value of equity/Total liabilities	0.73	0.6	0.44
Sales/Total assets	0.24	1	0.24
		Z score	1.35

8.29 Piotroski score

The Piotroski score is a discrete score between 0 and 9 which is an indicator of the firm's financial position. The score was named after the Chicago accounting Professor Joseph Piotroski. The cumulative points suggest whether the stock is a value stock or not. If the company achieves a score of 8 or 9, the stock can be considered strong. If the score ranges between 0 and 2, then the stock is considered weak.

8.29.1 Criteria for Piotroski score

SL	Profitability scores	Score points	Score for GE
1	Positive return on assets in current year	1	0
2	Positive operating cash flow in current year	1	1
3	Higher ROA in current year compared to previous year	1	0
4	Return on cash flow from operations greater than ROA	1	1

SL	*Profitability scores*	Score points	Score for GE
	Leverage, liquidity and sources of funds		
5	Lower ratio of long-term debt to average total assets in current year compared to previous year	1	0
6	Higher current ratio in this year compared to previous year	1	0
7	No new shares were issued in the last year	1	1
	Operational efficiency ratios		
8	A higher gross margin compared to the previous year	1	0
9	A higher asset turnover ratio compared to the previous year	1	0
Total		9	3

GE have a Piotroski score of 3 out of 9.

8.30 Graham number

It is a conservative method used for valuing a stock. It is a figure which measures a stock's fundamental value by taking into account the company's earnings per share and book value per share. Graham number is the upper bound of the price range which a defensive investor should pay for the stock. According to Graham number theory, any stock price below the Graham number is considered undervalued and hence worth investing in. Graham number is a combination of asset valuation and earnings power valuation.

The Graham number illustration is done with respect to year 2014 since the EPS in 2015 is negative.

EPS in year 2014 = 1.51.
Book Value per share = 13.42.

$$\text{Graham number} = \sqrt{22.5 \times (\text{Earning per share}) \times (\text{Book value per share})}$$
$$= \$21.35$$

The stock price during December 2014 was $24.23.

The detailed calculation and data for the analysis in each section of this chapter is given in the resources file *GE.xlsx*.

Further reading

[1] www.ge.com.
[2] http://www.alacrastore.com/mergers-acquisitions/General_Electric_Company-1006912.
[3] http://www.geaviation.com/aboutgeae/presscenter/other/other_20070504.html.

Strategies of wealth creation by Berkshire Hathaway

9

9.1 Introduction

Berkshire Hathaway is a holding company which owns a number of subsidiaries in diversified business activities which includes insurance and reinsurance, freight rail transportation, utilities and energy, finance, manufacturing, services, and retailing. Berkshire Hathaway Inc. consists of 60 subsidiaries. The subsidiaries of Berkshire Hathaway in the business of insurance underwriting and reinsurance are GEICO, General Re, Berkshire Hathaway Reinsurance Group. The subsidiaries involved in underwriting property and casualty insurance businesses are National Indemnity Company, Berkshire Hathaway Home State Insurance company, Medical Protective Company, Applied Underwriters, US Liability Insurance Company, Central States Indemnity Company, Bankers Surety, Cypress Insurance Company, Boat US, and the Guard Insurance Group. Berkshire Hathaway involve in both primary insurance and reinsurance of property/casualty, life and health risks. Insurance business consists of operations of underwriting and investing. The underwriting is the business responsibility of unit managers while investing decisions are responsibility of the CEO.

The powerhouse five is the collection of Berkshire's largest noninsurance businesses. The companies in this group are Berkshire Hathaway Energy (BHE), BNSF, IMC, Lubrizol, and Marmon. BNSF and BHE are regulated capital intensive businesses of Berkshire Hathaway. BNSF railroad system carries about 15% of all intercity freight in US.BHE's Utilities serve regulated retail customers in eleven states. BHE accounts for 6% of US's wind generation capacity and 7% of its solar generation capacity. Lubrizol Corporation is a technology driven complex specialty chemicals company. Marmon Group, part of Berkshire Hathaway is a global diversified industrial group which comprises three autonomous companies consisting of 13 diverse stand-alone business sectors and 185 independent manufacturing and service businesses. Shaw Industries is the World's largest manufacturer of tufted broadloom carpet. Benjamin More is manufacturer and retailer of architectural and industrial coatings. Acme Brick is the manufacturer of face brick and concrete masonry products. MiTek Inc. produces steel connector products and engineering software for building components market. Fruit of the Loom, Russell, Vanity Fair, Justin Brands, and Brooks Sports all manufacture, license and distribute apparel, and foot wear under a variety of brand names. FlightSafety International provides training to aircraft

Table 9.1 **List of operating companies in insurance business**

SL	Company	SL	Company
1	Applied Underwriters	7	GEICO
2	Berkshire Hathaway Home State Companies	8	General Re
3	Berkshire Hathaway Reinsurance Group	9	Guard Insurance Group
4	Berkshire Hathaway Specialty	10	Medical Protective
5	Boat US	11	National Indemnity Primary Group
6	Central States Indemnity	12	US Liability Insurance Group

operators. Nebraska Furniture Mart, R.C. Wiley Home Furnishings, Star Furniture are subsidiaries of Berkshire Hathaway which are retailers of home furnishing. Borsheims, Helzberg Diamond Shops and Ben Bridge are retailers of fine jewelry.[1]

9.2 Business segments

The operating businesses of Berkshire Hathaway can be segregated into large and diverse group of insurance, finance, manufacturing, service, and retailing businesses. Insurance is the core of Berkshire's operations. The major subsidiaries of Berkshire Hathaway in the business of insurance underwriting and reinsurance are GEICO, General Re, Berkshire Hathaway Reinsurance Group, and Berkshire Hathaway Primary Group. Table 9.1 lists the operating companies in insurance business of Berkshire Hathaway.

Business	Business activity
GEICO	Underwriting private passenger automobile insurance by direct response methods
General Re	Underwriting excess-of-loss, quota-share and facultative reinsurance worldwide
Berkshire Hathaway Reinsurance Group	Underwriting excess-of-loss and quota-share reinsurance for insurers and reinsurers
Berkshire Hathaway Primary Group	Underwriting multiple lines of property and casualty insurance policies for primarily commercial accounts
BNSF	BNSF operates one of the largest railroad systems in North America
Berkshire Hathaway Energy	Major regulated, electric and gas utility. Involved in power generation and distribution activities. The company is also involved in domestic estate brokerage and brokerage franchisor
McLane Company	Wholesale distribution of groceries and nonfood items
Manufacturing	Industrial, end user products, building products, and apparel

[1] Annual Report 2014.

Business	Business activity
Service and retailing	Providers of services for fractional aircraft ownership programs, aviation pilot training, electronic components distribution, and retailing
Finance and financial products	Manufactured housing and related consumer financing; transportation equipment, manufacturing and leasing; and furniture leasing

9.2.1 Government Employees Insurance Company (GEICO)

This division primarily writes private passenger automobile insurance which offers coverage to insured in all 50 states and the District of Columbia. The division aims to be a low cost auto insurer in which the policies are marketed mainly by direct response method via internet or telephone. Government Employees Insurance Company (GEICO) have 12 million auto policies in force and insured more than 18 million vehicles. It is considered as the third largest private passenger auto insurer in United States. In 1996, GEICO became the wholly owned subsidiary of Berkshire Hathaway. The affiliate companies of GEICO are GEICO Insurance company, GEICO Indemnity Company, GEICO Casualty Company, GEICO Advantage Insurance Company, GEICO Choice Insurance Company, and GEICO Secure Insurance Company. GEICO have consistently obtained AA++ from AM Best, a leading analyst of insurance industry and Standard and Poor.

GEICO suffered its single largest loss in 2012 due to Hurricane Sandy which cost GEICO more than three times the loss from the Katrina. GEICO had insured 46,906 vehicles which were destroyed or damaged in the storm.

9.2.2 Products offered by GEICO

9.2.2.1 Auto insurance

GEICO offers auto insurance. The auto insurance policy offered by GEICO is a package of several primary coverages like bodily injury liability coverage, property damage liability coverage, medical payments, no fault or personal injury coverage, uninsured motor coverage, comprehensive physical damage coverage, and collision coverage. In bodily injury coverage, GEICO pays for bodily injury or death resulting from an accident at which the client is at default and provides with a legal defense. Property damage liability coverage provides protection if the vehicle of insurance holder accidently damages another person's property along with legal defense in most cases. In underinsured motorist coverage, property damage caused by an uninsured or a hit and run driver is also included. In addition to these basic coverage, GEICO also offers Emergency Road Service, Rental Reimbursement, and Mechanical Breakdown Insurance. Rental Reimbursement is an optional coverage which facilitates insurance holders to pay rental car costs when the vehicle is being repaired as a result of a covered claim. The rental reimbursement coverage would be subject to a daily and per claim limit.

9.2.3 Motorcycle insurance

GEICO insures most types of motorcycle through coverage like accessories coverage, bodily injury liability coverage, collision coverage, comprehensive physical damage coverage, medical payments, and property damage liability coverage. ATV Insurance is underwritten by GEICO indemnity company.

9.2.4 Umbrella insurance

GEICO provides extra liability insurance termed Umbrella insurance. This insurance is designed to protect the policy holder from major claims and lawsuits. In this scheme, additional liability coverage is provided above the limits of the homeowners, auto and boat insurance policies. It provides coverage for bodily injury liability, property damage liability, and owners of rental units against cost of liability claims.

9.2.5 Home owner's insurance

GEICO provides homeowners insurance policy which offers different protection. The standard policies offered include broad coverage for damages for houses and permanent structures on properties. Limited coverage for an amount in range of $200–$2000 is provided for theft of jewellery. Coverage is also provided for personal liability exposures that arise from being a homeowner.

9.2.6 Other insurances

Other insurances include Renters Insurance, Condo Insurance, Coop Insurance, Recreational Vehicle (RV) Insurance, life Insurance, boat Insurance, personal watercraft insurance (PWC), flood insurance, mobile home insurance, overseas insurance, commercial auto insurance, business insurance, snowmobile, and pet insurance.

Renters insurance provide protection for household articles and named perils like theft, fire or lighting. Condominium association insurance covers the condominium building, commonly owned property and liability insurance for the association. Most condo insurance policy covers for losses arising from fire or lightning, smoke, theft or vandalism. Coop insurance covers the co-op building, commonly owned property, and liability insurance for the cooperative apartment corporation but excludes losses due to theft, fire etc. GEICO offers enhanced motorized RV and towable RV insurance policy. RV insurance coverage include features like total loss replacement, replacement cost personal effects. In total loss replacement coverage, a new equipped RV is provided if the RV is totaled within first four models. In replacement cost personal effects, the coverage pays for the replacement of personal items in RV. Vacation liability coverage pays for bodily injury and property damage losses at vacation sites. The emergency expense coverage pays for expenses for hotels and transportation due to a covered loss. An amount of $1000 for emergency expense coverage is automatically covered at no additional cost with comprehensive and collision coverage. GEICO covers motorized recreational vehicles including Type A motorhomes, Type B motorhomes (van campers), Type C motorhomes, and sport utility recreational vehicles. Towable RV insurance policy includes conventional travel trailers and truck campers. The boat insurance policy insures the holder and the boat against liability and damage in the event of an accident. PWC insurance ensures coverage for personal watercraft against accidents, vandalism and liability.

GEICO offers three business insurance products of general liability insurance, business owners policy and professional liability insurance. General liability insurance provides coverage for operations of business. Business Owners Policy (BOP) provides liability insurance and property damage coverage which are pooled together in a package policy. Professional liability insurance known as errors and omissions is coverage for businesses that offer personal and professional services. This insurance protects policy holders in the event that a client is harmed. GEICO's military center is dedicated to the sales and service of military policies.

9.2.7   General re corporation

General Re Corporation the subsidiary of Berkshire Hathaway is the holding company for global reinsurance and other operations. General Re owns Reinsurance Corporation and General Reinsurance AG. Gen Re is one of the leading global property casualty and life health reinsurer in the world. The company has 40 offices globally supported by approximately 1900 employees. In 1998, Berkshire Hathaway acquired General Re Corporation. In 2003, General Re and Cologne Re began marketing globally under the brand name Gen Re. By 2009 General Re acquired Cologne Re and renamed the company to General Reinsurance AG.

General Re conducts reinsurance business by offering property and casualty and life and health coverage to clients globally. Property and casualty reinsurance are written in North America on a direct basis through General Reinsurance Corporation and globally through German based General Reinsurance AG and wholly owned affiliates. Life and health reinsurance is written in North America through General Re Life Corporation and globally through General Reinsurance AG General.

9.2.8   Reinsurance solutions

9.2.8.1   Life/health solutions

General Re offers life and health reinsurance protection in lines of business like critical illness, group LTD and Group Life/AD&D, individual disability, individual life, and medicare supplement. Gen Re is one of the leading reinsurers of critical illness insurance globally. Critical illness provides lump sum cash payment upon diagnosis of costly conditions for diseases like cancer, heart attack, stroke, kidney failure, and major organ transplant. Gen Re provides solutions for products like long term disability (traditional and voluntary), group life and AD&D (basic, supplemental, and voluntary), long term disability conversion and life portability administration. Gen Re provides a variety of individual life reinsurance coverage solutions on products such as term, whole life, universal life (indexed, variable, and traditional) Individual, joint and last survivor products, supplement benefits and riders, corporate and bank owned life insurance. General Re also provides sophisticated risk management techniques through its worldwide network of actuaries, underwriters, marketers, and claim management specialists.

General Re's in house underwriting and actuarial teams in collaboration with clients' underwriting and pricing resources aims for comprehensive underwriting and pricing strategy. Gen Re provides reliable information for assessment of risk through online life and health underwriting manuals.

9.2.9   Property/casualty insurance

General Re provides solutions for a wide range of auto/motor exposures and coverage which includes auto/motor liability, auto physical damage/motor own damage, accident and transportation liability. The company also provides solutions for a broad range of property, marine, and engineering coverages.

The solutions include property exposures for boiler and machinery/machinery breakdown and commercial property in mining, oil and petrochemicals, semiconductor, and power generation. Inland marine, ocean marine solutions are also offered. The casualty underwriters also provides coverages such as directors and officers liability, employment practices liability, homeowners/householders liability, medical professional liability, personal accident, personal injury liability, and products liability. The solutions for property, marine and engineering coverages include casualty per occurrence facultative, casualty per occurrence excess of loss treaty, casualty per risk excess of loss treaty and quota share treaty. Gen Re offer wide range of services and solutions for surety and bond strategies. The services and solutions are offered for contract surety/construction bonds, court bonds, federal and public official, licenses and permit. The surety/bond reinsurance solutions include bonding per quota share, bonding per excess of loss and crime insurance facultative.

9.2.10   Family of companies under General Re

Company	Major role
Gen Re (Direct Reinsurance Operations)	Major global direct reinsurer in property/casualty, life/health
Gen Re Intermediaries	Reinsurance intermediary and risk advisor with specialization in delivering global reinsurance market solutions for Property Catastrophe, Aviation, Worker's Compensation, Catastrophe, and Casualty clash exposures
GR-NEAM	Global investment advisor which specializes in offering capital and investment management services basically to the insurance industry. By 2013, GR-NEAM had managed $61.8 billion in global unaffiliated assets under management for 100 insurance company clients. Investment accounting services were provided to 66 insurance clients with $80 billion in assets accounted. The comprehensive product offerings include

Company	Major role
	asset management, enterprise risk and capital management, investment technology solutions, and investment accounting and reporting services
General Star	Underwrite excess, surplus and specialty property and casualty insurance on an admitted and nonadmitted basis through appointed wholesale brokers. General Star also provides certain underwriting, claims and administrative services on behalf of General Star Indemnity Company and General Stat National Insurance Company
Genesis	It is the premier alternative insurance provider which provides innovative solutions. The underwriting division serves the public by providing insurance and reinsurance solutions for municipalities, counties, special districts, public and private colleges and universities and schools
United States Aircraft Insurance Group (USAIG)	A leading provider of insurance to all segments of aviation and aerospace industry. The group offers comprehensive ranges of coverages in areas like corporate aviation, commercial aviation, pleasure and business aircraft, helicopters, airlines, airport liability, aviation products liability, and workers compensation
Faraday	Faraday Group consists of Faraday Reinsurance and Faraday Syndicate 435. Underwriting business is carried out through teams of aviation, casualty, and property

9.2.11 Berkshire Hathaway Reinsurance Group and Berkshire Hathaway Primary Group

Berkshire Hathaway Reinsurance Group (BHRG) and Berkshire Hathaway Primary Group (BHPG) are the two subsidiaries of General Re. BHRG conducts business through group of subsidiaries which include National Indemnity Company (NICO) and Columbia Insurance Company. Primarily BHRG provides principally excess and quota share reinsurance to other property and casualty insurers and reinsurers. The underwriting activities of BHRG which includes life reinsurance and life annuity business are carried out by Berkshire Hathaway Life Insurance Company of Nebraska. The financial guarantee insurance is written through Berkshire Hathaway Assurance Corporation. BHRG also provide catastrophe excess of loss treaty reinsurance contracts. BHRG also provides individual coverage for individual risks covering terrorism, natural catastrophe and aviation risks. These catastrophe and individual risk policies provide amounts of indemnification per contract. As a result, a single loss event could produce losses under a number of contracts. BHRG also underwrites traditional noncatastrophe insurance and reinsurance coverage which are usually referred to as multiline property/casualty businesses.

Berkshire Hathaway Primary Group consists of a group of independently managed insurance businesses which provides a range of insurance coverage to the insured. National Indemnity Company and certain affiliates underwrite motor vehicle and general liability insurance to commercial enterprises on both an admitted and excess and surplus basis. US Investment Corporation through its four subsidiaries led by United States Liability Insurance Company (USIC) underwrite specialty insurance which covers commercial, professional and personal lines insurance. The policies offered by USIC are marketed in all states through wholesale and retail insurance agents. The USIC companies underwrite and market approximately 110 distinct specialty property and casualty insurance products. The Berkshire Hathaway Homestate Companies (BHHC) is a group of six insurance companies that provides commercial multiline insurance which includes worker's compensation, commercial auto and commercial property coverages. Medical Protective Company (MedPro) and Princeton Insurance Company provides healthcare malpractice insurance to physicians, dentists and other healthcare providers. Applied underwriters provides compensation solution for integrated workers. Boat US is a writer of insurance for owners of boats and small watercraft. Central States Indemnity provides credit and disability insurance to clients through the financial institutions. The total employees in the insurance business group was 40,061 in year 2014. Tables 9.2 gives the list of operating companies of Berkshire Hathaway in noninsurance business.

9.3   Growth of Berkshire Hathaway—Strategic perspective

The strength of property casualty business lies in its financial characteristics in which property casualty insurers receive premiums upfront and pay claims later. This model is known as pay—later model. In the case of some worker's compensation accidents, the payments stretch over decades. The pay later model results in holding large sums of money called float (Table 9.3).

Berkshire major strength is its unmatched collection of businesses. The Berkshire Group consists of 60 subsidiaries. The major financial strength of Berkshire Hathaway is due to its large and reliable stream of earnings, massive liquid assets, and no significant near term cash requirements.

Berkshire Hathaway through the insurance and reinsurance businesses of GEICO, General Re, Berkshire Hathaway Reinsurance Group, and Berkshire Hathaway Primary Group involve in both primary insurance and reinsurance of property/casualty, life and health risks. In primary insurance the company assume defined portions of the risks of loss from persons or organizations which are directly subject to the risks. In reinsurance activities, defined portions of similar or dissimilar risks that other insurers or reinsurers have been subjected is assumed. Insurance business can be categorized as underwriting and investing. Underwriting decisions are the responsibility of unit managers while investing decisions are responsibility of top management. Berkshire Hathaway evaluate performance of underwriting operations without any allocation of investment income or investment gains. The timing and amount of catastrophe losses could result in significant volatility in underwriting results. Catastrophe losses are considered significant if the pretax losses incurred from a single event or series of related events exceed $100 million on a consolidated basis.

Table 9.2 List of operating companies in noninsurance business

SL	Company	SL	Company
1	Acme	40	Iscar
2	Adalet	41	Johns Manville
3	Affordable Housing Partners	42	Jordan's Furniture
4	Alta Link	43	Justin Brands
5	Alta quip	44	Kern River Gas
6	Ben Bridge Jeweler	45	Kriby
7	Benjamin Moore	46	Larson Juhl
8	BH Energy	47	Lubrizol
9	BHE Renewables	48	Lubrizol Specialty Products Inc
10	BHE US Transmission	49	Marmon Group
11	BH Media Group	50	McLane Company
12	Borsheims	51	Metalogic Inspection Service
13	Brooks Sports	52	Mid American Energy
14	BNSF	53	MiTek Inc
15	The Buffalo News	54	Nebraska Furniture Mart
16	Business Wire	55	NetJets
17	CalEnergy Philippines	56	Northern Natural Gas
18	Campbell Hausfeld	57	Northern Powergrid Holdings
19	Carefree of Colorado	58	NV Energy
20	Charter Brokerage	59	Oriental Trading
21	Clayton Homes	60	PacifiCorp
22	Cleveland Wood Products	61	The Pampered Chef
23	CORT	62	The Precision Steel Warehouse
24	CTB	63	Richline Group
25	Dairy Queen	64	Russell
26	Douglas/Quikut	65	Other Scott Fetzer Companies
27	Fechheimer	66	See's Candies
28	FlightSafety	67	Shaw Industries
29	Forest River	68	Stahl
30	France	69	Star Furniture
31	Fruit of the Loom	70	TTI, Inc
32	Garan	71	United Consumer Financial Services
33	H H Brown Shoe Group	72	Vanity Fair Brands
34	Halex	73	Wayne Water Systems
35	Heinz	74	Western Enterprises
36	Helzberg Diamonds	75	R C Willey Home Furnishings
37	Home Services of America	76	World Book
38	Intelligent Energy Solutions	77	WPLG Inc
39	XTRA		

Table 9.3 **Float in million dollars**

Year	Float in US dollar millions
1970	$39
1980	237
1990	1632
2000	27,871
2010	65,832
2014	83,921

A major marketing strategy of the insurance businesses is the maintenance of extraordinary capital strength. This surplus is aimed to create opportunities to enter into insurance and reinsurance contracts. Berkshire Hathaway's operating businesses are managed on a decentralized basis. There are no centralized or integrated business functions like sales, marketing, purchasing, legal or human resources.

GEICO aims to become the lowest cost auto insurer. The company primarily write private passenger automobile insurance in 50 states and the District of Columbia. GEICO policies are marketed directly by direct response methods in which customers apply for coverage directly to the company via the Internet or over the telephone. Premium written and earned in 2014 amounted to $21 billion and $20.5 billion. This represented an increase of 9.8% and 10.4 % compared to premiums written and earned in 2013.

Berkshire Hathaway conduct reinsurance business offering property and casualty, life and health coverage to clients worldwide through General Re. The property and casualty reinsurance are written on a direct basis through Genera Re in North America. These reinsurances are written internationally through Germany based General Reinsurance and other wholly owned affiliates. The property/casualty premiums written and earned in year 2014 was $285 million and $96 million, respectively. There had been an increase of 9.6% in premium written and 3.2% in premium earned in year 2014 compared to the previous year 2013. In 2014, the pretax underwriting gains of the combined property and casualty business was $170 million compared to $148 million in 2013. The casualty /workers compensation business had pretax underwriting losses of $296 million in 2014 as compared to $5 million in 2013. In 2014, the premium written and earned in health and life insurance amounted to $170 million and $184 million which represented an increase of 5.7% and 6.2% compared to the previous year. The life/health operations had underwriting gains of $107 million in year 2014 compared to $135 million in year 2013. BHRG underwrite excess of loss reinsurance and quota share coverages on property and casualty risks for insurers and reinsurers worldwide. Retroactive reinsurance policies provide indemnification of losses and loss adjustment expenses with respect to past loss events and related claims. The life and annuity premiums earned in year 2014 declined by 19% compared to premiums earned in year 2013. The investment income received by Berkshire Hathaway consists of interest and dividends earned on investments by insurance businesses. The investment income amounted to $4357 million in year 2014.

Table 9.4 Equity investments

SL	Company	Percentage of company owned
1	American Express	14.8
2	Coca Cola	9.2
3	DaVita HealthCare Partners	8.6
4	Deere and Company	4.5
5	DIRECTV	4.9
6	The Goldman Sachs Group Inc.	3
7	IBM	7.8
8	Moody's Corporation	12.1
9	Munich Re	11.8
10	The Procter and Gamble Company	1.9
11	Sanofi	1.7
12	US Bancorp	5.4
13	USG Corp.	30
14	Walmart Stores	2.1
15	Wells Fargo	9.4

Source: Annual Report 2014, Page 17.

BNSF operates one of the largest railroad systems in North America consisting of approximately 32,500 route miles of track in 28 states and three provinces in Canada. The major business groups of BNSF are classified by the type of products shipped and can be divided into consumer products, coal industrial products, and agricultural products. BHE's domestic regulated utility companies are PacifiCorp, MidAmerican Energy Company, and NV Energy. McLane deals with wholesale distribution business which provides grocery and non food products to retailers, convenience stores, and restaurants. The service businesses of Berkshire Hathaway include NetJets which are the world's leading provider of fractional ownership programs for general aviation aircraft and Flight Safety which provides high technology training to operators of aircrafts.

Investment gains/losses arise primarily from the sale or redemption of investments or when investments are carried at fair value. Derivative gains/losses represent the changes in fair value of the derivative contracts like credit default and equity index put option contracts.

9.4 Equity Investments

Equity investments are a major source of investments for Berkshire Hathaway. The major 15 equity investments of Berkshire Hathaway as of 2014-year end are given below (see Table 9.4).

Berkshire's cost of investments was $55,056 million. The market value of these investments amounted to $117,470 million in year-end 2014. Thus it can be stated that the value of these investments rose approximately 2.13 times in year 2014. In year 2014, Berkshire increased its ownership interest in its big four major investments—American Express, Coca-Cola, IBM, and Wells Fargo. Berkshire increased its ownership from 6.3% to 7.8% in IBM. Equity ownership increased to 9.2% in Coca Cola, 14.8% in American Express and 9.4% in Wells Fargo. In addition to its existing investments in Bank of America, Berkshire Hathaway have the option to buy 700 million shares any time prior to September 2021 for $5 billion. In 2014 end, these shares were worth $12.5 billion.

Berkshire Hathaway generally makes equity investments in businesses that have at least $75 million of pretax earnings, otherwise the business must fit into one of its existing units. The equity investments are made in companies which earn good returns on equity with little or no debt.

9.4.1 Investment in fixed maturity securities

Berkshire Hathaway invests in US Treasury, US government corporations and agencies, states, municipalities and political subdivisions securities, foreign government bonds, corporate bonds, and mortgage backed securities.

Investments in foreign government securities include securities issued by national and provincial government entities as well as instruments that are unconditionally guaranteed by such entities. As of December 31 2014, approximately 93% of foreign government holdings were rated AA or higher by at least one of the major rating agencies. Approximately 77% of foreign government holdings were issued or guaranteed by the United Kingdom, Germany, Australia, Canada, Netherlands.

In 2014, the investments in stocks, bonds and cash equivalents totaled $158 billion in market value by year end 2014. The insurance float held in the insurance operations was used to fund investments worth $66 billion. The second major component of Berkshire Hathaway's earnings was derived from the 68 noninsurance companies. According to the Annual Report 2014, the compounded annual increase in per share investments was approximately 20% over the 40-year period (see Tables 9.5 and 9.6).

Table 9.5 Per share investments

Year	Per share investments
1970	$66
1980	$754
1990	$7798
2000	$50,229
2010	$94,730

Source: Annual Report 2014 page 125.

Table 9.6 **Compounded annual interest in per share investment**

Year	Compounded annual interest in per share investment (%)
1970–80	27.5
1980–90	26.3
1990–2000	20.5
2000–10	6.6

Source: Annual Report 2014 page 125.

9.5 Restructuring—Mergers and acquisitions

In 1967, Berkshire acquired National Indemnity and its sister company, National Fire and Marine, for $8.6 million. Berkshire carried out a spin-off in 1979 as a result of new regulations for holding company to divest a bank in Rockford Illinois. In 2013, Berkshire and H J Heinz Holding Corporation acquired H J Heinz Company. Berkshire and 3G (the parent company of Heinz Holding) each made equity investments in Heinz Holding which together with debt financing obtained by Heinz Holding was used to acquire Heinz for approximately $23.25 billion. Berkshire own a 50% interest in a joint venture Berkadia Commercial Mortgage with Leucadia National Corporation. Berkadia is the servicer of commercial real estate loans in the US. In 2014, Berkshire entered into a definitive agreement with Procter & Gamble to acquire the Duracell battery business from P&G which include $1.7 billion in cash. P&G would receive shares of its common stock currently held by Berkshire subsidiaries with value of $4.8 billion as of December 31, 2014.

In 2012, the subsidiary company McLane acquired Meadowbrook Meat Company, Inc. which was a large foodservice distributor for national restaurant chains. In 2014, Berkshire Hathaway acquired Alta Link a regulated electric transmission only company based in Canada for $2.7 billion. This acquisition was financed through loans from insurance subsidiaries of Berkshire Hathaway and the issuance of $1.5 billion of senior unsecured notes due in 2020, 2025, and 2045.

9.6 Corporate governance

Majority of the directors of the company are independent. There are no tenure or retirement policies which limit the director to be nominated for reelection. The governance, compensation and nominating committee is responsible for nominating directors for election or reelection. The board presently has 13 members (two management directors, two nonmanagement but not independent directors and nine independent directors). The board has three committees: (1) audit; (2) governance, compensation and nominating; and (3) executive. The audit and governance, compensation and nominating committees each consist solely of independent directors. Each director has full and free access to the officers and employees of the company and its subsidiaries. The governance, compensation and nominating committee conducts an annual evaluation to determine whether the board and its committees are functioning effectively and reports its conclusions to the board.

9.7 Equity share holding

Berkshire Hathaway has two classes of common stock designated as class A and class B. Class B common stock has the rights of 1/1500th of a share of class A common stock except that a class B share has 1/10,000th of the voting rights of a class A share (rather than 1/1500th of the vote). Each share of a class A common stock is convertible at any time, at the holder's option, into 1500 shares of class B common stock. Class B stocks cannot be converted into class A stocks. The class B can never sell for anything more than a tiny fraction above 1/1500th of the price of A. In a situation when it rises above 1/1500th, arbitrage takes place in which the NYSE specialist would buy the A and converts it into B. This pushes the prices back into a 1:1500 ratios. Berkshire had approximately 2700 record holders of its class A common stock and 21,500 record holders of its class B common stock as of February 16, 2015.

9.8 Financial highlights

The cash equivalents consist of funds invested in US treasury bills, money market account, demand deposits etc. In 2014, BNSF issued $3 billion of senior unsecured debentures with maturities in 2024 and 2044. Table 9.7 provides the financial highlights and Table 9.8 provides the revenue highlights of Berkshire Hathaway.

Table 9.7 Financial highlights of Berkshire Hathaway Inc. millions of dollars

Year	2010	2011	2012	2013	2014
Total revenues	136,185	143,688	162,463	182,150	194,673
Net earnings	12,967	10,254	14,824	19,476	19,872
Total assets	372,229	392,647	427,452	484,931	526,186

Table **9.8** **Revenue highlights of Berkshire Hathaway Inc. millions of dollars**

Year	2012	2013	2014
Insurance and others	121,514	138,492	146,879
Railroad utilities and energy	32,582	34,757	40,690
Finance and financial products	8367	8901	7104
Total	162,463	182,150	194,673

9.9 Risk management

The derivative contracts are entered by the finance and financial products and energy business divisions. The equity index put options (European style options) are written on four major equity indexes and would expire between June 2018 and January 2026. The value of the put options contracts was approximately $1.4 billion on December 2014. The credit default contract written in 2008 are related to approximately 500 zero coupon municipal debt issues with maturities ranging from 2019 to 2054. The regulated utility subsidiaries of Berkshire Hathaway are exposed to variations in the prices of fuel required to generate electricity. Derivative instruments used for hedging include forward purchases and sales, futures, swaps, and options. Derivative contract assets in railroad, utilities and energy businesses amounted to $108 million in year 2014. Equity index option contracts are based on the Black Scholes option valuation model. Berkshire Hathaway manage interest rate risk by regularly investing in bonds, loans or other interest rate sensitive instruments. The company rarely use derivative products such as interest rate swaps to manage interest rate risks. The company maintain high amounts of invested assets in exchange traded equity securities. Berkshire also faces equity price risk with respect to the equity index put option contracts. The company does not use derivative contracts to hedge foreign currency risks. The process of natural hedging occurs between the assets and liabilities denominated in foreign currencies in consolidated financial statements. Commodity price risks are managed through the pricing of the products and services. The energy subsidiary of Berkshire Hathaway uses derivative instruments like forwards, futures, options, swaps to secure future supply or sell future production generally at fixed prices.

9.10 Stock repurchase

Berkshire's board of directors has approved a common stock repurchase program under which Berkshire may repurchase its class A and class B shares at prices no higher than a 20% premium over the book value of the shares. It is proposed that Berkshire can repurchase shares in the open market or through privately negotiated transactions. The authorization of Berkshire's Board does not specify a maximum number of shares to be repurchased. It is stipulated that repurchases will not be made if they would reduce Berkshire's consolidated cash and cash equivalent holdings below $20 billion. The repurchase program does not obligate Berkshire to repurchase any dollar amount or number of class A or class B shares and there is no expiration date to the program. There were no share repurchases under the program in 2014.

9.11 Dividends

The payment of dividends by insurance subsidiaries are restricted by insurance statutes and regulations. Berkshire has not declared cash dividend since 1967. Table 9.9 gives the operating revenue highlights of insurance businesses of Berkshire Hathaway. Table 9.10 highlights the operating revenues of other business groups. Table 9.11 provides the net income highlights of different business segments. Table 9.12 gives the capital expenditure expenses of different business segments.

Table 9.9 Operating revenues of insurance groups in millions of dollars

Insurance group	2010	2011	2012	2013	2014
GEICO	14,283	15,363	16,740	18,572	20,496
General Re	5693	5816	5870	5984	6264
Berkshire Hathaway Reinsurance Group	9076	9147	9672	8786	10,116
Berkshire Hathway Primary Group	1697	1749	2263	3342	4377
Investment Income	5186	4746	4474	4735	4370
Total insurance group	35,935	36,821	39,019	41,419	45,623

Source: Annual Report 2014.

Table 9.10 Operating revenues of other business groups in millions of dollars

Other business segments	2012	2013	2014
BNSF	20,835	22,014	23,239
Berkshire Hathaway Energy	11,747	12,743	17,614
McLane Company	37,437	45,930	46,640
Manufacturing	32,105	34,258	36,773
Service and retailing	11,890	13,284	14,276
Finance and financial products	5933	6110	6526

Source: Annual Report 2014.

Table 9.11 **Net income highlights in millions of dollars**

Year	2012	2013	2014
Insurance underwriting	1046	1995	1692
Insurance—Investment income	3397	3708	3542
Rail road	3372	3793	3869
Utilities and Energy	1323	1470	1882
Manufacturing, service, and retailing	3357	3877	4468
Finance and financial products	899	1008	1243
Investment and derivative gains/losses	2227	4337	3321
Other	−797	−712	−145
Earnings available to Berkshire Hathaway shareholders	14,824	19,476	19,872

Table 9.12 **Capital expenditure in millions of dollars**

Business groups	2012	2013	2014
Insurance Group	61	89	94
BNSF	3548	3918	5243
Berkshire Hathaway Energy	3380	4307	6555
McLane Company	225	225	225
Manufacturing	1062	1037	1324
Service and retailing	381	488	591
Finance and financial products	1118	1023	1137
Total	9775	11,087	15,185

Table 9.13 **Premium and expense trends**

Year	2010	2011	2012	2013	2014	2015
Premium	30,749	32,075	34,545	36,684	41,253	40,251
Total benefits, claims, and expenses	117,134	128,374	140,227	153,354	166,568	173,854

9.12 Trend analysis

The values are given in millions of dollars. The average growth rate of premium during the five-year 2011−15 was approximately 6%. The highest year on year growth rate of 12.5% with respect to premium was registered in year 2014. The claim and expenses increase of approximately 11% was highest in year 2011. The average increase in claims and expenses during the five-year period 2011−14 was approximately 8% (see Table 9.13).

The values are given in millions of dollars except earnings per share. The average year on year growth rate of revenues during the 10-year period 2006−15 was 10%. The average growth rate of operating income during the 10-year period 2006−15 was 20%. The average growth rate of net income was 18% during the period 2006−15. The average growth rate of earnings per share during the 10-year period 2006−15 was 17%. On a comparative basis, the average growth rate of revenues during the five-year period 2006−10 was 11.4%. The average growth rate of revenues during the five-year period 2011−15 decreased to 8.8 %. The average operating income growth rate of 26% during the period 2006−10 declined to 14% during the period 2011−15 (see Table 9.14).

The profitability ratios have been fluctuating over the period 2005−15. The average operating margin have increased from 11.6% during the period 2005−10 to 14.14% during the period 2011−15. The net margin improved from 9% during the period 2005−10 to 9.6% during the period 2011−15. The average return on assets declined from 3.8% to 3.75% during the two period of analysis. The average return on equity declined from 8.7% during the period 2005−10 to 8.45% during the period 2011−15 (see Table 9.15).

Capital expenditure as % of sales have been fluctuating over the period 2005−15. Free cash flow (FCF) as % of sales have been fluctuating over the 11-year period (see Table 9.16).

Table 9.17 gives the turnover ratios.

9.13   Equity ownership

The equity consisted of 75% of the capital structure and the debt composed of 25% of the capital structure. Institutions owned 73.9% of the ownership of the company. Mutual funds owned 26% of the equity ownership. Insiders held 0.1% of the company equity ownership.

Top five funds held 2.59% of the total shares of the company. Top 10 institutions hold 9.36% of the share ownership of the company. The number of institutions owners were 832 and fund owners were 304 (see Tables 9.18 and 9.19).

9.14   Wealth creation by Berkshire Hathaway

The adjusted closing price of Berkshire Hathaway A share was $260 on March 17 1980. The adjusted closing price of Berkshire Hathaway A share was trading at $190,500 on January 4 2016. The closing prices are adjusted for dividends and stock splits. The analysis of stock returns during the period 1980−2015 representing 35 years reveal that the stock gave a cumulative return of 753.4% on the basis of estimation of monthly returns. The analysis was based on return analysis for 431 months representing the period 1980−2015.

Table 9.14 Income trends in millions of dollars

Year	2005	2006	2007	2008	2009	2010	2011	2012	2013	2014	2015
Revenues	81,663	98,539	118,245	107,786	112,493	136,185	143,688	162,463	182,150	194,673	207,260
Operating income	9189	12,934	16,523	7574	11,552	19,051	15,314	22,236	28,796	28,105	33,406
Net income	8528	11,015	13,213	4994	8055	12,967	10,254	14,824	19,476	19,872	22,760
Earnings per share	3.69	4.76	5.7	2.15	3.46	5.29	4.14	5.98	7.9	8.06	9.23

Table 9.15 Profitability ratios

Year	2005	2006	2007	2008	2009	2010	2011	2012	2013	2014	2015
Operating margin (%)	11.3	13.1	14	7	10.3	14	10.7	13.7	15.8	14.4	16.1
Net margin (%)	10.44	11.18	11.17	4.63	7.16	9.52	7.14	9.12	10.69	10.21	10.98
Return on assets (%)	4.41	4.93	5.07	1.85	2.85	3.87	2.68	3.62	4.27	3.93	4.28
Return on equity (%)	9.62	11.02	11.53	4.34	6.7	8.99	6.37	8.41	9.51	8.6	9.37

Table 9.16 Cash flow ratios

Year	2005	2006	2007	2008	2009	2010	2011	2012	2013	2014	2015
Cap Ex as a % of sales	2.69	4.64	4.54	5.69	4.39	4.39	5.7	6.02	6.09	7.8	8.11
Free cash flow/sales (%)	8.88	5.71	6.07	4.74	9.7	8.75	8.55	6.88	9.12	8.64	7.33

Table 9.17 Turnover ratios

Year	2005	2006	2007	2008	2009	2010	2011	2012	2013	2014	2015
Fixed assets turnover	11.65	4.83	3.4	2.65	2.45	1.95	1.49	1.57	1.59	1.5	1.52
Asset turnover	0.42	0.44	0.45	0.4	0.4	0.41	0.38	0.4	0.4	0.39	0.39

Table 9.18 Top funds

SL	Name	Percentage of total shares held
1	Fidelity Contrafund	1.43
2	VA College America Amercn Bal529E	0.53
3	VA College America Fundamental Invs529E	0.28
4	Davis NY Venture A	0.18
5	Sequoia	0.17

Table 9.19 Top Institutions

SL	Institutions	Percent of shares held
1	Frontier Wealth Management, LLC	3.84
2	Fidelity Management and Research Company	1.78
3	Capital World Investors	1.02
4	First Manhattan Company	0.92
5	Ruane, Cunniff & Goldfarb Inc	0.58
6	Gardner Russo & Gardner	0.31
7	Davis Selected Advisers	0.29
8	Vanguard Group Inc	0.21
9	Arnhold & S. Bleichroeder Advisers, LLC	0.21
10	Brown Brothers Harriman &Co	0.2

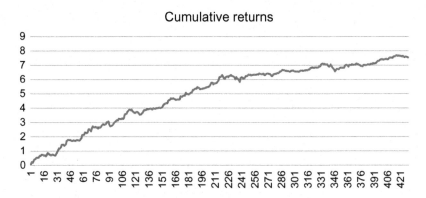

Cumulative returns

Suppose an investor had invested $1000 in the stock of Berkshire Hathaway in the year 1980. The investment would have been worth $7534 by 2015 based on above calculations.

Berkshire Hathaway registered the highest average returns in the year 2013. The company had an average yearly returns of 25% in year 2014 and 22% in year 2010. The average returns of Berkshire Hathaway stocks were negative in the year 2011 and 2015 (see Table 9.20).

The average monthly returns for Berkshire Hathaway and the market index DJIA (Dow Jones Industrial Average) was estimated for the period 2010−15 and then the

Table 9.20 Average yearly returns

Year	Average monthly returns (%)	Average yearly returns (%)
2010	1.8	22
2011	−0.3	−4
2012	1.3	16
2013	2.4	29
2014	2.1	25
2015	−1.05	−13

Table 9.21 Excess average yearly returns

Year	Berkshire Hathaway (%)	DJIA index (%)	Excess returns (%)
2010	22	15.34	7
2011	−4	6.31	−10
2012	16	7.47	9
2013	29	24.13	5
2014	25	7.60	17
2015	−13	−1.40	−11

Table 9.22 Holding period yield

Year	Holding period yield (%)
2010	5.1
2011	−6.3
2012	13.7
2013	22.0
2014	33.3
2015	−8.4

yearly average return was calculated. Excess return was estimated as the difference between the two yearly returns. Berkshire Hathaway outperformed the market index in the year 2010, 2012, 2013, and 2014, respectively. In 2014, Berkshire Hathaway's returns was 17% higher than that of DJIA Index. The excess returns for Berkshire Hathaway was 9% in year 2012. The market index outperformed the stock during the years 2011 and 2015. Hence it can be concluded that Berkshire Hathaway was not able to perform well in year 2015 compared to the previous years (see Table 9.21).

The holding period yield is based on the assumption that an investor buys a stock in the beginning of each year and sells by the end of year. For example, Berkshire Hathaway share is bought for $215,865 on January 2 2015 and sold on December 1 2015 for $197,800. The holding period yield is −8.4% in 2015. Berkshire Hathaway had the highest holding period yield of 33% in the year 2014 (see Table 9.22).

Table 9.23 **Average yearly returns**

Year	Monthly (%)	Yearly (%)
2010	1.9	22.6
2011	−0.3	−3.8
2012	1.4	16.6
2013	2.4	28.9
2014	2.1	24.8
2015	−1.0	−12.1

Table 9.24 **Excess market value creation in millions of dollars**

Year	2010	2011	2012	2013	2014	2015
Market value of equity	197,672	188,620	219,250	291,063	369,452	323,412
Book value of equity	157,318	16,4850	187,647	221,890	240,170	303,701.7
Excess value	40,354	23,770	31,603	69,173	129,282	19,710
BV asper cent of MV (%)	79.6	87.4	85.6	76.2	65.0	93.9

9.14.1   Return analysis of Berkshire Hathaway 's B shares

The cumulative monthly returns of B shares for the period 1996−2016 involving 237 months was approximately 219.75%. Suppose an investor invested $1000 in Berkshire Hathaway B share in the year 1996. The invested amount would have grown to $2197.5 by year 2015 based on the above calculations.

The Table 9.23 gives the yearly returns of Berkshire Hathaway B shares during the period 2010−15. The estimation was based on monthly returns and then yearly returns were estimated. The maximum yearly returns of approximately 29% was registered in year 2013.

Excess market value is calculated as the difference between the market value of equity and book value of equity. The highest excess value of $129.282 billion was in the year 2014. In 2014, book value of equity was 65% of the market value. The average book value as % of market value was 81% during the period 2010−15 (see Table 9.24).

9.15   Estimation of cost of capital

Cost of equity is estimated using the CAPM.
Cost of equity = Risk free rate + Beta (Return on market index − Risk free rate).

The yield of a 30 year US Treasury bond as on January 20 2016 was 2.18%.[2] This value is assumed as the risk free rate. Beta is estimated by regressing the daily stock returns of Berkshire Hathaway A shares on the market index S&P 500 daily returns during the two-year period 2014–15.

Beta = 0.86

Return on the market index is assumed as the average yearly returns of market index S&P 500 during the two-year period 2014–15.

The two-year return on market index S&P 500 = 9.3%

Risk premium = Return on market index − Risk free rate

= 9.3−2.81 = 6.49%

Cost of equity = 2.81 + 0.86 × 6.49 = 8.33 %.

9.15.1 Cost of debt estimation

Berkshire Hathaway has no bond issues. Hence yield of maturity to estimate the cost of debt is unavailable. The cost of debt is estimated in the following manner. The rating of Berkshire Hathaway given by standard rating agency Moody's Investors is first observed. Moody's current rating of Berkshire Hathaway is Aa2.[3] The default spread for rating Aa2 is 1.14%[4].

Cost of debt = Risk free rate + Default spread

= 2.81 + 1.14 = 3.32%.

The marginal federal corporate income tax rate on the highest income bracket of corporations (currently above USD 18,333,333) is 35%

After tax cost of debt = 3.32(1−0.35) = 3.32 × 0.65 = 2.16%

9.15.2 Estimation of Weighted Average Cost of Capital (WACC)

WACC is estimated based on market value weights.

Market value of equity = 323,412 million dollars

Book value of debt = 80,209 million dollars

Total value of firm = 403,621 million dollars

Weight of equity = 323,412/403,621 = 0.80

Weight of debt = 80,209/403,621 = 0.20

Weighted Average Cost of Capital (WACC) = Weight of equity × Cost of equity + Weight of debt × After tax cost of debt.

= 0.80 × 8.33 + 0.20 × 2.16 = 7.10%.

The WACC for Berkshire Hathaway is 7.10%.

9.16 Economic value

Economic value is estimated as net operating income after taxes (NOPAT) −Capital charge.

Profit before interest and tax − income tax = NOPAT.

Capital employed = Fixed assets + Working capital

---

[2] https://www.treasury.gov/resource-center/data-chart-center/Pages/index.aspx.

[3] https://www.moodys.com/credit-ratings/Berkshire-Hathaway-Inc-credit-rating-600046928.

[4] http://www.bondsonline.com/Todays_Market/Corporate_Bond_Spreads.php.

or

Capital employed = Total assets − Current liabilities.

or

Capital employed = Stock holder equity + Long term debt

Capital charge = Capital employed × WACC

Economic Value (EV) = NOPAT-Capital charge

Estimation of EV

NOPAT = PBIT − Taxes

NOPAT in 2015 = 36,943−10,321 = $26,622 million

Stock holder equity in year 2014 = $240,170 million

Long term debt in year 2014 = $80,209 million

Capital employed = $320,379 million.

Capital charge = 320,379 × 7.10% = $22,746.91 million

Economic value = NOPAT − Capital charge

= 26,622−22,746.91 = $3875 million.

EV created for Berkshire Hathaway = $3875 million.

9.17 Equity spread

Equity spread is a variation of the EV measures. Equity spread is the difference between the ROE and the required return on equity (cost of equity)

Equity value creation = (Return on equity in per cent −Cost of equity in percent) × Equity Capital.

Equity spread = (Return on equity − Cost of equity) × Equity capital

Return on equity = 9.37%

Cost of equity = 8.33%

Equity spread = (9.37%−8.33%) × 240,170 million = $2497.77 million.

Equity spread for Berkshire Hathaway = $2497.77 million.

9.18 Free cash flow valuation

During the past 13 years Berkshire Hathaway Inc. 's highest three-year average FCF per share growth rate was 31.10% per year.

Free cash flow = Cash flow from operations−Capital spending (see Table 9.25).

Table 9.25 Estimation of free cash flow

Year	2005	2006	2007	2008	2009	2010	2011	2012	2013	2014	2015
Cash flow from operations	9446	10,195	12,550	11,252	15,846	17,895	20,476	20,950	27,704	32,010	32,008
Capital spending	2195	4571	5373	6138	4937	5980	8191	9775	11,087	15,185	16,816
Free cash flow	7251	5624	7177	5114	10,909	11,915	12,285	11,175	16,617	16,825	15,192

Table 9.26 **Estimation of reinvestment rate**

Year	2011	2012	2013	2014	2015
Cash flow from operations	20,476	20,950	27,704	32,010	32,008
Capital Spending	8191	9775	11,087	15,185	16,816
Reinvestment	0.40	0.47	0.40	0.47	0.53

Table 9.27 **Estimation of growth rate from fundamentals**

Year	2011	2012	2013	2014	2015
Return on capital	0.11	0.08	0.09	0.08	0.10
Reinvestment rate	0.40	0.47	0.40	0.47	0.53
Growth rate	0.04	0.04	0.04	0.04	0.05
Average growth rate	0.04				

The values are given in millions of dollars. The average growth rate of cash flow from operations was approximately 15% during the five-year period 2010−14. The average growth rate of FCF during the five-year period 2010−14 was 10.6%.

Estimation of growth rate from fundamentals
Reinvestment rate = Capital spending/Cash flow from operations
Return on Capital Employed (ROCE) = Earnings before interest and tax (EBIT)/Capital employed
Capital employed = Stock holder equity + Long term debt
Growth rate = Reinvestment rate × ROCE.

The average reinvestment rate during the period 2011−15 was 45% (see Table 9.26).

The average growth rate from fundamentals was estimated as 4% (see Table 9.27). We assume the growth rate in FCF valuation model as the five-year average fundamental growth rate of 4%.

9.18.1 Two stage FCF valuation

It can be assumed that Berkshire Hathaway's operating earnings will grow at 4% at high growth period of 10 years and then will grow at the stable growth rate of US economy forever. The historical average growth rate of operating cash flow during the five-year period 2011−15 is assumed as the growth rate of earnings in high growth period.

High growth period = 10 years
Growth rate in high growth period = 4%
Reinvestment rate = Average reinvestment rate during the period 2011−15 = 45%
Cash flow from operations (current year) = 32,008 million dollars
WACC = 7.1%.

The sum of the present value of FCF in high growth phase = $150,316.6 million (see Table 9.28).

Table 9.28 **Present value of free cash flow in high growth phase**

Year	1	2	3	4	5	6	7	8	9	10
OCF	33,288.3	34,619.9	36,004.6	37,444.8	38,942.6	40,500.3	42,120.3	43,805.2	45,557.4	47,379.7
Reinvestment	14,979.7	15,578.9	16,202.1	16,850.2	17,524.2	18,225.1	18,954.2	19,712.3	20,500.8	21,320.8
Free cash flow	18,308.6	19,040.9	19,802.6	20,594.7	21,418.4	22,275.2	23,166.2	24,092.8	25,056.6	26,058.8
PV	17,094.8	16,600.0	16,119.5	15,653.0	15,199.9	14,759.9	14,332.7	13,917.9	13,515.0	13,123.8
Sum	150,316.6									

9.18.2   Stable stage inputs

The average growth rate of US economy during the past four years[5] is assumed to be the growth rate of cash flows of Berkshire Hathaway in the stable period.

Year	Annual GDP growth
2011	1.6
2012	2.3
2013	2.2
2014	2.4
Average	2.13

The average growth rate of 2.13% is assumed to be the growth rate of Berkshire in stable period.

Return on capital of the industry sector = 9.2%[6]

Growth rate = Reinvestment rate × ROCE

2.13% = Reinvestment rate × 9.2%

Reinvestment rate = 2.13%/9.2% = 23%

The reinvestment rate in stable growth period = 23%

Cash flow from operations at the end of high growth period = $47,379.7 million

Cash flow from operations at beginning of stable growth period = 47,379.7 × 1.0213 = $48,388.85 million

Reinvestment = $48,388.85 × 0.23 = $11,129.43 million

FCF in stable period = 48,388.85 − 11,129.43 = $37,259.41 million.

Terminal value of FCF in stable period = FCF in stable period/(WACC − growth rate in stable period)

= 37,259.41/(0.071−0.0213) = $749,686.34 million

Present vValue of terminal value = $216,786.23 million

Value of Berkshire Hathaway = Present value of FCF in high growth phase + Present value of FCF in stable phase growth.

Value of Berkshire Hathaway = = $150,316.6 + 216,786.23 = $367,102.82 million.

Value of debt in 2014 = $802,609 million

Value of equity = 367,102.82−802,609 = $286,893.82 million.

The value of equity estimated through two stage FCF valuation model was $286.893 billion dollars. The value of firm is estimated as $367.102 billion in year 2014. The market capitalization of Berkshire Hathaway in year-end 2014 was $369.452 billion. In January 2016, the market capitalization was $313.4 billion.

The FCF valuation was also done on the basis of the assumption that the growth rate of operating cash flows would be based on the historical average growth rate of 15% during the period 2011−14. The value of equity was arrived at $778,134.95 million dollars. The details of the analysis are given in excel sheet FCF2 of *Berkshire Hathaway.xlsx*.

---

[5] http://data.worldbank.org/indicator/NY.GDP.MKTP.KD.ZG.

[6] http://biz.yahoo.com/ic/432.html.

9.19   Relative valuation

9.19.1   EBITDA per share

EBITDA is a cash flow measure that ignores changes in working capital. EBITDA is widely used in financial analysis since depreciation and amortization are not present day cash expenses (see Table 9.29).

EBITDA per share have been fluctuating over the period 2005−14. The highest growth rate of EBITDA per share of 47% based on year on year growth rate was registered in year 2010. The EBITDA per share decline by 49% in year 2008 compared to the previous year. In 2011, the EBITDA per share declined by 13% in year 2011 compared to the previous year. The average growth rate of EBITDA per share during the period 2006−10 was 18.5%. The average growth rate of EBITDA per share during the period 2011−14 declined to 12%.

9.19.2   Enterprise value multiples

Enterprise value is more real in reflecting how much an investor pays when buying a company. EV/EBIT ratio is calculated as enterprise value divided by its EBIT. EV/EBITDA ratio is estimated as enterprise value divided by its EBITDA. EV/revenues is estimated as enterprise value divided by its revenues. EV/EBITDA is a valuation multiple used in finance and investment to measure the value of a company. In order to determine the fair market value of a company, the EV/EBITDA is often used in conjunction with, or as an alternative to the P/E ratio. EV/revenue is a similar ratio to P/S ratio (see Table 9.30).

9.19.3   Price multiples

The price to book ratio measures the valuation of the stock relative to the underlying asset of the company. The other valuation ratios like P/E, P/S or Price to FCF measure the valuation of the stock relative to the earning power of the company. Price to book ratio suits best for businesses like banks and insurance companies that earn most of their profit from their assets. Price to earnings ratio is the most widely used ratio in the valuation of stocks. PEG ratio is P/E ratio divided by growth rate. The EBITDA growth rate for the past five-year period is assumed as the growth rate (see Table 9.31).

The values are given in millions of dollars. The revenues of Berkshire are 3.47 times of AIG. The market capitalization of Berkshire Hathaway was 4 times higher than that of AIG. The operating income of Berkshire Hathaway was 4.8 times higher than that of AIG (see Table 9.32).

The Table 9.33 gives the current valuation of Berkshire Hathaway in comparison with peer companies like Allianz, AXA, and AIG. The industry average values are also given. The data source is Morningstar.com. Berkshire Hathaway had the highest price to book ratio among the peer companies. Its price to book ratio was higher than the industry average. The price to sales ratio was highest for Berkshire Hathaway compared to other firms and the industry average. AIG had the highest price to cash flow ratio compared to the other peer firms of comparison.

The detailed calculations for all analysis are given in the resources excel file **Berkshire Hathaway.xlsx**.

Table 9.29 **EBITDA per share**

Year	2005	2006	2007	2008	2009	2010	2011	2012	2013	2014
EBITDA per share	9412.9	13,338.52	15,833.12	7970.95	10,748.55	15,823.96	13,733.94	18,247.12	23,178.22	23,571.5
Growth rate		0.417	0.187	−0.496	0.348	0.472	−0.132	0.328	0.270	0.0169

Table 9.30 **Enterprise value multiples**

Year	2005	2006	2007	2008	2009	2010	2011	2012	2013	2014
EV/EBIT	7.86	8.69	9.61	17.32	12.15	10.33	11.98	9.6	10.05	12.37
EV/EBITDA	7.86	8.69	9.61	17.32	9.04	8.62	9.5	7.96	8.33	10.02
EV/revenues	1.3	1.63	1.79	1.53	1.46	1.64	1.5	1.48	1.74	1.99

Table 9.31 **Price multiples**

Year	2005	2006	2007	2008	2009	2010	2011	2012	2013	2014	2015
P/B	1.49	1.56	1.82	1.37	1.17	1.26	1.14	1.17	1.31	1.53	1.3
P/E	15.9	15.39	16.63	29.91	19	15.14	18.42	14.98	15.01	18.63	14.3
P/S	1.66	1.72	1.86	1.39	1.36	1.44	1.31	1.37	1.6	1.9	1.5
P/CF	18.7	14.5	17.5	13.3	9.7	11	9.4	10.6	11.5	11.9	10.2
PEG	0.34	0.28	0.56	2.71	0	0	2.78	0.75	0.54	1.43	
P/FCF	18.7	30.17	30.55	29.22	14.01	16.55	15.35	19.89	17.59	21.98	

Table 9.32 **Comparison with competitor**

Company	Revenues	Market cap	Total assets	Operating income
Berkshire Hathaway	207,260	323,412	526,186	33,406
AIG	59,806	76,658	515,581	6942

Table 9.33 **Relative valuation—Comparison with peer group**

Company	P/E	P/B	P/S	P/CF
Berkshire Hathaway	13.7	1.3	1.5	9.8
Allianz	10.6	1.1	0.6	2.7
AXA	10.8	0.8	0.4	3.2
AIG	16.3	0.7	1.3	26.7
Industry average	14.4	1	1.2	9.6

Further reading

[1] http://www.geico.com/information/aboutinsurance/.
[2] http://www.genre.com/aboutus/meet-genre/?c=n.
[3] http://www.genre.com/reinsurance-solutions/?c=n.
[4] http://www.berkshirehathaway.com/2012ar/linksannual12.html, Berkshire Annual Report 2012.
[5] http://www.berkshirehathaway.
[6] http://www.reuters.com/finance/stocks/companyProfile?symbol=BRKa.

Analysis of wealth—Walmart

10

10.1 Introduction

Walmart is an American multinational retail corporation which operates one of the world's largest chain of hypermarkets, discount department stores and grocery stores. By 2014, Walmart employed more than 2.2 million associates worldwide. According to the Fortune 500 Global list, Walmart is the world's largest company by revenue and the biggest private employer in the world. Walmart is a family owned business controlled by the Sam Walton family. The heirs of Walton own over 50% of Walmart through the holding company Walton Enterprises and individual holdings.

The company serves approximately 260 million customers each week through stores and websites globally. The firm have more than 11,000 stores in 27 countries. The company had a consolidated revenue of $486 billion in the year 2015. The company returned $64 billion as dividends and buybacks to the shareholders. The EPS were $4.99 in 2015 which was approximately 3% increase compared to the previous year. Approximately 57% of employees are women. Walmart have 3600 global ecommerce associates throughout the world. Walmart have more than 150 distribution centers which service stores, clubs and customers. The transportation fleet of Walmart consists of 6100 tractors, 61,000 trailers and more than 7800 drivers. Each distribution center provides support to approximately 100 stores in a radius of 150 miles.

10.2 Milestones of Walmart

Year	Event
1962	Sam Walton opened the first Walmart store in Rogers, Ark
1967	Walton owns 24 stores
1969	Walmart stores incorporated
1970	Walmart became public traded company. First stock sold for $16.50 per share
1972	Walmart listed on NYSE. The company had 51 stores. The sales reached $ 78 million
1979	Walmart foundation established
1980	$ 1 billion in annual sales. Company had 275 stores and 21,000 associates
1983	Opened First Sam Club. Walmart replaces cash registers with computerized point of sale system
1987	Company installs the largest private satellite communication system in United States to link company's operations through voice, data and video communication.
1988	First Walmart supercenter opened to combine general merchandise and full scale super market
1990	Walmart becomes the number one retailer in United States
1991	Walmart goes global by opening Sam's Club through joint venture with Cifra, the Mexican retail company

Strategic Financial Management Casebook.

Year   Event

1992   Walmart have operations with 1928 stores and clubs. The company employs 371,000
        associates.
1993   Walmart have its first $1 billion sales week
1998   Neighborhood market format introduced in Arkansas
1999   Walmart expands operation into United Kingdom with the acquisition of ASDA
2000   Walmart.com was established enabling customers to shop online. Walmart have 1.1
        million associates in 3989 stores and clubs globally
2002   Walmart topped the Fortune 500 list of America's largest companies. Walmart
        enters into Japanese market through its investment in firm Seiyu
2006   Introduces $4 generic drug prescription program
2007   Walmart.com launches site to store service
2009   Walmart enters Chile through acquisition of a majority stake in D&S S A. Sales
        exceeds $400 billion in annual sales for first time
2010   Joint Venture Bharti Walmart open its first store in India
2011   Acquires Massmart in South Africa. Walmart have more than 10,000 retail units
        around the world

Source: Walmart.com.

10.3 Business segments

10.3.1 Walmart United States

Walmart had started its humble beginnings as a small discount retailer in Rogers
Arkansas. Walmart offers customers the experience of one stop shopping by offering
deep assortment of products offerings ranging from grocery and entertainment to
sporting goods and crafts. Customers can shop directly in the store or shop online at
Walmart.com through the mobile applications. Walmart stores are present in 50 states
in United States. The product assortment is offered through three formats namely—
supercenter, discount store, and neighborhood market. Supercenters or hypermarkets
were established by Walmart in the year 1988. At present the supercenter possess
182,000 square feet and employs around 300 associates. These supercenters are open
24 hours a day and offers specialty shops like banks, salons, restaurants etc.
Supercenters of Walmart offer one stop shopping experience by offering combination
of grocery store with fresh produce, bakery, deli and dairy products along with
apparel, toys, electronics, home appliances, and furnishing. Discount stores are much
smaller than Supercenters with area of 10,600 square feet. Discount stores employ
around 200 associates. Neighborhood markets were designed by Walmart to serve
communities who require pharmacy, groceries, and merchandise. Neighborhood market are of 38,000 square feet size and employs around 95 associates.

10.3.2 Walmart international

In 1991, Walmart became an international company and presently operates in 27
countries. Walmart operate through subsidiaries in regions like Africa, Argentina,

Brazil, Canada, Central America, Chile, China, India, Japan, Mexico, and United Kingdom. Walmart operates more than 6200 stores internationally.

10.3.3 Sam's Club

Walmart established Sam's Club to facilitate small businesses to save money on merchandise purchased in bulk quantities. There are 650 clubs in United States and 100 international clubs. Sam's Club offers bulk groceries, consumables, general merchandise, and specialty services. Sam's Club serves more than 500,000 small entrepreneurs every day. Sam's Club offer comprehensive portfolio of services which includes savings on key business operations like payroll, accounting, and online marketing support. Sam club provides innovative initiatives like truckload savings, exports, and Club Pickup ordering programs.

10.3.4 Global ecommerce

The global ecommerce of Walmart is based in California with operations in Bangalore, India and Sao Paulo, Brazil. This business segment provides all online and mobile innovation activities for Walmart. There are approximately 45 million visits on Walmart's website Walmart.com. The mobile applications of Global ecommerce provides shipping options like Home Free, Site to Store, Pickup Today etc. Walmart operates ecommerce websites in 10 countries like United States, Argentina, Brazil, Canada, Chile, China, Japan, Mexico, South Africa, and United Kingdom.

In United States, Walmart had a total of 4574 units as of January 31, 2016. The Walmart International accounted for 6299 total units (see Tables 10.1 and 10.2).

10.4   Strategy

Walmart's customer proposition is based on focuses on price, access, assortment, and experience to create value for the company. In a historical sense, Walmart emphasized on price and assortment to create value for customers. The modern trend indicates that customers have become channel agnostic whereby shopping in stores is done online or through use of mobile phones. Walmart's strength lies in its

Table 10.1 Walmart stores—region wise

Region	Number of units
US	4574
Latin America	4067
Canada &EMEA	1429
Asia	799
Total	11,528

Table 10.2 **Walmart stores—Country wise**

Country	Number of units
Argentina	108
Brazil	499
Chile	395
Costa Rica	225
El Salvador	91
Guatemala	223
Honduras	82
Mexico	2360
Nicaragua	88
Canada	400
United Kingdom	621
Africa	408
China	432
Japan	346
India	21

Source: Walmart website.

unique assets, stores, clubs, global supply chain, and associates. Walmart relies on the "Every Day Low Price" (EDLP) strategy to build customer trust. The accessibility of Walmart has increased through its 11,000 stores, websites and mobile applications. Walmart provides an assortment of approximately eight million items on Walmart.com in United States. Approximately 75% of Walmart.com sales revenues are accounted from nonstore inventory. For manpower development, Walmart have made increased investments in wages and training and development for associates. Walmart is focusing on strategic initiatives for the integration of e-commerce with stores with focus area on assortment. The company announced $1 billion investment in US hourly associates to give higher wages and more training. Sam's Club focuses on strengthening digital integration through initiatives like Club Pickup. Walmart have made investments in global technology platform to strengthen usability and conversion across the e commerce websites and mobile apps. All business segments are focusing on integration of e commerce and mobile assets with stores and clubs like the "Click & Collect" pickup points in major markets. Walmart emphasizes high quality fresh food experience by improving quality through locally sourced fresh fruits and vegetables. Supercenters provide a convenient one stop solution to save time and money for customers. Walmart is expected to add approximately 16 million total net retail square feet in year 2016. In 2015, Walmart implemented EDLC agenda in China through programs like "We Operate for Less" and "We Buy for Less" programs through which the company saved $150 million.[1] Walmart have adopted optimization techniques to reduce empty miles driven. In 2015, Walmart hauled logistics with over 161 million cases while increasing miles

[1] Annual Report Walmart 2015.

only by 24 million. Walmart improved the efficiency of its truck fleet system by 87.4% in year 2014 compared to the year 2005. The company focuses on growth in net sales, club sales, ecommerce sales and unit square feet growth. In the year 2016, Walmart have plans to add approximately 26−30 million square feet with focus on continued investment in neighborhood markets. The company announced plans to invest approximately $1.5 billion in ecommerce websites and mobile applications to support stores and clubs.

10.5 Challenges

Walmart faces strong challenges with respect to sales competition from other discount stores, department stores, dollar, variety and specialty stores, warehouse clubs, supermarkets, ecommerce, and catalog businesses. Walmart also faces competition from companies with respect to acquiring prime retail site locations and attracting quality employees. The company also faces challenges due to various macro-economic factors. The retail companies are generally affected by factors like competitive pressures, consumer disposal income, consumer debt level and buying patterns, consumer credit availability, exchange rate fluctuations, insurance costs, and cyber security attacks.

10.6 Sustainability activities

In 2014, Walmart Foundation gave $1.4 billion in cash and in kind contributions globally. Walmart Foundation's initiatives are focused on women, veterans and small entrepreneurs. The Walmart Foundation awards funding through its local, state, national, and international giving programs.

Walmart had announced five-year commitment to hire 100,000 veterans by year 2018. In the last five years, Sam's Club giving program have given approximately $18 million to national nonprofit organizations like Accion US, SCORE and the Institute for Veteran and Military Families. In 2015, Sam club started a new program called Small Business Economic Mobility Initiate which is a five year grant based investment in small businesses by providing capital and training to entrepreneurs. In 2015, Walmart and Walmart Foundation announced $16 million grants to seven nonprofit organizations to provide training and education to US retail workers. This grant is the first part of $100 million commitment to provide economic mobility to US retail workforce.[2] In 2015, Walmart provided $20 million to support veterans and families. Walmart also announced plans to provide another $20 million through 2019 to support reintegration activities for veterans. Walmart had provided $100 million in grants to provide training to 540,000 women as a part of Women's Economic Empowerment program. Walmart focuses on waste reduction in its operations. Approximately 81% of the materials from stores, clubs and distribution centers are diverted from landfills.

---

[2] http://giving.walmart.com/walmart-foundation/opportunity.

In Japan and United Kingdom, the diversion rate is about 90%.[3] In 2013, Walmart donated 571 million pounds of food to local food banks and hunger relief organizations like Feeding America. In 2013, Walmart United Kingdom introduced light version of private label Eden falls water bottles which are lighter. Walmart have partnership initiatives with organizations to make proper recycling of used electronics. In 2013, Walmart initiated a smartphone trade in program in partnership with CExhange which offers an immediate credit of range $50−$300 for more than 100 smartphones. Walmart also have a tablet trade in program for electronics. Walmart have invested more than $1.5 million to strengthen technology infrastructure for disaster management. In 2015, Walmart gave 46,000 grants of $47 million value to different organizations. Walmart provided $4.5 million to the teacher reward program which has benefited more than 90,000 teachers.

10.7 Acquisitions

In 1997, Walmart acquired a majority stake in Cifra. Walmart had invested more than $1 billion in Seiyu since the year 2002. In 2005, Walmart acquired Seiyu one of the largest supermarket chains in Japan which was established in 1963. Seiku became a wholly owned subsidiary of Walmart. The company had spent $878 million to buy out minority shareholders of Seiku. Walmart offered 140 yen per Seiyu common share in a tender offer which represented a 61% premium to the closing share price of 87 yen.

Walmart Mexico acquired Walmart's operations in Central America from Walmart Stores Inc. in the year 2009. In the same year Walmart acquired majority stake in Chile's leading food retailer Distribución y Servicio D&S S.A. Walmart Chile operates several formats like hypermarkets, supermarkets, and Ekono convenience stores.

In 2011, Walmart acquired majority stake in Massmart Holdings Ltd. Massmart have approximately 350 stores in South Africa and 12 sub Saharan countries. The deal was valued at $2.4 billion dollars. The brands acquired by Walmart include Game, Cambridge, Dion Wired, Makro Kangela, Builders Warehouse, Builders Superstores, Rhino Cash and Carry, Jumbo Cash and Carry. By year 2013, Walmart reduced plastic bag waste by 38% compared to year 2007. This represented a reduction of 10 billion bags annually.

10.8 Governance[4]

The number of directors are fixed by the board which are pursuant to the resolution adopted by majority of the board or by the stockholders. The number of directors in

---

[3] http://corporate.walmart.com/global-responsibility/sustainability/.

[4] http://stock.walmart.com/investors/corporate-governance/governance-documents/default.aspx.

the board at present is 15. The majority of directors meet the criteria for independence as required by the New York Stock Exchange. The outside director is expected to serve for at least six years. The board will meet at least five times per year. The board has a practice of segregating the offices of Chairperson of the board and the CEO.

The Board of Directors Committee consists of Audit Committee, Compensation, Nominating and Governance Committee, Executive Committee, Strategic Planning and Finance Committee, Technology, and e-commerce Committee. The audit committee assist the Board in monitoring the integrity of the financial reporting process and systems of internal controls. The executive committee exercises the powers and duties of the board between board meetings. The Compensation, Nominating and Governance Committee will conduct an annual review of the CEO's performance. The global compensation committee administer the company's variable compensation with respect to incentive compensation and equity based compensation awards. The strategic planning and finance committee review and analyze financial matters and assist the board in long range strategic planning. The technology and ecommerce committee assists the board to review and provide insights on matters relating to information technology and systems. It is required that within five years of joining Board, new nonmanagement director will be required to own an amount of shares, or stock units in value to five times the annual cash retainer offered to each director at the time the director joined the board. Walmart have stipulated a code of ethics for CFO and all senior financial officers relating to ethical conduct, conflicts of interests, and compliance with all laws. The statement of ethics applies to all associates at all levels of Walmart globally and all members of the board of directors of Walmart Stores Inc. The statement of ethics applies to all associates and directors of Walmart controlled subsidiaries. The global anticorruption policy of Walmart prohibits corrupt payment in all circumstances whether in dealings with government officials or individuals in the private sector. Walmart's government relations departments coordinate company interactions with elected officials and legislative and regulatory bodies at the federal, state, and local level.

10.9   Risk management

Walmart is exposed to market risks which include changes in interest rates and fluctuations in currency exchange rates. Walmart faces interest rate risk on account of short term borrowings and long term debt issuances. The firm hedges interest rate risk by managing the mix of fixed and variable rate debt and interest rate swaps. Walmart is also exposed to fluctuations in foreign currency exchange rates due to net investments and operations in countries outside United States. Walmart hedge foreign currency risk by entering into currency swaps and considering certain foreign currency denominated long term debt as net investment hedges. The company also evaluate long lived assets other than goodwill and assets with indefinite lives for indicators of impairment. Credit risk is managed through established approval procedures like setting concentration limits by counter party and review credit rating. Walmart is a party to receive variable rate, pay fixed rate interest rate swaps that the firm uses to hedge the interest rate risk of certain nonUS denominated debt.

10.10 Borrowings

The short term debt of Walmart consists of commercial papers and lines of credit. The committed lines of credit have maturity period between June 2015 and June 2019 and carries interest rates ranging between LIBOR plus 10 basis points and LIBOR plus 75 basis points with commitment fees ranging between 1.5 and 4 basis points. The company had trade and standby letters of credit totaling $4.6 billion in the year 2015. As of January 31st 2015, Walmart had $500 million in debt with embedded put options.

Credit rating agencies have given strong ratings for Walmart's commercial paper issues and long term debt. In 2015, the S&P gave A-1 + and AA ratings for the commercial paper and long term debt of Walmart. Moody's Investors Service gave rating of P-1 and Aa2 for the commercial paper and long term debt of Walmart. Fitch gave a rating of F1 + and AA rating for Walmart's commercial paper and long term debt. The company has future lease commitments for land and building for approximately 282 future locations. These lease commitments have lease terms which range from 1 to 30 years.

10.11 Walmart shares

Walmart's IPO was in the year 1970. Walmart offered 300,000 shares of its common stock to the public at a price of $16.50 per share. Walmart started trading on the New York Stock Exchange on August 25 1972.

Table 10.3 **Dividend history 2000−15**

Year	Dividend per share	Year	Dividend per share
2000	0.24	2008	0.952
2001	0.28	2009	1.092
2002	0.3	2010	1.212
2003	0.36	2011	1.46
2004	0.52	2012	1.592
2005	0.6	2013	1.88
2006	0.672	2014	1.92
2007	0.88	2015	1.96

Table 10.4 Stock splits

2:1 Stock splits	Shares	Cost per share	Market price on split date
Initial offering	100	$16.50	
May 1971	200	$8.25	$47
March 1972	400	$4.125	$47.50
August 1975	800	$2.0625	$23.00
November 1980	1600	$1.03125	$50.00
June 1982	3200	$0.515625	$49.875
June 1983	6400	$0.257813	$81.625
September 1985	12,800	$0.128906	$49.75
June 1987	25,600	$0.064453	$66.625
June 1990	51,200	$0.032227	$62.50
Feburary 1993	102,400	$0.016113	$63.625
March 1999	204,800	$0.008057	$89.75

10.12 Dividends

Walmart provided an annual cash dividend, which was paid quarterly to shareholders since the first dividend of $0.05 per share annual dividend paid in the year 1974. The company paid annual dividends of $5.4 billion, $6.1 billion and $6.2 billion during the years 2013, 2014, and 2015, respectively (see Table 10.3).

The average growth rate in dividend per share had been 15% during the period 2000–15. The dividend per share increased by 44% in year 2004 compared to the previous year. The dividend per share increased by 31% in year 2007 compared to the previous year. The dividend data was sourced from Yahoo finance.

10.13 Stock splits[5]

Since 1970, Walmart had undertaken 11 two for one stock splits (see Table 10.4).

10.14 Share repurchase

Walmart had undertaken share repurchase program at different periods of time. Walmart had on June 6 2013 replaced the previous $15 billion repurchase program which had approximately $712 million of remaining authorization for share repurchases as of that date, with a new $15 billion repurchase program which was announced on June 7 2013. This current repurchase program have no set expiration dates or restrictions regard to limit period. As of January 31 2015 the authorization for $10.3 billion of share repurchases remained under the current share repurchase

[5] http://stock.walmart.com/investors/stock-information/dividend-history/default.aspx.

Table 10.5 **Repurchase statistics during 2013−15**

	2013	2014	2015
Total number of shares repurchased (millions)	113.2	89.1	13.4
Average price paid per share	$67.15	$74.99	$75.82
Total cash paid for repurchases	$7600	$6683	$1015

Source: Annual Report 2015.

Table 10.6 **Unit counts**

Year	2011	2012	2013	2014	2015
Walmart US segment	3804	3868	4005	4203	4516
Walmart International segment	4191	5287	5783	6107	6290
Sam's Club segment	609	611	620	632	647
Total	8604	9766	10,408	10,942	11,453

program. The timing of share repurchase program are regularly reviewed in the context of factors like current cash needs, capacity for leverage, cost of borrowings and market price of the common stock (see Table 10.5).

10.15 Operational highlights

Walmart International counts had the largest share among the total number of counts in global terms (see Table 10.6).

The Walmart US sales accounted for approximately 60% of the total sales. The sales of Walmart International accounted for 28% of the total sales revenues. Sam's Club sales revenues accounted for 12% of the total sales during the three-year period 2013−15 (see Table 10.7). Table 10.8 gives the operating income of Walmart during the three year period 2013-2015. Table 10.9 shows the capital expenditure incurred by Walmart during the period 2014-2015.

10.16 Financial highlights

Table 10.10 shows the financial highlights of Walmart during the ten year period 2007-2016. The total revenues increased from $348.65 billion to $482.130 billion during the period 2007−16. The net income increased from $11.284 billion to $14.694 billion during the above period. The operating cash flow increased $20.164 billion to $27.389 billion during the above period. The total cash including cash, cash equivalents and marketable securities increased from $7.767 billion in 2007 to

Table 10.7 **Net sales in millions of dollars**

Year	2013	2014	2015
Walmart US	274433	279406	288049
Walmart International	134748	136,513	136160
Sam's Club	56423	57157	58020

Table 10.8 **Operating income in millions of dollars**

Year	2013	2014	2015
Walmart US	21,103	21,787	21,336
Walmart International	6365	5153	6171
Sam's Club	1859	1843	1976

Table 10.9 **Capital expenditures in million dollars**

Year	2014	2015
New stores and clubs, including expansions and relocations	5083	4128
Information systems, distribution, digital retail, and others	2539	3288
Remodels	1030	822
Total US	8652	8238
Walmart International	4463	3936
Total	13,115	12,174

Source: Walmart Annual Report 2015.

$8.705 billion in year 2016. The market capitalization values given are based on January in each year. The market capitalization increased from $197 billion in the year 2007 to $209.83 billion in the year 2016. The capital expenditure decreased from $15.666 billion in year 2007 to $11.477 billion in year 2016.

The year on year growth rate of revenues during the period 2008−16 reveal that revenue growth rate was highest in the year 2008 compared to the previous year. Revenues grew by 9% during the year 2008.The operating cash flow increased by 14% in year 2009.The net income increased by 14% during the year 2011. The total cash grew by approximately 25% in fiscal year 2015. The market capitalization increased by 14% in year 2015.The average growth rate of revenues during the period 2008−16 was 3.7%. The operating income and operating cash flow increased by 2% and 4% on average basis during the period 2008−16. The average growth rate in net income and total cash during the above period was 3%. The average growth rate in book value of equity and market capitalization was approximately 3 and 1% respectively. The total assets and total debt increased by 3 and 4% on average basis during the period 2008−16. In 2015, Walmart generated free cash flow of more than $16 billion.

Table 10.10 **Financial highlights in millions of dollars**

Year	2007	2008	2009	2010	2011	2012	2013	2014	2015	2016
Revenues	348,650	378,799	405,607	408,214	421,849	446,950	469,162	476,294	485,651	482,130
Operating income	20,497	21,996	22,798	23,950	25,542	26,558	27,801	26,558	27,147	24,105
Operating cash flow	20,164	20,354	23,147	26,249	23,643	24,255	25,591	23,257	28,564	27,389
Net income	11,284	12,731	13,400	14,335	16,389	15,699	16,999	16,022	16,363	14,694
Cash and cash equivalents	7767	5492	7275	7907	7395	6550	7781	7281	9135	8705
Book value of equity	61,573	64,608	65,285	70,468	68,542	71,315	76,343	76,255	81,394	80,546
Market capitalization	197,007	201,590	186,171	202,286	197,142	209,728	231,814	241,440	274,315	209,830
Total assets	151,587	163,514	163,429	170,407	180,663	193,406	203,105	204,751	203,490	199,581
Long term debt	30,735	33,402	34,549	36,401	43,842	47,079	41,417	44,559	43,495	44,030
Capital expenditure	15,666	14,937	11,499	12,184	12,699	13,510	12,898	13,115	12,174	11,477

Table 10.11 **Profitability ratios in percent**

Year	2007	2008	2009	2010	2011	2012	2013	2014	2015	2016
Gross margin	24.2	24.4	24.5	25.4	25.3	25	24.9	24.8	24.8	25.1
Operating margin	5.9	5.8	5.6	5.9	6.1	5.9	5.9	5.6	5.6	5
Net margin	3.24	3.36	3.3	3.51	3.89	3.51	3.62	3.36	3.37	3.05
Return on assets	7.8	8.09	8.2	8.58	9.33	8.39	8.57	7.86	8.01	7.29
Return on equity	19.67	20.18	20.63	21.08	23.53	22.45	23.02	21	20.76	18.15
Return on invested capital	12.77	13.26	13.52	14.22	15.4	14.11	14.44	13.3	13.57	12.51

10.17   Ratio analysis

The average gross margin during the period 2007−11 increased from 24.76% to 24.92% during the period 2012−16. The average operating margin and net margin during the period 2007−16 was approximately 6% and 4%, respectively. The average ROA, ROE, and ROIC during the period 2007−16 was 8%, 21%, and 13.7%, respectively. The comparison of the average profitability ratios during the two five year periods suggest that the profitability ratios on average have remained constant (see Table 10.11).

The average revenue per share was 121.06 during the period 2007−16. The average revenue per share during the five-year period increased from 99.82 to 142.30 during the period 2012−16. The average EBITDA per share during the period 2007−16 was 9.14. The average EBITDA per share increased from 7.6 to 10.67 during the two periods of comparison. The average EPS during the period 2007−16 was 4.14. The average EPS increased from 3.48 to 4.81 during the five-year period 2012−16 compared to the period 2007−11 (see Table 10.12).

The average book value per share was 20.40 during the period 2007−16. The two five-year period of comparison (2007−11 and 2012−16) suggest that the book value per share increased from 17.16 to 23.64. The average dividends per share during the period 2007−16 was 1.36. The average DPS increased from 0.96 to 1.76. The average DPO during the period 2007−16 was 32%. The average DPO increased from 27% to 37%. The average total debt per share during the period 2007−16 was 13.73. The average debt per share increased from 11.29 to 16.17 during the two five year periods of comparison (see Table 10.13).

The average price earnings ratio during the period 2007−15 was 14.91. The average price to book ratio and price to sales ratio during the period 2007−15 was 3.05 and 0.52. The average price to earnings growth ratio during the period 2007−15 was 1.52. The average price to free cash flow and price to operating cash flow was 23.74 and 9.24. The growth rate used for calculation of PEG was the five year EBITDA growth rate (see Table 10.14).

The average debt equity ratio was 0.68 during the period 2007−15. The average long term debt to assets during the period 2007−15 was 0.21. The average Interest Coverage Ratio (ICR) was 11.3 during the period 2007−15. The earnings ability to pay interest charges is quite comfortable for Walmart (see Table 10.15).

The average current ratio during the period 2007−15 was 0.88 and the quick ratio during the above period was 0.25. Both the current and quick ratio remained the constant during the entire period of analysis (see Table 10.16).

The days payable and days sales outstanding have been fluctuating over the period 2007−15. The average asset turnover ratio and inventory turnover during the period 2007−15 was 2.40 and 8.50. The average days' inventory during the period 2007−15 was 43 days while the average days' payable was 38.2. The average days' sales outstanding was 4.27 days (see Table 10.17).

The table 10.18 gives the growth rate of revenues in terms of year on year, five and 10-year average growth rates for each year. The source of data was Morningstar. com. The growth rate in revenues is declining over the period of analysis.

The table 10.19 gives the year on year, five and 10-year average growth rates of operating income. The growth rate in operating income is showing a declining period.

Table 10.12 Per share cash flow ratios

Year	2007	2008	2009	2010	2011	2012	2013	2014	2015	2016
Revenue per share	83.58	92.95	102.35	105.26	114.95	128.53	138.29	145.08	149.75	149.87
EBITDA per share	6.3	7.02	7.55	8.08	9.1	10.01	10.74	10.92	11.23	10.46
EPS	2.71	3.13	3.39	3.71	4.47	4.52	5.02	4.88	5.05	4.57

Table 10.13 Per share data

Year	2007	2008	2009	2010	2011	2012	2013	2014	2015	2016
Book value per share	14.91	16.26	16.52	18.61	19.49	20.87	23.04	23.59	25.22	25.47
Dividends per share	0.67	0.88	0.95	1.09	1.21	1.46	1.59	1.88	1.92	1.96
Dividend payout ratio	0.23	0.28	0.28	0.29	0.29	0.32	0.32	0.39	0.39	0.43
Total debt per share	9.45	11.24	10.69	10.91	14.18	15.63	16.34	17.52	15.54	15.82

Table 10.14 Price multiples

Year	2007	2008	2009	2010	2011	2012	2013	2014	2015
PE	17.61	16.24	13.89	14.37	12.49	13.57	13.93	15.3	16.82
PB	3.2	3.12	2.85	2.87	2.88	2.94	3.04	3.17	3.37
PS	0.57	0.55	0.46	0.51	0.49	0.48	0.51	0.52	0.57
PEG	1.17	1.23	1.2	1.46	1.45	1.47	1.5	1.68	2.54
Price to free cash Flow	46.35	38.04	16.01	14.76	18.86	19.86	18.73	24.25	16.82
Price to operating cash flow	9.97	10.18	8.05	7.91	8.74	8.8	9.29	10.57	9.65

Table 10.15 **Leverage ratios**

Year	2007	2008	2009	2010	2011	2012	2013	2014	2015
Debt equity ratio	0.63	0.69	0.65	0.59	0.73	0.75	0.71	0.74	0.62
Long term debt to assets	0.2	0.2	0.21	0.21	0.24	0.24	0.2	0.22	0.21
ICR	11.33	10.44	10.44	11.62	11.58	11.42	12.33	11.51	11.03

Table 10.16 **Liquidity ratios**

Year	2007	2008	2009	2010	2011	2012	2013	2014	2015
Current ratio	0.90	0.82	0.88	0.86	0.89	0.88	0.83	0.88	0.97
Quick ratio	0.25	0.22	0.26	0.28	0.27	0.23	0.22	0.24	0.28

Table 10.17 **Efficiency ratios**

Year	2007	2008	2009	2010	2011	2012	2013	2014	2015
Asset turnover ratio	2.40	2.40	2.47	2.45	2.40	2.39	2.36	2.34	2.38
Days inventory	45.35	43.88	41.82	40.30	40.00	41.97	43.78	45.19	44.99
Days payable	39.38	38.68	34.63	36.51	38.89	39.89	39.45	38.14	38.40
Days sales outstanding	2.98	3.51	3.52	3.71	4.40	4.85	5.27	5.12	5.09
Inventory turnover	8.05	8.32	8.73	9.06	9.12	8.70	8.34	8.08	8.10

Table 10.18 **Growth rate of revenues**

Growth rate in percent	2012	2013	2014	2015	2016
Year on year	5.95	4.97	1.52	1.96	−0.73
5 year	5.09	4.37	3.27	3.54	2.71
10 year	7.35	6.65	6.29	5.36	4.33

Table 10.19 **Growth rate of operating income**

Growth rate in percent	2012	2013	2014	2015	2016
Year on year	3.98	4.68	−3.34	1.02	−11.21
5 year	5.32	4.8	3.34	2.54	−1.15
10 year	8.2	7.38	5.99	4.74	2.67

10.18 Ownership characteristics

Approximately 65% of the capital ownership is composed of equity and debt comprises 35% of the capital ownership in year 2015.

Institutions held approximately 83 per of the equity ownership currently. Mutual funds held approximately 16% and insiders held approximately 1% of the equity ownership structure. The top 10 mutual funds held 10% of the total equity capital. The top 10 financial institutions held approximately 57% of the total equity capital. The data source was Morningstar.com.

John T Walton Estate Trust held 44.2% of the total shares held by the company. Vanguard Group and State Street Corp held 3 and 2%, respectively of the total shares of the company.

The top five mutual funds held 3.13% of the equity ownership of the company (see Tables 10.20–10.22).

10.19 Wealth creation by Walmart

The cumulative returns given by Walmart during the 44-year period (August 1972 to April 2016) is analyzed in this section. The analysis covers monthly returns

Table 10.20 **Equity ownership in year 2015**

Type	Value in million dollars
Institutions	166,174.68
Mutual funds	30,935.56
Insiders	1123.19
Total	198,233.43

Table 10.21 **Top institutions equity ownership**

SL	Institutions	Percent of shares held
1	John T. Walton Estate Trust	44.22
2	Vanguard Group Inc.	3.17
3	State Street Corp	2.18
4	Walmart Stores Profit Sharing	1.78
5	Berkshire Hathaway Inc.	1.75
6	BlackRock Fund Advisors	1.32
7	Dodge & Cox	0.97
8	Northern Trust Investments N A	0.56
9	State Farm Mutual Automobile Ins Co	0.52
10	State Street Global Advisors Ltd.	0.47
	Total	56.94

Table 10.22 Top mutual funds equity ownership

SL	Name of mutual fund	Percent of shares held
1	Vanguard Total Stock Mkt Idx	0.87
2	Vanguard 500 Index Inv	0.62
3	Dodge & Cox Stock	0.58
4	Vanguard Institutional Index	0.54
5	SPDR S&P 500 ETF	0.52

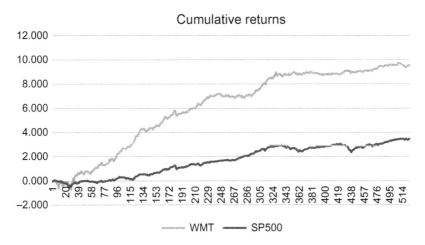

Figure 10.1 Comparison of cumulative returns 1972−2016.

involving 524 months during this 44-year period. Walmart stock generated cumulative returns of 954.95% during the 44-year period based on monthly returns. Suppose an investor invested $1000 in the stock of Walmart in August 1972. Based on active trading in which the stock is bought and sold every month, the Walmart investment would have increased to $10,550. The adjusted closing price of Walmart on August 8 1972 was $0.040. The adjusted closing price of Walmart on April 1 2016 was $69.15. The stock price increased by 1731.217 times during the above 44-year period. Consider the case of an investor who had invested an amount of $1000 during August 1972. If he had held his investment till April 2016, his investment would have grown to a value of $1,731,217.

The cumulative returns during the 44-year period for the market index S&P 500 reveals that the index had generated cumulative returns of 345.6% on the basis of monthly returns involving 524 months during August 1972 to April 2016 period (see Fig. 10.1).

The cumulative returns based on monthly returns for 44-year period for Walmart was approximately 955% while the cumulative returns for S&P 500 based on the

Table 10.23 Yearly returns in percent

Year	WMT	S&P500	Excess returns
2010	3.99	13.8	−9.81
2011	14.1	1.15	12.95
2012	17.31	13.16	4.15
2013	17.58	26.5	−8.92
2014	12.64	11.13	1.51
2015	−29.22	0.1	−29.32

Table 10.24 Holding period yield

Year	HPY in percent
2010	3.26
2011	9.50
2012	13.94
2013	15.26
2014	17.88
2015	−25.86

Table 10.25 Excess value added in millions of dollars

Year	2010	2011	2012	2013	2014	2015
Book value of equity	70,468	68,542	71,315	76,343	76,255	81,394
Market value of equity	202,286	197,142	209,728	231,814	241,440	274,315
BV as per cent of MV	0.348	0.348	0.340	0.329	0.316	0.297
Excess value	131,818	128,600	138,413	155,471	165,185	192,921

above period was approximately was approximately 345%. Walmart had outperformed the market index during the period of analysis.

The yearly returns of Walmart and S&P 500 are compared during the six-year period 2010−15 The Walmart stock had outperformed the S&P500 Index in three out of six years of analysis. Excess returns is estimated as the difference between returns of Walmart and S&P 500. Walmart had generated the highest excess returns of 12.95% in the year 2011. Though in the year 2013, Walmart generated returns of 17.58, the S&P 500 index returns was 26.5% in the same year. In 2015, Walmart had a negative return of 29.22% (see Table 10.23).

The holding period yield of 17.88% was highest in the year 2014. The holding period yield was 15.26% in the year 2013. The annual holding period yield was approximately 5% during the six-year period 2010−15 (see Table 10.24).

The average book value as % of market value during the five-year period 2010−15 was 33%. The average book value as% of market value was approximately 30% in the year 2015. The excess value is the difference between the market value and the book value of equity. The excess value in year 2015 amounted to $192.92 billion dollars (see Table 10.25).

10.20 Estimation of WACC

Cost of equity can be estimated using dividend discount model and capital asset pricing model.

Cost of equity using dividend discount model.

Cost of equity = Expected dividend next year/Current market price + growth rate

The five-year dividend growth rate is estimated as 10.09% based on geometric mean.

Current dividend = $1.96

Expected dividend next period = $1.96 \times 1.10 = \$2.16$

Current market price = $69.15

Cost of equity = 2.16/69.15 +0.10 = 13.12%

The cost of equity can also be estimated using the capital asset pricing model.

Cost of equity = Risk free rate + beta $\times$ Risk premium.

Risk free rate is the average yield to maturity on the 30-year treasury bond rate during the period 2014−16.[6]

Year	Yield to maturity on 30 year treasury bond
2014	3.55
2015	2.63
2016	2.63
Average	2.94%

Risk free rate = 2.94%

Beta is estimated by regressing Walmart monthly stock returns on monthly market index S&P500 returns during the three-year period 2014−15.

Beta = 0.373

Return on market index is the average returns on the S&P 500 index during the three-year period 2013−15.

Return on S&P 500 index during 2013−15 = 11.23%

Risk premium = Return on market index − Risk free rate = 11.23−2.94 = 8.29%.

Cost of equity = 2.94 + 0.373*8.29 = 6.03%.

For estimation purposes we assume cost of equity as 6.03% since CAPM model incorporates the risk characteristics.

Cost of debt is estimated based on the interest rate in the year 2015.

Interest paid in 2015 = $2461 million

Short term debt = $6402 million

Long term debt = $41,086 million

Total debt = $47,488 million

Interest rate = 2461/47,488 = 0.0518

Cost of debt = 5.18%

The effective tax rate during the three-year period 2013−15 was 32%.

After tax cost of debt = 5.18 $\times$ (1−0.32) = 3.52 %

[6] https://www.treasury.gov/resource-center/data-chart-center/interest-rates/Pages/Historic-Yield-Data-Visualization.aspx.

Market capitalization in year 2015 = $274,315 million
Book value of debt in year 2015 = $47,488 million
Total value = $321,803 million.
Weight of equity (We) = 274,315/321,803 = 0.85
Weight of debt (Wd) = 47,488/321,803 = 0.15
WACC = We × Cost of equity + Wd × After tax cost of debt
= 0.85 × 6.03 + 0.15 × 3.52 = 5.66%.
The weighted average cost of capital = 5.66%

10.21   Valuation of Walmart

10.21.1   Economic value

Economic value is estimated as net operating income after taxes (NOPAT) −Capital charge.
Profit before interest and tax (PBIT) − Income tax = NOPAT.
Capital employed = Stock holder equity + Long term debt
Capital charge = Capital employed × WACC
Economic Value (EV) = NOPAT − Capital charge (see Table 10.26).

The EV for Walmart in the year 2015 is estimated as $12.223 billion.

Table 10.26 Estimation of Economic Value (EV)

	in million dollars
PBIT in 2015	27,147
Income tax	7985
NOPAT	19,162
Stockholder equity	81,394
Long term debt	41,086
Capital employed	122,480
WACC	5.66%
Capital charge	6932.37
EV	12,229.63

Table 10.27 Equity spread

Stock holder equity	81,394
ROE IN 2015	20.76%
COE IN 2015	6.03%
Equity spread	11,989.34

Table 10.28 **Dividend trends**

Year	2010	2011	2012	2013	2014	2015
EPS	3.71	4.47	4.52	5.02	4.88	5.05
DPS	1.09	1.21	1.46	1.59	1.88	1.92
DPO	0.294	0.271	0.323	0.317	0.385	0.380

Table 10.29 **Estimation of growth rate from fundamentals for DDM**

Year	2010	2011	2012	2013	2014	2015
RR	0.71	0.73	0.68	0.68	0.61	0.62
ROE	0.21	0.24	0.22	0.23	0.21	0.21
Growth rate	0.15	0.17	0.15	0.16	0.13	0.13

Table 10.30 **Present value of dividends in high growth phase**

Year	1	2	3	4	5
EPS	5.797	6.654	7.638	8.768	10.065
DPO	0.328	0.328	0.328	0.328	0.328
DPS	1.901	2.183	2.505	2.876	3.301
PV	$1.79	$1.94	$2.10	$2.28	$2.46
SUM	$10.58				

10.21.2 Equity spread

Equity spread is a variation of the EV measures. Equity spread is the difference between the ROE and the required return on equity (cost of equity)

Equity spread = (Return on equity − Cost of equity) × Equity capital (see Table 10.27).

Equity spread for Walmart is estimated as $11,989.34 million.

10.21.3 Valuation of Walmart using DDM

The average growth rate of dividends during the period 2010−16 based on geometric mean was 10.3%. The average historical growth rate of earnings during the period 2010−16 was 3.5%.

The average DPO during the period 2010−15 was 32.8% (see Table 10.28).

Retention eatio = 1 − DPO
Growth rate = Retention ratio × Return on equity.
The average growth rate of earning estimated from fundamentals is calculated as 14.79% (see Table 10.29).

Two stage DDM

Two stage DDM is used to value Walmart stock. It is assumed that Walmart's earning per share will grow at a high growth rate of 14.79% for the next five years and thereafter at the stable growth of rate of US economy. The growth rate of US GDP during the period 2013−14 is 2.3%.[7]

High growth period inputs

High growth period = 5 years

High growth rate = 14.79%

EPS in year 2015 = 5.05

EPS in year 2016 = 5.05 × 1.1479 = $5.797

Average DPO = 32.8%.

Present value of dividends in high growth phase = $10.58 (see Table 10.30)

Stable period inputs

Growth rate in stable period = 2.3%

Growth rate = Retention ratio × Return on equity of industry sector.

Return on equity of the industry sector = 19.2%[8]

Retention ratio = Growth rate/Return on equity of industry sector.

  = 2.3/19.2 = 0.12

DPO = 1−0.12 = 0.88

Terminal value = DPS in stable period/(Cost of equity − growth rate in stable period)

EPS at end of high growth period	**10.065**
EPS at beginning of stable period	10.30
DPO	0.88
DPS in stable period	9.06
Terminal value	226.5754
PV	$166.93
Value of Walmart stock	$177.51

Value of Walmart stock = Present value of dividends in high growth phase + Present value of dividends in stable phase period = 10.58 + 166.93 = $177.51.

Table 10.31 Adjusted capital expenditure in millions of dollars

Year	2011	2012	2013	2014	2015	2016
Capital expenditures	12,699	13,510	12,898	13,115	12,174	11,477
Depreciation and amortization	7641	8106	8478	8870	9173	9454
Net capital expenditures	5058	5404	4420	4245	3001	2023
Net acquisitions	202	3548	316	15		
Adjusted net capital expenditures	5260	8952	4736	4260	3001	2023

[7] http://data.worldbank.org/indicator/NY.GDP.MKTP.KD.ZG.

[8] http://www.morningstar.com/stocks/XNYS/WMT/quote.html.

Table 10.32 Noncash working capital in millions of dollars

Year	2010	2011	2012	2013	2014	2015	2016
Total current assets	48,032	51,893	54,975	59,940	61,185	63,278	60,239
Cash and cash equivalents	7907	7395	6550	7781	7281	9135	8705
Noncash current assets	40,125	44,498	48,425	52,159	53,904	54,143	51,534
Total current liabilities	55,543	58,484	62,300	71,818	69,345	65,253	64,619
Short term debt	4919	6022	6348	12,719	12,082	6670	6004
Noninterest bearing current liabilities	50,624	52,462	55,952	59,099	57,263	58,583	58,615
Noncash working capital	−10,499	−7964	−7527	−6940	−3359	−4440	−7081
Change in noncash working capital		2535	437	587	3581	−1081	−2641

Table 10.33 Estimation of reinvestment rate for FCFE model

Year	2012	2013	2014	2015	2016
Adjusted net capital expenditure	8952	4736	4260	3001	2023
Change in noncash working capital	437	587	3581	−1081	−2641
Net debt issued	111	−1267	2104	1270	−4393
Reinvestment	9278	6590	5737	650	3,775
Net income	16,387	17,756	16,695	17,099	15,080
Reinvestment rate	0.57	0.37	0.34	0.04	0.25

Table 10.34 Estimation of FCFE

Year	2012	2013	2014	2015	2016
Net income	16,387	17,756	16,695	17,099	15,080
Adjusted net capital expenditure	8952	4736	4260	3001	2023
Change in noncash working capital	437	587	3581	−1081	−2641
New debt issued	5050	211	7072	5174	39
Debt repayment	4939	1478	4968	3904	4432
FCFE	7,109	11,166	10,958	16,449	11,305

Table 10.35 Estimation of growth rate from fundamentals for FCFE model

Year	2012	2013	2014	2015	2016
Reinvestment rate	0.57	0.37	0.34	0.04	0.25
Return on equity	0.225	0.230	0.210	0.208	0.182
Growth rate	0.127	0.085	0.072	0.008	0.045

Table 10.36 Present value of FCFE in high growth phase

Year	1	2	3	4	5
Net income	161,05	17,201	18,370	19,619	20,954
Reinvestment	5057	5401	5768	6161	6579
FCFE	11,048	11,800	12,602	13,459	14,374
PV of FCFE in high growth period	10,420	10,496	10,572	10,649	10,726
Sum	$52,862.25				

The cost of equity determined from the dividend model is estimated as 13.12% as given in the estimation of WACC. Based on this estimate of cost of equity, the value of Walmart on the basis of DDM is estimated as $61.71. See the worksheet *DDM of Walmart.xlsx* for detailed calculation.

10.22 Estimation of value of Walmart using Free Cash Flow to Equity (FCFE)

Net capital expenditures = Capital expenditures − Depreciation and amortization.
Adjusted net capital expenditure = Net capital expenditures + Net acquisitions (see Table 10.31).
Noncash current assets = Total current assets − cash and cash equivalents.
Noninterest bearing current liabilities = Total current liabilities − short term debt.
Noncash working capital = Noncash current assets − Noninterest bearing current liabilities (see Table 10.32).
The values except rates are given in millions of dollars.
Reinvestment = Adjusted net capital expenditure + Change in noncash working capital −Net debt issued
Reinvestment rate = Reinvestment/Net income
The average reinvestment rate during the five-year period 2012−16 was 31.4% (see Table 10.33).

The values of FCFE are given in millions of dollars. The amount of FCFE over the past five years have been fluctuating. The FCFE had been $11.305 billion in year 2016 (see Table 10.34).

Growth rate = Reinvestment rate × Return on equity
The average growth rate of net income estimated from fundamentals is 6.8% (see Table 10.35).
Two stage FCFE model
We use two stage FCFE model to value Walmart. It is assumed that the net income of Walmart will grow at 6.8% for five-year period.
High growth stage inputs
High growth period = 5 years
Growth rate in high growth period = 6.8%
Cost of equity = 6.03%
Average reinvestment rate = 31.4%
Net income in 2016 (Current income) = $15,080 million
Net income in the first year of high growth period = 15,080 × 1.068 = $16,105.44

FCFE = Net income − Reinvestment

The values are given in millions of dollars. The present value of FCFE in the high growth phase was estimated as $52,862.25 million (see Table 10.36).

Stable stage inputs

The growth rate of US GDP during the period 2013−14 is 2.3%.[9]

Growth rate in stable period = 2.3%

Growth rate = Reinvestment rate × Return on equity of industry sector.

Return on equity of the industry sector = 19.2%[10]

Reinvestment rate = Growth rate/Return on equity of industry sector.

= 2.3/19.2 = 0.12

Net income at the end of high growth period = $20,954 million

Net income at the beginning of stable period = 20,954 × 1.023 = $21,435.48 million

Reinvestment = 21,435.48 × 0.12 = $2567.79 million

FCFE = Net income −Reinvestment

= 21,435.48−2567.79 = $18,867.69 million

Terminal value = FCFE in stable period/(Cost of equity − growth rate in stable period)

= 18,867.69/(0.0632−0.023) = $471,692.23 million

Present value of terminal value = $347,530.08 million.

The value of operating assets of Walmart = 52,862.25 +347,530.08 = $400,392.33 million

Value of operating assets of Walmart = $400,392.33 million

Add cash and cash equivalents in 2016 = 8705 million

Value of equity of Walmart = $409,097.33 million

Number of shares = 3217 million

Value per share = $127.17

Table 10.37 Estimation of reinvestment rate for FCFF model

Year	2011	2012	2013	2014	2015	2016
EBIT	25,542	26491	27725	26872	27147	24105
Taxes	7579	7924	7958	8105	7985	6558
EBIT(1 − T)	17,963	18,567	19,767	18,767	19,162	17,547
Adjusted net capex	5260	8952	4736	4260	3001	2023
Change in noncash WC	2535	437	587	3581	−1081	−2641
Reinvestment	7795	9389	5323	7841	1920	−618
Reinvestment rate	0.43	0.51	0.27	0.42	0.10	−0.04

Table 10.38 Estimation of growth rate from fundamentals for FCFF model

Year	2011	2012	2013	2014	2015	2016
Reinvestment rate	0.43	0.51	0.27	0.42	0.10	−0.04
Return on capital employed	0.1612	0.1559	0.1588	0.1453	0.1484	0.1375
Growth rate	0.0700	0.0788	0.0428	0.0607	0.0149	−0.0048

[9] http://data.worldbank.org/indicator/NY.GDP.MKTP.KD.ZG.
[10] http://www.morningstar.com/stocks/XNYS/WMT/quote.html.

Table 10.39 **FCFF in millions of dollars**

Year	2011	2012	2013	2014	2015	2016
EBIT(1 − T)	17,963	18,567	19,767	18,767	19,162	17,547
Adjusted net Capex	5260	8952	4736	4260	3001	2023
Change in noncash working capital	2535	437	587	3581	−1081	−2641
FCFF	10,168	9,178	14,444	10,926	17,242	18,165

Table 10.40 **Present value of FCFF in high growth period**

Year	1	2	3	4	5
EBIT(1 − T)	18,477	19,456	20,487	21,573	22,717
Reinvestment	6282	6615	6966	7335	7724
FCFF	12,195	12,841	13,522	14,238	14,993
PV	$11,541.56	$11,502.24	$11,463.05	$11,423.99	$11,385.07
Sum	$57,315.91				

Value of Walmart per share is $127.174 according to FCFE model of valuation. The value of equity is estimated as $409.097 billion. The market capitalization of Walmart on April 18 2016 was 219.3 billion.

10.23 Valuation using FCFF model

Reinvestment = Adjusted net capital expenditure + Change in noncash working capital

Reinvestment rate = Reinvestment/EBIT(1 − T) where EBIT(1 − T) is the after tax operating income.

The average reinvestment rate is 34% during the five-year period 2011−15 (see Table 10.37).

Growth rate from fundamentals = Reinvestment rate *Return on capital employed
The average growth rate of earnings from fundamentals during the period 2011−15 was 5.3% (see Table 10.38)
Free Cash Flow to Firm (FCFF) = EBIT(1 − T) − Adjusted net Capex − Change in non-cash working capital.
The average FCFF for Walmart during the period 2011−16 was $13,354 million (see Table 10.39).
Two stage FCFF model
It is assumed that the earnings of the firm will grow at 5.3% for five years and thereafter at 2.3% (Average US GDP growth rate).
High growth period assumptions
Period of growth = 5 years

High growth rate = 5.3%
Reinvestment rate = 34%
WACC = 5.66%
Current EBIT$(1 - T)$ in year 2016 = $17,547 million
EBIT$(1 - T)$ in first year of high growth period = $17,547 \times 1.053$ = $18,477 million
The present value of FCFF in high growth phase is estimated as $57,315.91 million (see Table 10.40).
Stable stage inputs
The average growth rate of US GDP is assumed as the growth rate in the stable period
Growth rate = 2.3%
Growth rate = Reinvestment rate $\times$ Return on capital employed (ROCE) of the retail industry sector.
ROCE = 9.34%[11]
Reinvestment rate in the stable period = 2.3%/9.34% = 23.6%.
WACC = 5.66%
EBIT$(1 - T)$ at the end of five years = $22,717 million
EBIT$(1 - T)$ in the beginning of the stable period = $23,239.16 million
Reinvestment = $23,239.16 \times 0.236$ = $5484.44 million
FCFF in stable period = $23,239.16 - 5484.44$ = $17,754.72 million
Terminal value of FCFF = FCFF in stable period/(WACC−growth rate in stable phase) = $17,754.72/(0.0566-0.023)$ = $528,414.16 million
Present value of terminal value = $401,255.89 million
Value of operating assets = Present value of FCFF in high growth phase + Present value of FCFF in stable phase = $57,315.91 + $401,255.89 = $458,571.79 million
Value of Walmart = Value of operating assets + current cash and cash equivalents = $458,571.79 + 8705 = $467,276.79 million.
Value of equity = Value of Walmart − Value of debt = $467,276.79− $47,488 = $419,788.79
Value per share = 419,788.79/3217 = $130.49.

Summary of Discounted Cash Flow Valuation

Two stage DDM
Value of Walmart stock = $177.51 (Based on cost of equity estimated from CAPM model)
Value of Walmart stock = $61.71 (Based on cost of equity estimated from dividend growth model)
Two stage FCFE model
Value of Walmart = $127.17. The value of equity is estimated at $409.097 billion.
Two stage FCFF model
The value of Walmart is estimated as $467276.79 million. The value of equity is estimated at $419,788.79. The value per share according to FCFF model is arrived at $130.49.
The stock price of Walmart in NYSE on April 19 2016 was $69.65. The market capitalization was $219.2 billion. The 52 week range for Walmart stock was $56.30−$80.93.

---

[11] http://csimarket.com/Industry/industry_ManagementEffectiveness.php?ind=1305.

Table 10.41 Comparison with peer companies

Company	Walmart	Costco	Target	Dollar General
Total asset	203,706	33,440	41,404	11,224
Total debt	47,488	6147	12,796	2739
Capital expenditures	12,174	2393	1438	374
Revenues	485,651	116,199	72,618	18,910
Operating income	27,147	3624	4535	1769
Cash flow	36,433	4855	6664	2111
Total cash	9135	6419	2210	580
Net income	14,694	2377	3363	1165
Market capitalization	219,380	67,470	50,386	23,917

Table 10.42 Comparison of price multiples

Company	P/S	P/B	P/E	Dividend yield (%)
Walmart	0.5	2.7	15.3	2.8
Costco	0.6	6.1	29.4	1
Target	0.7	3.9	16	2.6
Dollar General Corp	1.2	4.4	21.2	1.1

Table 10.43 Price multiple comparison with Industry and market index

Ratios	Walmart	Industry average	S&P500
P/E	15.3	17.6	19.1
P/B	2.7	3.5	2.7
P/S	0.5	0.5	1.8
P/CF	8.2	9.8	11.8
Dividend yield (%)	2.8	2.3	2.4

Table 10.44 Enterprise value multiples

Company	Walmart	Costco	Target	Dollar General
Revenues	485,651	116,199	72,618	18,910
EBITDA	36,433	4855	6664	2111
EBIT	27,147	3624	4535	1769
Debt	47,488	6147	12,796	2739
Market value of equity	196,276	71,024	44,732	20,909
Cash and cash equivalents	9135	6419	2210	580
Enterprise Value (EV)	234,629	70,752	55,318	23,068
EV/REVENUES	0.48	0.61	0.76	1.22
EV/EBITDA	6.44	14.57	8.30	10.93
EV/EBIT	8.64	19.52	12.20	13.04

Table 10.45 Trend—EV multiples

Year	2007	2008	2009	2010	2011	2012	2013	2014	2015	2016
EV/revenues	0.66	0.64	0.55	0.58	0.57	0.58	0.60	0.62	0.48	0.53
EV/EBITDA	8.78	8.49	7.41	7.57	7.25	7.50	7.78	8.24	6.44	8.77
EV/EBIT	11.09	10.90	9.57	9.80	9.40	9.78	10.14	10.95	8.64	10.49

Table 10.46 Growth rate comparison of revenues

In percent	Walmart	Costco	Target	Dollar General Corp
5 year average	3.54	8.31	2.13	9.9
10 year average	5.36	8.18	4.48	9.46

Table 10.47 Growth rate comparison of operating income

In percent	Walmart	Costco	Target	Dollar
5 year average	−1.15	11.78	−0.6	13.16
10 year average	2.67	9.41	2.33	12.25

10.24 Relative valuation

The values are given in millions of dollars. The peer companies selected for comparison are Costco Wholesale Corporation, Target Corporation, and Dollar General Corporation. The data was taken from Morningstar.com. Cash flow is earnings before depreciation, interest and taxes. Net income and market capitalization are values for the year 2016. The values for other financial variables are based on year 2015. In terms of revenues, cash flows and earnings as well as asset sizes, Walmart is the largest company among the peer group of companies. Walmart had the highest market capitalization among the peer companies in year 2015. Walmart held the highest cash reserves compared to all competitors (see Table 10.41).

Walmart had the highest dividend yield among the peer companies. The multiple values are based on the current year of 2016. Walmart had the lowest price to sales, price to book and price to earnings ratio in comparison with other peer companies. With reference to investors, Walmart is an attractive stock to buy since its market price in relation to one dollar of earnings is the lowest compared to the other stocks. It can be interpreted that Walmart is the cheapest stock to buy among all the competitor firms analyzed. The earning yield is the highest for Walmart compared to all other companies taken for comparison. Earnings yield shows how much return shareholders' investment in the company earned over the past year. In terms of earning yield, Walmart is the most attractive stock (see Table 10.42).

The price multiples like price to earnings, price to book, price to sales, price to cash flow and dividend yield of Walmart are compared with the industry average and S&P500. The values of multiples are based on April 2016. Walmart had the lowest price to earnings ratio compared to the price earnings ratio of industry average and S&P500. The price to cash flow ratio is also the lowest for Walmart. The dividend yield is highest for Walmart compared to the industry average and S&P 500 (see Table 10.43).

The enterprise value multiples are estimated based on the year 2015 variable values. All financial variable values except ratios are given in millions of dollars (see Table 10.44).

Enterprise value = Market value of equity + Debt − Cash and Cash equivalents.

Lower the enterprise value multiples, the more undervalued and attractive a stock becomes for investment. Walmart have the least enterprise value multiples compared to the peer companies. Hence Walmart stock is the best attractive stock during the period of analysis.

The enterprise value multiples of EV/revenues, EV/EBIDA, and EV/EBIT have been fluctuating over the period 2007−16 (see Table 10.45).

The source of data was Morningstar.com. Dollar General corporation had the highest revenue growth rates both in terms of five years and 10-year average values. The basis of estimation was year 2015 (see Table 10.46).

Dollar General Corporation had the highest growth rate of operating income on the basis of five year and 10-year average estimates. The analysis was based on the year 2015 (see Table 10.47).

10.25   Performance indicators

10.25.1   Altman Z score

Investors can use Altman Z score to decide if they should buy or sell a particular stock based on the company's financial strength. The Altman Z score is the output of a credit strength test which gauges a publicly traded manufacturing company's likelihood of bankruptcy. Z score model is an accurate forecaster of failure up to two years prior to distress.

$$Z-Score = 1.2A + 1.4B + 3.3C + 0.6D + 1.0E$$

Where:

A = Working capital/Total assets
B = Retained earnings/Total assets
C = Earnings before interest and tax/Total assets
D = Market value of equity/Total liabilities
E = Sales/Total assets

The zones of discrimination are such that when Z score is less than 1.81, it is in distress zones. When the Z score is greater than 2.99, it is in safe zones. When the Z score is between 1.81 and 2.99, the company is in Grey Zone.

The financial values are given in millions of dollars.

Total assets	199,581		
Total liabilities	119,035		
Sales revenues	482,130		
Operating income	24,105		
Retained earnings	90,021		
Market value of equity	219,380		
Working capital	4380		
Ratios	**Values**	**Constant**	**Score**
Working capital/Total assets	0.02	1.2	0.03
Retained earnings/Total assets	0.45	1.4	0.63
Operating income/Total assets	0.12	3.3	0.40
Market value of equity/Total liabilities	1.84	0.6	1.11
Sales/Total assets	2.42	1	2.42
		Z score	4.58

On the basis of Altman Z score, it can be assumed that Walmart is in safe zone.

10.26 Piotroski score

The Piotroski score is a discrete score between 0 and 9 which is an indicator of the firm's financial position. The score was named after the Chicago accounting Professor Joseph Piotroski. The cumulative points suggest whether the stock is a value stock or not. If the company achieves a score of 8 or 9, the stock can be considered strong. If the score ranges between 0 and 2, then the stock is considered weak.

10.26.1 Criteria for Piotroski score

SL	Profitability scores	Score points	Score for Walmart
1	Positive return on assets in current year	1	1
2	Positive operating cash flow in current year	1	1
3	Higher ROA in current year compared to previous year	1	0
4	Return on cash flow from operations greater than ROA	1	1
	Leverage, liquidity and sources of funds		
5	Lower ratio of long term debt to average total assets in current year compared to previous year	1	0
6	Higher current ratio in this year compared to previous year	1	0
7	No new shares were issued in the last year	1	1
	Operational efficiency ratios		
8	A higher gross margin compared to the previous year	1	1
9	A higher asset turnover ratio compared to the previous year	1	1
Total		9	6

The stock has a cumulative point of 6 out of 9.

10.27   Graham number

It is a conservative method used for valuing a stock. It is a figure which measures a stock's fundamental value by taking into account the company's earnings per share and book value per share. Graham number is the upper bound of the price range which a defensive investor should pay for the stock. According to Graham number theory, any stock price below the Graham number is considered undervalued and hence worth investing in. Graham number is a combination of asset valuation and earnings power valuation.

EPS in year 2016 = 4.57

Book value per share = 25.16

$$\text{Graham number} = \sqrt{22.5 \times (\text{Earnig per share}) \times (\text{Book value per share})} = 50.86$$

Walmart was trading at $69.77 on April 20 2016.

Further reading

[1] www.walmart.com.
[2] Annual Reports Walmart.

Wealth analysis of Facebook

11.1 Introduction

Facebook is an online social networking service corporation founded by Mark Zuckerberg along with his Harvard College friends. Facebook enable people to connect and share through mobile devices and personal computers. Facebook facilitate people to share their opinions, ideas, photos and videos. The company is headquartered in Menlo Park, California in United States. The website of the company was launched on February 4 2004. The website's membership was initially given to Harvard students. Later on, it was expanded to colleges in Boston area, the Ivy League and Stanford University. Presently since 2006, anyone who is at least 13 years old is allowed to become a registered user of the website. Registered users can create a user profile and add other users as "friends," exchange messages, post status updates and photos, share videos, and use various apps. By August 2015, Facebook had over 1.59 billion monthly active users (MAUs). Facebook had its initial public offering (IPO) in May 2012 and initiated trading after three months of IPO. Facebook achieved the unique recognition as the fastest growing company in the Standard & Poor's 500 Index to achieve a market capitalization of $250 billion on July 13 2015. In the year 2005, Accel Partners invested an amount of $12.7 million in Facebook.[1] As of December 31 2015, Facebook have 12,691 employees. Facebook is available in more than 90 different languages and have offices or data centers in more than 30 different countries. Facebook is the leading social networking site based on monthly unique visitors. By May 2014 there were 151.8 million user members in United States, 108.9 million members in India, 70.5 million members in Brazil, 60.3 million members in Indonesia and 44.4 million members in Mexico.[2]

11.2 Products

Facebook is basically a mobile application and website which facilitate people to connect, share, discover, and communicate with each other on mobile devices and personal computers. By December 2015, on average Facebook had 1.04 billion daily active users (DAUs) which was an increase of 25% compared to the previous period December 2014. The most striking feature of Facebook is the News Feed which displays an algorithmically ranked series of stories and advertisements which are individualized for each individual.

[1] "Company Info | Facebook Newsroom." *Facebook*.
[2] Leading countries based on number of Facebook users as of May 2014 (in millions)".statista.com.

Strategic Financial Management Casebook.

Instagram is a mobile application which enables individuals to take photos or videos which are customized with filter effects and shared with friends and followers in a photo feed or send directly to friends.

Messenger is a messaging application which is available for mobile and web on a variety of platforms and devices. WhatsApp is a reliable mobile messaging application used on a variety of mobile platforms. Oculus is a technology and content platform product which facilitate people to play games, consume content and connect with people.

11.3 Strategy

Facebook generate revenues from selling advertising placements to marketers. Marketers can place advertisements which appear in multiple places like Facebook, Instagram and third party applications, and websites. Facebook focuses on different stages of advertising campaign cycle from pre purchase decision making to real time optimizations to post campaign analytics. Facebook associates with traditional advertising agencies, specialized agencies and partners. Advertising accounted for 89%, 92%, and 95% of the revenues during the years 2013, 2014, and 2015, respectively. Facebook generate all of the payment revenues from developers that use Facebook on personal computers. Facebook's key strategies involve prioritizing product developments investments which create interactions between users, developers and advertisers. Facebook invest significantly in improvement of core products like news feed, timeline, and photos. Facebook enables creating new platforms apps and website integrations. Facebook estimates its revenues by user geography based on its estimate of the geography in which advertisement impressions are delivered or virtual and digital goods are purchased. Average revenue per user (ARPU) is the total revenue in a given geography during a given quarter divided by the average number of MAUs in the area at the beginning and end of the quarter.[3] Facebook facilitates payments from its users to its platform developers wherein users can transact and make payments on the Facebook platform by using credit cards, Paypal or other payment methods available on its website. Facebook collects fees from its platform developers when users make purchases using the payments infrastructure. Facebook has also facilitated the use of its payments infrastructure for game apps on Facebook and fees which are generated exclusively from games. The fees revenues are also derived from user promoted posts, advertisement serving and measurement products. In 2012, Facebook launched mobile discovery platform Mobile Games Publishing which enabled small and medium developers to promote their games across the Facebook's mobile apps. In Facebook, the advertisers can specify the types of users they want to reach based on information that users chose to share. Advertisers can also use products such as Facebook Exchange and Custom Audiences to target their desired audiences. Advertisers and agencies use cookie

[3] http://marketrealist.com/2014/01/facebook-revenue-advertising/.

based demand side platforms to reach audiences through Facebook Exchange. Google have partnered with Facebook to offer its clients access to Facebook Exchange inventory through Double Click Bid Manager. Custom Audiences facilitate advertisers to find offline audiences among people who have Facebook account.

Facebook incurred R&D expenses of $1.42 billion, $2.67 billion, and $4.82 billion during the years 2013, 2014, and 2015, respectively.

11.4   Competition

Facebook faces competition from businesses which provides tools to facilitate communications, companies which enable marketers to display advertising and firms which facilitate development platforms for application developers. Facebook faces competition from companies which develop mobile applications for social or communications functionality such as messaging, photo and video sharing and micro blogging. Facebook faces competition from companies which provide web and mobile based information and entertainment products and services. Facebook faces a number of intellectual property lawsuits. The products and internal systems of Facebook rely on software, which include software developed or maintained internally or by third parties which are highly technical and complex.

11.5   Acquisitions

Facebook had acquired more than 50 companies. Most of the companies acquired by Facebook are based in the United States. Most of the acquisitions done by Facebook are talent acquisitions. In 2014, Facebook completed its acquisition of WhatsApp—the mobile message service for $22 billion in cash and stock. This acquisition was termed as the largest acquisition undertaken by Facebook. The initial deal was announced for $19 billion but later on the value increased on account of the Facebook's share price. Facebook paid $4.59 billion in cash and issued 178 million shares of class A common stock. In 2014 Facebook acquired virtual reality startup Oculus VR for $2 billion. The acquisition of Oculus involved payment of $400 million in cash and issue of 23 million shares of class B common stock. The stock was roughly $1.6 billion in value based on $69.35 share price average from the 20 trading days preceding the acquisition date. The deal also specified an additional $300 million in cash and stock if the company Oculus hits certain milestones. This acquisition of Oculus was aimed on building products and developing partnerships to support more games. In November 2010, Facebook acquired the domain name fb.com from the American Farm Bureau Federation. In April 2012 Kevin and Mike sold their 13 people startup, Instagram to Facebook.Facebook purchased the photo filter app 18 months after its launch for a value of $1 billion. This purchase involved $300 million in cash and the rest in the shares of Facebook. The photo sharing network of Instagram had about 30 million users at the time of the buyout deal. By 2013 there were more than 100 million MAUs who were posting more than 40 million photos per day. During March 2016, Facebook announced plans to buy Masquerade which was one of the most popular apps in the App Store. Masquerade possessed a app called MSQRD with world class imaging technology for video. Facebook had also purchased ConnectU. In 2009, Facebook bought FriendFeed, a real time feed aggregator which serves up updates from social networking sites, blogs or other type of RSS. FriendFeed was acquired for $15 million in cash and $32.5 million in Facebook shares. The FriendFeed team was a major asset for Facebook as it included ex Googlers and Gmail creator Paul Buchhe. In 2010, Facebook acquired the Nextstop for its engineering talent and assets. In 2010, Facebook acquired Hot Potato a New York based startup which specialized in social activity updates. Again in the same year Facebook acquired the assets of Drop.io a startup firm which allowed users to privately share files through a drag and drop interface with additional options like phone calls and faxing. In 2009, Facebook acquired Friend.ly whose social Q&A website allows users to post questions on different subjects and get them answered. Facebook acquired Android photo sharing app developer Lighbox for its employees. In 2012, Facebook acquired mobile gift giving app Karma for approximately $80 million. Facebook had also acquired Israeli startup which specialized in facial recognition technology known as Face.com. In 2014, Facebook acquired the fitness tracking application Moves and its ProtoGeo Oy development company. Facebook's acquisition strategy is to provide multiple and different experiences and to "unbundle the big blue (see Table 11.1)."

11.6 Stock ownership

Facebook is entitled to issue both class A and class B common stock. Facebook is authorized to issue 5000 million shares of class A common stock and 4141 million shares of common stock with a par value of $0.000006 per share. Both class A and class B common stock are entitled to dividends when declared by the board of directors. Shares of class B common stock are convertible into an equivalent number of shares of class A common stock and generally convert into shares of class A common stock upon transfer. There were 2293 million shares and 552 million shares of class A common stock and class B common stock issued and outstanding as of the year 2015.

The founder Chairman and CEO can exercise voting rights with respect to majority of voting power of the outstanding capital stock. Mark Zuckerberg had 28% ownership of the equity capital. The trading price of class A common stock had been volatile. The stock price had ranged from $17.55 to $110.65 through the year 2015. Facebook has never declared or paid cash dividends on the capital stock. Facebook have a dual class structure of common stock to ensure concentrated voting control is vested with CEO and certain other holders of the class B common stock. The class B common stock has ten votes per share and class A common stock

Table 11.1 **Acquisitions by Facebook**

Year	Company, business operations, and deal value in millions of dollars
2005	AboutFace (Facebook.com domain name; Deal value = $0.2 million)
2007	Parakey (Offline applications/Web desktop)
2008	ConnectU (Social networking; Deal value = $31 million)
2009	FriendFeed (Social networking aggregator; Deal value = $47.5 million)
2010	Octazen (Contact importer), Divvyshot (Photo management); Friendster patents (Intellectual property/patents, Deal value = $40 million), ShareGrove (Private conversations/forums), Nextstop (Travel recommendations, Deal value = $2.5 million), Chai labs (Internet applications, Deal value = $10 million), Hot Potato (Check—ins/status updates, Deal value = $10 million), Drop.io (File hosting and Sharing, Deal value = $10 million), FB.com domain name (American Farm Bureau federation, Deal value = $8.5 million)
2011	Relation (Mobile advertising); Beluga (Group messaging); Snaptu (Mobile app developer, Deal value = $70 million); RecRec (Computer vision); DayTum (Information graphics); Sofa (software design); MailRank (Email prioritization); Push Pop Press (Digital Publishing); Friend.ly (Social casual Q&A service app); Strobe (HTML5 mobile apps); Gowalla (Location based service)
2012	Instagram (Photo sharing, Deal value = $1000 million); Face.com (Face recognition platform, Deal value = $100 million); Tagtile (Customer loyalty app); Glancee (Social discovery platform); Lightbox.com (Photo sharing); Karma (Social gifting); Spool (Mobile bookmarking and sharing content); Acrylic Software (RSS app Pulp and secure database app wallet); Threadsy (Social aggregator)
2013	Atlas (Atlas advertiser suite); Osmeta (Mobile software); Hot Studio (Design agency); Spaceport (Cross platform game framework); Parse (Mobile app backends, Deal value = $85 million); Monoidics (Automatic verification software); Jibbigo (Speech translation app); Onavo (Mobile analytics); SportStream (Sports conversation analysis)
2014	Little Eye Labs (Performance analysis and monitoring tools for Android, Deal value = $15 million); Branch (Web conversation platform, Deal Value = $15 million); WhatsApp (Mobile instant messaging, Deal value = $19 billion); Oculus VR (Virtual reality technology, Deal value = $2 billion); Ascenta (High altitude UAVs, Deal value = $20 million); ProtoGeoOy (Fitness tracking app Moves); LiveRail (Publisher Monetization Platform); WaveGroup Sound (Sound Studio)
2015	Wit.ai (Speech recognition); Quickfire (Video compression); TheFind (Ecommerce); Surreal vision (Computer vision augmented reality); Pebbles (Computer vision augmented reality, Deal value = $60 million)
2016	MSQRD (Visual effects)

has one vote per share. Stockholders who hold shares of class B common stock which includes executive officers, employees and directors hold a substantial majority of the voting power of the outstanding capital stock. The class A common stock has been listed on the NASDAQ Global Select Market under the symbol FB" since May 18 2012. In December 2013, Facebook completed a follow on offering in which Facebook issued and sold 27 million shares of Class A common stock at a public offering price of $55.05 per share. The selling stockholders sold 43 million shares of class A common stock. The total net proceeds from the above issue amounted to $1.48 billion.

11.7 Facebook IPO

Facebook had its IPO on May 18 2012. This IPO was termed as the biggest IPOs in technology and internet history with a peak market capitalization of over $104 billion. But the stock fell as soon as it opened and the share prices declined more than 50% in the ensuing couple of months. It took more than a year for the shares to trade above the listing price of $38. Facebook raised $16 billion through its IPO. The list price was originally set between the range of $28–$35. But citing heavy demand, three days before the IPO, the underwriters consisting of Morgan Stanley, JP Morgan and Goldman Sachs increased the IPO range to between $35 and $38. This was done in spite of criticism from large investors that Facebook was overpriced and the IPO was overhyped. Prior to the IPO offering, Facebook expanded its number of shares by 25% to 421.2 million. Retail or individual investors are usually allocated up to 20% of the total shares in an IPO. In the context of overvaluation of shares, this led to forced selling from investors when quick profits failed to materialize days after the IPO. On the day of the trading, the stock opening was delayed due to technical glitches as NADAQ's electronic trading platform was unable to handle high volume of trades. As a result, some investors failed to sell the stock during initial day of trading when the stock price fell and resulted in bigger losses when the trade finally went through. Facebook faced a number of lawsuits following its IPO.[4]

11.8 Stock option plans

Facebook have two share based employee compensation plans known as the 2012 Equity Incentive Plan (2012 Plan) and the 2005 Stock Plan. These plan provides for the issuance of incentive and nonstatutory stock options, restricted stock awards and stock appreciation rights.

11.9 Trends in key metrics

The key metrics for analysis of performance used by Facebook consists of the DAUs, mobile DAUs, MAUs, mobile MAUs, and ARPU. A DAU is considered as a registered Facebook user who had logged in and visited Facebook through the

[4] http://finance.yahoo.com/news/why-did-facebook-shares-fall-225006922.html.

Table 11.2 **Daily active users worldwide in millions**

Period	DAU in millions
December 31, 2012	618
December 31, 2013	757
December 31, 2014	890
December 31, 2015	1038

Source: 10 K Facebook 2015.

Table 11.3 **Mobile monthly active users worldwide in millions**

Period	DAU in millions
December 31 2012	680
December 31 2013	945
December 31 2014	1189
December 31 2015	1442

Source: 10 K Facebook 2015.

Facebook's website or a mobile device or the Messenger application on a given day. Facebook view DAUs and DAUs as a percentage of MAUs[5]. A mobile MAU is a user who have accessed Facebook via a mobile application or via mobile versions of Facebook website such as m.facebook.com whether on a mobile phone or tablet. On average basis, the worldwide DAUs of Facebook increased from 890 million during December 2014 to 1.04 billion during December 2015 which represented an increase of 17% in 2015 compared to the previous year (see Tables 11.2 and 11.3). The major growth markets included India, the United States, and Brazil. The ARPU during the year 2015 was relatively higher primarily due to the size and maturity of online and mobile advertising markets. The ARPU in the United States and Canada region was more than seven times higher than in Asia Pacific region. Facebook generate substantially all revenues from advertising which is generated by displaying products on Facebook properties which include mobile applications and third party affiliated websites or mobile applications. The major growth driver in advertising revenues is increase in revenues from advertisements in news feed. The news feed advertisement which are displayed more prominently have significantly higher levels of engagement and higher price per advertisement relative to other advertisement placement of Facebook. Facebook generated 47% of the revenues from marketers and developers in the United States. The majority of revenues outside of United States comes from regions like western Europe, China, Brazil, Canada, and Australia.

---

[5] 10 K Facebook Inc., 2015.

The R&D expenses as a percentage of revenues was 27% in the year 2015. The R&D expenses amounted to $2666 million and $4816 million in the year 2014 and 2015. The increase in R&D expenses was approximately 81% compared to the previous year.

11.10   Investments

The cash and cash equivalents, and marketable securities consist of cash, certificates of deposit, time deposits, money market funds, US government securities, US government agency securities, and corporate debt securities.

11.11   Risk management

Facebook is exposed to market risks like foreign currency exchange rates, interest rates and inflation. Facebook have foreign currency risks related to revenue and operating expenses denominated in currencies like Euro. Facebook have not entered into derivatives or other financial instruments to hedge foreign currency exchange risk. Facebook have exposures to changes in interest rates on account of interest earned and market value of cash and marketable securities.

11.12   Debt financing

In year 2013, Facebook entered into a five-year senior unsecured revolving credit facility which allowed Facebook to borrow up to $6.5 billion to fund working capital and general corporate purposes with interest payable on the borrowed amounts set at LIBOR plus 1% as well as an annual commitment fee of 0.10% on the daily undrawn balance of the facility. Facebook have entered into various capital lease arrangements to obtain property and equipment. These lease agreements are typically for three years except for building lease which is for 15 years with interest rates ranging from 1% to 13%.

11.13   Corporate governance

The board at Facebook act as the adviser for management and continually monitors the performance of management. The board selects and appoints the Chief Executive Officer and Chairman of the board. The CEO select and appoint all other officers of Facebook with approval of Board. The board comprise a majority of directors who qualify as independent directors. The board conducts at least four regularly scheduled meetings of the board every year. The Facebook board do not require the separation of the offices of the Chairman and CEO. When the posts of Chairman and CEO are held by the same person, the independent directors appoint a lead independent director. The retirement age of the directors is 70 years. In a scenario wherein the outstanding shares of class B common stock constitute a majority of the combined voting power of Facebook, then Facebook will not have a classified board of directors and all directors will be elected for annual terms. In scenarios when the shares of class B common stock represent less than a majority of the combined voting power of the common stock of Facebook, then Facebook will have a classified board of directors which consists of three classes of approximately equal size with staggered three year terms. There are no limits on the number of terms to be served by a director. The board has two standing committees the Audit Committee and Compensation & Governance Committee. The nonemployee directors are paid compensation that consists of cash and equity. The Compensation & Governance Committee recommends to the board the form and amount of cash based and equity based compensation to be paid to the nonemployee directors. The board has not adopted a policy requiring equity ownership by directors. The board encourages the members of management to be invited to board meetings. The Compensation & Governance Committee will annually review these corporate governance guidelines and proposes changes to the board for consideration. Presently there are eight members in the board.

11.14   Ownership structure

The capital structure composed of 99.5% equity and 0.05% debt. In 2016, the equity value amounted to $44,218 million and debt amounted to $307 million.

The insider equity ownership was 0.38% during the period 2015. In terms of equity ownership, the percentage owned by financial institutions was 54.49%, while the percentage owned by mutual funds was 31.53% and the equity ownership of insiders was 0.34%. The number of institution owners were 2193 while the number of fund owners were 3690 (see Table 11.4).

The top 10 funds constituted 8.26% of the total shares issued by the company. The top 10 institutions constituted 21.04% of the equity ownership (see Table 11.5–11.6).

The revenues for Facebook increased from $1.974 billion in year 2010 to $17.928 billion in the year 2015. The average growth rate of revenues during the

Table 11.4 **Current ownership during April 2016**

Type	Million dollars
Institutions	176,946.55
Mutual funds	102,403.75
Insiders	1067.94

Table 11.5 **Top fund equity ownership**

	Funds	Percentage of total shares held
1	Fidelity ContraFunds	1.84
2	Vanguard Total Stock Market Idx	1.48
3	Vanguard 500 Index Inv	1.02
4	Vanguard Institutional Index	0.84
5	SPDR S&P500 ETF	0.8
6	Powershares QQQETF	0.58
7	Vanguard Growth Index Inv	0.43
8	T. Rowe Price Growth	0.44
9	Fidelity Sparatan@500 Index Inv	0.41
10	VA CollegeAmericaGrth Fund of Amer529F	0.37
	Total	8.26

Source: Morningstar.

Table 11.6 **Top institutions equity ownership**

	Institutions	Percentage of total shares held
1	Fidelity Management & Research Company	4.64
2	Vanguard Group Inc.	4.6
3	State Street Corp.	2.96
4	T. Rowe Price Associates, Inc.	2.15
5	BlackRock Fund Advisors	2.02
6	J.P. Morgan Investment Management Inc.	1.02
7	Jennison Associates LLC	1.02
8	Northern Trust Investments N A	0.9
9	Baillie Gifford & Co Limited	0.88
10	Sands Capital Management, LLC	0.85
	Total	21.04

Source: Morningstar.

five-year period 2011−15 was 56%. The highest growth rate of revenues which was 88% was registered in the year 2011. The operating income increased from $1.032 billion in year 2010 to $6.225 billion by year 2015. The net income increased from 0.606 billion in year 2010 to $3.688 billion in year 2015. The operating cash flow increased by 78% in the year 2014 which was the maximum increase during the five-year period of analysis. The average growth rate of operating cash flow during the period 2011−15 was 74.9%. The capital expenditure increased from 0.293 billion in year 2010 to $2.523 billion by the year 2015. The market capitalization which was $63.143 billion in year 2012 increased to $296.606 billion in year 2015. The Research and Development expenses increased from $0.144 in year 2010 to $4.816 billion in year 2015. The average increase in total cash during the five-year period 2011−15 was 69%. The market capitalization increased by

Table 11.7 **Financial highlights in millions of dollars**

Year	2010	2011	2012	2013	2014	2015
Revenues	1974	3711	5089	7872	12,466	17,928
Operating income	1032	1756	538	2804	4994	6225
Operating cash flow	698	1,549	1612	4222	5457	8599
Net income	606	1000	53	1,500	2940	3688
Capital expenditure	293	606	1235	1,362	1,831	2,523
Market capitalization	–	–	63,143	139,194	216,740	296,606
Research and development	144	388	1399	1415	2666	4816
Total cash	1785	3908	9626	11,449	11,199	18,434
Long term debt	367	398	1991	237	119	107
Total assets	2990	6331	15,103	17,895	39,966	49,407
Total equity	2162	4899	11,755	15,470	36,096	44,218
Retained earnings	606	1606	1659	3159	6099	9787

120% in the year 2013 compared to the previous year 2012. The total assets increased by 83% during the year 2011−15. The book value of total equity increased by 90.8% on an average basis. The average growth rate of retained earnings was 82.5% during the period 2011−15 (see Table 11.7).

11.15 Ratio analysis

All the per share ratios have increased over the period 2012−15. The revenue per share increased from 2.35 to 6.28 during the period 2012−15. The earnings per share increased from 0.01 in year 2012 to 1.29 in year 2015. The EBITDA per share increased from 0.55 in year 2012 to 2.86 in 2015. The free cash flow per share and book value per share also increased during the period of analysis. The average revenue per share was 4.1 and the average earnings per share was 0.8 during the period 2012−15. The average EBITDA per share, average free cash flow per share and average book value per share was 1.8, 1.2, and 9.9. The average debt per share was 0.3 during the period 2012−15 (see Table 11.8).

The price to earnings ratio peaked during the year 2012. From the perspective of the investor, the high price to earnings ratio indicate that it is costly for an investor to buy a share for every one dollar of earnings the firm makes. The average price to book ratio was 6.8 during the period 2012−15. The average price to earnings ratio was 726.7 during the period 2012−15. The average price to sales and average price to tangible ratio was 16.2 and 11.1 during the period 2012−15. The average price to free cash flow was 79 during the period 2012−15 (see Table 11.9).

The gross margin and net margin have increased over the period of six years The average gross and operating margin during the period 2010−15 was 78% and 37% respectively. The earning before tax and net margin was 36% and 17% respectively during the six-year period of analysis (see Table 11.10).

Table 11.8 **Per share ratios**

Year	2012	2013	2014	2015
Revenue per share	2.35	3.13	4.68	6.28
Earnings per share	0.01	0.6	1.1	1.29
EBITDA per share	0.55	1.52	2.32	2.86
Free cash flow per share	0.17	1.14	1.36	2.13
Book value per share	4.96	6.07	12.99	15.6
Total debt per share	0.99	0.19	0.08	0.11

Table 11.9 **Equity price multiples**

Price multiple	2012	2013	2014	2015
Price to book ratio	5.37	9	6	6.71
Price to earnings ratio	2662	92.16	71.06	81.64
Price to sales ratio	14.14	17.45	16.5	16.65
Price to tangible ratio	6.09	10.12	15.28	12.93
Price to free cash flow	162.32	48.02	56.7	49.14

Table 11.10 **Margins in percent**

Year	2010	2011	2012	2013	2014	2015
Gross margin (%)	75	76.8	73.2	76.2	82.7	84
Operating margin (%)	52.3	47.3	10.6	35.6	40.1	34.7
EBT margin (%)	51.06	45.68	9.71	34.98	39.39	34.55
Net margin (%)	18.85	18	0.63	18.94	23.46	20.47

Table 11.11 **Profitability ratios**

Year	2010	2011	2012	2013	2014	2015
Return on assets (%)	12.44	14.33	0.3	9.04	10.07	8.19
Return on equity (%)	24.05	22.91	0.4	10.95	11.34	9.14
Return on invested capital (%)	19.07	19.92	0.59	10.08	11.18	9.03
Interest coverage ratio	46.82	41.36	10.69	50.18	214.48	270.3

The profitability ratios like ROA, ROE, ROC were fluctuating over the six-year period 2010–15. The interest coverage ratio (ICR) is showing an increasing trend. The ICR ratio increased by 5.8 times in 2015 compared to the period 2010 indicating the increased capacity of Facebook to pay fixed interest payments. The average ROA and ROE during the period 2010–15 was 9.1% and 13.1%, respectively. The average return on invested capital was 11.6% during the period 2010–15. The ICR averaged 105 times during the period of analysis (see Table 11.11).

Table 11.12 Liquidity ratios

Liquidity ratios	2010	2011	2012	2013	2014	2015
Current ratio	5.77	5.12	10.71	11.88	9.6	11.25
Quick ratio	5.55	4.96	10.26	11.46	9.04	10.91

Table 11.13 Leverage ratios

Leverage ratios	2010	2011	2012	2013
Debt equity ratio	0.24	0.09	0.17	0.02
Long term debt to total asset ratio	0.12	0.06	0.13	0.01

Table 11.14 Efficiency ratios

Year	2010	2011	2012	2013	2014	2015
Days sales outstanding	68.97	45.24	45.4	42.38	40.8	43.13
Payables period	21.47	19.52	17.13	14.79	22.29	23.68
Receivables turnover	5.29	8.07	8.04	8.61	8.95	8.46
Fixed assets turnover	3.44	3.62	2.63	2.99	3.64	3.71
Asset turnover	0.66	0.8	0.47	0.48	0.43	0.4

Table 11.15 Enterprise value multiples

Enterprise value multiples	2012	2013	2014	2015
EV/revenues	10.91	16.26	16.5	15.53
EV/EBITDA	46.53	33.5	33.29	34.12
EV/EBIT	102.04	45.56	41.68	44.79

The average current ratio during the period 2010−15 was 9.06 while the average quick ratio during the above period was 8.70 (see Table 11.12).

The average debt equity ratio was 0.13 and average long term debt to total assets ratio was 0.08 (see Table 11.13).

The day's sales outstanding has been decreasing over the period 2010−15. The average days' sales outstanding have been 47.65 days during the time period 2010−15. The payable period has been fluctuating over the period of analysis. The average payable period during the six-year period had been 19.81 days. The average receivable turnover and fixed asset turnover ratio was 7.90 and 3.34, respectively during the period of analysis. The average asset turnover ratio had been 0.54 during the period of analysis (see Table 11.14).

The enterprise value (EV) multiples were fluctuating over the period of analysis (see Table 11.15).

11.16   Shareholder wealth analysis of Facebook

Facebook was listed on NYSE on May 18 2012. The initial adjusted trading price
was \$29.60 on May 18 2012. On April 1 2016, the adjusted closing price of
Facebook was \$117.58. The cumulative return analysis of the stock during the period
May 2012–April 2016 involving 47 months' reveals that the stock generated cumulative monthly returns of 174% approximately. In other words, if the stock was
actively traded every month involving buying and selling every month, the investor
would have generated 174% cumulative returns approximately during the five-year
period. Similarly, the cumulative monthly returns generated by NASDAQ during the
same five-year period was only 55.68%. Facebook outperformed the stock market
index NASDAQ Composite during the period of analysis (see Fig. 11.1).

Since 2012, the stock price has increased approximately five times. The analysis
of holding period returns suggest that the returns generated was approximately
297%. Assume that an investor invested an amount of \$1000 in Facebook shares
during May 2012 when it was listed. If the shares were held till April 2016, the
amount invested would have become \$3970.

Facebook has outperformed the market index during the five-year period
2012–16. On the basis of monthly cumulative returns, the market index
NASDAQ composite index generated higher cumulative returns than Facebook
during the period May 2012–June 2013. After June 2013, Facebook cumulative
returns increased substantially compared to NASDAQ index and hence
Facebook's stock performance outperformed that of market index during the
period June 2013–April 2016.

In terms of average yearly returns, Facebook outperformed the market index
Nasdaq composite in all years except in the year 2012. The highest average returns
and excess returns for Facebook was in the year 2013. Facebook generated an

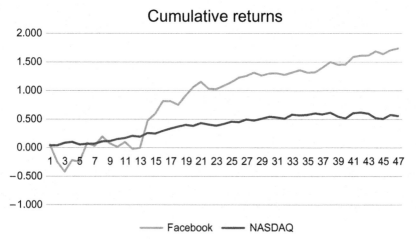

Figure 11.1 Cumulative returns.

average yearly returns of 88% in year 2013. During the first four months of year 2016, Facebook generated returns of 36.8% (see Table 11.16).

The holding period yield in percent for every year is estimated based on the assumption that the investor who buys the stock in January of every month hold it on till December of the year. The holding period yield of 76.4% in the year 2013 was the highest yield generated by Facebook during the period 2012–2015. The four-year annual holding period yield for Facebook during the period 2012–15 was approximately 37% (see Table 11.17).

The market value which was 4.9 times of the book value of equity in 2012 increased to 6.7 times in year 2015. The book value of equity which was 20% of market value of equity in year 2012 declined to 11 per in year 2013 and constituted 15% of market value of equity during the year 2015. The average book value as % of market value was 16% during the four-year period 2012–16. Excess value is estimated as the difference between market value and book value of equity. The excess value increased from $45.903 billion in 2012 to $252.388 billion in year 2015 (see Table 11.18).

Table 11.16 Average yearly returns in percent

Year	Facebook	Nasdaq composite	Excess returns
2012	5.4	13.8	−8.4
2013	88.2	1.15	87.1
2014	38.8	13.16	25.7
2015	31.4	26.5	4.9
2016	36.8	11.13	25.7

Table 11.17 Holding period yield in percent

Year	HPY in percent
2012	−10
2013	76.4
2014	24.7
2015	37.9

Table 11.18 Excess value added in millions

Year	2012	2013	2014	2015
Book value of equity	11,755	15,470	36,096	44,218
Market value of equity	57,659	139,191	216,740	296,606
BV as per cent of MV	20	11	17	15
Excess value	45,903.92	123,721	180,644	252,388

11.17   Estimation of cost of capital

The cost of equity is estimated using the capital asset pricing model.

Cost of equity = Risk free rate + Beta × Risk premium

Risk free rate is estimated as the average yield to maturity of 30 year US treasury bond during the period 2014−16.[6]

Year	Yield to maturity on 30 year treasury bond
2014	3.55
2015	2.63
2016	2.63
Average	2.94%

Risk free rate = 2.94%

Beta is estimated by regressing the weekly Facebook returns on the weekly market index NASDAQ returns during the period May 2012−April 2016.

Beta = 0.94

The return on market index is estimated as the average returns on the market index NASDAQ composite during the two-year period 2014−15.

Return on market index = 10.67%

Risk premium = Return on market index − Risk free rate

= 10.67%−2.94% = 7.73%

Cost of equity = 2.94 + (0.94*7.73) = 10.21%

The cost of equity is estimated as 10.21% for Facebook.

Cost of capital

Facebook have no bonds trading and hence the interest rate on the debt is assumed as the cost of debt.

Debt including capital leases in 2015 = $308 million

Interest expense in 2015 = $23 million

Interest rate = 7.47%

Cost of debt = 7.46%

Weight estimation

Market value of equity = $296,606 million

Book value of debt = $308 million

Total value = $296,914 million

Weight of equity = 0.999

Weight of debt = 0.0010

Weighted average cost of capital = 0.999 × 10.21% + 0.001 × 7.46% = 10.20%

The WACC of Facebook is calculated as 10.20%.

11.18   Valuation perspectives

This section estimates the value of Facebook using different methods like economic value, equity spread, Free Cash Flow to Equity (FCFE), and Free Cash Flow to Firm (FCFF) models.

[6] https://www.treasury.gov/resource-center/data-chart-center/interest-rates/Pages/Historic-Yield-Data-Visualization.aspx.

11.18.1   Economic value

Operating income in 2015 = $6225 million
Income tax = $2506 million
NOPAT = $3719 million
Stock holder equity = $44,218 million
Long term debt = $107 million
Capital employed = $44,325 million
WACC = 10.20%
Capital charge = 44,325 × 0.102 = $4521.15 million
Economic value = −802 million.

11.18.2   Equity spread

Stock holder equity in 2015 = $44,218 million
Return on equity in 2015 = 9.14%
Cost of equity in 2015 = 10.20 %
Equity spread = (Return on equity − Cost of equity) × Stock holder equity = (19.14−910.20) × 44218 = −$46871 million

11.18.3   Free Cash Flow to Equity (FCFE) valuation

Adjustments for FCFE valuation
Net capital expenditure = Capital expenditure − Depreciation and amortization
Adjusted net capital expenditure = Net capital expenditure + R&D expenses in current period − Amortization of research asset + Net acquisitions
Adjusted net income = Net income + Current year's R&D expenses−Amortization of research asset.
Adjusted book value of equity = Book value of equity + Value of research asset.

The research assets are amortized linearly over time. The life of research asset is assumed to be five years. The research assets are amortized 20% each year. The value of research asset and amortization expense for the year 2015 is given in the following table (see Table 11.19).

Amortization expense in year 2015 = $1202.4 million.
Value of research asset in year 2015 = $8435 million.
Adjusted net income in year 2015 = Net income + R&D expenses − Amortization expenses
 = 3688 + 4816−1202.4 = $7302 million.
Adjusted book value of equity in 2015 = Book value of equity + Value of research asset
 = 44,218 + 8435 = $52,653 million
Adjusted book value of capital = Adjusted book value of equity + Value of debt
 = 52,653 + 308 = $52,961 million
Adjusted ROE in% = 7302/52,961 = 0.14.
The adjusted ROE estimated as 14%.
Estimation of adjusted net capex
Adjusted net Capex = Net Capex + R&D expenses in current period−Amortization of research asset + Net acquisition.
Net Capex = Capex − Depreciation and amortization.

Table 11.19 **Estimation of amortization and value of research asset in year 2015**

Estimation of amortization and value of research asset in year 2015				
Year			Unamortized portion	Amortization this year (million $)
		%	(million dollars)	
Current year	4816	100	4816	
−1	2666	80	2132.8	533.2
−2	1415	60	849	283
−3	1399	40	559.6	279.8
−4	388	20	77.6	77.6
−5	144	0	0	28.8
	Value of research asset		8435	
	Amortization expense current year			1202.4

Table 11.20 **Adjusted net capital expenditure in millions of dollars**

Year	2015
Capex	2523
Dep and amortization	1945
Net Capex	578
R&D expenses in current period	4816
Amortization of research asset	1202.4
Net acquisitions	313
Adjusted net Capex	4504.6

The adjusted net capex for the year 2015 is estimated as $4504.6 million (see Table 11.20).

The change in noncash working capital amounted to $447 million in year 2015 (see Table 11.21).

Reinvestment = Adjusted net Capex + Change in noncash working capital
Reinvestment rate = Reinvestment/Adjusted net income.
The reinvestment rate is estimated as 68% in year 2015 (see Table 11.22).

Table 11.21 Estimation of noncash working capital in millions of dollars

Year	2014	2015
Total current assets	13670	21652
Cash and cash equivalents	11199	18434
Non cash current assets	2471	3218
Total current liabilities	1424	1925
Short term debt	0	201
Noninterest bearing current liabilities	1424	1724
Noncash working capital	1047	1494
Change in noncash working capital		447

Table 11.22 Estimation of reinvestment rate for FCFE model

Year	2015
Adjusted net Capex	4504.6
Change in noncash working capital	447
Reinvestment	4952
Adjusted net income	7302
Reinvestment rate	0.68

Table 11.23 Estimation of growth rate from fundamentals for FCFE model

Year	2015
Adjusted ROE	0.14
Reinvestment rate	0.68
Growth rate	0.09

Table 11.24 Estimation of FCFE in millions of dollars

Year	2015
Adjusted net income	7,302
Adjusted net Capex	4504.6
Change in noncash working capital	447
New debt issued	0
Debt repaid	119
FCFE	2,231

Growth rate = Adjusted ROE × Reinvestment rate = 9% (see Table 11.23).

Free Cash Flow to Equity (FCFE) = Adjusted net income − Adjusted net Capex − Change in noncash working capital + New debt issued−Debt repaid.

The FCFE in 2015 is estimated as $2231 million (see Table 11.24).

Table 11.25 Present value of FCFE in high growth phase

Year	1	2	3	4	5	6	7	8	9	10
Net income	7959	8676	9456	10,307	11,235	12,246	13,348	14,550	15,859	17,286
Reinvestment rate	0.68	0.68	0.68	0.68	0.68	0.68	0.68	0.68	0.68	0.68
FCFE	5412	5899	6430	7009	7640	8327	9077	9894	10,784	11,755
PV	4911	4858	4805	4753	4701	4650	4599	4549	4499	4450
Sum	46775									

Two stage FCFE model.
It is assumed that the net income of Facebook will grow at 9% for the next 10 years and thereafter at the stable growth rate of US economy.
High growth period inputs
Growth rate = 9%
Adjusted net income in 2015 = $7302 million
Reinvestment rate = 68%.
Cost of equity = 10.20%.
The present value of FCFE in the high growth period is estimated as $46,775 million (see Table 11.25).
Stable phase inputs
Growth rate in stable period = 2.3%[7]
Growth rate in stable period = Reinvestment rate × Industry ROE
Industry sector ROE = 7.3%
2.3% = Reinvestment rate × 7.3%
Reinvestment rate = 31.51%
Net Income at the end of high growth period = $17,286 million
Net Income at the beginning of stable period = 17,286 × 1.023 = $17,684.08 million
Reinvestment = 17,684.08 × 0.3151 = $5572.253 million
FCFE in stable phase = $17,684.08−$5572.253 = $12,111.83 million
Terminal value = FCFE in stable phase/(cost of equity − growth rate in stable phase)
= 12,111.83/ (0.1020−0.023) = $153,314.25 million
Present value of terminal value = $58,045.23 million
Value of operating assets = Present value of FCFE in high growth phase + Present value of FCFE in stable phase.
= $46,775 + $58,045.23 = $104,820.09 million
Value of equity = Value of operating assets + Value of cash and cash equivalents
= 104,820.09 + 18,434 = $123,254.09 million.
Number of shares in 2015 = 2853 million.
Value per share = $43.202.

11.18.4 Free Cash Flow to Firm (FCFF) valuation

FCFF = Adjusted EBIT(1 − T) − Adjusted net Capex − Change in noncash working capital.
Adjusted book value of capital = Adjusted book value of equity + Value of debt
= 52,653 + 308 = $52,961 million
Adjusted EBIT = EBIT(1 − T) + R&D expenses − Amortization of research asset

---

[7] Average US GDP growth rate during the period 2013−14.

Table 11.26 Estimation of reinvestment rate for FCFF model

Year	2015
Adjusted net Capex	4504.6
Change in noncash working capital	447
Reinvestment	4951.6
Adjusted EBIT(1 − T)	7,333
Reinvestment rate	0.68

Table 11.27 FCFF in year 2015

Adjusted EBIT(1 − T)	7,333
Adjusted net Capex	4504.6
Change in noncash working capital	447
FCFF	2,381

EBIT in year 2015 = $6225 million
Taxes in year 2015 = $2506 million
EBIT(1 − T) = $3719 million
Adjusted EDIT = 3719 | 4816 1202.40 − $7333 million.
Return on capital employed = Adjusted EBIT(1 − T)/Adjusted book value of capital
  = 7333/52,961 = 0.138
The adjusted return on capital employed is 13.8%.
The adjusted EBIT(1 − T) is estimated as $7333 million in year 2015.
Adjusted net capex + Change in noncash working capital = Reinvestment
Reinvestment rate = Reinvestment/Adjusted EBIT(1 − T)
The reinvestment rate is estimated as 68% (see Table 11.26).
Estimation of growth rate of operating income from fundamentals
Growth rate = Adjusted ROCE × Reinvestment rate
  = 0.138 × 0.68 = 0.0935
The growth of operating income estimated from fundamentals = 9.35%.
The FCFF in the year 2015 = $2381 million (see Table 11.27).
Two stage FCFF Model

It is assumed that the operating income of Facebook will grow at a growth rate of 9.35% for ten years and then at the stable growth rate which is assumed to be the GDP growth rate of US economy.

High growth inputs
High growth period = 10 years
Growth rate = 9.35%
Adjusted EBIT(1 − T) in year 2015 = $7333 million
Reinvestment rate = 68%
WACC = 10.20%.
The sum of FCFF in high growth phase = $22,493 million (see Table 11.28).
Stable phase inputs
US GDP growth rate during the two-year period 2014−15 is assumed as the growth rate in stable period.

Table 11.28 **Present value of FCFF in high growth phase**

Year	1	2	3	4	5	6	7	8	9	10
EBIT(1 − T)	8019	8768	9588	10,485	11,465	12,537	13,709	14,991	16,393	17,925
Reinvestment	5453	5962	6520	7130	7796	8525	9322	10,194	11,147	12,189
FCFF	2566	2806	3068	3355	3669	4012	4387	4797	5246	5736
PV	$2328	$2311	$2293	$2275	$2257	$2240	$2223	$2206	$2189	$2172
Sum	$22,493									

Growth rate = 2.3%

Return on capital employed of the internet information provider industry in year 2015 = 10.81%[8]

Growth rate = Reinvestment rate × ROCE of industry sector

Reinvestment rate = 2.3%/10.81% = 21.3%

The reinvestment rate in stable period is assumed to be 21.3%.

WACC = 10.20%

EBIT(1 − T) at the end of high growth period = $17,925 million

EBIT(1 − T) at the beginning of stable period = 17,925 × 1.023 = $18,337.7 million

Reinvestment = 0.213 × 18,337.7 = $3901.64 million

FCFF in stable period = 18,337.7−3901.64 = $14,436.1 million

Terminal value = 14436.1/(0.1020−0.023) = $182735.09 million

Present value of terminal value = $69,184.06 million

Value of operating assets = Present value of FCFF in high growth phase + Present value of FCFF in stable phase

  = $22,493 + $69,184.06 = $91,676.86

Value of Facebook company = Value of operating assets + Cash and cash equivalents in 2015

  = 91,676.86 + $18,434 = $110,110.86 million

Less value of debt = $308 million

Value of equity = $109,802.86 million

Number of shares = 2853 million

Value per share = $38.49

Summary of Discounted Cash Flow Valuation

FCFE model

Value of Facebook equity = $123,254.09 million.

Value per share = $43.202

FCFF model

Value of equity = $109,802.86 million

Value per share = $38.49

The year-end market capitalization of Facebook was $296,606 million in 2015. Facebook was trading at $104.66 in the first week of December 2015. The 52 week range for Facebook was $72.00−$120.79.

---

[8] http://csimarket.com/Industry/industry_ManagementEffectiveness.php?ind=1005.

11.19   Peer comparison

The financial parameters of Facebook are compared with companies like Alphabet, Tencent Holdings, LinkedIn, and Twitter Inc. Alphabet, the subsidiary of Google connects people with information and products which individuals uses frequently. Tencent Holdings provides internet value added services, mobile and value added services, online advertising services, and e commerce transactions services to users in the People's Republic of China. LinkedIn operates social networking website which is used for professional networking. Twitter Inc. is a platform for public self-expression and conversation in real time. Its services include live commentary, live connections and live conversations (see Table 11.29).

All values except EPS are stated in millions. The values for Tencent Holdings are stated in currency CNY. For all other firms, the values are in millions of dollars.

11.19.1   Growth rate comparison

The growth rate of revenues is estimated with respect to year 2015. Twitter had the highest five-year average growth rate of revenues followed by LinkedIn and Facebook. Tencent Holding had an average 10-year growth rate of revenues of 53.39% (see Table 11.30).

The growth rate of operating income is based on the year 2015. Facebook had the highest five-year average growth rate of operating income (see Table 11.31).

Table 11.29 Financial highlights—Comparison with competitors

Company	Facebook	Alphabet Inc.	Tencent Holdings Ltd.	LinkedIn Inc.	Twitter Inc.
Total asset	49,407	147,461	306,818	7011	6442
Total debt	308	5220	65,329	1082	
Capital expenditures	2523	9915	13,165	507	−347
Revenues	17,928	74,989	102,863	2991	2218
Operating income	6225	19,360	40,627	−151	−450
Cash flow	8162	24,818	44,400	257	−122
Total cash	18,434	73,066	44,636	3119	3495
Net income	3688	16,348	28,806	−166	−521
Stock holder equity	44,218	120,331	120,035	4469	4368
Market capitalization	296,606	521,615	1,434,098	29,722	16,062
EPS	1.29	23.11	3.06	−1.29	−0.79

Table 11.30 Growth rate of revenues

In percent	Facebook	Alphabet	Tencent holding	LinkedIn	Twitter
5 year average	55.47	20.66	39.25	65.2	139.28
10 year average		28.44	53.39		

Table 11.31 **Growth rate of operating income**

In percent	Facebook	Alphabet	Tencent holding
5 year average 10 year average	43.25	13.27 25.38	32.79 55.73

Table 11.32 **Comparison with price multiples as of April 2016**

Company	P/S	P/B	P/E	P/CF	Dividend yield (%)
Facebook	17	7.1	72.2	34.1	
Alphabet Inc.	7	4.3	33.2	20.2	
Tencent Holdings Ltd.	12.2	10.4	43.5	27.6	0.2
LinkedIn	5.1	3.6		18.3	
Twitter Inc.	4.4	2.3		25.3	

Table 11.33 **Price multiple comparison with Industry and Market index**

Ratios	Facebook	Industry average	S&P500
P/E	72.2	58.8	19.1
P/B	7.1	4.6	2.7
P/S	17	7.4	1.8
P/CF	34.1	15.2	11.8

11.20 Relative valuation

Facebook had the highest P/E ratio among the peer firms. Facebook also had the highest price to sales ratio and price to cash flow ratio among all the peer firms. Tencent Holdings had the second highest P/S, P/E, and P/CF ratios among the companies of comparison. Tencent Holdings Ltd. is the only dividend paying company among the peer group of firms. In terms of earning potential, Facebook is the most attractive stock as its PE ratio is 72.2 (see Table 11.32).

The price multiple comparison of Facebook with industry average and S&P500 is with respect to the period April 2016. Facebook had higher price multiples compared to the industry average and S&P 500. The price to earnings ratio was 72.2 for Facebook compared to 58.8 for industry average and 19.1 for S&P 500. The price to cash flow ratio for Facebook was 34.1 while it was 15.2 for industry average and 11.8 for S&P 500. The source of data was Morningstar.com (see Table 11.33).

The price multiples like P/E, P/B, and P/S is fluctuating over the four-year period of analysis. The price to cash flow ratio is consistently showing an increasing trend over the period of analysis (see Table 11.34).

Table 11.34 **Price multiple trends**

Year	2012	2013	2014	2015
P/E	1666.7	140.8	74.1	105.3
P/B	5.4	10.7	10.2	7.2
P/S	11.3	20.9	18.1	18.6
P/CF	35.7	39.2	39.7	40.3

Table 11.35 **Enterprise value multiples**

Company	Facebook	Alphabet	Tencent holding	LinkedIn	Twitter
Revenues	17,928	74,989	102,863	2991	2218
EBITDA	8162	24,818	44,400	257	−122
EBIT	6225	19,360	40,627	−151	−450
Debt	308	5220	65,329	1082	1455
Market value of equity	296,606	521,615	1,434,098	29,722	16,062
Cash and cash equivalents	18,434	73,066	44,636	3119	3495
Enterprise Value (EV)	278,480	453,769	1,454,791	27,685	14,022
EV/revenues	16	6	14	9	6
EV/EBITDA	34	18	33	108	−115
EV/EBIT	45	23	36	−183	−31

The lower the EV multiples are, the more attractive the stock is for buying. Enterprise value multiples are obtained by adding the book value of debt to the market capitalization and subtracting the cash and cash equivalents. The EVs are given in millions of dollars. The EV multiples are given for the year 2015 (see Table 11.35).

11.21 Performance indicators

11.21.1 Altman Z score

Investors can use Altman Z score to decide if they should buy or sell a particular stock based on the company's financial strength. The Altman Z score is the output of a credit strength test which gauges a publicly traded manufacturing company's likelihood of bankruptcy. Z score model is an accurate forecaster of failure up to two years prior to distress.

$$\text{Z-Score} = 1.2A + 1.4B + 3.3C + 0.6D + 1.0E$$

where:

A = Working capital/Total assets
B = Retained earnings/Total assets
C = Earnings before interest and tax/Total assets
D = Market value of equity/Total liabilities
E = Sales/Total assets

Table 11.36 **Determination of Altman score**

Total assets	49,407		
Total liabilities	5189		
Sales revenues	17,928		
Operating income	6225		
Retained earnings	9787		
Market value of equity	296,606		
Working capital	19,727		
Ratios	Values	Constant	Score
Working capital/Total assets	0.40	1.2	0.48
Retained earnings/Total assets	0.20	1.4	0.28
Operating income/Total assets	0.13	3.3	0.42
Market value of equity/Total liabilities	57.16	0.6	34.30
Sales/Total assets	0.36	1	0.36
		Z score	35.83

The zones of discrimination are such that when Z score is less than 1.81, it is in distress zones. When the Z score is greater than 2.99, it is in safe zones. When the Z score is between 1.81 and 2.99, the company is in Grey Zone (see Table 11.36).

Facebook have a very high Altman score of 35.83.

11.21.2 Piotroski score

The Piotroski score is a discrete score between 0 and 9 which is an indicator of the firm's financial position. The score was named after the Chicago accounting Professor Joseph Piotroski. The cumulative points suggest whether the stock is a value stock or not. If the company achieves a score of 8 or 9, the stock can be considered strong. If the score ranges between 0 and 2, then the stock is considered weak.

11.21.3 Criteria for Piotroski score

SL	Profitability scores	Score points	Score for Facebook
1	Positive return on assets in current year	1	1
2	Positive operating cash flow in current year	1	1
3	Higher ROA in current year compared to previous year	1	0
4	Return on cash flow from operations greater than ROA	1	1
	Leverage, liquidity, and sources of funds		
5	Lower ratio of long term debt to average total assets in current year compared to previous year	1	1
6	Higher current ratio in this year compared to previous year	1	1
7	No new shares were issued in the last year	1	0
	Operational efficiency ratios		
8	A higher gross margin compared to the previous year	1	1
9	A higher asset turnover ratio compared to the previous year	1	1
Total		9	7

The stock has a cumulative point of 7 out of 9.

11.21.4 Graham number

It is a conservative method used for valuing a stock. It is a figure which measures a stock's fundamental value by taking into account the company's earnings per share and book value per share. Graham number is the upper bound of the price range which a defensive investor should pay for the stock. According to Graham number theory, any stock price below the Graham number is considered undervalued and hence worth investing in. Graham number is a combination of asset valuation and earnings power valuation.

EPS in year 2015 = 1.29
Book value per share in 2015 = 14.62

$$\text{Graham number} = \sqrt{22.5 \times (\text{Earning per share}) \times (\text{Book value share})} = 20.60$$

Walmart was trading at \$117.78 on April 1 2016.

11.21.5 Peter Lynch valuation

Peter Lynch fair value is based on the assumption that it is advisable to buy the shares of the growth company at a P/E multiple which is equal to its growth rate. According to Peter Lynch, at fair value the PEG ratio of a growth company must be equal to one. The EBITDA growth rate is used as the earnings growth rate since this rate is less subject to management manipulations and distortion.

Peter Lynch fair value = PEG × Earnings growth rate × EPS
The EBITDA growth rate is 47.5%. Since the growth rate is more than 25%, we use 25% as growth rate for calculation purposes.
PEG = 72.2/0.25 = 288.8
EPS = 1.29
Peter Lynch fair value = 288.8 × 0.25 × 1.29 = \$93.14
Price to Peter Lynch fair value = 117.78/93.14 = 1.26.

*All detailed calculation and analysis are given in the resources file **Facebook. xlsx**.*

Wealth analysis of Procter and Gamble

12

12.1 Introduction

Procter &Gamble (P&G) was established by William Procter and James Gamble in the year 1837. P&G is one of the largest consumer goods company in the world. P&G is a global leader in fast moving consumer goods sector. By 2012, P&G's top 50 leadership brands accounted for 90% of P&G sales and more than 90% of the profits. Twenty-five of them are billion dollar brands. In 2015, P&G became a 178-year-old company. P&G have been consistently increasing dividends for the 59th year in a row. In the year 2015, P&G generated strong adjusted free cash flow of $11.6 billion and returned $11.9 billion to shareholders in the form of $7.3 billion as dividends and $4.6 billion as share repurchases. In the past five years, the company returned approximately 60 billion as dividends to shareholders. P&G products are sold in more than 180 countries through mass merchandisers, grocery stores, membership club stores, drug stores, department stores, salons, e commerce, high frequency stores (HFS), and pharmacies. The company have on the ground operations in approximately 70 countries. P&G have 21 billion dollar brands. In 2015, P&G made sales of value $70.7 billion. During the period 2013−15, sales to Walmart stores and its affiliates represented approximately 14% of the total revenues. During the above period, the top 10 customers accounted for approximately 33% of the total sales. The total R&D expenses amounted to $2 billion in year 2014 and 2015, respectively. Net sales in the United States accounted for approximately 37% of total net sales in the year 2015.

12.2 Organizational structure

P&G's organizational structure consists of the Global Business Units (GBUs), Selling and Market Operations (SMOs), Global Business Services (GBS), and Corporate Functions (CF). The GBUs are organized into four industry based sectors which consists of Global Beauty, Global Health and Grooming, Global Fabric and Home Care, Global Baby, Feminine and Family Care. GBUs are entrusted with the responsibility to develop the overall brand strategy, new product upgrades and marketing plans.

P&G is a global leader in the beauty, hair and personal care category.[1] In the beauty care sector, P&G offers a wide variety of products which includes deodorants, cosmetics, skin care. Brands like Olay brand is the top facial skin care brand

---

[1] P&G Annual Report 2014.

in the world with approximately 8% global market share. P&G is the global market leader in the retail hair care and color market with over 20% global market share. P&G is also a global market leader in the blades and razors market segment with market share of over 65%. In the health care segment, P&G have second position with global market share of approximately 20%. The Fabric Care and Home Care segment accounts for approximately 20% of the global market share. The Baby care segment have a market share of over 30%.

The SMOs develop and executive goto market plans at the local level. The SMOs consist of dedicated retail customer, trade channel and country specific teams. SMOs are divided into six regions namely Asia Pacific, Europe, Greater China, India, the Middle East, and Africa (IMEA). GBS provide the technology, processes, and standard data tools to serve consumers. GBS provide shared services such as payroll, purchases, real time data analytics, benefits, and facilities management.

CFs provides support for company level strategy and portfolio analysis and centralized functional support.

Table 12.1 gives the highlights of the major brands of P&G.The statistics in year 2015 suggest that the Fabric care and Home care accounts for 32% of the total net sales. Baby, Feminine and Family Care accounts for 29% of the sales. Beauty, Hair, and Personal Care accounts for 18% of the total net sales. Healthcare accounts for

Table 12.1 Major brands

Segment	Categories	Billion dollar brands
Beauty	Skin and Personal Care (Antiperspirant and Deodorant, Personal Cleansing, Skin Care); Hair Care	Head & Shoulders, Olay, Pantene SK II
Grooming	Shave Care (Female Blades & Razors, Male Blades & Razors, Pre- and Post-Shave Products, Other Shave Care); Electronic Hair Removal	Fusion, Gillette, Mach3, Prestobarba
Healthcare	Personal Health Care (Gastrointestinal, Rapid Diagnostics, Respiratory, Vitamins/Minerals/Supplements, Other Personal Health Care); Oral Care (Toothbrush, Toothpaste, Other Oral Care)	Crest, Oral-B, Vicks
Fabric Care and Home Care	Fabric Care (Laundry Additives, Fabric Enhancers, Laundry Detergents); Home Care (Air Care, Dish Care, P&G Professional, Surface Care)	Ariel, Dawn, Downy, Febreze, Gain, Tide
Baby, Feminine and Family Care	Baby Care (Baby Wipes, Diapers and Pants); Feminine Care (Adult Incontinence, Feminine Care); Family Care (Paper Towels, Tissues, Toilet Paper)	Always, Bounty, Charmin, Pampers

Source: http://www.pginvestor.com/PG-at-a-Glance/.

11% of the total sales. The developed nations account for 62% of the sales while the developing nations account for 38% of the sales. Region wise, North America accounts for 40% of the revenues, followed by Europe with 26% and Latin America with 10% of revenues. India, Middle East and Africa along with Greater China and Asia Pacific have 8% market share each. P&G own and operate 29 manufacturing sites located in 21 different states in United States. Additionally, P&G own and operate 100 manufacturing sites in 38 other countries Table 12.2 showcases the milestones achieved by P&G.

Table 12.2 **Milestones**

Year	Milestones
1937	William Procter and James Gamble combined their soap and candle businesses through partnership to form Procter and Gamble
1938	P&G gave its first print advertising for machine and lamp oil
1848	P&G achieves net sales of $37,000. Lard Oil, candles and soaps accounted for maximum of sales
1850	P&G officially adopts Moon and Star as the official trademark
1879	P&G introduces the Ivory soap. Ivory becomes the first branded soap and best-selling product
1884	Introduces Lenox soap
1886	Ivorydale factory established
1890	After 53 years of partnership, P&G incorporated as company to raise capital for growth. The total capital raised was $3 million out of which $2.5 million was stock capital. P&G establishes an analytical chemistry lab at Ivorydale
1891	P&G is listed on New York Stock Exchange
1894	The Richardon-Vicks Company introduce Vaporub which was purchased by P&G in 1985
1900	Ivory becomes the first P&G brand available outside the United States, with its introduction in the English market
1901	KC Gillette Razor the alternative to the straight razor introduced
1915	The company builds its first manufacturing plant outside United States in Hamilton Canada
1920	Soap production becomes the primary product. The company discontinue candle manufacturing. P&G introduces direct selling to retailers on the same terms it gave to wholesalers
1923	P&G pioneers advertising on commercial radio
1924	P&G becomes the first company to conduct data-based market research with consumers
1925	Coupons became an important marketing tool for P&G
1930	This period marks the end of day-to-day management by either of the Procter and Gamble families
1931	Creation of P&G Brand Management
1933	P&G launches "Ma Perkins," one of the world's first radio soap operas
1934	P&G makes entry into the haircare business with the introduction of Drene the first detergent based shampoo. P&G also introduces Teel, a dentifrice made in liquid form in the oral care category

(Continued)

Table 12.2 (Continued)

Year	Milestones
1939	P&G broadcasts its first television commercial for Ivory soap during the first televised major league baseball game
1941	P&G becomes one of the first company to establish Consumer Relations Department
1947	Tide, "the washday miracle," is introduced
1949	Oral-B introduces the first soft, flat-trimmed, nylon-bristled toothbrush to the market. Tide becomes the US market leader
1950	Logos for icons like Crest, Tide, Joy and Pampers created
1952	The company establishes P&G Fund to distribute money to charitable organizations
1954	Expands operation to United Kingdom, France and Belgium
1955	Builds detergent plants in Belgium. Toothpaste Crest introduced. It was the first toothpaste with fluoride clinically proven to fight cavities and help prevent tooth decay
1957	Crest Professional Program introduced to associate with young dentists
1958	Builds detergent plant in Italy
1961	P&G test markets Pampers, the first affordable disposable baby diaper. P&G introduces Head & Shoulders shampoo
1963	Pampers becomes the first affordable and successful disposable diaper
1967	P&G introduces Ariel, the first major laundry detergent to use enzyme technology
1968	P&G plays a pivotal role in championing the development of the bar code
1972	Dawn, a superior grease-cutting dish liquid is introduced. Bounce dryer sheets are introduced as a fresh alternative to liquid fabric softeners
1981	Researchers isolate the naturally occurring yeast that produced the "secret key" to beautiful skin. The ingredient was called Pitera and was the "secret key" to SK-II
1983	P&G introduces the first breakthrough in feminine protection -Always, using the proprietary "Dri-Weave" top sheet. Always/Whisper emerged as the global leader in its category just two years later
1984	Liquid Tide is introduced
1985	Herbal Vicks introduced in India
1986	P&G launched Pert Plus as the first "2-in-1" shampoo and conditioner on the market
1990	Victor Mills Society is created to felicitate P&G technologists for their technology innovations. The compact technology which was introduced in Japan with Cheer and Ariel brands is expanded to 36 brands in 20 different countries during the year
1991	Braun and Oral-B introduces the first power toothbrush clinically proven to clean better than a manual toothbrush. P&G introduces the Pantene Pro-V line of products. Pantene becomes the fastest growing shampoo in the world
1995	Health Care Research Center in Cincinnati is opened to serve as the worldwide hub for P&G's health care business
1996	P&G introduces its first website First PG.com
1997	P&G introduces its first ever P&G Shopper research center in Europe and North America. Introduces High Frequency Stores (HFS)

(Continued)

Table 12.2 **(Continued)**

Year	Milestones
1998	Introduces Febreze an odor eliminating fabric spray and Swiffer the cleaning system
2003	Olay brand which included Daily Facials, Total Effects, and Regenerate attains billion dollar businesses
2005	P&G adopts cold water technology to bring efficiency in Fabric care products. P&G creates a community management group to expand the potential for online conversations with consumers
2006	Introduces the mass mascara
2007	P&G brand the Mr. Clean Car Wash is extended into the service sector
2008	New technology is incorporated into Always Infinity pads
2010	The Gillette Fusion ProGlide razor is introduced
2012	Tide PODS is introduced in the laundry category
2013	Vicks and SK-II both became Billion Dollar Brands

Source: http://us.pg.com/who_we_are/heritage/history_of_innovation#.

Table 12.3 **Number of employees**

Year	Number of employees
2010	127,000
2011	129,000
2012	126,000
2013	121,000
2014	118,000
2015	110,000

Source: Annual Report 2015.

Table 12.3 gives the employment statistics of P&G during the period 2010-2015.

12.3   Restructuring by P&G

12.3.1   Gillette acquisition

In 2005, P&G acquired the Gillette Company—the largest acquisition in P&G history. The acquisition saw P&G gain access to Gillette brands such as Gillette, Oral-B, Duracell, and Braun. The acquisition created the world's biggest consumer products enterprise. The acquisition combined the marketing and distribution strengths of P&G whose products were marketed largely to women with the Gillette's high profit brands like razors which were marketed mainly to men. Through the acquisition, P&G entered into one of the most attractive categories in personal care and wet shaving segment. P&G also acquired the Duracell batteries and Braun small appliances of Gillette. The only major areas of overlap for both businesses was in the segments of deodorants and oral care. Gillette benefitted from P&G's formidable position in Japan, China, and Mexico. The deal gave P&G more control over shelf space at the major retailers and grocers. At the time of the deal, P&G was US's largest television advertiser while Gillette spends almost $1 billion a year on advertisement. The deal was aimed to get savings from broadcasters and other media companies on advertising purchases.

The acquisition enabled P&G to gain more dominating position in emerging markets like Brazil and India. Under the terms of the deal, P&G offered 0.975 of its shares for each outstanding share of Gillette. The offer was 17.6% above the Gillette's closing price of $45.85 on the New York Stock Exchange during the announcement period. For each one share of Gillette company, P&G issued 962 million shares of its common stock. The deal was valued at approximately $53.4 billion which included common stock, the fair value of vested stock options and acquisition costs. On the day of announcement of the deal, P&G stock price went down by 2% while Gillette's stock price jumped by 12%. As a result of the acquisition a new Grooming reportable segment was created. The Gillette oral care, batteries and personal care businesses were absorbed within the Health Care, Fabric Care and Home Care. At the time of the deal Gillette's largest shareholder was Warren Buffet who held 9% of the company.

Merrill Lynch & Co. was the investment adviser for P&G while Gillette was advised by UBS, Goldman Sachs and Davis Polk and Wardwell.

Table 12.4 provides the acquisition history of P&G.

Table 12.4 Restructuring by P&G

Year	Acquisitions
1930	P&G purchase Thomas Hedley & Co. Ltd. in England. The company becomes the first overseas subsidiary of P&G. Fairy Soap is one of Hedley's main products
1935	P&G expands into Philippines with the acquisition of the Philippine Manufacturing Company
1940−1950	P&G acquires operations for manufacturing detergents in Mexico, Venezuela and Cuba
1957	P&G acquires Charmin Paper mills which was a regional manufacturer of toilet tissue, towels, and napkins
1973	P&G acquires Nippon Sunhome Company in Japan
1982	P&G enters the over-the-counter health care business with the acquisition of Norwich Eaton Pharmaceuticals and its Pepto-Bismol brand
1985	P&G purchases the Richardson Vicks company
1988	P&G announces a joint venture to manufacture products in China
1991	P&G expands its operation into Eastern Europe with the acquisition of Rakona, a detergent company in Czechoslovakia.
1989−2003	P&G undertakes several acquisitions to expand its beauty care and feminine care portfolios. The company acquires Cover Girl in 1989; Old Spice in 1990; MaxFactor and Betrix in 1990; Tampax in 1997; Clairol in 2003 and Wella in 2003
2005	P&G acquires the Gillette Company which was the largest acquisition in P&G history

12.3.2   Divestitures

During the year 2014, the company streamlined its product portfolio by divesting or consolidating about 100 nonstrategic brands. As a result, the portfolio of about 65 key brands accounted for 85% of sales and 95% of after tax profit.

During July 2015, P&G entered into a definitive agreement with Coty Inc to divest four product categories which included 43 of its beauty brands to Coty Inc. The value of deal offered by Coty Inc. was $12.5 billion. During November 2014, P&G divested the batteries business via a split transaction with Berkshire Hathaway valued at $2.9 billion. It was proposed that P&G will exchange a recapitalized Duracell Company for Berkshire Hathaway's shares of P&G stock. P&G had completed the divestiture of its Pet Care business in the year 2015.

12.4   Strategy for growth[2]

P&G is focusing on portfolio transformation to create more value. P&G is focusing on 10 product category with about 65 brands. These 10 categories have been growing faster with higher operating margins. P&G is the market leader in seven of these brands. P&G have 21 brands with annual sales in the range of $1 billion–$10 billion. Eleven brands have sales within the range of $500 million-$1 billion. In 2014, P&G announced a plan to streamline its product portfolio by divesting or consolidating about 100 nonstrategic brands into a portfolio of 65 brands.

P&G aims for improving its strategic position by focusing on more focused business portfolio. P&G believes that there are significant growth opportunities in the developed markets as well as developing markets like China, Brazil, India, Russia and Mexico. For example, Power Oral Care business powered with Bluetooth technology and with annual turnover of over $ 1 billion have significant growth potential since the current household penetration is still low. Value creation in P&G is measured by the concept of Operating Total Shareholder Returns (TSR). TSR is a balanced measure of performance for all stakeholders of P&G. The fundamental building block of TSR are sales growth, gross, and operating margin improvement and asset efficiency. P&G focusses on organic sales growth. Significant investments in R&D have resulted in product innovations like the introduction of Pampers Swaddlers and Pants, Tide and Ariel PODS, Downy Unstoppables, Pantene conditioners with advanced Pro-V science, Gillette FlexBall, Venus Swirl, and Oral B Powerbrush. P&G is involved in implementing the biggest supply chain redesign in the firm's history. Through this restructuring, the firm aims to lower costs in overhead, cost of goods sold, marketing, and trade spending. The firm also is reorienting sales force to build profitable distribution and shell assortment. The company aims in investing in a more agile, flexible,

[2] Annual Reports, P&G Company.

and faster distribution network to reduce out of stocks and optimize inventory. The company have linked individual performance to each employee's contribution to Operating TSR at every level of the company.

Purposes, Values and Principles are the foundations for P&G's culture. P&G's growth was led through synthetic detergents in the 1950s and through paper products in the late 1960s and 1970s. P&G have built successful brands through important facets like cutting edge R&D, sophisticated marketing campaigns, strong distribution infrastructures and state of art market research. Each P&G product category provides a portfolio of innovation which includes a mix of commercial programs, product improvements and innovations. The productivity improvements focus on minimizing cost of goods sold, overhead reductions, and marketing efficiencies. Emphasizing the importance of retailers, P&G created the industry's first multinational customer teams in year 1991. In an initiative to partner closely with retailers, P&G had restructured its sales function and renamed it as Customer Business Development in the year 1994. By the year 2005, High Frequency Stores (HFS) became the largest customer channel for P&G. P&G through this 20 million stores across the world are able to connect to consumers with affordable products and packages. In 2011, P&G introduced Consumer Pulse, a scaled listening solution which enabled brands to monitor and measure influencers and consumer's perception about products in real-time. In the decade of 2000s, P&G focused on leading categories and brands with its largest retail customers in its developed markets while at the same time accelerated growth in health, beauty and personal care segments in developing markets. During the period 2000−6, the sales increased by more than 40% and the profits doubled. During this period, free cash flow of approximately $30 billion were generated. In 2003, P&G created the GYM the innovation and brainstorming facility. In the year 2007, P&G introduces Design Thinking, a methodology for using the mindsets and processes of design to unlock new solutions. P&G has also opened creative experimental environments and processes such as the Clay Street Innovation incubator and Loft Experiential Prototyping processes. Tide Dry Cleaning network locations cater to the needs of over 500,000 customers and process over 3.4 million garments. With a focus on improving shopper satisfaction, P&G introduced its first ever commercial strategy to link retailer's efforts to win at the "First Moment of Truth" (FMOT). In 2010, P&G created a community management group to expand the potential for online conversations with consumers. With the aim to focus on branding the company and not just the portfolio of brands, P&G led a successful sponsorship of the 2010 Olympics and the introduction of P&G's "Proud Sponsor of Moms" campaign. In the year 2010, P&G launched the Gillette Guard razor in India which was a cheaper version and more efficient razor targeted for rural Indians.

In the year 2012, the company initiated a productivity and cost savings plan to reduce costs and better leverage scale in the areas of supply chain, research and development, marketing and overheads. The company focuses on organic sales growth above the market growth rates in the categories and geographies in which they operate.

12.5 Corporate governance[3]

Presently there are 12 board members. Four committees help the board to fulfill its responsibilities. These committees are the Governance and Public Responsibility Committee, Audit Committee, Compensation and Leadership Development Committee, Innovation and Technology Committee. The Board's independent Governance and Public Responsibility Committee review the membership of each Board committee and recommends proposed membership lists for all Board committees to the full board. The Audit Committee maintains the integrity of the company's financial statements and its compliance with legal and regulatory requirements and overall risk management process. Audit Committee is composed exclusively of independent directors who meets regularly in private session with the company's independent auditors, Deloitte &Touché LLP. The internal control environment consists of rigorous business process controls which include written policies and procedures, segregation of duties etc. The Disclosure Committee is comprised of senior level executives who are responsible for evaluating disclosure implications of significant business activities and events. The Compensation and Leadership Development Committee have responsibility for the company's overall compensation policies. The Committee also assists the Board in the leadership development and evaluation of principal officers. The Innovation and Technology Committee provide counsel on aspects related to innovation and technology.

During 1887, P&G introduced a profit sharing program for employees. In fact, all employees own P&G stock or stock rights through various investment programs. The important feature of the Executive Share Ownership program is that senior executives can own shares of the company stock and/or restricted stock units (RSUs) valued at eight times base salary for CEO and five times base salary for other senior executives. The nonemployee directors of the firm must own firm stock and/or RSUs which are worth six times their annual cash retainer.

It is a mandatory requirement that every employee is required to be trained on the Company's worldwide business conduct manual. P&G's Global Government Relations & Public Policy (GGRPP) focuses on legislative and public policy issues which would affect the firm's bottom line and long term business interests. In United States, P&G engages in the political process by providing financial assistance to selected state ballot initiatives and advocacy campaigns.

12.6 Sustainability initiatives

P&G's sustainability activities are directed towards preservation of resources especially renewable resources. For example, the program Coldwater washing campaign reduced packaging, water usage, and increased recycled content in the packaging. The social programs of P&G include Children's Safe Drinking Water (CSDW)

---

[3] http://us.pg.com/who_we_are/structure_governance/corporate_governance/overview.

Program, the disaster relief efforts and brand programs like Pampers' partnership with the UNIC. In 2015, P&G have announced plans to reduce the absolute greenhouse gas emissions of the operations by 30% by 2020.

In 1990, P&G was one among nine other consumer product companies to be named as one of the Global 100 Most Sustainable Companies in the World. P&G product dawn dishwashing liquid had been a vital tool for wildlife conservation organizations. In the year 2004, P&G's Children's Safe Drinking Water Program (CSDW) is aimed at providing drinking water in developing countries. In the year 2004, P&G received the World Business Award from the United Nations Development Program and International Chamber of Commerce in recognition of UN's Millennium Development goals. By 2012, P&G had invested more than $35 million to deliver over five billion liters of clean drinking water through P&G Purifier of Water. In the year 2005, P&G created the Tide Loads of Hope program to assist families hit by natural disaster by providing laundry services. By the year 2012, it is estimated that the program had cleaned more than 34,000 loads of laundry for families affected by disasters like Hurricane, Katrina, San Diego wildfires and Hurricane Ike. In the year 2006, UNICEF and Pampers joined to provide tetanus vaccines to newborns in developing countries. P&G launched the "Thank You, Mom" campaign for the 2012 Summer Olympics where the company supported 150 global athletes and their Moms.P&G became the Olympic Worldwide Partner for the next decade. In 2013, approximately 45 P&G sites around the world achieved zero waste to landfill status. P&G have partnered with Constellation to build 50 megawatt biomass plant at Albany which makes the Charmin and Bounty products. This plant aims to produce 100% of the steam and up to 70% of the total energy for the site from renewable sources. P&G have announced plans to partner with EDF RE to build wind farm for electricity generation for Fabric and Home Care products such as Tide, Downy, Febreze, and Cascade in the US and Canada. Presently 68 sites have achieved zero manufacturing waste to landfill which was nearly half of P&G's global sites. On account of new packaging initiatives, P&G have saved more than 6000 tons of packaging which resulted in usage of 10% less plastic or saved 900 tons of plastic. P&G is focusing on achieving zero deforestation in the palm supply chain. In 2013, P&G made a commitment to move about 20% of the North America truck transportation to cleaner burning natural gas within two years. P&G have partnered with multinational companies in the Closed Loop Fund (CLF) initiative which is a social impact investment fund to provide cities with access to the capital required to build comprehensive recycling programs.

12.7 Dividends and stock splits

P&G has been paying a dividend for 125 consecutive years since its incorporation in 1890 and has increased its dividend for 59 consecutive years at an annual compound average rate of over 9% (see Table 12.5).

Total dividend payments to common and preferred shareholders were $7.3 billion in 2015 and $6.9 billion in 2014. The dividend yield was 3.08% in year 2011, 3.26% in 2012, 2.91%, 2.78% and 3.31% during the period 2013–15.

Table 12.5 Dividend trends

Year	1956	1966	1976	1986	1996	2006	2016
DPS split adjusted in $	0.01	0.03	0.06	0.16	0.40	1.15	2.59

Table 12.6 Stock splits

Year	Stock splits
1983	2 for 1 stock split
1989	2 for 1 stock split
1992	2 for 1 stock split
1997	2 for 1 stock split
2004	2 for 1 stock split

P&G had undertaken five stock splits during the period 1983−2004 (see Table 12.6).

P&G trades on the New York Stock Exchange and NYSE Euronext Paris under the stock symbol PG. There were approximately 2.6 million common stock shareowners which include participants in the P&G Shareholder Investment Program. The total share repurchases amounted to $6 billion and $4.6 billion in the year 2014 and 2015, respectively.

12.8 Long term debt

The total debt amounted to $30.4 billion and $35.4 billion in year 2015 and 2014, respectively. The short term credit ratings were P-1 (Moody's) and A-1 (Standard & Poor's) while the long term credit ratings were Aa3 (Moody's) and AA- (Standard & Poor's) in the year 2015. P&G maintain bank credit facilities to support its ongoing commercial paper program.

12.9 Risks and challenges

P&G faces numerous risks in operations and sales in international markets due to foreign currency fluctuations, currency exchange or pricing controls. P&G have sizable businesses and maintain local currency balances in a number of foreign countries with exchange import authorization, pricing or other controls. The profitability of P&G could be negatively impacted due to reduced demand such as slowdown in the general economy, reduced market growth rates, tighter credit markets for the suppliers, vendors or customers. P&G faces competitive pressures in the environments in which the company operate as well as challenges in maintaining profit margins. The businesses of P&G are subject to wide variety of laws and regulations involving intellectual property, product liability, marketing, antitrust, privacy, environmental issues across all the world. P&G faces cost pressures due to significant exposures to certain commodities such as oil derived materials like resins whose market prices are subject to much volatility. The net earnings could be affected by changes in United States or foreign government tax policies.

12.10 Risk management

P&G being a multinational company is exposed to market risks, such as changes in interest rates, currency exchange rates, and commodity prices. Interest rate swaps are used to hedge exposures to interest rate movement on underlying debt obligations. P&G uses forward contracts to manage exchange rate risk. P&G also uses certain currency swaps with maturities of up to five years to hedge the exposure to exchange rate movements on intercompany financing transactions. P&G uses futures, options, and swap contracts to manage commodity price fluctuations. To manage credit risk, P&G enter into transactions with investment grade financial institutions. The counterparty exposures are monitored daily and downgrades in counterparty credit ratings are reviewed on timely basis. P&G hedge certain net investment positions in foreign subsidiaries.

12.11 Employee benefit plans

P&G sponsor various post-employment benefits plans which include both defined contribution plans and defined benefit plans. P&G offers other post-employment benefit plans which consists of health care and life insurance for retirees. The stock based compensation plans of P&G offer annually grant stock option, restricted stock, RSU, and performance stock unit (PSU) to managers and directors. Since the year 2002, the key manager stock option awards granted during the period July 1998−August 2002 were vested after three years and have a 15-year life. The stock based compensation plan of P&G provides for issuance of a total of 185 million shares of common stock. The company incurred total stock based compensation expense for stock option grants of $249, $246, and $223 million during the period 2013, 2014, and 2015, respectively.

12.12 Ownership

In 2015, equity constituted 64% while debt composed 36% of the capital structure. Financial Institutions constituted 64.01% of the equity ownership of the company by May 2016. Approximately 29.75% of the equity ownership is held by the mutual funds. The insiders hold about 0.06% of the equity ownership. By May 2016, the number of institution owners were 2732 while the number of mutual fund owners were 3430. The top 10 institutions held 24.49% of the total equity ownership in May 2016. The top 10 mutual funds held 8.35% of the total equity ownership in May 2016 (see Tables 12.7 and 12.8).

Table 12.7 **Equity ownership—top five mutual funds**

	Name of fund	Percentage of total shares held
1	Vanguard Total Stock Mkt Idx	1.93
2	Vanguard 500 Index Inv	1.24
3	Vanguard Institutional Index	1.08
4	SPDRS&P500ETF	1
5	VA College America529E	0.64

Source: Morningstar.com.

Table 12.8 **Equity ownership—top financial institutions**

	Name	Percentage of total shares
1	Vanguard Group Inc.	6.37
2	State Street Corp	4.27
3	P&G Profit Sharing Trust and Employee Stock Ownership	3.11
4	BlackRock Fund Advisors	2.62
5	Berkshire Hathaway Inc.	1.95
6	Capital World Investors	1.85
7	Northern Trust Investments NA	1.27
8	Fidelity Management & Research Company	1.24
9	State Street Global Advisors (Aus) Ltd.	0.95
10	Norges Bank	0.86
	Total	24.49

Source: Morningstar.com.

Table 12.9 **Segmental revenues in year 2015**

Segment	Net sales revenues
Baby, Feminine, and Family Care	$20.2 billion
Fabric and Home Care	$22.3 billion
Beauty, Hair, and Personal Care	$18.1 billion
Health and Grooming	$15.2 billion

Tables 12.9–12.10 gives the segmental revenues and net earnings of P&G in year 2015.

12.13   Financial highlights

The values are given in millions of dollars. The revenues increased from $68.222 billion in year 2006 to $76.279 billion by the year 2015. The operating income of P&G

Table 12.10 Net earnings in year 2015

Segment	Net earnings
Baby, Feminine, and Family Care	$2938 million
Fabric and Home Care	$2635 million
Beauty, Hair, and Personal Care	$2584 million
Grooming	$1787 million
Health Care	$1167 million

declined from $13.249 billion in year 2006 to $11.79 billion by the year 2015. The market capitalization increased from $176.741 billion in year 2006 to $212.382 billion by the year 2015. The market capitalization is based on year-end closing price of the stock. The total cash increased from $7.826 billion in year 2006 to $11.612 billion by the year 2015. The year on year revenue growth rate of 12% was the highest in the year 2007 during the period 2006–15. The cash flow (EBITDA), operating income, operating cash flow and net income year on year growth rate was highest in the year 2007 during the period 2007–15. The average growth rate of revenues during the period 2007–15 was 1%. The average growth rate of operating income during the period 2007–15 was approximately 3%. The average growth rate of enterprise value and market capitalization was approximately 2% and 3% respectively during the period 2007–15. The average total cash and cash equivalents growth rate was approximately 13% during the period 2007–15 (see Table 12.11).

P&G had deconsolidated its local Venezuelan operations from the Consolidated Financial Statements with effective from June 30, 2015.

12.14   Ratio analysis

12.14.1   Performance ratios

The average gross margin during the period 2006–15 was 50.49%. The average gross margin during the period 2006–10 was 51.5% which declined to 49.48% during the period 2011–15. The average operating margin and earning before tax margin was 18.7% and 18% during the period 2006–15 period. The average net margin was 13.5% during the period 2006–15. The average operating margin declined from 20.16% during the period 2006–10 to 17.24% during the period 2011–15. The average net margin during the period 2006–10 declined from 14.54% to 12.46% during the period 2011–15 (see Table 12.12).

The average ROA during the period 2006–15 was 8.11%. The average return on equity (ROE) and return on invested capital (ROIC) was 17.6 % and 12.08 %. The average Interest Coverage Ratio (ICR) was 16.26. The average ROA, ROE, and ROIC declined in the period 2011–15 compared to the period 2006–10. The average ICR increased from 12.83 during the period 2006–10 to 19.68 during the period 2011–15 (see Table 12.3).

Table 12.11 Trend analysis

Year	2006	2007	2008	2009	2010	2011	2012	2013	2014	2015
Revenues	68,222	76,476	83,503	79,029	78,938	82,559	83,680	84,167	83,062	76,279
EBITDA	16,159	19,144	20,265	19,765	19,101	18,858	16,758	18,492	18,735	15,606
Operating income	13,249	15,450	17,083	16,123	16,021	15,818	13,292	14,481	15,288	11,790
Operating cash flow	11,375	13,435	15,814	14,919	16,072	13,231	13,284	14,873	13,958	14,608
Net income	8684	10,340	12,075	13,436	12,736	11,797	10,756	11,312	11,643	7,036
Total cash and equivalents	7826	5556	3313	4781	2879	2768	4436	5947	10,686	11,612
Retained earnings	35,666	41,797	48,986	57,309	64,614	70,682	75,349	80,197	84,990	84,807
Enterprise value	208,470	222,223	219,234	182,857	159,107	206,657	195,448	238,508	239,646	232,828
Market capitalization	176,741	190,959	184,516	149,059	170,553	175,816	168,315	211,130	213,042	212,382
Long term debt	35,976	23,375	23,581	20,652	21,360	22,033	21,080	19,111	19,811	18,329
Total equity	62,908	66,760	69,494	63,099	61,115	67,640	63,439	68,064	69,214	62,419

Table 12.12 Margin ratios

Year	2006	2007	2008	2009	2010	2011	2012	2013	2014	2015
Gross margin (%)	51.4	52	51.3	50.8	52	50.6	49.3	49.6	48.9	49
Operating margin (%)	19.4	20.2	20.5	20.4	20.3	19.2	15.9	17.2	18.4	15.5
EBT (%)	18.2	19.23	19.25	19.39	19.06	18.4	15.28	17.64	17.92	15.53
Net margin (%)	12.51	13.31	14.25	16.76	15.86	14.01	12.55	13.15	13.71	8.88

Table 12.13 Profitability ratios

Year	2006	2007	2008	2009	2010	2011	2012	2013	2014	2015
Return on asset (%)	8.66	7.44	8.44	9.5	9.52	8.68	7.76	8.15	8.03	4.95
Return on equity (%)	22.04	16.05	17.83	20.39	20.59	18.32	16.32	17.14	16.87	10.47
Return on invested capital (%)	13.32	11.08	12.65	14	14.02	12.98	11.62	12.09	11.75	7.31
ICR	11.84	11.85	11.64	11.87	16.94	19.03	17.28	21.71	21.56	18.83

12.14.2 Per share ratios (see Table 12.14)

The per share values are given in dollars. The average earnings per share was $3.56 during the period 2006−15. The average dividend per share was $1.88 during the period 2006−15. The average book value per share and EBITDA per share was $22.37 and $5.95. The average revenue per share and total debt per share during the period 2006−15 was $25.93 and $11.68. The average EPS increased from $3.54 during the period 2006−10 to $3.58 during the period 2011−15. The average DPS increased from $1.46 to $2.29 during the two comparative periods of analysis. The average book value per share increased from $20.99 to $23.76. The average EBITDA per share increased from $5.87 to $ 6.03 per share. The average revenue per share increased from $23.91 to $27.94 during the two periods 2006−10 and 2011−15. The total debt per share declined from $11.72 during the period 2006−10 to $11.63 during the period 2011−15.

12.14.3 Price multiples (see Table 12.15)

The average Price to Book (P/B) ratio during the period 2006−15 was 2.9. The average Price to Earnings (P/E) ratio was 19.1 during the period 2006−15. The average Price to Sales (P/S) ratio during the period 2006−15 was 2.5. The average Price to Cash Flow (P/CF) ratio during the period 2006−15 was 18.8. The average price multiple ratio values increased in the period 2011−15 compared to the period 2006−10. The average P/B ratio of 2.8 during the period 2006−10 increased to 3 during the period 2011−15. The average P/E ratio was 16.9 during the period 2006−10. The average P/E ratio increased to 21.2 during the period 2011−15. The P/S ratio which was 2.5 during the period 2006−10 increased to 2.6 during the period 2011−15. The price to cash flow ratio which was 17.1 during the period 2006−10 increased to 20.5 during the period 2011−15.

12.14.4 Leverage ratios (see Table 12.16)

The average long term debt to total assets during the period 2006−15 was 0.17. The average debt to equity ratio during the period 2006−15 was 0.52.

12.14.5 Liquidity ratios (see Table 12.17)

The average liquidity ratios increased during the period 2011−15 compared to the previous period 2006−10. The average current ratio increased from 0.85 during the period 2006−10 to 0.89 during the period 2011−15. The average quick ratio increased from 0.42 during the period 2006−10 to 0.44 during the period 2011−15.

Table 12.14 Per share ratios

Year	2006	2007	2008	2009	2010	2011	2012	2013	2014	2015
Earnings per share	2.64	3.04	3.64	4.26	4.11	3.93	3.66	3.86	4.01	2.44
Dividend per share	1.15	1.28	1.45	1.64	1.8	1.97	2.14	2.29	2.45	2.59
Book value per share	19.33	20.94	22.45	21.18	21.04	24.01	22.65	24.41	25.12	22.6
EBITDA per share	4.92	5.77	6.24	6.27	5.16	6.28	5.7	6.31	6.45	5.41
Revenue per share	20.76	23.06	25.18	25.06	25.47	27.5	28.45	28.72	28.6	26.45
Total debt per share	11.99	11.35	12.08	12.68	10.49	11.58	10.84	11.5	13.07	11.18

Table 12.15 Price multiples

Year	2006	2007	2008	2009	2010	2011	2012	2013	2014	2015
P/B	2.88	2.92	2.71	2.41	2.85	2.65	2.7	3.15	3.13	3.46
P/E	20.9	19.89	16.77	12.08	14.74	16.26	17.15	20.34	20.03	32.37
P/S	2.64	2.71	2.46	2.08	2.36	2.32	2.18	2.81	2.8	2.82
Price to cash flow	20.74	19.73	16.92	13.83	14.34	19.25	19.35	20.74	22.58	20.76

Table 12.16 Financial leverage ratios

Year	2006	2007	2008	2009	2010	2011	2012	2013	2014	2015
Long term debt to total assets	0.27	0.17	0.16	0.15	0.17	0.16	0.16	0.14	0.14	0.14
Debt to equity	0.61	0.53	0.53	0.59	0.49	0.47	0.47	0.46	0.51	0.49

Table 12.17 **Liquidity ratios**

Year	2006	2007	2008	2009	2010	2011	2012	2013	2014	2015
Current ratio	1.22	0.78	0.79	0.71	0.77	0.81	0.88	0.8	0.94	1
Quick ratio	0.68	0.4	0.33	0.34	0.34	0.33	0.42	0.41	0.51	0.55

12.14.6   Efficiency ratios (see Table 12.18)

The average days' sales outstanding during the period 2006–15 was 27.5 days. The average days' inventory and payable period during the period 2006–15 was 62.8 days and 64.2 days. The average receivables turnover ratio and inventory turnover ratio during the period 2006–15 was 13.3 and 5.8, respectively. The average fixed assets turnover and asset turnover ratio during the period 2006–15 was 4 and 0.6, respectively. The average days "sales outstanding during the period 2006–10 declined from 28 days to 27 days during the time period 2011–15. The average days" inventory during the period 2006–10 decreased from 66.2 days to 59.4 days during the period 2011–15. The average payable period during the above two periods of comparison shows that the payable period increased from 56 days to 72.3 days. The average receivable turnover ratio increased from 13.06 to 13.52. The average inventory turnover ratio increased from 5.52 to 6.15. The average fixed asset turnover ratio declined from 4.06 to 3.89 during the two periods of comparison. The average asset turnover ratio remained constant during the two periods of comparison.

12.14.7   Shareholder return analysis

In this section it is assumed that $100 was initially invested in P&G stock on June 30, 2010 and all the dividends were reinvested. The cumulative value of $100 investment through June 30 for five-year period for P&G, S&P 500 index, and S&P 500 Consumer Staples Index is given in the table (Table 12.19).

12.14.8   Stock wealth analysis

The wealth analysis was done based on monthly returns for a period of 46 years involving 11,694 months during 1970–2016. The cumulative returns of P&G stock during the period 1970–2016 based on monthly returns was 636.76%. On the basis of adjusted closing price, the price increased by 177 times in 2016 compared to the year 1970. The adjusted closing price of P&G stock was $0.46 on January 2, 1970. The adjusted closing price of P&G stock on May 6, 2016 was $82.13. The holding period return during the period 1970–2016 was 17,618.65%. Suppose an investor made an investment of $100 in P&G stock during January 1970. The investment if held till May 2016 would have become $17,718.65.

The average yearly returns and excess returns were calculated for the period 2010–15. In the year 2011, P&G stock had an excess return of 6.26% over the S&P 500 index returns. Except for the year 2011 and 2014, the market index S&P

Table 12.18 **Efficiency ratios**

Year	2006	2007	2008	2009	2010	2011	2012	2013	2014	2015
Days sales outstanding	26.51	29.48	29.26	29.09	25.83	25.66	26.92	27.27	28.33	26.91
Days inventory	62.24	65.22	68.32	71.77	63.84	61.61	60.7	58.63	58.75	57.33
Payables period	48	52.83	55.99	59.84	63.68	68.37	68.63	71.82	74.09	78.48
Receivables turnover	13.77	12.38	12.47	12.55	14.13	14.22	13.56	13.39	12.88	13.56
Inventory turnover	5.86	5.6	5.34	5.09	5.72	5.92	6.01	6.23	6.21	6.37
Fixed assets turnover	4.12	3.99	4.16	3.94	4.08	4.07	4.02	4	3.78	3.58
Asset turnover	0.69	0.56	0.59	0.57	0.6	0.62	0.62	0.62	0.59	0.56

Table 12.19 **Comparative wealth analysis**

Company	2010	2011	2012	2013	2014	2015
P&G	$100	$109	$109	$141	$149	$153
S&P500 Index	$100	$131	$138	$166	$207	$222
S&P 500 Consumer Staples Index	$100	$127	$145	$171	$197	$215

Source: P&G Annual Report 2015.

Table 12.20 Average yearly returns

Year	P&G	S&P500	Excess returns
2010	7.98	19.09	−11.11
2011	7.41	1.15	6.26
2012	5.95	13.16	−7.21
2013	22.51	26.54	−4.03
2014	15.12	11.14	3.98
2015	−9.36	0.11	−9.47

Table 12.21 Holding period yield in percent

Year	P&G
2010	6.96
2011	8.3
2012	10.45
2013	10.79
2014	21.72
2015	−3.39

Table 12.22 Excess wealth created in millions of dollars

Year	2011	2012	2013	2014	2015
Market value of equity	183,746	185,452	220,736	245,989	214,770
Book value of equity	67,640	63,439	68,064	69,214	62,419
BV asper cent of MV	37	34	31	28	29
Excess value	116,106	122,013	152,672	176,775	152,351

500 outperformed the P&G stock in all years of analysis. In the year 2013, P&G registered the highest average yearly returns of 22.51%. During the same year S&P 500 registered average yearly returns of 26.54% (see Table 12.20).

In holding period yield calculation, it is assumed that the investment period horizon is one year. The holding period yield was highest in the year 2014 with 21.72%. In the year 2015, the holding period yield for P&G was −3.39%. The six-year holding period yield (2010−15) was estimated as 7.55% (see Table 12.21).

The average book value as per cent of market value was 32% during the period 2011−15. The excess value determined as the difference between the market value and book value peaked in the year 2014 was $176.775 billion dollars (see Table 12.22).

Table 12.23 **Risk free rate**

Year	Yield to maturity on 30 year treasury bond
2014	3.55
2015	2.63
2016	2.63
Average	2.94%

12.15   Estimation of Weighted Average Cost of Capital (WACC)

The cost of equity is first estimated through the CAPM model.
Estimation of cost of equity using CAPM
Required rate of return = Risk free rate + Beta × (Return on market index − Risk free rate)
The risk free rate is assumed as the average yield to maturity on the 30-year treasury bond during the two-year period 2014−16.[4]

The risk free rate is 2.94% (see Table 12.23). Beta is estimated by regressing the weekly P&G stock returns on the market index S&P 500 weekly returns during the two-year period 2014−16 The beta value estimated is 0.56. The average returns on market index S&P500 during the period 2014−16 is taken as the returns on market index (Rm). Since the Rm−Rf is equal to 3.3%, we assume that the risk premium is equal to 5%.

Rm = 6.27%.
Cost of equity = Risk free rate + Beta × Risk premium
= 2.94 + 0.56 × (5) = 5.74%.
Cost of debt = Yield to maturity on the long term bond of P&G which matures on May 11, 2027[5].
The yield to maturity = 4.87%.
Income before taxes in year 2015 = $11,846 million
Tax expenses in year 2015 = $2916 million
Effective tax rate = 24.6%.
After tax cost of debt = 4.87 × (1−0.246) = 3.67%.

12.16   Estimation of WACC

Weights based on market value
Short term debt in year 2015 = $12,021 million
Long term debt in year 2015 = $18,329 million
Total debt = $30,350 million.
Market value of equity = $214,770 million
Total value of firm = 30,350 + 214,770 = $245,120 million
Weight of debt = 30,350/245,120 = 0.12

[4] https://www.treasury.gov/resource-center/data-chart-center/interest-rates/Pages/Historic-Yield-Data-Visualization.aspx.
[5] http://quicktake.morningstar.com/StockNet/bonds.aspx?Symbol=PG&Country=USA.

Weight of equity = 214,770/245,120 = 0.88
WACC = Weight of equity × Cost of equity + Weight of debt × After tax cost of debt.
= 0.88 × 5.74 + 0.12 × 3.67 = 5.48%.
The Weighted Average Cost of Capital (WACC) is estimated as 5.48%.

12.17 Valuation perspectives

12.17.1 Estimation of economic value of P&G in year 2015

Economic value is estimated as net operating income after taxes (NOPAT)−Capital charge.
Profit before interest and tax (PBIT) − Income tax = NOPAT.
Capital employed = Stock holder equity + Long term debt
Capital charge = Capital employed × WACC
Economic value (EV) = NOPAT − Capital charge (see Table 12.24).

The economic value for P&G in the year 2015 is estimated as $4449 million.

12.17.2 Equity spread

Equity spread is a variation of the EV measures. Equity spread is the difference between the ROE and the required ROE (cost of equity)

Equity spread = (Return on equity − Cost of equity) × Equity capital
Return on equity in year 2015 = 10.47%
Cost of equity = 5.74%
Equity spread = (10.47%−5.74%) × 62,419 million = $2952.419 million.
The value of equity spread for P&G is estimated as $2952.419 million.

12.17.3 Discounted cash flow valuation

The discounted cash flow valuation models used are dividend discount model (DDM), Free Cash Flow to Equity (FCFE) and Free Cash Flow to Firm (FCFF).

Table 12.24 Economic value in year 2015

PBIT in 2015	11,790
Income tax	2,916
NOPAT	8,874
Stockholder equity	62,419
Long term debt	18,329
Capital employed	80,748
WACC	5.48%
Capital charge	4424.99
EV	4,449

12.17.4 Dividend Discount Model (DDM)

The average dividend payout was 62% during the six-year period 2010−15 (see Table 12.25).

Retention ratio (RR) = 1 − DPO where DPO is dividend payout ratio.

Growth rate = Retention Ratio (RR) × ROE. The average growth rate estimated from fundamentals for the period 2010−15 was 7% during the period 2010−15 (see Table 12.26).

12.17.5 Two stage DDM

In this model it is assumed that the earnings per share of P&G will grow at 7% for the next 10 years and thereafter at the stable growth rate of US economy.

High growth period assumptions
High growth period = 10 years
Growth rate in high growth period = 7%
Average EPS during the period 2010−15 = $3.7
Average DPO = 62%
Cost of equity = 5.74% (Estimated from CAPM)
Cost of equity estimated using dividend growth model
Average growth rate of dividends during the period 2011−15 = 7.6%
DPS in year 2015 = $2.59
Current market price (P) = 82.50
Cost of equity = DPS/P + g = (2.59/82.50) + 0.076 = 10.73%
For estimation purposes, we find the average of the values of cost of equity obtained from CAPM model and dividend growth model.
Cost of equity for estimation purposes = 10.73 + 5.74/2 = 8.24%
The present value of dividends in the high growth phase = $21.54 (see Table 12.27)
Stable growth phase assumptions
Growth rate in stable period is assumed to be the growth rate of US economy. The average growth rate of US GDP for two-year period 2013−14 is taken for calculation. The GDP growth rate is estimated as 2.3%.[6]

Table 12.25 Dividend trends

Year	2010	2011	2012	2013	2014	2015
EPS	4.11	3.93	3.66	3.86	4.01	2.44
DPS	1.8	1.97	2.14	2.29	2.45	2.59
DPO	0.44	0.50	0.58	0.59	0.61	1.06

Table 12.26 Estimation of growth rate from fundamentals for DDM

Year	2010	2011	2012	2013	2014	2015
RR	0.56	0.50	0.42	0.41	0.39	−0.06
ROE	0.21	0.18	0.16	0.17	0.17	0.10
Growth rate	0.12	0.09	0.07	0.07	0.07	−0.01

[6] http://data.worldbank.org/indicator/NY.GDP.MKTP.KD.ZG.

Table 12.27 Present value of dividends in high growth phase

Year	1	2	3	4	5	6	7	8	9	10
EPS	3.96	4.24	4.53	4.85	5.19	5.55	5.94	6.36	6.80	7.28
DPO	0.62	0.62	0.62	0.62	0.62	0.62	0.62	0.62	0.62	0.62
DPS	2.455	2.626	2.810	3.007	3.217	3.443	3.684	3.942	4.217	4.513
PV	$2.27	$2.24	$2.22	$2.19	$2.17	$2.14	$2.12	$2.09	$2.07	$2.04
SUM	$21.54									

Table 12.28 Net capital expenditure in millions of dollars

Year	2011	2012	2013	2014	2015
Capex	3306	3964	4008	3848	3736
Dep and amortization	2838	3204	2982	3141	3134
Net Capex	468	760	1026	707	602
Net acquisitions	474	134	1145	24	137
Adjusted net Capex	942	894	2171	731	739

The ROE of consumer goods industry sector is 18.2%.[7]
Growth rate in stable period = 2.3%
Growth rate = RR × Industry ROE
2.3% = RR × 18.2%
RR = 2.3/18.2 = 0.13
DPO = 0.87
EPS at the end of high growth period = $7.28
EPS at the beginning of stable period = 7.28 × 1.023 = $7.45
DPO = 0.87
DPS in stable period = 7.45 × 0.87 = $6.50
Terminal value = DPS in stable period/(Cost of equity-growth rate in stable period)
= 6.50/ (0.0824−0.023) = $109.51
Present value of terminal value = $49.61
Value of P&G stock today = PV of dividends in high growth phase + PV of terminal value
= 21.54 + 49.61 = $71.15 P&G stock was trading at $82.50 in NYSE on May 11, 2016.
The 52 week range of the P&G stock was $65.02−$83.87 during May 2016.

12.17.6 FCFE valuation

Net capital expenditure = Capital expenditure − Depreciation and amortization
Adjusted net capital expenditure = Net capital expenditure + Net acquisitions.

The adjusted net capital expenditure declined from $942 million in year 2011 to $739 million in year 2015 (see Table 12.28).

Noncash current assets = Total current assets − Cash and cash equivalents
Noninterest bearing current liabilities = Total current liabilities − Short term debt

---

[7] http://www.morningstar.com/stocks/XNYS/PG/quote.html.

Table 12.29 Noncash working capital in millions of dollars

Year	2010	2011	2012	2013	2014	2015
Total current assets	18,782	21,970	21,910	23,990	31,617	29,646
Cash and cash equivalents	2879	2768	4436	5947	10,686	11,612
Noncash current assets	15,903	19,202	17,474	18,043	20,931	18,034
Total current liabilities	24,282	27,293	24,907	30,037	33,726	29,790
Short term debt	8472	9981	8698	12,432	15,606	12,021
Noninterest bearing current liabilities	15,810	17,312	16,209	17,605	18,120	17,769
Noncash working capital	93	1890	1265	438	2811	265
Change in noncash working capital		1797	−625	−827	2373	−2546

Table 12.30 Estimation of reinvestment rate for FCFE model

Year	2011	2012	2013	2014	2015
Adjusted net Capex	942	894	2171	731	739
Change in noncash working capital	1797	−625	−827	2373	−2546
Reinvestment	2739	269	1344	3104	−1807
Net income	11,797	10,756	11,312	11,643	7036
Reinvestment rate	0.232	0.025	0.119	0.267	−0.257

Table 12.31 Estimation of growth rate from fundamentals for FCFE model

Year	2011	2012	2013	2014	2015
Adjusted ROE	0.18	0.16	0.17	0.17	0.1047
Reinvestment rate	0.23	0.03	0.12	0.27	−0.26
Growth rate	0.04	0.00	0.02	0.04	−0.03

Noncash working capital = Noncash current assets − Noninterest bearing current liabilities (see Table 12.29).

The average reinvestment rate during the five-year period was 7.7% (see Table 12.30).

Reinvestment = Adjusted net capex + Change in noncash working capital.

Reinvestment rate = Reinvestment/adjusted net income.

Growth rate in net income = ROE × Reinvestment rate

The average growth rate estimated from fundamentals is equal to 3% (see Table 12.31).

FCFE = Adjusted net income − Adjusted net capex − Change in noncash working capital + new debt issued − debt repaid. The average FCFE generated by the company was $9451 million during the period 2011−15 (see Table 12.32).

Table 12.32 **Estimation of FCFE in millions of dollars**

Year	2011	2012	2013	2014	2015
Net income	11,797	10,756	11,312	11,643	7036
Adjusted net Capex	942	894	2171	731	739
Change in noncash working capital	1797	−625	−827	2373	−2546
New debt issued	1536	3985	2331	4334	2138
Debt repaid	55	2549	3752	4095	3512
FCFE	10,539	11,923	8547	8778	7469

12.17.7   Constant or single stage FCFE growth model

The growth rate of earnings estimated from fundamentals was 3% which is approximately equal to the growth rate of world economy.
Cost of equity = 5.74 %
Growth rate = 3%
Estimation of FCFE in the stable phase
Average net income during the period 2011−15 = $10,509 million
Net income in stable period = 10,509 × 1.03 = $10,824.06 million
Reinvestment rate = 7.7%
Reinvestment = 10,824.06 × 7.7% = $833.5 million
FCFE in stable period = 10,824.06−833.5 = $9990.61 million
Value of operating assets = FCFE in stable period/(Cost of equity − growth rate)
Value of operating assets = 9990.61/ (5.74%−3%) = $364,620.84 million
Cash and cash equivalents in year 2015 = $11,612 million.
Value of equity = 364,620.84 + 11,612 = $376,232.84 million.
Current number of shares = 2884 million
Value per share = $130.45.
According to FCFE constant growth model the value of P&G stock is arrived at $130.45.

12.17.8   FCFF valuation model

In FCFF valuation, the discount rate used is WACC.
In general form, FCFF = EBIT(1 − T) − Net capital expenditure − Change in working capital.

The average FCFF during the five-year period 2011−15 was $9725 million dollars (see Table 12.33).
Reinvestment rate = Reinvestment/Adjusted EBIT(1 − T).
Reinvestment = Adjusted net Capex + Change in noncash working capital.
The average reinvestment rate during the period 2011−14 based on geometric mean was 15.3% (see Table 12.34).[8]

---

[8] The reinvestment rate in year 2015 was not used for calculation of average since the rate was negative in this year.

Table 12.33 Estimation of FCFF in million dollars

Year	2011	2012	2013	2014	2015
EBIT	15,818	13,292	14,481	15,288	11,790
Taxes	3392	3468	3441	3178	2916
EBIT(1 − T)	12,426	9824	11,040	12,110	8874
Adjusted net Capex	942	894	2171	731	739
Change in noncash working capital	1797	−625	−827	2373	−2546
FCFF	9687	9555	9696	9006	10,681

Table 12.34 Estimation of reinvestment rate for FCFF model

Year	2011	2012	2013	2014	2015
Adjusted net Capex	942	894	2171	731	739
Change in noncash working capital	1797	−625	−827	2373	−2546
Reinvestment	2739	269	1344	3104	−1807
EBIT(1 − T)	12,426	9824	11,040	12,110	8874
Reinvestment rate	0.220	0.027	0.122	0.256	−0.204

Table 12.35 Estimation of growth rate of operating income from fundamentals

Year	2011	2012	2013	2014	2015
ROCE	0.13	0.12	0.12	0.12	0.073
Reinvestment rate	0.22	0.03	0.12	0.26	−0.20
Growth rate	0.029	0.003	0.015	0.030	−0.015

Growth rate of operating income = Return on Capital Employed (ROCE) × Reinvestment rate

The average growth rate of operating income during the period 2011−14 was approximately 2%. The year 2015 was excluded (see Table 12.35).

12.17.9 Single stage or constant growth FCFF model

Growth rate of operating earnings = 2%
Average reinvestment rate = 15.3%
EBIT(1 − T) in the year 2015 = $8874 million dollar
EBIT(1 − T) in the stable period = 8874 × 1.02 = $9051.48 million
Reinvestment = 9051.48 × 15.3% = $1384.88 million.
WACC = 5.48%
FCFF in stable period = 9051.48−1384.88 = $7666.60 million.
Value of operating assets = FCFF in stable period/(WACC − growth rate)
Value of operating assets = 7666.60/(5.48%−2%)
= $220,304.7 million

Cash and cash equivalents in year 2015 = $11,612 million
Value of firm = 220,304.7 + 11,612 = $231,916.7 million
Value of debt in year 2015 = $30,350 million
Value of equity = 231,916.7−30,350 = $201,566.7 million
Number of shares = 2884 million
Value per share = $69.89
According to FCFF single stage valuation model, the value of P&G stock is estimated as $69.89.

Summary of discounted cash flow valuation

Two stage DDM
 Value of P&G stock = $71.15
 One stage or constant growth FCFE model
 Value of equity = $376.23 billion
 Value per stock = $130.45.
 One stage or constant growth FCFF model
 Value of equity = $201.57 billion.
 Value per stock = $69.89
 The P&G stock was trading at $82.41 in NYSE as on May 13, 2016. As of this date, the 52 week range for P&G stock was $65.02−$83.87. The market capitalization of P&G on May 13, 2016 was $219.4 billion.

12.17.10 Peer comparison

The variables of comparison are for the year 2015 and stated in millions of dollars. P&G financial variables are compared with peer companies like Unilever NV, Reckitt Benckiser, and Colgate Palmolive. Unilever NV is a supplier of fast moving consumer goods. The focus areas of operations are personal care, home care, foods and refreshment. Reckitt Benckiser Group PLC is a consumer health and hygiene company which manufactures and sells branded products in the health, hygiene and home products. Colgate Palmolive, the consumer products company provides services such as oral care, personal care, home care and pet nutrition. P&G is the asset maximizer among all the peer firms. P&G also has the highest revenues, cash flow, operating income, net income, and total cash among all the peer firms of comparison. P&G has the highest market capitalization among the four companies (see Table 12.36).

The growth rate of revenues for the competitor firms are based on the year 2015. Unilever had the highest five-year average growth rate in revenues while Rickett Benickser had the highest 10-year average growth rate of revenues among the peer firms (see Table 12.37).

The analysis is based on the year 2015. Unilever had the highest five-year average growth rate of operating income. Rickett Benickser had the highest 10-year average growth rate of operating income among the competitor firms (see Table 12.38).

Table 12.36 Financial highlights—comparison with peer group

Company	P&G	Unilever	Rickett Benickser	Colgate Palmolive
Total asset	129,495	56,969	22,856	11,958
Total debt	30,350		3622	6571
Capital expenditures	3297	2259	268	691
Revenues	76,279	58,031	13,284	16,034
Operating income	11,790	8186	3355	2789
Cash flow	15,606	7515	3615	3345
Total cash	11,612	3418	1289	970
Net income	9078	5347	1743	1384
Stock holder equity	62,419	16,818	10,335	−299
Market capitalization	219,363	138,116	71,130	64,877
EPS	2.5	1.9	0.72	1.52

Table 12.37 Comparison of growth rates of revenues

In percent	P&G	Unilever	Rickett Benickser	Colgate Palmolive
5 year average	−0.68	3.78	0.98	0.6
10 year average	3	2.99	7.82	3.47

Table 12.38 Comparison of growth rates of operating income

In percent	P&G	Unilever	Rickett Benickser	Colgate Palmolive
5 year average	−5.95	3.46	1.02	−4.38
10 year average	0.76	3.53	10.31	2.33

Table 12.39 Price Multiples −Peer Comparison

Price multiple	P/S	P/B	P/E	Dividend yield (%)
P&G	3.3	3.8	26.8	3.2
Unilever	2.3	7.8	23.2	3
Rickett Benickser	5.7	7.1	29	2
Colgate Palmolive	4.2		47.9	2.1

12.17.11 Relative valuation

Price multiples comparison are based on the period May 2016. Rickett Benickser had the highest P/S ratio while Unilever had the highest P/B ratio among the peer firms. Colgate Palmolive had the highest P/E ratio. P&G had the highest dividend yield among the peer companies (see Table 12.39).

Table 12.40 Price multiples-industry and S&P 500 index comparison

Ratios	P&G	Industry average	S&P500
P/E	26.8	33.3	18.8
P/B	3.8	6.7	2.7
P/S	3.3	2.8	1.8
P/CF	15.4	16.4	11.7
Dividend yield (%)	3.2	2.7	2.4

Table 12.41 Price multiple trends

Year	2011	2012	2013	2014	2015
P/E	17.3	17.8	21.1	25.6	26.5
P/B	2.9	2.8	3.3	3.8	3.5
P/S	2.4	2.4	2.8	3.2	3.1
P/CF	15.4	13.8	16.9	17	15.7

Table 12.42 Enterprise value multiple comparison

Company	P&G	Unilever	Rickett Benickser	Colgate Palmolive
Revenues	76,279	58,031	13,284	16,034
EBITDA	15,606	7,515	3,615	3,345
EBIT	11,790	8,186	3,355	2,789
Debt	30,350	0	3,622	6,571
Market value of equity	219,363	138,116	71,130	64,877
Cash and cash equivalents	11,612	3,418	1,289	970
Enterprise Value (EV)	238,101	134,698	73,463	70,478
EV/REVENUES	3	2	6	4
EV/EBITDA	15	18	20	21
EV/EBIT	20	16	22	25

The price multiple comparisons are based on current valuation during May 2016. The P/E, P/B, P/CF was higher for the industry compared to P&G. The P/S and Dividend Yield was higher for P&G compared to the industry average. The source of data was Morningstar.com (see Table 12.40).

The P/E ratio and P/S have consistently increased over the five-year period 2011−15. The price to cash flow (P/CF) have been fluctuating over the five-year period of analysis. The source of data was Morningstar.com (see Table 12.41).

The values for variables are given in millions of dollars. The enterprise value multiple values are calculated for the year 2015. In terms of EV/EBITDA, P&G is the most attractive and undervalued stock among the peer firms. Unilever have the lowest EV/Revenues and EV/EBIT ratio among the peer firms (see Table 12.42).

Table 12.43 Enterprise value multiples

Enterprise value multiples	2011	2012	2013	2014	2015
EV/REVENUES	2.53	2.38	2.98	2.95	3.05
EV/EBITDA	11.01	11.84	13.38	13.07	14.92
EV/EBIT	12.97	14.7	16.07	15.77	18.67

The enterprise value multiples have been fluctuating over the period 2011–15. The EV/Revenues multiple increased from 2.53 in 2011 to 3.05 during the period 2015. The EV/EBITDA multiple increased from 11.01 in year 2011 to 14.92 in year 2015. The EV/EBIT increased from 12.97 in year 2011 to 18.67 in year 2015 (see Table 12.43).

12.18 Performance indicators

12.18.1 Altman Z score

Investors can use Altman Z score to decide if they should buy or sell a particular stock based on the company's financial strength. The Altman Z score is the output of a credit strength test which gauges a publicly traded manufacturing company's likelihood of bankruptcy. Z score model is an accurate forecaster of failure up to two years prior to distress.

$$Z\text{-Score} = 1.2A + 1.4B + 3.3C + 0.6D + 1.0E$$

Where:

A = Working capital/Total assets
B = Retained earnings/Total assets
C = Earnings before interest and tax/Total assets
D = Market value of equity/Total liabilities
E = Sales/Total assets

The zones of discrimination are such that when Z score is less than 1.81, it is in distress zones. When the Z score is greater than 2.99, it is in safe zones. When the Z score is between 1.81 and 2.99, the company is in Grey Zone (see Table 12.44).

The Altman score is estimated for the year 2015. The Altman score for P&G is estimated as 3.77. This score indicates that P&G is in safe zone.

12.18.2 Piotroski score

The Piotroski score is a discrete score between 0 and 9 which is an indicator of the firm's financial position. The score was named after the Chicago accounting Professor Joseph Piotroski. The cumulative points suggest whether the stock is a value stock or not. If the company achieves a score of 8 or 9, the stock can be considered strong. If the score ranges between 0 and 2, then the stock is considered weak.

Table 12.44 **Determination of Altman score**

Total assets	129,495		
Total liabilities	67,076		
Sales revenues	76,279		
Operating income	11,790		
Retained earnings	84,807		
Market value of equity	219,363		
Working capital	−144		
Ratios	Values	Constant	Score
Working capital/Total assets	0.00	1.2	0.00
Retained earnings/Total assets	0.65	1.4	0.92
Operating income/Total assets	0.09	3.3	0.30
Market value of equity/Total liabilities	3.27	0.6	1.96
Sales/Total assets	0.59	1	0.59
		Z score	3.77

12.18.3 Criteria for Piotroski score

SL	Profitability scores	Score points	Score for P&G
1	Positive return on assets in current year	1	1
2	Positive operating cash flow in current year	1	1
3	Higher ROA in current year compared to previous year	1	0
4	Return on cash flow from operations greater than ROA	1	1
	Leverage, liquidity, and sources of funds		
5	Lower ratio of long term debt to average total assets in current year compared to previous year	1	1
6	Higher current ratio in this year compared to previous year	1	1
7	No new shares were issued in the last year	1	1
	Operational efficiency ratios		
8	A higher gross margin compared to the previous year	1	1
9	A higher asset turnover ratio compared to the previous year	1	0
Total		9	7

The stock has a cumulative point of 7 out of 9. The Piotroski F score calculation is based on the year 2015.

12.18.4 Graham number

It is a conservative method used for valuing a stock. It is a figure which measures a stock's fundamental value by taking into account the company's earnings per share and book value per share. Graham number is the upper bound of the price range which a defensive investor should pay for the stock. According to Graham number theory, any stock price below the Graham number is considered undervalued and hence worth investing in. Graham number is a combination of asset valuation and earnings power valuation.

EPS in year 2015 = $2.44

Book value per share in 2015 = $22.71

$$\text{Graham number} = \sqrt{22.5 \times (\text{Earning per share}) \times (\text{Book value per share})} = \$35.31$$

P&G was trading at *trading at $82.41 in NYSE as on May 13, 2016.*

*All detailed calculation and analysis are given in the resources file **P&G.xlsx**.*

Wealth analysis of Wells Fargo

13

13.1 Introduction

Wells Fargo have a rich 164-year history. Wells Fargo was established in the year 1852. Wells Fargo & Company is a diversified financial services company with over $1.8 trillion in assets. The company was established in the year 1852 and headquartered in San Francisco. Wells Fargo provide banking, insurance, investments, mortgage, consumer and commercial finance services. The bank has offices in about 8700 locations in 36 countries and have 13,000 ATMS. According to statistics, Wells Fargo serve one in three households in the United States. Wells Fargo occupies the rank position of 30 on Fortune's ranking of America's largest corporations in the year 2015. The company was also ranked as the first in the market value of common stock among all US banks in the year 2015.

Wells Fargo Bank is one of the "Big Four Banks of the United States" along with JP Morgan Chase, Bank of America, and Citigroup. In March 2015, Wells Fargo became the world's biggest bank by market capitalization. The present day Wells Fargo was formed as a result of merger between San Francisco based Wells Fargo & Company and Minneapolis based Norwest Corporation. In the year 2008, Wells Fargo acquired Charlotte based Wachovia for $ 14.8 billion in an all-stock transaction. Wells Fargo had record earnings for the sixth consecutive year in year 2014. In 2014, Wells Fargo was the most profitable bank in the United States. Wells Fargo process more than 20,000 customer transactions like account openings or online bill payments every minute. The cross sell strategy of the bank is to increase the number of products the customers use by offering them financial products which satisfy their needs.

In the year 2015, Wells Fargo invested $7 billion for community development loans and investments. The bank had extended $18.8 billion to small business customers in the year 2015. The company allotted $281.3 million to nonprofit organizations in the year 2016.

In the year 2015, Wells Fargo generated $86.1 billion in revenue. In 2015, the total deposits reached a record $1.2 trillion. Wells Fargo gave back $12.6 billion to the shareholders through common stock dividends. In 2015, Wells Fargo had total equity of $193.9 billion, common equity tier one capital of $142.4 billion and a common equity tier one ratio of 10.77%. Wells Fargo have relationships with approximately three million small business owners.

Wells Fargo was ranked as No. 7 on Barron's 2015 ranking of the world's "100 Most Respected Companies." In 2015, Euromoney magazine named Wells Fargo as the "Best Bank in the US." In 2015, the Banker magazine had named Wells Fargo as the best global and US bank of the year.

Strategic Financial Management Casebook.
© 2017 Elsevier Inc. All rights reserved.

13.2 Business divisions

Wells Fargo have three operating segments—Community Banking, Wholesale Banking, and WIM.

Community banking offers a complete line of diversified financial products and services for consumers and small businesses which includes checking and savings accounts, credit and debit cards, auto, student, and small business lending. The community banking segment also include the results of corporate treasury activities. The community banking had registered net income of $13.5 billion in the year 2015.

Wholesale banking provides financial solutions to businesses throughout the world globally with annual sales generally in excess of $20 million. Products and business segments include Middle Market Commercial Banking, Government and Institutional Banking, Corporate Banking, Commercial Real Estate, Treasury Management, Wells Fargo Capital Finance, Insurance, Real Estate Capital Markets, Commercial Mortgage Servicing, Corporate Trust, Equipment Finance, Wells Fargo Securities, Principal Investments, Asset Backed Finance, and Asset Management. The Wholesale banking division reported net income of $8.2 billion in year 2015.

WIM formerly known as Wealth, Brokerage and Retirement division provides a full range of financial advisory services to clients. Wealth Management provides affluent and high net worth clients with a complete range of wealth management solutions, including financial planning, private banking, credit, investment management, and fiduciary services. Wells Fargo serve clients' brokerage needs, supply retirement and trust services to institutional clients. WIM had a reported net income of $2.3 billion in year 2015.

In 2015, Wells Fargo realigned its asset management business from Wholesale banking to Wealth Investment Management. The reinsurance business was realigned from WIM to Wholesale banking. The strategic auto investments, business banking and merchant payment services businesses was also restructured from community banking to wholesale banking.

13.3 Growth strategy of Wells Fargo

Wells Fargo focuses on strengthening its engagement with communities through operations, business practices, philanthropy, and community engagement. Wells Fargo focuses on new technology offerings and channels to gain competitive advantage. Wells Fargo focuses on innovative payment solutions like Apple Pay and Android Pay, initiatives for biometric customer authentication to attract retail customers. Wells Fargo have introduced YourLoanTrackerSM service in 2015 to enable customers to check the status of the loans using smartphones or tablets. In 2015, Wells Fargo formed a new cross functional Innovation Group to facilitate technological innovation in financial services. The Innovation Group focuses on research and development, payment strategies, design and delivery and analytics. Wells

Fargo focuses on the strategy of cross selling. The aim of this strategy is to understand the financial needs and innovate the products, services and channels of Wells Fargo. In the community banking sector, the cross sell metric highlights the relationship of all retail products used by customers in retail banking household.

A substantial portion of the revenues are generated from the interest and fees that are charged on the loans and products and services. A major chunk of the revenues and earnings also come from net interest income and fee income which are earned from the consumer and commercial lending and banking businesses which include mortgage banking businesses. Wells Fargo is the largest mortgage originator in the United States. The revenues are generated from the fees received for originating mortgage loans and servicing mortgage loans. The business and economic conditions could adversely affect the financial results for the fee based businesses which include investment advisory, mutual fund, securities brokerage, wealth management, and investment banking businesses. In the year 2015, approximately 26% of the revenues was fee income which included trust and investment fees, card fees, and other fees. The changes in the short term and long term interest rates would reduce Wells Fargo's net interest margin. The adverse changes in the credit ratings have a negative effect on the liquidity, cash flows, and financial results. Effective liquidity management also faces challenges in the context of financial market stress. The mortgage banking revenue are also subject to volatility as a result of changes in interest rates.

13.4   Mergers and acquisitions by Wells Fargo

In 1996 Wells Fargo acquired First Interstate Bancorp for $11.6 billion. The combined entity became the ninth largest bank in the United States. The combined bank had assets worth $116 billion, loans of $72 billion and deposits worth $89 billion. The acquisition resulted in Wells Fargo emerging as the main competitor to Bank America Corporation. The two banks controlled 40% of bank deposits in California at the time of the acquisition. The deal facilitated the entry of Wells Fargo outside California through First Interstate's subsidiaries in Western States. The deal saw the exchange of each share of First Interstate being exchanged for two thirds of a share of Wells Fargo. The deal valued at $11.6 billion which worked out to $152.33 a share.[1] In the year 1998, Norwest Corp and Wells Fargo merged to create a banking behemoth in the western region of United States. The deal was valued at $31.4 billion or $368.10 per share. The merger created the US's seventh largest bank during the period 1998. The combined bank had $191 billion in assets, 90,000 employees, 20 million customers and approximately 2800 branches in the west and mid-west region of United States. Northwest with headquarters in Minneapolis had approximately 1500 consumer finance outlets in different regions of United States.

---

[1] http://www.nytimes.com/1996/01/25/business/wells-fargo-wins-battle-for-first-interstate.html.

At the time of the deal, Norwest was largest originator and servicer of home mortgages in United States with more than 700 outlets. Wells Fargo received 10 Norwest common shares for each of its share. The merger resulted in Wells Fargo shareholders owning approximately 52.5% of the combined company and the Norwest shareholders owned 47.5 % of the combined firm. The merger was expected to generate cost savings of over $650 million for three years.

During the period 1999, Wells Fargo acquired 13 companies with total assets of $2.4 billion. These acquisitions included the buyout of Michigan Financial Corporation, National Bank of Alaska, First Commerce Bancshares etc. In 2000, Wells Fargo acquired First Security Corporation for $3 billion in stock. Through this acquisition, Wells Fargo became the largest banking franchise in the western region. During the period 2001, Wells Fargo acquired H D Vest Financial Services for $128 million. Wells Fargo divested the company for $580 million in the year 2015. In the year 2007, Wells Fargo acquired Placer Sierra Bank. In the same year Wells Fargo acquired Greater Bay Bancorp for $1.5 billion. In the year 2008, Wells Fargo acquired CIT's construction unit, United Bancorporation of Wyoming and Century Bancshares.

In October 2008, Wells Fargo bought out Wachovia for $15.1 billion all stock deal. The acquisition helped Wells Fargo gain entry into the big retail banking network. Under the terms of the deal, the Wachovia shareholders received 0.1991 shares of Wells Fargo common stock. The merger doubled the size of Wells Fargo and resulted in the creation of the fourth largest bank by assets in the year 2008. As a result of the acquisition, Wells Fargo had the US's largest branch network with more than 6600 offices in 39 states and possessed the largest retail brokerages. Wells Fargo expected approximately $5 billion in annual cost savings in year 2011 as a result of the acquisition. The combined banks had more than 70 million customer accounts. The combination resulted in the offerings of 80 different lines of businesses ranging from mortgage lending and credit cards to brokerage accounts and business loans.

13.5   Corporate governance

Wells Fargo is managed by the Board of Directors. The board delegates the conduct of business to the company's officers, managers and employees under the direction of the CEO. The Board's oversight responsibilities include succession planning for CEO and senior management, review, monitor and approval of the company's strategic plans and objectives, financial performance, risk management, and fostering of ethics. Board of Directors carries out its oversight function through seven standing committees. Risk Committee oversight includes providing enterprise wide risk management framework and structure. The Audit and Examination Committee is responsible for internal control over financial reporting. The Credit Committee's oversight includes credit risk which includes approval of the credit risk functional framework. The oversight of corporate responsibility committee includes matters related to the CSR activities. The Human Resources Committee's oversight includes planning of overall incentive compensation strategy and incentive compensation practices. This committee is also responsible for talent management and succession planning. The finance committee is responsible for annual financial plan. The oversight of the Governance and Nominating Committee include corporate governance compliance and Board committee performance. The board members are identified, evaluated and recommended by the Governance and Nominating Committee. Approximately 40% of the 15 director nominees elected in year 2016 are women. In 2015, Wells Fargo established the Office of Global Ethics and Integrity (GEI) to foster a culture of ethics and integrity in every department of the company. The board maintains significant majority of its members who meet the criteria for independence required by the NYSE. A lead director who will be independent under the rules of NYSE and the company's director independence standards is appointed by majority of independent directors annually. The nonmanagement directors of the board meet in regularly scheduled executive sessions without management. The human resources committee with full involvement of board plans for the succession to the position of CEO. Nonmanagement director's retirement age is specified as 72. Directors in Wells Fargo are required to own shares of the company's common stock. The stock ownership policy of the company states that each nonmanagement director after five years on the Board must own company common stock having a value equal to five times the annual cash retainer.

13.6 Sustainability initiatives

In the year 2015, Wells Fargo employees volunteered 1.8 million hours and contributed $98.8 million to nonprofits and schools. Wells Fargo have emerged as one of the top corporate cash donors in United States. During the period 2011–15, Wells Fargo had donated $1.4 billion for community engagement programs. Since 2012, Wells Fargo have contributed approximately $66 million to nonprofit organizations for education, job training and property. Wells Fargo have provided more than 300 mortgage free houses to wounded veterans and families. Wells Fargo employ more than 8000 self-identified veterans. Wells Fargo have partnered with Metropolitan Economic Development Association (MEDA) to provide assistance to approximately 19,000 entrepreneurs for startup of 500 businesses. Through the establishment of Wells Fargo Housing Foundation in 1993, the team members of Wells Fargo have volunteered more than 4.7 million hours to build and rehabilitate approximately 5600 homes. Since the year 2012, the LIFT program of Wells Fargo have facilitated in the creation of more than 10,725 homeowners in 39 communities by means of financial assistance in the form of about $278 million down payment. Wells Fargo initiated five-year grant program for environmental solutions for communities in the year 2012. This program has provided more than $9.8 million in grants to more than 250 nonprofit organizations for promotion of environmental sustainability. The US Green Building Council have named Wells Fargo as the "green building leader" among the financial institutions in the year 2015. About 20% of the total square footage of Wells Fargo's leased and owned buildings is LEED certified. Since 2008, Wells Fargo had 30% reduction in greenhouse gas emissions and the water efficiency increased by 47%. Wells Fargo had provided $15 billion in environmental loans and investments.

13.7   CSR initiatives[2]

Wells Fargo 2020 CSR strategy focuses on priority areas of diversity and social inclusion, economic empowerment and environmental sustainability. Wells Fargo have implemented various sustainability programs. The team members involve in annual engagement surveys, quarterly town meetings with CEO and senior leaders. Wells Fargo's EthicsLine is a 24/7 service where complaints and violations of code of conduct, company policies can be anonymously reported. Wells Fargo facilitate customers to provide feedback through website, social media and other channels like blogs for consumers and businesses. Well Fargo's investor outreach program include investor presentations, quarterly earnings investor calls, regulatory filings, and annual shareholder meeting. Wells Fargo engage with thousands of global suppliers through Supplier Diversity Program and Supplier Environmental Information Request process. Wells Fargo regularly engage with community leaders, advocacy groups and NGOs as part of the company's CSR efforts. Wells Fargo had provided $4 million in grants to GRID Alternatives, a nonprofit program which provide renewable energy and job training for low income communities since the year 2007. Through the LIFT program, Wells Fargo have provided approximately $278 million as down payment assistance and home education program. In the year 2015, the team members provided $98.8 million to 30,000 nonprofit organizations and schools. Wells Fargo provided $18.8 billion in new loan commitments to small business customers across the United States. Wells Fargo provides full range of products and services to more than 34.4 million households who are unbanked and underbanked. Wells Fargo have provided financial services to 1675 low and moderate income areas through 6100 retail banking stores across United States during the year 2015. Wells Fargo have provided $7.6 billion in community development loans and investments to support low and moderate income neighborhoods. Since the year 1998, Wells Fargo have invested more than $405 million in nonprofit microfinance schemes to help low and moderate income people in United States. Wells Fargo have invested $52 billion in environment lending and investments since the year 2012.

Wells Fargo have allocated $6 million across 69 nonprofits organization for neighborhood stabilization projects. In the year 2015, Wells Fargo donated

---

[2] https://www08.wellsfargomedia.com/assets/pdf/about/corporate-responsibility/corporate-social-responsibility-priorities.pdf.

$1.4 million to the American Red Cross and community based nonprofits organization to aid disaster relief.

Wells Fargo have plans to provide $100 billion in new small business loans during the period 2014–18. The bank aims to provide $150 billion in mortgage originations to minority households. Wells Fargo aims to provide approximately $75 million as grants and loans to Community Development Financial Institutions which serve small businesses by the stipulated year 2018. In recognition of the corporate culture, Wells Fargo was ranked as the seventh Most Respected Company in the World by Barron and ranked 22nd Most Admired Company in the World by Fortune during the year 2015. Since 2016, Wells Fargo have committed $2 million to Scholarship America for the Wells Fargo Veterans Scholarship Program and the Wells Fargo Veterans Emergency Grant Program.

Approximately 60% of the noninterest expense are accounted by Compensation and benefits. Wells Fargo have committed $1.2 million over two years to the US Hispanic Chamber of Commerce Foundation to establish training programs to diversified small businesses.

Wells Fargo support Bank On programs in 31 markets to serve underserved communities to enter into financial stream. During the year 2015, 3137 team members delivered Hands on Banking workshops to 165,700 individuals and families during the American Bankers Association's "Teach Children to Save" and Get Smart About Credit Campaigns. As part of the 2020 CSR commitment, Wells Fargo aims for a 45% reduction in absolute greenhouse gas emissions and 65% reduction in water use. In 2015, Wells Fargo delivered more than 800,000 electronic new account kits which facilitated the avoidance of more than 50 million sheets of paper. In 2015, the Environmental Solutions for Communities grant program supported 61 projects in 45 communities with total contributions of $2.5 million. The program funded a wide variety of projects in areas of sustainable agriculture and forestry, water and land conservation, and building of healthy urban ecosystems.

13.8   Investment securities

The available for sale securities portfolio mainly consists of liquid, high quality US Treasury and federal agency debt, agency mortgage backed securities (MBS), privately issued residential and commercial MBA, securities issued by US states and political establishments, corporate debt securities, and collateralized loan obligations. The held to maturity securities portfolio consist of high quality US treasury debt, agency MBA, asset backed securities (ABS) primarily collateralized by auto loans and leases and collateralized loan obligations.

13.9   Risk management

The company's risk management structure is under the oversight of the Board. The Risk Committee serves as the focal point for enterprise wide risk issues. The

Enterprise Risk Management Committee chaired by the Wells Fargo Chief Risk Officer manages all risk types across the company. The risk committee consists of a minimum of six members and meets at least quarterly. The governance committees for risk management consists of counterparty credit risk committee, credit risk management committee, enterprise technology governance committee, fiduciary and investment risk oversight committee and financial crimes risk committee, legal entity governance committee, market risk and model risk committee, operational risk management committee, and regulatory compliance risk management committee.

Wells Fargo maintain an effective operational risk management program to identify, measure, manage and report operational risks across all areas of Wells Fargo. The A&E committee of the board has the primary responsibility for oversight of operational risks.

Wells Fargo manage credit risk by establishing sound credit policies for underwriting new businesses and reviewing the performance of existing loan portfolios. The credit process consists of comprehensive credit policies, disciplined credit underwriting, extensive credit training programs, and continual loan review and audit process. Wells Fargo adopts the strategy of designation of certain portfolios and loan products as nonstrategic or liquidating after stopping their origination. Wells Fargo classify loans acquired with evidence of credit deterioration as purchased credit impaired (PCI) loans. For portfolio risk management, Wells Fargo aggregate commercial and industrial loans and lease financing on the basis of market segmentation and standard industry codes. The commercial and industrial loans and lease financing are subject to individual risk assessment using the internal borrower and collateral quality ratings. Most of the commercial and industrial loans and lease financing portfolio are secured by short term assets such as accounts receivables, inventory and securities and long lived assets such as equipment and other business assets. The monitoring and measurement of credit risk is a continuous process at Wells Fargo which tracks delinquencies, collateral values, FICO scores and economic trends by geographic areas. The risk mitigation strategies include the restructuring of repayment terms, securing collateral and guarantees and re underwriting of the loans. Wells Fargo also subject commercial and real estate loans to individual risk assessment through internal borrower and collateral quality ratings. The foreign country risk monitoring process is carried out using frequent dialogue with financial institutions, customers, counterparties, and regulatory agencies. The bank also establish exposure limits for each country by means of a centralized oversight process based on customer needs. Wells Fargo conduct periodic stress tests of country risk exposures and analyze the direct and indirect impact on the risk of loss from various macroeconomic and capital market scenarios. The real estate 1−4 family first and junior lien mortgage loans consists of loans which are associated as part of the asset liability management strategy. The credit monitoring of the real estate portfolio includes tracking delinquency, FIFCO scores and loan/combined loan to collateral values. In the year 2015, Wells Fargo completed more than 3600 proprietary and Home Affordability Modification Program (HAMP) Pick—a-Pay loan modifications. Wells Fargo applies a disciplined process and methodology to establish the allowance for credit losses each quarter. Many factors like historical and forecasted loss trends, loan level credit quality ratings and loan grade specific characteristics are incorporated in the process.

The primary oversight of the interest rate and market rate risk are vested with the Finance Committee of the Board of Directors. The interest rate risk is assessed by comparing outcomes under various earnings simulation using interest rate scenarios that differ in the direction of interest rate changes. The risk measures include both net interest income sensitivity and interest rate sensitive non-interest income and expense impacts. Wells Fargo uses investment securities portfolio and exchange traded and over the counter (OTC) interest rate derivatives to hedge the interest rate exposures. Wells Fargo uses derivatives to convert cash flows from selected asset and/or liability instruments/portfolios. Derivatives are also used to economically hedge mortgage origination pipeline, funded mortgage loans and Mortgage Servicing Rights (MSR) using interest rate swaps, swaptions, futures, forwards and options. The price risk of MSRs is hedged using a combination of highly liquid interest rate forward instruments which include mortgage forward contracts, interest rate swaps and interest rate options. Wells Fargo use derivatives to manage exposure to market risk, interest rate risk, credit risk, and foreign currency risk.

Wells Fargo engage in trading activities to act as a hedge to manage balance sheet risks. VaR is the primary market risk management measure for assets and liabilities which are classified as trading positions. Trading VaR is the measure of market risk of the company's trading positions which are classified as trading assets or trading liabilities in the balance sheet. Market risk are also measured by stress testing and sensitivity analysis.

13.10 Capital management

The total equity increased to $193.9 billion in year 2015 which was an increase of $8.6 billion compared to the previous year. Wells Fargo returned $12.5 billion in 2014 and $12.6 billion in 2015 in the form of stock dividends and net repurchases. In 2015, the common shares outstanding declined by 78.2 million shares through repurchase of common shares. Wells Fargo also entered into a $500 million forward repurchase contract with an unrelated third party in 2015. The common equity tier 1 ratio increased from 10.43% in the year 2014 to 10.77% in year 2015.

In 2015, Well Fargo planned to issue $100 billion in outstanding short term debt and $125 billion in outstanding long term debt. By December 2015, Wells Fargo Bank had availed $99.98 billion in short term debt issuance authority and $66.3 billion in long term debt issuance authority. In April 2015, Wells Fargo established $100 billion bank note program in which the bank has the option to issue $50 billion in outstanding short term senior notes and $50 billion in outstanding long term senior or subordinated notes. The planned long term capital structure of Wells Fargo was designed to meet regulatory and market expectations.

According to final Basel III capital rules, Wells Fargo currently target a long term CET1 capital ratio at or in excess of 10% which assumes a 2% G-SIB surcharge. In 2014, the board authorized the repurchase of 350 million shares of common stock. On the basis of that program, still 77 million shares are yet to be repurchased. In January 2016, the board authorized the repurchase of additional 350 million shares of common stock.

13.11   Stock plans

The participants can purchase shares of common stock at fair market value by reinvesting dividends or making optional cash payments. The Term Incentive Compensation Plan (LTICP) provides for awards of incentive and nonqualified stock options, stock appreciation rights, restricted shares, restricted stock rights and performance share awards and performance units and stock awards. The Wells Fargo &Company 401 (k) Plan is a defined contribution plan with an ESOP feature. The ESOP feature enables the 401 (k) Plan to borrow money to purchase the preferred or common stock. The ESOP preferred stock in the 401(k) Plan is released and converted into the common stock shares.

13.12   Dividends

The quarterly dividend payments by Wells Fargo was initiated from the year 1973 onwards. The table below gives the cumulative dividend payments each year during the period 1972−2015. The source of the data is yahoo finance (see Table 13.1).

In 1972, the DPS had been $0.016. The dividend per share was $0.060 in the year 1980. The dividend per share was $0.106 in year 1990. The dividend per share in the year 2000 was $0.450. In the year 2015, the dividend per share was $1.48. Table 13.2 gives the stock split details of Wells Fargo.

13.13   Ownership

The equity composed of 37% and debt composed of 63% of the capital structure by end of December 2015. Institutions accounted 69.7% of the equity ownership. Mutual funds held 30.3% of equity ownership while insiders held 0.03% of the equity ownership (see Tables 13.3 and 13.4).

The source of data was Morningstar.com. The top 10 financial institutions held 33.49% of the equity ownership of the company. The period of analysis was May 2016.

The top 10 mutual funds held 9.18% of the equity ownership of the bank.

Table 13.1 **Dividend trends**

Year	DPS	Year	DPS	Year	DPS
1972	0.016	1991	0.118	2010	0.2
1973	0.032	1992	0.135	2011	0.48
1974	0.033	1993	0.160	2012	0.88
1975	0.034	1994	0.191	2013	1.15
1976	0.036	1995	0.225	2014	1.35
1977	0.041	1996	0.263	2015	1.48
1978	0.046	1997	0.308		
1979	0.053	1998	0.350		
1980	0.060	1999	0.393		
1981	0.067	2000	0.450		
1982	0.070	2001	0.500		
1983	0.075	2002	0.550		
1984	0.075	2003	0.600		
1985	0.075	2004	0.930		
1986	0.075	2005	1.000		
1987	0.075	2006	1.080		
1988	0.081	2007	1.180		
1989	0.095	2008	1.300		
1990	0.106	2009	0.490		

Table 13.2 **Stock splits**

Date	Split amounts
31/3/1959	3 for 1
31/3/1969	2 for 1
17/5/1977	2 for 1
30/6/1988	3 for 2
21/7/1989	2 for 1
28/6/1993	2 for 1
10/10/1997	2 for 1
11/8/2006	2 for 1

13.13.1 *Financial highlights*

The bank had registered revenues of $86.1 billion in the year 2015. The net income amounted to $22.9 billion in the year 2015 and the EPS was $4.12. In the year 2015, Wells Fargo originated $213.2 billion in residential mortgage loans, $31.1 billion auto loans and $18.8 billion in new loan commitments to small business customers who had primarily less than $20 million in annual revenues. In 2015, the net losses in the commercial portfolio were $387 million or nine basis points of average loans. It is observed that approximately 67% of the consumer first

Table 13.3 Top financial institutions and equity ownership

Company	Percentage of total shares held
Berkshire Hathaway Inc.	9.93
Vanguard Group Inc.	5.39
State Street Corp.	3.82
Capital World Investors	2.96
Wellington Management Company LLP	2.51
BlackRock Fund Advisors	2.41
Fidelity Management & Research Company	2.15
J.P. Morgan Investment Management Inc.	1.49
Columbia Insurance Company	1.46
Dodge & Cox	1.37
Total	33.49

Table 13.4 Top mutual funds and equity ownership

Company	Percentage of total shares held
Vanguard Total Stock Mkt Idx	1.73
Fidelity Contrafund	1.2
Vanguard 500 Index Inv	1.15
Vanguard Institutional Index I	1.01
SPDR S&P 500 ETF	0.89
Vanguard Wellington Inv	0.8
Dodge & Cox Stock	0.8
VA CollegeAmerica WA Mutual 529B	0.64
Financial Select Sector SPDR ETF	0.5
Vanguard Windsor II Inv	0.46
Total	9.18

mortgage portfolio was originated after 2008 when new underwriting standards were implemented. The provision for credit losses was $2.4 billion in year 2015 compared with $1.4 billion in year 2014.

13.13.2 Earnings performance

Wells Fargo earn trust and investment management fees through managing and administering assets which include mutual funds, institutional separate accounts, personal trust, employee benefit trust and agency assets through the asset management, wealth and retirement businesses. The asset management business is conducted by Wells Fargo Asset Management that offers Wells Fargo proprietary mutual funds and manages institutional separate accounts. The trust and investment management fee income is earned from AUM.

Table 13.5 **Financial highlights**

Year	2010	2011	2012	2013	2014	2015
Net interest income	44,757	42,763	43,230	42,800	43,527	45,301
Noninterest income	40,453	38,185	42,856	40,980	40,820	40,756
Revenues	85,210	80,948	86,086	83,780	84,347	86,057
Provision for credit losses	15,753	7899	7217	2309	1395	2442
Noninterest expense	50,456	49,393	50,398	48,842	49,037	49,974
Net income	12,362	15,869	18,897	21,878	23,057	22,894
Investment securities	172,654	222,613	235,199	264,353	312,925	347,555
Loans	757,267	769,631	798,351	822,286	862,551	916,559
Assets	1,258,128	1,313,867	1,421,746	1,523,502	1,687,155	1,787,632
Deposits	847,942	920,070	1,002,835	1,079,177	1,168,310	1,223,312
Long term debt	156,983	125,354	127,379	152,998	183,943	199,536
Total equity	127,889	141,687	158,911	171,008	185,262	193,891

The net income for Wells Fargo in the year 2015 was $22.9 billion. The net interest income increased by $1.8 billion which was offset by a $1 billion increase in the provision for credit losses and $937 million increase in noninterest expense. The noninterest income amounted to $40.8 billion in year 2015. The efficiency ratio measured as noninterest expense as a percentage of revenue was 58.3% in the year 2013 and 58.1% in year 2014, respectively. The noninterest income is driven by the businesses which include credit and debit cards, mortgage, commercial banking, commercial real estate brokerage, multifamily capital, reinsurance, municipal products, and retail brokerage. Wells Fargo earn investment banking fees from underwriting debt and equity securities, arrangement of loan syndications, and other related advisory services. Brokerage advisory, commissions and other fees are received for providing full service and discount brokerage services basically from retail brokerage clients. The sources for mortgage banking income are net servicing income and net gains on loan origination and sales activities.

The financial data are given in millions of dollars except per share amounts (see Table 13.5). The revenues increased from $85.210 billion in the year 2010 to $86.057 billion in the year 2015. The average growth rate of revenues during the five-year period 2011−15 was 0.27%. The year on year growth rate analysis reveals that the revenue growth peaked in the 2012 with a growth rate of 6.3%. The growth rate of revenues was 2.6% in year 2013 compared to the previous year. The net interest income increased from $44.757 million in year 2010 to $45.301 million in the year 2015. The noninterest income increased from $40.453 billion in year 2010 to $40.756 billion in year 2015. The average growth rate of net interest income was 0.28% during the period 2011−15. The average growth rate of noninterest income during the period 2011−15 was 0.3% during the period 2011−15. The net income growth rate of 28% in the year 2011 was the highest growth rate of net income during the five-year period of analysis. The average growth rate of net income during the five-year period 2011−15 is 13.6%. The value of investment securities, loans and assets in the year 2015 was $347.56 billion, $916.56 billion and $1787.632 billion, respectively. The average increase in the value of investment securities was

Table 13.6 Performance measures in percent

Year	2013	2014	2015
ROA	1.51	1.45	1.31
ROE	13.87	13.41	12.6
Efficiency ratio	58.3	58.1	58.1
Stockholder's equity to assets	10.17	9.86	9.62
Total equity to assets	11.22	10.98	10.85
Common equity Tier 1	10.82	11.04	11.07
Tier 1 capital	12.33	12.45	12.63
Total capital	15.43	15.53	15.45
Tier 1 leverage	9.6	9.45	9.37

approximately 15% during the analysis period of five years. The loan amount increased by approximately 4% on average basis during the period 2011–15. The average growth rate of assets during the above period was approximately 7.2%. The average increase in deposits during the period 2011–15 was 7.6%. The average increase in long term debt was 6% during the five-year period of analysis. The average growth rate of total equity was 8.7% during the five-year period 2011–15.

The average net interest income as percent of revenues was 52% during the period 2010–15. The average noninterest income as % of revenues was 48% during the above period of analysis. The total interest expense as % of revenues was 5% in the year 2015. The total noninterest expense as % of revenues was 58% during the year 2015.

ROA and ROE have decreased over the period of three years. The efficiency ratio is noninterest expense divided by total revenue which consists of net interest income and noninterest income. The risk based capital ratios are common equity Tier 1, Tier 1 capital, total capital, Tier 1 leverage (see Table 13.6).

The trust and investment fees include brokerage advisory, commissions, trust and investment management, and investment banking fees. The other fees include charges and fees on loans, merchant processing fees, cash network fees, commercial real estate brokerage commissions, letters of credit fees. Mortgage banking fees include service income and net gains on mortgage loan origination (see Table 13.7).

Community banking accounted for the maximum segmental revenues followed by wholesale banking and WIM. The community banking revenues accounted for 54% of the total revenues on an average basis during the period 2013–15. The wholesale banking accounted for 29% of the total revenues on an average basis during the above period. The WIM accounted for 17% of the total revenues during the three-year period 2013–15 (see Tables 13.8 and 13.9).

The total nonperforming loans declined from $25.965 billion in the year 2011 to $12.807 billion in the year 2015. The nonaccrual loans as % of total loans was approximately 2% on average basis during the period 2011–15. The nonperforming loans as % of the total loans was 2.40% during the time period 2011–15. The nonaccrual loans consist of commercial and consumer loans. The commercial loans consist of commercial and industrial, real estate mortgage, real estate construction and lease financing. The consumer loans consist of real estate 1–4 family first

Table 13.7 **Noninterest income in millions of dollars**

Year	2013	2014	2015
Service charges on deposit accounts	5023	5050	5168
Total trust and investment fees	13430	14280	14468
Card and other fees	7531	7780	8044
Total mortgage banking	8774	6381	6501
Insurance	1814	1655	1694
Net gains from trading activities	1623	1161	614
Net gains (losses) on debt securities	−29	593	952
Net gains from equity investments	1472	2380	2230
Lease income	663	526	621
Life insurance investment income	566	558	579
All other	113	456	−115
Total	40980	40820	40756

Source: Annual Report 2015.

Table 13.8 **Segmental revenues in millions of dollars**

Year	2013	2014	2015
Community Banking	47,679	48,158	49,341
Wholesale Banking	25,847	25,398	25,904
Wealth and Investment Management	14,330	15,269	15,777
Others	−4076	−4478	−4965
Total	83,780	84,347	86,057

Source: Annual Report 2015.

Table 13.9 **Segment wise net income in millions of dollars**

Year	2013	2014	2015
Community Banking	12,147	13,686	13,491
Wholesale Banking	8752	8199	8194
Wealth and Investment Management	1766	2060	2316
Others	−787	−888	−1107
Total	21,878	23,057	22,894

Source: Annual Report 2015.

mortgage, real estate 1−4 family junior lien mortgage, automobile, and other revolving credit and installment. The foreclosed assets are classified as government insured and nongovernment insured (see Tables 13.10−13.12).

Market capitalization is based on the year-end values. Enterprise value is obtained as the sum of market value of equity plus value of debt minus cash and cash equivalents (see Table 13.13).

Table 13.10 **Average deposits in millions of dollars**

Year	2013	2014	2015
Community Banking	494.7	614.3	654.4
Wholesale Banking	353.8	404	438.9
Wealth and Investment Management	158.9	163.5	172.3
Others	− 65.3	− 67.7	− 71.5
Total	942.1	1114.1	1194.1

Source: Annual Report 2015.

Table 13.11 **Average loans in millions of dollars**

Year	2013	2014	2015
Community Banking	465.1	468.8	475.9
Wholesale Banking	329	355.6	397.3
Wealth and Investment Management	46.2	52.1	60.1
Others	− 37.6	− 42.1	− 47.9
Total	802.7	834.4	885.4

Source: Annual Report 2015.

Table 13.12 **Nonperforming assets in millions of dollars**

Year	2011	2012	2013	2014	2015
Total commercial loans	8197	5822	3475	2239	2424
Total consumer loans	13,107	14,664	12,193	10,609	8958
Total nonaccrual loans	21,304	20,486	15,668	12,848	11,382
Total foreclosed loans	4661	4023	3937	2609	1425
Total nonperforming loans	25,965	24,509	19,605	15,457	12,807

Source: Annual Report 2015.

Table 13.13 **Valuation and profitability position**

Year	2006	2007	2008	2009	2010	2011	2012	2013	2014	2015
Market capitalization	121,273	99,539	98,028	139,771	163,078	145,038	180,002	238,675	283,439	276,808
Enterprise value	206,190	237,880	484,061	366,576	369,588	312,920	356,936	442,770	531,410	577,868
Net income	8482	8057	2655	12,275	12,362	15,869	18,897	21,878	23,057	22,894

13.14   Ratio analysis

The average operating margin was 29.6% during the period 2006−15. The average net margin was 18.8% during the period 2006−15. The average return on assets was 1.2% and return on equity was 12.7% during the above period of analysis (see Table 13.14).

The average book value per share was $23.72 while the average DPS was $0.94 during the period 2006−15. The average EPS and EBITDA per share $2.78 and $4.99 during the period 2006−15. Revenue per share was $14.94 during the period 2006−15 (see Table 13.15).

The average price to book (P/B) during the period 2006−15 was 1.6. The average price to earnings (P/E) ratio during the period 2006−15 was 15.3. The average price to sales (P/S) and PEG ratio during the above period was 2.5 and 1.6. The growth rate was based on five year EBITDA growth rate (see Table 13.16).

The average EV/Revenues was 5.82 during the period 2006−15. The average EV/EBITDA was 22.98 and average EV/EBIT was 29.55 during the above period of analysis (see Table 13.17).

13.15   Stock wealth analysis

The data for share price analysis was based during the period June 1972 to May 2016. The share return analysis based on the period of 527 months reveals that Wells Fargo stock had a cumulative return of 723.77% during the period of analysis for 44 years. The cumulative returns for the market index S&P 500 during the above period was 346.7%. The adjusted closing price for Wells Fargo on June 1, 1972 was $0.196. The adjusted closing price for the stock on May 2, 2016 was $48.7. The increase in stock price during the above holding period was approximately 24,785.73%. Assume that an investor invested $1000 in the stock of Wells Fargo during July 1972 and held till May 2016. The investment would have increased to $248,857.3 during this holding period.

Wells Fargo outperformed the market index S&P 500 during the entire period of analysis (1972−2016) (see Fig. 13.1).

Wells Fargo outperformed the market index S&P 500 in all years of analysis except in the year 2011. The excess return was highest in the year 2012 where the average yearly returns for Wells Fargo was 25.34% (see Table 13.18).

The holding period yield estimation is based on the holding period of one year. The holding period yield of 33.21% was highest in the 2013. In the year 2014, the holding period yield was 24.27%. The six-year (2010−15) holding period yield was 13.91% (see Table 13.19).

The book value of equity increased from $127.889 billion in year 2010 to $193.891 billion in year 2015. The market value of equity increased from $163.078 billion in year 2010 to $276.808 billion in year 2015. The average book value as % of market value was 78.58% during the period 2010−15. Excess value is estimated as the difference between the market value of equity and the book value of equity (see Table 13.20).

Table 13.14 **Profitability ratios**

Year	2006	2007	2008	2009	2010	2011	2012	2013	2014	2015
Operating margin (%)	35.7	29.5	7.8	20.3	22.3	29.2	33.1	38.9	40.2	39.1
Net margin (%)	23.77	20.45	5.65	9.01	13.65	18.56	20.91	24.93	25.87	24.95
Return on assets (%)	1.76	1.52	0.25	0.63	0.93	1.17	1.32	1.42	1.36	1.24
Return on equity (%)	19.77	17.39	4.12	9.34	10.53	12.19	13.16	13.99	13.68	12.78

Table 13.15 **Per share ratio**

Year	2006	2007	2008	2009	2010	2011	2012	2013	2014	2015
Book value per share	13.47	14.31	20.38	19.95	22.37	24.48	27.47	29.27	31.95	33.54
DPS	1.08	1.18	1.3	0.49	0.2	0.41	0.78	1.15	1.35	1.48
EPS	2.49	2.38	0.7	1.75	2.21	2.82	3.36	3.89	4.1	4.1
EBITDA per share	4.68	3.89	1.45	4.57	3.98	4.86	5.85	6.69	6.84	7.09
Revenue per share	10.47	11.64	12.35	19.44	16.19	15.21	16.09	15.6	15.84	16.52

Table 13.16 **Price multiples**

Year	2006	2007	2008	2009	2010	2011	2012	2013	2014	2015
P/B	2.67	2.11	1.45	1.35	1.39	1.13	1.24	1.55	1.72	1.62
P/E	14.51	12.67	37.94	15.23	14.02	9.77	10.17	11.66	13.37	13.18
P/S	3.43	2.6	2.35	1.37	1.91	1.81	2.13	2.91	3.47	3.3
PEG	1.76	5.24	0	0	0	5.78	0.61	0.42	0.99	1.09

Table 13.17 **Enterprise value multiples**

Year	2006	2007	2008	2009	2010	2011	2012	2013	2014	2015
EV/Revenues	5.78	6.04	11.56	4.13	4.34	3.87	4.15	5.28	6.3	6.71
EV/EBITDA	12.99	18.08	97.42	17.59	17.66	12.1	11.41	12.33	14.59	15.65
EV/EBIT	16.3	20.46	146.69	20.37	19.45	13.23	12.54	13.57	15.67	17.18

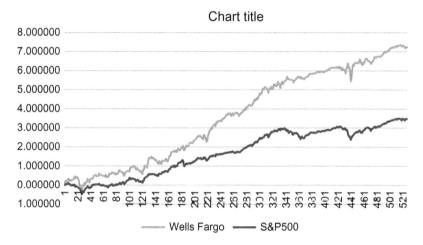

Figure 13.1 Cumulative returns of Wells Fargo versus S&P500

Table 13.18 **Average returns in percent**

Year	Wells Fargo	S&P500	Excess returns
2010	20.21	13.80	6.42
2011	−8.55	1.15	−9.70
2012	25.34	13.16	12.18
2013	32.22	26.54	5.68
2014	22.15	11.14	11.01
2015	2.76	0.11	2.65

Table 13.19 **Holding period yield in percent**

Year	HPY
2010	9.77
2011	−13.53
2012	20.15
2013	33.21
2014	24.27
2015	7.53

13.16   Estimation of cost of capital

The cost of equity is first estimated through the CAPM model.
Estimation of cost of equity using CAPM
Required rate of return = Risk free rate + Beta × (Return on market index − Risk free rate).
The risk free rate is assumed as the average yield to maturity on the 30-year treasury bond during the two-year period 2014−16 (see Table 13.21).[3]

Beta is estimated by regressing the monthly returns of Wells Fargo on the monthly returns of the market index S&P500 during the period January 2014−May 2016. The beta is estimated as 0.94. The risk premium is assumed to be 5%.

Cost of equity = Risk free rate + beta × Risk premium = 2.94% + 0.94 × 5% = 7.64%
The cost of equity is 7.64%.
Cost of debt is assumed is the yield to maturity on the long term bond which matures on April 22, 2016. The yield to maturity is 3.19%.[4]
Income before taxes = 33,641 million
Tax expenses = $10,365 million
Tax rate = 10,365/33,641 = 0.308
The tax rate is 30.8%.
After tax cost of debt = 3.19 × (1 − 0.308) = 2.21%
Total equity in 2015 = $193,891 million
Total debt in 2015 = $297,064 million

Table 13.20 Excess value added in millions of dollars

Year	2010	2011	2012	2013	2014	2015
Book value of equity	127,889	141,687	158,911	171,008	185,262	193,891
Market value of equity	163,078	145,038	180,002	238,675	283,439	276,808
BV as per cent of MV	78.42	97.69	88.28	71.65	65.36	70.05
Excess value	35189	3351	21091	67667	98177	82917

Table 13.21 Risk free rate

Year	Yield to maturity on 30 year treasury bond
2014	3.55
2015	2.63
2016	2.63
Average	2.94%

[3] https://www.treasury.gov/resource-center/data-chart-center/interest-rates/Pages/Historic-Yield-Data-Visualization.aspx.
[4] http://quicktake.morningstar.com/StockNet/bonds.aspx?Symbol=WFC&Country=USA.

Total capital = 193,891 + 297,064 = $490,955 million
Weight of equity = 193,891/490,955 = 0.39
Weight of debt = 297,064/490,955 = 0.61
WACC = 0.39 × 7.64 + 0.61 × 2.21 = 4.35%
Weighted Average Cost of Capital is 4.35%.

13.17 Valuation perspectives

The economic value is estimated as $17,822 million dollars (see Table 13.22).
    The equity spread is estimated as $9965.997 million dollars (see Table 13.23).

13.17.1 Dividend discount model

The average dividend payout ratio (DPO) was 24% during the period 2010−15 (see Table 13.24).

Retention Ratio (RR) = 1 − DPO
Growth rate = RR × Return on equity
The average growth rate during the period 2010−15 is estimated as 10% (see Table 13.25).

Table 13.22 Economic value in 2015

PBIT in 2015	45,301
Income tax	10,365
NOPAT	34,936
Stockholder equity	193,891
Long term debt	199,536
Capital employed	393,427
WACC	4.35%
Capital charge	17,114.07
EV	17,822

Table 13.23 Equity spread in 2015

Stock holder equity	193,891
ROE IN 2015	12.78%
COE IN 2015	7.64%
Equity spread	9965.997

Table 13.24 Dividend trends

Year	2010	2011	2012	2013	2014	2015
EPS	2.21	2.82	3.36	3.89	4.1	4.12
DPS	0.2	0.41	0.78	1.15	1.35	1.48
DPO	0.09	0.15	0.23	0.30	0.33	0.36

13.17.2   Two stage DDM

It is assumed that the earnings will grow at 10% for the next 10 years and thereafter at the
stable growth rate of US economy.
High growth period inputs
High growth period = 10 years
Cost of equity = 7.64%
Average DPO = 0.24
Growth rate = 10%
EPS in the current year (2015) = $4.12
EPS in the first year of high growth period = 4.12 × 1.10 = $4.532.
The present value of dividends in the high growth phase is estimated as $11.16 (see
Table 13.26).
Stable growth phase assumptions
Growth rate in stable period is assumed to be the growth rate of US economy. The
average growth rate of US GDP for two year period 2013−14. The GDP growth rate is
estimated as 2.3%.[5]
The return on equity of diversified financial service sector is 7.3%.[6]
Inputs for stable period
Cost of equity = 7.64%
Growth rate in stable period = 2.3%
Growth rate = RR × Industry ROE
2.3% = RR*7.3%
RR = 2.3%/7.3% = 32%
DPO = 1 − 0.32 = 0.68
EPS at the end of high growth period = $10.69

Table 13.25   Estimation of growth rate from fundamentals

Year	2010	2011	2012	2013	2014	2015
RR	0.91	0.85	0.77	0.70	0.67	0.64
ROE	0.11	0.12	0.13	0.14	0.14	0.13
Growth rate	0.10	0.10	0.10	0.10	0.09	0.08

Table 13.26   Present value of dividends in high growth period

Year	1	2	3	4	5	6	7	8	9	10
EPS	4.53	4.99	5.48	6.03	6.64	7.30	8.03	8.83	9.71	10.69
DPO	0.24	0.24	0.24	0.24	0.24	0.24	0.24	0.24	0.24	0.24
DPS	1.088	1.196	1.316	1.448	1.592	1.752	1.927	2.120	2.332	2.565
PV	$1.01	$1.03	$1.06	$1.08	$1.10	$1.13	$1.15	$1.18	$1.20	$1.23
Sum	$11.16									

[5] http://data.worldbank.org/indicator/NY.GDP.MKTP.KD.ZG.
[6] http://www.morningstar.com/stocks/XNYS/WFC/quote.html.

EPS at the beginning of stable period = 10.69 × 1.023 = $10.93
DPO = 0.68
DPS in stable period = 10.93 × 0.68 = $7.49
Terminal value = DPS in stable period/(Cost of equity − growth rate in stable period)
= 7.49/ (0.0764 − 0.023) = $140.22
Present value of terminal value = $67.15
Value of Wells Fargo stock = PV of dividends in high growth phase + PV of terminal value
= 11.16 + 67.15 = $78.32.
Wells Fargo stock was trading at $49.20 in NYSE on 25/5/2016. The 52 week range for Wells Fargo stock was $44.50−$58.76 during May 2016.

13.17.3   Peer group comparison

The peer comparison was based on the year 2015. Wells Fargo had the highest market capitalization among the four banks. Wells Fargo had the highest P/S, P/B, and P/E ratio among all the banks. Wells Fargo had the highest dividend yield among the four banks of comparison (see Table 13.27). The source of data was Morningstar.com.

13.17.4   Relative valuation (see Tables 13.28–13.31)

Table 13.28 compares the price multiples of Wells Fargo with that of industry average and S&P 500.

In terms of enterprise value multiples, JP Morgan Chase is the most undervalued stock among the peer financial institutions. Wells Fargo had the highest enterprise value multiple values compared to other peer banks like JP Morgan Chase, Bank of America, and Citigroup (see Table 13.29).

Table 13.27 Comparison with peer group

Banks	Market cap	Net income	P/S	P/B	P/E	Dividend yield (%)
Wells Fargo	249,790	22,552	2.9	1.4	12.1	3.1
JP Morgan Chase	236,000	24,048	2.6	1.1	10.9	2.7
Bank of America Corp	150,791	15,471	2	0.6	11.8	1.4
Citibank	134,595	15,973	1.8	0.6	9.1	0.4

Table 13.28 Price multiples

Bank	WFC	Industry average	S&P 500
Price/Earnings	12.1	12	18.8
Price/Book	1.4	0.9	2.7
Price/Sales	2.9	2.1	1.8
Price/Cash flow	14.5	4.5	11.7
Dividend yield (%)	3.1	3.6	2.4

Table 13.29 Enterprise value multiples

Banks	Wells Fargo	JP Morgan Chase	Bank of America	Citigroup
EV/Revenues	6.71	2.49	3.55	3.41
EV/EBITDA	15.65	6.53	12.01	9.18
EV/EBIT	17.18	7.16	13.3	10.47

Table 13.30 Enterprise value multiple trends

Year	2010	2011	2012	2013	2014	2015
EV/Revenues	4.34	3.87	4.15	5.28	6.3	6.71
EV/EBITDA	17.66	12.1	11.41	12.33	14.59	15.65
EV/EBIT	19.45	13.23	12.54	13.57	15.67	17.18

Table 13.31 Revenue growth rate comparison

In Percent	Wells Fargo	JP Morgan Chase	Bank of America	Citigroup
5 year average	20	− 1.85	− 5.63	− 2.49
10 year average	10.08	5.54	3.74	− 0.91

Table 13.30 gives the enterprise value multiple trends for Wells Fargo during the period 2010−2015.

The growth rate of revenues was based on the year 2015. The five-year and 10-year average growth rate of revenues was highest for Wells Fargo compared to the peer companies (Table 13.31).

13.17.5 Performance indicators

13.17.5.1 Graham number

It is a conservative method used for valuing a stock. It is a figure which measures a stock's fundamental value by taking into account the company's earnings per share and book value per share. Graham number is the upper bound of the price range which a defensive investor should pay for the stock. According to Graham number theory, any stock price below the Graham number is considered undervalued and hence worth investing in. Graham number is a combination of asset valuation and earnings power valuation.

EPS in year 2015 = $4.12
Book value per share in 2015 = $33.51

$$\text{Graham number} = \sqrt{22.5 \times (\text{Earning per share}) \times (\text{Book value per share})} = \$55.73$$

Wells Fargo was trading at $49.20 in NYSE on May 25, 2016.

13.17.5.2 Peter Lynch Fair valuation

Peter Lynch Fair value is basically applied to growth companies with growth rates in the range 10-20% a year. It is proposed that the fair P/E value for a growth company would be equal to its growth rate that is PEG = 1. The average growth rate used is five year EPS growth rate. The average growth rate in EPS is 17%. The PE ratio is estimated as 12.1. Hence PEG = 12.1/17 = 0.71.

Peter Lynch value = PEG × Five year EPS growth rate × EPS
= 0.71 × 17 × 4.21 = $49.72

Wells Fargo &Co was trading at $49.20 in NYSE on 25/5/2016. Wells Fargo & Co's Peter Lynch fair value is estimated as $49.72. The Wells Fargo &Co's Price to Peter Lynch Fair Value Ratio on May 25, 2016 was 0.99.

*All detailed calculation and analysis are given in the resources file **Wells Fargo. xlsx**.*

Wealth creation by Amazon

14

14.1 Introduction

Amazon.com, Inc. (Amazon), is an American-based electronic commerce company headquartered in Seattle, Washington. Amazon was established in 1994. Amazon have emerged as the largest Internet-based retailer in the United States. In initial years, Amazon established itself as an online bookstore. Later the company started selling DVDs, Blu-rays, CDs, video downloads/streaming, videogames, electronics, apparel, furniture, food, toys, and jewelry. Amazon has separate retail websites for different countries in the world. In 2015, Amazon became the fastest company ever to reach $100 billion in annual sales. In 2015, Amazon emerged as the largest wealth creator in the retail sector in United States in terms of market capitalization. Amazon have over 40 subsidiaries which include firms like Zappos, Diapers.com, Kiva Systems, Goodreads, etc. In 2014, Amazon announced plans to invest additional $2 billion in Indian market. Amazon have established software development centers in North America, Europe, Asia, and Africa which are operated by Amazon subsidiary called A2Z Development. Amazon's Fulfillment centers provide warehousing and order fulfillment for third-party sellers. In 1999, Amazon launched Web auctions service called amazon.com Auctions. In 2000, Auctions and zShops were converted into Amazon Marketplace. In 2002, Amazon launched Amazon Web Services (AWS). In 2005, Amazon introduced Amazon Prime which provides membership offering free two-day shipping on all eligible purchases for flat annual fee and discounted one-day shipping rates. In 2007, Amazon launched grocery service offerings Amazon Fresh. During November 2007, Amazon introduced e-book reader Amazon Kindle which provides download contents over "Whispernet" via Sprint's EV-DO wireless network. By July 2014, there were over 2.7 million e-books in the Kindle Store. In 2011, Amazon introduced Kindle Fire which marked its entry into tablet computer market. In 2012 and 2013, Amazon introduced the second- and third-generation tablets.[1] As of December 31, 2015, Amazon employed approximately 230,800 full-time and part-time employees.

14.2 Business segments

Amazon.com entered the World Wide Web in July 1995. Amazon business segment consists of consumers, sellers, developers, enterprises, and content creators.

---

[1] Annual Report 2015.

Amazon also provides advertising services and cobranded credit card agreements. Amazon offers platforms through its retail websites for selling dozens of product categories to millions of its consumers. Consumers are served directly through Amazon websites and through the mobile websites and applications. Amazon manufacture and sell electronic devices like Kindle e-readers, Fire tablets, Fire TVs, and Echo. Amazon Prime through the annual membership program offers unlimited free shipping on millions of items and access to unlimited instant streaming of thousands of movies and TV episodes. Amazon offers programs which facilitate sellers to advertise their products on Amazon websites and have own branded websites. Amazon serves developers and organizations which include government and academic institutions through AWS. AWS offers a broad set of global compute, storage, and database offerings. Amazon also serve authors and independent publishers through Kindle Direct Publishing. It is an online platform whereby independent authors and publishers can advertise and make available their book publications with 70% royalty option. Amazon programs also facilitate authors, application developers to publish and sell content.

14.3 Growth strategy of Amazon

The name Amazon reflected the vision of Jeff Bezos to create a large scale phenomenon like the Amazon river. Within a span of eight years since its inception, Amazon reached the milestone of $5 billion mark, a feat which Walmart took 20 years to achieve. The vision of Amazon is to emerge as the Earth's most customer-centric company. Amazon applied new technologies to gain competitive advantage. Amazon created a new business platform that organized and managed the commerce engine, its reviewer database and community, the apps community, and the cloud capability. The Amazon ecosystem is made up of writers, reviewers, publishers, apps developers, and market of commentators, feature writers, and analysts.

Amazon had transformed the retail landscape from brick and mortar shopping since it was established in 1994 as an online book store. The major growth catalyst for the company had been the Amazon Prime which provides customers with free two-day shipping as well as streaming music and videos. Amazon Prime was introduced in 2005. By 2014 approximately 30 million US households subscribed to Amazon Prime. Worldwide there were nearly 40 million subscribers to Amazon Prime in 2014. Many analysts believe by 2020, 50% of all US households will own an Amazon Prime subscription.[2] Another growth contributing segment of Amazon is the cloud computing service—AWS. The AWS segment reported year-on-year sales growth of 78% during 2015.The focus of Amazon's marketing efforts is on marketing channels.

---

[2] http://www.marketwatch.com/story/amazon-is-primed-for-growth-2015-12-17.

Amazon derives its revenues primarily from the sale of a wide range of products and services to customers. The products offered to the customers include the merchandise and content which were purchased for resale from vendors and those offered by third-party sellers. Amazon also manufacture and sell electronic devices. Amazon also offer services such as compute, storage, database offerings, publishing digital content subscriptions, advertising, and cobranded credit cards. Amazon focuses on revenue enhancement through sales of products and services through reduction of prices of products, improving delivery availability, and performance times. Amazon focuses on reduction of variable costs which include product and content costs, payment procession, transportation, and related transactions. The fixed costs control is aimed for efficient infrastructure features and web services. Amazon's technology and content investment and capital spending projects are meant to offer a variety of product and service offerings due to geographic expansion. Amazon design its websites to offer dozens of product categories to be sold to millions of customers through the firm channels and third parties. Amazon focuses on selection, price, and convenience for gaining competitive advantage. The pricing strategy of Amazon is to offer lowest prices possible to every product offering and improve operating efficiency. Amazon also focuses on easy-to-use functionality and timely customer service. The aim of communication strategy is to increase customer traffic to its websites, create awareness of products and services, promote repeat purchases, develop incremental product and service revenue opportunities, and strengthen the Amazon.com brand name.

In the 1990s, the Amazon platform did not include third-party sellers. Amazon sold all its books, music, and videos in the 1990s. In its globalization strategy to expand marketplace, Amazon built selling tools which enabled entrepreneurs in 172 countries to reach customers in 189 countries in 2015. These cross-border sales accounted for nearly a quarter of all third-party units sold on behalf of Amazon. For execution of this strategy, Amazon translated millions of product listing and facilitated conversion services among 44 currencies. Amazon allowed niche and small sellers to access the company's global customer base and global logistics network. Amazon had launched a program called Seller Flex in regions like India to offer Amazon's logistics capabilities with seller's selection at local neighborhood levels.

AWS offers more than 70 services for storage, databases, analytics, and enterprise applications in 33 Availability Zones across 12 geographic regions worldwide. AWS is used by more than one million customers worldwide.

Amazon have focused on price reduction to gain competitive advantage. Amazon have launched new lower cost services like Aurora, Redshift, Business Intelligence—QuickSight, Computer container service EC2, and server-less computing capability termed lambda. The e-commerce sector is propelling revenue growth for Amazon as the Kindle tablet plays a major role in the promotion of its merchandise sales. International markets hold the future for Amazon's growth. The Android devices can facilitate Amazon to promote its Kindle fire device ranges. Ever since Kindle was introduced the physical retail book stores had seen a huge revenue reduction.

Amazon faces competition from online, offline, multichannel retailers, publishers, vendors, and distributors of different products offers. Amazon also faces competition from publishers, producers, and distributors of physical, digital, and interactive media of different types. Amazon faces stiff competition from Web search engines, social networks, companies offering cloud based infrastructure, etc.

14.4   Innovation strategy[3]

In 2005, Amazon launched an innovative—"an all—you-can eat" express shipping membership program called Amazon prime. Amazon prime could offer two-day shipping which were guaranteed and unlimited when customers expected to pay for 4—6 business days. All—you-can-eat became feasible with a single annual membership. Amazon introduced Free Super Saver Shipping which lowered the cost of fast shipping. Amazon prime emerged as one of the most popular subscription services with millions of members throughout the world. Through Amazon prime, millions of members can have fast and free unlimited shipping on more than 20 million items. The other services provided include unlimited streaming of thousands of movies and TV episodes, hundreds of stations with million songs, unlimited photo storage in Amazon cloud drive, and access to more than 800,000 books to borrow from Kindle Owners' lending library. By January 2016, the total number of Amazon customers who subscribed to Amazon prime was estimated at 54 million.[4]

Amazon introduced Amazon Marketplace to facilitate sellers to list their products with no listing fee and also have the products featured alongside items carried by Amazon. Approximately 40% of units on Amazon are sold by third-party sellers globally on Amazon Market place. Initially Amazon launched Amazon Auctions which was later transformed into zShops. Later on zShops were morphed into Marketplace which were characterized as Single Detail Page. In 2014, approximately two billion units were ordered by customers from sellers.

In 2006, AWS was launched which provides technology infrastructure platform in the cloud. AWS offers a broad set of compute, storage, database, analytics application, and deployment services. AWS have a wide range of customers which include startups to large enterprises like Shell, BP, J&J, Philips, Comcast, Netflix, Adobe, etc. In 2015, Amazon launched Amazon Wind and solar Farms which was expected to provide 1.3 million MWh of wind power for AWS cloud datacenters. AWS is used by more than one million customers around the world. In 2014, Amazon introduced Echo, the device for query on information, music, news, sports scores, and weather. Again in 2014, Amazon launched Prime Now a program designed to get items within 1-h our delivery time period. Customers have the flexibility to download Prime Now App and order items from 6 a.m. to

---

[3] https://www.amazon.com/p/feature.
[4] http://www.nbcnews.com/tech/tech-news/amazon-prime-now-has-54-million-u-s-members-report-n505216.

midnight seven days a week with time period of 2-h delivery free and 1-h delivery for a price of $7.99. American Launchpad is a new program introduced in 2015 to facilitate startups to launch, market, and distribute products to customers globally. Amazon have provided crowd funding platforms to help more than 500 startups to launch over 750 products in the United States, the United Kingdom, and China. In its innovative pursuits, Amazon introduced Amazon Prime Air which is a future delivery system to provide packages to customers in a time of 30 min or less using small unmanned aerial vehicles. Customer reviews are a critical part of Amazon's innovation strategy. Customers can write reviews or upload images, answer other customer's question about a product, and rate one another's reviews on the Amazon site. Dash Button is Amazon's 1-Click, which was launched in March 2015. It can be used for reordering frequently used household items. In 2008, Amazon introduced "Frustration Free Packaging" for easy unpackage of products. Introduced in 2006, Fulfillment by Amazon (FBA) enables sellers to use more than 100 fulfillment centers and more than 15 sort centers to store, pack, and ship their products directly to customers. Sellers use FBA facilities to ship to about 185 countries. Amazon introduced Fire TV for providing streaming services such as Netflix, prime Instant Video, HBO GO, WatchESPN, and Hulu Plus. Amazon introduced AmazonFresh in 2007. Amazon introduced the first Fire tablet in November 2011 which enabled customers to gain access to millions of movies, TV shows, songs, apps, and games. Fire tablet have special features like free storage for Amazon content in the cloud, color touch screen, and powerful processor. The Mayday Button on Fire HDX tablets and Fire phone provides on device tech support throughout the year. In 2007, Amazon introduced the first Kindle which offered books in any language available within 60 s. Amazon's network of fulfillment centers has competitive technology with Amazon robotics, vision systems, and mechanical innovations. The US fulfillment network consists of 50 centers with over 15 sortation centers and more than 50,000 full-time Amazon employees. Amazon Fresh is Amazon's free same day delivery of fresh groceries and local produce. Amazon Dash creates own shopping list by using Amazon's own little gizmo that uses both voice recognition and a barcode scanner.

14.5 Acquisitions by Amazon.com

Amazon's biggest acquisitions included the purchase of Twitch, Zappos, Kiva Systems, Exchange.com, and Quidsi. Amazon acquired Twitch for $970 million in cash which was a video platform for video games in 2014. Twitch was the largest gameplay live streaming site which live stream video from pro-gaming tournaments, charity events. At the time of acquisition, Twitch was the fourth most trafficked site behind Netflix, Google, YouTube, and Apple. The acquisition enabled Amazon to host live broadcasted gaming related video for more than 55 million monthly viewers. The acquisition was aimed to create more focus toward media.

Amazon's Prime service offered Netflix like streaming functionality of shows and movies and intended to focus on game related videos which had a huge future potential. Strategically this acquisition by Amazon was aimed to become competitive with respect to other streaming videos like You Tube and Netflix. In 2009, Amazon acquired Zappos.com which was a leader in online apparel and footwear sales. The deal was valued at $928 million. Under the terms of the deal, Amazon acquired all the outstanding shares, options, and warrants of Zappos in exchange for approximately 10 million shares of Amazon stock. Zappos employees were offered $40 million in cash and restricted stock units. In 2012, Amazon acquired Kiva Systems the maker of robots that service warehouses in an all cash deal valued at $775 million. The acquisition added value to the vast network of warehouses in the context of improvement of margins. Amazon could use Kiva's technology to improve the productivity. This acquisition was significant in the context that Amazon was aggressively adding distribution centers to service its growing consumer base.[5] With Kiva in its Kitty, Amazon was looking at a more automated approach to fuel business in its fulfillment centers. In 1999, Amazon acquired Exchange.com, the premier online market place for hard to find books, at www.bibliofind.com and hard to find recordings and music memorabilia at www.music-file.com. The acquisition enlarged Amazon's core book and music store offerings. At the same time, independent dealers and retailers got the opportunity to sell and auction their books and memorabilia to Amazon's millions of online shoppers. In 2010, Amazon.com acquired Quidsi Inc., the parent company of Diapers.com and Soap.com for $545 million. The deal consisted of $500 million in cash and $45 million in debt and other liabilities. Online shopping of low value household goods like paper towels and laundry detergent were facing challenges due to the cost of shipping bulky items and also due to the competition from bricks and mortar stores which sell the products on a competitive basis. The synergy was expected on account of wide selection and free shipping with an efficient warehouse distribution system (Table 14.1).

In 2013, Amazon acquired different companies in cash transactions for an aggregate purchase price of $195 million. These acquisitions were aimed to expand the customer base and sales channels and obtain certain technologies to be used in product development. During 2014, Amazon acquired Twitch Interactive Inc. for approximately $842 million in cash. In 2015, Amazon acquired companies for aggregate purchase of $690 million.

14.6 Risk factors

Amazon faces competition from different industries like retail, e commerce services, digital content and electronic devices, Web and infrastructure computing services. Amazon faces regulatory constraints and license requirements which may

---

[5] http://dealbook.nytimes.com/2012/03/19/amazon-com-buys-kiva-systems-for-775-million/?_r=0.

Table 14.1 Acquisitions by Amazon

Year	List of companies
1998	Reminder service-based company PlanetAll based in Cambridge; XML-based data mining company Junglee ; UK-based online book retailer Bookpages.co.uk (now AmazonUK); German online store Telebook; Internet Movie database (IMDb)
1999	Database company—Alexa Internet; Financial services company-Accept. com; Acquires 40% stake in Drugstore.com; Acquires minority stake in wireless communication company Geoworks; Acquires stakes in Pets. com and Internet-based auction software Livebid.com. Incorporates e-Niche consisting of acquired companies like Exchange.com, Bibliofind.com, and Musicfile.com; Acquires 35 per stake in HomeGrocer.com; Acquires software firm Convergence Corporation and Mind Corps which develops applications for websites; Acquires Della.com, Back to Basics Toys, catalog toy store; Acquires 16.6% ownership in luxury products retailer—Ashford.com.; Acquires developer of CRM software Leep Technology Inc. Acquires Della.com which deals with gift registry and personalized gift suggestions
2000	Sells of Leep Technology Inc. to Overstock.com. Della.com merged with Wedding Channel.com
2003–2005	Purchases online music retailer CDNow; Chinese e-commerce website—Joyo.com; print on demand company BookSurge; e-book software company Mobipocket.com; on-demand DVD distributor CreateSpace. com; industrial component supplier—Smallparts.com
2006–2010	Acquires designer cloth retailer—Shopbop, digital photography review website—dpreview.com; Acquires publisher of Audiobooks-Brilliance Audio, Audible.com, Box Office Mojo, AbeBooks, BookFinder.com, Gojaba.com, and casual video game development company—Reflexive Entertainment. In 2009, Amazon acquired online shoe and apparel retailer—Zappos, Lexcycle, Image matching startup-SnapTell, and e-book reader Stanza. In 2010, Amazon purchased Touchco, Woot, Quidsi, BuyVIP, Amie Street, Toby Press
2011–2015	The companies acquired in 2011 include LoveFilm, The Book Depository, Pushbutton, and Yap. Amazon acquired Kiva Systems, Teachstreet, EV in 2012. In 2013, Amazon acquires IVONA Software, Goodreads, Liquavista, etc. In 2014, Amazon acquired Double Helix Games, comiXology, and Twitch. In 2015, Amazon acquires chip designer Annapurna Labs

restrict foreign investments and operation of Internet, IT infrastructure, and data centers in countries like China and India. To satisfy local ownership and regulatory licensing agreement, Amazon China is operated by People's Republic of China companies. Indian government restricts the ownership or control of Indian companies by foreign companies which are involved in online multibrand retail trading activities. Amazon India provide certain marketing tools and logistics services to third-party sellers to sell online and deliver to customers. Products and service offerings are exposed to foreign exchange rate fluctuations. Amazon is exposed to inventory risks which affect operating results due to seasonality, new product launches, changes in product cycles, and pricing. Restrictions on sales or distribution of certain products or services or uncertainty as a result of less Internet friendly legal systems and regulations by governments can adversely affect the revenues of Amazon. The operations of Amazon are subject to payment-related risks. Additional regulations and compliance requirements may result in significant costs. The reliance on third parties for certain payment methods which include credit and debit cards may lead to increase in costs.

Amazon faces interest rate risk due to the investment portfolio and long term debt. The market value of fixed income securities can be adversely affected due to rise in interest rates. The net sales from international segment accounted for approximately 33 per cent of the consolidated revenues during the period 2015. The revenues from these international segments are basically denominated in the functional currencies which include Euros, Japanese Yen and British Pounds. Amazon faces currency risk on account of these revenues. Amazon also faces foreign exchange risk related to foreign denominated cash, cash equivalents and marketable securities. Amazon faces foreign exchange risk related to intercompany balances denominated in different foreign currencies. Amazon faces investment risk due to its equity investments.

14.7 Corporate Governance

The majority of directors are independent directors in Amazon board. The chief executive officer also serves as a director of the board. The three committees of the board are Audit Committee, the Leadership Development and Compensation Committee, and the Nominating and Corporate Governance Committee. The audit committee have oversight responsibility with respect to the company's financial statement and financial reporting processes, performance of independent auditors, and the firm's internal audit functions along with compliance of legal and regulatory requirements. The Nominating and Corporate Governance Committee periodically review and assess the composition of the board, identify potential candidates for directorship, and provide leadership role with respect to corporate governance of the company.

The Nominating and Corporate Governance Committee nominates candidates for election to the board. The nominating and corporate governance committee annually reviews the tenure and performance of board members. One of the independent director serves as a lead director on the basis of the recommendation of the Nominating and Corporate Governance Committee. Every nonemployee director has to own company shares which are equal to at least three times the director's annual compensation as measured by the number of shares scheduled to vest annually. The board and the leadership development and compensation committee are responsible for succession planning which are reviewed annually. Leadership development and compensation committee evaluate the firm's programs and practices related to leadership development. The committee administer the company's equity based and other compensation plans. Amazon's Vice President of Global Public Policy reviews and approves political contribution and expenditure which are lawful and consistent with the firm's business objectives and public policy priorities. In 2015, Amazon spent approximately $9.1 million on federal lobbying activities. In the same year, Amazon spend $2.1 million to the company's US-based trade associations, coalitions, and social welfare organizations. In pursuant to SEC's conflict mineral rules, Amazon designed the due diligence on the source and chain of the gold, tin, tungsten, and tantalum meant for the Kindle/Fire products in accordance with the OECD's due diligence guidance for responsible supply chains of minerals. The Board has overall responsibility for risk oversight. The Board has delegated responsibility related to certain risks to the Audit Committee and Leadership Development and Compensation Committee.

14.8   Sustainability initiatives[6]

Amazon had provided aggregate funding of over $1.5 billion to micro, small, and medium business to regions like the United States, the United Kingdom, and Japan through the Amazon Lending program. The long-term aim of AWS is to achieve 100% renewable energy usage for the global infrastructure facilities. By April 2015, approximately 25% of the power consumed by the global infrastructure came from renewable energy sources. The new solar and wind farms are expected to generate more than 1.6 million MWh of additional renewable energy for AWS Cloud data centers. In summer 2014, AWS initiated the Amazon Climate research grant program to support the US Government's Climate Action Plan and White House Climate Data Initiative. AWS has committed to award a total of 50 million core hours of supercomputing using Amazon EC2 spot Instances. In 2015, Amazon signed the White House's American Business Act on Climate Pledge to express support for action on climate change and create a low carbon economy. In 2015, Amazon announced plans for construction of Amazon solar farm US East, Amazon Wind Farm, US Central, and Amazon Wind Farm US east. Amazon has also focused on improvements in the sustainability of packaging across supply chain system. Amazon have multiyear waste reduction initiatives like e commerce ready packaging and Amazon Frustration Free Packaging to promote easy to open and 100% recyclable packaging. In 2015, these initiatives have eliminated more than 36,000 tons of excess packaging. Amazon's offices in Germany have been gold certified as environmentally friendly by the German Green Sustainable Building Council. Amazon's fulfillment centers have sustainable and ecofriendly interiors and exteriors. In 2009, four of Amazon's fulfillment centers in Indiana, Pennsylvania, and Arizona had received LEED certification for their commercial interiors. Amazon had signed the Renewable Energy Buyers' Principles developed by over 50 corporate signatories with support of World Wildlife Fund and the World Resources Institute.

---

[6] https://aws.amazon.com/about-aws/sustainability.

14.9   Stock

The Amazon stock is traded on the NASDAQ Global Select Market. By January 2016, there were 2578 shareholders on record. Amazon have never declared or paid dividends on its common stock. Amazon had authorized 500 million shares of $0.01 par value preferred stock. The common shares outstanding plus shares underlying the outstanding stock awards amounted to 490 million in 2015. In 2010, Amazon announced repurchase of up to $2 billion of common stock with no fixed expiration. Still $763 million remained under $2 billion repurchase program.

14.10   Stock compensation plans

Amazon have used restricted stock units as the primary stock-based compensation plan since 2002. The fair value of restricted stock units is determined based on the number of shares granted. The fair value of stock options is estimated on the date of grant using a Black−Scholes model. The stock-based compensation amounted to $1.1 billion, $1.5 billion, and $2.1 billion during 2013, 2014, and 2015, respectively. Stock options outstanding obtained through acquisitions amounted to $0.2 million in 2015.

14.10.1   Investments

Amazon invests excess cash in investment grade short to intermediate term fixed income securities and AAA rated money market funds.

14.10.2   Capital structure

In June 2016, equity accounted for 64% of the equity ownership while debt held 36% of the capital structure.

14.11   Stock ownership

Altogether there are 2288 institutional owners and 3574 mutual fund owners for Amazon. The data is based on the period June 2016. The insiders hold 14 per cent of the stock ownership. The top ten funds held 11.81% of the total shares of the company. The top 10 financial institutions held 30.07% of the total shares of the institutions. Among the top 10 financial institutions, T. Rowe Price Associates Inc. and Vanguard Inc. held 4.85% and 4.81% of the total shares of the company. Among the top 10 mutual funds, VA College America Growth Fund of Amer 529F and Vanguard Total Stock Market Index held 2.83% and 1.55% of the total shares of Amazon (Table 14.2). Table 14.3 gives the details of stock splits undertaken by Amazon.

Table 14.2 **Stock ownership**

Market Cap in mil USD	339,452
No. of Institution owners	2288
No. of fund owners	3574
% owned by financial institutions	55
% owned by funds	32
% owned by insiders	14

Source: Morningstar.com.

Table 14.3 **Stock split**

Date	Split
9/2/1999	2:01
1/5/1999	3:01
6/2/1998	2:01

Table 14.4 **Net sales by region**

Year	2013	2014	2015
North America	41,410	50,834	63,708
International	29,934	33,510	35,418
AWS	3,108	4,644	7,880
Total	74,452	88,988	107,006

14.12   Trend analysis

The net sales during the three period of analysis are given in millions of dollars (Table 14.4). On average basis the North American region accounted for 57% of the net sales while the international sector accounted for 37% of the net sales. The AWS sector accounted for 6% of the net sales on average basis during the period 2013−2015. The sales increased by 22%, 20%, 20% during the 3-year period 2013−2015 in comparison with the previous periods. The cost of sales basically includes the purchase price of consumer products, digital media content. The fulfillment costs consist of costs incurred in operating and staffing the North America and International fulfillment and customer service centers and payment processing costs along with AWS payment processing and related transaction costs. The technology costs basically include research and development activities which include payroll and related expenses for employees which are involved in application, production, maintenance, operation, and platform development.

Amazon's revenue grew by approximately 10 times in 2015 compared to the revenues in 2006. The revenues increased from $10.711 billion in 2006 to $107.006 billion in 2015. The earnings before interest, tax, ,depreciation and amortization which was $0.66 billion in 2006 increased to $8.308 billion in 2015. Amazon's net income had been negative in 2012 and 2014. The Research and Development expenditure increased from $0.662 billion to $125.40 billion by 2015. The enterprise value increased from $15.584 billion to $312.719 billion by 2015. The total cash increased from $2.019 billion in 2006 to $19.808 billion in 2015. The market capitalization increased from $16.336 billion in 2006 to $318.344 billion by 2015 (see Table 14.5).

The year on year growth rate analysis shows that the growth rate in revenues was highest in 2011 (41%) during the period 2006−2015. The average growth rate of revenues during the period 2006−2015 was 29%. During the 9-year period 2007−2015, the average growth rate of EBITDA was 34%. The average growth rate of net income was negative during the period 2011−2015. The market capitalization increased by 172% in 2009 compared to the previous year. At the same time the enterprise value increased by 186% while total equity increased by 97%. The increase in total equity was 178% in 2007.The average growth rate of total assets, total equity, enterprise value, and market capitalization during the period 2007−2015 was 36%, 56%, 58%, and 56%, respectively. The average growth rate in cash reserves was 30% during the period 2007−2015. The increase in capital expenditure was 50% on average basis during the period 2007−2015.

14.13   Ratio analysis

The average gross margin, operating margin, and net margin during the 10-year period 2006−2015 was 25%, 2.7%, and 1.7%, respectively. The average ROA, ROE, and ROIC during the above 10-year period was 4.1%, 20.4 %, and 10.7%, respectively. The average ICR was 13.5. The analysis of profitability ratios during the two 5-year periods 2006−2010 and 2011−2015 reveals that the profitability ratios have declined on average basis expect the gross margin ratio. The average gross margin ratio during the time period 2006−2010 which was 22.5% increased to 27.4% during the period 2011−2015. On the contrary the average operating margin and average net margin declined from 4.2% and 3.1% to 1.2% and 0.4%, respectively. The average ROA, ROE, and ROIC declined from 7.5% to 37.9% and 18.8% to 0.8%, 2.8%, and 2.6%, respectively. The average ICR declined from 20.7 to 6.4 (Table 14.6).

The revenue per share increased by 8.9 times in 2015 compared to 2006. The average revenue per share, EBITDA per share, and earnings per share were $105.13, $6.2, and $1.02, respectively, during the period 2006−2015 (Table 14.7).

The average book value per share and total debt per share was $14.5 and $8.9 during the period 2006−2015. The book value per share increased by approximately 27 times in 2015 compared to 2006 (Table 14.8).

Table 14.5 Financial highlights in millions of dollars

Year	2006	2007	2008	2009	2010	2011	2012	2013	2014	2015
Revenues	10,711	14,835	19,166	24,509	34,204	48,077	61,093	74,452	88,988	107,006
EBITDA	660	983	1259	1573	2104	2082	2795	3900	4845	8308
Operating income	389	655	842	1129	1406	862	676	745	178	2233
Net income	190	476	645	902	1152	631	−39	274	−241	596
Total cash	2019	3112	3727	6366	8762	9576	11,448	12,447	17,416	19,808
Long term debt	1267	1344	533	252	641	1415	3830	5181	12,489	14,183
R&D expenditure	662	818	1033	1240	1734	2909	4564	6565	9275	12,540
Total assets	4363	6485	8314	13,813	18,797	25,278	32,555	40,159	54,505	65,444
Total equity	431	1197	2672	5257	6864	7757	8192	9746	10,741	13,384
Enterprise value	15,584	36,787	18,754	53,613	73,059	70,600	106,277	175,779	139,386	312,719
Market capitalization	16,336	38,538	21,948	59,727	81,180	78,761	113,895	183,045	144,313	318,344
Capital expenditure	216	224	333	373	979	1811	3785	3444	4893	4589

Table 14.6 Profitability ratios

Year	2006	2007	2008	2009	2010	2011	2012	2013	2014	2015
Gross margin %	22.9	22.6	22.3	22.6	22.3	22.4	24.8	27.2	29.5	33
Operating margin %	3.6	4.4	4.4	4.6	4.1	1.8	1.1	1	0.2	2.1
Net margin %	1.77	3.21	3.37	3.68	3.37	1.31	−0.06	0.37	−0.27	0.56
Return on assets %	4.72	8.78	8.72	8.15	7.07	2.86	−0.13	0.75	−0.51	0.99
Return on equity %	56.13	58.48	33.34	22.75	19.01	8.63	−0.49	3.06	−2.35	14.94
Return on invested capital %	12.06	22.02	21.7	20.65	17.56	7.6	−0.05	2.55	−0.68	3.39
Interest coverage	5.83	9.57	13.69	35.15	39.38	15.37	6.91	4.59	0.47	4.42

Table 14.7 Per share cash flow ratios

Year	2006	2007	2008	2009	2010	2011	2012	2013	2014	2015
Revenue per share	25.26	34.99	44.37	55.45	75.01	104.29	134.86	160.11	192.62	224.33
EBITDA per share	1.56	2.32	2.91	3.56	4.61	4.52	6.17	8.39	10.49	17.42
Earnings per share	0.45	1.12	1.49	2.04	2.53	1.37	−0.09	0.59	−0.52	1.25

Table 14.8 Book value and debt per share

Year	2006	2007	2008	2009	2010	2011	2012	2013	2014	2015
Book value per share	1.04	2.88	6.24	11.84	15.22	17.05	18.04	21.23	23.1	28.42
Total debt per share	3.06	3.27	1.25	0.57	1.42	3.11	8.44	11.29	26.86	30.11

Table 14.9 Price multiples

Year	2006	2007	2008	2009	2010	2011	2012	2013	2014	2015
PE	87.69	82.35	34.26	66.23	71.26	126.26	0	684.03	0	545.07
PB	37.91	32.2	8.21	11.36	11.83	10.15	13.9	18.78	13.44	23.7
PS	1.57	2.64	1.15	2.42	2.4	1.66	1.87	2.47	1.62	3
Price to free cash flow	34.31	33.35	16.38	20.39	32.69	38.29	258.9	91.55	71.97	44.35
Price to operating cash flow	23.8	28	13.14	18.07	23.52	20.48	26.98	33.68	20.87	27.14

The average PE during the period 2006−2015 was 169.7. The average price to book ratio, price to sales ratio, price to free cash flow, and price to operating cash flow during the period 2006−2015 was 18.1, 2.1, 64.2, and 23.6, respectively (Table 14.9).

Table 14.10 Leverage ratios

Year	2006	2007	2008	2009	2010	2011	2012	2013	2014	2015
DER	2.94	1.14	0.2	0.05	0.09	0.18	0.47	0.53	1.16	1.06
Long-term debt to assets	0.29	0.21	0.06	0.02	0.03	0.06	0.12	0.13	0.23	0.22

Table 14.11 Liquidity ratios

Year	2006	2007	2008	2009	2010	2011	2012	2013	2014	2015
Current ratio	1.33	1.39	1.3	1.33	1.33	1.17	1.12	1.07	1.12	1.08
Quick ratio	0.95	1.03	0.96	1	1	0.82	0.78	0.75	0.82	0.77

Table 14.12 Efficiency ratios

Year	2006	2007	2008	2009	2010	2011	2012	2013	2014	2015
Days sales outstanding	11.47	13.58	14.59	13.51	13.74	15.78	17.73	19.93	21.29	20.53
Days inventory	31.9	33.01	31.84	34.33	36.92	40.1	43.76	45.28	45.69	47.23
Payables period	70.35	73.29	78.28	88.46	93.83	93.95	97.12	95.83	91.88	93.87
Receivables turnover	31.83	26.88	25.02	27.01	26.57	23.13	20.59	18.31	17.15	17.78
Inventory turnover	11.44	11.06	11.46	10.63	9.89	9.1	8.34	8.06	7.99	7.73
Fixed assets turnover	26.61	29.67	27.44	22.86	18.47	14.08	10.65	8.27	6.38	5.52
Asset turnover	2.66	2.74	2.59	2.22	2.1	2.18	2.11	2.05	1.88	1.78

The average debt equity ratio during the period 2006−2015 was 0.78 while the average long-term debt to assets ratio was 0.14 during the above period (Table 14.10).

The average current ratio was 1.22 during the period 2006−2015. The average quick ratio during the period 2006−2015 was 0.89 (Table 14.11).

The day's sales outstanding and days inventory have increased over the 10-year period of analysis. The payables period has consistently increased over the period 2006−2015. The turnover ratios have declined over the period of analysis. The average days' sales outstanding and days inventory over the period 2006−2015 was 16.2 and 39 days. The average payable period was 87.7 days. The average receivables turnover, inventory turnover, fixed assets turnover and assets turnover ratio during the period 2006−2015 was 23.4, 9.6, 17, and 2.2 (Table 14.12).

Table 14.13 gives the growth rate of revenues in terms of year on year, 5- and 10-year average growth rates for each year. The source of data was Morningstar. com. The growth rate in revenues is declining over the period of analysis.

Table 14.14 gives the growth rate of operating income in terms of year on year, 5- and 10-year average growth rates for each year. The source of data was Morningstar.com. The year on year growth rate in operating income had been negative in 2011, 2012, and 2014, respectively. The five-year average growth rate in

Table 14.13 **Growth rate of revenues**

Growth rate (%)	2011	2012	2013	2014	2015
Year on year	40.56	27.07	21.87	19.52	20.25
5-year average	35.03	32.72	31.18	29.42	25.62
10-year average	31.45	31.56	30.33	29.1	28.84

Table 14.14 **Growth rate of operating income**

Growth rate (%)	2011	2012	2013	2014	2015
Year on year	−38.69	−21.58	10.21	−76.11	1154.49
5-year average	17.25	0.63	−2.42	−30.89	9.69
10-year average		26.56	10.66	−8.66	17.85

Table 14.15 **Comparative cumulative total return for year ended December 31**

Year	2010	2011	2012	2013	2014	2015
Amazon.com, Inc.	100	96	139	222	172	375
Morgan Stanley Technology Index	100	89	103	136	153	163
S&P 500 Index	100	102	118	157	178	181
S&P 500 Retailing Index	100	104	132	192	213	268

Source: Amazon Annual Report 2015.

operating income was negative during the period 2013 and 2014, respectively. The 10-year average growth rate in operating income was negative in 2014.

14.14 Stock performance analysis

Table 14.15 gives the performance of Amazon stock in terms of cumulative total returns in comparison with indexes like Morgan Stanley Technology Index, the S&P 500 Index, and S&P 500 Retailing Index during the period 2010−2015. It is assumed that $100 is invested in Amazon stock and the indexes in beginning of 2010 and the investment is measured during fiscal year end of each year.

14.15 Stock wealth analysis

The stock wealth analysis of Amazon.com was done for the period 1997−2016 based on the weekly returns of Amazon stock. The analysis covered 993 weeks during the 19-year period of analysis. The adjusted closing price of Amazon.com on

16/5/1997 was $1.73. The adjusted closing price of Amazon.com on 31/5/2016 was $725.54. The stock price increased by approximately 420 times during the 19-year period. If an investor invested $100 in Amazon stock in 1997, the investment would have increased to $41,959 by 2016. The cumulative weekly returns for Amazon during the 993 weeks were 725.54%. Suppose an investor invests $100 in Amazon stock during May 1997. If the investor involved in active trading of buying and selling every week, the investment would have grown to $72,654 based on cumulative returns by 2016. The cumulative returns registered for Nasdaq Composite during the period 1997−2016 was 188% (Fig. 14.1).

The weekly cumulative analysis was for the period May 1997−May 2016. The Amazon stock outperformed the market index Nasdaq Composite during the entire period of analysis.

In 2015, Amazon registered the highest average yearly returns of 84.06%. The average excess returns over the market index Nasdaq was also the highest in 2015. In 2012, the excess returns of Amazon over the market index Nasdaq Composite was 25.75%. Amazon outperformed the market index Nasdaq in all the years of analysis during the period 2010−2015 except in 2014 on the basis of excess returns (Table 14.16).

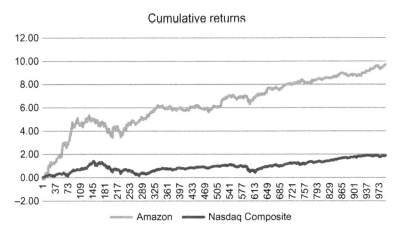

Figure 14.1 Cumulative Returns—Amazon Versus Market Index Nasdaq Composite.

Table 14.16 Average yearly returns in percent

Year	Amazon	Nasdaq Composite	Excess Returns
2010	34.05	17.54	16.51
2011	3.45	1.06	2.39
2012	43.91	18.16	25.75
2013	45.85	29.30	16.54
2014	−20.90	14.26	−35.16
2015	84.06	7.07	76.98

Table 14.17 **Holding period yield**

Year	Holding Period Yield (%)
2010	34.8
2011	−6.7
2012	41.9
2013	48.0
2014	−22.4
2015	127.6
2016	19.5

Table 14.18 **Market value added**

Year	2010	2011	2012	2013	2014	2015
Book value of equity	6864	7757	8192	9746	10,741	13384
Market value of equity	81,180	78,761	113,895	183,045	144,313	318,344
Excess value	74,316	71,004	105,703	173,299	133,572	304,960
BV as percent of market value	8.46	9.85	7.19	5.32	7.44	4.20

The holding period yield for each year is estimated based on the assumption of holding period of one year. The holding period in 2016 is based on the assumption of investment in stock during January 2016 and selling it in May 2016. The holding period yield was 127.6% in 2015. The holding period yield was negative in 2011 and 2014. The annual holding period yield during the period January 2010 to May 2016 was 29.75% for Amazon stock (Table 14.17).

Excess value is estimated as the difference between market value and book value of equity. The excess value increased from $74.316 billion in 2010 to $304.960 billion in the 2015. The book value of equity was only 4.2% of market value of Amazon stock in 2015. The average book value as percent of market value during the 6-year period 2010−2015 was 7.08%. (see Table 14.18)

14.16   Estimation of cost of capital

The first step for estimation of cost of capital is estimation of cost of equity. Cost of equity is estimated using the capital asset pricing model (CAPM).

Cost of equity = Risk free rate + Beta × Risk premium.

Risk free rate is the average yield to maturity on the 30-year treasury bond rate during the period 2014−2016.[7]

---

[7] https://www.treasury.gov/resource-center/data-chart-center/interest-rates/Pages/Historic-Yield-Data-Visualization.aspx.

Year	Yield to maturity on 30-year treasury bond
2014	3.55
2015	2.63
2016	2.63
Average	2.94%

Risk-free rate (Rf) = 2.94%

Beta is estimated by regressing Amazon's weekly stock returns on monthly market index Nasdaq Composite during the January 2014−May 2016 period

Beta = 1.14

Return on market index = Average yearly returns on market index Nasdaq Composite during the period 2014−2016

Return on market index (Rm) = 12.74%

Risk premium = Rm − Rf = 12.74% − 2.94% = 9.8%

Cost of equity = 2.94 + 1.14 × 9.8 = 14.11%

Cost of equity is estimated as 14.11%

Cost of debt

The yield on the long-term bond of Amazon with maturity date 12/5/2044 is taken as the cost of debt. The yield on the bond = 3.921%.[8] The price of the bond on 4/6/2016 was $117.39.

Average tax rate during the period 2014−2016 = 44.93%

After tax cost of debt = 3.921 × (1 − 0.4493) = 2.16%.

Book value of debt in 2015 = $8235 million dollars

Ratio of price of long-term bond to the face value of bond = 117.39/100 = 1.1739

Market value of debt = 8235 × 1.1739 = $9667.89 million

Market value of equity in 2015 = $318,344 million

Total value = 318,344 + 9667.89 = $328,011.9 million

Weight of equity = 318,344/328,011.9 = 0.97

Weight of debt = 9667.89/328,011.9 = 0.03

WACC = Weight of equity × Cost of equity + Weight of debt × After tax cost of debt
     = 0.97 × 14.11 + 0.03 × 2.16 = 13.76%

Weighted average cost of capital = 13.76%.

14.17   Valuation perspectives

14.17.1   Economic value

Economic value is estimated for the year ended 2015.

Economic value is estimated as net operating income after taxes(NOPAT)−Capital charge.

Profit before interest and tax (PBIT) − Income tax = NOPAT.

Capital employed = Stock holder equity + Long-term debt

Capital charge = Capital employed × WACC

Economic value (EV) = NOPAT − Capital charge

---

[8] www.finra.org.

Table 14.19 **Economic value in 2015**

	in million dollars
PBIT in 2015	2233
Income tax	950
NOPAT	1283
Stockholder equity in 2015	13,384
Long-term debt in 2015	8235
Capital employed	21,619
WACC	13.76%
Capital charge	2974.77
EV	−1691.77

Table 14.20 **Equity spread estimation**

Equity Spread	in million dollars
Stock holder Equity	13,384
ROE in 2015	14.94%
COE in 2015	13.76%
Equity Spread	157.93

The economic value in 2015 is estimated as −1691.77 million dollars (Table 14.19).

14.18   Equity spread

Equity spread is a variation of the EV measures. Equity spread is the difference between the ROE and the required return on equity (cost of equity)
Equity spread = (Return on equity − Cost of equity) × Equity capital

Equity Spread for 2015 is estimated as $157.93 million (Table 14.20).

14.19   Discounted cash flow valuation—FCFF model

Free cash flow to firm valuation model is used to value Amazon.com.
Net capital expenditures = Capital expenditures − Depreciation &amortization
Adjusted net capital expenditure = Net capital expenditures + Net acquisitions (Table 14.21)
The adjusted net capital expenditure was negative in 2015.
Noncash current assets = Total current assets − cash and cash equivalents
Noninterest bearing current liabilities = Total current liabilities − Short-term debt

Table 14.21 **Adjusted net capital expenditure in millions of dollars**

Year	2011	2012	2013	2014	2015
Capital expenditures	1811	3785	3444	4893	4589
Depreciation & amortization	1083	2159	3253	4746	6281
Net capital expenditures	728	1626	191	147	−1692
Net acquisitions	705	745	312	979	795
Adjusted net capital expenditures	1433	2371	503	1126	−897

Table 14.22 **Noncash working capital in millions of dollars**

Year	2011	2012	2013	2014	2015
Total current assets	17,490	21,296	24,625	31,327	36,474
Cash and cash equivalents	9576	11,448	12,447	17,416	19,808
Noncash current assets	7914	9848	12,178	13,911	16,666
Total current liabilities	14,896	19,002	22,980	28,089	33,899
Short-term debt	0	0	0	0	0
Noninterest bearing current liabilities	14,896	19,002	22,980	28,089	33,899
Noncash working capital	−6982	−9154	−10,802	−14,178	−17,233
Change in noncash working capital		−2172	−1648	−3376	−3055

Table 14.23 **Estimation of reinvestment rate**

Year	2011	2012	2013	2014	2015
EBIT	862	676	745	178	2233
Taxes	291	428	161	167	950
EBIT(1-T)	571	248	584	11	1283
Adjusted net capex	1433	2371	503	1126	−897
Change in noncash WC		−2172	−1648	−3376	−3055
Reinvestment	1433	199	−1145	−2250	−3952
Reinvestment rate	2.51	0.80	−1.96	−204.55	−3.08

Noncash working capital = Noncash current Assets − Noninterest bearing current liabilities (Table 14.22)

The reinvestment rate has been highly fluctuating over the five-year period of analysis (Table 14.23).

The FCFF is fluctuating over the period of analysis (Table 14.24).

On account of highly fluctuating reinvestment rate and FCFF, the growth rate estimation is not feasible in the correct sense. Hence the FCFF model is not used.

Table 14.24 Estimation of FCFF in millions of dollars

Year	2012	2013	2014	2015
EBIT(1-T)	248	584	11	1283
Adjusted Net Capex	2371	503	1126	−897
Change in Non-Cash Working Capital	−2172	−1648	−3376	−3055
FCFF	49	1729	2261	5235

Table 14.25 Estimation of reinvestment rate

Year	2011	2012	2013	2014	2015
Operating cash flow	3903	4180	5475	6842	11,920
Capital expenditure	1811	3785	3444	4893	4589
Reinvestment rate	0.46	0.91	0.63	0.72	0.38

Table 14.26 Present value of free cash flow in the high growth period

Year	1	2	3	4	5	6	7	8	9	10
Operating cash flow	14,423	17,452	21,117	25,552	30,917	37,410	45,266	54,772	66,274	80,192
Reinvestment	8798	10,646	12,881	15,586	18,860	22,820	27,612	33,411	40,427	48,917
FCF	5625	6806	8236	9965	12,058	14,590	17,654	21,361	25,847	31,275
PV	4945	5259	5594	5950	6329	6732	7160	7616	8100	8616
Sum	66,300									

14.20 Free cash flow model

The average reinvestment rate based on geometric mean during the period 2011−2015 was 61% (Table 14.25).

The growth rate of operating cash flow based on geometric mean during the period 2012−2014 is 21%.

We use two-stage FCF valuation model in which it is assumed that the operating cash flow of Amazon will grow at 21% for the next 10 years and thereafter at the stable growth rate of US economy assumed as 2.3%.

High growth stage inputs
Operating Cash flow in year 2015 = $11,920 million
Reinvestment rate = 61%
Growth rate in high growth period = 21%
High growth period = 10 years
Operating cash flow in first year of high growth period = 11,920 × 1.21 = $14,423.2 million
The present value of free cash flows in the high growth period = $66,300 million (see Table 14.26)

Stable period inputs

Growth rate in stable period = Growth rate of US economy during the period 2013–2015.

Growth rate = 2.3%

Growth rate = Reinvestment rate $\times$ Return on capital employed of retail specialty sector

Return on capital employed of retail specialty sector = 8.31%[9]

Reinvestment = 2.3%/8.31% = 27.7%

WACC = 13.76%

Operating cash flow at the end of high growth period = $80,191.8 million

Operating cash flow at beginning of stable growth period = 80,191.8 $\times$ 1.023 = $82,036.21 million

Reinvestment = 82,036.21 $\times$ 0.277 = $22,724.03 million

Free cash flow in stable period = 82,036.21 − 22,724.03 = $59,312.18 million

Terminal value of free cash flow = 59,312.18/ (0.1376 − 0.023) = $517,558.29 million

Present value of terminal value = $271,651.03 million

Value of operating assets = Present value of free cash flows at high growth phase + Present value of free cash flows at stable phase period

= 66,300 + 271,651.03 = $337,951.37 million

Value of equity = Value of operating assets − Value of debt

= 337,951.37 − 8235 = $329,716.37 million

No. of shares = 477 million

Value per share = 329,716.37/477 = $691.23

Amazon stock was trading at $725.54 at Nasdaq on 5/6/2016. The 52-week range for Amazon in May 2016 was $419.14 − $728.28

14.21 Relative valuation

14.21.1 Comparison with peer companies

The competitor companies chosen are Alibaba Group, eBay, and O'Reilly Inc. O'Reilly is a specialty retailer of automotive aftermarket parts, tools, supplies equipment, and accessories in the United States. Alibaba Group through its subsidiaries provide retail and wholesale marketplaces available through personal computer and mobile interfaces. Bay Inc. is an online market place for sale of goods.

The values for Amazon, eBay, and O'Reilly are given in millions of dollars while for Alibaba, the financial values are given in millions of CNY. The competitors' comparison is based on the latest year-end financial data available. Amazon have the highest revenues and market capitalization among all the peer companies (Table 14.27).

The year on year growth rate of revenues was based on 2015 compared to the previous year 2014. The 5-year and 10-year average comparison are based on 2015. Alibaba had the highest growth rate in revenues followed by Amazon on the basis of year on year, 5-year and 10-year average comparison. The data source is Morningstar.com (Table 14.28).

---

[9] http://csimarket.com/Industry/industry_ManagementEffectiveness.php?ind=1307.

Table 14.27 **Financial highlights of peer companies**

Company	Amazon	Alibaba	eBay	O'Reilly
Total asset	65,494	364,450	17,785	6677
Total debt	8235	57,771	6779	1390
Capital expenditures	4589	10,845	668	414
Revenues	107,006	101,143	8592	7967
Operating income	2233	29,102	2197	1514
Cash flow	8308	90,115	3237	1728
Total cash	19,808	115,696	6131	116
Net income	596	71,460	1725	931
Market capitalization	318,344	191,234	32,536	24,769

Table 14.28 **Growth rate comparison of revenues**

In percent	Amazon	Alibaba	eBay	O'Reilly
Year on year	20.25	32.73	−52.01	10.4
5-year average	25.62	91.27	−1.26	8.1
10-year average	28.84	59.25	6.56	14.56

Table 14.29 **Growth rate comparison of operating income**

In Percent	Amazon	Alibaba	eBay	O'Reilly
Year on year	1154.49	25.79	−37.48	19.18
5-year average	9.69	92	1.36	16.26
10-year average	17.85	65.91	4.3	19.61

Table 14.30 **Price multiple comparison**

Company	P/S	P/B	P/E
Amazon	3.1	23.3	300.4
Alibaba	12.9	5.8	18.2
EBay	3.4	4.4	14.8
O'Reilly	3.2	13.1	27.1

The year on year growth rate of operating income was based on 2015 compared to the previous year 2014. The 5-year and 10-year average comparison are based on 2015.The data source is Morningstar.com (Table 14.29).

In terms of P/S, Amazon is the most undervalued stock. The P/E ratio of Amazon is very high compared to the other firms. The period of comparison is current period May 2016. The source of data is Morningstar.com (Table 14.30).

Table 14.31 Comparison with industry average and S&P 500

Ratios	Amazon	Industry Average	S&P500
P/E	300.4	32.8	19.4
P/B	23.3	7.4	2.7
P/S	3.1	1.9	1.9
P/CF	31.1	8.7	12

Table 14.32 Price multiple trends

Year	2006	2007	2008	2009	2010	2011	2012	2013	2014	2015
P/E	57.5	82.6	34.4	65.8	71.4	91.7	–	1428.60	–	1000.00
P/B	83.3	32.2	8.2	11.4	11.8	10.1	13.9	20.2	14	25.6
P/S	1.7	2.6	1.2	2.4	2.4	1.8	1.9	2.6	1.7	3.2
P/CF	28.6	27.9	13.1	18.1	23.5	25.5	27.2	37	25.2	32.6

Table 14.33 Enterprise value multiple comparison

Company	Amazon	Alibaba	eBay	O'Reilly
Revenues	107,006	101,143	8592	7967
EBITDA	8308	90,115	3237	1728
EBIT	2233	29,102	2197	1514
Debt	8235	57,771	6779	1390
Market value of equity	318,344	191,234	32,536	24,769
Cash and cash equivalents	19,808	115,696	6131	116
Enterprise value (EV)	306,771	133,309	33,184	26,043
EV/REVENUES	2.87	1.32	3.86	3.27
EV/EBITDA	36.92	1.48	10.25	15.07
EV/EBIT	137.38	4.58	15.10	17.20

Amazon had very high P/E ratio compared to industry average and S&P500. The comparison is for the period May 2016. The price to book ratio, price to sales, and price to cash flow were higher for Amazon compared to the industry average and S&P500 (Table 14.31). Table 14.32 gives the price multiple trend during the period 2006-2015.

The enterprise value multiples are based on 2015. The lower the enterprise value multiples, the more underpriced and attractive the stock becomes for buying (Table 14.33).

Enterprise value = Market value of equity + Debt-cash and cash equivalents

The enterprise value multiples have been fluctuating over the 10-year period (2006−2015) of analysis (Table 14.34).

Table 14.34 **Enterprise value multiple trends**

Year	2006	2007	2008	2009	2010	2011	2012	2013	2014	2015
EV/Revenues	1.45	2.48	0.98	2.19	2.14	1.47	1.74	2.36	1.57	2.92
EV/EBITDA	23.54	37.42	14.91	34.08	34.74	33.91	38.04	45.07	28.77	37.64
EV/EBIT	34.1	49.91	19.31	44.9	47.6	70.67	174.8	271.26	1422.30	154.2

14.22 Performance indicators

14.22.1 Altman Z-score

Investors can use Altman Z-score to decide if they should buy or sell a particular stock based on the company's financial strength. The Altman Z-score is the output of a credit strength test which gauges a publicly traded manufacturing company's likelihood of bankruptcy. Z-score model is an accurate forecaster of failure up to two years prior to distress.

$$\text{Z-Score} = 1.2A + 1.4B + 3.3C + 0.6D + 1.0E$$

where

A = Working capital/Total assets; B = Retained earnings/Total assets; C = Earnings before interest & tax/Total assets; D = Market value of equity/Total liabilities; E = Sales/Total assets

The zones of discrimination are such that when Z-score is less than 1.81, it is in distress zones. When the Z-score is greater than 2.99, it is in safe zones. When the Z-score is between 1.81 and 2.99, the company is in gray zone.

The variable values are given in millions of dollars.

Total assets	65,494.00		
Total liabilities	52,060.00		
Sales revenues	107,006		
Operating income	2233		
Retained earnings	2545		
Market value of equity	318,344		
Working capital	2575		
Ratios	Values	Constant	Score
Working capital/Total assets	0.04	1.2	0.05
Retained earnings/Total assets	0.04	1.4	0.05
Operating income/Total assets	0.03	3.3	0.11
Market value of equity/Total liabilities	6.11	0.6	3.67
Sales/Total assets	1.63	1	1.63
		Z-score	5.52

Amazon in the year end 2015 had a Z-score of 5.52 indicating that the company is in safe zone.

14.23   Piotroski score

The Piotroski score is a discrete score between 0 and 9 which is an indicator of the firm's financial position. The score was named after the Chicago accounting Professor Joseph Piotroski. The cumulative points suggest whether the stock is a value stock or not. If the company achieves a score of 8 or 9, the stock can be considered strong. If the score ranges between 0 and 2, then the stock is considered weak.

14.23.1   Criteria for Piotroski score

SL	Profitability scores	Score points	Score for Amazon
1	Positive return on assets in current year	1	1
2	Positive operating cash flow in current year	1	1
3	Higher ROA in current year compared to previous year	1	1
4	Return on cash flow from operations greater than ROA	1	1
	Leverage, liquidity, and sources of funds		
5	Lower ratio of long-term debt to average total assets in current year compared to previous year	1	1
6	Higher current ratio in this year compared to previous year	1	0
7	No new shares were issued in the last year	1	0
	Operational efficiency ratios		
8	A higher gross margin compared to the previous year	1	1
9	A higher asset turnover ratio compared to the previous year	1	0
Total		9	6

The analysis is based on 2015. Amazon has a score of 6 out of 9.

14.24   Graham number

It is a conservative method used for valuing a stock. It is a figure which measures a stock's fundamental value by taking into account the company's earnings per share and book value per share. Graham number is the upper bound of the price range which a defensive investor should pay for the stock. According to Graham number theory, any stock price below the Graham number is considered undervalued and hence worth investing in. Graham number is a combination of asset valuation and earnings power valuation.

EPS in 2015 = $1.25
Book value per share = $28.42
Graham number = $\sqrt{22.5 \times \text{(Earning per share)} \times \text{(Book value per share)}}$
= $28.27

Amazon was trading at $725.54 in Nasdaq on 5/6/2016.

14.25   Peter Lynch Fair valuation

Peter Lynch Fair value is fundamentally applicable to growth companies. The ideal range for the growth rate is between 10 and 20% a year. According to this valuation criteria, the fair P/E value for a growth company must equals its growth rate that is PEG = 1. The earnings are the trailing twelve month (TTM) earnings.

Amazon's Peter Lynch Fair value is calculated in the following manner
Peter Lynch Fair value = PEG × 5-year EBITDA growth rate × EPS
The 5-year EBITDA growth rate during the period 2011−2015 is arrived at 31.6%. As per Peter Lynch value criteria, we use the growth rate as 25. The price to earnings ratio (PE) is 545.67
PEG = 545.67/25 = 21.08. The TTM EPS in 2015 was $1.25
Peter Lynch Fair value = 21.08 × 25 × 1.25 = $681.34
According to Peter Lynch fair value model, the value of Amazon stock is $681.34. The 52-week range of Amazon stock during May 2016 was $ 419.14−$728.28.

*The detailed calculation for all analysis is given in the excel file **Amazon.xlsx**.*

Wealth analysis of AT&T

15

15.1 Introduction

The origin of American Telephone and Telegraph Company (AT&T) can be traced to the period when in 1876 Alexander Graham Bell invented the telephone. AT&T have a legacy of 140 years. The AT&T network is the largest communication company in the world. AT&T is a fully integrated service provider. AT&T offer advanced mobile services, next-generation TV, high-speed Internet, and smart solutions. AT&T provides advanced services to 3.5 million businesses which involve nearly all of the Fortune 1000 businesses. AT&T's high-speed mobile Internet network covers over 365 million people and businesses across North America and Mexico. AT&T Network carries 117.4 petabytes of data traffic on an average business day.[1] Approximately 99% of the people in America are covered by AT&T. The company have invested over $140 billion in wireless and wireline networks over the period 2011—2015. Approximately 1,053,240 route miles of fiber are owned and operated globally by AT&T. There are approximately 139.6 million wireless customers in the United States and Mexico. AT&T's 4G LTE network are accessed by 365 million people in the United States and Mexico. AT&T have operations in more than 200 countries where AT&T offers services to talk, text, and data coverage. AT&T provide satellite video service through subsidiary DIRECTV whose satellites are licensed by the Federal Communications Commission (FCC). By 2015, AT&T had approximately 8.7 million wireless subscribers in Mexico and 12.5 million video connections in Latin America.

AT&T are the world's largest provider of pay TV with approximately 25 million video subscribers. AT&T provides high-speed fiber to about one million business locations and high-speed Internet to about 57 million customer locations. Innovations at AT&T Labs have resulted in 8 Nobel Prizes and more than 12500 patents worldwide. AT&T is a Fortune 500 company which is listed on the New York Stock Exchange. AT&T workforce in 2015 was 280,000.

AT&T have been named as the Most Admired Telecommunications Company in the world by Fortune magazine in 2016 which was second time in a row. AT&T was also ranked in J D Powerless Purchase Experience Study six consecutive times.

15.2 Business segments

AT&T have four reportable segments. They are Business Solutions, Entertainment Group, Consumer Mobility and International Division. Business solutions is the largest segment which contributed over $71 billion of total revenues in 2015.

---

[1] http://www.att.com/gen/investor-relations?pid=5711.

Strategic Financial Management Casebook.

The business segment contributed 49 % towards the operating revenues in 2015. AT&T provides services to business, government, wholesale customers and individual subscribers who have access to wireless services through employer sponsored plans. AT&T provide advanced Internet protocol (IP)-based services which include virtual private networks, Ethernet-related products and broadband, data, and voice products. The business solution segment through wireless and wired network provide complete communication solution to business customers. The Entertainment group accounted for 24% of the total segment revenues in 2015. This segment provides video, Internet, and voice communication services to residential customers in the United States. This segment uses the wired network and satellite technology. The Consumer Mobility segment accounted for 24% of the operating revenues in 2015.Consumer Mobility segment provides nationwide wireless service to consumers, and wireless wholesale and resale subscribers. The segment uses wireless network to provide voice and data services which include high-speed Internet, video entertainment, and home monitoring services. The international segment accounted for 3% of the 2015 total segment operating revenues. This segment provides entertainment services in Latin America and wireless services in Mexico. Video entertainment services are provided to residential customers using satellite technology. The international segment consists of Latin America operations of Direct TV which were acquired in 2015.

15.3 Strategy of growth

During the period 2007−2014, the mobile data traffic on AT&T network have increased 100,000%. Huge amounts of bandwidth with streaming video are being used by millions of people. Wired connections are being replaced by mobile devices. The change in networking strategy is revolutionizing the economy in digital age. AT&T is a leader in the fast growing technology of connectivity. Currently AT&T have certified more than 2200 types of devices to connect to AT&T network.

The smartphone era has been transformed into a new phase where billions of devices have been connected to networks globally. AT&T strategically focuses on emerging as the world's premier integrated communications company by focusing on key areas. The future lies for integrated communications company which can provide end to end connectivity for meeting new demands.

AT&T focuses on key areas to emerge as the premier integrated communications company in global context. AT&T's primary focus is on providing connectivity and integrated solutions. It is vital for companies to offer premier network assets for integrated mobile, video, and data solutions for clients. Wireless LTE, WiFi, satellite, IP networks, and fiber optics are technological means through which customer can access the content. AT&T provides high-speed fiber connections to more than one million US business centers. AT&T provides high-speed Internet connections to more than 57 million customers in the United States. AT&T possess satellites which deliver HD and Ultra HD video to customers in the United States and Latin America. The strategy of the company is to serve the customers globally with the focus on industry leading cost structure. AT&T aims to transform network from hardware to software centric. AT&T focuses on delivering the most networked traffic at the lowest marginal cost in the industry. AT&T focuses on offering integrated wireless, video, and wireline services and fixed strategic services for its growth pursuits. Another area of focus is on equipment revenues. Traditional service revenues are showing a declining trend. The wireless services provided by AT&T are increasingly subject to governmental regulations. In 2015, FCC reclassified both fixed and mobile consumer broadband Internet access services as telecommunication services were subject to comprehensive regulation under the Telecom Act. AT&T and other providers of broadband Internet access services have challenged the FCC's decision before the US Court of Appeals for the DC Circuit. With respect to international regulation, AT&T is involved in multiple initiatives with foreign regulators to open markets and reduce network costs.

AT&T divested subsidized mobile handsets to improve EBITDA margins. AT&T expects to realize annual synergies of amount $2.5 billion by 2018 on account of the integration of DIRECTV. AT&T have invested over $140 billion of capital investments in building wireless and wireline networks and acquisitions of wireless spectrum and operations. These initiatives were aimed to create one of the most advanced wireless fiber and IP networks in the world. AT&T have launched different plans like Mobile Share and AT&T Next to attract and retain subscribers in maturing markets as wireless growth depends on the ability to offer innovative services plans and devices. On account of AT&T Next and Mobile Share plans, the average revenue per average wireless subscriber of postpaid phone decreased by 4% in 2015. The postpaid subscribers increased by 1.8% in 2015. AT&T Next program facilitated postpaid subscribers to purchase certain devices in installments over a period of up to 30 months. In addition, the subscribers after a specified period of time will also have the right to trade in the original device for a new device with a new installment plan.

The existence of robust competition in the wireless industry would put pressure on the service revenue and ARPU. The strategy of the Next program is to generate growth in equipment revenue which could also impact the services revenues.

The connected devices of AT&T include data centric devices such as session-based tablets, monitoring devices, and automobile systems. Connected device subscribers increased by 25% in 2015. In this context, AT&T added approximately 3.9 million "connected" cars through agreements with various carmakers. This strategic step is aimed at creating future relationships with the car owners. In 2015, AT&T had expected to connect nearly half of new US passenger vehicles and expected to have more than 10 million vehicles on the network by end of 2017.

AT&T expect the future growth to come from IP-based broadband services, video entertainment, and wireless services from the North American base. With the acquisition of DIRECTV and wireless properties, AT&T aims to provide integrated services to diverse groups of customers on different technological platforms. The strategic plan of AT&T is to develop and provide unique integrated video, mobile, and broadband solutions. From January 2016, AT&T started offering an unlimited mobile data plan to customers who purchase DIRECTV or U verse service through which customers could view video anywhere in the world. As a part of its strategic plan to leverage next-generation converged services which combines technologies and services, AT&T have entered into agreements with automobile manufacturers to provide vehicle-embedded security and entertainment services.

AT&T faces competition from brands like Verizon Wireless, Sprint, T-Mobile/ Metro PCS, and a number of regional service providers of cellular, PCS, and other wireless communication services. AT&T faces competition from providers offering voice, text messaging, and other service applications on data networks. The subsidiaries of AT&T face competition from multiple providers like wireless, satellite, cable, and other "voice over Internet protocol" (VoIP) providers.

15.3.1 Corporate restructuring by AT&T

AT&T had its origin in American Bell Telephone Company. In 1881, American Bell Telephone Company had a controlling stake in the Western Electric Company. In 1899, AT&T bought the assets of American Bell. AT&T gained monopoly status due to a number of regulatory actions by the government. AT&T focused on purchasing companies within specific geographic areas which increased its effective control of the telephone system market. In 1926, AT&T started to focus on the telephone business as a communication common carrier and sold its broadcasting subsidiary Broadcasting Corporation of America to RCA. In 1925, AT&T created the research and development unit called Bell Telephone Labs. In due course of time AT&T increased its control of the telephone system through its leasing arrangements for telephones and telephone equipment made by its subsidiary Western Electric. In most of the 20th century, AT&T subsidiary, AT&T Long Lines had near total monopoly on long distance telephone service in the United States. AT&T controlled 22 Bell Operating Companies which provided local telephone service to most of the United States. AT&T and the bell companies together constituted the Ma Bell System. The telephone monopoly of AT&T ended in 1982 when the United States Department of Justice settled the antitrust suit against AT&T. Under the settlement, AT&T's (Ma Bell) local operations were split into seven independent Regional Bell Operating Companies known as "Baby Bells." In 1984, AT&T divested its local telephone operations but retained its long distance R&D and manufacturing divisions. SBC Communications was created as a result of this divestiture. Following the breakup of AT&T in 1984, the industry witnessed an intense accelerated horizontal diversification. Many new players entered the telecommunications sector offering new options for telephone service in a tightly focused niche market.

AT&T and the Bell System lost considerable revenues which were earned from phone leasing by local Bell companies during eighties. Western Electric had to close all of its US phone manufacturing plants. Western Electric renamed as AT&T Technologies was split into different customer focused groups like AT&T Network Systems and AT&T Consumer Products. In 1991, these groups along with

Bell Labs were merged into AT&T. In the same year AT&T discontinued telegraph services. In 1991, AT&T acquired NCR Corporation to gain access to the personal computer and Unix networked server markets. AT&T took over NCR in a hostile takeover. As a result of the deregulation of US telecom industry in 1996, NCR was divested by AT&T. During this period, majority of AT&T Technologies and Bell Labs was spun off as Lucent technologies. During the 1990s, much restructuring took place in the telecommunication industry due to deregulation, technological advances, and reduction of demand and pricing power in the telecommunication sector. In 1994, AT&T acquired cellular carrier McCaw Cellular for $11.5 billion and gained access to 2 million subscribers. In 1995, AT&T acquired long distance provider Alaska Communications System and operated it as an AT&T subsidiary on account of regulatory stipulations. AT&T became the largest provider of cable television in the United States through acquiring stakes in TCI and Media One. In 1997, AT&T acquired TCI in a $48 billion all stock transaction which included the assumption of $16 billion of debt. AT&T acquired MediaOne for $54 billion in cash and stock after bidding contest with Comcast. AT&T acquired the Olivetti Research Lab from Olivetti and Oracle research Lab from Oracle Corporation in 1999. Again in 1999, AT&T acquired IBM's Global Network business for $5 billion. Under the purchase agreement IBM gave AT&T a five-year $5 billion contract to service IBM's networking needs. In reciprocity, AT&T outsourced some of its applications processing and data management work to IBM.

In 2001, AT&T spun off AT&T Wireless Services through IPO. In the same year the company spun off AT&T broadband and Liberty Media which possessed cable TV assets. AT&T Broadband was later acquired by Comcast in 2002. In 2004, AT&T Wireless and Cingular Wireless merged to form Cingular. In 2007, Cingular became AT&T Mobility.

Southwestern Bell Corporation (SBC) was one of the new companies created as a result of the breakup of AT&T. In 2005, Southwestern Bell acquired AT&T and took over the AT&T's name and branding. In 2007, AT&T acquired Dobson Cellular which provided services in US rural areas under the brand Cellular One for $2.8 billion. AT&T had also acquired the outstanding debt of AT&T for $2.3 billion. In 2008, AT&T acquired Wayport Inc. provider of Internet hotspots in the United States. The acquisition enabled AT&T to enhance its public Wi Fi deployment to 20,000 hotspots in the United States. In 2011 AT&T purchased $1.93 billion worth of spectrum from Qualcomm. In 2013, AT&T acquired Leap Wireless for $1.2 billion and gained access to Leap's towers, stores, and 5.3 million subscribers. In 2015, AT&T completed the acquisition of DIRECTV which gave AT&T the access to the Mexican wireless market.

On March 20, 2011, AT&T and Deutsche Telekom entered into a stock purchase agreement under which AT&T agreed to acquire the T-Mobile subsidiary of Deutsche Telekom in exchange for approximately $39 billion. But AT&T ended its effort to buy T-Mobile US, as it could not overcome the stiff opposition by the administration to form the nation's biggest cell phone service provider. During January 2015, AT&T acquired GSF Telecom the Mexican wireless company of GSF Telecom Holdings for $2500 which included net debt of approximately $700.

In April 2015, AT&T acquired the subsidiaries of NI Holdings Inc. (Nextel Mexico) which operated wireless business in Mexico for $1875 million.

15.3.2   Major mergers and acquisitions

15.3.2.1   SBC–AT&T merger[2]

In 2006, SBC bought AT&T and became the largest telecommunications company in the world. Twenty-one years after federal regulators forced the old AT&T to split up, Ma Bell has come full circle. SBC Communications, a so-called Baby Bell acquired venerable Ma Bell AT&T signifying the reunion of the two companies after the court mandated breakup decades ago. SBC was one of the most ambitious of the so-called Baby Bells and had about 50 million local telephone customers at the time of merger. AT&T because of federal decisions was not able to get back into the local market and connect up its local service with its long distance service. The merger was approved by the federal agencies FCC and the United States Department of Justice. SBC renamed itself as AT&T. AT&T shareholders received 0.77942 shares of SBC common stock for each common share of AT&T. The deal was valued at $16 billion or $19.71 per share. The merger of two telecom giants brought together the local, global, and wireless network resources under one entity and set the standard for innovations. The transaction combined the AT&T's global systems capabilities, business and government customers, and fast-growing Internet protocol (IP)-based business with SBC's extraordinary local exchange, broadband, and wireless solution. SBC and AT&T had complementary world-class assets and industry-leading capabilities. AT&T bought to the combined company the world's most advanced communications network to meet the sophisticated data communication needs of large businesses with multiple locations. Beyond network capabilities, AT&T had complementary assets that allowed SBC to bring a full range of innovative voice and data services to customers around the world. These included a broad, high-end enterprise customer base, proven sales expertise in complex communications solutions, and an advanced product portfolio including a broad range of IP-based services.[3] AT&T Labs had more than 5600 patents at the time of merger. The synergies were expected to be realized from network operations and IT. It was expected to realize 15% of synergies from eliminating duplicate corporate functions.

15.3.2.2   Cingular wireless/AT&T wireless services merger

Cingular became one of the Regional Bell Operating Companies as a part of the Bell System divestiture. In 1984, Cingular Wireless was founded as a joint venture (60:40) of SBC Communications and Bell South. The joint venture created United States' second largest carrier. In 2004, Cingular Wireless and AT&T Wireless

---

[2] http://news.cnet.com/SBC-closes-AT38T-acquisition/2100-1036_3-5961206.html;   http://people.stern. nyu.edu/igiddy/cases/sbc-att.htm; http://knowledge.wharton.upenn.edu/article.cfm?articleid=1134.

[3] Rajesh Kumar, Mega Mergers and Acquisitions, Case Studies from Key Industries, Palgrave Macmillan ISBN 978-1-137-00589-2.

merged to create the United States' biggest wireless carrier in terms of subscribers. The deal was valued at $41 billion. As Cingular was jointly owned by Baby Bells, SBC Communications, and Bell South Corp, SBC and BellSouth contributed $25 billion and $16 billion for AT&T wireless. Cingular had to divest itself of wireless customers and other assets in 13 US markets in order to gain Justice Department approval for the merger. At the time of the deal, the merged entity called Cingular Wireless became the largest wireless carrier much ahead of Verizon Wireless with about 46 million subscribers. AT&T wireless had 22 million subscribers and Cingular had 24 million subscribers. It also had licenses to operate wireless service in 49 of 50 US states, and served the top 100 US metropolitan areas. The combined company offered network resources to customers free of roaming charges.

15.3.2.3   AT&T Bell South Merger[4]

Bell South Corporation was one of the world's largest communications companies, serving close to 34 million customers in the United States and in 18 other countries, with a particularly large market in Latin America. Bell South provided local telecommunications as well as wireless local and long distance service, long distance access, cable and digital television, Internet access, and other electronic commerce. BellSouth was formed in 1983 as part of the court-ordered breakup of the AT&T. AT&T had often used the Bell South as the testing ground for new technologies, which gave BellSouth a lead in high-technology services, such as using telephone lines to monitor gas meters. The $87 billion merger of AT&T and Bell South created the largest phone company in the United states with Verizon and AT&T being the two major players. The merger reunited large parts of AT&T's former domain by folding Bell South's nine state territories into AT&T's existing operations spanning the Midwest, Southwest, and West Coast in the United States. The merger helped the Cingular, BellSouth, and AT&T networks into a single fully integrated wireless and wireline IP network offering a full range of advanced solutions. The merger facilitated the merged firm to speed the convergence of new and improved video services which facilitated the industry's shift to the next-generation IP-based technologies.

AT&T and BellSouth offered conventional telephone service in different regions of the country. AT&T operated in the Southwest, Far West, and the Midwest. BellSouth provided telephone service in the Southeast. Both companies were losing subscriber lines rather rapidly as consumers switched to cellular phones or VoIP provided by the cable companies or independent providers, such as Vonage. The new broadband (DSL) Internet services offered by AT&T and BellSouth have not been sufficient to offset the revenue losses from traditional telephone services. Combining these two companies provided some useful synergies in their battle to compete with the cable television companies. The total synergies expected was estimated to be over $2 billion in 2008. BellSouth received 1.325 shares of AT&T for each BellSouth or $37.09 per share. At the time of merger, AT&T had 71 million

[4] http://money.cnn.com/2006/03/06/technology/business2_att_telecom/; http://www.nytimes.com/2006/12/30/business/30tele.html.

access lines and 9.8 million broadband subscribers ahead of Comcast's 8.5 million cable modem subscribers. This merger was a strategic attempt by AT&T to seek a real alternative to cable monopolies in the VoIP market and in the "triple play"— broadband voice, data, and video service plans.

AT&T and BellSouth are also closely aligned when it comes to their wireline broadband strategies, which could mean speedier IPTV deployments for BellSouth customers. The main reason for this is that the companies have built their networks around a similar architecture.

With the acquisition, AT&T brought BellSouth, which had no video strategy, into its broadband services picture. The merger had put AT&T back on top as the largest telecommunications company in the United States after it was broken up into eight smaller companies by the federal government in 1984.

15.3.2.4 Acquisition of DIRECTV

In July 2015, AT&T completed the acquisition of DIRECTV which is a leading digital television entertainment services provider in the United States and Latin America. AT&T acquired DirecTV for $49 billion making it the largest pay TV company in the United States. The acquisition was aimed at creating cost and revenue synergies from bundling and integrating services. The acquisition was expected to deliver distribution scale for AT&T by means of offering consumers attractive services by combining video, high-speed broadband and mobile services. The acquisition would result in the combined company emerging as a content distribution leader across mobile, video, and broadband platforms. Under the terms of the merger agreement, each share of DIRECTV stock was exchanged for $28.50 cash plus 1.892 shares of AT&T stock. AT&T issued 954 million shares to DIRECTV shareholders. DIRECTV shareholders held 16% stake in the new combined company.

AT&T had plans to rejuvenate DirecTV by making content more accessible on more platforms and bring in cost savings of $ 2.5 billion. The deal was expected to bring in substantial savings on content costs.[5] In a scenario of market saturation and competition in US wireless business, the acquisition of DirecTV provided AT&T more scale in television and leverage to offer new video services over the top and on mobile devices. The deal was approved by FCC subject to several conditions. The regulatory requirement stipulated AT&T to expand its fiber optic broadband service and offer stand-alone broadband services at set prices to low-income individuals who meet the criteria. AT&T was also expected to apply any broadband data caps it imposes on customers to its own over the top video service and content.

15.3.2.5 Divestitures

AT&T had divested its stake in Connecticut for $2018 in 2014. In the same year, AT&T sold of the remaining stake in America Movil for approximately $5885 million.

---

[5] http://www.wsj.com/articles/at-t-defends-directv-acquisition-even-as-pay-tv-subscriptions-fall-1439411700.

15.4   Corporate Governance at AT&T[6]

The corporate governance guidelines were adopted by the Board of Directors on the recommendation of the Corporate Governance and Nominating Committee. Under the AT&T Bylaws, the Board is entrusted with the responsibility to fix from time to time the size of the board. The size of the Board range from 11 to 14 members. The composition of the Board encompasses a broad range of skills, expertise, industry knowledge, and contacts relevant to AT&T's business. A substantial majority of directors of the Board are independent in accordance with the listing standards of the New York Stock Exchange. Directors are elected annually to one-year terms and retirement age is 72 years. No director is allowed to serve on more than four other boards of publicly traded companies except under exceptional situations approved by Corporate Governance and Nominating Committee. The lead director shall be selected by the nonmanagement directors from among the committee chairpersons to serve two-year terms. The nonmanagement directors will meet in executive session with no management directors or management personnel present which is no less frequently than quarterly. The Board appoints the following primary Committees: Audit Committee, Corporate Development and Finance Committee, Corporate Governance and Nominating Committee, Executive Committee, Human Resources Committee, and Public Policy and Corporate Reputation Committee. The Corporate Governance and Nominating Committee, the Audit Committee, and the Human Resources Committee is composed of at least three Directors who are independent in accordance with the listing standards of the New York Stock Exchange. Each Director who has served on the Board for at least five years should own shares of common stock (including deferred shares and stock units where the value is based on the price of the common stock) equal to at least five times the annual base retainer. The Audit Committee shall meet as often as it determines, but not less than six times a year. The Corporate Development and Finance Committee assist the Board in its oversight of the Company's finances, the payment by the Company of dividends, the Company's capital investment policies, and the Company's strategic planning. The Corporate Governance and Nominating Committee is appointed by the Board of Directors to identify individuals qualified to serve members as Board of Directors. The Executive Committee is appointed by the Board of Directors of AT&T Inc. to act on behalf of the Board in the intervals between meetings of the Board. The Human Resources Committee is appointed by the Board of Directors of AT&T Inc. to discharge the Board's responsibilities relating to compensation of the Company's executives and other compensation matters. The Public Policy and Corporate Reputation Committee assist the Board in its oversight of policies related to protecting the Company's reputation, including its public policy positions, social responsibility efforts, and the Company's brands. The Public Policy and Corporate Reputation Committee reviews the federal, state, and local lobbying expenditures on an annual basis. AT&T in appropriate circumstances would seek restitution of bonus, commission, or compensation received by any employee as a result of the

[6] http://www.att.com/gen/investor-relations?pid=5609.

employee's intentional or knowing fraudulent or illegal conduct. AT&T aims to follow highest standards of business ethics and support of global anti bribery initiatives. AT&T stipulates that all employees and suppliers acting on AT&T's behalf with government officials must follow the antibribery laws, regulations, and international conventions in countries where AT&T have business operations. FCPA due diligence process complies with FCPA laws. The prospective merger targets must be reviewed by AT&T for history of FCPA and antibribery compliance.

15.5   Citizenship and sustainability initiatives[7]

AT&T is creating initiatives to realize the goal of sustainable world by providing connecting cars and homes, smarter and more resilient energy grids and tools to reduce pollution. For supporting these initiatives, AT&T have invested approximately $140 billion in mobile and wired networks since 2009.

AT&T introduced the no texting while driving campaign It Can Wait in 2010 to educate millions of wireless users, employees, and general public about dangers of texting while driving. In 2014, AT&T had more than 1.4 million activations of the DriveMode mobile app. AT&T have focused on digital and social media through the voice of influencers and a new Twitter handle, @ItCanWait to attract teens toward the safe driving campaign. AT&T Smart Controls is an all-in-one online destination which offers customers access to helpful tips and tools for staying safe and connected. Smart Limits is a service that enables customers to provide their children with the freedom and security of a mobile phone, while setting sensible boundaries for the phone's use. AT&T FamilyMap is a convenient tool which assists customers to see the location of family members on an interactive map from their AT&T wireless phone, tablet, or computer. AT&T have partnered with institutions like Family Online Safety Institute, iKeepSafe, ConnectSafely, and the National Cyber Security Alliance to promote online safety education and awareness.

AT&T have financial partnership with iKeepSafe to develop a program, in conjunction with LULAC and Dialogue on Diversity, to enhance the Latino community's digital literacy. To address the gap in technology skills for older adults, AT&T have contributed $3 million per year to the Oasis Institute.

AT&T technology powers Hydropoint a solution which provides users the ability to track weather patterns and reduce water use. As a result of the implementation of the program, Hydropoint's customers were able to cut 15 billion gallons of water and 62 million KWh of electricity. AT&T have partnered with GE to develop smart energy solutions for developing more connected energy network. AT&T foundry for innovation have initiated more than 200 projects. AT&T surveys its suppliers annually using a supplier sustainability scorecard to monitor environmental issues like greenhouse gas emissions and social issues. AT&T is a signature education initiative focused on high school success and career goals. AT&T involve in initiatives

---

[7] http://about.att.com/csr.

such as ConnectED to bring Internet connectivity and educational resources to more students across America. AT&T have partnered with education technology provider Udacity to launch online Nanodegree programs to provide instruction in industry relevant skills. AT&T have invested more than $600 million in network disaster recovery program since 1992.

AT&T has contributed $1.1 million to Télécoms Sans Frontières, the world's leading emergency telecommunications organization since 2003. AT&T provides financial support and volunteer time for the AdvanceNet Labs Centers of Excellence—a workforce development program helping to provide today's youth with the skills they need to succeed in careers in technology AT&T has provided contributions worth $140,000 to Childnet International a UK-based children's charity which focuses on making Internet a safe place for kids since 2008. AT&T focuses on enhancing the participation of minority, women, and LGBT-owned business enterprises by purchasing their materials and services. The Prime Supplier Program is an important AT&T Supplier Diversity program in which the prime suppliers increase the use of diverse businesses in supply chain through subcontracting and value-added reseller arrangement. In 2014, AT&T had corporate spend of $16.5 billion for minority, women, and disabled veterans business enterprises. AT&T is a founding member of the 100,000 Jobs Mission, launched in 2011 by JPMorgan Chase and 10 other companies to commit to hiring 100,000 veterans by 2020.

15.6 Risk management

AT&T faces market risks basically from changes in interest rates and foreign currency exchange rates. AT&T manages market risk using interest rate swaps, interest rate locks, foreign currency exchange contracts, and cross currency swaps. AT&T do not use derivatives for trading or speculative purposes. Interest rate risk arises for AT&T due to the financial debt instruments like medium and long-term fixed rate notes and debentures. AT&T uses interest rate swaps to manage interest rate risks. AT&T have established interest rate risk limits to monitor interest rate sensitivities in the debt and interest rate derivative portfolios. The interest rate and foreign currency exchange risk with respect to interest and principal payments of foreign denominated long-term debt are hedged using cross currency swaps. AT&T enters into interest rate locks to partially hedge the risk of increases in the benchmark interest rate during the time of probable issuance of fixed rate debt. AT&T is exposed to foreign currency exchange risk through foreign affiliates and equity investments in foreign companies. AT&T employs sensitivity analysis to determine the effects of market risk exposures on the fair value of financial instruments and results of operations.

15.7 Financing activities

AT&T paid dividends of $10,200 million in 2015. The increase of dividends in 2015 was basically due to increase in shares outstanding due to acquisition of

DIRECTV. During 2015, AT&T received net proceeds of $33,969 million from the issuance of $34,129 million in long-term debt in various markets with average weighted maturity of approximately 12 years and a weighted average coupon of 27%. The debt issued included February 2015 issuance of $2619 of 4.6% global notes which are due in 2045. AT&T also have March 2015 borrowings under a variable rate term loan facility due in 2020 and variable rate 18-month credit agreement due in 2016, together totaling $11,155 million. In 2015, AT&T redeemed $10,042 million as repayment of various senior notes. In the same year AT&T entered into a five-year $12,000 million revolving credit agreement with Citibank NA. In 2015, AT&T entered into a $9155 million syndicated credit agreement which contains a $6286 million term loan facility (the Tranche A Facility) and a $2869 term loan facility (the Tranche B Facility) with banks like Mizuho Bank Ltd. AT&T had outstanding debt with estimated value of $26,221 million in 2015. These debts are denominated in currencies like Euro, British pound sterling, Canadian dollar, Swiss franc, and Brazilian real.

15.7.1 Investment activities

The cash used for investing activities in 2015 consisted of acquisition of spectrum licenses, capital expenditures, acquisitions of DIRECTV, GSF Telecom, Nextel Mexico. AT&T's capital expenditures are incurred on communications networks, video services, and support systems for digital entertainment services. AT&T investment securities include equities, fixed income bonds, and other securities. The alternate investments include investments in private equity, real estate, mezzanine and distressed debt, limited partnership interests, and fixed income securities.

15.7.2 Equity investments

AT&T have equity investments in SKY Mexico, Game Show Network, Otter Media Holdings, YP Holdings, Major League Baseball (MLB) Network, and NW Sports Net. AT&T hold a 41% interest in Sky Mexico which was acquired as a part of DIRECTV. The company also hold 42% stake in GSN which is a television network with focus on game-related programming and Internet interactive game. AT&T hold a 43.4% in Otter Media Holdings which was a joint venture between the Chernin Group and AT&T. Otter provides the top subscription video services. AT&T also holds a 47% stake in YP Holdings, an online advertising company and directory publisher. AT&T holds 16.7% stake in MLB and 39% stake in NW Sports. Both MLB and NW Sports acquisition were a part of the DIRECTV acquisitions.

15.8 Retirement and ownership plans

AT&T provide supplemental retirement plans to senior and middle management employees with nonqualified, unfunded supplement retirement and savings plans.

These plans have assets in a designated nonbankruptcy remote trust which are independently managed. In addition, these plans provide compensation deferral plans. AT&T also maintain contributory savings plan for all employees. These savings plan match in cash or company stock as stated percentage of eligible employee contributions which are subject to a specified ceiling. AT&T also have share-based payments. Under these plans, senior and other management employees and nonemployee directors can receive non invested stock and stock units. On account of acquisition of DIRECTV, the restricted stock units of DIRECTV were converted to AT&T shares which were vested for a period of 1−4 years. AT&T grant performance stock units which could be noninvested stock units based on the stock price at the date of grant and awarded in the form of AT&T common stock and cash at the end of a three-year period under the condition of achievement of certain performance goals.

15.9   Equity repurchase program

AT&T often repurchase shares of common stock for distribution through the employee benefit plans or in connection with certain acquisitions. In 2013, AT&T repurchased 300 million shares which were authorized by the Board in 2012. In 2013, the Board approved a second authorization involving repurchase of 300 million shares which were completed in 2014. The third authorization to repurchase up to 300 million shares of common stock was approved in 2014. By December 2015, AT&T have repurchased approximately 48 million shares and 8 million shares for distribution through the employee benefit plans in 2014 and 2015. These authorizations are implemented through open market repurchase programs.

There are 14 billion authorized common shares of AT&T stock and 10 million authorized preferred shares of AT&T stock. As of December 31, 2015 and 2014, no preferred shares were outstanding. As a part of the acquisition of DIRECTV, AT&T issued 954,407,524 shares to DIRECTV shareholders.

15.10   Stock split and dividends

Table 15.1 gives the stock split statistics of AT&T. AT&T pays quarterly dividends. The year 2016 dividends are forecasted based on two instalments of dividends paid in 2016. AT&T paid a dividend of $0.12 per share during 1984. By 2015, the dividend

Table 15.1 **Stock split**

Year	Split information
1987	3 for 1 common stock split
1993	2 for 1 common stock split
1998	2 for 1 common stock split

Table 15.2 **Dividend history—1984–2016**

Year	DPS	Year	DPS	Year	DPS
1984	0.12	1995	0.82	2006	1.33
1985	0.38	1996	0.85	2007	1.42
1986	0.52	1997	0.89	2008	1.60
1987	0.42	1998	0.92	2009	1.64
1988	0.61	1999	0.96	2010	1.68
1989	0.64	2000	1.01	2011	1.72
1990	0.68	2001	1.02	2012	1.76
1991	0.71	2002	1.07	2013	1.80
1992	0.73	2003	1.37	2014	1.84
1993	0.75	2004	1.25	2015	1.88
1994	0.78	2005	1.29	2016	1.92

paid per share increased to $1.88 per share. The average growth rate of dividend per share during the period 1984–2016 on the basis of year on year analysis was 13% (Table 15.2). The average growth rate of dividend per share during the period 2009–2016 period was 2%. In 2008, AT&T dividend per share increased by 13% compared to the previous year 2007.

15.11 Ownership structure

Equity constituted 49% and debt composed of 51% of the capital structure in 2016. With respect to equity ownership 56.15% were owned by institutions, while 25.44% were owned by funds and insiders owned 0.03% of the equity ownership. The number of institution owners were 2707 and the number of fund owners were 3043. The top five funds held 5.96% of the total shares (Table 15.3). The top 10 institutions held 22.88% of the total shares held by the company (Table 15.4).

The ownership statistics is based during the period June 2016. The source of data is Morningstar.com.

Table 15.3 **Equity ownership top mutual funds**

SL	Mutual funds	Shares held (%)
1	Vanguard Total Stock Mkt Idx	1.94
2	Vanguard 500 Index Inv	1.26
3	Vanguard Institutional Index I	1.11
4	SPDR S&P 500 ETF	0.99
5	VA CollegeAmerica Cap Inc Bldr 529E	0.66
	Total	5.96

Source: Morningstar.com.

Table 15.4 **Equity ownership—financial institutions**

SL	Institutions	Shares held (%)
1	Vanguard Group Inc.	6.08
2	State Street Corp	4.18
3	Evercore Trust Company, NA	3.31
4	BlackRock Fund Advisors	2.96
5	Capital Research Global Investors	1.51
6	Fidelity Management and Research Company	1.2
7	Northern Trust Investments NA	1.15
8	Dimensional Fund Advisors, Inc.	0.85
9	Geode Capital Management, LLC	0.84
10	State Street Global Advisors (Aus) Ltd	0.8
	Total	22.88

Source: Morningstar.com.

15.12 Segmental operational and financial highlights

The total wireless customers increased by 9% and 14% approximately during 2014 and 2015. The average increase in wireless customers during the period 2012–2015 was 7.5%. The number of video connections increased by 538% in 2015 (Table 15.5).

Table 15.5 **Operating data**

Year	2011	2012	2013	2014	2015
Total wireless customers (000)	103,247	106,957	110,376	120,554	137,324
Video connections (000)	3791	4536	5460	5943	37,934
In region network access lines in service (000)	34,054	29,279	24,639	19,896	16,670
Broadband connections (000)	16,427	16,390	16,425	16,028	15,778
Number of employees	256,420	241,810	243,360	243,620	281,450

Source: Annual Report 2015.

The revenues are given in millions of US dollars. The business solutions accounted for 49% of the total segment revenues while the Entertainment group and consumer mobility segments accounted for 24% each of the total revenues. The international segment accounted for 3% of the total revenues (Table 15.6).

The operating and support expenses incurred in 2015 are given in millions of dollars (Table 15.7). The business solutions and entertainment group accounted for 46 and 29% of the total operations and support expenses (Table 15.8). The consumer mobility and international segment accounted for 22 and 4% of the total segmental revenues.

Table 15.6 Segment revenues in 2015

Segment	Revenues
Business solutions	71,127
Entertainment group	35,294
Consumer mobility	35,066
International	4102
Segment total	145,589
Corporate and other	1297
Acquisition-related items	−85
Certain significant items	
Total	146,801

Source: Annual Report 2015.

Table 15.7 Operations and support expenses in 2015

Segment	Operations and support expenses
Business solutions	44,946
Entertainment group	28,345
Consumer mobility	21,477
International	3930
Segment total	98,698
Corporate and other	1057
Acquisition related items	1987
Certain significant items	−1742
Total	100,000

Source: Annual Report 2015.

Table 15.8 Business solutions—operating revenues

Year	2013	2014	2015
Wireless service	29,696	30,182	30,687
Fixed strategic services	8444	9666	10,910
Legacy voice and data services	21,669	19,857	18,019
Other service and equipment	3878	3860	3558
Wireless equipment	3960	7041	7953
Total segment operating revenues	67,647	70,606	71,127

Source: Annual Report 2015.

The values are given in thousands. The connected devices include data centric devices such as session-based tablets, monitoring devices, and automobile systems. The business wireless postpaid churn rate was 0.99% in 2015. The churn rate is calculated by dividing the aggregate number of wireless subscribers who cancelled service during a period divided by the total number of wireless subscribers at the beginning of that period. The churn rate for the period is equal to the average of the churn rate for each month of that period. The business IP Broadband connections in 2013, 2014, and 2015 were 631,000, 822,000, and 911,000, respectively (Table 15.9).

Table 15.9 Business solutions—key performance measures

Year	2013	2014	2015
Postpaid	40,811	45,160	48,290
Reseller	−1	11	85
Connected devices	16,326	19,943	25,284
Total business wireless subscribers	57,136	65,114	73,659

Source: Annual Report 2015.

The operating revenues are given in millions of dollars. The total entertainment group operating revenues increased from $21.542 billion in 2013 to $35.294 billion in 2015 (Table 15.10). The operating revenues from video entertainment increased by 196% in 2015 compared to the previous year. The operating revenues from high-speed Internet increased by 30% in 2014 compared to 2013. The operating revenues from legacy voice and data services is showing a declining trend over the three-year period 2013–2015.

Table 15.11 gives the statistics of the video connections. The figures are in thousands.

Table 15.10 Entertainment group-operating revenues

Year	2013	2014	2015
Video entertainment	5810	6826	20,271
High-speed Internet	4219	5522	6601
Legacy voice and data services	9667	7592	5914
Other service and equipment	1846	2293	2508
Total segment operating revenues	21542	22,233	35,294

Source: Annual Report 2015.

Table 15.11 Entertainment group—key performance measures (video connections)

Year	2013	2014	2015
Satellite			19,784
U verse	5257	5920	25,398
Total video connections	5257	5920	45,182

Source: Annual Report 2015.

Table 15.12 Entertainment group—key performance measures (broadband connections)

Year	2013	2014	2015
IP	9484	11,383	12,356
DSL	4829	3061	1930
Total broadband connections	14,313	14,444	14,286

Source: Annual Report 2015.

Table 15.12 gives the statistics of the broadband connections. The figures are in thousands.

Table 15.13 Entertainment group—key performance measures (consumer voice connections)

Year	2013	2014	2015
Retail consumer switched access lines	12,013	9243	7286
U verse consumer VoIP connections	3701	4759	5212
Total retail consumer voice connections	15,714	14,002	12,498

Source: Annual Report 2015.

Table 15.13 gives the statistics of the consumer voice connections. The figures are in thousands.

Table 15.14 Consumer mobility—operating revenues

Year	2013	2014	2015
Postpaid wireless	27,140	24,282	22,030
Prepaid wireless	2317	4205	4662
Other service revenue	2399	2363	2458
Equipment	4387	5919	5916
Total segment operating revenues	36,243	36,769	35,066

Source: Annual Report 2015.

The operating revenues of consumer mobility segment are highlighted in Table 15.14. The figures are given in thousands. The consumer mobility post-paid churn was 1.24% while the total consumer mobility churn was 1.95% on an average basis during the three-year period 2013–2015 (see Table 15.15).

The value of operating revenues accounted by international segment amounted to $4102 million (see Table 15.16).

15.13 Financial trend analysis

All the values are stated in millions of dollars. The revenues of AT&T increased from $63.055 billion in 2006 to $146.801 billion by 2015. The operating cash flow

Table 15.15 Consumer mobility—key measures of performance

Year	2013	2014	2015
Postpaid	31,827	30,610	28,814
Prepaid	5817	9965	11,548
Reseller	14,028	13,844	13,690
Connected devices	1567	1021	929
Total consumer mobility subscribers	53,239	55,440	54,981

Source: Annual Report 2015.

Table 15.16 International segment—operating revenues

Year	2015
Video entertainment	2150
Wireless	1647
Equipment	305
Total segment operating revenues	4102

Source: Annual Report 2015.

increased from $10.288 billion in 2006 to $24.785 billion by 2015. The net income increased from $7.356 billion in 2006 to $13.345 billion by 2015. The total cash increased from $2.418 billion in 2006 to $5.121 billion in 2015. The total cash includes cash, cash equivalents, and marketable securities. The total assets increased from $270.634 billion in 2006 to $402.672 billion by 2015. The long-term debts have been showing an increasing trend over the 10-year period (2006–2015) of analysis. The average growth rate of revenues, operating income, operating cash flow, free cash flow, and net income during the period 2007–2015 was approximately 12%, 30%, 14%, 17%, and 37%, respectively. The total cash increased by 31% on average basis during the period 2007–2015. The average increase in total assets during the nine-year period of analysis was 5%. The short-term and long-term debts increased by 5% and 11% on average basis during the period 2007–2015. The average increase in capital expenditure during the above period was 14%. The book value of equity and market capitalization increased by 2% and 1% on average basis during the period of analysis. The growth rate in earnings was highest in 2007. The revenues and operating income increased by 89% and 98% in 2007 compared to the previous year. The operating income registered the highest growth rate of 111% in 2015 compared to the previous year. The total cash increased by 112% in 2011 compared to the previous year. The total assets grew by 36% in 2015 (Table 15.17).

Table 15.17 Financial highlights

Year	2006	2007	2008	2009	2010	2011	2012	2013	2014	2015
Revenues	63,055	118,928	124,028	123,018	124,280	126,723	127,434	128,752	132,447	146,801
Operating income	10,288	20,404	23,063	21,492	19,573	9218	12,997	30,479	11,746	24,785
Operating cash flow	15,615	34,072	33,656	34,445	34,993	34,648	39,176	34,796	31,338	35,880
Free cash flow	7295	16,355	13,321	17,110	14,691	14,538	19,711	13,852	9905	15,865
Net income	7356	11,951	12,867	12,535	19,864	3944	7264	18,249	6224	13,345
Total cash	2418	1970	1792	3741	1,437	3045	4868	3,339	8603	5121
Total assets	270,634	275,644	265,245	268,312	269,391	270,442	272,315	277,787	296,834	402,672
Short-term debt	9733	10,431	17,968	11,531	7,196	3453	3486	5498	6056	7636
Long-term debt	50,063	57,255	60,872	64,720	58,971	61,300	66,358	69,290	75,778	118,515
Capital expenditure	8320	17,717	20,335	20,335	20,335	20,335	20,335	20,335	20,335	20,335
Year end market capitalization	223,035	251,170	167,951	165,431	173,668	179,218	188,149	183,757	174,228	211,447
Book value of equity	115,540	115,367	96,347	101,564	111,647	105,534	92,362	90,988	89,716	122,671

15.14   Ratio analysis

On average basis the profitability ratios have declined over the five-year period 2011−2015 compared to the five-year period 2006−2010 (Table 15.18). The average gross margin of 58.9% during the period 2006−2010 decreased to 56% during the period 2011−2015. Similarly, the operating margin and net margin decreased from 17.1% and 11.7% to 13.4% and 7.4%, respectively. The average ROA, ROE, and ROIC of 5%, 12.5%, and 8.8 % during the period 2006−2010 decreased to 10.1%, 7%, and 5%, respectively, during the period 2011−2015. The average ICR decreased from 6.4 to 5 during the two periods of comparison.

The per share ratio values are given in US dollars. The average EPS declined from $2.29 during the period 2006−2010 to $1.77 during the period 2011−2015. The average book value per share increased from $16.10 during the period 2006−2010 to $17.96 during the period 2011−2015. The free cash flow per share improved from $2.43 to $2.72 during the period of analysis. The EBITDA per share declined from $6.81 to $6.78 during the two periods of analysis (Table 15.19).

The average P/B ratio during the period 2006−2010 was 1.81. The average P/B ratio declined to 1.88 during the period 2011−2015. The average P/E ratio which was 15.27 during the period 2006−2010 increased to 25.37 during the period 2011−2015. The average P/S ratio declined from 1.69 to 1.41 during the two periods of comparison. The price to cash flow ratio have been fluctuating over the period of analysis (Table 15.20).

Table 15.21 provides the enterprise value multiple highlights. The average current ratio during the period 2006−2015 was 0.68. The average quick ratio during the period 2006−2015 was 0.49 (see Table 15.22).

The debt intensity of the company has been increasing over the period 2006−2015. The average debt equity ratio has increased from 0.55 during the period 2006−2010 to 0.78 during the period 2011−2015. The average long-term debt to total assets have increased from 0.22 to 0.25. The total debt per share have increased from 11.66 to 14.81 during the period of analysis (Table 15.23).

The fixed asset turnover ratio remained constant at 1.2 during the two periods of comparison. The average asset turnover ratio increased from 0.4 during 2006−2010 to 0.5 during the period 2011−2015. The average receivable turnover ratio increased from 7.3 to 9.6 during the two periods of comparison. The average days' payable has declined from 54.9 days to 38.4 days (Table 15.24).

15.15   Estimation of cost of capital

The cost of equity is estimated using CAPM.

Required   rate   of   return = Risk-free   rate + Beta × (Return   on   Market Index − Risk-free rate)

The risk-free rate is assumed as the average yield to maturity on the 30-year treasury bond during the two-year period 2014−2016.[8]

[8] https://www.treasury.gov/resource-center/data-chart-center/interest-rates/Pages/Historic-Yield-Data-Visualization.aspx.

Table 15.18 Profitability ratios

Year	2006	2007	2008	2009	2010	2011	2012	2013	2014	2015
Gross margin (%)	56.63	61.27	59.77	59.03	57.95	54.72	56.67	60.03	54.24	54.33
Operating margin (%)	16.32	17.16	18.59	17.47	15.75	7.27	10.2	23.67	8.87	16.88
Net margin (%)	11.67	10.05	10.37	10.19	15.98	3.11	5.7	14.17	4.7	9.09
Return on assets (%)	3.53	4.38	4.76	4.69	7.39	1.46	2.68	6.63	2.18	3.84
Return on equity (%)	8.64	10.35	12.16	12.65	18.6	3.63	7.34	19.91	7.02	12.77
Return on invested capital (%)	6.41	8.03	8.49	8.39	12.59	3.49	5.87	12.73	5.14	7.7
Interest coverage ratio	5.58	5.82	6.87	6.62	7.09	2.9	4.03	8.05	3.76	6.02

Table 15.19 Per share performance ratios

Year	2006	2007	2008	2009	2010	2011	2012	2013	2014	2015
Earnings per share	1.89	1.94	2.16	2.12	3.35	0.66	1.25	3.39	1.19	2.37
Book value per share	8.88	19.09	16.35	17.27	18.89	19.17	16.55	16.4	17.86	19.83
Free cash flow per share	1.89	2.65	2.24	2.89	2.47	2.53	3.39	2.92	2.16	2.61
EBITDA per share	5.82	7.02	7.25	7.11	6.84	4.81	5.5	9.31	6.1	8.2

Table 15.20 Market value multiples

Year	2006	2007	2008	2009	2010	2011	2012	2013	2014	2015
P/B	1.93	2.18	1.74	1.63	1.56	1.7	2.04	2.02	1.94	1.72
P/E	19.04	21.6	13.26	13.66	8.81	46.38	27.88	10.22	27.76	14.6
P/S	2.2	2.15	1.37	1.35	1.4	1.42	1.55	1.48	1.32	1.29
P/OCF	8.9	7.46	5.03	4.82	4.98	5.18	5.03	5.46	5.6	5.3

Table 15.21 Enterprise value multiples

Year	2006	2007	2008	2009	2010	2011	2012	2013	2014	2015
EV/Revenues	4.45	2.66	1.98	1.94	1.92	1.9	1.99	1.99	1.87	2.27
EV/EBITDA	12.39	7.32	5.63	5.75	5.88	8.42	7.91	5.07	7.74	7.13
EV/EBIT	22.04	14.6	10.36	10.89	11.24	23.53	18.26	7.99	17.99	13.47

Table 15.22 Liquidity ratios

Year	2006	2007	2008	2009	2010	2011	2012	2013	2014	2015
Current ratio	0.63	0.63	0.53	0.66	0.59	0.75	0.71	0.66	0.86	0.75
Quick ratio	0.46	0.46	0.42	0.51	0.44	0.55	0.55	0.46	0.62	0.45

Table 15.23 Financial leverage ratios

Year	2006	2007	2008	2009	2010	2011	2012	2013	2014	2015
Debt/Equity	0.43	0.5	0.63	0.64	0.53	0.58	0.72	0.76	0.88	0.97
Long-term debt to total assets	0.19	0.21	0.23	0.24	0.22	0.23	0.24	0.25	0.26	0.29
Total debt per share	9.59	11.2	13.38	12.92	11.19	10.93	12.51	14.31	15.78	20.53

Table 15.24 Efficiency ratios

Year	2006	2007	2008	2009	2010	2011	2012	2013	2014	2015
Fixed assets turnover	0.82	1.25	1.27	1.24	1.22	1.21	1.18	1.17	1.18	1.24
Asset turnover	0.3	0.44	0.46	0.46	0.46	0.47	0.47	0.47	0.46	0.42
Receivables turnover	4.94	7.35	7.69	7.93	8.69	9.31	9.7	10.07	9.65	9.45
Days payable	92.34	55.94	50.63	0	51.54	0	79.83	81.99	90.23	114.58
Days sales outstanding	93.74	49.67	47.22	44.05	39.97	38.11	36.25	36.62	40.03	41.1

Year	Yield to maturity on 30-year treasury bond
2014	3.55
2015	2.63
2016	2.63
Average	2.94%

The risk-free rate is estimated as 2.94%. Beta is estimated by regressing the daily returns of AT&T on the daily returns on market index S&P 500 during the two-year period May 2014–May 2016. The beta value was estimated as 0.61. The annual market returns are estimated on the basis of the average daily returns of market index S&P 500 during the two-year period May 2014–May 2016. The market return = 8.94%.

Cost of equity = 2.94% + 0.61 × (8.94%−2.94%)
= 6.6%

The yield to maturity of the long-term bond which matures on 15/5/2046 is assumed as the cost of debt. The yield to maturity on this long-term bond was 4.72%.[9] The price of this bond on 12/6/2016 was 100.5

The pretax income in 2015 was $20,692 million and the tax expenses amounted to $7005 million. Hence the effective tax rate was 33.85%

After tax cost of debt = 4.72 × (1 − 0.3385) = 3.12%

Market value weights

Market value of equity in 2015 = $211,447 million

Book value of debt in 2015 = Short-term debt + Long-term debt = 7636 + 118,515 = $126,151 million

Market value of debt = (Book value of debt) × (Ratio of price of the long-term bond to the face value of bond)

Ratio = 100.50/100 = 1.005

Market value of debt = 126,151 × 1.005 = $126,781.8 million

Market value of equity = = $211,447 million

Total value of the firm = 126,781.8 + 211,447 = $338,228.8 million

Weight of equity (We) = 211,447/338,228.8 = 0.63

Weight of debt (Wd) = 126,781.8/338,228.8 = 0.37

WACC = We × Cost of equity + Wd × After tax cost of debt
= 0.63 × 6.6 + 0.37 × 3.12 = 5.3%

Weighted Average Cost of Capital (WACC) of AT&T is estimated as 5.3%

15.16   Valuation perspectives

15.16.1   Estimation of economic value of AT&T

Economic value is estimated as net operating income after taxes(NOPAT)−Capital charge
Profit before interest and tax (PBIT) − Income tax = NOPAT
Capital employed = Stock holder equity + Long-term debt

[9] http://quicktake.morningstar.com/StockNet/bonds.aspx?Symbol=T&Country=USA.

Capital charge = Capital employed × WACC
Economic value (EV) = NOPAT − Capital charge
Estimation of economic value (EV) in 2015
PBIT in 2015 = $24,785 million
Income tax in 2015 = $7005 million
NOPAT = 24,785 − 7005 = $17,780 million
Stock holder equity = $122,671 million
Long-term debt = $118,515 million
Capital employed = $241,186 million
WACC = 5.3%
Capital charge = 241,186 × 0.053 = $12,782.86 million
Economic value = 17,780 − 12,782.86 = $4997 million

The economic value for AT&T is estimated as $4997 million

15.16.2 Equity spread

Equity spread is a variation of the EV measures. Equity spread is the difference between the ROE and the required return on equity (cost of equity)

Equity spread = (Return on equity − Cost of equity) × Equity capital
Return on equity in 2015 = 12.77%
Cost of equity = 6.6%
Equity spread = (12.77% − 6.6%) × 122,671 million = $7568.801 million

The value of equity spread for AT&T is calculated as $7568.801 million in 2015

15.16.3 FCFE valuation model

Net Capital Expenditures = Capital Expenditures − Depreciation AND amortization
   Adjusted net capital expenditure = Net capital expenditures + Net acquisitions
(see Table 15.25)

Table 15.25 Adjusted capital expenditure in millions of dollars

Year	2010	2011	2012	2013	2014	2015
Capital expenditures	20,302	20,110	19,465	20,944	21,433	20,015
Depreciation and amortization	19,379	18,377	18,143	18,395	18,273	22,016
Net capital expenditures	923	1733	1322	2549	3160	−2001
Net acquisitions	2906	2368	828	4113	4982	30,676
Adjusted net capital expenditures	3829	4101	2150	6662	8142	28,675

Noncash current assets = Total current assets − Cash and cash equivalents
   Noninterest bearing current liabilities = Total current liabilities − Short-term debt

Table 15.26 Non-cash working capital in millions of dollars

Year	2010	2011	2012	2013	2014	2015
Total current assets	20,854	22,985	22,706	23,196	33,606	35,992
Cash and cash equivalents	1437	3045	4868	3339	8603	5121
Noncash current assets	19,417	19,940	17,838	19,857	25,003	30,871
Total current liabilities	34,854	30,892	31,787	34,995	37,282	47,816
Short-term debt	7196	3453	3486	5498	6056	7636
Noninterest bearing current liabilities	27,658	27,439	28,301	29,497	31,226	40,180
Noncash working capital	−8241	−7499	−10,463	−9640	−6223	−9309
Change in noncash working capital		742	−2964	823	3417	−3086

Noncash working capital = Noncash current Assets − Noninterest bearing current liabilities (see Table 15.26)

The values except rates are given in millions of dollars.

Reinvestment = Adjusted net capital expenditure + Change in noncash working capital−Net debt issued

Table 15.27 Estimation of reinvestment rate

Year	2010	2011	2012	2013	2014	2015
Adjusted net capital expenditure	3829	4101	2150	6662	8142	28,675
Change in noncash working capital	0	742	−2964	823	3417	−3086
Net debt issued	5467	362	4753	9138	5633	23,927
Reinvestment		4481	−5567	−1653	5926	1662
Net income	19,864	3944	7264	18,249	6224	13,345
Reinvestment rate		1.14	−0.77	−0.09	0.95	0.12

Reinvestment rate = Reinvestment/Net income

The reinvestment rate has been hugely fluctuating over the five-year period 2011−2015. The average reinvestment rate based on arithmetic mean was 27% (see Table 15.27).

The average FCFE during the five-year period 2011−2015 is estimated as $8835 million (see Table 15.28).

Table 15.28 **Estimation of FCFE in million dollars**

Year	2011	2012	2013	2014	2015
Net income	3944	7264	18,249	6224	13,345
Adjusted net capital expenditure	4101	2150	6662	8142	28,675
Change in noncash working capital	742	−2964	823	3417	−3086
New debt issued	7,936	13,486	18,312	16,033	33,969
Debt Repayment	7574	8733	9174	10,400	10,042
FCFE	−537	12,831	19,902	298	11,683

FCFE = Net income-Adjusted net capital expenditure − Change in noncash working capital + New debt issued−Debt repaid

The average growth rate estimated from fundamentals during the period 2011−2015 is 1% (see Table 15.29)

Table 15.29 **Estimation of growth rate from fundamentals**

Year	2011	2012	2013	2014	2015
Reinvestment rate	1.14	−0.77	−0.09	0.95	0.12
Return on equity	0.036	0.073	0.199	0.070	0.128
Growth rate	0.041	−0.056	−0.018	0.067	0.016

The growth rate of US GDP during the period 2013−2014 is 2.3%[10]

Growth rate in stable period = 2.3%

Constant growth stage FCFE model

It is assumed that the net income will grow at the stable growth rate of US economy which is 2.3%

Net income in 2015 = $13,345 million

Net income in stable period = 13,345 × 1.023 = $13,651.94 million

Reinvestment rate = 27%

Reinvestment = 0.27 × 13,651.94 = $3686.02 million

FCFF = 13,651.94 − 3686.02 = $9965.91 million

FCFF in stable period = $$9965.91million

Cost of equity = 6.6%

Value of operating assets = FCFF in stable period/(Cost of equity − Growth rate in stable period)

= 9965.91/(6.6% − 2.3%) = $231,765.4081 million

Value of equity = Value of operating assets + Total cash in 2015

= 231,765.4081 + 5121 = $236,886.41 million

[10] http://data.worldbank.org/indicator/NY.GDP.MKTP.KD.ZG.

Number of shares in 2015 = 5646 million
Value of equity = $236.886 billion
Value per share = $41.96
The 52-week range for AT&T during May/June 2016 was $30.97 − $40.43. The market capitalization for AT&T on June 12, 2015, was $248.3 billion.

15.16.4   FCFF valuation model

Reinvestment = Adjusted net capital expenditure + Change in noncash working capital
Reinvestment rate = Reinvestment/EBIT(1-T) where EBIT(1-T) is the after tax operating income (Table 15.30).

Table 15.30 Estimation of reinvestment rate

Year	2011	2012	2013	2014	2015
EBIT	9218	12,997	30,479	11,746	24,785
Taxes	2532	2900	9224	3442	7005
EBIT(1-T)	6686	10,097	21,255	8304	17,780
Adjusted net capex	4101	2150	6662	8142	28,675
Change in noncash WC	742	−2964	823	3417	−3086
Reinvestment	4,843	−814	7485	11,559	25,589
Reinvestment rate	0.72	−0.08	0.35	1.39	1.44

The average reinvestment rate during the period 2011−2015 was 66%.

Table 15.31 Estimation of growth rate from fundamentals

Year	2011	2012	2013	2014	2015
Reinvestment rate	0.72	−0.08	0.35	1.39	1.44
Return on capital employed	0.0349	0.0587	0.1273	0.0514	0.077
Growth rate	0.0253	−0.0047	0.0448	0.0715	0.1108

Growth rate from fundamentals = Reinvestment rate × Return on capital employed
The average growth rate during the period 2011−2015 based on geometric mean was estimated as 5% (Table 15.31).

Table 15.32 FCFF in millions of dollars

Year	2011	2012	2013	2014	2015
EBIT(1-T)	6686	10,097	21,255	8304	17,780
Adjusted net capex	4101	2150	6662	8142	28,675
Change in noncash working capital	742	−2964	823	3417	−3086
FCFF	1843	10,911	13,770	−3255	−7809

Free cash flow to firm (FCFF) = EBIT(1-T) − Adjusted net capex-change in noncash working capital

The average FCFF during the period 2011−2015 was $3092 million (see Table 15.32)

Two-stage FCFF model

Two-stage FCFF model is used to value AT&T in this section

It is assumed that the earnings of the firm will grow at 5% for five years (based on fundamentals) and thereafter at 2.3% (average US GDP growth rate)

First-stage growth inputs

First-stage growth period = 5 years

Growth rate in first-stage growth period = 5%

WACC = 5.3%

Reinvestment rate − 66%

Current EBIT(1-T) in the 2015 = $17,780 million

EBIT(1-T) in the first year of estimation = $17,780 × 1.05 = $18,669 million

The present value of FCFF in the first stage = $29,968.64 million (see Table 15.33)

Table 15.33 Present value of FCFF in the first stage

Year	1	2	3	4	5
EBIT(1-T)	18,669	19,602	20,583	21,612	22,692
Reinvestment	12,321.5	12,937.6	13,584.5	14,263.7	14,976.9
FCFF	6347.5	6664.8	6998.1	7348.0	7715.4
PV of FCFF	$6027.98	$6010.80	$5993.68	$5976.60	$5959.58
Sum	$29,968.64				

Stable stage inputs

The average growth rate of US GDP is assumed as the growth rate in the stable period

Growth rate = 2.3%

Growth rate = Reinvestment rate × Return on capital employed (ROCE) of the communication services industry

ROCE of communication services industry = 8.56%[11]

Reinvestment rate = 2.3/8.56 = 0.2687

The reinvestment rate in stable period = 26.87%

---

[11] http://csimarket.com/Industry/industry_ManagementEffectiveness.php?ind=905.

WACC = 5.3%
EBIT(1-T) at the end of five-year estimation period = $22692 million.
EBIT(1-T) at the beginning of the stable period = 22,692 × 1.023 = $23,214.2 million
Reinvestment = 23,214.2 × 0.2687 = $6237.7 million
FCFF in stable period = 23214.2-6237.7 = $16976.6 million
Terminal Value of FCFF = FCFF in stable period/(WACC − growth rate)
  = 16,976.6/(0.053 − 0.023) = $565,885.029 million
Present value of terminal value = $437,105.58 million
Value of operating assets of AT&T = = $29,968.64 + $437,105.58 = $467,074.22 million
Value of AT&T = Value of operating assets + Total cash
Value of AT&T = 467,074.22 + 5121 = $472,195.22
Value of equity = Value of AT&T − Value of debt in 2015
  = 472,195.22 − 126,151 = $346,044.22 million
Number of shares in 2015 = 5646 million
Value per share = 346,044.22/5646 = $61.29

Summary of Discounted Cash Flow Valuation

Constant growth stage FCFE model
Value of equity = $236.886 billion
Value per share = $41.96
Two stage FCFF model
Value of equity = $346,044.22 million
Value per share = $61.29
The 52-week range for AT&T during May/June 2016 was $30.97 − $40.43.
The market capitalization for AT&T on June 12, 2015, was $248.3 billion.

15.16.5 Peer comparison and relative valuation

The financial highlights for AT&T and Verizon Communication are given in millions of dollars. The financial highlights of China Mobile are given in millions of CNY and that of NTTDOCOMO are given in millions of Japanese Yen (Tables 15.34).

The price multiples are based on the period June 2016. AT&T have the lowest P/S ratio and P/B ratio among the peer companies. AT&T have the highest dividend yield among the competitor firms. The source of data is Morningstar (Table 15.35).

The price multiples comparison is based on the period June 2016. The source of data is Morningstar.com. AT&T's dividend yield is higher than that of the industry average and S&P 500 (Table 15.36).

The price multiples are fluctuating over the 10-year period (2006−2015). The average P/E, P/B, P/S, and P/CF are 19.09, 2.04, 1.56, and 5.74, respectively, during the 10-year period of analysis (Table 15.37).

Table 15.34 **Financial highlights peer comparison**

Company	AT&T	Verizon communication	China mobile	NTTDOCOMO
Total asset	402,672	24,4640	1,427,895	7,146,340
Total debt	126,151	110,194	4995	222,651
Capital expenditures	20,015	27,717	172,455	596,500
Revenues	146,801	131,620	668,335	4,383,397
Operating income	24,785	33,060	102,922	639,671
Cash flow	46,828	49,177	281,295	1,304,467
Total cash	5121	4820	99,009	349,310
Net income	13,345	17,879	108,539	520,691
Market capitalization	211,447	214,698	232,888	101,853

Table 15.35 **Price multiples**

Company	P/S	P/B	P/E	Dividend yield (%)
AT&T	1.5	2	17.1	4.7
Verizon	1.6	11.5	12	4.3
China mobile	2.3	1.7	14.1	3.1
NTTDOCOMO	2.4	2	20.6	1

Table 15.36 **Price multiple comparison with S&P 500 and industry average**

Ratios	AT&T	Industry average	S&P 500
P/E	17.1	19.4	19.4
P/B	2	2	2.7
P/S	1.5	1.4	1.9
P/CF	6.4		12
Dividend yield (%)	4.7	3.5	2.4

Table 15.37 **Price multiple trends—AT&T**

Year	2006	2007	2008	2009	2010	2011	2012	2013	2014	2015
P/E	19.2	21.5	13.2	13.2	9.1	15.4	27	25.8	10.3	36.2
P/B	4	2.2	1.7	1.6	1.6	1.6	2	2.1	1.9	1.7
P/S	2.3	2.2	1.4	1.3	1.4	1.4	1.5	1.5	1.3	1.3
P/CF	9	7.5	5	4.8	5	4.9	5	5.2	5.3	5.7

Table 15.38 **Enterprise value multiples**

Company	AT&T	Verizon	China mobile	NTTDOCOMO
Revenues	146,801	131,620	668,335	4,383,397
EBITDA	46,828	49,177	281,295	1,304,467
EBIT	24,785	33,060	102,922	639,671
Debt	126,151	110,194	4995	222,651
Market value of equity	211,447	214,698	232,888	101,853
Cash and cash equivalents	5121	4820	99,009	349,310
Enterprise value (EV)	332,477	320,072	138,874	−24,806
EV/REVENUES	2.26	2.43	0.21	−0.01
EV/EBITDA	7.10	6.51	0.49	−0.02
EV/EBIT	13.41	9.68	1.35	−0.04

The financial variables of AT&T and Verizon are given in millions of dollars while that of China Mobile is given in millions of CNY and that of NTTDOCOMO is given in millions of JPY. The enterprise value multiples are estimated based on 2015 variable values.

Enterprise value = Market value of equity + Debt − Cash and cash equivalents.

Lower the enterprise value multiples, the more undervalued and attractive a stock becomes for investment (Table 15.38).

Table 15.39 **Growth rate comparison of revenues**

In Percent	AT&T	Verizon	China mobile	NTTDOCOMO
Year on year	10.84	3.57	4.19	1.56
5-year average	3.39	4.31	6.61	1.73
10-year average	12.84	5.77	10.64	0.24

The source of data was Morningstar.com. The basis of estimation was 2015. AT&T had the highest growth rate in revenues among the peer companies in 2015 compared to the previous year. AT&T also had the highest 10-year average growth rate of revenues compared to the other competitor firms (Table 15.39).

The source of data was Morningstar.com. The analysis was with respect to 2015. AT&T had the highest growth rate of 111.01% in operating income in 2015 compared to the previous year. AT&T had the highest 10-year average growth rate in operating income compared to the peer firms (Table 15.40).

Table 15.40 Growth rate comparison of operating income

In percent	AT&T	Verizon	China mobile	NTTDOCOMO
Year on year	111.01	68.68	− 12.28	− 10.64
5-year average	4.84	17.69	− 7.35	− 0.6
10-year average	14.92	8.36	3.4	− 1.12

15.16.6 Performance indicators

15.16.6.1 Piotroski score

The Piotroski score is a discrete score between 0 and 9 which is an indicator of the firm's financial position. The score was named after the Chicago accounting Professor Joseph Piotroski. The cumulative points suggest whether the stock is a value stock or not. If the company achieves a score of 8 or 9, the stock can be considered strong. If the score ranges between 0 and 2, then the stock is considered weak.

Criteria for Piotroski Score

SL	Profitability scores	Score points	Score for AT&T
1	Positive return on assets in current year	1	1
2	Positive operating cash flow in current year	1	1
3	Higher ROA in current year compared to previous year	1	1
4	Return on cash flow from operations greater than ROA	1	1
	Leverage, liquidity, and sources of funds		
5	Lower ratio of long-term debt to average total assets in current year compared to previous year	1	0
6	Higher current ratio in this year compared to previous year	1	0
7	No new shares were issued in the last year	1	1
	Operational efficiency ratios		
8	A higher gross margin compared to the previous year	1	1
9	A higher asset turnover ratio compared to the previous year	1	0
Total		9	6

The analysis is based on 2015. The stock has a cumulative point of 6 out of 9.

15.16.6.2 Graham number

It is a conservative method used for valuing a stock. It is a figure which measures a stock's fundamental value by taking into account the company's earnings per share and book value per share. Graham number is the upper bound of the price range which a defensive investor should pay for the stock. According to Graham number theory, any stock price below the Graham number is considered undervalued and hence worth investing in. Graham number is a combination of asset valuation and earnings power valuation.

EPS in 2015 = $2.37

Book value per share in 2015 = $19.83

Grahamnumber $= \sqrt{22.5 \times (\text{Earning per share}) \times (\text{Book value per share})} = 32.52$

The closing price of AT&T in NYSE was $40.34 on 13/6/2016.

15.17   Stock wealth analysis

Table 15.41 compares the cumulative returns of AT&T Inc., S&P 500 Index, and S&P 500 Integrated Telecom Index over each of the five-year period. The comparison above assumes $100 invested on December 31, 2010, in AT&T common stock, S&P 500, and Standard & Poor's 500 Integrated Telecom Index (S&P 500 Integrated Telecom). Total return equals stock price appreciation plus reinvestment of dividends.

Table 15.41 Comparison of five-year cumulative total return

Year	2011	2012	2013	2014	2015
AT&T	109	128	141	142	153
S&P 500 Integrated Telecom Index	108	124	138	141	145
S&P 500 Index	102	118	157	178	181

Source: Annual Report 2015.

15.17.1   Stock return analysis

AT&T was trading at $1.15 in NYSE on 19/7/1984. The adjusted closing price of AT&T was $40.33 on 1/6/2016. The stock price increased by 35 times during these two periods. The return analysis during the period July 1984−June 2016 reveals that the cumulative returns generated by AT&T was 433.50%. The analysis involved 384 months during the 32-year period. During the same period the cumulative returns generated by S&P 500 amounted to 301.07%. Suppose an investor invested $1000 in AT&T stock on 19/7/1984. If the stock was held till 1/6/2016, the investor would have received an amount of $35,069.57. On the basis of cumulative returns, an investor who invested an amount of $1000 in 1984 would see his investment grow to $5335 by 2016. The assumption made in this case is that the investor involves in active buying and selling every month during the 32-year period.

AT&T stock have outperformed the market index S&P 500 during the entire period of 383 months of analysis (Fig. 15.1).

Excess return is estimated as the difference between AT&T and S&P 500 index average yearly returns. The excess return amounted to 8.7 % in 2015. AT&T had

Figure 15.1 Cumulative Returns of AT&T and S&P 500 Index.

Table 15.42 **Average yearly returns in percent**

Year	AT&T	S&P 500	Excess return
2011	9.6	1.1	8.4
2012	17.3	13.2	4.1
2013	10.2	26.5	−16.3
2014	1.5	11.1	−9.6
2015	8.8	0.1	8.7

the highest average yearly returns of 17.3% in 2012. S&P 500 index outperformed the AT&T stock during the period 2013 and 2014, respectively (see Table 15.42).

The holding period is assumed to be one year. The holding period yield was highest in 2012 based on five years of analysis. The annual holding period yield during the five-year period 2011−2015 was 10.02% (Table 15.43).

Table 15.43 **Holding period yield**

Year	Holding period yield
2011	14.72
2012	19.05
2013	4.96
2014	4.82
2015	8.98

Table 15.44 **Excess value created**

Year	2011	2012	2013	2014	2015
Market value of equity	179,218	188,149	183,757	174,228	211,447
Book value of equity	105,534	92,362	90,988	89,716	122,671
BV as percent of MV	58.89	49.09	49.52	51.49	58.02
Excess value	73,684	95,787	92,769	84,512	88,776

The market value, book value, and excess value are stated in millions of dollars. The average book value as percent of market value was 53.4 during the period 2011−2015. The book value as percent of market value was 49 in 2012. The highest excess value found out as the difference between market value and book value of equity was registered in 2012 (Table 15.44).

*The detailed calculation for all analysis is given in the excel file **AT&T.xlsx**.*

Wealth creation by Boeing

16

16.1 Introduction

Boeing is the largest aerospace company in the world which manufactures commercial jetliners, defense, space and security systems. In 2016, Boeing completes one century flying in the sky. The products and services offered by Boeing include commercial and military aircraft, satellites, electronic and defense systems, launch systems, advanced information and communication systems. Boeing has headquarters in Chicago. The company employs about 160,000 people in United States and other 65 countries. Boeing is one of the largest defense contractor in the world. Boeing is also the largest exporter in the United States by dollar value for about decade. Boeing stock is a component of the Dow Jones Industrial Average. Boeing was ranked 27th on the Fortune magazine "Fortune 500" list in the year 2015. Boeing had returned $30 billion to shareholders since 2010.[1] Boeing Commercial Airplanes had reported revenues of $66 billion in the year 2015. According to Boeing statistics, the company holds record unit backlog of approximately 5800 airplanes with value of $432 billion. Boeing provides products and service support to customers in more than 150 countries. Approximately 70% of commercial airplane revenues are accounted from customers outside the United States. The revenues in the year 2015 amounted to $96 billion. Boeing has manufacturing, service, and technology partnership with firms throughout the world. Boeing has contracts with more than 20,000 suppliers and partners globally. Boeing offers a family of airplanes and wide portfolio of aviation services for passenger and cargo carriers. About half of the world's fleet are Boeing airplanes with more than 10,000 jetliners in service. The Defense Space and Security division designs, builds, and supports net enabled platforms and systems for government and commercial customers.

16.1.1 Boeing history—milestones

Year	Events
1910	William Boeing buys Heath's shipyard in Seattle which was converted into the first airplane factory. The first airplane flight is made over Seattle
1916	Final assembly of the B&W seaplane. William Boeing takes Bluebill, the first B&W on its maiden flight. Pacific Aero Products Co. is incorporated for $100,000. Boeing purchases 998 of the issued 1000 stocks. Boeing Airplane established in year 2016
1917	Pacific Aero Products changed into Boeing Airplane Co.

---

[1] Boeing Annual Report 2015.

Strategic Financial Management Casebook.

Year	Events
1918	U.S. Navy orders 50 of the seaplane trainers. Boeing Airplane Co. signs contract with Navy for value of $116,000 to build 50 HS-2Ls. The Martin MB-1 bomber, the first US designed and built bomber, enters production stage
1919	The first Boeing designed commercial aircraft makes its first flight.
1920	Boeing BB-1 and Boeing BB-L6 make its first flight
1921	The first airplane to lift a useful load which exceeded its own weight named the Cloudster makes its maiden flight. Boeing Airplane gets a contract to build 200 Thomas Morse MB-3A pursuit fighters. Boeing Airplane Co. armored Army ground-attack biplane (GA-2) makes its first flight
1923	The Boeing NB-1, a two-seat seaplane trainer, makes its first flight
1926	The Boeing Airplane Co. receives an order from the Army for 25 PW-9C fighters
1928	Boeing Air Transport acquires 73% of Pacific Air Transport's stock. The Boeing Model 80, a 12-passenger trimotor biplane transport, makes its first flight
1929	The Boeing P-12 fighter makes its first flight
1930	The first Boeing commercial monoplane makes its first flight
1933	North American Aviation (NAA) buys General Aviation Manufacturing Corp. NAA reorganizes, disposes of interests in TWA, Douglas Aircraft and Western Air Express, and becomes an aircraft manufacturing company
1935	The Douglas A-17/8A Nomad attack bomber, designed by Northrop's El Segundo team, makes its first flight. The Douglas Sleeper Transport (DST) makes its first flight
1936	The Boeing Airplane Co. signs a contract with Pan American Airways to build six Model 314 Clippers
1940	Boeing delivers its first Model 307 Stratoliners to Pan American Airways
1941	The Boeing-built Douglas DB-7B attack bomber makes its first flight
1942	The Boeing XPBB-1 Sea Ranger which is a long-range seaplane patrol bomber makes its maiden flight
1944	The Boeing Model 345 (B-29) bomber makes its maiden flight. The Boeing C-97 Stratofreighter prototype, Model 367, makes its first flight in Seattle
1945	The Boeing B-29 Enola Gay drops an atomic bomb on Hiroshima, Japan. Three days later, the B-29 Bockscar bombs Nagasaki, Japan
1946	Boeing signs a contract to design the B-52, a long-range heavy bomber
1949	The Boeing B-47 covers 2289 miles in 3 hours, 46 minutes, at an average speed of 607.8 mph which is a transcontinental speed record
1951	The first Boeing B-52 bomber is rolled out at the Seattle plant
1952	The Douglas A3D (A-3) Skywarrior, the biggest and heaviest aircraft, makes its first flight
1953	The Boeing B-47E jet bomber makes its first flight at Wichita, KS.
1955	20 Boeing Model 707 jet transports are ordered by Pan American World Airways
1956	The last Boeing-produced B-47 is delivered to the Air Force from Wichita Eight Boeing B-52s complete a record nonstop flight of 17,000 miles over the North Pole
1958	The U.S. Air Force orders three Boeing 707-120s for use by the president and other high-ranking officials. The Air Force selects Boeing to assemble and test the Minuteman intercontinental ballistic missile (ICBM)
1959	American Airlines starts service from New York to Los Angeles for the first transcontinental jetliner route using Boeing 707. Boeing starts developing the manned orbiting craft called Dyna-Soar

Year	Events
1960	Boeing acquires the Vertol Aircraft Corp. of Philadelphia and its subsidiaries to form Vertol Division of Boeing
1963	A Boeing 727 completes a 76,000-mile world tour to 26 countries
1964	Boeing and Lockheed are selected to design the supersonic transport program
1965	The first Boeing-built Saturn S-1C first-stage rocket booster rolled out. Boeing receives the largest commercial order at that time when United Air Lines orders 66 jetliners with options for 39 more and leasing of another 25
1966	Boeing plans to build a 490-passenger 747 transport. The Boeing Company celebrates its 50th anniversary. The first Boeing-built Lunar Orbiter is launched. Boeing wins the contract to design, develop, and test the short-range attack missile (SRAM)
1967	The Model 737 makes its first flight. The 1000th Boeing Minuteman missile is installed in its silo. First unmanned Saturn V is launched from Kennedy Space Center, Florida. The Saturn V and the Apollo modules were built by the combined resources of Boeing, McDonnell Douglas and North American
1969	The Boeing 747-100 makes its first flight
1970	The Boeing 747 makes its first commercial flight from New York to London for Pan American Airlines. Boeing becomes the prime contractor for the airborne warning and control system (AWACS)
1971	The federal government cancels funding for the Boeing SST. The first Boeing Lunar Roving Vehicle is used by astronauts on the moon
1972	The first Boeing AWACS plane, a modified 707-320B, makes its first flight
1973	Boeing-built Mariner 10 is launched on its flight to photograph and collect data from Venus and Mercury
1974	NASA awards Boeing a contract to build some components of Hubble Space Telescope which was launched in 1990. Boeing Marine Systems launches its first commercial JETFOIL
1976	The Boeing YC-14 military STOL transport makes its first flight
1977	A modified Boeing 747 is delivered for use as a delivery vehicle for the Space Shuttle
1978	NASA launches the Boeing Applications Explorer Mission 1 (AEM-1). Boeing begins production of the 757 and 767
1979	The Boeing Chinook CH-47D makes its first flight.
1981	The Boeing 767-200 makes its first flight.
1982	Boeing designs a solar power satellite system with a capacity to provide power to 1 million homes. The Boeing 757-200 makes its first flight. NASA launches the first Boeing IUS which places two communication satellites in orbit
1985	Boeing begins preliminary designs for the International Space Station
1988	The simultaneous rollout of the Boeing 737-400 and the 747-400 takes place. The first Boeing 767-300ER is delivered to American Airlines
1990	The Boeing 737 becomes the world's best-selling jetliner. The 6000th Boeing jetliner, a 767, is delivered to Britannia Airways. A new Air Force One, a modified Boeing 747-200B, is delivered to the Air Force for the President of United States
1993	The Boeing 747-400 freighter rolls out
1994	The Boeing 777 twinjet, the newest member of the Boeing jet family rolled out
1995	NASA and Boeing officials enter into a $5.63 billion contract to design and develop the International Space Station. The Boeing 767 Freighter makes its first flight

Year	Events
1997	Boeing offers 767-400ERX for sale to airlines. The first Next-Generation Boeing 737, a 737-700, makes its first flight
	The Boeing Company, along with its North American component, merges with McDonnell Douglas Corp.
1999	First flight of the 757-300 and 737-600 takes place
2000	Boeing announces plans to acquire Hughes' space and communications business for $3.75 billion in cash
	The first 737-900 rolls out. The net orders for Boeing commercial jetliners crosses above the 15,000 mark
2001	Boeing wins a $235 million contract to produce 11,054 JDAM kits for the U.S. Air Force
	Boeing Satellite Systems completes the launch of its 200th commercial communications satellite
2002	Boeing delivers the 1000th 757
2003	China Airlines orders 10 Boeing 747-400s. Boeing announces the decision to cease production of the 757 jetliner in late 2004
2005	People's Republic of China announces plans to purchase 60 Boeing 787 Dreamliners
	Boeing and Lockheed Martin Corp. form the United Launch Alliance for the launches of Boeing Delta and Lockheed Martin Atlas rockets
2006	Boeing gets its largest satellite contract in 9 years for three satellites. The 5000th 737 comes off the production line. The 737 becomes the most-produced large commercial jet airplane in aviation history with the production of the 5000th 737 jetliner. Emirates orders 10 747-8 Freighters. The first production CH-47F Chinook helicopter successfully completes its first flight
	Boeing sets total of 1044 net orders
2007	Boeing receives NASA contract valued at approximately $514.7 million to produce the upper stage of the Ares I crew launch vehicle. Boeing had 1413 net commercial airplane orders in 2007
2008	Boeing delivers its 1400th 747, a 747-400 Freighter to GE Commercial Aviation Services. The first Boeing 777 Freighter makes its first flight
	The Missile Defense Agency awards Boeing a $250 million contract to maintain ground-based midcourse defenses against long-range ballistic missiles
	Boeing acquires Insitu Inc., a pioneer in the unmanned air systems market
	Boeing delivers its 200,000th JDAM tail kit
2009	Boeing delivers the Emirates' 78th 777. The Dubai-based Emirates Airlines becomes the world's largest operator of the 777
	Boeing delivers its 25,000th Combat Survivor Evader Locator Search and Rescue Communications System to the U.S. joint services
	The first 787 Dreamliner makes its first flight from Paine Field in Everett
2010	The Boeing 747-8—the third generation of the legendary 747 jetliner family—makes its first flight
	Phantom Eye—the first unmanned liquid hydrogen-powered high-altitude long endurance demonstrator aircraft introduced
	ScanEagle Compressed Carriage unmanned airborne system makes its first flight
	Boeing launches InFlight Optimization Services, which helps airline customers save fuel in real time with its Direct Routes and Wind Updates services, which provide up-to-the-minute information to flight crews and airlines enabling adjustments en route
	The Boeing P-8I team begins fabricating the first part for the Indian Navy's first long-range maritime reconnaissance and antisubmarine warfare aircraft

Year   Events
2011   The new 747-8 Intercontinental unveiled
        The 747-8 Intercontinental successfully completes its first flight. The Space Shuttle
        makes its final launch
        Boeing signs a deal with Ministry of Defense, India to acquire 10 Boeing C-17
        Globemaster III airlifters
        Boeing and Dubai-based Emirates Airline announce an order for 50 777-300ERs
        (Extended Range) plus options for an additional 20. The order, with a value of
        $18 billion, makes this the single largest commercial airplane order in Boeing's
        history to date. The 787 Dreamliner establishes two new world records
        completing the longest flight for an airplane in its weight class
        Boeing and Southwest airlines announce a firm order for 150 737 MAX airplanes
2012   The first Boeing 787 Dreamliner to be assembled in South Carolina rolls out of final
        assembly in North Charleston
2013   Acalis develops microprocessors that provide onboard security for Boeing aerospace
        and defense platforms
        The 787-9 Dreamliner makes its first flight
        Boeing and the U.S. Air Force complete the first unmanned QF-16 flight
        Etihad Airways announces an order for 30 787-10 Dreamliners. 787 Dreamliners
        reaches 1000 sales faster than any other wide body airplane in aviation history
2014   Boeing announces the launch of the Boeing Business Jet (BBJ) MAX family of
        airplanes
        Boeing surpasses the 2000th order for the 737 MAX. The 737 MAX reaches 2000
        orders faster than any other Boeing airplane to date
        Boeing delivers to Lufthansa airlines the 1500th 747 to come off the production line
        Boeing and Qatar Airways finalize an order for 50 777-9Xs, valued at $18.9 billion
        at list prices. This is the largest product launch in commercial jetliner history to
        date
        Boeing receives its first commercial order for the 502 Phoenix small satellite
Source: http://www.boeing.com/history/.

16.2   Business segments

There are two main business segments within Boeing-Commercial Airplanes and
Defense, Space and Security (BDS). The supporting segments are Boeing Capital
Corporation, Shared Services Group, and Boeing Engineering and Operations &
Technology. Boeing Capital Corporation is the global provider of financing solutions; Shared Services Group provides a broad range of services to Boeing worldwide; Boeing Engineering, Operations & Technology helps to develop, acquire,
apply, and protect innovative technologies and processes.

16.2.1   Commercial airplanes

Boeing had been the major manufacturer of commercial jetliners for many years.
Boeing manufactures the families of airplanes such as the 737, 747, 767, 777,
and 787 along with the Boeing Business Jet range. The new product

development offerings include the Boeing 787-10 Dreamliner, the 737 MAX, and the 777X. Boeing has built over 10,000 commercial jetliners which are in operation globally. Approximately 90% of the world's cargo is carried onboard through Boeing aircraft. Commercial Aviation Services business offers full range of customer support, aftermarket parts, engineering modifications, logistics and information services to customers globally. The services offered also include the maintenance, repair, and overhaul facilities for passenger and cargo airlines.

16.2.2   Defense, Space & Security

Boeing is the world's largest manufacturer of military aircraft. Boeing is the world's largest provider of commercial and military satellites and service provider to NASA. The Defense, Space & Security segment provides leading solutions for the design, production, modification, and support of military-based wing aircraft, rotorcraft, weapons, and satellite systems. The segment also offers a set of portfolio like 702 family of satellites, AH-64 Apache helicopter, cybersecurity, EA-18G electronic attack aircraft, and KC-46 aerial refueling aircraft.

Boeing's Space and Communications group offers an array of advanced technology products in four major markets: launch services, information and communications, human space flight and exploration, and missile defense and space control. Boeing is NASA's leading contractor, the lead integrator for the 16-nation International Space Station, the builder of the Delta family of launch vehicles, and the lead systems integrator for the National Missile Defense program. Boeing also designs and builds advanced Rocketdyne rocket propulsion systems and global positioning system satellites known as GPS IIF. Boeing is a partner in Sea Launch, the four-nation joint venture that launches satellites from a floating platform in the Pacific near the equator.

16.2.2.1   Boeing military aircraft segment

This aircraft segment engages in the research, development, production, and modification of manned and unmanned military aircraft and weapons systems. The products include fighter aircraft and missile systems which consist of rotorcraft and tilt rotor aircraft, autonomous systems, mobility surveillance, battle management, airborne, antisubmarine, transport, and tanker aircraft. The major programs in the military aircraft segment consist of EA-18G Growler Airborne Electronic Attack, F/A-28E/F Super Hornet, F-15 Strike Eagle, CH-47 Chinook, AH-64 Apache and V-22 Osprey, KC-46A Tanker, etc.

16.2.2.2   Network & Space Systems

This segment is involved in the research, development, production, and modification of products and related services such as electronics and information solutions. These include command, control, communications, computers, intelligence, surveillance and reconnaissance, cyber and information solutions, intelligence systems, strategic missile and defense systems, satellites and commercial satellite launch vehicles and space exploration. The major programs in this segment include strategic missile and defense system-based Ground-based Midcourse Defense (GMD), commercial, civil and military satellites for space and intelligence systems, Space exploration-based Space Launch System (SLS), Commercial crew and International Space Station.

16.2.2.3 Global Services & Support segment

This segment provides full range of services for aircraft and systems. The segment provides integrated logistics, supply chain management, engineering support, maintenance, modification, and upgrades for aircraft, training systems, pilot, and maintenance training. Integrated logistics addresses the complete life cycle of aircraft and systems. Aircraft modernization and sustainment is carried out at different global centers. Major programs include C-17 Globemaster III Integrated Sustainment Program, Airborne Early Warning and Control, and Airborne Early Warning and Control Systems (AWACS).

16.2.3 Boeing Capital Corporation

Boeing Capital Corporation is the financing arm which provides financing solution to Boeing customers. By end-2015, Boeing Capital Corporation had a portfolio value of $3.4 billion. BCC's portfolio includes equipments under the category of operating leases, finance leases, notes and other receivables, assets held for sale or re lease and investments. The gross customer financing and investment portfolio amounted to $3459 million during the year 2015.

16.2.4 Shared services

The shared services support Boeing's global operations. The services offered include maintenance and protection of Boeing's worldwide sites, managing the sale and acquisition of all leased and owned property, purchase of nonproduction equipment and supplies, recruitment and management of finances, etc. Global Services & Support provides training, maintenance, and other services to government customers worldwide.

16.3 Strategy of growth[2]

Boeing has a leadership position in the aerospace market. The company focuses on the expansion of its product line through innovation. Boeing focusses on the creation of efficient commercial aircraft, design and integration of military platforms

---

[2] http://www.boeing.com/; Annual Report 2015.

and defense systems, adoption of advanced technology solutions and innovative customer financing options. The strategy of Boeing is focused on its healthy core businesses of Commercial Airplanes and Defense, Space & Security (BDS) which is supplemented by Boeing Capital. BDS through its integration of resources in defense, intelligence, communications, security, space, and services focusses on the delivery of solutions to customers at reduced cost. The BDS strategy is to leverage the core businesses to capture key next-generation programs and expand the presence in international markets. This strategic focus helps Boeing to offset the cyclicality of commercial and defense markets. Boeing facilitates, arranges, and provides selective financing solutions to the Boeing customers.

The commercial airplane market offers substantial growth opportunity for Boeing as fleet expansions and replacement demand will drive the need for approximately 38,0000 airplanes worldwide over the next 20 years. The expected demand along with the record unit backlog would provide opportunities for earnings growth for Boeing in the future ahead. The combination of range and fuel efficiency has enabled Boeing's 787 to have more than 90 new nonstop routes between cities soon. The demand for twinaisle airplane, the 777X, which has a backlog of 306 orders from 6 customers is expected to be ready for delivery by the year 2020. Boeing also has a backlog of more than 200 current model 777s. Boeing has introduced fastened automation technology on the 777 program to reduce cost and flow time in assembly. In the highly competitive single aisle market, the 737 family have a total program at year end-2015 of nearly 4400 planes. The commercial airplane output of Boeing is expected to grow approximately by 30% over the next 5 years since 2015.

Boeing forecasts that approximately 48% of the global traffic would come from the Asia Pacific region. It is estimated that about 9540 narrow body and 3570 wide body planes are required for the next 20 years. Boeing predicts that the majority of the requirement would be for single aisle jets. Hence there exist enough potential for single aisle jets like the BA 737 and 737 Max families. Market liberalization in Europe and Asia is enabling low-cost airlines to continue gaining market share. These airlines are increasing the pressure on airfares. The reengineered 737 MAX is estimated to be 14% more fuel efficient than competing jets. Hence airlines could offer lower fares to passengers. In the wide body segment, the focus of Boeing's strategy is on its 787 Dreamliner, 777, and 777X aircraft.

The Boeing Defense, Space & Security had registered revenues which totaled $30.4 billion in the year 2015. In the year 2015, the division delivered 186 aircraft along with 15,787 weapon systems and four satellites. The international customers accounted for 40% of current backlog and one-third of revenues in the year 2015. The major milestones achieved in defense-related projects in the year 2015 include NASA's completion of the critical design review of the Space Launch System which includes core rocket stage and avionics system and 12 successful launches by the United Launch Alliance joint venture. The portfolio of products and services, disciplined investments in innovations, leverage of enterprise capabilities and technologies for future programs like the T-X trainer, JSTARS recapitalization and unmanned systems are the major strengths of the defense and space business segments.

Industry projections indicate that the space and communications market will grow primarily driven by growth in commercial and government information and communications systems and services. Boeing is focusing its growth in space and communications in areas that include classified government program opportunities, new space-based air traffic management systems, the movement of broadband information on and off mobile platforms, and integrated military battlefield and defense systems. Boeing has extensive customer support services network which spans the life cycle of the airplane which includes aircraft acquisition, service, maintenance and engineering, upgradation and transition to next model.

Boeing faces intense competition from competitors like Airbus, Embraer, and Bombardier. Boeing is focused on improving its processes and cost reduction efforts. Boeing Defense and Security system faces competition from Lockheed Martin Corporation, Northrop Grumann, Raytheon Company, and General Dynamics Corporation. Other competitors include BAE Systems.

16.4   Regulations

Boeing deals with various U.S. government agencies, U.S. military, NASA, Federal Aviation Administration, and Department of Homeland Security. The Boeing businesses are heavily regulated in most of the markets in which they operate. The commercial aircraft products are required to comply with FAA regulations governing production and quality systems, airworthiness and installation approvals and operational safety. The international sales are subject to U.S. and non-U.S. governmental regulations and procurement policies and practices, regulations related to import/export control, exchange control, and repatriation of earnings.

16.5   Mergers and acquisitions

Boeing has become the world's leading aerospace company through a series of strategic mergers and acquisitions. Boeing 7 series family of airplanes are the market leaders in the industry. Commercial Aviation Services support carriers worldwide (Table 16.1).

16.5.1   Acquisition of defense assets of Rockwell

In 1996, Boeing and Rockwell International Corporation entered into a definitive agreement under which Boeing acquired the aerospace and defense businesses of Rockwell International Corporation for $3.2 billion. Boeing issued approximately $860 million of its common stock and retained $2.165 billion of Rockwell debt and certain retiree obligations of Rockwell. Rockwell transferred its businesses like Automation, Avionics, Communications, Semiconductor systems, Automotive Components systems to a new company with the same name Rockwell. The new

Table 16.1 **Boeing—Combination of pioneering companies**

Boeing Airplane Co. established in 1916
Douglas Aircraft Co. established in 1921
Stearman Aircraft Co. established in 1927
North American Aviation established in 1935
Piasecki Helicopter established in 1940
McDonnell Aircraft established in 1945
Hughes Space and Communications established in 1948
McDonnell Douglas established in 1967
Rockwell International established in 1968

Rockwell company became virtually debt free and positioned to make investments in its remaining businesses. The acquired units became a wholly owned subsidiary of the Boeing Company with the name Boeing North American Inc. The major product groups of the acquired divisions were the ICBM systems, tactical missiles, sensors, B-1B bomber commercial aero structures, aircraft and helicopter modifications, rocket propulsion, global positioning system satellites, etc. The Boeing Defense & Space Group virtually has all of the company's business with the U.S. Department of Defense, NASA, and international defense customers. The acquisition strengthened Boeing's position as a prime contractor and enhanced the strategic capabilities in the space systems which included space transportation, satellite and space station programs. The acquisition cemented the strategic aim of Boeing for the fusion between space technology and consumer air travel.

16.5.2 Merger of McDonnell Douglas with Boeing

McDonnell Douglas, the major American aerospace manufacturing corporation and defense contractor, was formed by the merger of McDonnell Aircraft and Douglas Aircraft company in the year 1967. McDonnell Aircraft produced well-known commercial aircraft and military aircraft such as the DC-10 airliner and F-15 Eagle air superiority fighter. In 1996, the two aerospace giants Boeing and McDonnell Douglas Corp announced plans to merge in a $13.3 billion stock for stock transaction. At the time of merger, the new combined firm named Boeing surpassed Lockheed Martin as the US largest defense contractor with estimated annual revenues of $48 billion and combined backlog of $120 million.[3] The merger united the world's largest commercial jet manufacturer with a military aircraft powerhouse. On the day of announcement of the deal, McDonnell's shares gained 20% while Boeing's share rose by 4.5%. The Seattle-based Boeing and St. Louis-based McDonnell Douglas together accounted for more than 60% of the world market for large commercial jetliners and range of military planes like the U.S. Navy's F/A-18, US Air Force's F-15 fighter. The major defense segment competitor

[3] http://www1.american.edu/ted/hpages/aero/BAMD.HTM.

Lockheed Corporation had in the same year merged with Martin Marietta Corporation and Loral Corporation.

The merger with McDonnell brought much need capacity for Boeing to compete with Airbus Industrie. The merger with McDonnell also bolstered Boeing's defense business as it was a strategy to diversify risks and counterbalance the boom and bust cycles of its commercial jet lines. McDonnell Douglas had faced series of setbacks in both commercial and defense lines. In the period of merger, Boeing along with Lockheed Martin were selected to develop new generation of fighter jet for all three services of US defense system. The combination of Boeing and McDonnell created competitive pressures for the Airbus Industrie consortium which was the world's second biggest maker of commercial airliners. The McDonnell's headquarters and fighter jet factories were transformed into a Boeing unit termed the McDonnell Defense Systems Group which boosted Boeing's bid for the development of next-generation light fighter. The Douglas Aircraft commercial jet unit became a division of Boeing's airline division. The space products division of the combined company merged to focus on the development of rockets and international space station.[4]

Under the terms of merger agreement, Boeing offered $63 a share to be paid out in Boeing stock for each McDonnell share. The deal amounted to a premium of approximately 17% above the closing price of $52 a share for McDonnell on the New York Stock Exchange on the day of merger announcement. CS First Boston was the adviser for Boeing and JP Morgan & Co was McDonnell Douglas's advisor for the deal.

16.5.3   Acquisition of Hughes Electronics

In the year 2000, Boeing announced plans to purchase Hughes Electronics Corp for $3.75 billion in an all cash transaction. The acquisition was aimed to strengthen Boeing's position as the leader in integrated space-based information and communications. The acquisition provided the opportunity for Boeing to expand growth opportunities in classified government programs, space-based air traffic management, and broadband delivery systems for mobile platforms. The deal made Boeing the world's largest producer of commercial communication satellites while transforming Hughes electronics into an entertainment and communications company through its DirecTV satellite television operation. On account of lower profit margins in satellite manufacturing services than in communication services, the acquisition resulted in a scenario whereby Hughes could make more focused investment in DirecTV and in its planned Spaceway system to provide internet services from satellites. Fast-growing DirecTV delivered scores of digital television channels to home dish antennas to about 8 million customers in the year 1999. Hughes was also a key provider of communications services for businesses. Hughes owned 81% of PanAmSat, one of the largest operator of communications satellites in the United States. The acquisition of Hughes operation was aimed at expanding the Boeing's

---

[4] http://www.wsj.com/articles/SB850664260619716000.

space and communication division by approximately 30%. The acquisition enabled Boeing to develop satellite communications services for the delivery of internet or video to airplanes or ships. At the time of deal, Hughes was the world's technological leader in space-based communications, reconnaissance, surveillance, and imaging systems. It was also the world's leading manufacturer of communication satellites. Under the terms of the definitive agreement, Boeing also acquired Hughes Electron Dynamics which was a leading supplier of electronic components for satellites and Spectrolab which was a provider of solar cells and panels for satellites. The acquired business unit became part of the Boeing Space and Communications group and was named Boeing Satellite Systems.

16.5.4 Other acquisitions

In 1960, Boeing acquired the Vertol Aircraft Corporation of Philadelphia and its subsidiaries to form the Vertol division of Boeing. The twin-rotor CH-47 Chinook, produced by Vertol, took its first flight in 1961. In 2000, Boeing acquired Jeppesen Sanderson Inc. the world's leading provider of flight information services for $1.5 billion cash. Jeppesen acquisition was a part of Boeing's growth strategy to enter into aviation services. Jeppesen became the wholly owned subsidiary of Boeing reporting to the Commercial Aviation Services business unit of Boeing Commercial Airplanes Group (BCAG). Jeppesen provides full range of print and electronic flight information services which includes navigation data, computerized flight planning, aviation software products, aviation weather services, pilot training systems and supplies. Jeppesen's NavData Services uses sophisticated databases to develop many products like the Flight Information Master Database which contains more than 1 million records. The flight information analysts at Jeppesen edit and verify an average of approximately 30,000 pieces of information each month which are compiled from more than 180 agencies worldwide.[5] This database is widely recognized by airlines, corporate flight departments, and major avionics manufacturers.

In July 2008, Boeing Company entered into an agreement to acquire Insitu Inc., a pioneer in the unmanned air system (UAS) and leader in the design, development, and manufacture of low-cost UAS which are used for intelligence, surveillance, and reconnaissance. Boeing and Insitu have partnered to develop the ScanEagle UAS program which had more than 100,000 operational flight hours with the U.S. Department of Defense and international customers. The acquisition was aimed to increase Boeing's presence in the unmanned systems market. In 2009, Boeing acquired the business and operations conducted by Vought Aircraft Industries at its South Carolina facility and initiated building of key structures for the 787 Dreamliner. In the same year, Boeing had acquired Alenia North America's half of Global Aeronautic LLC which was a fuselage subassembly facility for Boeing's 787 Dreamliner. Alenia North America is the subsidiary of

---

[5] http://boeing.mediaroom.com/2000-10-05-Boeing-Concludes-Purchase-of-Jeppesen-Sanderson-Inc.

Italy's Alenia Aeronautica. In 2011, Boeing entered into an agreement to acquire Solution Made Simple Inc (SMSi) which is an information services provider for the US government and the Intelligence community. In 2012, Boeing entered into an agreement to acquire Inmedius which was a provider of software applications and services for managing and sharing information and learning content. Inmedius was integrated into Boeing subsidiary Continental Data Graphics in support of Boeing's Digital airline strategy. The acquisition gave Boeing an expanded portfolio of technical services and solutions for aerospace, defense, and manufacturing markets. The acquisition of Inmedius solutions was aimed to bring efficiencies to technical content management across commercial and defense programs. This acquisition contributed to Boeing's Digital Airline strategy of facilitating customers use information, airplane technology, and industry first solutions. In 2013, Boeing acquired the CPU Technology Inc.'s Acalis business. The Acalis microprocessors contain unique hardware and software which can guard mission critical onboard systems in Boeing platforms. The acquisition of Acalis enabled Boeing to pursue its strategy of increasing Boeing's vertical depth to enhance its differentiation with respect to its offerings and provide long-term value for its global aerospace and defense customers. In 2014, Boeing announced an agreement to acquire ETS Aviation, which provides fuel efficiency management and analytics software based in Bristol, UK.

16.6   Strategic collaborations

In May 2005, Boeing Company and Lockheed Martin established a joint venture termed United Launch Alliance to combine the production, engineering, test, and launch operations of U.S. government launches of Boeing Delta and Lockheed Martin. The alliance was structured as a 50–50 joint venture between Boeing and Lockheed Martin by combining services which were earlier provided separately by Boeing Integrated Defense Systems Expendable Launch Systems division and Lockheed Martin's Space Systems company. The annual savings on account of the joint venture were estimated to be approximately $100–$150 million. Under the terms of the agreement, Boeing's Delta and Lockheed Martin's Atlas rockets would continue to be available as alternatives on individual launch missions. Upon vehicle selection, the United Launch Alliance team will carry out the mission which included vehicle integration and payload processing. Morgan Stanley served as the financial advisor to Boeing and JP Morgan served as the financial advisor to Lockheed Martin.

In 2012, Boeing and SELEX Sistemi Integrati entered into a collaborative agreement for the European air traffic modernization program titled Single European Sky ATM Research (SESAR). SELEX Sistemi Integrati is a leading industry supplier of air traffic management and airport systems. The focus area of collaboration is research in flight data modeling and data link communication for all phases of flight and system-wide information management.

Largest defense deals in the 1990s

In March 1993, Lockheed Corporation acquired General Dynamics Corp's military aircraft business for $1.52 billion. In April 1993, Martin Marietta Corp acquired the aerospace assets of General Electric for $3.05 billion. In December 1993, Loral Corp acquired the Federal Systems Division of IBM for $1.57 billion. During the period May 1994, Northrop Corp acquired Grumman Corp for $2.17 billion. In December 1994, Martin Marietta Corp merges with Lockheed Corporation for a value of approximately $10 billion. In 1996, Raytheon Co. acquires E-Systems for $2.3 billion. During March 1996, Northrop Grumman Corp acquires the defense electronic assets of Westinghouse Electric Corp for $3.2 billion. In April 1996, Lockheed acquired the bulk of the assets of Loral Corp in a deal valued at approximately $9 billion. In December 1996, Boeing acquired the defense businesses of Rockwell International Corporation for $3.2 billion. In the same year, Boeing and McDonnell Douglas Corporation announced plans to merge based on a transaction value of $13.3 billion.

16.7   Corporate Governance[6]

The Governance, Organization and Nominating ("GON") Committee periodically evaluates and makes recommendations to the Board regarding the appropriate size of the Board. The Board has stipulated that presently the Board's optimum size is between 10 and 14 members. At least 75% of the Board has to satisfy the New York Stock Exchange criteria for independence. The Board's oversight responsibilities include evaluating succession plan for the CEO and senior management, review of long-range strategic plans and approving policies of corporate conduct. A director may not serve on the boards of more than four other public companies or, if the director is an active CEO or equivalent of another public company, on the boards of more than two other public companies. If the Chairman is not an independent director, the independent directors shall designate from among them a Lead Director. The lead director serves as liaison between the Chairman and the independent directors. The Board have established the standing committees like Audit, Compensation, Finance, GON, and Special programs. The GON Committee oversees an annual self-evaluation of the Board to determine the performance of the board. The Board has also established stock (including stock equivalents) ownership requirements for senior executives. The ownership requirements should be attained within 5 years of becoming a senior executive and are based on a multiple of base salary. The total number of shares of stock of all classes which the Corporation shall have authority to issue is 1,220,000,000 shares, of which 20,000,000 shares shall

---

[6] http://www.boeing.com/company/general-info/corporate-governance.page.

be Preferred Stock of the par value of $1 each (hereinafter called "Preferred Stock") and 1,200,000,000 shares shall be Common Stock of the par value of $5 each (hereinafter called "Common Stock").

16.8   Risk management

The commercial airline business of Boeing depends on commercial airlines and hence the company faces unique risks. The demand for Boeing aircraft depends on airline profitability, availability of aircraft financing, availability of aircraft financing, world trade policies, technological factors, fuel prices, factors like terrorism and environmental regulations. The airline industry is cyclic and faces significant profit swings and cost competitive. Boeing has firm-fixed price aircraft sales contracts with indexed price escalation clauses which are subject to losses if Boeing incurs cost overruns or if increases in its cost exceed the applicable escalation rates. The commercial aircraft sales are basically entered years before the aircraft are delivered. The changes in the escalation factors significantly impact the revenues and operating margins of the commercial airplane business of Boeing. The commercial aircraft business being extremely complex requires extensive coordination and integration with U.S. and non-U.S. suppliers and stringent regulatory requirements. The introduction of new aircraft programs involves risks with respect to development, testing, production, and certification schedules. Boeing focusses on planned production rate and productivity improvement targets to maintain profitability. Operational issues such as delays or defects in supplier components, failure to meet internal performance plans, or delays to achieve regulatory certifications can result in increased production costs or delayed deliveries. Boeing derives substantial portion of revenues from the defense-related programs of the U.S. government. Changes in the level of U.S. government defense spending could negatively impact the financial position and results of operations. The sales to the U.S. government are subject to the extensive procurement regulations and the changes to regulations will increase Boeing's cost. For the defense and space businesses, Boeing enters into fixed price contracts. The contracts of Boeing in the commercial satellite industry and some government-related satellite contracts include in-orbit incentive payments. Contracts in the commercial satellite industry and certain government satellite contracts include in-orbit incentive payments. These in-orbit payments may be paid over time after final satellite acceptance or paid in full prior to final satellite acceptance. In both cases, the in-orbit incentive payment is at risk if the satellite does not perform to specifications for up to 15 years after acceptance.[7]

In the year 2015, non-U.S. customers accounted for approximately 59% of the revenues. Changes in domestic and international governmental policies, fluctuations in international currency exchange rates also contribute to significant risks for Boeing's businesses. The fixed rate debt obligations of Boeing are subject to

[7] Boeing Annual Report 2015, Page 26.

interest rate risk along with customer financing assets and liabilities. Boeing Capital uses interest rate swaps with certain debt obligations to manage exposure to interest rate changes. Boeing also faces currency exchange rate risk due to receipts from customers and payments to suppliers in foreign currencies. Boeing uses forward contracts to hedge price risk associated with foreign-denominated payments and receipts. The firm uses fair value hedges to manage market risks.

16.9   Research and development

Research and development expenditure is involved in experimentation, design, development, and test activities for defense systems, new and derivative jet aircraft which includes both commercial and military, advanced space and company-sponsored product development. The total research and development expense amounted to $3.1 billion, $3 billion, and $3.3 billion in the years 2013, 2014, and 2015, respectively. There are 11 research and development centers, plus 17 consortia and 72 joint research centers established by Boeing around the world. Boeing holds 15,600 plus active patents throughout the world.

16.10   Citizenship initiatives[8]

Boeing's primary areas of contribution are in the sectors of Education, Environment, Military, and Veteran support. Boeing had 183 humanitarian delivery flights, in partnership with more than 50 airline customers since 1992. In the year 2015, nearly 28,000 pounds of relief supplies were delivered to global communities. Approximately 53% of the Boeing's charitable contributions were devoted towards education programs and organizations. In 2015, Boeing contributed $190 million to charities. About $39 million was donated by employees through giving programs which included the Employees Community Fund which was one of the largest employee-owned funds in the world. About 11,000 military service veterans are employed by Boeing. Approximately 15% of the workforce of Boeing still serve the National Guard and Reserve. About 11,055 community partners worldwide engage with Boeing annually through the charitable programs. About 500 Boeing employees provided mentorship to more than 7500 students in FIRST teams in 2015 to promote interest in engineering and science. About 85,000 teachers and students in China engaged in engineering through the Soaring with Your Dream Program of Boeing in the year 2015.

Boeing engineers have associated with several leading educational partners to co-create K-12 learning resources for students and teachers to prepare the next generation of innovators with the critical skills. Boeing engineers also volunteered to develop resources alongside Boeing nonprofit partners like Iridescent and Teaching

[8] Corporate Citizenship Report 2015.

Channel. Boeing has partnered with the Ounce of Prevention organization for developing solutions to provide children with early childhood learning and development skills. Boeing has partnered with "New Leaders" for leadership development of teachers, principals, and principal supervisors. Boeing provides support for MIND Research Institute for the development of instructional consulting for mathematical learning experiences.

Approximately 54 Boeing locations across 5 countries have been ISO 14001 Certified. About 170,000 native plants have been installed through Boeing's Lower Duwamish Waterway restoration project. About 6.5 million plus acres of land worldwide are being preserved with the help of Boeing and its environmental partner organizations. In the jet age, Boeing has focused on improving the efficiency of its products. The airplanes of Boeing are 70% more fuel efficient and have 90% smaller noise footprint than the first phase jets. Boeing has achieved 40% reduction in operational noise footprint in 737 MAX family of airplanes. Boeing aims for 20% reduction in fuel consumption and carbon dioxide emissions in new airplanes.

Boeing and aviation industry partners are involved in biofuel development which have the scope to reduce carbon dioxide emissions by 50−80% compared with conventional petroleum fuel. Boeing, RSB, South African Airways, SKYNRG, and Sunchem Holdings are involved in a project titled "Project Solaris" to develop aviation biofuel supply chain in South Africa using an energy-rich tobacco plant called Solaris. In 2010, Boeing initiated an environmental cleanup and habitat restoration project in Seattle. Boeing, Masdar Institute of Science and Technology, Etihad Airways, and Honeywell's UOP have established a research institution in Abu Dhabi to use saltwater agricultural systems for the development and commercialization of plant-based aviation biofuels and other products. Boeing has also begun the construction of 2.3-acre salmon habitat in Seattle. In 2013, Carbon Disclosure Project, an international nonprofit environmental organization, named Boeing as one of the leading companies for initiating actions to improve environmental performance and report climate change strategy. In 2014, The US Environmental Protection Agency awarded Boeing with Climate Leadership Award for the recognition of its efforts to reduce greenhouse gas emissions.

In 2015, Boeing awarded subcontracts worth $5 billion plus to small and diverse businesses. Approximately $50 billion was paid by Boeing to more than 14,800 businesses in the year 2015. Boeing also supports aircraft maintenance training programs to address youth training and employment needs. Boeing has partnered with higher education institutions since the year 1917. Every year, Boeing provides about 17,000 internships to US and international university students. Boeing conducts 25 plus sponsored competitions for creating solutions for designing and engineering challenges for university students around the world. Boeing and Carnegie Mellon university have established Aerospace Data Analytics Lab to use artificial intelligence and big data to capitalize on the amount of data generated in the design, construction, and operation of modern aircraft.

Table 16.2 gives the annual orders of Boeing during the period 2003−2015. The orders given are gross orders which do not include cancellations or conversions. During the period 2003−15, the gross orders amounted to 11,795. The maximum

Table 16.2 **Annual aircraft orders**

Year	717	737	747	757	767	777	787	Total
2003	8	197	4	7	11	13		240
2004	8	152	10		9	42	56	277
2005		574	48		19	153	235	1029
2006		733	72		8	77	160	1050
2007		850	25		36	143	369	1423
2008		488	4		29	54	94	669
2009		197	5		7	30	24	263
2010		508	1		3	76	37	625
2011		625	7		42	202	45	921
2012		1184	7		23	75	50	1339
2013		1208	17		2	121	183	1531
2014		1196	2		4	283	65	1550
2015		666	6		49	58	99	878
Total	16	8578	208	7	242	1327	1417	11,795

Source: http://www.boeing.com/company/general-info/index.page#/overview.

orders were for 737 airplanes which accounted for approximately 73% of the total gross orders during the period 2003−15. The maximum increase in gross orders was registered in the year 2005 where the increase was 271% compared to the previous year. The net orders in 2016 by June 7, 2016, were 269.

16.11   Dividends & share repurchases

Cash dividends have been paid on common stock every year since 1942. In 2015, Boeing announced a new repurchase plan for $14 billion of common stock which replaced the repurchase plan of the year 2014. In 2015, Boeing purchased an aggregate of 5,292,358 shares of the common stock in the open market as a part of repurchase plan 2014. During 2015 and 2014, Boeing repurchased 46.7 million and 46.6 million shares totaling $6.8 billion and $6.0 billion through the open market share repurchase program.

In 1962, the dividend per share was $0.03. In 2015, the dividend per share increased to $3.64. During the period 1980−85, the dividend per share remained constant at $0.21. During the period 1991−95, the dividend per share remained constant at $0.5. In the period 1997−2001, the DPS was constant at $0.56. During the period 2009−11, the DPS remained at $1.68. The DPS has been steadily increasing over the period 2012−15. The DPS increased by 50% in the year 2014. The growth rate of dividends had been 5% and 10% in the years 2012 and 2013, respectively. The average growth rate of dividends had been 22.5% during the period 2012−15. The average growth rate of dividends during the period 1962−2015 had been 13% (see Table 16.3).

Table 16.3 Dividend history

Year	DPS	Year	DPS	Year	DPS	Year	DPS	Year	DPS
1962	0.03	1971	0.01	1981	0.21	1991	0.5	2001	0.56	2011	1.68
1963	0.03	1972	0.01	1982	0.21	1992	0.5	2002	0.68	2012	1.76
1964	0.03	1973	0.01	1983	0.21	1993	0.5	2003	0.68	2013	1.94
1965	0.04	1974	0.02	1984	0.21	1994	0.5	2004	0.77	2014	2.92
1966	0.05	1975	0.03	1985	0.21	1995	0.5	2005	1	2015	3.64
1967	0.04	1976	0.04	1986	0.27	1996	0.55	2006	1.2		
1968	0.04	1977	0.06	1987	0.31	1997	0.56	2007	1.4		
1969	0.03	1978	0.04	1988	0.26	1998	0.56	2008	1.6		
1970	0.01	1979	0.07	1989	0.39	1999	0.56	2009	1.68		
		1980	0.21	1990	0.48	2000	0.56	2010	1.68		

16.12   Financing resources

Many non-U.S. customers finance purchases through the Export Import bank of the United States. Boeing has commercial paper program which is a potential source of short-term liquidity. By 2015, Boeing had $5 billion of unused borrowing capacity on revolving credit line agreements which serve as backup liquidity. The financing commitments totaled $16.7 billion in year 2014 and $16.3 billion in year 2015. Boeing has entered into standby letters of credit and surety bonds with financial institutions which were meant for guarantee on certain contract. In 2015, the contingent liabilities on outstanding letters of credit agreement and surety bonds amounted to $4968 million. Boeing has issued credit guarantees to facilitate the sale and/or financing of commercial aircraft. The commercial aircraft credit guarantees are collateralized by the underlying commercial aircraft and certain other assets. In 2015, Boeing had issued fixed rate senior notes.

16.13   Pension plans

Boeing union and nonunion employees have participated under defined pension plans. Boeing provides various forms of share-based compensation to employees. Employees who have participated in defined pension plans can make the transition to a company funded defined contribution retirement savings plan in the year 2016. Postretirement benefit plans provided by Boeing consist principally of healthcare coverage to eligible retirees and qualifying dependents. Major pension plans are funded through trusts. Retiree healthcare is provided principally until age 65 for approximately half those retirees who are eligible for healthcare coverage. The funded status of the plans is measured as the difference between the plan assets at fair value and the projected benefit obligation (PBO).

16.13.1   Investment strategy of pension funds

The investment strategy of the pension fund is to earn a rate of return over time to satisfy the benefit obligations of the pension plans and maintain sufficient liquidity to pay benefits and address other cash requirements of the pension fund. Boeing periodically updates its long-term strategic asset allocations. Boeing uses various analytics to determine the optimal asset mix and consider plan liability characteristics, liquidity characteristics, funding requirements, expected rates of return, and distribution of returns. Investments are made in asset classes of fixed income, global equity, private equity, real estate and real assets, hedge funds, etc.

16.14   Share-based compensation plan

Under the 2003 Incentive Stock Plan, Boeing awards nonqualified stock options, stock appreciation rights, restricted stock or units, performance shares, performance-restricted stock or units, performance units, and other stock- and cash-based awards to employees, officers, directors, consultants, and independent contractors. In 2013, Boeing offered 6,591,968 options to executives. The options were granted with an exercise price equal to the fair market value of the Boeing stock on the date of grant and expire 10 years after the date of grant. The stock options vest over a period of 3 years, with 34% vesting after the first year, 33% vesting after the second year, and the remaining 33% vesting after the third year. The restricted stock units (RSUs) are the part of the long-term incentive program with grant date fair values of $154.64, $129.58, and $75.97 per unit, respectively. Performance-Based Restricted Stock Units (PBRSUs) are stock units that pay out based on the Boeing's total shareholder return as compared to a group of peer companies over a 3-year period. The award payout can range from 0% to 200% of the initial PBRSU grant but will not exceed 400% of the initial value (excluding dividend equivalent credits). The PBRSUs granted under this program will vest at the payout amount and settle in common stock (on a one-for-one basis) on the third anniversary of the grant date.

16.15   Ownership

Equity constituted 29% and debt constituted 71% of the total capital structure by June 2016. In June 2016, equity amounted to $4043 million and debt amounted to $9964 million. Institutions held 65.9% of the equity ownership, while mutual funds and insiders held 34% and 0.1% of the equity ownership. There were 2025 institution owners and 2372 fund owners. The top 10 institutions held 40.99% of the total shares while the top 5 mutual funds held 8.68% of the total shares (Tables 16.4 and 16.5).

16.16   Operational highlights

Boeing had revenues of $96.1 billion and total backlog of $489.299 billion in the year 2015. In the year 2015, Boeing delivered 762 commercial airplanes and 186 military aircraft along with 15,787 weapons system and four satellites. In the year 2015, Boeing had a diverse backlog of approximately 5800 airplanes with the value of $432 billion. The space and security backlog amounted to $58 billion in 2015.

Table 16.4 Equity ownership top mutual funds

	Funds	Percent of shares held
1	VA College America WA Mutual 529B	2.79
2	Vanguard Total Stock Mkt Idx	1.94
3	VA CollegeAmerica Fundamental Invs 529E	1.39
4	VA CollegeAmerica Amercn Bal 529E	1.31
5	Vanguard 500 Index Inv	1.25
	Total	8.68

Source: Morningstar.com.

Table 16.5 Equity ownership top financial institutions

	Institutions	Percent of shares held
1	Capital World Investors	6.85
2	Evercore Trust Company, N.A.	6.73
3	Vanguard Group Inc.	6.06
4	T. Rowe Price Associates, Inc.	5.81
5	State Street Corp	4.34
6	Royal London Asset Management Ltd	2.96
7	BlackRock Fund Advisors	2.9
8	Capital Research Global Investors	2.66
9	Fidelity Management and Research Company	1.36
10	Jennison Associates LLC	1.32
	Total	40.99

Source: Morningstar.com.

Table 16.6 Financial highlights in millions of US dollars

Year	2011	2012	2013	2014	2015
Revenues	68,735	81,698	86,623	90,762	96,114
Core operating earnings	6340	7189	7876	8860	7741
Core operating margin	9.20%	8.80%	9.10%	9.80%	8.10%
Core earnings per share	5.79	5.88	7.07	8.6	7.72
Operating cash flow	4023	7508	8179	8858	9363
Contractual backlog	339,657	372,355	422,661	487,092	476,595
Total backlog	355,432	390,228	440,928	502,391	489,299

The major new contracts in this segment included awards from NASA for two commercial human space flights of CST-100 Starliner to the International Space Station: contracts for 15 EA-18G Growlers for the U.S. Navy and contracts for 43 AH-64E Apache helicopters for the U.S. Army. Other orders included 22 Apaches and 15 Chinook heavy lift helicopters from India, 5 V-22 tiltrotor aircraft for Japan. There had been a $1.5 billion contract with U.S. Navy for the P-8A Poseidon. The total backlog amounted to $489.299 billion in the year 2015 (Table 16.6).

The major commercial airplane milestones in the year 2015 included the deliveries of the 100th 747-8 and 350th 787 airplanes. The major milestones achieved by the Defense, Space & Security segment included the first test flights of a fully equipped KC-46A tanker, the launch and successful on-orbit operation of the first all-electric propulsion satellites and rollout of the first 12 EA-18G Growlers for Australia's armed forces.

The revenues accounted by the commercial airplanes segment have been increasing over the 5-year period 2011–15. The growth rate of revenues accounted by the commercial airplanes segment has increased by approximately 35% in the year 2012 compared to the year 2011. The average growth rate of revenues for the

Table 16.7 Revenue highlights in millions of dollars

Year	2011	2012	2013	2014	2015
Commercial Airplanes	36,171	49,127	52,981	59,990	66,048
Defense, Space & Security					
Boeing Military Aircraft	14,100	15,373	15,275	13,500	13,482
Network & Space Systems	8964	7911	8512	8003	7751
Global Services & Support	8912	9323	9410	9378	9155
Total Defense, Space & Security	31,976	32,607	33,197	30,881	30,388
Boeing Capital	547	468	408	416	413
Unallocated items, eliminations, and others	41	−504	37	−525	−735
Total revenues	68,735	81,698	86,623	90,762	96,114

Source: Annual Report 2015.

Table 16.8 Contractual backlog in millions of dollars

Year	2011	2012	2013	2014	2015
Commercial Airplanes	293,303	317,287	372,980	440,118	431,408
Defense, Space & Security					
Boeing Military Aircraft	22,091	27,878	23,580	21,119	20,019
Network & Space Systems	9429	10,078	9832	8935	7368
Global Services & Support	14,834	17,112	16,269	16,920	17,800
Total Defense, Space & Security	46,354	55,068	49,681	46,974	45,187
Total Contractual Backlog	339,657	372,355	422,661	487,092	476,595

commercial airplane sector had been 17% approximately during the 5-year period 2011−15. The Defense Space & Security (BDS) segment revenues have shown a declining trend over the 5-year period 2011−15. The total BDS revenues declined from $319.76 billion in 2011 to $303.88 billion in 2015. The revenues accounted by the BDS segment registered a negative growth of 1% during the period 2011−15 on an average basis. The commercial airplane segment accounted for 62% of the total revenues on an average basis during the period 2011−15. The BDS segment accounted for 38% of the total revenues on an average basis during the period 2011−15. The cost of sales as percent of revenues was 84.6% during the year 2014 and 85.4% of revenues during the period 2015 (Table 16.7).

The commercial airplanes backlog increased from $293.303 billion in the year 2011 to $431.408 billion in the year 2015. The total contractual backlog increased from $339.657 billion in the year 2011 to $476.595 billion in the year 2015. Total backlog is comprised of contractual backlog, which represents work which Boeing is contracted to perform with receipt of funds, and unobligated backlog, which represents the work which Boeing is on contract to perform for which funding has not yet been authorized (Table 16.8).

16.17   Financial highlights: trend analysis

The revenues have increased from $61.53 billion in the year 2006 to $96.114 billion by the year 2015. The operating income increased from $3.014 billion in the year 2006 to $7.443 billion by the year 2015. The operating cash flow increased from $7.499 billion to $9.363 billion by the year 2015. The net income and total cash increased by 2.34 and 1.88 times during the period of analysis. The average growth rate of revenues during the period 2007−15 was approximately 5%. The average growth rate of revenues which was 1% during the period 2007−10 increased to 8% during the period 2011−15. The average growth rate in operating income was 22% during the period 2006−15. The average increase in total cash and total assets was 26% and 7%, respectively, during the period 2007−15. The average increase in market capitalization had been 7% during the period 2007−15. The capital expenditure also increased by 7% on an average basis during the period 2007−15. The average increase in the short-term debt has been 11% while the increase in long-term debt had been 3% during the period 2007−15 on an average basis (Table 16.9).

16.18   Ratio analysis

The average gross margin which was 18.3% during the period 2006−10 declined to 16.02 during the period 2011−15. The average operating margin which was 6.2% during the 5-year period 2006−10 increased to 7.94% during the period 2011−15. The average net margin of 4.2 during 2006−10 increased to 5.5 during the period 2011−15. The average ROA increased from 4.7% to 5.2% during the two period of comparison. The average ROE declined from 121.3% to 74.1% during the analysis period. The average return on investment capital increased from 20.6 to 27.4 during the period of analysis. The average ICR increased from 16.6 to 18.4 during the two periods of comparison. Most of the profitability ratios have increased during the period of analysis (Table 16.10).

The cash flow ratios on average basis have improved in the period 2011−15 compared to the period 2006−10. The average earnings per share increased from 3.62 during the period 2006−10 to 6.25 during the period 2011−15. The average free cash flow per share, revenue per share, and EBITDA per share increased from 4.63, 85.94, and 7.71 during the period 2006−10 to 7.30, 114.58, and 11.57, respectively (Table 16.11).

The payout amounted to 90% in the year 2009. The average DPO during the period 2006−15 was 0.43 (Table 16.12).

The average price to book ratio, price to earnings ratio, price to sales have declined during the period 2011−15 compared to the period 2006−10. The average price to book ratio declined from 11.62 to 11.59 during the two 5-year period of comparison. The average price to earnings and price to sales ratios declined from 20.98 and 0.79 to 17.65 and 0.96, respectively. The average price to cash flow ratio

Table 16.9 Financial highlights in millions of dollars

Year	2006	2007	2008	2009	2010	2011	2012	2013	2014	2015
Revenues	61,530	66,387	60,909	68,281	54,306	68,735	81,698	86,623	90,762	96,114
Operating income	3014	5830	3950	2096	4971	5844	6311	6562	7473	7443
Operating cash flow	7499	9584	−401	5603	2952	4023	7508	8179	8858	9363
Free cash flow	5818	7853	−2253	4417	1825	2310	5798	5941	6622	6913
Net income	2215	4074	2672	1312	3307	4018	3900	4585	5446	5176
Total cash	6386	9308	3279	11,223	10,517	11,272	13,558	15,258	13,092	12,052
Total assets	51,794	58,986	53,779	62,053	58,565	79,986	88,896	92,663	92,921	94,408
Short-term debt	1381	762	560	707	948	2353	1436	1563	929	1234
Long-term debt	8157	7455	6952	12,217	11,473	10,018	8973	8072	8141	8730
Capital expenditure	1681	1731	1852	1186	1127	1713	1710	2238	2236	2450
Year end market capitalization	70,072	67,173	43,193	39,331	47,983	54,624	56,944	102,010	91,861	96,387
Book value of equity	4739	9004	−1294	2128	2766	3515	5867	14,875	8665	6335

Table 16.10 Profitability ratios

Year	2006	2007	2008	2009	2010	2011	2012	2013	2014	2015
Gross margin (%)	18	19.6	17.3	17.2	19.4	18.7	16	15.4	15.4	14.6
Operating margin (%)	4.9	8.8	6.5	3.1	7.7	8.5	7.7	7.6	8.2	7.7
Net margin (%)	3.6	6.14	4.39	1.92	5.14	5.85	4.77	5.29	5.99	5.38
Return on assets (%)	3.96	7.36	4.74	2.27	5.06	5.41	4.62	5.05	5.67	5.34
Return on equity (%)	28.04	59.29	69.31	314.63	135.15	127.94	83.14	44.21	46.22	68.96
Return on invested capital (%)	13.2	26.69	23.94	14.8	24.38	28.25	26.15	23.88	26.96	31.56
Interest coverage	14.31	32.21	20.78	6.11	9.73	11.83	13.76	17.15	22.43	27.02

Table 16.11 Per share ratios

Year	2006	2007	2008	2009	2010	2011	2012	2013	2014	2015
Earnings per share	2.85	5.28	3.67	1.84	4.45	5.34	5.11	5.96	7.38	7.44
Book value per share	13.98	11.72	−1.28	2.93	3.76	8.01	7.76	11.98	20.53	10.11
Free cash flow per share	7.44	10.17	−3.09	6.19	2.45	0.89	7.61	11.74	3.87	12.39
Revenue per share	78.12	85.94	83.55	95.71	86.4	91.27	107.29	112.85	123.2	138.29
EBITDA per share	6.32	10.1	7.8	5.24	9.07	10.03	10.75	11.02	12.73	13.33

Table 16.12 **Payout trend**

Year	2006	2007	2008	2009	2010	2011	2012	2013	2014	2015
Dividend payout ratio	0.42	0.27	0.44	0.9	0.38	0.32	0.34	0.33	0.4	0.49

Table 16.13 **Market value multiples**

Year	2006	2007	2008	2009	2010	2011	2012	2013	2014	2015
P/B	14.79	7.46	0	18.48	17.35	15.54	9.71	6.86	10.6	15.22
P/E	31.46	16.57	11.79	30.43	14.63	13.7	14.72	22.83	17.56	19.44
P/S	1.13	1.02	0.51	0.56	0.75	0.8	0.7	1.21	1.06	1.05
P/OCF	9.24	7.07	0	6.85	16.47	13.74	7.65	12.85	10.84	10.72

Table 16.14 **Enterprise value multiples**

Year	2006	2007	2008	2009	2010	2011	2012	2013	2014	2015
EV/Revenues	1.19	1	0.78	0.6	0.78	0.81	0.66	1.11	0.97	0.98
EV/EBITDA	14.71	8.47	8.36	11.01	7.38	7.4	6.6	11.4	9.38	10.19
EV/EBIT	21.32	10.47	11.34	19.87	9.95	9.51	8.48	14.58	11.78	12.7

increased from 7.93 during the period 2006−10 to 11.16 during the period 2011−15 (Table 16.13).

The average EV/Revenues increased from 0.87 to 0.906 during the two periods of analysis. The average EV/EBITDA and EV/EBIT declined from 9.98 and 14.59 during the period 2006−10 to 8.99 and 11.41 during the period 2011−15 (Table 16.14).

The average current ratio during the period 2006−15 was 1.12 The average quick ratio during the above period was 0.46 (Table 16.15).

The debt equity ratio has increased on average basis during the two 5-year periods of comparison. The average debt equity ratio increased from 1.53 during the period 2006−10 to 1.71 during the period 2011−15. The average long-term debt to total assets declined from 0.16 to 0.10 while the average total debt per share increased from 12.98 to 14.21 during the two periods of comparison (Table 16.16).

The efficiency ratios are compared on average basis for the two periods 2006−10 and 2011−15. The average fixed assets turnover ratio increased from 7.6 to 8.3 while average asset turnover ratio declined from 1.1 to 1.0. The average receivable turnover ratio increased from 11.6 to 13.1 during the two periods of comparison. The average turnover ratio decreased from 4.5 to 1.8. The average days' payable decreased from 74.8 days to 50.2 days. The average days' sales outstanding decreased from 31.6 days to 29.5 days. The average days' inventory increased from 91.9 days to 198.8 days (Table 16.17).

Table 16.15 Liquidity ratios

Year	2006	2007	2008	2009	2010	2011	2012	2013	2014	2015
Current ratio	0.77	0.86	0.84	1.07	1.15	1.21	1.27	1.26	1.4	1.35
Quick ratio	0.5	0.56	0.34	0.56	0.46	0.43	0.43	0.43	0.44	0.42

Table 16.16 Financial leverage ratios

Year	2006	2007	2008	2009	2010	2011	2012	2013	2014	2015
Debt/equity	2.01	0.91	−5.81	6.07	4.49	3.52	1.77	0.65	1.05	1.57
Long-term debt to total assets	0.16	0.13	0.13	0.2	0.17	0.13	0.1	0.09	0.09	0.09
Total debt per share	12.09	10.7	7.42	17.79	16.89	16.61	13.78	12.89	12.83	14.95

16.19 Stock wealth analysis

Cumulative 5-year total shareholder return estimation assumes $100 invested and includes reinvestment of dividends. The average returns for Boeing during the 5-year period 2011−15 was 23.3% while the average returns for S&P500 Aerospace and Defense and S&P500 Index was 18.3% and 13.11% during the same period (Table 16.18).

The analysis of monthly returns involving 653 months during the period 1962 to June 2016 shows that average yearly returns was approximately 16.8%. The adjusted closing price of Boeing stock on 2/1/1962 was $0.235. The adjusted closing price of Boeing stock on 1/6/2016 was $129.82. The stock price increased by 552.7 times during the holding period of 54 years. Suppose an investor invested $100 in Boeing stock on 1/6/2016. The investment would have increased to $55,271.25 by the period July 2016. The cumulative returns for Boeing stock based on monthly returns during the 53.5-year period was approximately 915.41%. Suppose an investor had invested $100 on 2/1/1962 and involved in active trading of buying and selling the stock every month till 1/6/2016, his investment would have grown to $1015.41. The cumulative returns of market index S&P500 during the same period 1962−2016 based on monthly returns was 401.84%.

Boeing stock has outperformed the market index S&P500 during the entire period of analysis except in the initial months of analysis (Figure 16.1).

The yearly returns are estimated on the basis of average monthly returns. The year 2016 returns are based on the period January 2016−June 2016 and then forecasted for yearly average. Excess returns are estimated as the difference between Boeing returns and market index S&P 500 returns. Boeing had the highest average yearly returns of 64% in the year 2013. The excess returns amounted to 37.7% in the year 2013. On the basis of average yearly returns, Boeing outperformed the market index S&P500 in 4 out of 7 years of analysis (Table 16.19).

Table 16.17 Efficiency ratios

Year	2006	2007	2008	2009	2010	2011	2012	2013	2014	2015
Fixed assets turnover	7.65	8.33	7.15	7.78	7.26	7.54	8.61	8.71	8.55	8.33
Asset turnover	1.1	1.2	1.08	1.18	0.99	0.93	0.97	0.95	0.98	1.03
Receivables turnover	11.69	12.04	10.74	11.99	11.48	12.26	14.33	14.25	12.72	11.69
Inventory turnover	6.31	6.05	4	3.47	2.51	1.98	1.96	1.82	1.71	1.75
Days payable	117.24	113.98	42.56	45.81	54.32	54.92	49.95	47.32	50.73	48.02
Days sales outstanding	31.35	31.56	33.57	30.92	30.78	30.76	25.05	27.58	31.08	33.09
Days inventory	57.83	60.38	91.25	105.05	145.21	184.75	186.08	200.92	213.21	209.01

Table 16.18 **Comparison of cumulative 5-year total shareholder return**

Company/index	Base period 2010	2011	2012	2013	2014	2015
Boeing	100	115.2	121.23	223.96	218.3	248.97
S&P500 Aerospace & Defense	100	105.28	120.61	186.85	208.21	219.52
S&P500 Index	100	102.11	118.45	156.82	178.29	180.75

Source: Boeing Annual Report 2015.

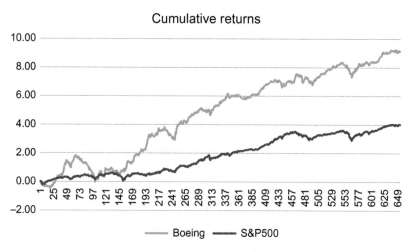

Figure 16.1 Cumulative Monthly Returns during the period January 1962–June 2016.

Table 16.19 **Average yearly returns in percent**

Year	BA	S&P500	Excess returns
2010	25.5	13.8	11.7
2011	16.3	1.1	15.1
2012	6.1	13.2	−7.1
2013	64.2	26.5	37.7
2014	−1.1	11.1	−12.2
2015	15.3	0.1	15.2
2016	−13.5	3.4	−16.9

Table 16.20 Holding period yield in percent

Year	Holding period yield in percent
2010	10.38
2011	8.15
2012	4.04
2013	88.45
2014	6.19
2015	1.99
2016	9.96

Table 16.21 Excess value added in millions of dollars

Year	2010	2011	2012	2013	2014	2015
Book value of equity	2766	3515	5867	14,875	8665	6335
Market value of equity	47,983	54,624	56,944	102,010	91,861	96,387
Excess value	45,217	51,109	51,077	87,135	83,196	90,052
BV as percent of MV	5.8	6.4	10.3	14.6	9.4	6.6

The holding period yield estimation is based on the assumption of holding period of 1 year. The holding period yield for Boeing was highest in the year 2013. The second highest yield was registered in the year 2010. The 2010–July 2016 annual holding period yield for Boeing was estimated as 15.2% (Table 16.20).

The average book value as percent of market value was 8.8% during the period 2010–15. Excess value is estimated as the difference between the market value and book value of equity (see Table 16.21).

16.20 Estimation of cost of capital

The cost of equity is estimated using CAPM.

Cost of Equity = Risk-Free Rate + Beta*Risk Premium.

The yield to maturity on the long-term U.S. treasury bond is assumed as the risk-free rate. The risk premium is assumed to be 5.5%. Beta is estimated by regressing the weekly stock returns of Boeing stock on weekly market index S&P500 returns during the period January 2014 to June 2016.

Beta = 1.088.

Table 16.22 **Estimation of risk-free rate**[10]

Year	Yield to maturity on 30-year treasury bond
2014	3.55
2015	2.63
2016	2.63
Average	2.94%

Risk-free rate = 2.94% (see Table 16.22).

Cost of Equity = 2.94 + 1.088*5.5 = 8.92%.

Cost of debt is assumed to be the yield to maturity on the long-term bond issued by Boeing which matures on 15/2/2040. The yield to maturity of this bond on 19/6/2016 was 3.6%. The price of the bond was 136.1.[9]

The latest 2-year effective tax rate was 25.675%.

After tax cost of debt = 3.6*(1 − 0.2568) = 2.68%.

WACC is estimated using market value weights of equity and debt. To find the market value of debt, the book value of debt is multiplied by the ratio of market price of the long-term bond to the face value of the bond.

Ratio = 136.1/100 = 1.361.

Book Value of debt in the year 2015 = $9964 million

Market Value of debt in 2015 = 9964*1.361 = $13,651 million

Market Value of Equity in 2015 = $96,387 million

Total Value = Market Value of Equity + Market Value of Debt = 96,387 + 13,651 = $109,948 million

Weight of Equity (We) = 96,387/109,948 = 0.88

Weight of Debt (Wd) = 13,561/109,948 = 0.12

WACC = We*Cost of Equity + Wd*After tax cost of debt

    = 0.88*8.92% + 0.12*2.68% = 8.15%

Weighted Average Cost of Capital (WACC) is estimated as 8.15%.

16.21 Valuation perspectives

16.21.1 Estimation of economic value of Boeing

Economic Value is estimated as net operating income after taxes (NOPAT) − Capital Charge.

Profit before interest and tax (PBIT) − Income tax = NOPAT.

Capital Employed = Stock holder Equity + Long-term debt

Capital Charge = Capital Employed * WACC

Economic Value (EV) = NOPAT − Capital Charge

Estimation of Economic Value (EV) in the year 2015

PBIT in the year 2015 = $7443 million

---

[9] http://quicktake.morningstar.com/StockNet/bonds.aspx?Symbol=BA&Country=usa.

[10] https://www.treasury.gov/resource-center/data-chart-center/interest-rates/Pages/Historic-Yield-Data-Visualization.aspx.

Income tax in the year 2015 = \$1979 million
NOPAT = 7443 − 1979 = \$5464 million
Stock holder Equity = \$6335 million
Long-term debt = \$8730 million
Capital Employed = \$15,065 million
WACC = 8.15%
Capital charge = 15,065*0.0815 = \$1227.798 million
Economic Value = 5464 − 1227.798 = \$4236 million.

The economic value for Boeing is estimated as \$4236 million.

16.22 Equity spread

Equity spread is a variation of the EV measures. Equity spread is the difference between the ROE and the required return on equity (cost of equity).

Equity Spread = (Return on Equity − Cost of Equity)*Equity Capital
Equity capital in 2015 = \$6335 million
Return on equity in 2015 = 68.96%
Cost of equity in 2015 = 8.92%
Equity Spread = \$3803.534 million

The value of equity spread for Boeing is calculated as \$3803.534 million in the year 2015.

16.23 Dividend discount model valuation

The average growth rate of earnings per share during the 5-year period 2011−15 was approximately 11%. The average growth rate of dividends during the 5-year period 2011−15 was approximately 17% based on geometric mean. The average dividend payout during the 5-year period was 37.4% (Table 16.23).

Table 16.23 Dividend trends

Year	2010	2011	2012	2013	2014	2015
EPS	4.45	5.34	5.11	5.96	7.38	7.44
DPS	1.68	1.68	1.76	1.94	2.92	3.64
DPO	0.378	0.315	0.344	0.326	0.396	0.489

The average growth rate of earnings estimated from fundamentals is estimated as 53% (Tables 16.24). Since this growth rate is too high, we proceed for DDM-based valuation based on the historical growth rate of earnings.

Table 16.24 Estimation of growth rate from fundamentals

Year	2010	2011	2012	2013	2014	2015
RR	0.62	0.69	0.66	0.67	0.60	0.51
ROE	1.35	1.27	0.83	0.44	0.46	0.69
Growth rate	0.84	0.87	0.54	0.30	0.28	0.35

Two-stage DDM model

In this model, it is assumed that earnings will grow at the historical growth rate of 11% for the next 10 years and thereafter at the stable growth rate of US economy. The historical growth rate of earnings for the period 2011–15 is assumed as the growth rate in the high growth period.

High growth stage inputs
High growth period = 10 years
Growth rate = 11%
Cost of Equity in 2015 = 8.92%
Average DPO = 37.4%
EPS in the current year (2015) = $7.44.

EPS in the first year of high growth period = 7.44*1.11 = $8.26.

Table 16.25 Present value of dividends in high growth phase

Year	1	2	3	4	5	6	7	8	9	10
EPS	8.258	9.167	10.175	11.294	12.537	13.916	15.447	17.146	19.032	21.125
DPO	0.374	0.374	0.374	0.374	0.374	0.374	0.374	0.374	0.374	0.374
DPS	3.089	3.428	3.806	4.224	4.689	5.205	5.777	6.413	7.118	7.901
PV	$2.84	$2.89	$2.95	$3.00	$3.06	$3.12	$3.18	$3.24	$3.30	$3.36
SUM	$30.92									

Present Value of dividends in high growth phase = $30.92 (Table 16.25).

Stable period inputs

The growth rate in stable period is assumed to be the growth rate of US economy. The average growth rate of U.S. economy during the period 2013–14 is estimated as 2.3%.[11]

Growth rate in stable period = 2.3%.
Growth rate = Retention Ratio*Return on Equity of aircraft industry sector
Return on Equity of aircraft industry sector = 26.3%[12]
Retention Ratio = 2.3%/26.3% = 9%
DPO in stable phase = 1 − 0.09 = 0.91

[11] http://data.worldbank.org/indicator/NY.GDP.MKTP.KD.ZG.
[12] http://www.morningstar.com/stocks/XNYS/BA/quote.html.

EPS at the end of high growth period = \$21.125
EPS at the beginning of stable period = \$21.125*1.023 = \$21.61
DPO in stable period = 0.91
DPS in stable period = 21.61*0.91 = \$19.67
Terminal Value = DPS in stable period/(Cost of equity − growth rate in stable period)
= 19.67/(8.92% − 2.3%) = \$297.068
Present Value of terminal value = \$126.41
Value of Boeing stock = Present value of dividends in high growth phase + Present value of dividends in stable phase
= 30.92 + 126.41 = \$157.33
Value of Boeing stock = \$157.33.

Boeing was trading at \$129.37 on 20/6/2016. According to the DDM valuation, Boeing is undervalued in the stock market.

16.24   FCFE valuation model

FCFE is the residual cash flow available to shareholders. It is the residual cash flow after taxes, interest expenses, and reinvestment needs.

FCFE = Net Income − Capital Expenditure + Depreciation and Amortization − Change in Noncash Working Capital + New debt issued − Debt Repayment.
Boeing have research and development expenses. The following adjustments are made in the FCFE valuation.
Net Capital Expenditure = Capital Expenditure − Depreciation and Amortization.
Adjusted Net Capital Expenditure = Net Capital Expenditure + R&D Expenses in current Period − Amortization of research asset + Net Acquisitions (Table 16.26).
Adjusted Depreciation and Amortization = Depreciation and Amortization + Amortization of Research Asset.

Research assets are amortized linearly over time. The life of research asset is assumed to be 25 years and straight line depreciation is used.

Table 16.26 **Adjusted net capital expenditure in millions of dollars**

Year	2010	2011	2012	2013	2014	2015
Capital Expenditures	1127	1713	1710	2238	2236	2450
Depreciation & Amortization	1727	1660	1811	1844	1906	1833
Net Capital Expenditures	−600	53	−101	394	330	617
R&D Expenses in current period	4121	3918	3298	3071	3047	3331
Amortization of research asset	164.84	156.72	131.92	122.84	121.88	133.24
Acquisitions	932	42	124	26	163	31
Adjusted Net Capital Expenditure	4288	3856	3189	3368	3418	3846

Table 16.27 **Estimation of noncash working capital in millions of dollars**

Year	2010	2011	2012	2013	2014	2015
Total Current Assets	40,572	49,810	57,309	65,074	67,767	68,234
Cash and Cash Equivalents	10,517	11,272	13,558	15,258	13,092	12,052
Noncash Current Assets	30,055	38,538	43,751	49,816	54,675	56,182
Total Current liabilities	35,395	41,274	44,982	51,486	48,233	50,412
Short-term debt	948	2353	1436	1563	929	1234
Noninterest bearing current liabilities	34,447	38,921	43,546	49,923	47,304	49,178
Noncash Working Capital	−4392	−383	205	−107	7371	7004
Change in noncash working capital		4009	588	−312	7478	−367

Noncash working capital = Non cash current assets − Noninterest bearing current liabilities (Table 16.27).
Noncash current assets = Total current assets − cash and cash equivalents
Noninterest bearing current liabilities = Total current liabilities − short-term debt.

Table 16.28 **Estimation of reinvestment rate for FCFE Model**

Year	2011	2012	2013	2014	2015
Adjusted Net Capital Expenditure	3856	3189	3368	3418	3846
Change in noncash working capital	4009	588	−312	7478	−367
Net debt issued	−131	−2016	−1434	−1601	861
Reinvestment	7996	5793.08	4490.16	12,497.12	2618
Net Income	4018	3900	4585	5446	5176
Reinvestment Rate	1.99	1.49	0.98	2.29	0.51

The values except rates are given in millions of dollars.
Reinvestment = Adjusted net capital expenditure + Change in noncash working capital − Net debt issued
Reinvestment rate = Reinvestment/Net income.

The average reinvestment rate is estimated to be 122% during the period 2011−2015. For estimation purposes, we assume the reinvestment rate of 51% (year 2015) in the high growth period (Table 16.28).

Table 16.29 **Estimation of FCFE in millions of dollars**

Year	2011	2012	2013	2014	2015
Net Income	4018	3900	4585	5446	5176
Adjusted net capital expenditure	3856	3189	3368	3418	3846
Change in noncash working capital	4009	588	−312	7478	−367
New debt issued	799	60	0	0	1746
Debt Repayment	930	2076	1434	1601	885
FCFE	−3978	−1893	95	−7051	2558

FCFE = Net Income − Adjusted net capital expenditure − change in noncash working capital + new debt issued − debt repaid (Table 16.29).

Table 16.30 **Estimation of growth rate from fundamentals**

Year	2011	2012	2013	2014	2015
Reinvestment rate	1.99	1.49	0.98	2.29	0.51
Return on Equity	0.225	0.230	0.210	0.208	0.182
Growth Rate	0.447	0.342	0.206	0.476	0.092
Average growth rate	0.313				

The average growth rate estimated from fundamentals during the period 2011−15 is 31.3% (Table 16.30). For estimation purposes, we assume the historical growth rate of net income during the 5-year period 2011−15. The historical growth rate of net income during the period 2011−15 was 9.3% based on geometric mean.

Two-stage FCFE model
High growth period assumptions

High growth period = 10 years
High growth rate = 9.3% (Based on 5-year historical growth rate)
Reinvestment rate = 51% (Reinvestment rate in year 2015)
Net Income in year 2015 = $5176 million
Net Income in the first year of high growth period = 5176*1.094 = $5662.544 million.

Table 16.31 **Present value of FCFE in high growth period**

Year	1	2	3	4	5	6	7	8	9	10
Net Income	5662.5	6194.8	6777.1	7414.2	8111.1	8873.6	9707.7	10620.2	11,618.5	12,710.6
Reinvestment	2887.9	3159.4	3456.3	3781.2	4136.7	4525.5	4950.9	5416.3	5925.4	6482.4
FCFE	2774.6	3035.5	3320.8	3633.0	3974.4	4348.0	4756.8	5203.9	5693.1	6228.2
PV of FCFE	2547.4	2558.6	2569.9	2581.2	2592.6	2604.0	2615.5	2627.0	2638.6	2650.3
Sum	$25,985.3									

The values are given in millions of dollars. The sum of the present value of FCFE in high growth phase is estimated as $25.985 billion (Table 16.31).

Stable period inputs

Growth rate of US economy is assumed to be the growth rate in the stable period.
Growth rate in stable period = 2.3%.
Growth rate = Reinvestment Rate*Return on Equity of aircraft industry sector
Return on Equity of aircraft industry sector = 26.3%[13]
Reinvestment rate in stable period = 2.3/26.3 = 9%

Net Income at end of high growth period	12,710.6
Net Income at beginning of stable period	12,710.6*1.023
	13,002.99
Reinvestment rate in stable period	0.09
Reinvestment in stable period	13,002.99*0.09
	1170.27
FCFE in stable period	13,002.99 − 1170.27
	11,832.72
Terminal Value = FCFE in stable period/(cost of equity − growth rate)	
11,832.72/(0.0892 − 0.023) =	178,741.96
Present Value of terminal value	$76,058.93
Value of operating assets = PV of FCFE in high growth phase + PV of FCFE in stable phase	
25,985.3 + 76,058.93	$102,044.3
Adding the value of cash	12,052
Value of Boeing equity	$114,096.3
Number of shares	695 million
Value per share	164.17

All values except per share are given in millions of dollars. The value of Boeing equity is estimated as $114.096 billion. The value per share is calculated as $164.17.

16.25 FCFF valuation

Table 16.32 Estimation of reinvestment rate for FCFF Model

Year	2011	2012	2013	2014	2015
EBIT	5844	6311	6562	7473	7443
Taxes	1382	2007	1646	1691	1979
EBIT(1 − T)	4462	4304	4916	5782	5464
Adjusted net capex	3856	3189	3368	3418	3846
Change in noncash WC	4009	588	−312	7478	−367
Reinvestment	7865	3777	3056	10,896	3479
Reinvestment rate	1.76	0.88	0.62	1.88	0.64

---

[13] http://www.morningstar.com/stocks/XNYS/BA/quote.html.

The reinvestment rate for calculation purpose is assumed to be the reinvestment rate of 64% in the year 2015 (Table 16.32).

Reinvestment = Adjusted net capital expenditure + Change in noncash working capital
Reinvestment rate = Reinvestment/EBIT(1 − T) where EBIT(1 − T) is the after tax operating income.

Table 16.33 Estimation of growth rate from fundamentals

Year	2011	2012	2013	2014	2015
Reinvestment rate	1.76	0.88	0.62	1.88	0.64
Return on Capital Employed	0.2825	0.2615	0.2388	0.2696	0.3156
Growth rate	0.4980	0.2295	0.1485	0.5081	0.2009

Growth rate = Reinvestment rate*Return on Capital Employed.

The average growth rate estimated from fundamentals is calculated as 31% based on geometric mean during the period 2011−15 (see Table 16.33).

For estimation purposes, we assume the historical growth rate of operating income after taxes since the growth rate estimated from fundamentals is very high. The average growth of operating income after taxes during the period 2011−15 is estimated as 5.7%.

Table 16.34 Estimation of FCFF in millions of dollars

Year	2011	2012	2013	2014	2015
EBIT(1 − T)	4462	4304	4916	5782	5464
Adjusted net capex	3856.28	3189.08	3368.16	3418.12	3845.76
Change in noncash WC	4009	588	−312	7478	−367
FCFF	−3403.28	526.92	1859.84	−5114.12	1985.24

Free Cash Flow to Firm (FCFF) = EBIT(1 − T) − Adjusted Net Capex − Change in noncash working capital.

The average FCFF for Boeing during the period 2011−15 was $13,354 million (see Table 16.34).

Two-stage FCFF model

It is assumed that the operating income will grow at 5.7% for next 10 years and thereafter at the stable growth rate of U.S. economy.

High growth period inputs

High growth period	10 years
Growth rate	5.70%
Reinvestment rate	0.64
WACC	8.15%

High growth period	10 years
EBIT(1 − T) in the year 2015	5464
EBIT(1 − T) in the first year of high growth period	
5464*1.057	5775.45

Table 16.35 Present value of FCFF in high growth period

Year	1	2	3	4	5	6	7	8	9	10
EBIT(1 − T)	5775	6105	6453	6820	7209	7620	8054	8514	8999	9512
Reinvestment rate	0.64	0.64	0.64	0.64	0.64	0.64	0.64	0.64	0.64	0.64
Reinvestment	3696	3907	4130	4365	4614	4877	5155	5449	5759	6088
FCFF	2079	2198	2323	2455	2595	2743	2900	3065	3240	3424
PV of FCFF	$1922	$1879	$1836	$1795	$1754	$1714	$1676	$1638	$1600	$1564
Sum	$17,379									

The sum of the present value of FCFF in high growth phase = $17,379 million (Table 16.35).

Stable period inputs

Growth rate in stable period = 2.3% (US GDP growth rate during the 2-year period 2013−14)

Growth rate = Reinvestment rate*Aerospace and Defense Industry ROCE

Aerospace and Defense Industry ROCE = 9.86%[14]

Growth rate = Reinvestment rate*ROCE

Reinvestment rate = 2.3/9.86 = 0.233

Reinvestment rate = 23.3%

Growth rate of operating income in stable period	2.30%
Reinvestment rate	23.30%
EBIT(1 − T) at end of high growth phase	9512
EBIT(1 − T) at the beginning of stable phase	
9512*1.023	9730.776
Reinvestment = 9730.776*0.233	2269.86
FCFF in stable period = 9730.776 − 2269.86	7460.92
Terminal Value = FCFF in stable period/(WACC − growth rate in stable period)	
7460.92/(8.15% − 2.3%)	127,537.09
PV of terminal value	$58,260.10
Value of Operating assets = PV of FCFF in high growth period + PV of FCFF in stable period	
17,379 + 58,260.10	$75,638.91
Adding Cash and Cash Equivalents in 2015	12,052
Value of Boeing Firm	$87,690.91
less value of debt in 2015	9964
Value of Equity	$77,726.91
Number of shares in million	695
Value per share	111.837

[14] http://csimarket.com/Industry/industry_ManagementEffectiveness.php?ind=201.

Value of Equity = $77,726 million.

Summary of Discounted cash flow valuation

Two-stage DDM
Value per stock = = $157.33.
Two-stage FCFE
Value of equity = $114.096 billion
Value per share = $164.17.
Two-stage FCFF
Value of Boeing firm = $87.691 billion
Value of Equity = $77.727 billion
Value per stock = $111.84.
Boeing was trading at $132.75 on 21/6/2016 in NYSE. The 52-week range as of 21/6/2016 was 102.10−150.58. The market capitalization on 21/6/2016 was $84.6 billion.

16.26   Peer comparison and relative valuation

Table 16.36 **Financial highlights—peer comparison**

Company	Boeing	Airbus group	Lockheed Martin	General dynamics
Total Asset	94,408	106,681	49,128	31,997
Total Debt	9964	8737	15,261	3399
Capital Expenditures	2450	2924	939	569
Revenues	96,114	64,450	46,132	31,469
Operating Income	7443	2901	5436	4178
Cash Flow	9263	6392	6492	4682
Total Cash	12,052	10,857	1090	2785
Net Income	5176	2696	3605	2965
Market Capitalization	96,387	49,384	66,231	42,992

The peer companies selected for comparison are Airbus, Lockheed Martin, and General Dynamics. Lockheed Martin is a global security and aerospace firm which focuses on the research, design, development, manufacture, integration and sustainment of advanced technology systems, products, and services. Airbus group is a European consortium which produces the Airbus family of passenger aircraft, corporate jet, beluga supertransport, and military transport. General Dynamics is a global aerospace and defense company which produces gulf stream business jets, submarines, wheeled combat vehicles, and communication systems (Table 16.36).

Table 16.37 Price multiple comparisons

Company	P/S	P/B	P/E	Dividend yield%
Boeing	0.9	20.9	17.9	3
Airbus	0.6	5.2	18	2.5
Lockheed Martin	1.6	22.9	21.1	2.7
General Dynamics	1.4	4.1	15.2	2

The price multiple comparison of peer companies is done with respect to the period June 2016. Boeing had the highest dividend yield among the peer companies. Lockheed Martin had the highest P/S, P/B, and P/E ratios among the peer companies. The source of data was Morningstar.com (Table 16.37).

Table 16.38 Price multiple comparison with industry and S&P500

Ratios	Boeing	Industry average	S&P500
P/E	17.9	17.7	19.4
P/B	20.9	4.6	2.7
P/S	0.9	1.3	1.9
P/CF	8.6	12.5	12
Dividend Yield%	3	2.1	2.4

The price multiples of Boeing are compared with S&P500 and Industry average based on the period June 2016. Boeing had higher P/B ratio compared to industry average and S&P500. Similarly, Boeing had the higher dividend yield compared to the industry average and S&P500. The source of data was Morningstar.com (Table 16.38).

Table 16.39 Price multiple trends

Year	2006	2007	2008	2009	2010	2011	2012	2013	2014	2015
P/E	41.5	16.6	11.7	29	14.6	14.5	14.7	24.2	18.6	18.2
P/B	6.4	7.5	−33.3	18.5	17.4	9.2	9.7	11.4	6.3	14.3
P/S	1.2	1	0.5	0.6	0.8	0.8	0.7	1.2	1.1	1.1
P/CF	9.4	7	−77.5	6.9	16.4	24.9	7.6	9.6	18.5	9.1

The average P/E, P/B, P/S, and P/CF were 20.36, 6.74, 0.9, and 3.19 for Boeing during the period 2006−15 (Table 16.39).

Table 16.40 Enterprise value multiples

Company	Boeing	Airbus	Lockheed Martin	General dynamics
Revenues	96,114	64,450	46,132	31,469
EBITDA	9263	6392	6492	4682
EBIT	7443	2901	5436	4178
Debt	9964	8737	15,261	3399
Market Value of Equity	96,387	49,384	66,231	42,992
Cash and Cash Equivalents	12,052	10,857	1090	2785
Enterprise Value (EV)	94,299	47,264	80,402	43,606
EV/Revenues	0.98	0.73	1.74	1.39
EV/EBITDA	10.18	7.39	12.38	9.31
EV/EBIT	12.67	16.29	14.79	10.44

The enterprise value multiples are estimated based on the year 2015. The lower the enterprise value multiples, the more attractive the stock would be (Table 16.40).

Table 16.41 Growth rate comparison of revenues

In percent	Boeing	Airbus	Lockheed Martin	General dynamics
Year on Year	5.9	6.16	1.17	2
5-year average	8.37	7.09	0.14	−0.62
10-year average	5.77	6.54	2.17	4.01

The comparison of the revenues for peer companies is based on the year 2015. Boeing had the highest 5-year average growth rate of revenues which amounted to 8.37% (Table 16.41).

Table 16.42 Growth rate comparison of operating income

In percent	Boeing	Airbus	Lockheed Martin	General dynamics
Year on Year	−0.4	5.04	−2.79	7.43
5-year average	8.41	23.24	5.82	1.15
10-year average	10.22	2.21	6.17	6.64

The growth rate of operating income for the firms is based on the year 2015. Boeing had the highest 10-year average growth rate of operating income based on the year 2015 (Table 16.42).

16.27 Performance indicators

16.27.1 Altman Z score

NYU Stern Finance Professor, Edward Altman, developed the Altman Z score formula in the year 1967. In the year 2012, he released an updated version called the Altman Z Score Plus which can be used to evaluate both public and private companies. Investors can use Altman Z score to decide if they should buy or sell a particular stock based on the company's financial strength. The Altman Z score is the output of a credit strength test which gauges a publicly traded manufacturing company's likelihood of bankruptcy. Z score model is an accurate forecaster of failure up to 2 years prior to distress.

$$Z\text{-Score} = 1.2A + 1.4B + 3.3C + 0.6D + 1.0E$$

where

A = Working Capital/Total Assets, B = Retained Earnings/Total Assets, C = Earnings Before Interest & Tax/Total Assets, D = Market Value of Equity/Total Liabilities, and E = Sales/Total Assets.

The zones of discrimination are such that when Z-Score is less than 1.81, it is in distress zones. When the Z-Score is greater than 2.99, it is in safe zones. When the Z-Score is between 1.81 and 2.99, the company is in Grey Zone.

Altman Z-Score for Boeing is estimated as 2.74 based on the year 2015.

16.28 Piotroski score

The Piotroski score is a discrete score between 0 and 9 which is an indicator of the firm's financial position. The score was named after the Chicago accounting Professor Joseph Piotroski. The cumulative points suggest whether the stock is a value stock or not. If the company achieves a score of 8 or 9, the stock can be considered strong. If the score ranges between 0 and 2, then the stock is considered weak.

16.28.1 Criteria for Piotroski score

SL	Profitability scores	Score points	Score for Microsoft
1	Positive return on assets in current year	1	1
2	Positive operating cash flow in current year	1	1
3	Higher ROA in current year compared to previous year	1	0
4	Return on cash flow from operations greater than ROA	1	1
	Leverage, liquidity and sources of funds		

SL	Profitability scores	Score points	Score for Microsoft
5	Lower ratio of long-term debt to average total assets in current year compared to previous year	1	1
6	Higher current ratio in this year compared to previous year	1	1
7	No new shares were issued in the last year	1	1
	Operational efficiency ratios		
8	A higher gross margin compared to the previous year	1	0
9	A higher asset turnover ratio compared to the previous year	1	1
Total		9	7

Boeing has a Piotroski score of 7 out of 9. The analysis based on the year 2015 suggests that Boeing is a stable firm.

16.29 Graham number

It is a conservative method used for valuing a stock. It is a figure which measures a stock's fundamental value by taking into account the company's earnings per share and book value per share. Graham number is the upper bound of the price range which a defensive investor should pay for the stock. According to Graham number theory, any stock price below the Graham number is considered undervalued and hence worth investing in. Graham number is a combination of asset valuation and earnings power valuation.

EPS in year 2015 = $7.44
Book Value per share = $10.11
Graham Number = $\sqrt{22.5 * (\text{Earning Per Share}) * (\text{Book Value Per Share})}$
= $41.14

Boeing was trading at $132.75 on 21/6/2016 in NYSE.

16.30 Peter Lynch valuation

Peter Lynch Fair Value applies to growing companies. The ideal range for the growth rate is between 10% and 20% a year. Peter Lynch Fair Value is based on the assumption that it is advisable to buy the shares of the growth company at a P/E multiple which is equal to its growth rate. According to Peter Lynch, at fair value the PEG ratio of a growth company must be equal to one. The EBITDA growth rate is used as the earnings growth rate since this rate is less subject to management manipulations and distortion.

Peter Lynch Fair Value = PEG*Earnings Growth Rate*EPS
The EBITDA growth rate is 5.3%.
PE ratio = 19.44
PEG = 19.44/0.053 = 366.79
EPS = $7.44
Peter Lynch Fair Value = 366.79*0.053*7.44 = $144.63
Price to Peter Lynch Fair Value = 132.03/144.63 = 0.91
The price of Boeing on 21/6/2016 was $132.03.

The detailed calculation for all the analysis is given in the resources file *Boeing.xlsx*.

Analysis of wealth— Time Warner Inc.

17

17.1 Introduction

Time Warner is a global leader in media and entertainment with the focus on television networks and film and TV entertainment. The operating divisions like Home Office Inc., Turner and Warner Bros. have emerged as symbols of creativity and excellence. Home Box Office (HBO) along with its sister channel Cinemax have become the world's leading premium pay television and subscription video on demand (SVOD) service. Turner possesses premier portfolios of advertising supported cable networks and related brands. Warner Bros is the world's leading producer of television programming and filmed entertainment. Time Warner employed approximately 24,800 people by December 2015. Time Warner has a long tradition of innovation which dates back to the early days of motion pictures and includes milestones like the first talking feature film, the invention of premium television services, and the first 24-hour news channel (Table 17.1).

17.2 Business segments

17.2.1 Turner Broadcasting System, Inc. (Turner)

Turner owns and operates portfolio of domestic and international cable television networks which provides entertainment, sports, kids, and news programming on television and digital platforms for consumers throughout the world. Turner operates more than 180 channels globally. The major network brands of Turner include TNT, TBS, Adult Swim, truTV, Turner Classic Movies, Turner Sports, Cartoon Network, Boomerang, Cable News Network (CNN), and HLN. Turner's digital properties include bleacherreport.com, NBA.com, NCAA.com, PGA.com, and the CNN digital network. Turner businesses are offered in more than 200 countries. Turner's programming is basically distributed by cable system operators, satellite service distributors, telephone companies, and other distributors which are known as affiliates. Some affiliates of Turner offer smaller bundles of networks and streaming services. Turner also uses nontraditional distribution options for its programming like SVOD and other over-the-top (OTT) services which include DISH's Sling TV and Sony PlayStation. Turner's digital properties constitute its own websites and websites Turner manages or operates for sports leagues for which Turner holds the related programming rights. Turner's CNN digital network is the leading

Table 17.1 **Milestones Time Warner**[a]

Year	Events
1923	Time, a weekly magazine is founded by Henry Luce and Briton Hadden. First issue of Time had less than 20,000 subscribers
1927	Warner Bros. released the world's first feature-length talking picture, The Jazz Singer
1930	Fortune a monthly magazine is published
1936	Life, a weekly photo journal is published with circulation of more than 5 million in less than 4 weeks. Company diversifies into radio, newsreels, book publishing, oil products
1960	Approximately 90% of Time's revenues accounted from magazines
1964	Time Inc. trades from NYSE
1967	Revenue reaches $600 million
1972	Life ceases publication. Money is launched. HBO a new form of pay TV is introduced. Kinney National Company spun off its nonentertainment assets and renamed itself Warner Communications Inc.
1974	People magazine is launched
1975	HBO is the owner of 52 cable systems in USA. HBO had 287,000 customers. HBO became the first TV network to broadcast nationally. Warner formed a joint venture with American Express named Warner Amex Satellite Entertainment
1976	Warner Communication buys Atari Inc.
1980	Profit from Time's video divisions exceed those from magazines for the first time. One of the 10 television households receives HBO. Warner purchases The Franklin Mint for about $225 million which was later sold to American Protection Industries Inc.
	Turner launched CNN, the first 24 hour all news network
1985	AOL is incorporated under the original founding name Quantum Computer Services registered in Delware
1986	Warner buys out American Express share of Warner-AMEX Cable for $400 million
1988	Warner acquires Lorimar Tele pictures
1989	Time merges with Warner Communications. America Online service is launched for Macintosh and Apple II
1992	America Online goes public on the NASDAQ market at original price of $11.50
1993	Windows version of America Online launched
1994	AOL reaches 1 million members
1996	Time Warner acquires Turner Broadcasting System. AOL have 5 million members
1997	Ten million members for AOL
1998	American Online (AOL) completes acquisition of CompuServe. AOL included in S&P500 Index
1999	Time Warner establishes joint venture with AT&T to offer telephone service in 33 states. AOL completes its acquisition of Netscape Communication Corporation. AOL tops 20 million subscribers

(*Continued*)

Table 17.1 (Continued)

Year	Events
2000	Time Warner and America Online announce $181 billion merger
2006	CBS Corporation and Time Warner create a new broadcast network, The CW
2010	Time Warner's Latin American division bought Chilean nationwide terrestrial television Chilevision

[a]http://money.cnn.com/2000/01/10/deals/aol_warner/timeline.htm.

digital new destination. Bleacherreport.com of Turner is the number two digital sports destination. Turner's digital properties had approximately 115 million average monthly domestic multiplatform unique visitors during the year 2015.

The domestic entertainment networks of Turner provide a blend of original and acquired series, movies, sports, and reality programming. In the year 2015 TNT, TBS, and Adult Swim emerged as the 3 of the top 10 primetime advertising supported cable networks among the adults in the age group of 18−49 in the United States. The focus of TNT is on drama and syndicated series, sports, and network premier motion pictures. TBS focuses on contemporary comedies, as well as original series, sports, and acquired television series and movies. Adult Swim is an evening and overnight block of programming airing on Turner's Cartoon Network. truTV focuses on entertainment programming aimed at adult audiences with the tag line "Way More Fun." Turner Classic Movies is a commercial-free network that presents classic films from some of the largest film libraries in the world. Cartoon Network is the number one advertisement supported network focused on children of ages 6−11. CNN is the original 24-hour news network and the number one digital source of political news to global audiences. HLN is the "news and views" network of Turner which brings viewers breaking news and in-depth coverage.

17.2.2 Home Box Office

HBO offers original productions that includes series, films documentaries, championship boxing, concerts, and family as well as Hollywood blockbusters. HBO is the most watched pay service in the United States which provides hit Hollywood films to global consumers across a wide range of platforms and offerings. Cinemax services feature more than 1000 movie titles annually as well as new and exclusive primetime high impact series.

HBO and Cinemax Branded Services include HBO, HBO NOW, HBO GO, HBO on Demand, HBO2, HBO Signature, HBO Family, HBO Comedy, HBO Zone, HBO Latino, etc. CINEMAX include Cinemax, MAX GO, Cinemax on Demand, More Max, Action Max, 5 Star Max, Max Latino, Outer Max, and Movie Max. HBO and Cinemax branded networks are available in more than 60 countries including United States and other regions like Latin America, Central America and the Caribbean Basin, Europe, and Asia.

17.2.3   Warner Bros.

Warner Bros. is an entertainment industry leader with business focus in feature films, television, home entertainment, video games, and consumer products. Warner Bros. Home Entertainment was the industry leader with 19% market share. The Warner Bros. Television Group spans the entire portfolio of Warner Bros.' television businesses which include worldwide production, traditional, and digital distribution and broadcasting. The Warner Bros. Television Group (WBTVG) produces primetime, first run cable and animated series. The group aired more than 70 programs during the year 2015. Warner Bros. Television is the leading supplier of network programming as well as major producer for cable. WBTVG includes Warner Horizon Television, Tele pictures, Shed Media, Warner Bros. Animation, and Blue Ribbon Content. Warner Horizon Television is the producer of scripted cable programs. Tele pictures possesses the first run syndicated programming. Shed Media is the producer of unscripted cable programs. Warner Bros. Animation produces animation series like "Mike Tyson Mysteries," "Teen Titans Go!" "The Tom and Jerry Show," and Wabbit. Blue Ribbon Content is the producer of live action and animated short form digital series (Table 17.2).

Warner Bros. Consumer products deals with the intellectual properties of Warner Bros. Entertainment's film and television library. The division holds more than 3700 active licensees worldwide. The well-known icons include DC Comics, Batman, Superman, Green Lantern, Wonder Woman, and Supergirl along with blockbuster film franchise Harry Potter and Hanna-Barbera properties like Yogi Bear and Tom & Jerry.

DC Entertainment (DCE) has iconic brands like DC Comics, Vertigo, and MAD. Vertigo deals with high concept stories such as Sandman, Fables, and American Vampire. MAD is subversive humor parodying pop culture and events. DCE is the largest English language comic publisher in the world which publishes comic books, graphic novels, and magazines.

Warner Bros. Studio facilities oversees the physical operations of Warner Bros. Studios which is one of the leading motion picture and television production and

Table 17.2 Warner Bros. Entertainment Brands

Warner Bros. Entertainment Inc.
Home Entertainment, Warner Home Video, Warner Bros. Advanced Digital Services, Warner Bros. Interactive Entertainment, Warner Bros. Technical Operations, Warner Bros. Anti-Piracy Operations
Motion Pictures
Warner Bros. Pictures, New Line Cinema
Television
Warner Bros. Television Group, Warner Bros. Television, Telepictures Production, Warner Horizon Television, Warner Bros. Animation, Warner Bros. Domestic Television Distribution, Warner Bros. International Television Distribution, Warner Bros. International Television Production, Warner Bros. International Branded Services, Studio 2.0, The CW Television Network

postproduction facilities in the world. Warner Bros. Theatre Ventures is the live stage play division that develops and produces first class musicals and other stage productions.

17.3   Growth strategy[1]

Time Warner's strategy is to become the world's leading video content company. Time Warner focusses on expansion in the most attractive global territories to take advantage of growing demand for content worldwide.

Time Warner focuses on using its industry leading operating scale and brands to create, package, and deliver high quality content globally. Over the past years, Time Warner has transformed its business to focus on the production and distribution of high quality video content. The businesses of Time Warner focuses on leveraging strong brands, distinctive intellectual property, and global scale. Time Warner have been following the strategy of making investments in the world's best and most engaging video content. Divisions of Time Warner like Warner Bros, HBO, and Turner is an industry leader. Time Warner create products and services by harnessing technology to entertain audiences in new ways to provide new experiences. The "Content Everywhere" initiatives provides consumers with access to high quality con tent across platforms and devices. Time Warner is strategically placed to address the developments in television industry, growth of new video services, and shifting con sumer habits. Time Warner is a leader in enhancing the value of traditional pay tele vision subscriptions for consumers and affiliates within the traditional TV ecosystem. The company focuses on high quality distinctive programming and sports program ming. Time Warner focuses on making more of its content available on demand and on a growing variety of devices and invests in technology to improve consumer expe rience. Time Warner supports the development of better user interfaces for on demand viewing of programming offered through affiliates. Turner develops new advertisement offerings designed using data analytics that facilitate advertisers to better reach their target audiences. Time Warner emphasizes on new growth opportu nities outside the traditional ecosystem by focusing on new investments in new digital products and technologies like SVOD and "OTT" services. The company has also been investing in content. Time Warner focuses on increasing the digital sales and rentals of its film and television content.

Turner became the only programming group with 3 of the top 10 advertisement supported cable networks in primetime among adults in the age group 18−49 years. Over the period of time, Turner has expanded its presence outside the traditional TV ecosystem with CNN Digital occupying the top position in news for multiplat form views. In 2015, CNN grew primetime ratings by 29% in its key demographic segments. In 2015, Turner launched new digital initiatives—Great Big Story and Super Deluxe. In 2015, HBO had received 43 Primetime Emmy awards. The major sources of revenues for Turner are programming revenues obtained from affiliates

[1] Annual Report 2015.

who distribute the programming to subscribers, the sale of advertising on its networks and digital properties that Turner owns or manages for other companies. Turner also derives revenues from licensing of its original programming to SVOD and other OTT services and its brands for consumer products. Turner is improving its competitive position through strategic regional launches, partnerships, and acquisitions in key territories.

The strategy of Turner is to strengthen the programming on its cable television networks by focusing on high quality original programming, modifying the mix of programming on its networks, and repositioning or rebranding of some of its networks. Turner had broadened the scope of CNN programming to include programs on important events, long form documentaries. The truTV network has been rebranded to focus on light hearted comedy at adults. Turner is repositioning TNT and TBS to focus on distinctive original programming aimed at young audiences. Additional investments are being made in new digital products and technology. In the year 2015, Turner launched Super Deluxe, the digital production studio to develop original short form digital content. In the same year CNN launched Great Big Story, an independent news brand which distributes its content via digital properties for mobile devices and social networks. In Latin America, Turner is the number one provider of multichannel television in the region.

Turner sports programming provides revenue sources through higher affiliate fees, ratings, and advertising rates. Turner Sports produces award winning sports programming and content for Turner's TNT, TBS, truTV networks, etc. Turner's sports have licenses to feature programs from the National Basketball Association through the period 2024—25.

Turner's Cartoon Network and Boomerang provides original, acquired, and classic animated and live action entertainment for kids in different parts of the world. Turner have focused on expansion of its global kids business by forming strategic partnership with Warner Bros. in the year 2015 to produce and distribute 450 half-hour episodes of original animated programming across the Cartoon Network and Boomerang networks. By 2015, Cartoon Network had 94.3 million domestic television households. Boomerang offers exclusive new original content from Warner Bros. as well as classic animated entertainment from the Warner Bros., Hanna-Barbera, MGM, and Cartoon Network libraries.

Turner focusses on maintenance of CNN's leadership position in worldwide breaking-news and political coverage. By 2015, CNN had 94.3 million domestic television households. As of December 2015, CNN managed 41 news bureaus and editorial operations. CNN had approximately 300 million households outside the US by December end 2015.

HBO focuses on investing in technology to enhance the overall consumer experience on the HBO GO, MAX GO, and HBO NOW streaming services. Home Box's office's premium pay television service is distributed by affiliates. HBO NOW is distributed by third parties that include digital distributors and some traditional affiliates. HBO also sells its original programming in both physical and digital formats and licenses some of its programming to the Amazon Prime SVOD service. HBO distributes its programming internationally through distribution models like premium pay and basic tier television services distributed by affiliates, licensing, and streaming services distributed by third parties and direct to consumer streaming services. HBO's original programming is offered to customers in over 150 countries. A major portion of HBO and Cinemax services are derived from uncut and uncensored feature films. HBO have licensing agreements with major film studios and producers and distributors like Warner Bros., Twentieth Century Fox, Universal Pictures, and Summit Entertainment. These agreements give HBO the exclusive right to exhibit and distribute on its premium pay television services and digital platform the feature films theatrically released in the United States by these studios. Internationally a major portion of the programming on HBO's premium pay, basic tier television, and streaming services consists of feature films which were licensed from major studios in the United States. In 2015, HBO had approximately 49 million domestic premium pay subscribers which included HBO NOW and HBO. HBO licenses its programs to television networks and SVOD services in over 150 countries. Warner Bros. Entertainment Inc. is the largest television and film studio in the world on the basis of studio revenues in year 2015. Warner Bros. is the number one producer of primetime television series for the United States broadcast networks for the year 2015. Warner Bros. is following the strategy of increasing digital sales and rentals of its film and television content. By December 2015, Warner Bros. content library comprises of over 75,000 hours of programming which included over 7000 feature films and 5000 television programs. Warner Bros. have built strong global franchise properties from its brands and characters like the Batman and Harry Potter series and The Hobbit and The Lord of the Rings trilogies. Warner Bros. is also the global leader in television production and distribution businesses. Warner Bros. focuses on developing programs specifically tailored for local audiences through its global network of production companies. Warner Bros. is a leader in the feature film business and produces feature films under its Warner Bros. and New Line Cinema banners. Warner Bros. derives revenues from the home entertainment distribution of its film and television content in physical and digital formats. Warner Bros. focuses on increasing revenues electronic sell through (EST) sales and transactional VOD rentals of its film and television content. Warner Bros. develops, publishes, and distributes video games, including mobile and console games.

The demand for digital distribution offers immense strategic opportunities for Warner Bros. Entertainment segment. Home Entertainment focuses on enhancing the value of the studio's content while deriving the benefits of emerging technologies. Warner Bros. Pictures crossed the $3 billion mark of revenues for the ninth consecutive year in 2015. Time Warner derives a major chunk of revenues from its cable networks, premium pay television services, production, and licensing of television programming and premium pay television services. Developments in technology leading to new video services and shift in consumer viewing patterns creates challenges for Time Warner. Disruptions in the traditional television content delivery model by video streaming services are critical risk factors for the company. The United States television industry has been experiencing declines in subscribers due to shift of subscribers to multichannel video services and industry wide declines in ratings for programming. Multichannel video services offer smaller bundles of networks to counteract the subscriber's declines which present risks to Time Warner's businesses. Time Warner addresses these risks by strategically investing in high quality original programming along with investment in technology. Time Warner also partners with affiliates to enhance the value of multichannel video subscriptions to consumers and selectively licenses its content to SVOD services.

17.4   Corporate restructuring by Time Warner

Time Warner Inc. has engaged in a number of mergers, acquisitions, and other corporate actions over the years.

17.4.1   Time Inc. merger with Warner Communications[2]

In 1990, Time Inc. merger with Warner Communication (WCI) to form Time Warner Inc. The merger in which Time acquired Warner was valued at $18 billion. Time exchanged 12.5% of its shares for about 10% of Warner share. Each Warner share was exchanged tax free for a 0.465 share of Time Inc. common stock with an indicated market value of $50.74 based on Time's closing stock price of $109.125 a share on the day before the announcement of deal. The combined company had $10.7 billion debt. The merger was billed as merger of equals.

The WCI holders received 0.7188774 of a share of Time Warner Inc. Series C8 ¾% Convertible Exchangeable Preferred Stock (Series C) and 0.5421044 of a share of Time Warner Inc. Series D11% Convertible Exchangeable Preferred Stock Series D and 0.15166 of a share of Class A common stock of BHC Communications. The Series C and Series D preferred stock have been redeemed for cash. Time Inc. and Warner Communication merged to create a world power in the field of media and entertainment. The merger created the largest media and entertainment conglomerate in the world. Time was a leading book and magazine publisher with extensive cable television holdings. Warner was a major producer of movies and records and has a large cable television operation. The merger made Time Warner as one among the few global media giants which were able to create and distribute information in virtually any medium. The merger positioned Time Warner to compete against major European and Asian companies. At the time of merger, the merged entity had a stock market value of $15.2 billion and revenue of $10 billion.

Time brought to the combination Time magazine and other publications such as Life, People, Money, and Sports Illustrated. It also controlled the second largest cable system in the United States, American Television and Communications, and

[2] Kathryn Harris and Paul Richter, Time Warner merger creates a world power, http://articles.latimes. com/1989-03-05/news/mn-471_1_time-warner; Douglas Gomery, http://www.museum.tv/eotvsection. php?entrycode=timewarner; Randall Rothenberg, The media business; Time Warner's merger payoff, a http://www.nytimes.com/1990/12/31/business/the-media-business-time-warner-s-merger-payoff.html? pagewanted=all&src=pm

HBO, the nation's largest cable programming service, which included HBO and Cinemax. Time also maintained a significant presence in book publishing with its Book-of-the-Month Club, Time-Life Books, and Little.

Warner Communications was established in 1971 when Kinney National Company spun off its nonentertainment assets due to a financial scandal. It was the parent company for Warner Bros Pictures and Warner Music Group during the 1970s and 1980s. It also owned DC Comics and Mad. In the 1970s, Warner formed joint venture with credit card company American Express named Warner Amex Satellite Entertainment which held cable channels like MTV, Nickelodeon, and Showtime. Later in 1984, Warner bought American Express stake in the joint venture and sold it to Viacom which was renamed as MTV Networks. In 1982, Warner purchased Popular Library from CBS Publications. In 1983, Warner was a takeover target of the News Corporation which was thwarted by offering larger stake in Warner to Chris Craft. Warner Communications had also acquired Lorimar Telepictures Corp, a pre-eminent supplier of television programs such as Dallas and Falcon Crest.

The new entity owned USA's most lucrative recorded music and magazine publishing businesses, the largest television programming operation for both pay cable and primetime network television. The merger elevated Time Warner as the biggest television company in the world. The merger provided the scale for Time Warner to position against Japanese conglomerates like Sony and Matsushita. This merger was also significant as it underscored the network companies' vulnerability to competition. The network companies are not allowed to own cable television systems. The merger facilitated Time Warner to create television programming, distribute it over its own cable system and syndicate it around the world. For the combined firm, half of its revenues came from television related subsidiaries. The other half came from movie making, owing and operating one of the top six major music labels and publishing string of magazines which included Time, Fortune, and Money. After the merger, Time had packaged advertisements for its newest magazine in Warner videotapes; Warner's Looney Tunes cartoon characters appeared in books published by Time. Synergy benefits were realized through Time Warner Direct which oversees the Book of the Month Club and the Quality Paperback Book club as well as the television offers for parapsychology books that sell by mail or telephone. Access to Time Warner's database of 13 million direct marketing customers enabled Warner Bros. to promote their major movies. Warner also became the source of numerous new products promoted by Time's direct marketing operations which included videotape series featuring Warner Bros.'s properties as World War II movies, Clint Eastwood films, and Looney Tunes cartoons.

17.4.2   Time Warner Turner Broadcasting merger[3]

In 1995, Time Warner merged with Turner Broadcasting. This merger boosted Time-Warner's position as the world's largest entertainment and media

[3] Geraldine Fabrikant, Holders back Time Warner Turner merger, http://www.nytimes.com/1996/10/11/business/holders-back-time-warner-turner-merger.html, Oct 11, 1996.

conglomerate. Under the merger agreement, Time-Warner purchased 82% of Turner Broadcasting, in a deal worth an estimated $7.5 billion. The merger gave Time-Warner access to the important brands of Ted Turner which included the CNN, the Cartoon Network, the Atlanta Braves baseball team, and two movie studios. Ted Turner, the chairman of Ted Turner, became a major shareholder and vice chairman of Time-Warner. The merger faced stiff competition from major shareholders of Turner like Comcast Corporation, Continental cablevision Inc., and US West the regional Bell telephone company. US West filed a lawsuit to block the merger. US West's investment in Time Warner consisted of a 25.5% stake in the Warner Bros. Studio, Time Warner Cable, and HBO. Turner wholly owns a number of cable networks including CNN, Headline News, Turner Network Television (TNT), WTBS, Cartoon Network and Turner Classic Movies. Under the terms of deal, the combined entity was expected to have annual revenues of about $18.5 billion, surpassing that of Walt Disney Company. The combined company accounted for about 40% of all cable programming in United States at the time of merger. At the time of merger, Time Warner was second largest cable distributor behind Tele-Communications Inc. with 11.5 million cable subscribers representing 17% of all United States cable television households. Under the terms of all stock deal, Turner Broadcasting's shareholders received three-quarters of a Time Warner share for each Turner class A or B share.

17.4.3   American Online and Time Warner merger[4]

America Online and Time Warner completed their historic merger on January 2001. Time Warner was taken over by AOL at a 71% premium to its share price on the announcement date. AOL had proposed the acquisition in October 1999. The deal valued at $164 billion became the largest merger on record up to that time. The merger was structured as a stock swap. Time Warner shareholders received 1.5 shares of the new company for every share of Time Warner stock they owned. AOL shareholders received one share of the new company for every AOL shares they held. The shareholders of AOL and Time Warner held 55% and 45% of the new company, respectively. The combined entity had a market capitalization of $350 billion.

Founded in 1985, AOL was a leader in providing interactive services, web brands, internet technologies, and electronic commerce services. AOL operates two subscription-based Internet technologies. At the time of merger announcement, AOL had 20 million subscribers plus another 2 million through CompuServe. At the time of merger, AOL had less than one-fifth of the revenue and workforce of Time Warner, but had almost twice the market value.

The merger created the world's largest vertically integrated media and entertainment company. Basically there was little overlap between the two businesses. Time Warner was a media and entertainment company, whereas AOL was largely an

---

[4] http://archipelle.com/Business/AOLTimeWarner.pdf; Knowledge@Wharton. "Giving Up on AOL Time Warner". March 2, 2003. http://news.com.com/2009-1069-990592.html?tag=fd_nc_1

Internet service provider offering access to content and commerce. The combination of Time Warner's broadband systems, media contents, and subscriber base was expected to create significant synergies and strategic advantages with AOL's online brand and Internet infrastructure. AOL had the brand and credibility to capitalize upon the growth of broadband Internet but lacked the infrastructure. As the leading provider of cable television, Time Warner had the distribution capabilities AOL needed. For Warner, merging with AOL was more effective way to distribute its contents via online channels as opposed to building its own capabilities. The new merged entity was expected to provide an important new broadband distribution platform for America Online's interactive services and drive subscriber growth through cross-marketing with Time Warner's preeminent brands. Through this acquisition, AOL got more direct path into broadband transmission as Time Warner Cable systems served 20% of United States markets at the time of merger. The cable connection facilitated the introduction of AOL TV which was designed to deliver access to the Internet through the TV transmission. At the time of acquisition announcement, AOL had 22 million subscribers; Time Warner had 28 million magazine subscribers, 13 million cable subscribers, and 35 million HBO subscribers.

AOL's subscriber base and advertising revenues were growing exponentially until the dotcom crash of 2000 occurred. As a part of a put option contract with German media giant Bertelsmann, AOL had to borrow $600 million in order to buy AOL Europe. By 2002, the total debt of the combined company reached $28 billion. The total loss including write down of goodwill for 2002, reached $100 billion. On the merger announcement date, AOL and Time Warner had market values of $165 billion and $76 billion respectively. By 2004, the combined market value of the firm fell to about $78 billion. The downfall of this merger is symbolic for the burst of the Internet bubble. At the time of the merger AOL's stocks were overvalued mainly due to the Internet bubble.

The merger faced integration challenges as the culture at the two organizations was entirely different. A key part of the merger strategy was to position AOL as the major global provider of high speed services. Time Warner's cable competitors were reluctant to open up their networks for AOL as they feared that AOL could deliver video over the Internet and take away their core television customers. The cable companies were competing with AOL's dial up and high speed services by offering a tiered pricing system giving subscribers more options than AOL. AOL Time Warner though the global leader in digital revolution, failed to build the business model of Internet telephony or Voice over IP (VoIP) which was the emerging trend. The combined entity was not able to promote their idea of a combined music-platform. In 2003, Time Warner decided to drop AOL from its name. In 2009, AOL had about 6 million paying subscribers in the United States, down from 13 million at the end of 2006. AOL revenues were down to $4.2 billion in 2009 compared to $9.1 billion in 2002. In 2009, Time Warner completed the separation of AOL from Time Warner through a spin-off involving a pro rata dividend distribution of all of the AOL common stock held by Time Warner to Time Warner stockholders.

17.4.4 Other acquisitions

In August 2015, Turner acquired a majority interest in in iStreamPlanet Co., LLC ("iStreamPlanet"), a provider of streaming and cloud-based video and technology services. This acquisition was aimed at improving Turner's digital streaming capabilities.

17.4.5 Spin offs

17.4.5.1 Spin off of AOL

In the year 2009, Time Warner completed the spinoff of AOL Inc. One share of AOL common stock was distributed for every 11 shares of Time Warner common stock as of record date of November 27, 2009. Stockholders received cash payment instead of fractional AOL shares. The AOL spin-off was structured as a tax-free dividend to Time Warner stockholders for U.S. federal income tax purposes, except for the cash received in lieu of fractional shares. The spinoff of AOL was aimed to streamline Time Warner's portfolio of businesses by focusing on creating, packaging, and distributing branded content. The spin off gave Time Warner and AOL greater strategic and operational flexibility. AOL Time Warner merger was termed as one of the most disastrous corporate mergers in history. AOL has steadily lost subscribers for its dial-up Internet access business. The spin off was aimed to make AOL a standalone public company with the focus to strengthen its core businesses and develop innovative products and services.

17.4.5.2 Spin off of Time Warner Cable

On March 12, 2009, Time Warner Inc. announced the separation of Time Warner Cable Inc. through a tax-free spin-off. Warner affected a 1 for 3 reverse stock split. 0.083670 share of Time Warner Cable common stock was distributed for each share of Time Warner common stock holders. Time Warner Cable is the second-largest cable provider in the United States after Comcast Corp with 13.3 million video subscribers. After the spun off, Time Warner wanted to focus on cable network, entertainment, and publishing operations. Time Warner had emerged more of a full-fledged telecommunication business with expansion into high-speed Internet access and digital phone service with different needs that did not fit as well with Time Warner's traditional media businesses. Cable operators typically have a more highly leveraged capital structure than pure content companies like entertainment and media companies, since they usually have to invest heavily in infrastructure. Time Warner Cable paid special cash dividend to holders of its common stock which amounted to $10.27 a share or $9.25 billion. Time Warner held 80% of the Time Warner Cable.

17.4.5.3   Spin off of Time Inc.

On June 6, 2014, Time Warner Inc. completed the spin-off of Time Inc. on June 6, 2014. Time Warner distributed all outstanding shares of Time Inc. common stock to Time Warner shareholders at a distribution ratio of one share of Time Inc. common stock for every eight shares of Time Warner common stock held on the May 23, 2014 record date. The spin off was aimed to position Time Warner as the world's leading video company. Time was the United States's largest magazine publisher in terms of profit. Though Time Magazine was still profitable, other brands like Fortune and Entertainment Weekly are not making large contribution. The advertising revenues from titles like Time, People, and Sports Illustrated have been declining over the period of time. Time Warner decided to spin off its entire Time Inc. magazine group after talks with Meredith Corp failed over the proposed merger of most of their titles. The spin off took place in a scenario whereby there appeared a permanent decline in newsstand sales and protracted advertisement slump.

17.5   Strategic investments

Time Warner makes strategic investments in early to mid-stage companies that generate strategic value for Time Warner. Time Warner Investments seeks to acquire minority equity stakes in private companies and targets an investment size of up to $25 million.

Time Warner hold an approximately 49.4% voting interest in Central Media Enterprises Ltd., a publicly traded broadcasting company that operates leading television networks in Bulgaria, Croatia, and other East European countries. The CW is a 50-50 joint venture between Warner Bros. and CBS Corporation which offers primetime lineup of advertising supported original programming. During the period February 2016, Warner Bros. and NBCUniversal Media, LLC ("NBCUniversal") entered into an agreement under which Warner Bros. agreed to sell its Flixster business in exchange for a 25% interest in Fandango Media, LLC, a subsidiary of NBCUniversal ("Fandango"). In August 2015, Turner acquired a majority ownership interest in iStreamPlanet Co., LLC ("iStreamPlanet"), a provider of streaming and cloud-based video and technology services, for $148 million, net of cash acquired (Table 17.3).

17.6   Stock split

America Online, Inc. declared seven 2-for-1 stock splits after becoming a public company in March 1992 (Table 17.4).

Table 17.3 **Select investment portfolio**

Company	Description
Adaptly	Social media buying and optimization platform for advertisers
AUDIENCESCIENCE	Online advertising company that provide services like integrated brand management, audience targeting, and campaign execution technology to brand advertisers
BUSTLE	Digital content company focused on the 18–34-year-old females which focusses on events, entertainment, lifestyles, fashion, and beauty
Conviva	Real-time big data processing platform that enables the delivery of TV-quality experiences over the Internet
Crowdstar	Developer and publisher of games geared toward the female demographic
Dynamic Signal	Focuses on Employee Advocacy
EPOXY	Platform that facilitates content owners to effectively distribute their videos across the social web
FanDuel	Daily fantasy sports platform in which users compete in daily contests to win cash prizes
Fuse	Provides entertainment and lifestyle content across traditional and digital platforms
gaiga	Hybrid social networking site which targets 13–24 year olds
Joyous	Video e-commerce company which features female premium products in fashion, food, beauty and life style
Kamcord	Mobile application and web platform which enables users to broadcast live videos from their mobile phones
Krux	Data management platform that provides publishers and advertisers a technology platform to measure and analyze their first party audience data on any online platform
SIMULMEDIA	Advertising technology that provides web-like ad targeting and measurement to TV
TRION	Developer and publisher of premium games
Vessel	Premium video service that provide short form videos
Weloveit	Image-based social network
Yieldmo	Mobile advertising technology company
Hammer Chisel	Provider of voice and text messaging service for gamers
Mashable	Digital content company
NextVR	NextVR provides the transmission of live, long-form virtual reality content

Table 17.4 **American Online stock splits**

Date	Ratio of split
November 23, 1994	2 for 1
April 27, 1995	2 for 1
November 28, 1995	2 for 1
March 16, 1998	2 for 1
November 17, 1998	2 for 1
Febraury 22, 1999	2 for 1

Table 17.5 **Historic TW Inc. stock splits**

Date	Ratio of split
October 1, 1976	2 for 1
October 1, 1981	2 for 1
September 10, 1992	4 for 1
December 15, 1998	2 for 1

Table 17.6 **Dividend history**

Year	DPS
2005	0.29
2006	0.60
2007	0.68
2008	0.72
2009	4.70
2010	0.82
2011	0.90
2012	1.00
2013	1.10
2014	1.25
2015	1.40

Source: The source of data was yahoo finance.

Historic TW Inc. stock split four times between 1976 and its merger with America Online. The 1976 and 1981 splits mentioned are for Historic TW Inc.'s predecessor, Time Inc. (Table 17.5).

17.7 Dividend trends

The average growth rate of dividends during the 5-year period, 2011–15 was approximately 11% (Table 17.6).

17.8 Ownership structure

According to the statistics, by the period June 2016 equity and debt constituted 50.2% and 49.8% of the total capital structure. With respect to equity ownership, there were 1492 institutional owners and 2411 fund owners. Currently institutions hold 66.3% and mutual funds hold 33.6% of the equity ownership. The insiders hold 0.1% of the equity ownership. The top 10 funds hold 11% of the total shares. The top 10 financial institutions hold 31.73% of the equity ownership. Dodge & Cox mutual fund held 2.82% of the total shares in June 2016 (Table 17.7).

Table 17.7 **Top 10 financial institutions**

	Name	Percent of total shares held
1	Vanguard Group Inc.	5.72
2	MFS Investment Management KK	5.31
3	Dodge & Cox	4.83
4	State Street Corp	3.94
5	BlackRock Fund Advisors	3.09
6	J.P. Morgan Investment Management Inc.	2.79
7	Royal London Asset Management Ltd.	1.8
8	Capital World Investors	1.79
9	Capital Research Global Investors	1.28
10	Longview Partners (Guernsey) Ltd.	1.18
	Total	31.73

Source: Morningstar.com.

17.9 Corporate governance

The board of directors consists of 12 members who are drawn from varied fields of business and public service. The three standing committees are the Audit and Finance Committee, the Compensation and Human Development Committee, and the Nominating and Governance Committee. These committees are composed of independent directors. According to Time Warner's corporate governance policy, the lead independent director shall preside at meetings of the Board at which the Chairman is not present. The Board of Directors have adopted charters and policies for each of its three standing committees. The Audit and Finance Committee have a policy on auditor rotation. The board has also adopted a policy regarding director nominations which outlines the processes whereby director nominees are selected. The company's By-Laws are one of the company's foundational governance documents.

17.10 Corporate social responsibility activities[5]

In 2007, Time Warner expanded the scale of greenhouse gas emissions assessment to include the Scope 1 and 3 emissions as defined by the World Resource Institute's Greenhouse Gas Reporting Protocol. In 2011, HBO's communication facility in New York was designed and build for environmental efficiency with green roof and approximately 80% of the building set below the ground level. Warner Bros. received a LEED Gold rating for Stage 23 from the U.S. Green Building Council in 2009. In 2010, Warner Bros. developed a scorecard designed to help productions set goals and track results. Carbon calculators are also used to

[5] CSR Report Time Warner.

measure emission related to activities such as fuel use, air and automotive travel, utilities and solid waste. In the year 2010, Warner Bros., established green production baselines, developed metrics and reporting frameworks for broader sustainability initiatives. Warner Bros. have provided materials to over 100 schools and nonprofit organizations through its material donation program called Encore. This program was established in the year 1996 to provide like new and lightly used materials such as furniture, construction materials, clothing, equipment, and office supplies to local community partners. Time Warner partners with international vendors who specialize in sustainable asset recovery and disposal to replace electronic equipment. Time Warner provides grant funding to institutions like Brooklyn Academic of Music, City Park Foundation, Lincoln Center, and Apollo Theater for promotion of arts. The Time Warner Foundation is a private nonprofit foundation that seek innovative and powerful ways to discover and nurture the next generation of storytellers. For example, the Time Warner Foundation Fellowships is a full tuition award to the American Film Institute (AFI) conservatory for students of exceptional promise from statistically underrepresented communities. In the year 2005, Time Warner became the first major US-based media and entertainment company to publish a comprehensive corporate social responsibility.

17.11   Debt financing

During 2015, Time Warner issued $3.0 billion and €700 million aggregate principal amount of debt securities in three separate offerings under its shelf registration statement. In June 2015, Time Warner purchased $687 million aggregate principal amount of the $1.0 billion aggregate principal amount outstanding of its 5.875%. Notes due 2016 (the "2016 Notes") through a tender offer. On December 18, 2015, Time Warner amended its $5.0 billion of senior unsecured credit facilities (the "Revolving Credit Facilities"), which consist of two $2.5 billion revolving credit facilities, to extend the maturity dates of both facilities from December 18, 2019 to December 18, 2020.

17.12   Dividends and share repurchases

In 2015, Time Warner returned close to $5 billion to shareholders in share repurchases and dividends. In 2016, Time Warner increased dividend by 15% which was the seventh straight year of double digit increases in dividend. During the period 2008−15, Time Warner registered total return to shareholders of over 140%. On the basis of stock repurchase plans, the number of shares repurchased in 2013, 2014, and 2015, amounted to 60 million, 77 million, and 45 million respectively. In January 2016, Time Warner's Board of Directors authorized up to $5 billion of share repurchases. Purchases under the stock repurchase program may be made from time to time on the open market and in privately negotiated transactions.

17.13   Equity shares

By December 31, 2015, the shareholders' equity of Time Warner included 795 million shares of common stock net of 857 million shares of common stock held in treasury. As of December 31, 2015, Time Warner is authorized to issue up to 8.33 billion shares of common stock and 750 million shares of preferred stock.

17.14   Equity compensation plans

The company has one active equity plan, the Time Warner Inc. 2013 Stock Incentive Plan. Under the 2013 Stock Incentive Plan, Time Warner is authorized to grant equity awards to employees and nonemployee directors that covers an aggregate of approximately 36 million shares of company's common stock. Stock options and RSUs have been granted to employees and nonemployee directors of the company. Generally, stock options are granted with exercise prices equal to the fair market value on the date of grant, vest in four equal annual installments and expire 10 years from the date of grant. Time Warner has a PSU program for executive officers who are awarded a target number of PSUs who represent the contingent (unfunded) right to receive shares of company common stock at the end of a 3-year performance period based on performance level of the company.

17.15   Revenue highlights

Segmental revenue highlights are given in Tables 17.8–17.12.

Table 17.8 **Total revenue highlights in millions of dollars**

Year	2013	2014	2015
Turner	9983	10,396	10,596
Home Box Office	4890	5398	5615
Warner Bros.	12,312	12,526	12,992
Intersegment eliminations	−724	−961	−1085
Total revenues	26,461	27,359	28,118

Source: Annual Report 2015.

Table 17.9 **Home Box Office revenue highlights in millions of dollars**

Year	2013	2014	2015
Subscription	4231	4578	4748
Content	659	820	867
Total Revenues	4890	5398	5615

Source: Annual Report 2015.

Table 17.10 Warner Bros. total revenue highlights in millions of dollars

Year	2013	2014	2015
Theatrical product	6119	5839	5143
Television product	4690	5099	5635
Video games and others	1503	1588	2214
Total revenues	12312	12526	12992

Source: Annual Report 2015.

Table 17.11 Theatrical product revenues in millions of dollars

Year	2013	2014	2015
Film rentals	2158	1969	1578
Home video and electronic delivery	2118	1913	1717
Television licensing	1652	1686	1579
Consumer products and other	191	271	269
Total revenues	6119	5839	5143

Source: Annual Report 2015.

Table 17.12 Television product revenues in millions of dollars

Year	2013	2014	2015
Television licensing	3628	4121	4650
Home video and electronic delivery	719	584	529
Consumer products and other	343	394	456
Total revenues	4690	5099	5635

17.16   Financial trend analysis

In the year 2009, AOL was spun off from Time Warner. The year-end capitalization increased by 11% on average basis during the period 2011–15 while the average market capitalization declined by 7% during the period 2006–10 (Table 17.13).

Table 17.13 **Financial highlights in millions of dollars**

Year	2006	2007	2008	2009	2010	2011	2012	2013	2014	2015
Revenues	44,224	46,482	46,984	25,785	26,888	28,974	28,729	29,795	27,359	28,118
Operating income	7362	8949	−15957	4545	5428	5805	5918	6605	5975	6865
Operating cash flow	8598	8475	10,332	4709	3290	3432	3442	3714	3681	3851
Free cash flow	4457	4045	5955	4148	2659	2660	2799	3112	3207	3428
Net Income	6552	4387	−13,402	2468	2578	2886	3019	3691	3827	3833
Total cash	1549	1516	1099	4733	3663	3476	2841	1816	2618	2155
Total assets	131,669	133,830	114,059	66,059	66,524	67,801	68,089	67,999	63,146	63,848
Short-term debt	64	126	2041	862	26	23	749	66	1118	198
Long-term debt	34,933	37,004	19,855	15,346	16,523	19,501	19,122	20,061	21,263	23,594
Capital expenditure	4141	4430	4377	561	631	772	643	602	474	423
Year-end market capitalization	55,783	39,128	23,806	32,327	33,893	33,749	42,742	59,822	71,069	51,413
Book value of equity	60,389	58,536	42,288	33,396	32,940	29,957	29,796	29,904	24,476	23,619

17.17   Ratio analysis

The profitability ratios have improved over the 10-year period of analysis. The profitability ratios have improved during the period 2011−15 compared to the period 2006−10. All profitability ratios except gross margin were negative in the year 2008. The average gross margin increased from 42.8% during the period 2006−10 to 43.66% during the period 2011−15. The average operating margin which was 8% during the period 2006−2010 improved to 21.8% during the period 2011−15. The average net margin increased from 3% to 12% during the comparative period. The return on assets, return on equity, and return on invested capital increased from 0.9%, 1.1 %, and 2.7% to 5.2%, 12.3%, and 8.8% on average basis during the time period 2011−15 compared to the period 2006−10. The average ICR increased from 1.9 to 4.7 during the two periods of comparison (Table 17.14).

The average EPS increased from 0.25 during the period 2006−10 to 3.74 during the period 2011−15. The average book value per share decreased from 38.16 to 31.51 during the two periods of comparison. The average cash flow per share ratios have increased during the period 2011−15 compared to the period 2006−10. The average free cash flow per share, revenue per share and EBITDA per share increased from 3.12, 30.57, and 7.94 to 3.29, 30.63 and 9.08 during the period of comparison (Table 17.15).

The values for price multiples have increased during the period 2011−15 compared to the period 2006−10 on average basis. The average price to book, price to earnings, price to sales, and price to operating cash flow have increased from 0.83, 9.15, 1.17, and 6.44 to 1.93, 15.76, 2.02, and 16 respectively (Table 17.16).

The enterprise value multiple values have increased over the 10-year period. The average EV/Revenues, EV/EBITDA, and EV/EBIT have increased from 1.8, 6.6, and 4.5 during the period 2006−10 to 2.6, 8.6, and 11.6 during the period 2011−15 (Table 17.17).

The average current ratio and quick ratio during the period 2006−15 was 1.34 and 1.02. respectively (Table 17.18).

The leverage intensity has increased over the period 2011−15 compared to the period 2006−10. The average debt equity ratio increased from 0.61 during the period 2006−10 to 0.77 in the period 2011−15. The average long-term debt to total asset increased from 0.24 to 0.32. The average total debt per share increased from 21.08 to 24.14 (Table 17.19).

The efficiency ratios are compared on an average basis during two time periods of 2006−10 and 2011−15. The average fixed assets turnover increased from 3.5 to 8.3. The asset turnover ratio remained at 0.4. The average receivable turnover ratio decreased from 5.7 to 3.6 and inventory turnover ratio decreased 11.3 to 8.5 respectively. The average days' payable decreased from 20.3 to 17 days. The average days' sales outstanding and average days' inventory increased from 68.2 and 34.7 days to 102.8 and 43.1 days (Table 17.20).

Table 17.14 Profitability ratios

Year	2006	2007	2008	2009	2010	2011	2012	2013	2014	2015
Gross margin, %	43.07	41	41.92	44.01	44.13	43.7	44.54	45.53	41.98	42.55
Operating margin, %	16.65	19.25	−33.96	17.63	20.19	20.04	20.6	22.17	21.84	24.41
Net margin, %	14.82	9.44	−28.52	9.57	9.59	9.96	10.51	12.39	13.99	13.63
Return on assets, %	5.16	3.3	−10.82	2.75	3.9	4.3	4.44	5.42	5.83	6.03
Return on equity, %	10.64	7.38	−26.58	6.52	7.77	9.18	10.09	12.35	14.08	15.94
Return on invested capital, %	8.83	6.12	−13.05	4.9	6.82	7.45	7.76	8.99	9.89	9.84
Interest coverage	3.74	3.57	−5.76	3.52	4.25	4.39	4.72	5.15	4.42	4.97

Table 17.15 Per share ratios

Year	2006	2007	2008	2009	2010	2011	2012	2013	2014	2015
Earnings per share	4.65	3.51	−11.22	2.07	2.25	2.71	3.09	3.92	4.34	4.62
Book value per share	47.73	48.88	35.37	28.85	29.97	32	32.06	33.44	30.32	29.75
Free cash flow per share	1.57	3.23	4.99	3.47	2.32	2.12	2.87	3.62	3.55	4.28
Revenue per share	31.4	37.06	39.34	21.58	23.48	27.22	29.43	31.61	31	33.9
EBITDA per share	10.92	15.46	−8.04	10.21	11.17	6.21	6.85	15.63	7.67	9.05

Table 17.16 Price multiples

Year	2006	2007	2008	2009	2010	2011	2012	2013	2014	2015
P/B	0.92	0.67	0.56	0.97	1.03	1.13	1.43	2	2.9	2.18
P/E	9.17	9.36	0	13.54	13.68	12.72	15.29	17.03	19.78	13.98
P/S	1.4	0.89	0.9	1.32	1.32	1.29	1.77	2.33	2.78	1.92
P/OCF	7.14	4.85	2.31	7.11	10.79	10.81	15	19.43	20.76	14

P/B, Price to book ratio; P/E, Price to Earning; P/S, Price to Sales; P/OCF, Price to operating cash flow.

Table 17.17 Enterprise value multiples

Year	2006	2007	2008	2009	2010	2011	2012	2013	2014	2015
EV/Revenues	2.13	1.7	1.81	1.73	1.74	1.72	2.36	2.87	3.32	2.6
EV/EBITDA	6.09	4.7	11.96	3.68	6.45	3.65	5.21	11.16	13.43	9.73
EV/EBIT	11.17	8.89	− 16.52	9.65	9.18	8.77	11.08	12.52	15.06	10.7

EBITDA, Earning before interest, tax and depreciation; EBIT, Earning before interest and tax.

Table 17.18 Liquidity ratio

Year	2006	2007	2008	2009	2010	2011	2012	2013	2014	2015
Current ratio	0.85	1.02	1.19	1.48	1.52	1.51	1.35	1.53	1.43	1.56
Quick ratio	0.6	0.72	0.92	1.13	1.17	1.17	1.04	1.16	1.12	1.2

Table 17.19 Financial leverage ratio

Year	2006	2007	2008	2009	2010	2011	2012	2013	2014	2015
Debt/equity	0.58	0.63	0.89	0.46	0.5	0.65	0.64	0.67	0.87	1
Long-term debt to total assets	0.27	0.28	0.17	0.23	0.25	0.29	0.28	0.3	0.34	0.37
Total debt per share	27.04	31	18.31	14.01	15.06	20.05	21.32	22.49	26.9	29.93

Table 17.20 Efficiency ratios

Year	2006	2007	2008	2009	2010	2011	2012	2013	2014	2015
Fixed assets turnover	2.9	2.67	2.58	2.3	6.86	7.39	7.27	7.67	8.44	10.71
Asset turnover	0.34	0.35	0.38	0.29	0.41	0.43	0.42	0.44	0.42	0.44
Receivables turnover	7.04	6.91	5.93	3.77	4.67	4.35	4.02	3.52	2.97	3.24
Inventory turnover	13.54	13.65	13.33	7.66	8.12	8.56	8.07	7.94	8.52	9.36
Days payable	19.89	18.86	18.8	25.53	18.53	20.22	19.84	16.46	14.57	13.86
Days sales outstanding	51.84	52.8	61.57	96.72	78.22	83.99	90.88	103.63	122.78	112.53
Days inventory	26.96	26.74	27.38	47.63	44.94	42.63	45.24	45.97	42.86	39.01

17.18   Stock wealth analysis

The stock wealth analysis of Time Warner was based on monthly returns for 292 months during the period March 1992–June 2016. Time Warner stock generated cumulative return of 824.71% during this 292-month period of analysis. The average yearly returns for the stock was 34% during the period March 1992–June 2016. The adjusted closing price of Time Warner was $0.23 on March 19, 1992. The adjusted closing price of Time Warner was $70.72 on June 01, 2016. The stock price increased by approximately 305 times during this period of analysis. Assume that an investor invested $100 in Time Warner on March 19, 1992. On the basis of holding period returns, the investment would have grown to $30470.68 by June 2016. The same investment of $100 would have become $924.71 on the basis of cumulative returns in which the investor is involved in active trading every month till June 2016. The cumulative returns for the market index S&P500 for the same period involving 292 months were 187.7% (Fig. 17.1).

Time Warner stock have outperformed the S&P500 index in terms of monthly cumulative returns during the entire period of analysis (March 1992–June 2016).

It is assumed that $100 is invested in Time Warner, the S&P500 and peer group index on December 31, 2010. The cumulative returns calculation includes the reinvestment of dividends (Table 17.21).

The average monthly returns are estimated and then the yearly returns were estimated. For the year 2016, the average monthly returns for the period January 2016–June 2016 were estimated and then the yearly forecast was made. The average yearly returns of 41.38% was highest for Time Warner in the year 2013. The excess returns of Time Warner over the S&P500 index amounted to 19.60% in the year 2012 (Table 17.22).

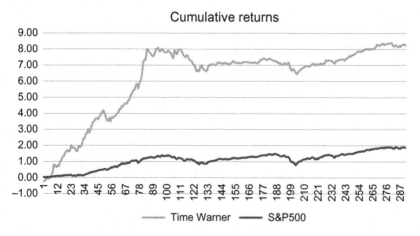

Figure 17.1 Cumulative monthly returns of Time Warner versus market index S&P500.

Table 17.21 **Cumulative total returns**

Year	December 2010	December 2011	December 2012	December 2013	December 2014	December 2015
Time Warner	$100	115	157	233	303	234
S&P 500 Index	$100	102	118	157	178	181
Peer Group Index	$100	114	154	245	271	253

Source: Annual Report 2015.

Table 17.22 **Average yearly returns (in percent)**

Year	Time Warner	S&P500	Excess returns
2010	15.44	13.80	1.65
2011	19.07	1.15	17.92
2012	32.77	13.16	19.60
2013	41.38	26.54	14.84
2014	29.55	11.14	18.41
2015	− 22.28	0.11	−22.40
2016	22.70	0.14	22.56

Table 17.23 **Holding-period yield (in percent)**

Year	Holding-period yield
2010	20.63
2011	18.18
2012	32.50
2013	40.70
2014	44.31
2015	− 15.49
2016	1.56

The holding-period yield was highest in the year 2014 with yield of 44.31%. Only in the year 2015, the holding-period yield was negative. The holding-period yield calculation is based on 1-year period. For 2016 estimations, the holding period is the period January 2016—June 2016. The annual holding-period yield for Time Warner stock during the period January 2010—June 2016 was 19% (Table 17.23).

The excess value estimated as the difference between market value and book value of equity amounted to $46,593 million in the year 2014. The average book value as percent of market value was 64.3% during the period 2010—15 (see Table 17.24).

Table 17.24 **Excess value in millions of dollars**

Year	2010	2011	2012	2013	2014	2015
Book value of equity	32,940	29,957	29,796	29,904	24,476	23,619
Market value of equity	33,893	33,749	42,742	59,822	71,069	51,413
Excess value	953	3792	12946	29918	46593	27794
BV as percent of MV	97.2	88.8	69.7	50.0	34.4	45.9

17.19 Estimation of cost of capital

The cost of equity is estimated using CAPM. According to CAPM:

Cost of equity = Risk free rate + Beta × Risk premium.

The yield to maturity on the long term US treasury bond is assumed as the risk free rate (see Table 17.25). The risk premium is assumed to be 5.5%. Beta is estimated by regressing the weekly stock returns of Time Warner stock on weekly market index S&P500 returns during the period January 2014–June 2016.

Beta = 0.76

Table 17.25 **Estimation of risk-free rate[a]**

Year	Yield to maturity on 30 year treasury bond
2014	3.55
2015	2.63
2016	2.63
Average	2.94%

[a]https://www.treasury.gov/resource-center/data-chart-center/interest-rates/Pages/Historic-Yield-Data-Visualization.aspx.

Cost of equity = 2.94% + (0.76 × 5.5%) = 7.12%.

Cost of debt is assumed to be the yield to maturity on the long term bond issued by Time Warner which matures on November 15, 2036. The yield to maturity of this bond on June 26, 2016 was 4.82%. The price of the bond was 121.7.[6]

The latest 2-year average tax rate is 23.55%.

After tax cost of debt = 4.82(1 − 0.2355)
= 3.69%

WACC is estimated using market value weights of equity and debt. To find the market value of debt, the book value of debt is multiplied by the ratio of market price of the long-term bond to the face value of the bond.

---

[6] http://quicktake.morningstar.com/StockNet/bonds.aspx?Symbol=TWX&Country=USA

Ratio = 121.7/100 = 1.217
Book value of debt in year 2015 = $23792 million
Market value of debt in 2015 = 23792 × 1.217 = $28954.86 million.
Market value of equity in 2015 = $51413 million
Total value = Market value of equity + Market value of debt = 51413 + 28954.86 = $80367.86 million
Weight of equity (We) = 51413/80367.86 = 0.64
Weight of debt (Wd) = 28954.86/80367.86 = 0.36
WACC = We × Cost of equity + Wd × After tax cost of debt
= 0.64 × 7.12% + 0.36 × 3.69% = 5.88%

Weighted Average Cost of Capital (WACC) is estimated as 5.88%.

17.20 Valuation perspectives

17.20.1 Estimation of economic value of Time Warner

Economic Value (EV) is estimated as net operating income after taxes (NOPAT) − Capital Charge.

Profit before interest and tax (PBIT) − Income tax = NOPAT.
Capital employed = Stock holder Equity + Long-term debt
Capital charge = Capital employed × WACC
EV = NOPAT − Capital Charge

Estimation of EV in year 2015.

PBIT in year 2015 = $6865 million
Income tax in year 2015 = $1651 million
NOPAT = 6865 − 1651 = $5214 million
Stock holder equity = $51413 million
Long-term debt = $23594 million
Capital employed = $75007 million
WACC = 5.88%
Capital charge = 75007 × 0.0588 = $4410.412 million
EV = 5214 − 4410.412 = $804 million.

The economic value for Time Warner is estimated as $804 million in the year 2015.

17.20.2 Equity spread

Equity spread is a variation of the EV measures. Equity spread is the difference between the ROE and the required return on equity (cost of equity).

Equity spread = (Return on equity − Cost of equity) × Equity capital
Equity capital in 2015 = $51,413 million
Return on equity in 2015 = 15.94%
Cost of equity in 2015 = 7.12%
Equity spread = $4534.627 million.

The value of equity spread for Time Warner is calculated as $4534.627 million in year 2015.

17.20.3 Dividend Discount Model valuation

The average growth rate of earnings per share during the 5-year period 2011–15 was approximately 15.5%. The average growth rate of dividends during the 5-year period 2011–15 was approximately 11%. The average dividend payout during the 5-year period 2011–15 was 31.5% (Table 17.26).

Table 17.26 Dividend trends

Year	2010	2011	2012	2013	2014	2015
EPS	2.25	2.71	3.09	3.92	4.34	4.62
DPS	0.82	0.9	1	1.1	1.25	1.4
DPO	0.364	0.332	0.324	0.281	0.288	0.303

Table 17.27 Estimation of growth rate from fundamentals

Year	2010	2011	2012	2013	2014	2015
RR	0.64	0.67	0.68	0.72	0.71	0.70
ROE	0.08	0.09	0.10	0.12	0.14	0.16
Growth rate	0.05	0.06	0.07	0.09	0.10	0.11

Growth rate = Retention ratio × Return on equity
Retention ratio = 1 − Dividend payout ratio

The average growth rate of earnings estimated from fundamentals during the period 2010–15 is 8% (Table 17.27).

Two-stage DDM: In this model, it is assumed that earnings will grow at the high growth rate of 11% for the next 10 years and thereafter at the stable growth rate of US economy. The historical growth rate of earnings for the period 2011–15 is assumed as the growth rate in the high growth period.

High growth stage inputs

High growth period = 10 years
Growth rate = 8%
Cost of Equity in 2015 = 7.12%
Average DPO = 31.5%
EPS in the current year (2015) = $4.62
EPS in the first year of high growth period = 4.62 × 1.08 = $4.99

Table 17.28 **Present value of dividends in high-growth phase**

Year	1	2	3	4	5	6	7	8	9	10
EPS	4.990	5.39	5.820	6.285	6.788	7.331	7.918	8.551	9.235	9.974
DPO	0.315	0.315	0.315	0.315	0.315	0.315	0.315	0.315	0.315	0.315
DPS	1.572	1.697	1.833	1.980	2.138	2.309	2.494	2.694	2.909	3.142
PV	$1.47	$1.48	$1.49	$1.50	$1.52	$1.53	$1.54	$1.55	$1.57	$1.58
Sum	$15.23									

Present value of dividends in high growth phase = $15.23 (Table 17.28)

Stable period inputs
The growth rate in stable period is assumed to be the growth rate of US economy. The average growth rate of US economy during the period 2013–14 is estimated as 2.3%.[7]

Growth rate in stable period = 2.3%.
Growth rate = Retention ratio × Return on equity of media and entertainment industry sector
Return on equity of media and entertainment industry sector = 19.3%[8]
Retention ratio = 2.3%/19.3% = 12%
DPO in stable phase = 1 − 0.12 = 0.88
EPS at the end of high growth period = $9.974
EPS at the beginning of stable period = $9.974 × 1.023 = $10.20
DPO in stable period = 0.88
DPS in stable period = 10.20 × 0.88 = $8.98
Terminal value = DPS in stable period/(Cost of equity-growth rate in stable period)
= 8.98/(7.12% − 2.3%) = $186.286
Present value of terminal value = $93.64
Value of Boeing stock = Present value of dividends in high growth phase + Present value of dividends in stable phase
= 15.23 + 93.64 = $108.87

Value of Time Warner stock = $108.87. Time Warner was trading at $70.72 in NYSE on June 26, 2016. According to the DDM valuation, Time Warner is undervalued in the stock market. The 52-week range for Time Warner on June 26,2016 was $55.53–$91.34.

17.20.4 Free Cash Flow to Firm Valuation Model

See Tables 17.29–17.31.

Net Capital Expenditure = Capital Expenditure − Depreciation and Amortization.
Adjusted Net Capital Expenditure = Net Capital Expenditure + Net Acquisitions (see Table 17.29).
Reinvestment = Adjusted net capital expenditure + Change in noncash working capital
Reinvestment rate = Reinvestment/EBIT(1-T) where EBIT(1-T) is the after tax operating income.

[7] http://data.worldbank.org/indicator/NY.GDP.MKTP.KD.ZG.
[8] http://www.morningstar.com/stocks/xnys/twx/quote.html.

Table 17.29 Adjusted net capital expenditure in millions of dollars

Year	2010	2011	2012	2013	2014	2015
Capital expenditures	631	772	643	602	474	423
Depreciation and amortization	7601	922	892	8148	733	681
Net capital expenditures	−6970	−150	−249	−7546	−259	−258
Net acquisitions	934	365	668	485	950	672
Adjusted net capital expenditures	−6036	215	419	−7061	691	414

Table 17.30 gives the estimation of non-cash working capital.

Table 17.30 Estimation of noncash working capital in millions of dollars

Year	2010	2011	2012	2013	2014	2015
Total current assets	13,138	13,432	13,264	12,531	13,180	12,513
Cash and cash equivalents	3663	3476	2841	1816	2618	2155
Noncash current assets	9475	9956	10,423	10,715	10,562	10,358
Total current liabilities	8643	8922	9799	8388	9204	8002
Short-term debt	26	23	749	66	1118	198
Noninterest bearing current liabilities	8617	8899	9050	8322	8086	7804
Noncash working capital	858	1057	1373	2393	2476	2554
Change in noncash working capital		199	316	1020	83	78

Table 17.31 Estimation of reinvestment rate

Year	2011	2012	2013	2014	2015
EBIT	5805	5918	6605	5975	6865
Taxes	1484	1526	1749	785	1651
EBIT(1-T)	4321	4392	4856	5190	5214
Adjusted net capex	215	419	−7061	691	414
Change in noncash working capital	199	316	1020	83	78
Reinvestment	414	735	−6041	774	492
Reinvestment rate	0.10	0.17	−1.24	0.15	0.09

The average reinvestment rate is estimated as 12.75%. The year 2013 reinvestment rate was excluded from the calculation of average value (Table 17.31).

The average growth rate of operating income after taxes was approximately 4.9% during the period 2011−15.

The average Free Cash Flow to Firm (FCFF) during the period 2011−15 was $5519.8 million (Table 17.32).

Two-stage FCFF.

Table 17.32 FCFF in millions of dollars

Year	2011	2012	2013	2014	2015
EBIT(1-T)	4321	4392	4856	5190	5214
Adjusted net capex	215	419	−7061	691	414
Change in noncash working capital	199	316	1020	83	78
FCFF	3907	3657	10,897	4416	4722

High-growth period inputs	
High-growth period	10 years
Growth rate	4.90%
Reinvestment rate	0.1275
WACC	5.88%
EBIT(1-T) in year 2015	5214
EBIT(1-T) in the first year of high-growth period	
5214 × 1.049	5469.49

Table 17.33 Present Value of FCFF in high-growth phase

Year	1	2	3	4	5	6	7	8	9	10
EBIT(1-T)	5469	5737	6019	6314	6623	6947	7288	7645	8020	8413
Reinvestment Rate	0.1275	0.1275	0.1275	0.1275	0.1275	0.1275	0.1275	0.1275	0.1275	0.1275
Reinvestment	697	732	767	805	844	886	929	975	1022	1073
FCFF	4772	5006	5251	5509	5778	6062	6359	6670	6997	7340
PV of FCFF	$4507	$4465	$4424	$4383	$4343	$4302	$4263	$4223	$4184	$4145
Sum	$43,239									

The sum of the present value of FCFF in high growth phase = $43239 million (Table 17.33).

Stable Phase Inputs

Growth rate in the stable period = 2.3%. The growth rate is assumed to be the growth rate of US economy during the 2-year period 2013−14.

Growth rate = Reinvestment rate × Media and entertainment industry ROCE

Return on capital employed of media and entertainment industry = 13.82%[9]

Reinvestment = 2.3/13.82 = 0.166

Reinvestment = 16.6%

Growth rate of operating income in stable period	2.30%
Reinvestment rate	16.60%
EBIT(1-T) at end of high-growth phase	8413
EBIT(1-T) at the beginning of stable phase	
8413 × 1.023	8606
Reinvestment = 8606 × 0.166	1428.68
FCFF in stable period = 8606 − 1428.68	7177.82
Terminal Value = FCFF in stable period/ (WACC − growth rate in stable period	
7177.82/(5.88% − 2.3%)	200497.77
PV of terminal value	$113,232.27
Value of Operating assets = PV of FCFF in high-growth period +PV of FCFF in stable period	
43239 + 113232.27	$156,471.70
Adding cash and cash equivalents in 2015	2,155
Value of Time Warner	$158,626.70
less value of debt in 2015	23,792
Value of equity	$134,834.70
Number of shares in million	830
Value per share	162.45

Summary of discounted cash flow valuation

Two-stage Dividend Discount Model

Value of Time Warner stock = $108.87.

Two-stage FCFF Model

Value of Time Warner equity = $134.835 billion

Value per share = $162.45

Time Warner was trading at $70.72 in NYSE on June 26, 2016. The 52-week range for Time Warner on June 26, 2016 was $55.53 − 91.34. The market capitalization of Time Warner was $55.6 billion on June 27, 2016.

---

[9] http://csimarket.com/Industry/industry_ManagementEffectiveness.php?ind=902.

17.21   Peer comparison and relative valuation

Table 17.34 **Financial highlights—peer comparison**

Company	Time Warner	Walt Disney	Twenty First Century Fox	CBS Corp
Total asset	63,848	88,182	50,051	23,765
Total debt	23,792	17,336	19,039	8448
Capital expenditures	423	4265	424	193
Revenues	28,118	52,465	28,987	13,886
Operating income	6865	13,224	5906	2417
Cash flow	7509	16,487	6642	2679
Total cash	2155	4269	8428	323
Net income	3833	8382	2275	1492
Market capitalization	51,413	155,300	51,031	24,917

The year of comparison was 2015. The values are given in millions of dollars. The peer companies selected for comparison are Walt Disney, Twenty First Century Fox, and CBS Corp. Walt Disney Company with its subsidiaries is a diversified entertainment company with operations in five business segments of Media Networks, Parks and Resorts, Studio Entertainment, Consumer Products and Interactive. Twenty-First Century Fox Inc. is a diversified media and entertainment company which operates in business segments of Cable Network Programming, Television, and Filmed Entertainment. CBS Corp is a major media and entertainment company with segments which include the CBS Television Network, cable networks, content production and distribution, television and radio stations, Internet-based businesses, and consumer publishing.

Walt Disney was the most asset intensive company among the peer group. Walt Disney was the highest revenue maximizer among the competitor firms. The operating income, cash flow, net income and market capitalization were highest for Walt Disney compared to the other competitor firms (Table 17.34).

The price multiple comparison was based on the current period June 2016. Walt Disney had the highest P/S ratio. CBS Corp had the highest P/B ratio. Twenty First Century Fox had the highest P/E ratio. Time Warner had the highest dividend yield among the competitor firms (Table 17.35).

Table 17.35 **Price multiple comparison**

Company	P/S	P/B	P/E	Dividend yield%
Time Warner	2	2.3	14.3	2.1
Walt Disney	2.9	3.5	17.6	1.4
Twenty First Century Fox	2	3.5	23.2	1.1
CBS Corp	1.8	4.5	17.7	1.1

Source: The source of data was Morningstar.com.

The comparison is based on the period June 2015. The price to cash flow was higher for Time Warner compared to the industry average and S&P 500 (Table 17.36).

Table 17.36 Price multiple comparison with Industry and S&P500

Ratios	Time Warner	Industry average	S&P 500
P/E	14.3	16.5	19.4
P/B	2.3	3.2	2.7
P/S	2	2	1.9
P/CF	16.1	12.9	12
Dividend Yield%	2.1	1.4	2.4

Source: Data source was Morningstar.com.

The price multiple ratios have been fluctuating over the 10-year period 2006–15. The average P/E, P/B, P/S, and P/CF were 16.1, 1.5, 1.7, and 12.2 respectively during the 10-year period (Table 17.37).

Table 17.37 Price multiple trends

Year	2006	2007	2008	2009	2010	2011	2012	2013	2014	2015
P/E	19.1	15.3	–	16.8	14.3	13.7	15.5	17.6	17.8	14.9
P/B	1.4	1	0.9	1	1.1	1.1	1.5	2.1	2.8	2.2
P/S	2.1	1.3	0.8	1.4	1.4	1.4	1.6	2.3	2.5	1.9
P/CF	15.9	7.3	3.5	7.4	11.2	12.7	13.6	16.7	20.1	13.6

All variable values are given millions of dollars. The enterprise value multiple calculations are based on the year 2015. The lower the enterprise value multiples, the more undervalued the stocks would be (Table 17.38).

Table 17.38 Enterprise value multiples comparison

Company	Time Warner	Walt Disney	Twenty First Century Fox	CBS Corp
Revenues	28,118	52,465	28,987	13,886
EBITDA	7509	16,487	6642	2679
EBIT	6865	13,224	5906	2417
Debt	23,792	17,336	19,039	8448
Market value of equity	51,413	155,300	51,031	24,917
Cash and cash equivalents	2155	4269	8428	323
Enterprise Value (EV)	73,050	168,367	61,642	33,042
EV/REVENUES	2.60	3.21	2.13	2.38
EV/EBITDA	9.73	10.21	9.28	12.33
EV/EBIT	10.64	12.73	10.44	13.67

Enterprise Value = Debt + Market Value of Equity − Cash and cash equivalents.

The comparison of the revenues for peer companies is based on the year 2015. Walt Disney had the highest year on year, 5-year average and 10-year average growth rate in the year 2015 (Table 17.39).

Table 17.39 Growth rate comparison of revenues

In percent	Time Warner	Walt Disney	Twenty First Century Fox	CBS Corp
Year on tear	2.77	7.48	0.69	0.58
5 year average	0.9	6.63	−0.27	−0.25
10 year average	−4.3	5.09		−0.46

The growth rate of operating income for the firms are based on the year 2015. Twenty First Century Fox had the highest year on year growth rate of operating income in 2015. Walt Disney had the highest 5- and 10-year average growth rate of operating income in year 2015 (Table 17.40).

Table 17.41 Altman score for Time Warner in year 2015

Total assets			63848.00
Total liabilities			40229.00
Sales revenues			28118.00
Operating income			6865.00
Retained earnings			77381.00
Market value of equity			51413.00
Working capital			4511.00
Ratios	**Values**	**Constant**	**Score**
Working Capital/Total Assets	0.07	1.20	0.08
Retained Earnings/Total Assets	1.21	1.40	1.70
Operating Income/Total Assets	0.11	3.30	0.35
Market Value of Equity/Total liabilities	1.28	0.60	0.77
Sales/Total Assets	0.44	1.00	0.44
		Z Score	3.34

17.22 Performance indicators

17.22.1 Altman Z Score

NYU Stern Finance Professor, Edward Altman developed the Altman Z score formula in the year 1967. In the year 2012, he released an updated version called the Altman Z Score Plus which can be used to evaluate both public and private companies. Investors can use Altman Z score to decide if they should buy or sell a particular stock based on the company's financial strength. The Altman Z score is the output of a credit strength test which gauges a publicly traded manufacturing company's likelihood of bankruptcy. Z score model is an accurate forecaster of failure up to two years prior to distress.

$$Z - Score = 1.2A + 1.4B + 3.3C + 0.6D + 1.0E$$

Where

A = Working Capital/Total Assets
B = Retained Earnings/Total Assets
C = Earnings Before Interest and Tax/Total Assets
D = Market Value of Equity/Total Liabilities
E = Sales/Total Assets

The zones of discrimination are such that when Z Score is less than 1.81, it is in distress zones. When the Z score is greater than 2.99, it is in safe zones. When the Z Score is between 1.81 and 2.99, the company is in Grey Zone (Table 17.41).

Table 17.40 Growth rate comparison of operating income

In percent	Time Warner	Walt Disney	Twenty First Century Fox	CBS Corp
Year on Year	14.9	14.59	67.71	− 16.54
5 year average	4.81	15.42	− 4.2	5.88
10 year average	4.27	12.42		

The financial variables are given in millions of dollars. The Altman Z score for Time Warner is estimated as 3.34 in year 2015.

17.22.2 Piotroski score

The Piotroski score is a discrete score between 0 and 9 which is an indicator of the firm's financial position. The score was named after the Chicago accounting Professor Joseph Piotroski. The cumulative points suggest whether the stock is a value stock or not. If the company achieves a score of 8 or 9, the stock can be considered strong. If the score ranges between 0−2, then the stock is considered weak.

Criteria for Piotroski Score

SL	Profitability scores	Score points	Score for Microsoft
1	Positive return on assets in current year	1	1
2	Positive operating cash flow in current year	1	1
3	Higher ROA in current year compared to previous year	1	1
4	Return on cash flow from operations greater than ROA	1	1
	Leverage, liquidity, and sources of funds		
5	Lower ratio of long-term debt to average total assets in current year compared to previous year	1	0
6	Higher current ratio in this year compared to previous year	1	1
7	No new shares were issued in the last year	1	1
	Operational efficiency ratios		
8	A higher gross margin compared to the previous year	1	1
9	A higher asset turnover ratio compared to the previous year	1	1
	Total	9	8

Boeing have a Piotroski score of 8 out of 9. The analysis based on the year 2015 suggests that Time Warner is a strong stock.

17.22.3 Graham number

It is a conservative method used for valuing a stock. It is a figure which measures a stock's fundamental value by taking into account the company's earnings per share and book value per share. Graham number is the upper bound of the price range which a defensive investor should pay for the stock. According to Graham number theory, any stock price below the Graham number is considered undervalued and hence worth investing in. Graham number is a combination of asset valuation and earnings power valuation.

Graham number	
Constant	22.5
EPS in year 2015	4.62
Book Value per share in 2015	29.75
	3092.5125
Graham number	55.61

$$\sqrt{22.5 \times (\text{Earning Per Share}) \times (\text{Book Value Per Share})} = \$55.61$$

Time Warner was trading at $70.72 in NYSE on 26/6/2016.

All detailed calculation and analysis is given in the excel worksheet *Time Warner.xlsx*.

Index

Note: Page numbers followed by "*f*," "*t*," and "*b*" refer to figures, tables, and boxes, respectively.

Printed in the United States
By Bookmasters